PENGUIN BO

THE TRIAL OF THE CANNIBAL D

Anne Salmond is a Distinguished Professor and Pro-Vice-Chancellor at the University of Auckland. One of New Zealand's most prominent anthropologists and historians, Professor Salmond is the author of the award-winning *Hui: A Study of Maori Ceremonial Gatherings, Eruera: Teachings of a Maori Elder* and *Amiria: The Life Story of a Maori Woman*. Her other major works are *Two Worlds: First Meetings Between Maori and Europeans, 1773–1815*. She received the CBE for services to literature and the Maori people in 1988 and was made Dame Commander of the British Empire for services to New Zealand history in 1995.

ANNE SALMOND

The Trial of the Cannibal Dog

Captain Cook in the South Seas

PENGUIN BOOKS

To Jeremy, with love and pride

PENGUIN BOOKS

Published by the Penguin Group
Penguin Books Ltd, 80 Strand, London WC2R ORL, England
Penguin Putnam Inc., 375 Hudson Street, New York, New York 10014, USA
Penguin Books Australia Ltd, 250 Camberwell Road, Camberwell, Victoria 3124, Australia
Penguin Books Canada Ltd, 10 Alcorn Avenue, Toronto, Ontario, Canada M4V 3B2
Penguin Books India (P) Ltd, 11 Community Centre, Panchsheel Park, New Delhi – 110 017, India
Penguin Books (NZ) Ltd, Cnr Rosedale and Airborne Roads, Albany, Auckland, New Zealand
Penguin Books (South Africa) (Pty) Ltd, 24 Sturdee Avenue, Rosebank 2196, South Africa

Penguin Books Ltd, Registered Offices: 80 Strand, London WC2R ORL, England

www.penguin.com

First published by Allen Lane 2003
Published in Penguin Books 2004

1

Typeset by Rowland Phototypesetting Ltd, Bury St Edmunds, Suffolk
Printed in England by Clays Ltd, St Ives plc

Contents

Imperial histories and the trap of Cyclops. Cross-cultural dynamics over
Cook's three Pacific voyages.

1. How Englishmen Came to Eat Dogs   1
Cook's return to Queen Charlotte Sound, early in the third Pacific voyage;
the killing and eating of his men at the end of the previous voyage.
Kahura's portrait by Webber; Maori contempt because the Europeans
failed to take revenge. Mock court martial of the cannibal dog on board
the *Discovery*.

2. Rule Britannia!   10
A brief account of Cook's home society, Georgian England, as a
background to shipboard dynamics during his three Pacific voyages.

3. The Wooden World of the *Endeavour*   22
James Cook's background and previous career; the Royal Navy; how the
voyage came together. Joseph Banks's life story before joining the
expedition. The *Endeavour* leaves England.

4. High Priest of 'Oro   34
The *Dolphin*'s visit to Tahiti in 1767. The Society Islands in the decades
before the Europeans' arrival. The *arioi*, and their sexual practices; the
war god 'Oro. Tupaia, the high priest navigator, and his background.
Bougainville's visit; and war in Tahiti. The *Endeavour* sails from
Portsmouth.

Kalani'opu'u. The second return to Hawai'i. The attack on Cook; the
reactions of Lieutenant Williamson and the marines; Cook's death at
Kealakekua.

The aftermath of Cook's death, on shore and on board his ships. The
attack on the priests at Kealakekua. Hawai'ian veneration of Cook's
bones after his death; parallels with Tahitian veneration of Cook's
portrait. The significance of the long-run history of the voyages, and their
cross-cultural dynamics.

List of Illustrations

Black and White Illustrations

Colour Plates

List of Maps

Cartographer: Jan Kelly

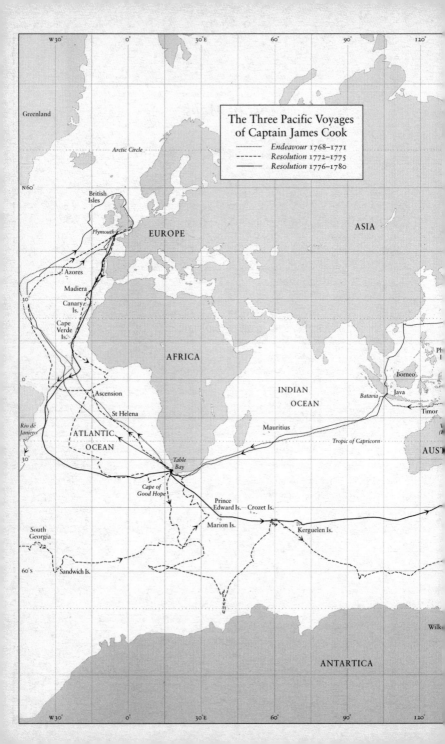

The Three Pacific Voyages
of Captain James Cook

.... *Endeavour 1768–1771*
- - - - - - - *Resolution 1772–1775*
————— *Resolution 1776–1780*

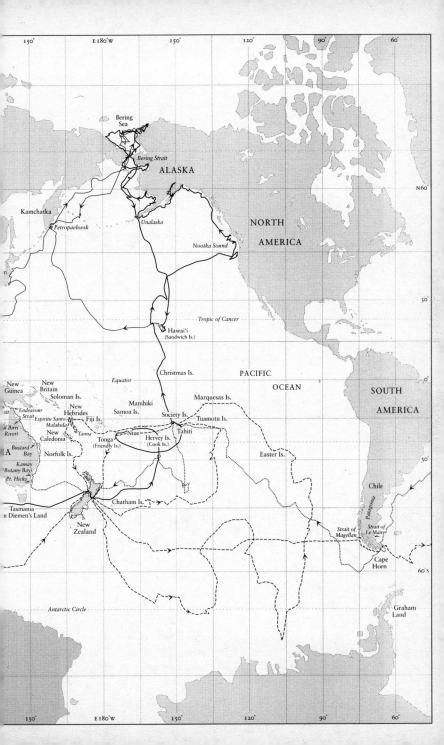

Acknowledgements

Writing a book about Captain James Cook is, in its own way, a voyage of discovery. While retracing Cook's steps, I came in touch with people in a number of countries and received a great deal of help, including some spectacular acts of generosity. I would like to thank Douglas Oliver, formerly professor of Anthropology at Harvard, for lending me his card index of early missionary sources in Tahiti, and his astute commentary on the manuscript. Roger Green, emeritus professor of Anthropology at the University of Auckland, advised on the original proposal, discussed research issues, and read and corrected the final version. Marshall Sahlins, professor of Anthropology at the University of Chicago, gave valuable and insightful comments on the paper which led to this book, as did Gananath Obeyesekere, professor of Anthropology at Princeton, who also acted as a referee for the project. I want to thank these two scholars for their generosity and a riveting debate over the death of Cook, which echoed in many ways the passion and gusto of the eighteenth-century controversies which surrounded the voyages.

Nicholas Thomas, during his time as Director of the Centre for Cross-Cultural Research at the Australian National University, helped to inspire this work, and supported the original proposal. Margarette Lincoln, Director of Research at the National Maritime Museum in Greenwich, backed the project from its inception. Glyndwr Williams, former professor of History at the University of London, offered warm hospitality and helpful comments on the final manuscript. Herb Kane, artist and scholar, shared his insights into the events which surrounded Cook's death during two unforgettable visits to Kealakekua Bay. Harold Carter, the biographer of Joseph Banks, despatched copies of Banks's letters, and shared with me the thrill of his discovery that some of the sketches from the first voyage had been painted by Tupaia, the Ra'iatean high priest-navigator.

Many other scholars around the world shared their specialist knowledge of various places visited by James Cook, and the objects collected during his voyages. For Tahiti, I would like to thank Serge Dunis, Danielle Carlsson, Robert Koenig and Mark Eddowes for their assistance and advice during trips to the archipelago; and Hank Driessen for access to his fine unpublished thesis on early Tahitian beliefs and rituals. For Tonga, I gained much from a meeting of the Tongan Historical Association in Tongatapu in 1999, and discussions with Futa Helu. I am grateful to Melenaite Taumoefolau and Konai Thaman for their counsel, Meredith Filihia for excellent research assistance and advice, Arne Perminow for material on traditional Tongan agriculture, and Phyllis Herda for checking the final manuscript. For Niue, Tom Ryan checked the account of Cook's visit to the island against his own historical research, and a field trip to the landing sites.

For Hawai'i, I am indebted to David Chappell and Kalani Meinecke for acts of kindness. John Charlot commented on the reconstruction of Cook's visits to Hawai'i, drawing on his expert knowledge of traditional Hawai'ian society. Elizabeth Lindsey arranged a memorable meeting with Mau Pialug, the navigator who taught a new generation of Pacific explorers, while John Longley invited me to Kealakekua Bay in 1999 for the visit by the *Endeavour* replica. I will never forget the sense of time collapsing as the *Endeavour* sailed around the point, the rituals of healing that followed, and a feast shared with Hawai'ian elders (including Herb Kane, Fern Pule and Rubellite Johnson) below decks as the ship rocked at anchor. Afterwards, David Hume of the *Endeavour* Foundation kept in touch, and sent helpful research materials. For New Zealand, Patu Hohepa, Peggy Kaua, Darcy Ria, Ngawhira Fleet, Atholl Anderson, Waerete Norman, Margaret Mutu, Sir Hugh and Lady Freda Kawharu, John Mitchell and many other experts and elders gave inspiration and information, and checked two earlier works on Captain Cook's encounters with Maori (*Two Worlds: First Meetings Between Maori and Europeans 1642–1772* and *Between Worlds: Early Exchanges Between Maori and Europeans 1773–1815*), which underpin the New Zealand sections.

For Australia, Fiona Powell, Deborah Bird Rose, David Martin, Bryce Barker, Peter Sutton, Gillian Cowlishaw, Kate Glaskin and Chris Gregory gave generous responses to inquiries about the *Endeavour* contacts with Aboriginal people; and John Macdonald made helpful comments on the Australian section of the manuscript. For Polynesian voyaging, Ben Finney shared insights into Tupaia's geographical knowledge, while Marshall Weissler sent various papers on pre-contact voyaging in the Pacific.

In Germany, Volker Harms arranged a visit to the ancestral *poupou* (wall-panel) collected by Cook in Tolaga Bay, New Zealand, and sent his unpublished paper on its provenance; Anke Scharrahs introduced Jeremy and me to the carving while it was being restored in Dresden. In Russia, Geoff Ward arranged a visit to the Great Museum of Anthropology and Ethnography in St. Petersburg, where Mariya Vladimirovna Stanyukovich and Yuri K. Chistov, the Director of the Museum, allowed us to inspect their marvellous collection of Tahitian and Hawai'ian artefacts, presented by Captain Clerke to the Governor of Kamchatka at the end of the third voyage.

For the Royal Navy at the time of Cook, I am grateful to Paul Turnbull of the *Endeavour* project; Nigel Rigby at the National Maritime Museum in Greenwich for generous help; Con Flinkenberg for insights into the nature of military command; Michael Phillips for detailed advice about naval artillery; and Linda Bryder for information about eighteenth-century medical knowledge. For Cook's Yorkshire background, my thanks to John and Judith Warren of Countersett, Yorkshire for taking Jeremy and me to the Countersett Meeting House, and illuminating discussions about the possible influences of Quakerism on Cook. For insights into eighteenth-century popular culture in England and the esoteric mysteries of animal trials, I am indebted to Joe Zizek, and Barry Reay, who checked that section of the manuscript.

Such a project must be funded, and I am very grateful to the New Zealand Government and the Marsden Fund of the Royal Society of New Zealand for their generous support. The University of Auckland and the Vice-Chancellor, Dr John Hood, granted the research leave without which this book would not have been written. My colleagues in the Department of Anthropology at Auckland, Mark Mosko and Christine Dureau, and Bronwen Douglas at the Australian National University offered early feedback on the project. The Interloan section of the University of Auckland Library scoured the world for obscure texts; and archivists in various libraries in New Zealand, Australia, the United Kingdom and the United States gave expert assistance during visits to their institutions. Ben Howe and Monique Ward did excellent work on the original manuscripts from the voyages, and Felicity Stewart checked the bibliographical sources and quotes in the final manuscript. I would also like to acknowledge the great Cook scholars J.C. Beaglehole, Andrew David, Bernard Smith and Rudiger Joppien for their magnificent work on Cook's three Pacific voyages; and two marvellous editors at Penguin, Geoff Walker and Simon Winder.

My family have been pivotal to this project. Jack Thorpe, my father, and his father William told me stories about our forebears in Whitby, where James Cook first went to sea. Jeremy, to whom this book is dedicated, shared most of the fieldwork, took innumerable photographs and engaged with the research from beginning to end. Stephen brought his graphic skills to bear on the manuscript; Tim and my mother Joyce Thorpe gave support and encouragement; and Amiria, now assistant curator at the Museum of Ethnology and Archaeology at Cambridge University, gave insights into the material exchanges which surrounded the voyages from her own research and writing.

I would like to thank Merimeri Penfold for illuminating conversations about Cook and Tupaia, and her friendship over many years, and my teachers Eruera and Amiria Stirling, who took me in hand when I was young, and led me into the world of Maori knowledge.

To all of these people, my aroha.

> *E paru i te tinana, e ma i te wai,*
> *E paru i te aroha, ka mau tonu e.*

> If you're touched with mud, you can wash it off
> If you're touched with aroha, it lasts always.

Preface

Without doubt, Captain James Cook was one of the world's great explorers. During his three Pacific journeys his wooden ships circled the world, navigating the ice-bound fringes of the Antarctic and Arctic circles, where sails froze solid and the rigging hung with icicles; sailed into tropical seas, where they survived hurricanes, lightning strikes and volcanic eruptions; edged around uncharted lands and islands, always in danger of shipwreck; and in one harbour after another, found unknown people. For any time and in any culture, these were remarkable voyages, like the journeys of Odysseus, or the Polynesian star navigators.

At the same time, Captain Cook has become an icon of imperial history. His voyages epitomise the European conquest of nature, fixing the location of coastlines by the use of instruments and mathematical calculation, classifying and collecting plants, animals, insects and people. As the edges of the known world were pushed out, wild nature – including the 'savages' and 'barbarians' at the margins of humanity – was brought under the calm, controlling gaze of Enlightenment science, long before colonial domination was attempted.

Cook's Pacific voyages, and his life and death, thus provoke reflection about the nature of history, and the impartiality of its explanations. Tales of the European discovery of the world are still shaped by imperial attitudes; and accounts of the great voyages of exploration are often written as epics in which only the Europeans are real. They travel in seas which had been traversed for centuries, 'discovering' places long inhabited by others. Yet *Terra Nullius*, the 'empty lands', were only empty because their people had been reduced to 'savages' without the power to shape the future, to influence the Europeans and to change them.

Such presumptions have helped to craft our disciplinary divisions. History, for instance, looks at the way the future has been shaped, within and across nations, while the discipline of anthropology has often analysed the customs of indigenous peoples as timeless structures, outside of history. Consequently, it has been difficult to imagine the great European voyages

Captain James Cook, painted by Nathaniel Dance

of exploration as cross-cultural encounters, in which Europeans and Pacific Islanders alike were historical agents. On the whole, the historians have studied the European explorers, and the anthropologists have studied the islanders at those moments of contact, thus accomplishing a kind of disciplinary apartheid. Yet when the voyages are bisected in this way, understanding of their dynamics is radically impoverished.

This book tries to avoid the trap of Cyclops, with his one-eyed vision. It is based on the perception, shared by James Cook himself, that in his journeys of Pacific exploration, Europeans and 'natives' alike were only human. On each side, there was savagery and kindness, generosity and greed, intelligent curiosity and stupidity. Maori, Tahitians and other Pacific Islanders engaged with Cook's men in ways that were defined by their cosmology and culture, just as Cook's men were shaped by the cosmology and culture of Georgian England. With this idea in mind, *The Trial of the Cannibal Dog* investigates the social background of these voyages in England and Polynesia, and their cross-cultural dynamics over time, both on board the ships and in visits to various Pacific islands.

In many parts of the Pacific, the islanders were stunned when Cook's ships first arrived, as though a spaceship had landed in their harbour. At first they were not certain whether the British were human beings or not; and this sparked a process of inquiry that changed their world for ever. They forged relationships with the sailors, and eventually some Pacific Islanders joined the ships for long periods and travelled to many islands, including Great Britain. They learned to speak English, to eat European food and wear European clothes, and had exotic experiences (including those with other Pacific Islanders).

At the same time, Cook and many of his men were deeply influenced by their experiences ashore, and their relationships with Pacific Island shipmates. They were surprised and entranced by the islanders' sexuality, infuriated by their attitudes to property, and shocked by human sacrifice and cannibalism. Again, curiosity led to inquiry, and relationships were forged across cultural boundaries. Over a decade of voyaging, many of the sailors acquired tattoos, and Pacific Island friends and lovers; they learned to eat Pacific delicacies, and to speak Polynesian languages. Cook himself engaged in ceremonial friendships with high chiefs in Tahiti, Tonga and Hawai'i, exchanging names and gifts with them.

Increasing intimacy between islanders and explorers led to heightened risk, as relationships on shore and on the ships were endangered by these unpredictable exchanges. Ashore in the islands, familiarity with the explorers bred contempt as well as friendship, while on the ships, familiarity with the islanders was often regarded with suspicion. As these tensions increased over time, shipboard discipline was sometimes threatened. Throughout the first two voyages Cook was determined to act as an 'enlightened' leader, but during the third voyage, his resolve faltered. After a tense and difficult visit to Queen Charlotte Sound in New Zealand during 1777, floggings of his own men doubled, and Pacific Islanders were treated with unprecedented severity. Ears were cropped and high chiefs were held hostage. At both Tonga and Tahiti, local people tried to kill him in revenge for such actions. In Hawai'i, they succeeded.

It would be easy but wrong to describe Cook's behaviour during the last voyage as imperialist brutality, however. The impact of Polynesia had played its part in his transformation. In various island groups, Cook was granted the status of an *ariki* [high chief], and like a high chief, he came to treasure his *mana* [prestige and power]. As one of his men put it, '[he] was born to deal with savages and he was never happier than in association with them.

He loved them and understood the languages of the different islanders and had the art of captivating them with his engaging manner. This was probably the reason that they honoured and at times even worshipped him, and also further reason that when they ceased to honour him, or sometimes even ridiculed him, he burned with rage.'[1] In the chapters that follow, the explosive cross-cultural processes that led to Captain Cook's disenchantment and death are traced over his three Pacific voyages, from their beginnings in Georgian England to their violent climax in 1779, on a rock-strewn beach at Kealakekua Bay in Hawai'i.

I

How Englishmen Came to Eat Dogs

During Captain Cook's third and last Pacific voyage, Alexander Home was a master's mate on board the consort ship, *Discovery*. In his old age, he used to spin a yarn about an incident that happened at Queen Charlotte Sound, New Zealand in 1777, a moment of 'glorious fun' amidst the hardships of the voyage:

When we were in New Zealand, Neddy Rhio, one of my messmates had got hold of a New Zealand dog, as savage a devil as the savages from whom he got it, and this same dog he intended to bring home to present to the Marchioness of Townsend, his patroness. But one day, when Neddy was on shore on duty, a court-martial was held on the dog, and it was agreed *nem.con.* that, as the dog was of cannibal origin, and was completely a cannibal itself, having bit every one of us, and shewn every inclination to eat us alive if he could, that he should be doomed to death, and eat in his turn, we being short of fresh provisions at the time.

The sentence was immediately executed, the dog cooked, dressed, and eat, for we could have eat a horse behind the saddle, we were all so confoundedly hungry; but, considering that Neddy had the best right to a share, we put past his portion in a wooden bowl, and by way of having some sport, we cut a hole in the dog's skin, and as Neddy came up the side, I popped his own dog's skin over his head with the tail hanging down behind, and the paws before. He looked the grin horrid, told us we were all a set of d—d cannibals, as bad as the New Zealanders we were amongst, and dived down below quite in the sulks.

I had locked up his share, and went down after him to see if hunger would overcome his delicacy, and sure enough, after growling and grumbling and swearing a reasonable time, he looks at me very woefully and says, 'D—n you, did you not even leave me a share?' 'That I did', says I, 'Neddy, my boy, and here it is for you.' So poor Rhio munched up his dog, cursing all the while as heartily as we were laughing at him. Ah! Those were the glorious days; but we are all going now. Rhio, poor fellow, came to be a post-captain, and fell at the taking of Copenhagen.[1]

Home and his messmates found this episode hilarious, yet cannibalism was no laughing matter during their visit to New Zealand. Just three years earlier during Cook's second Pacific voyage, the ships had been separated in a storm and the *Adventure* took refuge in Queen Charlotte Sound, where local Maori attacked a boatload of her crew and killed them all. Cook's ships had often returned to the Sound since their first arrival there in 1770, and there had been violent clashes with local people, including several shootings. Revenge, when it came, though, was shocking. A launch commanded by the *Adventure*'s second lieutenant, James Burney, sent out to search for the missing cutter, found rowlock ports and a shoe, and then human flesh bundled up in flax food baskets in a small bay, and the tattooed hand of one of the sailors. Rounding the point to the next bay they found Grass Cove 'throng'd like a Fair', attacked the crowd with muskets and wall-guns (swivel guns like small cannons), landed, and found cooking fires burning and dogs chewing on the roasted hearts, lungs, heads, hands and feet of their comrades.

This 'shocking scene of Carnage and Barbarity' was described in detail in Burney's report, and imprinted on shipboard memory. Cook's men had known about Maori cannibalism since their first visit to New Zealand, but had not expected to encounter it so closely. This was the stuff of sailors' nightmares, a tale of man-eating 'savages' come true. When Cook sailed into the Sound several months later, looking for the *Adventure*, his sailors avidly traded for human bones while local Maori concealed the killing of the *Adventure*'s men from him. Rumours reached him of a fight between the crew of a shipwrecked European vessel and local people, but these were garbled and inconsistent. Upon asking a chief about the *Adventure*, Cook was assured that the ship had been there ten months earlier, and that it had safely left the Sound. This was true, except for the fact that some of her crew had been killed and eaten. Cook accepted the chief's story, and spent a peaceful three weeks in the Sound on his way back to England. When news of the fate of the *Adventure*'s boat crew finally reached him at the Cape of Good Hope, Cook thought that the sailors might have been responsible. In his journal at the time, he commented:

I shall make no reflections on this Melancholy affair untill I hear more about it. I must however observe in favour of the New Zealanders that I have allways found them of a Brave, Noble, Open and benevolent disposition, but they are a people that will never put up with an insult if they have an opportunity to resent it.[2]

Now, early in the third voyage, Captain Cook was back in Queen Charlotte Sound, and still keeping an open mind about the killings. Until he knew what had provoked local Maori, he was determined to do nothing to harm them:

It appeared to me that they were apprehensive we were come to revenge the death of Captain Furneaux's people: seeing Omai on board whose first conversation with them generally turned on that subject; they must be well assured that I was no longer a stranger to that unhappy affair, and I did all in my power to assure them of the continuence of my friendship, and that I should not disturb them on that account.[3]

For local Maori, though, his response was difficult to grasp. The warriors in the Sound regarded Cook's assurances of friendship with bemusement, for as he had noted earlier, they would 'never put up with an insult if they have an opportunity to resent it'. To kill and ritually eat members of another group was the epitome of insult, 'biting the head' of their ancestors, an act which attacked their mana, their capacity to act effectively in the world. A true *rangatira* (leader) was bound to retaliate with all the force at his command to such an insult, or his gods would withdraw their presence, leaving both leader and people bereft and defenceless. Mai (Omai), a young Raiatean who had been on the *Adventure* and had since spent two years in England, understood this very well, and reacted to Cook's restraint with incredulity. During this stay in the Sound both Mai, and local Maori who regarded themselves as friends to the British, often urged Captain Cook to exact retribution from those who were responsible for the killings.

Many of the sailors, too, were thirsty for revenge. They were outraged that people who had cooked and eaten their comrades should walk about unscathed. Lieutenant Burney, who commanded the launch which had discovered the feast at Grass Cove, was back in the Sound for the first time since that horrific experience. In addition to Burney and Mai, there were many old Polynesian hands on board the ships: Cook's first lieutenant John Gore and Charles Clerke, the captain of his consort vessel the *Discovery*, both now on their fourth voyage to the Pacific; eight others who had been on *Endeavour* and then the *Resolution* during Cook's first and second Pacific voyages; and several more sailors from the *Adventure*. Some of these men could now speak Polynesian languages quite well, and they had also learned something about mana. In discussing the killing of the *Adventure*'s men with various of the groups in the Sound, they must have frequently been urged to take *utu* (or equal return) against the offenders.

Cook's inaction was all the more inexplicable because Kahura, the man primarily responsible for killing his men, had visited the camp at Ship Cove and boarded his ships on several occasions. In Maori terms, this was provocative behaviour. At Grass Cove, the sailors' heads and hearts had been cut from their bodies and eaten in the *whangai hau* ceremony, destroying the mana of the victims and leaving their kinsfolk bereft of ancestral protection. Each time Kahura visited Cook's ships, he was flaunting the power he had gained by killing their compatriots. The other Maori groups in the Sound watched with bated breath, waiting for the British to retaliate. According to Cook 'many of them said he was a very bad man and importuned me to kill him, and I believe they were not a little surprised that I did not, for according to their ideas of equity this ought to have been done.'[4]

Towards the end of their visit, therefore, when Cook let Kahura sit in his cabin on board the *Resolution* and had the ship's artist, John Webber, paint his portrait, this was too much for his men. When Mai was asked to bring Kahura to the great cabin, he exclaimed furiously, 'There is Kahura, kill him!' Cook ignored him so Mai walked out in disgust, only to return soon afterwards, vehemently protesting:

Why do you not kill him, you tell me if a man kills an other in England he is hanged for it, this Man has killed ten and yet you will not kill him, tho a great many of his countrymen desire it and it would be very good![5]

Cook had promised Kahura he would do him no harm, however, and he was determined to act as an 'enlightened' leader. He wrote, 'As to what was past, I should think no more of it as it was some time sence and done when I was not there, but if ever they made a Second attempt of that kind, they might rest assured of feeling the weight of my resentment.'[6] He had been told that the sailors (particularly Rowe, who commanded them that day) had provoked the attack, and although Clerke agreed that there was no purpose to be served by killing Kahura, many of the sailors were of a mind with Mai, and found their impotence galling. Burney spoke for them when he wrote:

It seemed evident that many of them held us in great contempt and I believe chiefly on account of our not revenging the affair of Grass Cove, so contrary to the principals by which they would have been actuated in the like case.[7]

The scene was now set for the mock trial of the dog on board the *Discovery*. James Burney, the living witness of what had happened at Grass Cove and the ship's first lieutenant, was chafing at Cook's failure to act. The *Discovery* was Cook's consort ship, so the trial was staged at a safe distance from their commander. It was a marvellous way of letting Cook and Clerke know what the sailors (and some of their officers) thought of Maori cannibals, and how they ought to be handled.

*

John Webber's portrait of Kahura

Such exemplary trials of animals were not unprecedented in Europe. In *The Great Cat Massacre*, Robert Darnton tells a tale of eighteenth-century printer's apprentices in Paris who lived a hard life with their master, sleeping in a filthy, freezing room, working long hours and being beaten and abused. The master's wife in this workshop adored her cats, especially *la grise* (the gray), a favourite, and fed them well, while the cook gave the apprentices cat's food – old, rotting scraps of meat. Finally the apprentices rebelled. For several nights one of their number, who had a gift for mimicry, yowled and meowed above the master's bedroom until he and his wife thought they were bewitched. In desperation they ordered the apprentices to get rid of the cats, except of course her favourite, who must on no account be frightened. The apprentices, armed with weapons, went after every cat they could find, beginning with la grise, beat them until they were half-dead, then dumped their bodies in the courtyard where the entire workshop staged a trial. The cats were charged with witchcraft, tried, convicted and hung.

When their mistress came out and saw a bloody cat dangling from a noose, she let out a great shriek, to the joy of all the workers. For weeks afterwards the apprentices re-enacted their trial and killing of the cats with roars of laughter and 'rough music', running their composing sticks across the type cases, thumping their mallets and pounding the cupboards.[8] They had managed to let their master and mistress know just what they thought of them, without exposing themselves to punishment, and the memory was both hilarious and intensely satisfying.

Animal trials, not always burlesque, had in fact been held in Europe for centuries. As Jean Duret, a French jurist, explained in 1610, 'If beasts not only wound, but kill and eat any person . . . they should pay the forfeit of their lives and be condemned to be hanged and strangled, in order to efface the memory of the enormity of the deed.'[9] Pigs, dogs or wolves might thus be accused and tried in a civil court. In 1712, for example, a dog in an Austrian garrison town which bit a municipal councillor was solemnly tried and sentenced to one year's imprisonment in an iron cage in the marketplace.[10] At mid-century a cow and an ass were tried in France for crimes against people.[11] In England in 1779, Tom Paine told the tale of a Sussex farmer whose dog was sentenced to be hanged by local judges, who disliked the way his master had voted in a parliamentary election.[12]

On board British ships, too, as Joseph Banks recounted for the *Endeavour* voyage in 1769, animals were involved in similar rough rituals. Dogs and cats as well as men who had not yet 'Crossed the Line' were ceremonially ducked from the yardarm on crossing the equator, unless someone paid in rum to redeem them. This was a dangerous proceeding, evocative of the old custom of ducking witches; and on that occasion Banks paid in brandy to save himself, his servants, his greyhound and a nondescript mongrel he called his 'Bitch Lady' from being dropped into the ocean.[13]

The trial of the cannibal dog, then, was not aberrant behaviour for eighteenth-century Europeans. It was 'rough humour', and like all such carnival antics, not quite a joke. During this period in Europe, animals such as cats and dogs were often treated as part of human society, as metonyms (partial representations) of their masters.[14] Many people still believed in witches at this time, and cats, dogs and other creatures were thought to act as 'familiars', carrying out evil deeds for their masters and mistresses.[15] In the trial of the *kuri* (Polynesian dog), Cook's sailors were treating the dog as a stand-in for local Maori, since the dog had exhibited the same fearful tastes as its original owners. By trying and convicting the dog of cannibalism, they could show how they felt about Kahura and his compatriots, while laughing at their own horror. The trial was on board ship, though, where captains were the masters. The *Discovery*'s men were also telling Cook and

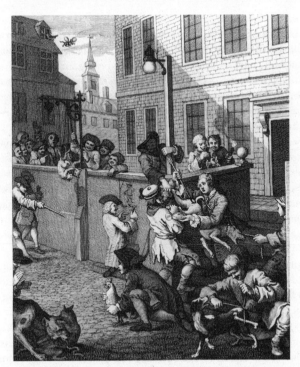

'Rough humour' involving animals, sketched by
William Hogarth in 1751

Clerke what they thought of their failure to take revenge for the murder of
their shipmates, sending a message to their commanders at least as much as
to anyone on shore. The beauty of such burlesque was that it could be
excused as a practical joke (rather than mutinous comment), and that made
it all the more funny.

If the shipboard trial was not weird behaviour, though, eating the dog
certainly was, in European terms. As representatives of their mistresses and
masters, cats and dogs in Europe were under a dietary taboo.[16] The thought
of eating their flesh was abhorrent, akin to cannibalism. How, then, could
Neddy Rhio's messmates eat his pet dog?

Kuri were not exactly like European dogs; they also resembled foxes.
They had long bodies, thick tails, short legs, and fox-like heads; and like
foxes, they never barked, but cried. Like their masters, they appeared to be
on a borderline between nature and culture, half tame and half savage. On
shore, these dogs were docile, but when they were brought out to the British

vessels, they frequently bit the sailors. Like their masters, they seemed to have a taste for European flesh. Still, foxes in Europe were not eaten either. This difference between Polynesian and European dogs cannot explain what happened on board the *Discovery*.

Rather, it may have been that Cook's sailors (or some of them) were no longer purely 'European'. Nor was this the first time that Cook's men had eaten dogs in Polynesia. During the *Endeavour*'s first visit to Tahiti in 1769, they had learned to eat dog flesh as feast food, served by hospitable chiefs. As Cook noted at the time, 'Dogs . . . we learned to eat from them and few were there of us but what allowe'd that a South Sea Dog was next to an English lamb.'[17] They learned, too, that Polynesians kept dogs in their houses, fed them with vegetables, tied them with strings around the belly and even buried them in special burial grounds.[18] Polynesian dogs had personal names (from the same series of names as people, unlike most European dogs), and provided clothing, festive food and sometimes sacrifices for chiefs and ancestor gods.

During the *Endeavour*'s voyage, just before they rounded the far southern end of New Zealand, the crew celebrated the birthday of one of the officers with a feast of dog meat: the hindquarters roasted, the forequarters in a pie, and the guts made into a haggis.[19] On the second voyage, after their first visit to Queen Charlotte Sound, a black dog from the Cape was cooked and eaten in the gunroom, leading Johann Forster to muse upon the European prejudice that treated cats and dogs as unclean animals, unfit to eat. And when Cook fell desperately ill off Easter Island and they despaired of his life, Forster sacrificed another dog to feed him. Cook commented later:

A favourite dog belonging to Mr Forster fell a Sacrifice to my tender Stomack; we had no other fresh meat whatever on board and I could eat of this flesh as well as broth made of it, when I could taste nothing else, thus I received nourishment and strength from food which would have made most people in Europe sick.[20]

Thus, by the third voyage, far from feeling sick at the thought of eating dog meat (whether European or Polynesian), the sailors' mouths had begun to water. They had come under Polynesian influence – not surprisingly, since some of them had spent more time in the Pacific than anywhere else in recent years, forming close relationships with Polynesian friends and lovers on shore as well as shipmates at sea. Cook's men had learned to eat dogs, and much more about Polynesia. They had learned about the power of mana, how to resent an insult, and how to express that resentment. Polynesian dogs also served as metonyms of their masters, even in societies (such as the

Society Islands) where the people did not eat human flesh. After almost a decade of visits to Polynesia, if Cook's sailors could eat a dog after convicting it of cannibalism, that is no great cause for amazement.

2

Rule Britannia!

By 1777, Cook's ships were not pure exemplars of Europe – far from it. During successive encounters with Polynesians over almost a decade, British voyagers and Polynesians alike had been transformed. In those meetings, perceptions and practices were *mutually* altered. Both sides were caught up in contradictory influences, and in this 'space of wondering' they were vulnerable to confusion.[1] By the third Pacific voyage, Cook had a long history of engagement with Polynesians, which had significantly changed him. In order to understand this process of cultural shift and exchange, the lives of both British voyagers and Polynesians in the eighteenth century must be investigated, and understood. Our ethnographic account of Cook's ships and the complex transformations on board therefore begins with a sketch of their home society, Georgian England.

Georgian England

> Rule Britannia! Britannia rule the waves
> Britons never will be slaves.
> *(From the masque* Alfred *by Thomas Arne, 1740)*

By the mid-eighteenth century, Great Britain was in an ebullient mood, confident, materialistic and worldly. The Royal Navy ruled the world's oceans and guarded Britain's shores, protecting her freedom and prosperity. The British had won mighty and lucrative victories in the War of Spanish Succession (1702–13) and the Seven Years' War (1756–63) against more populous European opponents, and 'John Bull' was feeling triumphant. Across the channel, Voltaire observed with envy:

As trade enriched the citizens in England, so it contributed to their freedom, and this freedom on the other side extended their commerce, whence arose the grandeur of the state. Trade raised by insensible degrees the naval power, which gives the English a superiority over the seas, and they are now masters of very near two hundred ships of war.[2]

It was gratifying to be granted superiority (especially by a Frenchman), for at this time the world was intensely hierarchical. The 'Great Chain of Being' ordered the universe, from God in His Heaven to the lowliest of His creatures. The King, George III, sat at the apex of British society, followed by the peers, princes of the Church, gentry and rich merchants, through the 'middling orders' to the great mass of the labouring people, including most sailors. Below the labourers were the slaves (for there were slaves from the West Indies in Britain at this time, and many of the wealthiest families were involved in the African slave trade).

Outside of England there were other 'civilised' kingdoms, with which it vied for dominance, but there were also 'barbarians' and 'savages' – in the Scottish Highlands and Ireland as well as parts of Europe, Africa, the Americas and the Pacific. Below the human order were the ranked orders of the animal kingdom, from apes to 'half-reasoning' elephants, dogs and beavers, through birds to fish and insects. Beyond the animals were the plants (the vegetable kingdom), and finally rocks, stones and earth (the mineral kingdom), which were inanimate.[3]

This vast cosmological scheme made sense of the world, and its rank orderings were everywhere visible. The fields and commons in the country-side, the architecture and decoration of English buildings, the ranks in the Army and Navy, the rituals of the Court, the Church and the Law, and the etiquette of everyday life all echoed its patterns. As elsewhere in Europe, the structures of privilege were formidable. A clique of noble families controlled the offices of Church and State, dispensing patronage and favours to the lower orders. The grandees were not numerous – fewer than 300 peers – but they were fabulously rich and controlled great political power, and perhaps 20 per cent of England's land.

The place of individuals in these structures was not immutable. Except at the very highest levels, the social hierarchy depended on wealth at least as much as birth, and men (and, more rarely, women) could rise up by patron-age and their own efforts. As Daniel Defoe's 1709 classification of English society made clear, status followed prosperity:

1 The Great, who live profusely.
2 The Rich, who live very plentifully.
3 The Middle Sort, who live well.
4 The Working Trades, who labour hard, but feel no Want.

5 The Country People, Farmers etc; who fare indifferently.

6 The Poor, that fare hard.

7 The Miserable, that really pinch and suffer Want.[4]

According to Joseph Massie in 1759, only 310 families in England had six thousand pounds a year or more, and only about 1 per cent of families had incomes of more than four hundred pounds. Naval officers were among the top 10 per cent of income earners, with an average 80 pounds a year by his calculation. Half of the families lived on less than 25 pounds a year, including the wives and children of ordinary sailors, who earned between 10 and 14 pounds a year. Labourers, cottagers and soldiers had less; and the families of paupers and vagrants had almost nothing.[5] While it was possible to rise in this finely graded society, it was also possible to fail, and fall. Although some men improved their lot and that of their families, others sank into penury and the poorhouse.[6]

At mid-century, however, great changes were under way. The old hierarchies were still taken for granted, but their foundations were shifting. Much of Britain's wealth was founded on international trade; and convoys of ships sailed around the world, linking Great Britain with a network of colonies and trading stations, and circulating new ideas and discoveries as well as cargoes of goods, slaves and raw materials. Felons were often transported to America where they became ardent advocates of liberty; while those who wanted to improve their lot migrated to colonial settlements or foreign trading ports, where they came in contact with exotic ways of living. This sense of expanding frontiers fired a hope that discovery and exploration might open up new possibilities, especially if these processes were ruled by reason; and this vision inspired a growing devotion to experimental procedures and Enlightenment science, with its challenges to the old cosmic order.

By the mid-eighteenth century, this willingness to try new ways of doing things led to widespread ferment in Britain. In many parts of England, for example, customary rights were under siege in the name of 'improvement'. In the countryside, mediaeval landscapes of winding tracks and footpaths, small, irregular fields and thick, tangled hedges were being replaced by large square fields cut through the land with a ruler. As landowners enclosed the commons, and built turnpikes and canals, new landscapes of big villages and thin hawthorn hedges were emerging. Wastelands were divided up and cultivated, fallowing was increasingly replaced by manuring and fodder crops, new staples (including maize and potatoes) were introduced. Some tenant farmers became rich, but many of the minor gentry and small farmers found life difficult, and cottagers and squatters were driven off the land.

Local crops were sent to London or overseas by the new roads and canals, and the poor, who were no longer able to gather food, firewood and building materials on the commons, suffered terribly in times of poor harvests.

They did not sit quietly under these impositions. Villagers and townsfolk pulled down fences and hedges around enclosures, killed dogs belonging to local landowners, destroyed toll-gates on turnpikes, and attacked farmers, middlemen and millers who hoarded grain and tried to drive up prices. In times of dearth, they were driven to desperation. In 1762, for example, John Bailey, the JP at Rossendale received an anonymous letter from villagers in his district, demanding that he enforce the old laws against market profiteering:

If You don't put those good Laws in Execution against all Those Canables or Men Slayers That have the Curse of God and all honest Men both by Gods Laws and Mens Laws so take Notice Bradshaw Bailey and Lloyd the biggest Rogue of all Three I know You all have Power to stop such vilonas Proceedings if You please and if You don't amaidatley put a Stopp and let hus feel it the next Saturday We will murder You all that We have down in Ower List and Wee will all bring a Faggot and burn down Your Houses and Wait Houses and make Your Wifes Widdows and Your Children Fatherless for the Blood of Shull de hill lyes cloose at Ower Harts and Blood for Blood We Require.

Take Care. Middleton.[7]

When new taxes on local produce were introduced, there were further outbursts of popular fury. In Exeter in 1763, where the townspeople were infuriated by a new Cider Tax, they made an effigy of George III's Scottish Prime Minister, Lord Bute, dressing it in a star and plaid bonnet. A gallows was set up on a cart, where the effigy was ceremoniously hanged. Afterwards a man riding an ass, wearing a placard on his back which read 'From the Excise and the Devil good Lord deliver us', led a mock funeral procession through the town. Forty men marched behind the ass carrying white wands, each with an apple on top, followed by the cart with the gallows. This was followed by a cider hogshed covered with a funeral pall, shouldered by six men in black cloaks. Thousands of people ran shouting and hallooing through the streets, and that night a bonfire was lit, and the effigy was burned to ashes.[8]

Other protests at this time were provoked by the introduction of new industrial technologies. Many rural families combined work on the land with 'cottage industries' – spinning, weaving, wool-combing, nailing, scythe-making, shoe-making or lace-making. When Richard Arkwright invented a power-driven spinning machine and set up large textile factories, the factory

*Burning an effigy of the Earl of Bute, from a ballad sheet
published in 1763*

system of labour got under way, transforming family life and work practices. Some profited from these new opportunities. Merchants, bankers and middlemen were enriched by increasing commerce and trade. Manufacturers and inventors became wealthy. As communications improved, more people were able to travel. Many tradespeople, small businessmen and professionals did well in this bustling, business-like climate. And as labourers left the land, they often became more free, escaping the controls of the 'lords of the manor'.

At the same time, however, they also became more vulnerable in this shifting economy. Workers of this kind – porters and bargees, textile workers and artisans, labourers and colliers – became involved in a rash of riots which broke out in England in 1740, 1756–7, 1766–7, 1769 and 1773, protesting about high food prices, low wages and poor working conditions. As Benjamin Franklin noted in 1769:

I have seen, within a year, riots in the country, about corn; riots about elections; riots about work-houses; riots of colliers, riots of weavers, riots of coal-heavers; riots of sawyers; riots of Wilkesites; riots of government chairmen; riots of smugglers, in which custom house officers and excisemen have been murdered, the King's armed vessels and troops fired at.[9]

He might also have mentioned sailors, for in 1768 when the price of wheat skyrocketed, there was a great strike of merchant seamen. After the Seven Years' War, over 150,000 men had been discharged from the Army and Navy and thrown on the labour market. It was suggested that they might be employed in the Scottish fishing industry, or settled in uncultivated commons, wastes and forests, and they were allowed to work in trades without serving an apprenticeship, but many found themselves unemployed, and smarting at the injustice. Industries that had expanded during the War were scaled down, leading to large-scale job losses. Owners of merchant ships, taking advantage of this situation, hired many apprentices and drove down the wages of experienced seamen.

On 5 May 1768, as the *Endeavour* was preparing to sail from England, a great body of sailors assembled at Deptford and took over the ships, reefing their topsails and demanding that the owners raise their wages. On 7 May there was a mass meeting of sailors in St George's Fields, who marched in two groups to St James's, colours flying, drums beating and fifes playing, to present a petition to the King. Two days later, thousands of sailors marched en masse to the Royal Exchange, where they presented a petition to Parliament. When they were sent away without major concessions, their leaders went into a dockside pub to write out their grievances. According to his account, when the pubkeeper told them their actions were treasonable, they retorted:

Seamen: 'Most of us have ventured our lives in defence of His Majesty's Person, Crown and Dignity and for our native country and on all occasions have attacked the Enemy with courage & Resolution & have been Victorious. But since the conclusion of the [Seven Years'] War We Seamen have been slighted and our Wages reduced so low & Provisions so Dear that we have been rendered uncapable of procuring the common necessaries of Life for ourselves & Familys, and to be plain with you if our Grievances is not speedily redressed there is Ships & Great Guns enough at Deptford and Woolwich we will kick up such a Dust in the Pool as the Londoners never see before . . . We are determined to unmast every ship in the River & then bid you, & Old England adieu & steer for some other country.'[10]

Over the days that followed, London was brought to a standstill as sawyers, ship carpenters, watermen, weavers, coal-heavers, journeymen tailors and hatters joined the protests. People were forced to illuminate their houses in support of John Wilkes, the populist MP and advocate of 'Liberty'; every ship on the Thames was unrigged and the masters of colliers and corn-ships were made to keep their cargoes on board; while 'every Person they found doing the least Business they made ride (as they term it) the Wooden Horse, which is carrying them upon a sharp Stick, and flogging them with Ropes, Sticks, and other Weapons, till they are tired with their own Cruelty.'[11]

Despite all this uproar, however, the ruling families stood firm. The English social hierarchy proved extremely resilient. In the case of the merchant seamen, they gained some concessions, including higher wages. Elsewhere, local gentry and JPs met with angry crowds, listened to their complaints, and promised to take some action. Sometimes they read the Riot Act, and resolutely faced the mob down. As the Chief Justice remarked, 'The laws, executed with spirit, will always suppress a mob: the magistrates did it with ease in this case. The undaunted courage of an individual . . . disperses or assuages these fevers of the people: experience, as well as history, shews it.'[12] Most of these crowds were not intent on rebellion, however. They acted to uphold customary rights, not to tear down the social order. Many of the 'middling sort' and more fortunate workers, who shared in England's prosperity, had a growing stake in 'improvement'. The ruling elite had patronage to dispense, and if all else failed, they controlled Parliament and the Law, and could enforce respectful behaviour.

During this century, Parliament passed laws so draconian that capital offences multiplied from 50 to 200. There were fewer actual executions, because many juries refused to convict a person for the new capital crimes, and the prerogative of mercy was often exercised; but in their defence of property, the ruling classes bore hard on the poor.[13] Offenders were clapped into stinking, feverish gaols, and theft, poaching, forgery, burning hayricks, destroying turnpikes or sending threatening letters to the powerful were harshly punished, as sessions reports from the Old Bailey demonstrate:

The same day, at noon, the Sessions ended at the Old Bailey, when the 2 following persons received sentence of death, viz. John Turner, for breaking into the apartments of Mrs Turner, who was an intimate of his father's, near Queenhithe, and stealing from thence 1 guinea, 5 pounds 1 shilling in silver, a several wearing apparel; and Anne Palmer, alias Hinks, for stealing 8 pounds 1 shilling in money, and goods to the value of 38 shillings, the property of Mr. Sam. Ruffel . . . Five were burnt in the hand, and 30 were cast for transportation . . . Seven were burnt in the hand and about 20 were ordered for transportation . . . Eight were burnt in the hand.[14]

In these riotous times, there was a growing gap between the elite and the lower orders in Britain. Many of the grandees simply withdrew from casual contacts with the poor. In the cities, especially in London, they constructed elegant new squares with lighting, paved streets and walled gardens. In the countryside, they built great houses guarded by high gates and lodges, and surrounded by deer-parks, grottoes and ha-has. These mansions had commanding views of their grounds, so that their owners could enjoy 'that charm which only belongs to ownership, the *exclusive right* of enjoyment, with the power of refusing that others should share our pleasure', as the landscape designer Humphry Repton put it.[15]

The sons of landowning families were often raised on these estates; and then went to schools such as Eton, Harrow and Winchester, where they fagged and were flogged, studied Greek, Latin, grammar and history, and were exposed to gambling and drinking. After school, younger sons might join the Army or Navy, or attend either Oxford or Cambridge in preparation for the Church. A wealthy young heir might travel to one of the European universities, followed by a Grand Tour of France, Italy, Germany and Holland. Some of these travellers, dubbed 'macaronis' or 'dilettanti', brought Continental fashions back to England and enthused about French culture and literature, Italian art and music, and antiquities. In the Society of Dilettanti, founded in 1743, they promoted Italian opera and art, drank quantities of alcohol and boasted about their sexual exploits; at Almack's and White's huge sums of money were gambled; while at the Hellfire Club, wealthy rakes enjoyed a raunchy, libertine subculture.

Upper-class women had less freedom. They were taught the graceful arts at home, and required to make suitable marriages. While their husbands might have mistresses and bastards, or visit bordellos and bagnios, wives were expected to be refined and domestic. Not all of them observed these punctilios, however; the Duchess of Devonshire had a child by Lord Grey, for instance, and Lady Harley was said to have become pregnant by so many different men that her offspring were known as the 'Harleian Miscellany'.[16]

During the season, when the gentry congregated in London, they enjoyed balls and receptions, masquerades, concerts and plays, and visited the pleasure gardens at Vauxhall and Ranelagh. They went shopping, collected art works, antiquities, curiosities and books, visited each other, gossiped and arranged marriages for their children. At this time London was the country's financial powerhouse, home of the Court, Parliament and Government, and one of the fastest-growing cities in the world. As Tobias Smollett remarked:

London is literally new to me; new in its streets, and even in its situation; as the Irishman said, 'London is now gone out of town.' What I left open fields, producing hay and corn, I now find covered with streets and squares, and palaces, and churches.

I am credibly informed, that in the space of seven years, eleven thousand new houses have been built in one quarter of Westminster, exclusive of what is daily added to other parts of this unwieldy metropolis.[17]

In this sprawling city, a lively 'polished' society was emerging. Women such as Mrs Elizabeth Montagu, Mrs Hester Thrale and Hannah More held 'salons' for literary discussion, musical performances and witty conversation. In the 1760s, a series of concerts organised by J.C. Bach featured Mozart and other European composers, and Handel's oratorios attracted large audiences. The theatres at Covent Garden and Drury Lane in the West End performed a repertoire of British plays ranging from Shakespeare to John Gay's *The Beggar's Opera*, featuring actors such as David Garrick and Susannah Cibber, or musical comedies by Thomas Arne and Samuel Arnold. William Hogarth printed and sold engravings as a commercial venture, and when the Royal Academy of Arts was established in 1768, it exhibited works by Joshua Reynolds, Benjamin West and Thomas Gainsborough.

Novels by Samuel Richardson, Tobias Smollett, Henry Fielding and Fanny Burney, books of history and exploration, and works by Daniel Defoe, Oliver Goldsmith and Dr Johnson had an avid readership. Men met at the coffee houses and taverns to read the newspapers, hear the latest gossip and engage in debate and discussion; and attended the meetings of various clubs and societies. There was the British Museum to visit, and the meetings and lectures organised by the various learned and scientific associations, including the Society of Antiquaries and the Royal Society. As newspapers and magazines circulated more widely, as the arts were commercialised and travel became more rapid and easy, this polite, 'refined' culture spread to the 'middling sort' and the more prosperous tradesmen; and to provincial cities and towns, where London fashion, pleasure gardens, concerts, balls, book clubs, circulating libraries and learned societies flourished.

Life among the poor was very different, however. In London, where about one-quarter of the population were linked in some way with the maritime trades, the dwellings of the gentry were in stark contrast with the sinks and stews inhabited by impoverished families. As Archenholz noted in 1780:

. . . the east end, especially along the shores of the Thames, consists of old houses, the streets there were narrow, dark and ill-paved; inhabited by sailors and other workmen who are employed in the construction of ships and by a great part of the Jews. The contrast between this and the West end is astonishing: the houses here are mostly new and elegant; the squares are superb, the streets straight and open . . . If all London were as well built, there would be nothing in the world to compare with it.[18]

Hanover Square in London, sketched in 1787

Because they inhabited different parts of the city, the wealthy saw little of the domestic miseries of the poor. Henry Fielding remarked in 1753:

. . . the sufferings of the poor are indeed less observed than their misdeeds; not indeed from any want of compassion, but because they are less known; and this is the reason why they are so often mentioned with abhorrence and so seldom with pity . . . They starve and freeze and rot among themselves, but they beg, steal and rob among their betters.[19]

Many aspects of popular culture were condemned as criminal, or as savage and irrational. In the urban tenements, and in rural hamlets and villages, people believed in witches and ghosts at a time when most of the 'better sort' scoffed at such superstitions. In 1763 Parliament declared that witchcraft was not a crime, and banned attacks against people (usually old women) who were suspected of being witches. Nevertheless, in a village in Wiltshire in 1773, a crowd of around 100 people ducked an old woman in a mill pond for witchcraft. Her clothes kept her afloat, 'proving' that she was guilty. A year later, an old couple accused of bewitching cattle were swum in the same village. In other villages, witches were being swum, or scratched in the face to destroy their magical powers.[20] In the countryside, and in the urban alleys and warrens, people used divination rituals and love charms, and resorted to folk remedies to cure their ailments.

Fairs, feasts, festivals and pageants staged at this time also evoked a pagan past – rush-bearings, well-dressings, Jack-a-Lent, hobbyhorses, mummers, harvest homes and Maypole dancing. These celebrations were rowdy, sometimes finishing with bear-baiting, cock-fighting, prize-fighting and wrestling, naked foot-races, drinking and gambling. Although many of the elite enjoyed such activities, attempts were made to put them down, often to no avail. 'I could not suppress these Bacchanals,' moaned the Reverend John de la Flechere of the Shropshire Wakes in 1761, 'the impotent dyke I opposed only made the torrent swell and foam, without stopping the course.'[21]

'Rough humour' was part of this robust, rambunctious folk tradition. Mock trials (like the court martial of the cannibal dog on Cook's consort ship) and elections were held in which unpopular figures of authority were ridiculed. Rituals known as 'skimmington' or 'riding the stang' were also used to humiliate cuckolds and adulterers, who were made to ride back-to-front on asses or horses, while their tormenters clashed pots and pans together, tooted on horns, and bellowed out satirical verses. In Aveton Gifford in 1737, for instance, a group of villagers:

Assembled before the doors of the dwelling house of Charles Jones, Gent. Did make an Assault upon Mary his wife and in a sporting maner did demand where the black Bull was, meaning the said Charles Jones, and in such Riotous manner did run up and down the Church Town of Aveton Gifford with black and Disguised Faces carrying a large pair of Rams Horns tipt like Gold and adorned with Ribbons and Flowers with a mock child made of raggs, and having an Ass whereon the said John Macey [a miller] and John Pinwell [a labourer] rid, dressed in a Ludicrous manner, back to back, with beating of Drums and winding of Hunting Horns, and throwing of lighted Squibbs, and Reading a Scandalous Libellous paper, making loud Huzzahs Hallows and out Cries and so continuing for the space of 5 hours.[22]

Offenders against popular opinion might be impersonated or represented by effigies, and mock hangings and burnings were common. As E.P. Thompson has noted, such rough humour 'brushes the carnival at one extreme and the gallows at the other; . . . is about crossing forbidden frontiers or mixing alien categories; . . . [it] traffics in transvestism and inversion.'[23]

In the Age of Enlightenment, however, such uproarious pleasures were under siege. The poor were decried as 'a people not only without delicacy but without government, a herd of barbarians or a colony of Hottentots', as Dr Johnson put it; while their culture was dismissed as 'rude' and 'backward'. Many thought that the polite arts should be more widely cultivated among ordinary folk, because 'it is universally allowed, that in proportion as these are encouraged or discountenanced, the manners of the people are civilized and improved, or degenerate into brutal ferocity, and savage moroseness.'[24]

As notions of 'polished' and 'enlightened' behaviour spread through the academies and charity schools, and many more people gained access to newspapers, periodicals and books, their loyalty to traditional ways of thinking was weakened. In provincial towns, as lecturers performed experiments and extolled the findings of Newtonian science, 'improvement' – technical, scientific and moral – became a matter of popular enthusiasm. John Wesley and many Dissenters (including the Quakers) urged the virtue of lives based on peaceful conduct, piety, industry, thrift and sobriety. Laws were passed to license public houses, raise the duties on liquor, control brothels and disorderly houses; the public hangings at Tyburn were stopped, and in 1766 the gaping crowds were shut out of Bedlam. As the Dissenting physician James Currie declared, 'the labouring poor demand our constant attention. To inform their minds, to repress their vices, to assist their labours, to invigorate their activity, and to improve their comforts – these are the noblest offices of enlightened minds in superior stations.'[25] Or as David Hume put it, 'The minds of men, being once roused from their lethargy and put into fermentation, turn themselves on all sides, and carry improvements into every art and science.'[26]

Many Englishmen from humble backgrounds – and Captain James Cook was one – were inspired by this kind of vision. Driven by the threat of poverty and obscurity, they sought to improve themselves through education, hard work and self-discipline. Although some failed, others succeeded, giving Great Britain the reputation among its European peers as a remarkably open and free society. These tensions in its collective life – between merit and inherited privilege, between 'polite' and popular culture, between superstition and science – made British society dynamic, if confusing. The same contradictions played themselves out during James Cook's three great voyages of discovery, shaping the relationships among the scientists and sailors on board his ships, and their exchanges with the Pacific peoples they encountered.

3

The Wooden World of the *Endeavour*

James Cook was an unlikely hero, born to a humble family in Yorkshire on the north-east coast of England, with its rocky cliffs and deep, sheltered harbours, winding lanes, stone-walled moorlands, fertile downs and valleys.[1] Cook's father was a farm labourer who had migrated there from Scotland, while his mother was a local woman. When James was born on 27 October 1728, his family lived in a two-roomed cob cottage in Marton-in-Cleveland, described as 'a few farm houses and cottages, ranged irregularly on the summit of a gentle elevation'.[2] James Senior was sober and industrious, and when he was appointed as bailiff on a farm near Great Ayton, his sons worked alongside him. Young James was clever, so the squire sponsored him at the village school where he learned to read and write, and mastered the rudiments of mathematics. He had no wish to stay in the countryside, however, and after working for a grocer in Staithes, a fishing village tucked in a steep-sided coastal cleft, he was apprenticed in his teens to a Quaker shipowner in the ancient port of Whitby, Captain John Walker, who became his lifelong friend and patron.

Walker sent James to sea as a servant on one of his colliers, the *Freelove*, a flat-bottomed 'cat' with a narrow stern, projecting quarters and a deep waist, a stubby and unglamorous vessel. Over the next nine years Cook sailed on ships of this kind in the North and Baltic Seas, and along the rocky, shoal-strewn eastern coastline of England, learning the practical arts of 'Lead, Latitude and Look-out'. Between voyages he studied navigation and mathematics at night, living in Walker's household, which followed Quaker ideals of plain speaking and living, purity and peacefulness. The Quakers disliked the pomp of the established Church and denounced drunkenness, slavery and excesses of state-sanctioned violence;[3] and during these years Cook was influenced by their values. Under Walker's guidance he worked his way up to the rank of mate until finally he was offered the command of his own vessel. As Walker observed, however, 'he had always an ambition to go into the Navy', and in 1755, at the age of 27, Cook joined the Royal Navy as an able seaman. He was soon promoted to master's mate and fought in several battles during the Seven Years' War, including a bloody engagement in the Channel where his ship the HMS *Eagle* attacked and defeated a French ship at point-blank range, leaving the *Eagle*'s hull riddled with shot, and ten of her crew dead and eighty wounded.

After this engagement, John Walker approached his local MP, seeking Cook's promotion to lieutenant. Although the MP gave his support, Cook's captain on the *Eagle*, Hugh Palliser, a member of the Yorkshire gentry, could not grant the request because Cook had not served the requisite six years in the Navy. Instead, he was promoted to boatswain, then master, the most senior deck-working seaman on board a ship, responsible for boats, rigging and sails, surveying anchorages, rivers and bays, and accurate pilotage and navigation. In 1758 Cook sailed as master of HMS *Pembroke* in a British expeditionary force sent to drive the French out of Canada, where he added surveying to his seafaring skills and helped to chart the St Lawrence river for the attack on Quebec. After Quebec was taken he served on the *Northumberland* under Lord Colville, painstakingly charting the coasts of Nova Scotia and Newfoundland. Lord Colville also had a high regard for Cook, writing to the Admiralty in London, 'From my experience of Mr. Cook's Genius and Capacity, I think him well qualified for the Work he has performed, and for greater Undertakings of the same kind.'[4]

Although Cook had won high praise from his commanders, however, his dream of a naval commission was proving elusive. Like British society itself in the mid-eighteenth century, the Royal Navy was very hierarchical. Its men were finely graded, from the First Lord of the Admiralty through the ranks of admirals, commodores, captains, commanders and lieutenants, to the warrant and petty officers; down through the ratings of able and ordinary seamen. In the Georgian Navy, naval rank usually mirrored social status, for most commissioned officers came from land-owning or professional families, with only 7 per cent from labouring backgrounds. The younger sons of the gentry, unlike their eldest brothers, had to earn a living, and they often entered the Navy because it did not require capital or a university education. Most of these men went to sea very young, about 10 to 14 years old, and while they had to master their trade, they could rely on a network of family and friends to get them ships and positions. If they were successful at sea, there was wealth to be won, especially prize money when enemy ships were captured, and officers contended eagerly for promotion. A high-ranking admiral could become rich and influential, and a member of 'polite society'.

These spoils, however, were usually reserved for the privileged classes. Most sailors and their families belonged to the 'labouring poor',[5] and their poverty (with wages of eleven pounds a year for an ordinary seaman and fourteen pounds a year for an able seaman) kept them in that position. A man who rose from the lower decks to the wardroom had to be gifted and lucky, and his progress was likely to be slow and painful. James Cook, with his labouring background, was no exception – as he wryly noted in the preface to the account of his second Pacific expedition: '[I am] a man, who has not the advantage of Education, acquired, nor Natural abilities for writing; but . . . one who has been constantly at sea from his youth and who, with the Assistance of a few good friends has gone through all the Stations belonging to a Seaman, from a prentice boy in the Coal Trade to a Commander in the Navy.'[6]

In 1762, when Cook was appointed to assist in surveying the coastline of Newfoundland, he was still a warrant officer, but at least his income was improving. On 10 shillings a day, he earned better wages than many lieutenants. Now Cook could marry, and he soon courted and wed Elizabeth Batts, a woman from the outskirts of London, although for the next five years he spent much of his time away from England. He bought a small house at Mile End in Stepney for his growing family, and each winter returned to London where he completed a marvellous set of charts of the Newfoundland coasts, drawn at large scale up to 10 feet long and 5 feet wide, showing shoals, islands, harbours, lakes and rivers in meticulous detail. His work and its links with the contested Newfoundland fisheries brought him to the attention of the First Lord of the Admiralty, Lord Egmont, who discussed his observations with him.

In 1764 Cook was given command of a small schooner, the *Grenville*, to carry on his surveys, suffering his first major accident when a large powder-horn blew up in his hand, leaving a cruel scar that would still be prominent fifteen years later. Cook was now a master of his craft, and in 1766 he carried out astronomical observations of an eclipse of the sun in Newfoundland which were published in the Royal Society's *Philosophical Transactions*. By the time he was finally commissioned as lieutenant and made commander of the *Endeavour* in 1768, Cook was 40 years old, quite old for such a promotion. Perhaps the Admiralty was making a limited investment in this voyage, despite the herculean tasks it had been set. They had made a ship's master lieutenant and given him a Whitby collier to sail around the world, to conduct observations of the 1769 Transit of Venus, and to discover and chart the coastlines of *Terra Australis Incognita*, the Unknown Southern Continent.

Preparations for the *Endeavour* Voyage

At the time of the *Endeavour* voyage, Enlightenment science was in an expansive phase, studying the stars, classifying the earth's plants and animals, and charting its continents and islands. The Pacific Ocean, a vast watery expanse covering more than a third of the earth's surface, was still largely unknown, except for the lands to the west, a scatter of islands across the track of the Spanish galleons, and further south, an enigmatic squiggle representing Abel Tasman's 1642 voyage up the western coastline of New Zealand. The southern, western and northern coasts of Australia had been sketched by Dutch navigators, and some maps included a speculative line across the south Pacific, marking the edge of the fabled continent of 'Terra Australis'.

The Royal Society, an influential body of wealthy patrons and scientists at the forefront of scientific discovery, had a strong interest in maritime exploration, and at one of its gatherings in 1716, the astronomer William Halley urged that when the planet Venus crossed the sun in 1761 and 1769, English scientists should be stationed at different parts of the world to measure its passage. From their observations the distance of the sun from the earth and Venus, and thus the size of the universe, could be calculated, to the great improvement of 'natural knowledge' and navigation. In 1761, at the height of the Seven Years' War, when 120 European scientists set off around the world to observe the Transit of Venus, however, there were only eighteen Englishmen among them.

The astronomers' calculations were inconclusive, and in 1766, after the great victories of the War, the Royal Society was determined that Britain should play a leading role in the 1769 observations. The President, the Earl of Morton, sent a memorial to their patron, King George III, declaring that 'The British Nation have been justly celebrated in the learned world, for their knowledge of Astronomy, in which they are inferior to no Nation upon Earth, Ancient or Modern; and it would cast dishonour upon them should they neglect to have correct observations made of this important phenomenon.'[7] The King agreed, and granted the Society 4000 pounds for its expenses. The Admiralty was commanded to provide a ship and its company to carry the observers to the South Pacific, where the Marquesas Islands and Amsterdam Island (Tongatapu) had been identified as possible locations. The Royal Society suggested Alexander Dalrymple, an employee of the East India Company with a passion for exploration and an obsession with finding Terra Australis, as leader of the expedition. When Dalrymple insisted that he would only go if he could command the ship, however, he

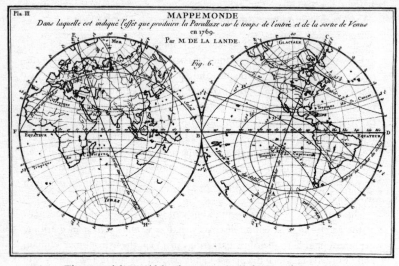

The map of the world for the 1769 transit of Venus observations

was roundly rebuffed by the Admiralty, which declared that his terms were 'totaly repugnant to the regulations of the Navy'.

Meanwhile, the *Earl of Pembroke*, a Whitby-built 'cat' of 370 tons, was purchased by the Navy Board and renamed the *Endeavour*. The ship was sent to the dry dock at Deptford and given an extra skin of boards studded with nails as a matter of 'utmost despatch'. In early May, however, the great merchant seamen's strike broke out, throwing the dockyard into chaos, and the *Endeavour* was left on the stocks for several weeks in the heat, suffering considerable damage. At this time, James Cook was living at his home in Mile End in Stepney, where many of the strike meetings were held, counting his blessings. He had steady, well-paid work, unlike so many other sailors, and was preparing for a new season of surveying in Newfoundland. While he was busy working on his charts, the Admiralty was looking around for a suitable naval officer to command the Royal Society expedition to observe the Transit of Venus in the Pacific. Cook had learned to sail on Whitby cats, his observations of a transit of the sun had recently been published in *Philosophical Transactions*, he was an expert surveyor, he was known to be sensible and discreet, and above all, he was in London and available. The Secretary of the Navy, Philip Stephens, put forward his name for the post, supported by Cook's patron Hugh Palliser, now the commanding officer at Newfoundland. Cook sat and passed his lieutenant's examination, and on 25 May the Lords of the Admiralty sent him his certificate. Cook had got his commission at last, and the *Endeavour* had found her captain.

At the same time, the Royal Society settled on Charles Green, a York-shireman who had assisted two Astronomers Royal at Greenwich, as primary observer for the expedition. Green, a cheerful, dedicated man who had sailed to Barbados to help test John Harrison's chronometer in 1768, seemed ideally suited for the task. On 5 May the Council resolved to appoint him with a gratuity of 200 guineas (and 100 guineas a year extra if the voyage lasted for longer than two years), and Cook, whose observations of a transit of the sun they had recently published, was made second observer with a gratuity of 100 guineas.[8]

The very next day, however, events took a new turn. The *Dolphin* under Captain Samuel Wallis anchored in the Downs after her second circumnavigation of the world, with news of a discovery that decided the *Endeavour*'s destination. Although Wallis's men had been sworn to secrecy, the news soon got out that they had found a marvellous island in the Pacific with high mountains, bright rivers and waterfalls, coral reefs fringed with coconut palms, and with beautiful, amorous women. They had named it 'King George's Island' and fixed its position by astronomical observations, and by good fortune it turned out to be almost at the centre of the area specified by the Astronomer Royal for observing the Transit of Venus. There was a song that the *Dolphin*'s sailors sang about this island in the inns and taverns of London:

> Then we plow'd the South Ocean, such land to discover
> As amongst other nations has made such a pother.
> We found it, my boys, and with joy be it told,
> For beauty such islands you ne'er did behold.
> We've the pleasure ourselves the tidings to bring
> As may welcome us home to our country and King.
>
> For wood, water, fruit, and provision well stor'd
> Such an isle as King George's the world can't afford.
> For to each of these islands great Wallis gave name,
> Which will e'er be recorded in annals of fame.
> We'd the fortune to find them, and homeward to bring
> These tidings as a tribute to country and King.[9]

There were many experienced sailors eager for work and this Paradise in the South Seas, where the Transit of Venus was to be observed, sounded enticing.

❋

Most of the *Endeavour*'s crew were appointed by the Admiralty, rather than by James Cook, who was after all just a brand-new lieutenant. He was allowed a few 'followers' from the *Grenville*, his previous command, but when he protested about being given a one-handed cook, John Thompson, his arguments were summarily overridden. Sensibly enough, the Admiralty assigned six *Dolphin* volunteers to the *Endeavour*, men who had previously sailed across the Pacific. John Gore, 33, an American-born veteran who had twice circumnavigated the world on the *Dolphin*, was appointed the ship's third lieutenant. Charles Clerke, 25, who was made master's mate, had sailed on the *Dolphin*'s first voyage to the Pacific under Byron. He was a high-spirited, amusing young man, fond of practical jokes, who had written a straight-faced account of the 'Giants' in Patagonia and published it in the *Philosophical Transactions*. Molyneux, 22, a master's mate under Wallis who joined the *Endeavour* as her master, was later described by his captain as 'a young man of good parts but had unfortunately given himself up to extravecancy and intemperance which brought on disorders that put a pirod to his life'.[10] Richard Pickersgill, 19, another *Dolphin* veteran, was a cheerful young sailor from Yorkshire who became master's mate and learned to draw good charts on the voyage, although he drank far too much on occasion. Then there was Francis Wilkinson, an AB, and Francis Haite, a carpenter's yeoman. Between them these men had a rich store of memories of 'Otaheite' and Pacific voyaging, and their collective experience helped to shape the *Endeavour* expedition.

Among the other crew, Zachary Hicks, who joined the ship as Cook's second lieutenant, had not sailed in the Pacific before, but he was an experienced, steady officer, although already infected with the tuberculosis that would kill him during the voyage. William Brougham Monkhouse, the ship's surgeon, was a disorganised fellow who drank far too much, but he was well-educated and a superlative observer. There were a few foreign sailors among the crew, including James Magra, another American, who later published an unauthorised account of the voyage, and a number of boys who served as officers' servants. In addition, Cook added his two small sons to the muster-roll, an illegal but time-honoured way of earning boys sea-time while they stayed safely at home. In all, the *Endeavour* ended up with a crew of eighty-five men and boys, including twelve marines, one of whom (Samuel Gibson) later distinguished himself by learning to speak Polynesian languages fluently, and by trying to desert at Tahiti. Most of the sailors on the *Endeavour* were in their twenties, and from labouring backgrounds. James Cook, at the ripe old age of 40, was one of the most experienced men on board, although he had never commanded a crew of any size before, nor sailed on a very long voyage. As a captain who had 'come in through the hawse-hole'[11] (i.e. up from the lower deck), he had no aristocratic 'polish' to bolster his authority. He would have to win the respect of his men by sheer competence and force of personality.

In late July, when the Admiralty formally appointed a wealthy young botanist, Joseph Banks, and his entourage to join the *Endeavour* expedition, the challenges facing Cook became even more formidable.[12] Banks came from the upper reaches of English society, the opposite end of the social spectrum from Cook, and while he was engaging and good-humoured, he could also be haughty and demanding. Banks had been born at Revesby Abbey, a mansion surrounded by hundreds of flat acres of deer-park, woods and gardens on the edge of the Lincolnshire fens, and educated at Harrow and Eton. At Eton he had acquired a passion for botany, avidly collecting plants and learning to describe them. At 17 he went up to Oxford, where the Professor of Botany professed but did not teach the subject, so Banks hired a tutor from Cambridge, who ran a summer course in botany to the great applause of his students. When his father died the next year, Banks inherited estates that yielded 6000 pounds a year, at the upper end of annual incomes in Georgian England. Although his family was not aristocratic, Banks was related by a network of marriages to the Earl of Exeter, the Earl of Chatham, Lord Stanhope of Lincolnshire, and to William Pitt the Younger and William Wyndham Grenville, both of whom became Prime Ministers of Britain.

When he came down from Oxford, Banks met Lord Sandwich (First Lord of the Admiralty 1748–51, 1771–82, and Secretary of State 1763–5, 1770–71), and despite the difference in their ages, they became close friends, going fishing and enjoying women together. Sandwich was a leading light in the Society of Dilettanti and a notorious libertine, a member of the Hellfire Club nicknamed 'Jemmy Twitcher' by the London mobs, and under his tutelage Banks acquired a measure of sexual sophistication. At the same time he pursued his study of natural history, making short botanical trips and spending time at the Chelsea Physic Garden in London with Philip Miller, the chief gardener and friend of the great Swedish naturalist Carl Linnaeus.

Banks also haunted the British Museum, where he met Daniel Solander, a favourite student of Linnaeus's. In 1763 Solander was engaged in cataloguing the Museum's natural history collections by the Linnaean method, and Banks was fascinated by his erudition. When Banks went on his first expedition in 1766, to Labrador and Newfoundland on HMS *Niger*, he got to know William Brougham Monkhouse, surgeon of this ship and later surgeon on the *Endeavour*. During a visit to St Johns in Newfoundland, it is possible that he also briefly met James Cook, who had been surveying the coastline and arrived in the port two days after the *Niger*. By the time he joined the *Endeavour* expedition Banks was 25 years old, an amateur botanist with a growing reputation and a Fellow of the Royal Society.

Just as Alexander Dalrymple was being dismissed from the voyage, Banks became entranced with its prospects. When he was asked whether he intended to travel to Europe, he declared 'Every blockhead does that; my Grand Tour shall be one around the whole globe!' As he later explained to one of his friends, upon reading an account of the *Dolphin*'s first Pacific voyage, 'it immediately occurd to me that it would be a most desirable one for me to Engage in, the Whole tract of the South Seas & I may say all South America is Intirely unknown to a Naturalist, the South at least has Never been visited by any man of Science in any branch of Literature.'[13] And when Banks heard that during the *Dolphin*'s second voyage, on the approach to Tahiti some of Wallis's men claimed to have seen the high, misty mountains of Terra Australis Incognita, 'often talkd of, but neaver before seen by any Europeans', an excursion to the Pacific seemed even more enticing.

Some geographers (including Dalrymple) believed that there must be a great land mass in the south to balance the weight of the northern continents, and in the mid-eighteenth century, the search for this hidden continent had intensified. France hoped to overcome her humiliating defeat in the Seven Years' War by discovering gold and silver and rich trade opportunities in the Great Unknown Southern Continent, while Britain was determined to maintain her maritime and colonial supremacy. It was argued that because gold and silver had been discovered in these latitudes in South America, Terra Australis must be fabulously wealthy. In 1756 Charles de Brosses published a plan for the French exploration and settlement of this great continent, which heralded its likely marvels:

How many people differing among themselves and certainly very dissimilar to us in appearance, manners, customs, ideas, religion. How many animals, fossils and metals. There are doubtless, in all fields, countless of species of which we have not even a notion, since that world has never had any connection with ours and is, so to speak, almost as alien as if it were another planet.[14]

De Brosses suggested that a French expedition of cartographers, astronomers, botanists, painters and surgeons should be sent to explore the coastlines of this last great land mass and document its natural and cultural wonders. The Lords of the Admiralty, however, were determined that Great Britain should claim Terra Australis, not France, and they sent out first Byron (1764–1766) and then Wallis in the *Dolphin* to search for the southern continent, although these expeditions failed to find it. Like the Admiralty, the Royal Society was eager to forestall its French rivals in making such discoveries, and Banks (who had studied de Brosses's plan) was willing to invest some of his personal fortune to ensure that this happened. This was the first major maritime expedition promoted by the Royal Society, and they intended its science to be exemplary.

By early 1768, it seems that Lord Sandwich had successfully pulled strings at the Admiralty, and Banks's dream of joining the *Endeavour* voyage received an official blessing. Over the next few months he assembled a travelling party which included Sydney Parkinson, a serious, well-read young Quaker who had worked as a botanical draughtsman on his Newfoundland collection; Alexander Buchan, a skilled landscape artist but also an epileptic; two young footmen from Revesby, two black servants, and Nicholas Young, a boy who later made the first sighting of the east coast of New Zealand. At a dinner held in London, when the company began to talk about the scientific fame to be won on the expedition, Daniel Solander leaped to his feet and proposed to join Banks's party. His botanical skills were augmented by those of Herman Diedrich Spöring, his clerk, a good naturalist and instrument-maker. As Banks and Solander assembled their equipment and supplies for the voyage, their peers watched with awe and some envy. Another Fellow of the Royal Society reported to Linnaeus:

No people ever went to sea better fitted out for the purpose of Natural History. They have got a fine library of Natural History: they have all sorts of machines for catching and preserving insects; all kinds of nets, trawls, drags and hooks for coral fishing, they have even a curious contrivance of a telescope, by which, put into the water, you can see the bottom at a great depth, when it is clear . . . In short Solander assured me this expedition would cost Mr Banks 10,000 pounds.[15]

While Banks was making these preparations, Cook was getting the *Endeavour* ready for her long voyage. When he received his formal appointment to the ship in May 1768, and his Admiralty instructions two months later, he must have felt a sense of achievement and exhilaration. The first set of instructions ordered him to proceed to Tahiti in the *Endeavour* to observe the Transit of Venus, while the second set ordered him to search for the Great Unknown Southern Continent:

SECRET

Whereas there is reason to imagine that a Continent or Land of great extent, may be found to the Southward of the Tract lately made by Captn Wallis in His Majesty's Ship the Dolphin (of which you will herewith receive a Copy) . . .

You are to proceed to the southward in order to make discovery of the Continent above-mentioned until you arrive in the Latitude of 40 degrees unless you sooner fall in with it. But not having discover'd it or any Evident signs of it in that Run, you are to proceed in search of it to the Westward between the Latitude before mentioned and the Latitude of 35 degrees until you discover it, or fall in with the Eastern side of the Land discover'd by Tasman and now called New Zeland.[16]

According to these instructions, Cook was to explore the coasts of Terra Australis, and, failing that, of New Zealand; to describe the soil, animals and birds, fish, mineral resources and flora; to cultivate a friendship with the inhabitants and observe their 'Genius, Temper, Disposition and Number'. He must gain their consent for possession to be taken of convenient situations in the country for King George III of Great Britain. All logbooks and journals were to be collected at the end of the voyage and sealed for delivery to the Admiralty. None of the crew was permitted to discuss the voyage with anyone until they were given permission to do so.

Over the next three months, Cook's years of experience as a master proved invaluable. Miracles of refurbishment and stowage were performed on the ship as her crew was assembled. The *Endeavour* was a small ship, only 106 feet long and 29 feet wide, and such 'cats' were usually managed by crews of about twenty sailors.[17] As plans for the voyage evolved, extra men were added to her crew until it reached a grand total of eighty-five. A new Lower Deck was built for the sailors and marines, and small cabins were constructed below the Quarter Deck for the officers. When Green and his servant, and Banks and his entourage were added to the contingent, the ship's internal layout had to be altered again. The Great Cabin, which would normally have been Cook's private preserve, became the working place for Banks's party, and they took over the officers' cabins. The officers were shifted to cabins aft on the new lower deck, so that the usual patterns of authority on board were disrupted. In the hold, room was found for Banks's equipment and supplies, although it was already jam-packed with spare anchors, cork jackets, swivel guns, carriage guns and ammunition, astronomical instruments, tiers of water casks, tools, 'trifles' for the natives, ready-made clothes and supplies for 18 months at sea – 21,000 pounds of bread in bags, 13,000 pounds of bread in butts, 9000 pounds of flour in barrels, 1200 gallons of beer in puncheons, 4000 pieces of beef in casks, 6000 pieces of pork in ditto, brandy and arrack, suet and raisins, malt in hogsheads, pease in butts, oatmeal and wheat, mustard seed, oil, sugar and vinegar, and various kinds of anti-scorbutics for experimental use during the voyage.

Many captains would have resented the loss of the Great Cabin, and the requirement to share so small a ship with so many civilians. Cook had just

The sailors' farewell, by Thomas Rowlandson

won his first command as a commissioned officer, however, and he was in no mood to quibble. In his youth he had learned to defer to the gentry, and Banks was a wealthy young scion of the ruling elite with 'interest' and patronage at his disposal. Furthermore, his presence gave an added cachet to the voyage, assuring an influential audience for its achievements. On 14 August, when Cook arrived in Plymouth on the *Endeavour*, he sent an express message to London telling Banks and Solander to come there directly. When Banks received the message the next day he was at the opera with a young lady, Harriet Blosset, who according to the gossips was desperately in love with him. Banks drank heavily that evening to disguise his emotions,[18] but the next day he and Solander left London in tearing high spirits, and travelled to Plymouth to join the *Endeavour*. There were all kinds of last-minute arrangements to complete, the weather was foul and the sailors had their own ardent farewells to make, but on 26 August 1768, Cook wrote this laconic entry in his journal:

At 2pm got under sail and put to sea having on board 94 persons including Officers, Seamen Gentlemen and their servants, near 18 months provisions, 10 carriage guns 12 swivels with a good store of Ammunition and stores of all kinds.

On a fresh, breezy day, under a cloudy sky, the *Endeavour* sailed from Plymouth at last, bound for the South Seas and Tahiti.

4

High Priest of 'Oro

Tahiti, the *Endeavour*'s destination, is a jewel of a tropical island – jagged volcanic mountains of black rock rising out of a blue-green sea, waterfalls tumbling through forests of flowering and fruiting trees, bright birds flying across the clearings – a world away from Yorkshire and London. The island is edged by a rim of flat land dotted with clusters of thatched houses, groves of coconut palms and large, twisted trees, and encircled by lagoons where brilliant fish dart through the water. These lagoons are protected by a ring of coral reefs, where the wild, spraying surf thunders during stormy weather. The first voyagers to the island took their canoes through gaps in this reef where freshwater rivers run out to the sea, and opposite these gaps they built *marae*, stone temples to their ancestors.

The remote forbears of the islanders left Taiwan about five thousand years ago, sailing eastwards across the Pacific. In a wave of migrations they had settled one island after another, finally reaching West Polynesia by about 950 BC. Their long-range voyaging into Polynesia, based on sophisticated craft and navigational expertise, preceded the Viking oceanic explorations out of Europe by about two thousand years.[1] After a period in West Polynesia (the islands around Tonga and Samoa), they began to explore East Polynesia (including the Cooks, the Austral Islands, the Society, Tuamotu and Marquesas archipelagos), where by AD 800 a network of communities linked by inter-island voyaging were flourishing.[2] From there, expeditions sailed to Hawai'i to the north, Easter Island in the east, and New Zealand to the south, the extremities of the so-called 'Polynesian Triangle'.

Until recently details of their navigational techniques were obscure, because most European explorers lacked the linguistic expertise to discuss these matters with island navigators. The surviving evidence and modern experiment, however, indicate that these voyagers marked out familiar seas by 'sea-paths' between known features, located under a series of named horizon stars which rose or set over given destinations. Navigators took back bearings from landmarks as they set off on a voyage, orientating themselves by a 'star compass' at night, and by the sun during the daytime. Prevailing winds and particular swells with their deflection patterns off particular islands were also identified, and these, together with land clouds and reflections from the land, the flight paths of land-roosting birds at dawn and dusk, land debris floating on the sea and patterns of underwater luminescence streaking out from islands, helped to expand identifiable targets at sea by a radius of perhaps twelve to thirty miles.

Voyages of exploration were often sailed upwind or using wind shifts, allowing a safe and rapid downwind journey home. In unfamiliar waters a skilled navigator could recognise and name new swells by studying the sea hour after hour, and the star-path (or succession of guiding stars), the wind and current patterns and numerous other items of navigational information were memorised for the return voyage. During such expeditions the navigator slept as little as possible, ceaselessly scanning the sea and the night sky and keeping watch for land clouds and homing birds. It was said that you could always recognise a star navigator by his bloodshot eyes.[3]

According to early Tahitian accounts, these navigators saw the Pacific Ocean as a vast watery plain, joined around the edges of the horizon by the layered spheres of the sky, which encircled its clusters of known islands. It was also a marae, a sacred place where people went to cleanse themselves in times of spiritual trouble. The islands were fixed on Te Tumu, the 'rock of foundation', and below this rock and beyond the tiered arch of the sky was Te Po, a cosmic darkness inhabited by gods and ancestors. When the world began, a generative source produced Te Po, and then space, the shooting stars and the moon were created, and the sun and comets. As the star ancestors emerged one by one they sailed in canoes across the sky, and on their voyages of exploration, new stars were created. A star god eventually created 'the kings of the chiefs of the earth . . . and the chiefs in the skies', each with their own star, whose boundaries were marked by a marae, a great stone temple. The arched heavens were supported by star-pillars between sky and earth, and some of the carved boards on marae represented the stars which stood above them. Thus when Tahitian navigators sailed from a marae at the edge of the land, they were retracing the sky voyages of their star ancestors.[4]

It is not surprising, therefore, that Polynesian voyaging was closely linked with the ancestor gods. At the time of the first European arrival in Tahiti in 1767, the Society Islands were in an uproar, because the worship of a great war-god, 'Oro, was being carried from island to island. 'Oro demanded human sacrifices, and his marae were dark, awesome places, associated with Te Po and regarded with dread and terror. 'Oro's temple, Taputapuatea, stood in the district of Opoa on Ra'iatea, an island which had emerged at

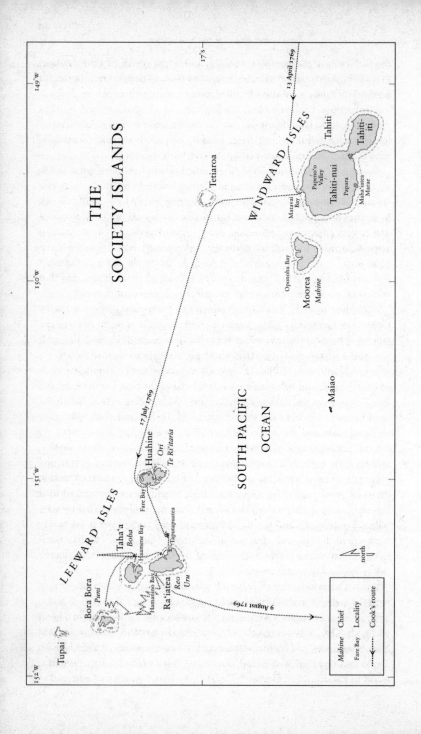

THE
SOCIETY ISLANDS

WINDWARD ISLES

13 April 1769

Tetiaroa

Tahiti

Papeno'o
Valley

Matavai
Bay

Tahiti-nui   Tahiti-
iti

Papara

O
Maha'iatea
Marae

Moorea

Mahine

Oponohu Bay

LEEWARD ISLES

17 July 1769

Tupai

Bora Bora
Puni

Taha'a
Boba

Haamene Bay

Huahine

Ori
Te Ri'itaria

Fare Bay

Hamanino Bay

Ra'iatea

Reo
Uru

Taputapuatea

Maiao

SOUTH PACIFIC
OCEAN

9 August 1769

north

Mahine	Chief
Fare Bay	Locality
....	Cook's route

17°S

149 W   150 W   151 W   152 W

the beginning of the cosmos. Ra'iatea was also called Havai'i, the homeland, the place from which the other Society Islands had been settled. According to an early European visitor to the island:

[At Taputapuatea] human victims, ready slain, were sent [from every shore] to be offered on the altar of Oro, the god of war, whose principal image was worshipped here . . . Opoa was also the residence of the kings of this island, who, besides the prerogatives of royalty, enjoyed divine honors, and were in fact living idols among the dead ones, being deified at the time of their accession to political supremacy here. These sovereigns (who always took the name of Tamatoa) were wont to receive presents from the kings and chiefs of adjacent and distant islands, whose gods were also considered tributary to the Oro of Raiatea, and their princes owing homage to its monarch, who was Oro's hereditary high priest, as well as an independent divinity himself.[5]

The navigators who carried the worship of 'Oro to other islands were members of the *arioi*, an exclusive society of priests, voyagers, warriors, orators and famed lovers dedicated to 'Oro. Among the arioi were artists who tattooed, painted bark-cloth and performed music, dance and drama on their expeditions from island to island. Although many of their songs and dances were bloodthirsty, others graphically extolled the delights of sexual pleasure (although members of this society were not permitted to have children). Only attractive, gifted men and women could become arioi, and their ranks were marked by the clothing they wore and the tattoo patterns on their bodies.

The highest grade of arioi were singled out by red bark-cloth garments and their black tattooed legs, and these men and women enjoyed great influence and a privileged lifestyle. Large houses were built to accommodate them on their travels, and feasts were staged for their entertainment. They were lavished with gifts, presented with bed-companions and took what they wanted. On their expeditions, a fleet of canoes assembled, and travelled under 'Oro's protection to other islands.[6] The missionary William Ellis, who lived in the archipelago during the early nineteenth century, gave a vivid description of the arrival of an arioi flotilla:

[The canoes] advanced towards the land, with their streamers floating in the wind, their drums and flutes sounding, and the Areois, attended by their chief, who acted as their prompter, appeared on a stage erected for the purpose, with their wild distortions of person, antic gestures, painted bodies, and vociferated songs, mingling with the sound of the drum and the flute, the dashing of the sea, and the rolling and breaking of the surf . . . the whole . . . presented a ludicrous imposing spectacle.[7]

On this occasion they came to entertain the locals, but when the arioi travelled en masse to the ceremonies at Taputapuatea, their fleets of large, carved canoes carried images of the gods, and pairs of dead men and fish (including sharks and turtles) lay on their prows as sacrifices for 'Oro. As they landed at the marae, drums and conch trumpets sounded, and the bodies of 'Oro's sacrificial victims were hung in trees by ropes strung through their heads, or laid as rollers under the keels of the sacred canoes as they were dragged up the beaches.

The great temple of Taputapuatea still stands on the beach at Opoa. The site is dominated by the ruins of the main marae – an oblong pile of tumbled rocks edged by huge upright slabs, with ferns and trees growing between them. A wide pavement with a few upright stones lies in front of this structure, surrounded by a scatter of smaller marae along the shoreline, where the sandy soil is pockmarked by the burrows of coconut crabs. On a small huddle of rocks nearby, backed by a fan-shaped stone slab, a new generation of island voyagers have placed tributes of shell necklaces, anchor stones braided with sinnet rope, and stones from their home islands. On another stone pavement, next to the sea, a red-pillared sacrificial platform carries a sun-dried offering of bananas and yams; while a third pavement at the water's edge is dedicated to the navigators. Although the trees that once hid the marae in dark secrecy have been removed, Taputapuatea is still an eerie place, echoing with its memories of royal high priests and the ceremonies dedicated to 'Oro.

According to Society Island traditions, by the mid-eighteenth century Taputapuatea had become the centre of a great voyaging network which reached across the archipelago, south to the Cook and Austral Islands, north to the Marquesas and east to the Tuamotus; a history which powerfully shaped the way that the Tahitians reacted when Captain Wallis and the *Dolphin* arrived, and how they received Captain Cook shortly afterwards. High priest navigators from Opoa, it is said, established a 'Friendly Alliance' between these far-flung islands, and periodically they met at Taputapuatea. Long-range voyaging in Eastern Polynesia had been commonplace during the early settlement period, and although such journeys were now infrequent, the arioi still had the means and the motivation to travel.[8] Around 1740, the island of Tahiti joined the 'Alliance' when a high-ranking arioi named Mahi carried the worship of 'Oro to the south end of the island.[9] He was followed twenty years later by another arioi, the high priest-navigator Tupaia, who carried an image of 'Oro from Ra'iatea to the district of Papara, on the west side of Tahiti.[10] Tupaia is an important figure in our story, for in later years he would sail across the Pacific with Captain

Cook on the *Endeavour*, guiding the expedition through the Society Islands and around the coastline of New Zealand. He was a leading arioi, born in about 1725 to a high-ranking Ra'iatean family, and in his youth he had travelled to other island groups on arioi expeditions.[11] As he grew older Tupaia became a priest of 'Oro, playing a significant role in affairs of state on his home island.

In about 1740 there was a battle in Tahiti, and some of the defeated fled to Ra'iatea. One of these women, a sister of the high chief of Papara (a man named Amo), married the high chief of Opoa, Ari'i Ma'o (the Shark King), and they had a son. In the 1750s, however, there was a series of attacks on Ra'iatea by warriors from Borabora, and Ari'i Ma'o was killed. When the Boraborans finally occupied the island, his son decided to return to his mother's lands at Papara, on the west side of Tahiti. His family approved of this plan, and a feathered girdle and an image of 'Oro were made and consecrated. Tupaia (who had lost his lands in the Borabora conquest) was put in charge of the sacred relics, and in about 1760 he took the young high chief, the red feather girdle and the image of 'Oro on the god's sacred canoe, and carried them off to Tahiti. When the image and the girdle were installed on the marae at Papara, Tupaia became the high priest of 'Oro in the district. He joined the local arioi, and later became lover to Purea, Amo's wife, a high-born woman who was related to many of the chiefs of Tahiti and Ra'iatea.[12] He acted as counsellor and strategist for Purea and her family; and in 1767, when the *Dolphin* brought the first Europeans to the island, they described Tupaia as Purea's 'right-hand man'; and Purea as the 'Queen' of Tahiti.[13]

The arrival of HMS *Dolphin* in Tahiti, which heralded Cook's *Endeavour*, had been foretold by one of the priests at Taputapuatea. During the Borabora invasion of Ra'iatea, marauding warriors went to the marae where they chopped down one of the great trees which guarded its secrets. Distraught at this desecration a priest named Vaita entered a trance, and announced that a new kind of people were coming to the island:

> The glorious offspring of Te Tumu
> will come and see this forest at Taputapuatea.
> Their body is different, our body is different
> We are one species only from Te Tumu.
> And this land will be taken by them
> The old rules will be destroyed
> And sacred birds of the land and the sea

Will also arrive here, will come and lament
Over that which this lopped tree has to teach
They are coming up on a canoe without an outrigger.[14]

Such a prophecy was too ominous to be ignored, and in June 1767, when the *Dolphin* – a 'canoe without an outrigger' – appeared off the coast of Tahiti, many of those who saw it remembered Vaita's vision.[15] As he had foretold, the European 'discovery' of Tahiti would change life on the island forever, shaping all future encounters between the islanders and 'the glorious offspring of Te Tumu', including their subsequent meetings with Cook's men on the *Endeavour*.

It began with a moment of pure bewilderment. On the evening of 18 June, the *Dolphin*'s crew saw 'a great high mountain' covered with clouds to the south of their ship, and rejoiced, thinking they were the first Europeans to discover the Unknown Southern Continent. The next morning when they approached the south-east extremity of Tahiti, a thick bank of fog shrouded the vessel. As it lifted, the sailors were astonished to find the ship surrounded by a hundred or more canoes, their crews 'hallowing and Hooting' and gazing at them in amazement. The Tahitians held up branches of plantain (representations of human bodies as sacrificial offerings), and after a long, perplexed discussion, a priest made a speech and threw his branch into the ocean. One young man climbed up the mizzen chains onto the *Dolphin* and jumped up on the awning, where he stood staring and laughing. More canoes came out, more speeches were made and more plantain branches were thrown into the water.

After these ceremonies of peacemaking, a number of people climbed on board the *Dolphin*, including a 'Stout & a noble looking Man', who seemed to be a chief, talking loudly and gesturing in an effort to communicate with the Europeans. The sailors did not understand a word, but held up cloth, knives, beads and ribbons, and produced hogs and fowl, grunting like pigs and crowing like cocks to indicate what they wanted. The Tahitians did not seem surprised by this since they had pigs and chickens on shore, and imitated these noises, but when sheep and goats were produced and a billy-goat butted one of them in the haunches, they leaped overboard in terror.

These visitors were avidly eager for iron, and despite their fear they soon climbed back on board, where they grasped eagerly at the nails they were offered and tore at stanchions and ring-bolts, trying to take them. As Tupaia would later tell Cook's men, a European ship had been wrecked on a nearby island some years earlier (one of Roggeveen's vessels, wrecked in the Tuamotus in 1722), and iron from the wreck had been salvaged and sent to

Tahiti, where the Tahitians soon learned its uses. When the sailors stopped them from taking iron objects from the ship, the people in the canoes grew 'surly' and began to threaten them, so Captain Wallis ordered a nine-pounder fired over their heads to deter them from attacking the vessel, and his visitors leaped overboard again (although one man managed to seize a midshipman's gold-laced hat before jumping off the taffrail into the ocean).

The *Dolphin* now stood out to sea while the canoes paddled back to shore, their crews smarting from this encounter. That afternoon the ship's cutter went in to sound a nearby bay, where it was surrounded by another large fleet. The officers on the ship fired a nine-pounder, signalling the cutter to return; but when it tried to come back to the ship the canoes paddled to cut it off, pelting its crew with large stones and hurting several of the sailors. John Gore, a master's mate who would later sail with Cook, fired his musket in reply, wounding a warrior in the shoulder who dived into the sea with his comrades, and driving the canoes back to shore in consternation. That afternoon as the *Dolphin* sailed south along the eastern coastline of Tahiti, the sailors exclaimed at the beauty of the island. Thousands of men, women and children stood lined up along the beaches, staring at them in amazement. As William Robertson, master of the *Dolphin*, wrote that night:

We saw the whole coast full of Canoes, and the country had the most Beautiful appearance it's possible to Imagine. From the shore side, one two and three miles Back, there is a fine Level country that appears to be all laid out in plantations, and the regular-built Houses seem to be without number; all along the Coast, they appeared like long Farmer's Barns, and seemed to be all very neatly thatched, with Great Numbers of Cocoa-Nut Trees ... This appears to be the most populous country I ever saw, the whole shore-line was lined with men, women and children all the way that we sailed along.[16]

The *Dolphin* stood on and off the island, and the following afternoon as the ship approached the large and deep valley of Papeno'o on the north-east coast, they saw canoes sailing very fast along the coast to warn their neighbours about the imminent arrival of this strange vessel. The next morning off the mouth of the Papeno'o River, another huge crowd gathered. Wallis sent in the boats at daybreak to take soundings, and they soon found a safe anchorage for the *Dolphin* on clean, sandy ground. Canoes came out to barter pigs, chickens, plantains, coconuts, yams, sugar cane and mangoes for nails, old iron and trinkets. After some peaceful exchanges, disputes broke out in which several sailors were struck by angry Tahitians. When the ship's boats, filled with armed marines and sailors, were sent to take soundings along the coast, they were pursued by large sailing canoes, their crews hooting and yelling.

On the beaches people beckoned to the sailors, who mistook this for an invitation to come ashore, although in Tahiti this was a gesture of dismissal. As the boats continued sounding along the coastline hundreds of large and small canoes gathered around them, and then suddenly three large canoes rammed the cutter, carrying off a spar and tearing the mizzen sail, while others attacked the barge in a concerted manoeuvre. The crew of the cutter fired two muskets over the warriors' heads but they just laughed, so they fended them off with their bayonets and picks while the marines on the barge fired at their attackers, wounding one man and killing another. When the people in his canoe tried to make this man stand or sit upright, they discovered that he was stone-dead, killed by these mysterious weapons. As Robertson recorded:

They now understood the use of Musketry and made signs that we had killed two of their partners. The way they took to make us understand them was this; they called loudly bonbon, then smote their breast and foreheads and laid backward with their eyes fixed and without motion.[17]

According to Tahitian histories, some of these people decided that the *Dolphin* was Vaita's 'canoe without an outrigger', which had burst through their sky from Te Po. Others thought that this was a sacred island, drifting along their coastline.[18] When they saw the red-coated marines sighting down the barrels of their muskets, they thought that the strangers were blowing into their weapons, and thus they called the muskets *pupuhi roa*, breath which killed at a distance.[19]

Over the next few days there were repeated confrontations with the Tahitian warriors, as the *Dolphin*'s men looked for an anchorage off the island. Both Captain Wallis and his first lieutenant were stricken with stomach disorders and could hardly crawl about the ship, while at least thirty of the sailors were confined to their hammocks in the late stages of scurvy, limbs ulcerated, gums bleeding, breath putrid and stinking. Although the sight of them would not have impressed the Tahitians, the men were all desperate to get ashore, to obtain fresh food and water. On 22 June, John Gore was sent with the ship's boats to try and persuade the Tahitians to fill water barrels at a nearby river. In the morning some of them swam out to the boats, bringing water in large bamboos and calabashes for the sailors, but in the afternoon when Gore sent some barrels ashore, offering nails and iron hoops if the local people would fill them with fresh water, they refused to co-operate and kept two of the casks. Gore fired a musketoon (a large, bell-mouthed firearm) into the sea in an attempt to frighten them into doing what he wanted, but they only laughed at him. After this some beautiful young girls were brought to the waterside where they played 'a great many droll wanton tricks' to divert and entice the sailors, and when Gore ordered his men to row back to the ship instead of going ashore, the girls pelted them with fruit and yelled in derision.

On 23 June, as the *Dolphin* approached 'Port Royal' (Matavai) Bay to the north with the boats sounding out ahead, looking for a safe place to anchor, they were surrounded by a milling crowd of hundreds of canoes. In the confusion, the officers misread the signals from the boats and grounded the ship on a rock, to the huge delight of the Tahitians. After several futile efforts to free the vessel, the *Dolphin*'s sails were turned to an offshore wind which carried her safely out to sea, to the 'Unspeakable Joy' of the sailors. Later that afternoon when they returned to anchor in Matavai Bay, Wallis put his crew on alert, dividing them into four armed watches and ordering them to load and prime all of the ship's weapons. His precautions were timely, for as soon as the *Dolphin* was at anchor, the Tahitians decided to try and capture the vessel.

Very early the next morning as the sailors warped the ship up the harbour, chanting and heaving on the capstan, hundreds of canoes came out to watch. Soon a fleet of 500 canoes, carrying about four thousand people and led by 'the King of the Island' sitting on a canopy in a large double canoe about fifty feet long, surrounded the vessel. This was probably the sacred high chief of the district, borne upon the platform of the sacred canoe which carried the gods into battle.[20] Conches and flutes were played, and men sang in hoarse voices, while some of them tried to haul up the ship's stream anchor. The large canoe approached the side of the *Dolphin*, where their leader handed up a bunch of red and yellow feathers (a way of summoning the gods to battle) to Captain Wallis. As some canoes paddled through the fleet, distributing stones to those who had none, other canoes came out with women lined up on their platforms who postured provocatively, exposing their genitals to the sailors. This performance was at once a diversion and an outrageous challenge. When the women stood in this way, exposing the dark passage through which all men are born from Te Po (the realm of spirits and the dead), they were suggesting that their enemies would soon be back in Te Po, the victims of battle, while inciting their own gods to action.[21]

Such subtle implications, however, were wasted on Wallis's men, who had seen no women for months. They crowded on the decks, watching avidly. As Wilkinson remarked, 'As our men is in good Health & Spirits

*Matavai Bay in Tahiti, with an arioi warrior-priest on a sacred
canoe, by William Hodges*

and begin to feel the Good Effect of the fresh Pork we T[h]ank God for it.
It is Not to be wondred that their Attention Should be Drawn to A Sight so
Uncommon to them Especially as their woman are so well Proportisned.'[22]
While the crew of the *Dolphin* were thus preoccupied, the large canoe
withdrew to a safe distance where the high priest made a signal by waving
a coconut branch around his head. The warriors let out a 'strange kind of
Hallow', and the sailors were caught unawares as a barrage of rocks flew at
them from all sides, hurled by warriors with slingshots.

In a fury the sailors ran to their guns – and muskets, deck guns loaded
with smallshot, cannons loaded with round- and grapeshot were fired into
the canoes, tossing their crews into the water and sending out a lethal spray
of splinters. As the surviving canoes rushed to rescue their comrades, the
sailors turned their guns on the shore where great crowds had gathered on
the hillsides and beaches, causing havoc and killing many people. When
Wallis ordered a pause in the firing, the 'King of the Island' hoisted white
streamers on his great canoe to rally the fleet. A large number of canoes
paddled back to the ship's stern where they were fired on again, and the
great canoe was cut in half by a cannon-ball as grapeshot swept through
its crew, hurling shattered bodies into the bloodstained water. Later that
afternoon, while the sailors carried on sounding the bay, a woman's body

floated past the ship with a shot through her belly. Robertson wrote in his journal that night:

How terrible must they be shocked, to see their nearest and dearest of friends Dead, and torn to pieces in such a matter as I am certain they never beheld before. To Attempt to say what these poor Ignorant creatures thought of us, would be taking more upon me than I am able to perform.[23]

The next day, the local people seemed chastened, and frightened. A few of them came out to the *Dolphin* in a 'solemn procession', carrying plantain branches, and tried to make peace with the British. When one of their number made a long speech, they listened in a subdued fashion and then threw their branches into the sea, looking beseechingly at the sailors.

According to Robertson, his messmates thought that they were now regarded 'as Demi-gods, come to punish them for their past transgressions'. The sailors behaved haughtily towards the Tahitians, allowing only two or three to come alongside at any one time. Indeed, many of the local people had probably decided that the European ship was associated with 'Oro, the great war god, for all the signs pointed in that direction. Thunder and lightning were the signs of his power, and human sacrifices were his tribute. When the *Dolphin* – the canoe without an outrigger – arrived in Matavai Bay, there had been loud noises, clouds of smoke and brilliant flashes of light, and many people were torn to pieces. Red was 'Oro's colour, a sign of his presence; and the *Dolphin*'s marines wore scarlet coats, just as the arioi wore red bark-cloth garments and the high chiefs wore the *maro 'ura*, the red feather girdle. This great frigate, with its thunder and lightning, and its red-painted gun carriages and striped sides, must have seemed a strange version of 'Oro's sacred canoe, the 'Rainbow'.

That afternoon, Wallis sent an armed party to 'take possession' of the island. They landed at Matavai Bay, where the red-jacketed marines went through their drill and Lieutenant Tobias Furneaux turned a sod, renaming Tahiti 'King George the Third's Island' and claiming it for Great Britain. As the sailors hoisted a pennant of red bunting and drank grog in honour of the occasion, a large crowd of Tahitians gathered on the opposite side of the river, holding up plantain branches. Furneaux beckoned to two old men, and when one of them crept across the river on his hands and knees (a sign of obeisance), bearing gifts of a small pig and a plantain bough, Furneaux gave him a return gift of hatchets, nails and toys. As the armed party rowed back to the ship, they saw this white-bearded old man dancing around the red pennant. He was soon joined by other people who crowded around the pole, laying down their green branches; but when a breeze blew up and the pennant snapped over their heads, they panicked and scattered.

At dusk more people gathered around the flag, kneeling on one knee as they approached it, although one man threw a stone at it. An offering of two large pigs and more plantain branches was placed at the foot of the pole and then carried out to the ship, where the old man presented these gifts to the sailors. As he returned to the beach the red pennant was ceremoniously lowered and carried away, while conches, drums and flutes sounded and fires flared up along the coastline. The next morning a crowd of about four thousand people paraded with the red banner flying above their heads, and surrounded the ship's boats at the watering-place. Fearing that his men were about to be attacked again, Wallis ordered the ship's guns to be fired, killing many more people, and sent the ship's carpenters ashore with their axes to destroy all the canoes hauled up on the beaches.

From that time on, the power of Wallis and his men was no longer seriously challenged. That afternoon a large crowd of men and women, one man wading in the sea up to the waist and carrying a child in his arms, appeared at the watering-place. They carried green boughs which they stuck in the sand, and then returned with eight large hogs, four pigs, a dozen chickens, fruit, bales of bark-cloth, and two fat dogs with their forefeet trussed above their heads, which they presented as a peace offering to Lieutenant Furneaux.[24] The sailors took the pigs, chicken and fruit, and put down hatchets and nails in return, but freed the dogs and left the cloth lying there. The Tahitians seemed unhappy about this, and it was not until the sailors carried the bales of cloth out to the ship that they would accept the gifts laid down by the British. Some old men now hustled a group of young women (although these did not include women of high rank) onto the beach and made them stand in a line, offering them to the sailors with graphic gestures. Arioi warriors were sexually voracious, and it seems that the *Dolphin*'s men were being treated as conquerors. Although some of the women were reluctant and afraid, the sailors were in no mood to wait, and one Irish marine, determined to take 'the Honour of having the first', fornicated with a woman on the beach in front of his shipmates. Although they later thrashed him for this shameless behaviour, they also slept with the women under trees and behind the houses. From this time on, the sailors were all 'mad for the shore', leaving the ship at every opportunity.

The impression that the *Dolphin*'s men, like the arioi, were closely linked with the gods must have been reinforced by a strange episode on 5 July, when some of the sailors caught a large female shark and shot it in the head with their muskets. For some reason, they decided to tow this shark ashore,

and left it on the beach at the watering-place. They had no idea that the
Teva people (who included the Papara clans) claimed descent from a Shark
God, who had slept with the wife of a high chief while he was away collecting red feathers for his son's feather girdle.[25] This circumstance probably
explains the local reaction to the creature, however, which Robertson
observed from the *Dolphin* through his spyglass:

The Natives assembled in a great body near where the Shark was lying ... They
made the first stop at about twenty yards distance, and then advanced at a very slow
pace until they came within about ten yards of her, then stopped a long time, until
several of them went up for Green boughs to make peace with this Sea Monster.
When they came down with the Green Boughs, two of them stepped up to the dead
creature very slowly, and laid down the Green boughs at its head and started back
some paces, where they stood some minutes, and made some sort of speech and
looked very steadfastly on the dead shark ... This ceremony of making peace with
this Sea Monster continued near an hour.[26]

Some days after this performance, a fleet of very large canoes arrived in the
bay, flying coloured streamers, and soon a tall, fine-looking woman named
Purea whom the British quickly dubbed the 'queen' of the island, appeared
on the scene for the first time with her 'right-hand man' Tupaia. As we
noted earlier, Tupaia was the high priest who had brought the 'Oro cult to
Tahiti, while Purea, a high-born woman with a 'most majestic bearing', was
the former wife of Amo (a fellow arioi and high chief of the district of
Papara). In about 1762 Purea had given birth to a son, but refused to kill
the child as the rules of the arioi dictated. Such a child assumed the titles
and status of both of his parents as soon as he was born, and Amo had been
infuriated by his wife's decision. He fell out with Purea, and when they were
both stripped of their rank as 'black leg' arioi (the highest grade in the
society), he left her. After Purea took Tupaia as her lover she and Amo
became friends again, transferring their ambitions to their son and seeking
to set him up as the paramount chief of the island.

By the time Wallis arrived at Tahiti in 1767, Amo, Purea and Tupaia were
building a great marae at Papara on the west coast of Tahiti, as the centre
of 'Oro worship on the island. Human sacrifices (five to ten from each
district) had been buried beneath its foundations, and the stone walls were
slowly rising.[27] Tupaia already held the red feather girdle and the red feather
image of 'Oro from Ra'iatea in his possession, and it is said that the
Dolphin's red pennant was also taken to this marae. This was a matter of
great ritual importance, for the Tahitians thought that this flag was imbued
with the power of the strangers' gods, just as the red feather girdles of their

high chiefs were imbued with the mana of 'Oro. Now that the power of the gods of the Europeans and the gods of the archipelago had been joined, Purea, Amo and Tupaia hoped to make their new temple the ruling marae of the island.

Certainly, Purea seemed to feel a particular affinity with the British, and she showered them with gifts and attention. Her favourites included Captain Wallis; the ship's gunner, William Harrison; the red-coated Sergeant of Marines; and the *Dolphin*'s sailing master, George Robertson. When Purea first came out to the ship on 11 July she gave the gunner a gift of several large pigs, and Captain Wallis presented her with a looking glass, ribbons, beads and a long blue mantle tied with ribbons. Seeing that Wallis was ill, Purea urged him to visit the arioi house where she was staying. When he came ashore the next day, she ordered her servants to carry him across the river to the house (which Wallis described as 327 feet long and 42 feet wide, with fourteen pillars, several of them finely carved), where she made her people kiss his hand, commanded four young girls to massage his body and legs to ease his pain, presented him with a pregnant sow, and dressed him and his companions in bark-cloth garments. It was probably because Wallis and many of his men were so ill when they arrived at Tahiti that local people thought their white skin might be a symptom of some strange disease.[28] They were also amazed at their boots and trousers, and when the ship's doctor took off his wig in this house to cool himself on this occasion, the crowd gasped in astonishment.

After this visit Purea came out to the ship several times, examining its layout with close attention. On one occasion when Robertson escorted her to the Great Cabin she squeezed his leg muscles, inspecting his thighs and arms to see if they were tattooed and showing great surprise when she found that his chest was hairy. She also examined various items of equipment on board the ship, paying particular attention to the spit and coppers in the galley. When Tupaia joined her for one of these visits, he prayed to his gods and made a solemn offering of bread before he would eat with the British; although Purea would never eat or drink on the vessel.

In return for their hospitality, Purea entertained Wallis and his men ashore, and during one of these visits she tied a plaited necklace of her own hair around Wallis's neck, gave him fine mats, put a bunch of red feathers on his hat, and presented him with another pregnant sow. This ritual evoked the actions of the god 'Oro's brothers at his marriage to a beautiful woman, when he changed his brothers into a sow in litter and a red feather bunch as gifts for his wife's family.[29] It was intended to bind Wallis and Purea together as fellow arioi and *taio* or ceremonial friends, a relationship which almost amounted to a partial exchange of social identities.[30]

Other bonds which were being forged between the strangers and their hosts were much less ceremonial in nature. As soon as the Tahitians and the British stopped fighting, they started having sex, and some of these relationships became commercial. The crew of the *Dolphin* were having a glorious time, concealing each other's absences ashore from the officers, and stealing iron from the ship to pay for sexual favours. As Francis Wilkinson remarked, 'The Women were far from being Coy. For when A Man Found A Girl to his Mind, which he Might Easly Do Amongst so many, their was Not much Cermony on Either Side, and I Belive Whoever Comes here hereafter will find Evident Proofs that they are not the first Discoverys.'[31] He also noted that some of these 'Women', who were very young (no more than 10 or 11 years old), had been brought by their male kinsmen to the Europeans.

Over the weeks the 'old trade' (as the sailors called it) turned into a competitive frenzy. By 20 July the carpenter reported that every wooden cleat in the ship had been drawn, and that most of the hammock-nails had been stolen.[32] Some men were now paying for sex with spike nails (nails four inches or more long, used to fasten the ship's planks to its frame), putting the vessel at risk and ruining the terms of trade for provisions. When the officers tried to find out who was responsible, however, the sailors closed ranks, refusing to identify the culprits. That night there was a brawl below decks, as they meted out their own kind of justice. Worse, when the captain ordered a sailor who had been caught stealing a cleat-nail to run the gauntlet, his shipmates struck him so lightly that the punishment was almost farcical. On shore, too, the 'old trade' was having destructive consequences. Although the ship's surgeon had sworn on his honour to Wallis that none of the crew suffered from venereal diseases, he was wrong, for many of the women who slept with the English sailors contracted lymphogranuloma venereum and perhaps also gonorrhoea.[33] In that period, it was not known that some venereal diseases remained infectious for years after visible signs of their presence had vanished. When the symptoms began to appear, these newly introduced diseases were called the 'English sickness', and the islanders blamed them on the malevolent powers of the Europeans, or the wrath of their own gods, infuriated by the strangers' transgressions of various tapu (sacred restrictions).[34]

On 22 July, fearing that discipline on his ship was at risk, Wallis cancelled all shore leave and decided to leave the island. When he told Purea, she wept bitterly and begged him to stay for ten days longer and go inland with her, but he could not accept the invitation. To console her, he sent ashore a splendid gift of turkeys, geese, guinea-hens, a cat in litter, china, bottles, shirts, needles and thread, cloth and ribbons, peas and garden seeds, iron pots, knives, scissors, spoons and bill-hooks; and Purea sent a return gift of large quantities of fruit and livestock out to the vessel. As preparations were made for their departure, Robertson, the ship's master, and the purser (a good mathematician) carried out observations of an eclipse of the sun. Tupaia and Purea watched their performance with intent curiosity, and when Robertson showed them how to look at the eclipse through the dark glass, and gave them a glimpse of their friends about five miles off through the telescope, this 'surpris[ed] them beyond measure'. In Tahiti, an eclipse was a sign that the gods were attacking the sun in revenge for some wrongdoing, so the Europeans' interest in this celestial display must have provoked much speculation.[35]

On 25 July Wallis sent John Gore inland with an armed party, to examine the interior of the island. They entered the valley behind Matavai Bay where the local inhabitants gave them a feast, and in the mountains high above the river, they found tributary valleys scattered with houses and villages, and surrounded by groves of trees planted in neat rows, lush, irrigated plantations and walled gardens. The next morning when Purea came out to the *Dolphin* for the last time, she asked Wallis when he would come back to the island. He told her that he could not return before fifty days had passed, and again she wept bitterly and begged him to come back in thirty. That night she slept on the beach, and according to Robertson when she came out in her canoe to make her final farewells, 'This Great friendly Woman took no manner of notice of what she got from us, but . . . wept and cried, in my opinion with as much tenderness and Affection as any Wife or Mother could do, at the parting with their Husbands or children.'[36]

Purea's distress was not entirely altruistic, however. As her new ceremonial friend, she must have hoped that Captain Wallis would help with the preparations for the new marae, and the associated struggle for supremacy on the island. Although his departure shattered these dreams, in the months that followed the red pennant from the *Dolphin* was joined to the red feather girdle at Papara, thus binding the power of the gods of Europe to the mana of 'Oro. With this girdle and others representing ancient high titles, Purea and Amo intended to install their son on their new marae as the paramount chief of the island.

As the *Dolphin* sailed away from Matavai Bay, the sailors made signs that they would return, and Purea's people, after following them for a time in their canoes, went up onto the mountains and lit fires as a farewell signal. In the months that followed the *Dolphin*'s departure, the Papara people continued their labours at Maha'iatea marae. They were determined that this would be the largest and most splendid stone structure in the archipel-

Maha'iatea marae in Papara, sketched by William Wilson

ago, and it was built with eleven great steps, faced with coral and basalt, in front of a wide stone forecourt. When the stonework was finished, the god houses and platforms were completed, and carved images of the gods were erected on the marae. The people celebrated its completion by chanting:

> Look at Maha'i-atea!
> Papara now has two mountains,
> One is Mount Tamaiti [a high hill in Papara]
> The other is Maha'i-atea !³⁷[37]

In April 1768, however, their labours were interrupted by a brief flurry of excitement when two European ships arrived on the opposite side of the island. Purea hoped that this was her taio Captain Wallis returning to the island, but instead they proved to be French ships, whose crews were quite unaware of her ambitions. Louis Antoine de Bougainville, their commander (who had fought on the opposite side to James Cook during the battle of Quebec), was a warm-hearted, sophisticated man of the world with a passion for science – soldier, diplomat, noted mathematician and a Fellow of the Royal Society of London. Early in the voyage he had handed over a French colony on the Falkland Islands to Spain, and now, like Wallis, he was searching for the Unknown Southern Continent. Bougainville's ships anchored off the district of Hitia'a for just ten days. During this brief visit he and his men were oblivious to the political controversies on the island, being distracted by other, more seductive aspects of life in Tahiti. The people of Hitia'a had learned how to please Europeans from the *Dolphin*'s men, and almost as soon as the ships had anchored off the east coast of the island, they tried to establish taio relationships with the French sailors by bringing out beautiful naked young women. As Bougainville wrote in his journal:

I ask you, how was one to keep four hundred young French sailors, who hadn't seen women in six months, at their work in the midst of such a spectacle? Despite all the precautions which we took, a young girl got on board and came onto the forecastle and stood by one of the hatchways which are over the capstan. The girl negligently let fall her robe and stood for all to see, as Venus stood forth before the Phrygian shepherd; and she had the celestial shape of Venus. The sailors and soldiers rushed to get at the hatchway, and never was a capstan turned with such eagerness. We managed to restrain these bedeviled men, however, but it was no less difficult to control oneself.[38]

The local people had already dismissed the idea of attacking the French, and that afternoon when the ships' officers landed, they were greeted with displays of warm hospitality. The local chief, Reti, gave them bark-cloth and ornamental feather gorgets, although his old father watched them with evident suspicion. An arioi sang while another blew on a nose flute, and that night when a group of islanders visited the ships, they were treated to a concert of flutes, base-viols and violins, and a spectacle of skyrockets and fire-snakes.

After some negotiations about how long they would stay on the island, Reti gave permission for the French to set up a camp on the beach, overriding his father's objections. Once the sailors came ashore, however, it was almost impossible to control them. They ranged around the neighbourhood, intently watched by the Tahitians, who discovered (to Bougainville's amazement, since he had no idea) that the naturalist Commerson's 'assistant' was a young woman in disguise. When the sailors slept with the women, they were watched by fascinated spectators, and when things were filched from their pockets, disputes broke out with the local people. Before long a Tahitian was shot, and several days later three more islanders were shot or bayoneted. All of Reti's people fled into the mountains after this episode, and after a violent storm in which his ships lost most of their anchors and were almost wrecked on the reef, Bougainville decided to leave the island. He formally took possession of Tahiti for France, and as they were about to set sail Reti, who had made peace with them after the storm, brought a friend of his out to the ship who wanted to go with the Europeans. Bougainville's parting comments about Tahiti described it as a glorious Arcadia:

Nature had placed the island in the most perfect climate in the world, had embellished it with every pleasing prospect, had endowed it with all its riches, and filled it with large, strong, and beautiful people . . . Farewell, happy and wise people; remain always as you are now. I will always remember you with delight, and as long as I live I will celebrate the happy island of Cythera [the island of Aphrodite, the goddess of love]: it is the true Utopia.[39]

Although Bougainville's brief visit to Tahiti made little immediate impact on the island's political affairs, his tales of an island Eden in the South Pacific created a sensation upon his return to Europe. Ahutoru, the young Tahitian who sailed with Bougainville to France, was fêted in Parisian society, and a letter from Commerson and a leaflet giving idyllic accounts of life in Tahiti were widely circulated, fuelling philosophical speculations about 'the state of nature', including Diderot's sardonic commentary on colonial ventures and Jean Jacques Rousseau's dreams of the 'noble savage'. Bougainville, however, had already begun to corrupt his 'true Utopia', infecting its people with new and fatal diseases. Almost as soon as he set sail for France, a virulent epidemic raged in Hitia'a (probably plague, carried by flea-ridden rats from his ships). Although he described venereal diseases as 'naturalised among them' (in fact introduced by the English),[40] his men also introduced an array of venereal disorders including syphilis, which in its advanced stages caused its victims to lose their nails and hair while suffering acute intestinal disturbances.[41] Again, the Tahitians concluded that these afflictions were due to the anger of their gods, provoked by the strangers' impious transgressions.

As Bougainville sailed back to France across the Pacific, and James Cook on the *Endeavour* was crossing the Atlantic on his way to the South Seas, a vicious conflict broke out on the 'happy island of Cythera'. During Bougainville's brief visit to the east coast of the island, Purea and Amo's grandiose schemes for their son Te Ri'i rere were reaching a climax. As the finishing touches were given to their new marae, Purea and Amo declared a general *rahui* (ceremonial restriction) over the whole of Tahiti. This required each district to set aside the bulk of their provisions for a great feast, to consecrate the new marae and install their son with the red feather girdle.[42]

Almost at once, other senior women rose up to challenge Purea and Amo's claim to ascendancy. First Purea's sister-in-law, enraged by her presumption, tried to break the rahui in the name of her son, Te Ri'i Vaetua, taking her canoe through the sacred pass in the reef opposite the new temple. According to Tahitian etiquette, Purea should have greeted her and given her a feast, breaking the ceremonial restriction, but instead she came out and rudely sent her away. As she was paddled away, her sister-in-law slashed her head with a shark's tooth, making the blood flow in shame and anger. Next, Purea's niece 'Itia, repeated the challenge in the name of her brother, Te Ri'i Vaetua.[43] When she came through the sacred pass she disembarked on the beach, and when she slashed her head she made the blood flow into a hole in the sand, a sign that blood would have to be shed in atonement. One of Purea's senior relatives came out and wiped the blood from her face, trying to avoid a feud in the family, but again Purea refused to acknowledge the claims being made on behalf of her nephew, insisting that only her son Te Ri'i rere would be recognised.[44]

While these challenges were occurring, Tupaia advised Purea and Amo to send a sacred flag around the island, as a sign that their son would soon be invested with the red feather girdle from Ra'iatea (now joined with the red pennant from the *Dolphin*). As the breadfruit ripened on the trees, the 'Season of Plenty' was approaching; and in about December the districts would gather for the Matahiti, a festival which celebrated 'the ripening of the year', a fitting time for a young chief's installation.[45] Most of the districts in Tahiti decided to send representatives to the investiture, as did the high chiefs of other islands, including Mo'orea, Borabora, Maupiti and Ra'iatea; but in the southern district of Taiarapu in Tahiti, the fighting chief Vehiatua struck the sacred flag down and declared war on the Papara people. Before the investiture could take place, their enemies descended upon Papara. Devastating raids by the warriors from the south were followed by an onslaught by their affronted kinsmen from the north and the west. The warriors from the west, led by the fighting chief Tutaha, threw down the stones of the new marae and seized its sacred relics – the image of 'Oro, and the red feather girdle of Papara, carrying them off to Atehuru.

In the final battle in December 1768, so many people were killed around Maha'iatea that the beaches were covered with their bones; and in the thick of the fighting Tupaia was wounded by a priest who urged on the enemy troops, wielding the tail of a stingray as his weapon. As his *Endeavour* shipmates later reported, he had numerous scars on his body, including one where a spear tipped with a stingray's tail had gone right through his chest.[46] Tupaia, with Purea and all of her family, fled to the mountains while rampaging warriors cut down the trees, destroyed gardens and set fire to the houses and canoes of Papara, which burned red in the sky behind them. After this battle, Vehiatua had Amo's brother killed and cooked in an earth oven, an ultimate degradation. When the warriors finally returned to their homes, Purea's family and Tupaia were allowed to return to Papara, but their power had been greatly diminished.[47]

Like Taputapuatea in Ra'iatea, the great marae of Maha'iatea still stands on its original site in Papara. Once the largest and most impressive stone structure in the Society Islands, this tumbled pile of rubble now hides on a small rocky beach, reached by an obscure winding dirt pathway.[48] In many ways, its sombre remains are a fitting monument to Purea and Amo's ambitions. Like this great temple, they had their moment of glory, but at its height they were overthrown, and all their schemes fell into ruins. Of course, Wallis did not return to the island in fifty days, as he had promised, or even in five hundred. Although his arrival in Tahiti and his friendship with Purea had fuelled her ambitions, he was not there to help his taio in her time of trial. Instead, he sailed back to England in time to hand over his charts, journals and a prized milking goat to James Cook, who left England just months before the great battle of Papara.

All the same, the *Dolphin*'s visit to Tahiti created an enduring link between the islanders and the British. A number of men from the *Dolphin* joined the *Endeavour* expedition, and their memories of 'the queen of Tahiti' and her 'right-hand man' Tupaia became part of shipboard lore. As they set sail from Portsmouth on 26 August 1768, the *Endeavour*'s crew dreamed in their hammocks about the beautiful, amorous women of Tahiti, inspired by the boastful yarns of their *Dolphin* shipmates. And back in Tahiti, Purea, Amo and Tupaia still remembered their British friends, whom they regarded as part of their extended family. When Cook and his men arrived in Tahiti, Vehiatua was poised to attack Purea and Amo once more, in an attempt to finally destroy them. The arrival of the *Endeavour* at Matavai Bay forced him to put his campaign on hold, however. This relationship between the British and Purea, Amo and their high priest Tupaia would powerfully shape Cook's reception by all of the other lineages in the Society Islands.

5

Tupaia's Paintbox

The *Endeavour*, James Cook's ship, was small, only 106 feet long, and when she sailed from England she was packed to the gunwales with tons of ballast, timber, sails, kegs of spirits, supplies, and items of seafaring and scientific equipment. The officers had been relegated to hutches of cabins on the lower deck, where they lived alongside the sailors and marines, who slept packed tight in swaying rows of hammocks. Below the quarterdeck, Cook shared his working space with Joseph Banks and his scientific party, and their clutter of sketch-books and paint-pots, leather-bound *Voyages* and travel accounts, microscopes, dissections of fish and birds, and plant presses. In various nooks and crannies, cattle, sheep and goats, chickens and ducks bleated and squawked in their pens, while dogs and cats ran underfoot and rats and cockroaches swarmed through the vessel.

Despite the stresses and strains of overcrowding, however, the *Endeavour* was a happy ship. James Cook soon established his authority over the crew, and forged a good working relationship with the 'Gentlemen' whose papers and specimens spilled out into the Great Cabin. Joseph Banks was young and ebullient, full of the joys of exploration; while his scientific friend Dr Solander was amusing, friendly and uncomplaining. Although Banks's party had occupied the officers' cabins aft, and invaded the captain's private space with their scientific equipment and library, Cook had acquired intelligent, good-natured companions for the voyage.

A Royal Naval captain was often a Jovian figure, remote, stern and isolated. The Great Cabin was his inner sanctum, guarded by a marine, where the captain mostly dined alone; and when he walked on the quarterdeck, the officers moved out of his way, and did not speak to him unless they were spoken to. On the *Endeavour*, however, things were different. Cook had the respect of his crew for his formidable skills as a seaman and surveyor, but he shared the promenade on the quarterdeck with the 'Gentlemen', and they dined with him daily in the Great Cabin, sharing their interests and discoveries.

This was, after all, the Royal Society's expedition, and in addition to his instructions from the Admiralty, Cook carried written 'Hints' from the Earl of Morton, the President of the Society, about how to conduct the voyage. The Earl of Morton was a natural philosopher imbued with Enlightenment ideals, and it is likely that he had studied the *Dolphin* journals before he wrote his 'Hints' for the Royal Society expedition. This document gave Cook and his companions advice about their conduct on the voyage, and especially how to treat any natives they might meet on their travels:

To exercise the utmost patience and forbearance with respect to the Natives of the several Lands where the Ship may touch.

To check the petulance of the Sailors, and restrain the wanton use of Fire Arms.

To have it still in view that sheding the blood of those people is a crime of the highest nature: – They are human creatures, the work of the same omnipotent Author, equally under his care with the most polished European; perhaps less offensive, more entitled to his favor.

They are the natural, and in the strictest sense of the word, the legal possessors of the several Regions they inhabit. No European Nation has a right to occupy any part of their country, or settle among them without their voluntary consent. Conquest over such people can give no just title; because they could never be the Agressors . . .

There are many ways to convince them of the Superiority of Europeans, without slaying any of these poor people . . . Upon the whole, there can be no doubt that the most savage and brutal Nations are more easily gained by mild, than by rough treatment. If during an inevitable skirmish some of the Natives should be slain; those who survive should be made sensible that it was done only from a motive of self defence; But the Natives when brought under should be treated with distinguished humanity, and made sensible that the Crew still considers them as Lords of the Country.[1]

Cook studied the Earl of Morton's 'Hints' with care, noting his support for native rights and his repugnance for casual violence; and the presence of Joseph Banks and his party on board ensured a punctilious observance of naval regulations during this voyage. There was no outbreak of flogging as the new captain sought to assert his authority, and the atmosphere seems to have been good-humoured and equable. Most of the crew were old hands, who settled into the rhythm of daily life at sea with 'great chearfullness and readyness'. On 1 September, shortly after they sailed from Plymouth, the *Endeavour* faced her first test when violent gales battered the ship, sweeping the boatswain's boat off the deck and drowning most of the poultry; but the ship handled well and there were no other disasters. In the calms that followed, Joseph Banks and his co-workers began to establish their own working routine: studying books during the morning from the ship's library, sharing their dinner with Cook at midday, and in the afternoon returning to the Great Cabin, where Sydney Parkinson sketched specimens caught over the ship's side, while Banks and Solander wrote scientific descriptions of them.

On 10 September, after less than three weeks at sea, the *Endeavour* approached the coast of Madeira. Giving a passing thought to Harriet Blosset (who had retired to the English countryside, to work waistcoats for him in melancholy seclusion), Banks wrote in his journal:

Today for the first time we dind in Africa, and took our leave of Europe for heaven alone knows how long, perhaps for Ever; that thought demands a sigh as a tribute due to the memory of friends left behind and they have it; but two cannot be spard, twold give more pain to the sigher, than pleasure to those sighd for.[2]

As they came to anchor at Funchal harbour in Madeira, a master's mate got entangled in a buoy rope and was dragged overboard and drowned, the first casualty of the voyage. Over the next few days Banks and Solander roamed about the neighbourhood, collecting plants and examining the fish and shells brought to them by local people; and when the Governor came to visit them, an Electrical machine was brought ashore at his request and they 'shockd him full as much as he chose'.[3] At the same time Cook was busy in the port, buying supplies of onions, wine and beef in his role as the ship's purser, and when two of the crew refused to eat the fresh meat he had supplied, he ordered them to be punished with twelve lashes each to deter any further displays of disobedience.

On 18 September the *Endeavour* set sail again. During the passage to Rio de Janeiro, Banks and his servants rowed around the ship in the calms, fishing for sharks and netting tiny sea creatures. When Cook exercised the midshipmen and mates with small arms, as Green noted with amusement, 'they behaved like the London Trane Band with their [weapon] sometimes on one Shoulder and then on the other.'[4] Some days later when Banks tried to exercise with ropes in his cabin, he slipped and crashed on his head, giving himself a mild case of concussion. He quickly recovered, however, roaring with laughter when the ship heeled in a squall and all of Sydney Parkinson's paint-pots flew off the table.

When the ship reached the equinoctial line on 25 October, the ceremony of 'Crossing the Line' was conducted. Everyone on board (including the ship's dogs and cats) was examined, and all of the novices were put on a list drawn up by the sailors. Although Captain Cook, Dr Solander, Joseph

Banks and his dogs paid a hefty fine of spirits and were let off the ordeal, when the ship hove to, twenty-two men and boys were each lashed to a cross-piece on a rope slung from the main yard and dropped three times into the sea, emerging half-suffocated and choking, or 'grinning and exulting in their hardiness'.[5] That night they all got immensely drunk to celebrate the occasion.

On 12 November the *Endeavour* arrived at Rio de Janeiro. The Portuguese Viceroy was unimpressed with Cook's claims that his ship was a naval vessel sent on a scientific mission, suspecting that they were military spies or smugglers. He sent a guard boat to patrol the ship and ordered its passengers not to land. Banks was outraged, and helped Cook to draft a Memorial of protest. In defiance of these restrictions, he and Dr Solander went ashore in disguise while other members of his party sneaked out at night to collect plants and insects for the scientists. These glimpses of new flora and fauna only increased Banks's frustration, however, which he vented in a letter to a friend back in England:

O Perrin you have heard of Tantalus in hell you have heard of the French man laying swaddled in linnen between two of his Mistresses both naked using every possible means to excite desire but you have never heard of a tantalized wretch who has born his situation with less patience than i have done mine I have cursd swore ravd stampd & wrote memorials to no purpose in the world, they only laugh at me![6]

During this stay at Rio, another sailor fell overboard and was drowned, and four more men were punished, each with twelve lashes – one for refusing to work, the second for swearing at the officer of the watch, the third for attempting to desert, and the fourth for not doing his duty in laying on the lashes. As Wallis and innumerable other captains could testify, it was much easier to maintain discipline at sea than when the ship was at anchor. When the *Endeavour* finally set sail from the port on 5 December, a thick cloud of butterflies fluttered around her masts and rigging as the fort fired its cannons at the ship, one shot just missing the main mast – apparently because its commander had not received the order telling him that the *Endeavour* was free to leave Rio.

As the *Endeavour* sailed south along the coast of South America, the weather began to deteriorate, and Cook put his men on 'watch and watch', allowing them only four hours sleep at a time, although they had been on three watches for most of the voyage, which gave each watch eight hours' sleep every day. On Christmas Day, as Banks noted, 'all hands get abominably drunk so that at night there was scarce a sober man in the ship, wind thank god very moderate or the lord knows what would have become of

A flogging at sea, by George Cruikshank

us'.[7] As the weather became colder, woollen jackets and trousers were issued to the crew and Banks donned his flannel waistcoat and jacket. In stormy seas off Tierra del Fuego one memorable night, Banks's bureau was tossed on its side as the ship smashed into a wave, throwing his books onto the floor where they skidded about all night, while his cot knocked against the sides of the cabin. The *Endeavour* coped well with this weather, however. As Banks noted: 'The ship during this gale has shewn her excellence in laying too remarkably well, shipping scarce any water tho it blew at times vastly strong; the seamen in general say that they never knew a ship lay too so well as this does, so lively and at the same time so easy.'[8]

By 14 January 1769 they were off the Strait of Le Maire; Banks and Solander were desperate to go ashore to collect plants, after their frustrations in Rio. Cook yielded to their entreaties and lowered them overboard in their boat near Cape St. Vincent, where they collected about 100 new species of plants in just four hours. Banks was ecstatic but Cook was a little testy, since he had put the ship at some risk of shipwreck to satisfy their curiosity. That night he wrote in his journal:

I sent a Boat with an officer a Shore to attend on Mr Banks and People who was very desireous of being aShore at any rate, while I kept plying as near the shore as possible with the Ship. At 9 they return'd on board bringing with them several Plants Flowers &c most of them unknown in Europe and in that alone consisted their whole Value.[9]

The next day when the ship anchored in the Bay of Good Success, Cook landed with Banks and Solander. Some local people appeared and were given beads and ribbons. They were so pleased that they came out to the ship, where the sailors clothed them in jackets and gave them bread and beef in the Great Cabin.

The next morning, Cook conducted a survey of the bay while Banks and Solander went ashore again with their party. This was a disastrous expedition. Banks had decided to search for alpine plants in the hills, and he and Solander set out with their servants, accompanied by Buchan the artist, Monkhouse the ship's surgeon, Green the astronomer, two sailors and his greyhound. They climbed for hours, clambering over dense thickets of low, tangled bushes. Eventually Buchan, who was an epileptic, had a fit and collapsed in exhaustion. A fire was kindled and some of the party stayed with him, while Banks carried on up the mountain with Solander, Green and Monkhouse. It started to snow, and as they began their descent Solander began to suffer from hypothermia. He lay down in the snow, roused himself and staggered down the hill for a while, and then lay down again and slept, where he was joined by Richmond, one of the black servants. At dusk Banks sent Green and Monkhouse ahead to build a fire, and then half-carried Solander down the hill to join them. Richmond would not stir, so Banks was forced to leave him behind with the other black servant and a sailor. At midnight Banks and several of his companions, roused by the sailor, climbed back up the hill to check on Richmond, but found him and the other black servant lying insensible. They had consumed all of the party's liquor, and could not be aroused. Eventually they covered them with boughs and returned downhill to the fire, huddling together all night in freezing conditions. The next morning they found the two men frozen to death in the snow, Banks's greyhound lying beside them; and retracing their tracks they found that they had spent most of the previous day walking in circles.

Despite this ordeal Banks's enthusiasm was undimmed, and while his companions retired to their cots as soon as they got back to the ship, he had the boat lowered and went off fishing. Several days later he took a party inland to visit an encampment of Ona Indians, who lived in flimsy, open shelters on a knoll surrounded by mud. Buchan sketched one of these families in their hut; as Cook remarked, 'We could not discover that they had any head or chief, or form of Government, neither have they any usefull or neccessary Utentials except it be a Bagg or Basket to gather their Muscels into: in a Word they are perhaps as miserable a set of People as are this day upon Earth.'[10] The *Endeavour* was soon well supplied with fresh water and wood, and Cook set sail again 'to the Joy of all hands'. On 25 January they rounded Cape Horn, where Cook and Green determined the longitude by cross-checking their solar and lunar observations. The *Endeavour* had doubled the Cape in thirty-three days, without encountering the terrifying storms which made the Horn a byword among sailors, battering the *Dolphin* for three interminable months during her passage through the Straits of Magellan.

The *Endeavour* was now in the South Seas at last, heading westwards to search for Terra Australis Incognita. By this stage in the voyage, their shared experiences had forged the civilians and the sailors into a tight shipboard community. Banks's high spirits and intelligent curiosity made him popular among the officers and men, and Dr Solander was gregarious and chatty. As well as handling the ship, the sailors often helped with the collection of specimens, and the Great Cabin became a travelling learned society where charts and specimens were studied, journals were written, and the aims and findings of the voyage were debated. As they entered the South Pacific, Cook, already sceptical about the existence of the fabled continent, noted the absence of the currents usually associated with large land masses. As the miles passed, even Banks (an ardent advocate of Terra Australis) began to be doubtful. Sightings of land proved to be no more than fog banks or clumps of low-lying clouds – 'Cape Flyaway', the sailors called them; and Banks mused: 'The number of square degrees of the [geographers'] land that we have already chang'd into water . . . teaches me at least that till we know how this globe is fixd in that place which has been since its creation assignd to it in the general system, we need not be anxious to give reasons how any one part of it counterbalances the rest.'[11]

As the days and weeks passed and the weather grew warmer, the ship's company changed into light clothing and went back to three watches. On 25 March the monotony of this passage over the blue-green rolling sea was broken when a quarrel broke out between a young marine, William Greenslade, and one of Cook's servants. While Greenslade was on sentry duty outside the Great Cabin, the servant had left a seal-skin in his charge, and intending to make a tobacco pouch, the young marine cut a piece from the skin and hid it. When this theft was discovered, Greenslade was hauled before his comrades who gave him such a tongue-lashing for dishonouring their Corps that he ran up on deck and, in an agony of shame, threw himself into the ocean and drowned.

By this time scurvy was beginning to afflict the crew, making them argumentative and moody. When Banks got ulcers in his mouth and his glands swelled up, he 'flew to the lemon juice', while Cook ordered sauerkraut and portable broth (made from blocks of meat essence boiled in water) to be served to the crew as anti-scorbutics. At first they refused to eat the sauerkraut, but when it was served daily in the Great Cabin where the officers and gentlemen ate it with relish, the sailors asked eagerly for their servings. As Cook drily observed, 'Such are the Tempers and disposissions of Seamen in general that whatever you give them out of the Common way, altho it be ever so much for their good yet . . . you will hear nothing but murmurings gainest the man that first invented it; but the Moment they see their Superiors set a Value upon it, it becomes the finest stuff in the World and the inventer an honest fellow.'[12]

On 4 April, Banks's servant Peter Briscoe sighted land, to the delight and relief of his shipmates. This proved to be a small atoll, one of the Tuamotu Islands [Vahitahi], which Cook named 'Lagoon Island'. Several naked, dark-skinned warriors came to the shore to watch the ship passing, carrying long weapons, but retired as soon as they realised that the Europeans did not intend to land on their island. Over the next few days as the *Endeavour* sailed through the archipelago, no direct contact was made with the islanders, although at another small island, Ravahere, two canoes put off and the people on shore beckoned to them with their weapons (in fact, a gesture of defiance and rejection). In his journal, Banks reflected upon the debates in the Great Cabin about how islanders should be handled:

Our situation made it very improper to try them farther, we wanted nothing, the Island was too trifling to be an object worth taking possession of; had we therefore out of mere curiosity hoisted out a boat and the natives by attacking us oblige us to destroy some of them the only reason we could give for it would be the desire of satisfying a useless curiosity. We shall soon by our connections with the inhabitants of Georges Island [Tahiti] (who already know our strength and if they do not love at least fear us) gain some knowledge of the customs of these savages; or possibly persuade one of them to come with us who may serve as an interpreter, and give us an opportunity hereafter of landing where ever we please without running the risk of being obligd to commit the cruelties which the Spaniards and most others who have been in these seas have often brought themselves under the dreadfull nescessity of being guilty of, for guilty I must call it.[13]

Now that the *Endeavour* was approaching Tahiti, Cook drew up a set of Rules based on Captain Wallis's experience and the Earl of Morton's instructions. He was determined that, during their stay, his expedition would do as little harm to the local people as possible. In the 'Rules', Cook instructed his crew to 'endeavour by every fair means to cultivate a friendship with the Natives and to treat them with all imaginable humanity'. He informed them that 'a proper person or persons' would be appointed to control all trade, ordered that 'No Sort of Iron, or any thing that is made of

Iron, or any sort of Cloth or other usefull necessary articles are to be given in exchange for any thing but provisions,' and warned them that any man who lost his arms or tools ashore would have their value charged against his wages.[14]

The sailors heard these instructions with regret, since the barter of iron for sexual delights in Tahiti had become legendary among them. As the island came into sight they gazed longingly at the shore, which Parkinson vividly described as 'uneven as a piece of crumpled paper, being divided irregularly into hills and valleys; but a beautiful verdure covered both, even to the tops of the highest peaks.'[15] When some canoes came out to the ship, their crews calling out *'Taio! Taio!'* [Friend! Friend!], the sailors responded with unfeigned pleasure.

As it happened, there was no immediate need for forbearance. During Wallis's visit on the *Dolphin*, his men had after all fired cannons into an unruly crowd, blowing a number of people to pieces. As a result, the Tahitians were terrified of guns, and on 13 April 1769 when the anchors splashed down in Matavai Bay, a white-bearded old man named Owhaa [Fa'a], the *Dolphin*'s 'old man', came out while a crowd of canoes surrounded the vessel. They began to trade peacefully, offering coconuts, breadfruit, small fish and Tahitian apples for nails, beads and buttons. Like Wallis and Bougainville, Cook found these people incorrigibly light-fingered, and as they climbed up the sides and swarmed all over the ship, the sailors' pockets were picked and things filched from the cabins. Hiro, the god of thieves, was highly esteemed on the island, and as the Tahitians later explained to the missionaries, 'We thought, when we were pagans, that it was right to steal when we could do it without being found out. Hiro, the god of thieves, used to help us.'[16] The islanders were amiable, however, and as they recognised former *Dolphin*s among the crew, greeted them warmly.

After this reassuring welcome, Cook, Gore and the 'Gentlemen' with an armed party of marines went ashore, where hundreds of the 'meaner sort of inhabitants' lined up to greet them. An envoy came forward with a plantain branch, creeping almost on hands and knees, a sign of utmost respect and veneration. Forewarned by Lieutenant Gore, the *Dolphin* veteran who had played a key role during Wallis's visit to Tahiti, each of the *Endeavour* party picked up a green bough, and walked with the Tahitians to a place about half a mile away, where their guides scraped an area clear of greenery and laid down their branches. On a signal from Cook, the red-coated marines stood to attention and then each marched forward to put his plantain branch on the pile of greenery, followed by the officers and gentlemen.

Once this ritual of peacemaking was over, Gore led Cook and his com-

The shore at Matavai Bay from the Endeavour, *by*
Sydney Parkinson

panions several miles through the woods to the great arioi house where
Purea, the 'Queen of the Island', had stayed during the *Dolphin*'s visit. As
they walked along beneath the forest canopy, Banks was enraptured: '[The]
groves of Cocoa nut and bread fruit trees [were] loaded with a profusion of
fruit and giving the most gratefull shade I have ever experienced, under
these were the habitations of the people most of them without walls: in
short the scene we saw was the truest picture of an arcadia of which we
were going to be kings that the imagination can form.'[17] Like Bougainville, he
found the Tahitian countryside idyllic, describing it as an Elysium (although
Bougainville was a much more accomplished classicist than Banks, who had
loathed the subject at Eton). There was trouble in Arcadia, however, for
when they came to the site where Purea's arioi house had once stood, it had
been abandoned. Lieutenant Gore was stunned to find that the fine houses,
the marae with their carvings, the pigs and chickens and the lush gardens
were all gone, and the fine canoes which had once lined the bay had vanished.
Early the next morning, several double canoes came out to the ship

carrying two dignified elders, who were escorted to the Great Cabin. As these men approached Cook and Joseph Banks, they took off their bark-cloth garments and, dressing their guests in Tahitian clothing, invited them ashore. The boats were hoisted out and the elders guided them to a long house at the south-west end of the bay, where several hundred people had gathered. This was the arioi house at Point Utuhaihai belonging to Tutaha, the leader of the Pare-Arue districts, who had allied himself with Vehiatua and defeated Purea and Amo just six months earlier. As they entered the house, Cook and Banks were seated in front of Tutaha. He was a tall, sturdy old man whom Banks, much impressed by his robust physique and fine looks, dubbed 'Hercules' in his journal. Eyeing his visitors gravely, Tutaha presented them with a cock and a hen, and two lengths of perfumed bark-cloth. When Banks took off a large lacy silk neckcloth and a linen handkerchief and presented these in return, the old chief was delighted and immediately put them on. By these exchanges Cook, Banks and Tutaha became taio or ceremonial friends, and potential military allies.[18]

According to Tahitian histories, after their defeat at the battle at Maha'ia-tea, Purea, Amo and Tupaia had escaped into the mountains, crossing to the eastern districts where the chief (Amo's nephew) gave them refuge. After some time a truce was negotiated in which Purea and Amo retained their high rank and Tupaia remained a high priest of 'Oro, while Tutaha was recognised as Regent of Tahiti-nui, the northern part of the island, on behalf of his great-nephew Tu (properly known as Tu Nui e A'a i te Atua). Purea and Amo were still important figures in Tahitian society, however, and Captain Wallis had been Purea's taio. If she could forge a close relationship with Captain Cook, as she had done with Wallis, the British might help her to renew her ambitions. To forestall such a threat, Tutaha had hastened to make Cook and Banks ceremonial friends of his own; and as they wandered through his settlement after the ceremony, the women beckoned enticingly and offered them sexual hospitality. A taio had free access to his friend's wives and possessions; but the Englishmen were unaccustomed to making love in such conditions. As Banks remarked:

We walkd freely about several large houses attended by the ladies who shewd us all kind of civilities our situation could admit of, but as there were no places of retirement, the houses being intirely without walls, we had not an opportunity of putting their politeness to every test that maybe some of us would not have faild to have done had circumstances been more favourable; indeed we had no reason to doubt any part of their politeness, as by their frequently pointing to the matts on the ground and sometimes by force seating themselves and us upon them they plainly shewd that they were much less jealous of observation than we were.[19]

In frustration, Banks tore himself away from these alluring companions, to join Cook and the rest of their party. They strolled about a mile along the beach, where they were greeted by another group of Tahitians, headed by a middle-aged chief named 'Tubourai Tamaide' [better known as Te Pau] who came hurrying up to greet them. Te Pau, a stately, good-humoured man with thick black frizzled hair and an air of 'natural majesty', was Purea's eldest brother and the *ari'i rahi* or high chief of her lineage, although he had allied himself with Tutaha in the recent quarrels.[20] Again, plantain branches were presented, and the leaders of each party put their hands on their chests and said 'Taio' (friend). Te Pau invited his new friends to eat with him, and soon they were dining on a feast of raw and cooked fish, breadfruit, coconuts and plantains. Te Pau's wife sat close to Joseph Banks, feeding him by hand, but when Banks spied a pretty girl 'with a fire in her eyes that I had not before seen in the countrey' he invited her to sit beside him and showered her with gifts, offending the older woman.

While Banks was thus engrossed, Solander and Monkhouse discovered that their pockets had been picked, and that Solander had lost an opera glass while Monkhouse's snuff-box had been taken. Banks immediately leaped to his feet, striking the butt of his gun on the ground, and complained to the chief who began to throw things at the people who had crowded into his house, quickly dispersing them. Te Pau hastily offered bales of bark-cloth in compensation for the thefts, and when these were refused he went off to recover the stolen items, which he eventually succeeded in doing. As Banks commented, 'We returnd to the ship admiring a policy at least equal to any we had seen in civilizd countries, excercisd by people who have never had any advantage but meer natural instinct uninstructed by the example of any civilizd countrey.'[21] For his sense of justice, Banks named Te Pau 'Lycurgus', yet another classical allusion.

Having established friendly relationships with the two leading chiefs at Matavai, Cook went ashore the next morning with Banks to lay out a site on a sandy point, where the tents could be pitched and a small fort built to protect the observatory. The site of this fort is still visible at Matavai Bay, although the narrow promontory is covered with tarseal and grass, and a white lighthouse surrounded by a grove of swaying palm trees. While the sailors erected a small tent on 'Point Venus', as Cook named it, Banks drew a line in the sand and told the Tahitians not to cross it. Late that afternoon, Cook and Banks walked off into the woods with the *Dolphin*'s 'old man', looking for supplies, and Banks amazed his companions by killing three ducks with one shot. During their absence, a sentinel who was on guard outside the tent was shoved over, and a man stole his musket. As the rest of the Tahitians fled from the scene, the midshipman in charge ordered the marines to open fire, shooting the thief dead and wounding a number of these people. Parkinson noted with dismay:

A boy, a midshipman [Jonathan Monkhouse, the surgeon's brother], was the commanding officer, and, giving orders to fire, they obeyed with the greatest glee imaginable, as if they had been shooting at wild ducks ... What a pity, that such brutality should be exercised by civilized people upon unarmed ignorant Indians!

When Mr. Banks heard of the affair, he was highly displeased, saying, 'If we quarrelled with those Indians, we should not agree with angels;' and he did all he could to accommodate the difference, going across the river, and, through the mediation of an old man, prevailed on many of the natives to come over to us, bearing plantain-trees, which is a signal of peace amongst them; and, clapping their hands to their breasts, cried Tyau, which signifies friendship. They sat down by us; sent for cocoa nuts, and we drank the milk with them. They laughed heartily, and were very social, more so than could have been expected, considering what they had suffered in the late skirmish.[22]

Although it was considered meritorious in Tahiti to steal if one could escape undetected, thieves who were caught in the act were often killed in vengeance. Nevertheless, Banks and his party were outraged by these shootings; and when they returned to the ship, they were further distressed to learn that Buchan had suffered another epileptic fit, and that Dr Monkhouse did not expect him to recover. The following night when the young man died, Banks suggested that he should be buried at sea, since the digging of a grave might offend the local people. His sorrow at the young landscape artist's death was genuine but self-centred: 'I sincerely regret him as an ingenious and good young man, but his Loss to me is irretrevable, my airy dreams of entertaining my friends in England with the scenes that I am to see here are vanishd. No account of the figures and dresses of men can be satisfactory unless illustrated with figures: had providence spard him a month longer what an advantage would it have been to my undertaking but I must submit.'[23]

Over the next few days as the British fort began to rise on Point Venus, both Tutaha and Te Pau regularly came out to the ship with gifts of pigs, chickens, coconuts, bananas, yams and breadfruit. Cook put Banks and Solander in charge of barter with the local people, in an effort to control the terms of trade and ensure that the Earl of Morton's 'Hints' were scrupulously followed. A set of trading guidelines were established – a spike nail for a small pig; a hatchet for a hog; a small spike nail for a chicken; twenty coconuts or breadfruit for a forty-penny nail; ten for a white glass bead and six for an amber one. Banks's tents were erected in the fort, and on 18 April he and Solander slept ashore for the first time, guarded by sentries.

The next morning Te Pau and his family arrived at Matavai Bay, where they erected temporary shelters. When Banks went to visit them, the chief took him to a place in the woods where a canoe awning was pitched, and clothed him in red cloth and a fine mat, the costume of a high-born arioi. Afterwards he introduced Banks to his son, showing him the same friendship that his sister Purea had extended to Captain Wallis. In return, Banks invited Te Pau to dinner the next day in his tent. The chief arrived with a gift of Tahitian delicacies; and when he was served, he ate his food delicately with a knife and fork, although his wife (like all Tahitian women, because of a food taboo[24]) ate separately from the menfolk. The following day Banks returned to Te Pau's camp, where the chief ordered two boys to play the flute, while another sang. In response Parkinson showed him some of his portraits of Tahitians, which he greatly admired, 'pronouncing their names as soon as he saw them'. Parkinson had taken over Buchan's duties as the expedition's portrait artist, and he now set up his easel on shore, attracting great interest from the Tahitians, but the flies swarmed over the specimens he was painting and ate the paint off the paper almost as fast as he could lay it on. In desperation the artist had himself swathed in mosquito net, with a fly trap set inside to capture the offending insects.

Encouraged by these amiable exchanges, on 23 April Cook gave his sailors liberty to go on shore, providing that they did not leave the bay, or hurt and molest the local people. This was a difficult situation to manage. If he tried to keep his men on the ship after so many months at sea, he would have a mutiny on his hands; but once they were ashore it would be almost impossible to control them. The men were often out of sight of their officers; and officers, gentlemen and sailors alike were soon sleeping with Tahitian women. After only five days of shore leave, unmistakeable symptoms of venereal diseases (gonorrhoea and perhaps also chancroid), first introduced by the *Dolphin* and now established on shore, began to appear among the crew. Before their arrival on the island, William Monkhouse had assured Cook that only one of the sailors was still infected with VD, but Cook remained deeply concerned about this matter:

I had reason (notwithstanding the improbability of the thing) to think that we had brought [VD] along with us which gave me no small uneasiness and did all in my power to prevent its progress, but all I could do was to little purpose for I may safely say that I was not assisted by any one person in ye Ship; . . . and the Women were so very liberal with their favours, or else Nails, Shirts &c were temptations that they could not withstand, that this distemper very soon spread it self over the greatest part of the Ships Compney but now I have the satisfaction to find that the Natives all agree that we did not bring it here. However this is little satisfaction to them who must suffer by it ... and may in time spread it self over all the Islands in the South Seas, to the eternal reproach of those who first brought it among them.[25]

As Cook suspected, it seems certain that some of the *Endeavour*'s crew were still infectious with venereal diseases, and there was also tuberculosis among the sailors, for Lieutenant Hicks suffered from consumption (i.e. pulmonary tuberculosis), and it seems probable that he had infected others among his shipmates by this stage in the voyage. There were no signs of concern that this disease might also be passed on to the islanders, however, because in the eighteenth century, it was thought that consumption was hereditary, not transmitted by infection.[26] Hints of Bougainville's visit to the east coast of the island had already reached Cook, and he was quick to blame the introduction of VD to Tahiti on the French ships (although based on local descriptions of the flag which the strangers had flown, he thought that they were Spanish).

Apart from the introduction of exotic diseases, there were numerous causes for tension with the local people. The British found it difficult to recognise religious sentiment amongst the Tahitians, showing a blithe disregard of their sacred restrictions. On 21 April, for instance, when Green and Monkhouse were out walking, they came upon the corpse of the man that the sentry had shot, laid out on a burial platform with offerings of food beside it. Their Tahitian companions were uneasy, indicating that they should leave the body alone, but they insisted on inspecting it closely, and later Cook and then Banks followed their example. Although the Europeans made themselves unclean by this act and angered the gods with their impiety, Cook was not much concerned: 'If it is a Religious ceremoney we may not be able to understand it, for the Misteries of most Religions are very dark and not easily understud even by those who profess them.'[27] The Tahitians were appalled, however, associating these offences with the new diseases, for in Tahiti illness was seen as a punishment from the gods, visited upon them for such breaches of tapu.

Like other Europeans in the mid-eighteenth century, the *Endeavour* party generally took it for granted that they were superior to 'savages'. Although they recognised that Tahiti was an aristocratic society, their conduct towards local leaders was sometimes cavalier and arrogant. On 25 April, for example, despite their growing intimacy, Banks accused Te Pau of stealing his knife. The night before, Dr Solander had loaned his knife to one of Te Pau's women, who forgot to return it, and when his own knife went missing

Banks jumped to conclusions. He accused Te Pau of the theft, who flatly denied it and began to search everywhere for the missing object, which one of Banks's servants soon produced, saying that he had picked it up for safekeeping. Upon this discovery, Te Pau burst into tears, and Banks had to abase himself. As he noted, 'I became the guilty and he the innocent person, his looks affected me much. A few presents and staying a little with him reconcild him intirely; his behaviour has however given me an opinion of him much superior to any of his countrymen.'[28]

Two days later, after dining with Banks, Te Pau returned in a fury to report another insult. The ship's butcher had offered his wife a nail in exchange for a stone hatchet, and when she refused, he threatened to cut her throat with a reap-hook. Banks promised him that the butcher would be punished, although when the offender was stripped in front of them two days later, and tied to the ship's rigging and flogged, Te Pau and his wife wept loudly and begged Cook to put an end to this barbarous punishment. Discipline was always difficult to maintain in port, and it was harder still in Tahiti, where people were so seductive and sympathetic. Cook, however, was determined that his men should not ill-treat the Tahitians, and 'explained the nature of his Crime in a most lively manner, and made a very Pathetick speech to the Ship's Company during his punishment'.[29]

On 28 April, two weeks after the *Endeavour*'s arrival at Tahiti, about thirty double canoes arrived at Matavai Bay and Purea, 'the Queen of Tahiti', finally made her appearance. When she arrived at Banks's bell tent, accompanied by Tupaia and her former husband Amo, no one knew who she was, but when Molyneux (who had sailed on the *Dolphin*) arrived, he recognised Purea and welcomed her warmly. As Banks wrote:

Our attention was now intirely diverted from every other object to the examination of a personage we had heard so much spoken of in Europe: she appeard to be about 40, tall and very lusty, her skin white and her eyes full of meaning, she might have been hansome when young but now few or no traces of it were left.[30]

Purea was invited to go out to the ship, and when she entered the Great Cabin with Tupaia, Cook and Gore (another former *Dolphin* veteran) greeted her with pleasure. Cook, who was beginning to understand something about Tahitian politics, described Purea as 'head or Chief of her own Family or Tribe but to all appearance hath no authority over the rest of the Inhabitants whatever she might have had when the Dolphin was here'.[31] They tried to converse for a while, and then Cook presented her with a doll, whimsically telling her that this was a portrait of his wife. Purea was delighted, holding up the doll in triumph. When they went ashore together she presented him with a pig and some plantains and led him in a procession, her people bearing these gifts before them. Tutaha, who had just arrived on the beach, was so infuriated by this display that he was hastily given a doll of his own. The toys were probably thought to be ancestral images,[32] but Tutaha's concern was more fundamental. He was engaged in a deadly struggle with Purea and Amo for control of the island, and was disconcerted to see his rival hobnobbing with the British. If Purea could forge a close relationship with Captain Cook, this might undermine his standing with his new ceremonial friends, and his status as Regent of Tahiti-nui.

Cook tried to remain neutral in these struggles for power, but Banks was much less discreet. Over the next few days he spent much of his time with Purea, and began a passionate affair with one of her women, Tiatia.[33] At the same time, his relationship with Te Pau continued to be intense. On 29 April when Banks went to visit Te Pau's family, he found them all weeping. Apparently Fa'a (the *Dolphin*'s 'old man') had prophesied that in another four days, the *Endeavour* would fire on them with its guns. Nothing that Banks could say would comfort them, so he left and returned to the fort, where he reported this conversation to the officers. They immediately ordered the sentries at the fort to be doubled, and the men to sleep with their weapons beside them. While the fort was being completed, two four-pounders and six swivel guns had been mounted on its walls, arousing suspicion among the local people. The next morning, though, Purea went out to the ship without any signs of concern, and later that day Te Pau's wife came to Banks's tent to implore him for his help, saying that her husband was dying. Banks went with her at once and found Te Pau vomiting in agony, but upon discovering that his friend had swallowed a chew of tobacco, soon cured him with a dose of coconut milk.

On 2 May, lurking tensions between the Tahitians and the *Endeavour* party came to a head. That morning when Cook and Green went to set up the astronomical quadrant in the observatory, they discovered that the quadrant was missing. They were amazed, because it was stored in a hefty packing case and kept in a tent with a sentry outside the entrance. The theft of the quadrant was devastating, because it was essential for the observations of the Transit of Venus, but the Tahitians regarded this as a great coup, thinking this was some kind of ritual treasure. Cook consulted with his officers and decided to seize Tutaha and the other principal chiefs, and to detain all of the canoes in the bay until the quadrant had been returned; while Banks hurried off to find Te Pau in an effort to mediate the situation. Te Pau told him that the quadrant had been taken to the east, and Banks asked him to guide him there so they could recover it.

Te Pau, Banks, Green and a midshipman set off in pursuit of the thief, sometimes walking and sometimes running in the intense heat, and in this manner they travelled seven miles along the coast, armed only with Banks's two pocket pistols. In Georgian England it was thought that a gentleman, by courage and sheer force of character, could control an unruly mob, and Banks was quite fearless in this situation. When they arrived at their destination, one of Te Pau's people arrived with parts of the quadrant in his hand and a large crowd gathered ominously around them. Banks brandished his pistols, and order was soon restored. The pieces of the quadrant were packed in grass to protect them, and on their way back to the ship they met Captain Cook, chasing after them at the head of an armed party of marines. They returned to the fort together, well pleased with the outcome of their excursion.

Back at Point Venus, however, Cook was dismayed to find Tutaha under guard and in a state of intense fear, convinced that he was about to be executed. During their absence, the Tahitians (including Purea) had fled from the bay; and when Tutaha and his people set off by canoe, they were intercepted by one of the ship's boats. Tutaha had dived overboard in an attempt to escape, but was pulled out of the water by his hair and handled very roughly by the boatswain. This was an appalling insult, for the head and hair of a chief, where the sacred power of his ancestors abided, was intensely tapu. The sailors shoved and hustled him to the fort where the first lieutenant detained him, although Cook had given orders before he left that Tutaha should not be molested, since it seemed certain that he had had nothing to do with the theft of the quadrant. As soon as Cook arrived at the fort he ordered the chief be released, and Tutaha presented him with two pigs, although he was seething with rage about the way he had been treated. Cook was his ceremonial friend, and such conduct towards a taio was a disgrace. The next morning, all supplies to the ship dried up as the local people furiously complained about the way that their leader had been insulted.

The next day Tutaha's servants came to collect his canoe, and Tupaia arrived to make certain that Purea's canoe had not been damaged. That night he slept in her canoe, and as Banks enviously remarked, 'not without a bedfellow tho the gentleman cannot be less than 45'.[34] This must have been the woman named 'Obubu' [Pupu], whom Solander described as 'Tupaia's Dolly' in his list of Tahitians (along with such delightful characters as 'Sniggle mouthed Jack', 'Square Kate', 'Mrs. Yellow face' and 'Fine wild woman'!).[35] From this time on Tupaia spent much of his time with the British, and especially with Banks and his party. He was gratified that his enemy Tutaha had been humiliated by the British; and Banks's retinue, with their scientific and artistic equipment and skills, seemed fascinating. Banks was wealthy and well born, with elegant clothes and an amorous disposition – just like an arioi; while Tupaia was one of the most intelligent and knowledgeable men in the archipelago – like a natural philosopher. He was intensely curious about Cook's men, and as communications improved he tried to instruct Banks and his companions about Tahitian navigation, the locations of islands in the surrounding seas, and Tahitian beliefs and customs. Tupaia was enthralled with Sydney Parkinson's sketches and paintings, and soon struck up a friendship with him. Parkinson began to learn Tahitian, and collected vocabulary items with Tupaia's assistance; while he and the other Tahitians began to learn the Englishmen's names, although they found the consonants difficult to pronounce – so Cook became 'Tute', Banks 'Topane', Solander 'Tolano', Parkinson 'Patini', Gore 'Toaro', Molyneux 'Boba' (or Bob), while Hicks was known as 'Hete'.[36]

Despite his anger with Cook's men, Tutaha did not cut off his ties with the British, fearing that they might ally themselves instead with Purea and Amo. Upon his release Tutaha had given Cook two pigs and Cook had promised an axe and a shirt in return; and on 4 May Tutaha sent a messenger to remind him of this promise. The next morning Cook, Banks and Solander set off with an armed party in the pinnace, and went to Pare where Tutaha and about 500 of his people were waiting. As they landed, a man wearing a large turban and wielding a white stick drove the people back by throwing stones and 'laying about him unmercifully'. When they approached Tutaha, who sat under a tree surrounded by venerable old men, the people crowded around crying out 'Taio Tutaha' – 'Friends of Tutaha!' As the axe and the shirt were ceremoniously presented to Tutaha, along with a broadcloth tunic, Purea and several other women came and sat beside the Europeans as though they were part of their retinue.

After these exchanges Cook and Banks were ushered to a courtyard where a wrestling match was staged for their entertainment. Before such contests (*taupiti maona*), which were often arranged in honour of distinguished visitors, the contestants visited their own marae to ask the gods for assistance. When they entered the wrestling ring, they challenged each other by slapping themselves on the left forearm and chest, making a loud clapping noise, and grappling together in pairs until one threw the other onto his back.[37] Although Tutaha invited the Europeans to sit beside him, Banks sat with Purea instead, annoying Tutaha intensely. He did not invite his guests to join the feast held after the wrestling, but instead asked himself to dinner on the *Endeavour*, ordering his people to load a small roasted pig into the pinnace. As they were rowed the four miles back to the ship, Cook and Banks, who by now were famished, were tantalised by the delicious aroma of roasted pork, feasting on Tutaha's gift as soon as they got back to the vessel.

Although Tutaha resumed his regular visits to the ship and the fort, Cook still found it difficult to obtain foodstuffs on the island. A rahui (ceremonial ban) had been placed on supplies to the sailors, and whenever the *Endeavour* men tried to trade for pigs, chickens or vegetables, no matter how far they travelled along the coast, they were told that these were all reserved for Tutaha.[38] Nevertheless, members of the ruling families flocked from all parts of the island to visit the Europeans. On 12 May, for instance, a man and two women arrived in a double canoe off Point Venus, asking to see Joseph Banks. The man, who carried a small bunch of parrots' feathers and a dozen plantain branches, offered the plantain branches to Banks one by one, speaking briefly as he made each presentation. Tupaia (who acted as master of ceremonies on this occasion) received these gifts and put them in the boat. The man then laid a length of bark-cloth on the ground, and one of the women, who was swaddled in bark-cloth, turned towards Banks, spinning herself slowly around until all of the bark-cloth was unwound, and she stood naked before him. This ceremony, which was repeated three times, was a mark of great honour for a distinguished guest, but carried no implication of sexual availability. Banks did not understand this, however, and led the two women into his tent, where he tried to persuade them to stay, but they soon departed. Fortunately for him, Purea appeared shortly afterwards with his 'flame' Tiatia, to console him for this disappointment.

Over the following days, there was much casual coming and going between the Europeans and Tahitians. Purea and Tiatia, and Te Pau and his wife often slept in Banks's tent, while Tupaia firmly attached himself to Banks's party. In true arioi style, Purea made advances to Banks, but he was not tempted. As he remarked, 'I am at present otherwise engag'd; indeed was I free as air her majesties person is not the most desireable.' During this period, too, Tupaia learned to paint in the English style, probably from both Parkinson and Spöring, since they often sketched the same subjects as Tupaia. A series of 'naïve' water-colour paintings survive from the voyage; and although these have previously been attributed to Joseph Banks, a letter from Banks recently came to light which makes it plain that one of these images (and by implication, the entire series) was drawn by Tupaia:

Tupaia the Indian who came with me from Otaheite Learned to draw in a way not Quite unintelligible. The genius for Caricature which all wild people Possess Led him to Caricature me & he drew me with a nail in my hand delivering it to an Indian who sold me a Lobster.[39]

Tupaia's sketch of ariori musicians

Some male arioi were skilled in painting and dyeing bark-cloth, and Tupaia may have been among them. It is suggestive that his images use red, brown and black, the predominant colours of bark-cloth painting, and it is said that arioi men sometimes made special bark-cloth capes adorned with 'fantastic figures'.[40] The motifs, however, are more likely to have come from Tahitian tattooing, where naturalistic images of plants and people were common. In his turn, Sydney Parkinson learned the names of the Tahitian dyes and the plants from which they were made, while Parkinson, Banks and others of his party acquired arioi tattoos – so the process of artistic instruction was mutual.[41] Other artistic exchanges occurred when Banks and his companions were invited to an arioi performance, where some of the arioi played flutes while others drummed and sang songs in praise of the Englishmen, while Parkinson and Tupaia sat together and sketched the performers. When Banks and his companions sang in their turn, the arioi were delighted, and according to Banks, '[we] receivd much applause, so much so that one of the musicians became desirous of going to England to learn to sing.'[42]

During this time too, Cook decided that Divine Service should be conducted on shore, delegating this duty to William Monkhouse.[43] Tutaha, Te Pau and his wife, and Purea and Tiatia attended these rituals, which they understood to be the English equivalent of marae ceremonials. On two Sundays in a row, Monkhouse conducted services at Matavai Bay, the

Tahitians taking their cue from Joseph Banks, standing, sitting or kneeling at different stages in the ritual. This enhanced Monkhouse's status among the Tahitians, who evidently concluded that the ship's surgeon was some kind of *tahu'a* (priest), since priests were also healers in Tahiti. Banks, who had a tempestuous relationship with Te Pau, felt that Monkhouse was getting too close to the chief; and it may have been Te Pau who invited the surgeon to participate in the more private (and sexually explicit) arioi celebrations, which he later described to his captain. Although Cook's account of these ceremonials was oblique, some arioi dances included genital displays, including phallic distortions which left the sailors gaping. These were reported by later observers, including Captain Bligh of the *Bounty*:

The Heiva began by the Men jumping and throwing their Legs and Arms into violent and odd motions, which the Women keep time with, and as they were conveniently cloathed for the Purpose, their persons were generally exposed to full view, frequently standing on one Leg and keeping the other up, giving themselves the most lascivious and wanton motions.

Out of compliment the Women were directed to come nearer, and they accordingly advanced with their Cloaths up, and went through the same Wanton gestures which on their return ended the Heiva.[44]

In 1792, James Morrison, one of the *Bounty* mutineers, added an important caveat to these descriptions:

[These] gestures, however, are not merely the effects of Wantoness but Custom, and those who perform thus in Publick are Shy and Bashful in private, and seldom suffer an freedom to be taken by the Men on that account. The Single Young Men have also dances wherein they shew many indecent Gestures which would be reproachable among themselves at any other time but at the dance, it being deemd shameful for either Sex to expose themselves Naked even to each other, and they are more remarkable for hiding their Nakedness in Bathing then many Europeans.[45]

It seems that arioi performances sometimes included the sexual act itself, because after the first Divine Service was conducted on shore, Cook reported that some of the sailors saw a young man six foot tall making love to a very young girl in front of the fort, while Purea and her women instructed her in her duties. Although Cook later recounted the story to James Boswell in London, it seems unlikely that Boswell was shocked, for in his journals he confessed to copulating with prostitutes in the streets and on bridges, and these and other libertine practices were commonplace in Georgian England. When ships were in port, for example, public love-making was a familiar sight, and orgiastic displays were a regular feature in the gatherings of groups like the Hellfire Club, and in the London brothels.[46]

On 28 May, Cook, Banks and Solander went to Atehuru on the north-west side of the island, in response to an urgent message from Tutaha, asking them to visit him. The Wallis maro 'ura (red feather girdle) had been kept at this place since the battle of Maha'iatea, and there may have been a ritual reason for summoning the British. At about this time each year, the Pleiades sank below the horizon, indicating that the Season of Scarcity had begun and the Season of Plenty had ended. Although Cook doubted Tutaha's good will, he was eager to obtain fresh supplies for his men, and decided to accept this invitation. Upon his arrival at Atehuru, he presented Tutaha with a petticoat of yellow fabric and other gifts, but received only one pig in return, and the chief did not offer them lodgings.

Banks chose to spend the night in Purea's canoe (no doubt with Tiatia), and as he lay down to rest, Purea volunteered to look after his white waistcoat and his jacket decorated with silver frogs, with a powder-horn and a pair of pistols in its pockets. At about 11 pm, however, Banks woke up and suddenly realised that his clothes were missing. Candles were lit, and Tutaha, who was sleeping in the next canoe, rushed off with Purea to look for the missing garments. Tupaia, who had also been woken, took Banks's musket and stood guard while Banks lay down again, convinced that Purea and Tutaha were doing everything they could to recover the stolen items. Soon after, however, he was aroused by lights and music, and when he went to investigate he found Tutaha's musicians singing for Captain Cook, who sat there looking disconsolate. He had lost his stockings while he slept, and the two midshipmen with him had each lost a jacket. When Banks woke up the next morning, he found Tupaia sitting beside him, still holding his musket and guarding the rest of his clothes. Tutaha and Purea appeared soon afterwards, but refused to do anything further to recover the missing objects, so that Banks suspected that they had conspired to take them. Later that morning when Dr Solander rejoined their party, they found that he had been more fortunate. He had slept peacefully all night in a house about a mile away, and none of his possessions had gone missing.

While Cook and Banks were furious about these thefts, the British and the islanders had very different ideas about 'property'. Although Cook's men were protective of their own possessions, they frequently took Tahitian property without permission, cutting down their trees, taking fruit and fishing in their lagoons. In addition, they often failed to make an adequate return for gifts and hospitality. As the *Bounty* mutineer James Morrison observed in 1792, in Tahiti, such stinginess invited retribution:

It is no disgrace for a Man to be poor, and he is no less regarded on that account, but to be Rich and Covetous is a disgrace to Human Nature & should a Man betray such a sign and not freely part with what He has, His Neighbours would soon put Him on a level with the Poorest of themselves, by laying his posessions waste and hardly leave him a house to live in – a Man of such a discription would be accounted a hateful Person.[47]

The daring and stealth of Hiro, the god of theft, were also often emulated in Tahiti. Above all, European goods were irresistably tempting, especially iron (including nails, which were used for woodworking) and items which seemed ritual in nature. Banks's and Cook's clothes were probably taken for this reason, since the garments of chiefs were thought to be imbued with their mana. It is likely that Tutaha and Purea wanted these items for the ceremonies at Atehuru, to invoke the Europeans' gods for their own purposes. When Cook's party returned to the boat, still blaming the chiefs for their misfortune, they saw ten or twelve Tahitians riding high waves on the stern of an old canoe, who seemed 'most highly entertaind with their strange diversion'.[48] For the first time, Europeans witnessed the Polynesian pastime of surfing, marvelling at their skill and courage.

On 1 June, still smarting from these thefts, Cook made his final preparations for observing the Transit of Venus. Lieutenant Gore was sent with Banks, Monkhouse and Spöring to the nearby island of Mo'orea to make one set of observations, accompanied by Te Pau and his wife, while Clerke, Pickersgill and a midshipman were dispatched to a small island off Hitia'a, where Bougainville's ships had anchored, to take another set of readings. Captain Cook himself, Charles Green and Dr Solander stayed at the fort to observe the Transit from the observatory.

The day of the Transit, 3 June, dawned bright and clear, but the observations themselves proved very frustrating. The times for its onset and ending recorded by each group of observers varied considerably, because of an indistinct haze around the edge of the planet. Cook and his scientific companions had travelled around the world to make these observations, and it was infuriating to discover that they could not make accurate measurements. At Mo'orea, the high chief Ta'aroa and his sister visited the observers, bringing a gift of pigs, a dog and some fruit which they gave to Banks, who presented them with return gifts and allowed them to watch the Transit through his telescope. Again, the Europeans' scrutiny of the stars and planets provoked avid curiosity. That evening, three beautiful young women arrived at Banks's tent, and with very little persuasion agreed to spend the night with him. The following day, when the King's birthday was celebrated at the fort with a feast, and ample supplies of liquor, Banks invited several of the local people, including Tupaia, to dinner; and according to Banks, Tupaia drank all of the toasts to 'Kihiargo' (King George), getting 'enormously drunk . . . to shew his Loyalty'.[49]

During Banks's absence at Mo'orea, an old female relative of Te Pau's wife had died, and soon after his return to the fort, Banks went to inspect the burial platform, with its offerings. A group of her relatives had gathered, slashing themselves with sharks' teeth and weeping. Te Pau was acting as chief mourner on this occasion, and his elaborate costume was kept in a special shelter.[50] As part of the mourning rituals, he donned this costume every evening and rampaged through the village, slashing at anyone who got in his way with a lethal weapon edged with sharks' teeth. Banks was fascinated by this performance, and on 9 June he asked Te Pau if he could join him when he next ran. Te Pau agreed, and when Banks joined Te Pau and his wife the next evening, the women stripped off his clothes and daubed him with charcoal and water, putting a strip of bark-cloth around his waist while Tupaia and Spöring sketched Te Pau in his costume. After this, according to Banks:

To the fort then we went, to the surprize of our freinds and affright of the Indians who were there, for they every where fly before the *Heiva* [mourning party] like sheep before a wolf. We soon left it and proceeded along shore towards a place where above 100 Indians were collected together. We the *Ninevahs* had orders from the *Heiva* to disperse them, we ran towards them but before we came within 100 yards of them they dispers'd every way, running to the first shelter, hiding themselves under grass or whatever else would conceal them.[51]

After several hours of this entertainment, they went home and scrubbed themselves clean, while the Chief Mourner removed his fantastic costume. Te Pau had obviously enjoyed this escapade, because the next day he came to the fort to challenge John Gore (who had a passion for all field sports) to an archery contest. Archery was a chief's sport in Tahiti, but Tahitians valued long distance shooting rather than accuracy. Since Te Pau prided himself on the distance he could fire an arrow, while John Gore considered himself an expert marksman, their competition proved to be frustrating.

Although Cook's ships had now been anchored in Matavai Bay for almost two months, discipline among his men had been good. They were eating well and spending time ashore, enjoying themselves tremendously with the Tahitian women. Two men had been given twelve lashes each for disobedience during the first days at Tahiti, and the butcher Jeffs was similarly punished for insulting Te Pau's wife, but all through May there had been no floggings. There had been a brief outbreak of mutinous murmurs on board (inspired by one or two men who reckoned that life in Tahiti would be better than life as a sailor), but Molyneux had secured promises of good conduct from the offenders and Cook excused them from punishment with a warning. Captain Wallis had ordered at least seven floggings during the four weeks he had spent in Tahiti, and Cook by comparison had been very moderate.

On 3 June, however, while Cook and his officers were away from the ship observing the Transit of Venus, one of the men stole a large quantity of spike nails from the vessel with the assistance of some of his shipmates, whom he refused to identify. Cook was furious and ordered this man to be given a flogging of twenty-four lashes, in an effort to deter similar offences. After the archery contest, two sailors robbed some Tahitians of bows and arrows and some plaited hair ornaments, and they were also given twenty-four lashes each – an ominous sign that discipline on board the *Endeavour* was fraying.

At the same time, relationships with the local people were beginning to deteriorate. On 13 June, William Monkhouse was attacked as he picked a flower from a tree on a burying ground, breaking a sacred restriction. A man came behind him and hit him, and when Monkhouse attempted to retaliate, two other men seized him by the hair and rescued their companion. The next day, perhaps in retaliation for Monkhouse's offence, a coal-rake used in the bread oven was stolen from the fort. As Cook remarked:

I was very much displeased with them as they were daily either commiting or attempting to commit one theft or other, when at the same time (contrary to the opinion of every body) I would not suffer them to be fired upon, for this would have been putting it in the power of the Centinals to have fired upon them upon the most slightest occasions as I had before experienced.[52]

Cook's determination to avoid unnecessary killings was no doubt largely prompted by the Earl of Morton's instructions. His orders that the Tahitians should not be harmed, however, like his efforts to prevent the transmission of venereal disease to the islanders, put him at odds with his men, leaving him isolated. Something had to be done to deter further thefts, so Cook ordered an entire flotilla of fishing canoes which had just landed in the Bay to be captured. Twenty-five large sailing canoes filled with fish were seized, and Cook threatened to burn them unless the coal-rake was returned. It was immediately brought back, but Cook then demanded the return of a number of other things that had been stolen from his party – Banks's pistols, a sword, a water cask and the marine's musket. When he heard about it, Banks disagreed with Cook's action, since there was no guarantee that the sailing canoes belonged to those responsible for the thefts. Tutaha was also furious, blaming Purea for taking these things, and ordered that all supplies of food to the sailors should be stopped until further notice.

Over the days that followed, most of the Tahitians moved away from Point Venus, and only Tiatia, Te Pau and his wife, and Tupaia remained faithful. On 18 June Tutaha's sense of injury was compounded when an officer sent to collect ballast for the ship began to take the stones from a marae, despite furious protests by the local people.[53] The next day another sailor was flogged, this time for stealing rum; and that night after dark, Purea returned to the fort with a double canoe loaded with provisions. Since she had brought none of the stolen goods with her, Cook refused to accept her gifts and Banks would not let her sleep in his tent, offending her deeply. The next morning, however, they both relented. Cook received her presents, some breadfruit and plantain, a pig and a very fat dog; and Banks invited Purea and her female attendants, including Tiatia, to sleep in his marquee during the heat of the day.

In order to celebrate this reconciliation Tupaia decided to prepare a chiefly meal, and killed the dog by smothering it, singed the hair off over a fire, scraped the body clean with a shell and then butchered it, cooking it in an earth oven. After four hours in the oven the meat was beautifully cooked, and Cook, Banks and Solander ate it with relish. Parkinson said it had a strong, unpleasant smell, however, and only tasted a mouthful; and the sailors would not even touch it. As Cook remarked, 'It was the opinion of every one who taisted of it that they Never eat sweeter meat, we therefore resolved for the future not to despise Dogs flesh.'[54] After this meal, tempers flared when Monkhouse and one of the ship's lieutenants took over Banks's tent to make love with the young women. Monkhouse pushed one of these girls out of the tent, upsetting all the others including Tiatia, who cried bitterly. Banks, who was already a little jealous of Monkhouse, yelled angrily at the surgeon, and as Parkinson drily commented, 'I expected that they would have decided it by a duel, which, however, they prudently avoided.'[55] That night Banks went off in a huff, leaving his tent to sleep with Purea and Tiatia in their canoe.

Purea hoped that she had now made her peace with Captain Cook, and sought to seal her alliance with the British. The next morning her former husband Amo arrived at the fort with their son, the high chief Te Ri'i rere (who was about seven years old) and a young woman. When they appeared Purea and her companions went out to meet them, stripping themselves to the waist as a sign of respect to the boy. The young chief, who carried the prestige of both of his parents, was carried on a man's back, a sign that he was intensely sacred.[56] Although Te Ri'i rere had not been invested as the paramount chief of Tahiti, he still played a key role in the ritual life of the island, and was

A portrait of Potatau, high chief of Atehuru, by William Hodges

treated with great respect by his people. Purea assured Cook that her son was the 'Heir apparent to the Sovereignty of the Island', and that only the ari'i rahi (high chief) was as sacred, although he was no friend to the English and would not come to see them. This was a mischievous reference to Tu, Tutaha's nephew, who after the battle of Maha'iatea had been installed with the highest titles on the island.

Purea and her ex-husband spent all of the next day with Cook and Banks. Amo asked a number of shrewd questions about England, and its manners and customs. Purea was irrepressible in her ambitions for her son, and this meeting was very provocative. It was intended to demonstrate Purea's friendship with the British, and clearly infuriated Tutaha. The next day he sent his men to kidnap one of the seamen, a Portuguese, promising him all kinds of good things if he would stay with him, although when an axe was offered for his release, the man was soon returned to the *Endeavour*. The next day Te Pau came to Banks with a large bale of bark-cloth for his sister Sophia, followed by Potatau, a tall, burly, powerful man with great presence who was the high chief of Atehuru, and his wife, who later claimed Cook as her 'brother'.[57] As more of the leading men and women aligned themselves with Cook and the *Endeavour* party, the balance of power in Tahiti was shifting. By this time, at least as far as Tutaha and his allies were concerned, the British had outstayed their welcome on the island.

6

Cook's Tour of Tahiti

On 26 June 1769, Captain Cook made a surprising decision. Although relationships with the Tahitians at Matavai Bay had become fraught, he decided to leave his ship and the fort, and make a circuit of the island. Accompanied by Joseph Banks and a Tahitian guide, Tuahu, and leaving Lieutenant Hicks in command, he set off eastwards in the pinnace. Cook wanted to draft a chart of the island, with soundings of its harbours, while Banks hoped to gather more natural and artificial 'curiosities' (i.e. specimens and artefacts) for his collections. This was glorious adventure, rowing down the eastern coast as bright-coloured fish darted through the coral below, and high mountains, luxuriant forests, and thatched houses and canoe sheds glided past along the shoreline. Early that morning they reached the mouth of the Papeno'o valley where the local chief gave them breakfast, and Banks met two young people who had acted as his fellow mourners several weeks earlier, who eagerly joined Cook's party.

After breakfast, Cook and Banks set out on foot to Hitia'a, where Bougainville's ships had anchored. Despite the long months at sea they were in good physical condition, walking almost twenty kilometres while the pinnace rowed offshore, taking soundings. At Hitia'a, they were greeted by the local chief Reti, a tall, active man with a cheerful manner, who showed them where the 'Spaniards' (in fact Bougainville and his men) had pitched their tents, and where their ships had anchored. After sharing a quick meal with Reti, Banks asked one of his young friends to guide them to the southern end of the island. At first the young man refused, saying that the people there owed no allegiance to Tutaha, and would kill him. His caution was not surprising, since they were heading straight for Tautira, the headquarters of Vehiatua, the great warrior leader of Tahiti-iti, at the southern end of the island. As soon as he saw them loading ball into their muskets, however, he changed his mind and agreed to go with them. They climbed on board the pinnace and rowed along the coast until nightfall, landing at the Taravao isthmus where some of their acquaintances from Matavai, who

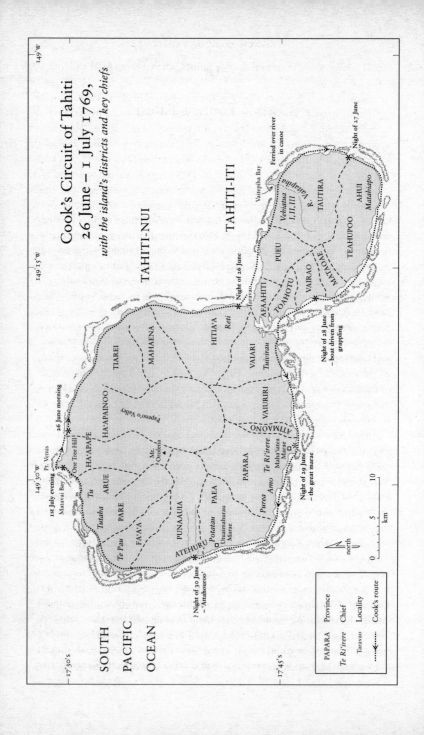

Cook's Circuit of Tahiti
26 June – 1 July 1769,
with the island's districts and key chiefs

SOUTH
PACIFIC
OCEAN

149° W

149°15′W

149°30′W

17°30′S

17°45′S

TAHITI-NUI

TAHITI-ITI

Pt. Venus

Matavai Bay — 26 June morning

1st July evening

One Tree Hill

Tu
Tutaha

Te Pau

ARUE

PARE

FA'A'A

HA'APAPE

HA'APAINOO

TIAREI

MAHAENA

Papeno'o Valley

Mt. Orohena

PUNAAUIA

PAEA

ATEHURU

? Night of 30 June –
'Attahouroo'

Potatau
Unaimahurau Marae

Purea
Amo

PAPARA

Te Ri'irere

Mahaiatea
Marae

VAIURIRI

ATIMAONO

VAIARI
Tutirrau

VAIRAO

MAYAOE

TOAHOTU

AFAAHITI

HITIA'A

Reti

Tarava

Night of 26 June

Night of 29 June –
the great marae

Night of 28 June –
boat driven from
grappling

PUEU

Vehiatua
I, II, III

Vaitepiha Bay

R.
Vaitapiha

Ferried over river
in canoe

TAUTIRA

TEAHUPOO

AHUI
Matahiapo

Night of 27 June

Legend

PAPARA	Province
Te Ri'irere	Chief
Taravao	Locality
·········	Cook's route

north

0   5   10
km

had arrived there in several double canoes, offered them food and lodgings for the night.

Taravao is a narrow, boggy isthmus, almost dividing Tahiti into two separate islands. When they got up at daybreak, Cook and Banks were told that the isthmus was crossed by a canoe portage, dividing the land into two great provinces. To the north (where Tutaha ruled) was Tahiti-nui [Great Tahiti], while the land to the south (where Vehiatua ruled) was called Tahiti-iti [Little Tahiti] or Taiarapu. These two parts of the island were divided into numerous districts, each with its own mountain and rivers, assembly ground, marae, arioi house and school of learning, and chiefly leader.[1] After exploring the marshlands for a while, the travellers carried on down the coast to Anuhi (now Pueu), the first district on the east coast of Tahiti-iti, where the local chief gave them food and exchanged a large hog for a hatchet. In a nearby house, they saw two 12-pound cannon balls, one marked with the English broad arrow – presumably a trophy from the *Dolphin*'s visit, although they were told that these had been a gift from the 'Spanish' leader, Bougainville. Again they set off on foot, walking about seven kilometres to Tautira, Vehiatua's headquarters on the south-east coast of the island. There they crossed a broad river, the Vaitepiha, where as Banks remarked with wry humour:

We were oblig'd to ferry over in a canoe and our Indian train to swim, which they did with as much facility as a pack of hounds taking the water in much the same manner.[2]

This valley is a spectacular place, encircled by high, misty mountains, where the Vaitepiha winds its way out of a precipitous gorge into a fertile plain, and a wide, sunlit harbour. As they reached the opposite bank of the river their companions dried themselves off, while Cook and Banks carried on to the easternmost point of the bay, where they found the warrior chief Vehiatua sitting under a decorated canoe awning. He was a thin, old man with very white hair and a beard, accompanied by his wife, a beautiful, high-born young woman named Purahi, who according to local histories was one of the key instigators of the war against Purea and Amo.[3]

Although Vehiatua was the ari'i rahi or paramount chief of Tahiti-iti, famed throughout the archipelago for his military prowess, their meeting with him was brief and unceremonious. He was still at war with Cook's friends, and uncertain about his visitors' intentions. Nevertheless, he greeted them courteously and sent his eldest son, Te Ari'i (also known as Ta'ata Uraura), to take them on the next stage of their journey.[4] Their guide Tuahu remained behind, and Te Ari'i took them further along the eastern coast,

The Vaitepiha River in Tahiti-iti, by William Hodges

where they saw many large houses in ruins, evidence of an enemy raid some time earlier.[5] In places, stone walls had been built to protect the plain from the sea; and it was intensively cultivated, with gardens watered by streams running along narrow stone channels. Fleets of large canoes, their awnings on pillars, lay hauled up on the beaches, and these were longer, with higher, more richly carved sterns than those in Tahiti-nui. On almost every point there was a marae or a burial place, ornamented with carvings; and these, too, were more elaborate than those in Tahiti-nui. As Banks noted:

[They were] raisd into the form of a roof of a house, but these were cleaner and better kept and also ornamented with many carvd boards set upright, on the tops of which were various figures of birds and men; on one particularly a figure of a cock painted red and yellow in imitation of the feathers of that bird [most likely the red and yellow feathers of 'Oro]. In some of them were figures of men standing on each-others heads which they told me was the particular ornament of Burying grounds [these were ancestor images].[6]

Despite the obvious wealth of this district, however, they were unable to obtain breadfruit, for all of the trees had been stripped of their fruit. The season of scarcity had begun, although the Tahitian chestnut or *mape* trees along the coast had begun to fruit profusely.

By now Cook and Banks were footsore and weary. It was a relief when the pinnace picked them up from one of the eastern beaches. At nightfall, they stopped in a bay on the south coast opposite a small island, anchoring the pinnace in a snug harbour with a freshwater rivulet. Banks wandered off into the woods, where he found an empty long-house. The Tahitians lit a fire, roasting just one breadfruit, some chestnuts, several ducks and a few curlews for their dinner. During the season of plenty, a chiefly person might be served several baked breadfruit, two or three fish, a large bunch of plantains and a quart of mashed pudding at a sitting, and the British had become accustomed to this kind of banquet. That night, Banks slept under the awning of Te Ari'i's canoe while Cook went to sleep in the long-house, lulled by the sound of the surf on the reefs off the islet. Some time during that night, their guide Tuahu arrived in the bay, found his way to the long-house and lay down beside him.

When they woke in the morning, Cook and his companions were ravenous. Banks wandered along the beach, looking for someone to give them food, but found no one. Again he and Cook set off on foot, walking about three miles to a bay where they found a number of large canoes hauled up on the beach, with a crowd of their acquaintances from Matavai sitting around them. The coconut palms in this bay were laden with nuts, and they asked their friends to climb up and pick some. When no one made a move, Banks threatened to cut down one of the trees unless they would do as he asked, but they simply sat there and stared at him. Eventually he and Cook realised that these people were strangers in the area with no rights to the palms, and traded for coconuts with some locals.

After this encounter they rejoined the pinnace, and the sailors rowed them west along the barren, rocky southern shoreline. When they reached a bay with some flat land and a river, their guide told Cook that this was the district of Ahui, ruled by a chief called Matahiapo.[7] As they landed on the beach, Matahiapo hurried out to greet them, gazing at them in astonishment. His people presented their visitors with bunches of coconuts but were reluctant to give them breadfruit, bartering about twenty at a very dear rate while the chief exchanged a pig for a glass bottle. At Matahiapo's settlement, Banks noticed an English goose and a turkey cock wandering about, relics from the *Dolphin* voyage and both immensely fat, which the people treated with great affection. The long-house in the village had fifteen underjawbones hung on a semicircular board at one end of its gable. Although these jawbones seemed quite fresh and undamaged, the local people would tell him nothing about them.

When they returned to the pinnace, Matahiapo asked if he could go with them, suggesting that Cook should visit a friend of his, a 'great man' to the north. Cook agreed, so Matahiapo climbed aboard the boat, urging them to stop and go ashore at every possible moment. After landing about five or six times along the west coast of Tahiti-iti to meet the local people, who showered them with gifts of breadfruit, coconuts, fish and plantains, they reached the western side of the Taravao isthmus. Matahiapo suggested that they should land there for the night, and they stopped in the district of Vaiari, where his friend, Tuivirau, welcomed them to his long-house.

As they settled down for the night, Banks stayed close to the women, hoping that one of them would offer him a place to sleep. For once this ploy did not work; for as he ruefully observed, 'They were very kind, too much so for they promisd more than I ask'd, but when they saw that we were resolvd to stay they dropd off one by one and at last left me jilted 5 or 6 times and obligd to seek out for a lodging myself.'[8] Before lying down to sleep, Banks sent his clothes off to the boat for safekeeping and wrapped himself in a length of bark-cloth. When Matahiapo complained about the cold, Cook sent a sailor to fetch him a cloak, but soon after this, the chief vanished. At first they supposed that he had gone off to wash, as the Tahitians always did before sleeping; but when their guide reported that Matahiapo had run off with the cloak, Banks jumped up in a fury, brandishing his pocket pistol and urging the Tahitians to chase the thief and recover the stolen garment. Shocked by his anger, they began to edge out of the house until he grabbed a man who seemed to be of aristocratic rank, and threatened to shoot him unless the cloak was recovered. Escorted by this man (who proved to be Tuivirau's brother), Cook and Banks ran out of the house to chase the thief. Although the cloak was brought back to them about ten minutes later, Banks was furious that Matahiapo had got away, thus escaping a 'severe thrashing'. He returned to the long-house where he and Cook settled down for the night, after persuading Tuivirau and his family to come back and sleep with them.

Early the next morning the sentry woke Cook in a panic, reporting that the pinnace was missing. He had seen it about half an hour earlier, riding on the grappling, but when he thought he heard the sound of oars splashing some time later and looked out to sea, he realised that it had vanished. Cook and Banks ran to the beach, but the boat was nowhere to be seen. Looking at each other in consternation, they realised that they had only one musket, two pocket pistols and limited ammunition between the three of them. If they were attacked, it would be difficult to defend themselves. Fortunately for their peace of mind, about fifteen minutes later the pinnace drifted back into view, having been driven off her grappling by the current. After a good breakfast, they set off on their journey again, making a brief stop in the last district on the west side of Tahiti-iti. The chief of this district, Moe, was in the process of building a house and was eager to trade for a hatchet, but unfortunately they had none left in the pinnace. After some negotiations Cook agreed to give Moe a hatchet if he would deliver a large pig to the *Endeavour*, and carried on to Vaiari [or Papeari] on the other side of the isthmus.

At Vaiari, they were joined by a group of their friends from Matavai, including Tupaia, who was overjoyed to see them safely back in Tahiti-nui. Tupaia took them straight to the local marae, which Cook described as a stone pavement with a pyramid about five feet high, covered entirely with palm nuts. Beside the pyramid sat the skulls of three men, 'very white and clean and quite perfect', and a little thatched roof sheltering a small stone image. An altar nearby carried the skulls of twenty-six hogs and six dogs, the remains of earlier sacrifices. After this visit they went back to the pinnace and were rowed further up the coast, landing at a bay where Tupaia persuaded the local people to show them an image of the god Maui, the only one on the island. This was a wickerwork figure about seven feet high, covered with white feathers to represent its skin, and black feathers for its hair and tattoo patterns. The god was clothed in a loincloth which covered its genitals, with four small protuberances on his head which the people described as *ta'ata iti* [little people]. When they tried to explain the functions of the image to the Europeans, however, as Banks remarked in frustration, 'their language was totaly unintelligible and seemed to referr to some customs to which we are perfect strangers'.[9]

From this bay they rowed up the west coast to Papara, the home of Purea and Amo, where they intended to spend the night. Unfortunately their friends had gone to Matavai Bay, but in their absence Purea's father offered them hospitality. Purea's small house was not far from Maha'iatea, the marae which she and Amo had built for their son. The great monument loomed up on a sandy beach shaded by a clump of *toa* [ironwood] trees, and Tupaia took Cook and Banks to see it. As they measured its dimensions, Tupaia made a sketch of its layout. According to their descriptions, Maha'iatea was a pyramid made up of eleven steps, rising up all around 'like those leading to a sundial'. Each step was four feet high, made from a row of white squared coral rocks topped with rows of rounded polished stones (each shaped from basalt). On the apex of this pyramid, which measured 177 feet by 7, stood the figure of a bird carved in wood, and a broken stone image of a fish. Its base of squared reddish stone measured 267 feet long and 87 feet wide, with a wide stone pavement before it, edged by a stone wall, which they measured as 360 feet by 354 feet in total. Plantain and toa trees grew up from this pavement, sheltering it from the sun, and on other paved areas nearby stood raised altars on pillars about seven feet high, carrying the skulls of about fifty pigs and some dogs. Tupaia assured his companions that these skulls represented only a fraction of the sacrifices that had been offered to the gods since their conquest by Vehiatua and Tutaha; and as they walked across the beach, human bones (mainly ribs and vertebrae) crunched under their feet, a grisly reminder of the battle which had raged there six months earlier.[10]

During their visit to Maha'iatea, Tupaia told Banks and Cook that this place had been devastated during the month of *Varehu* (December–January 1768–9). Hundreds of people had been killed, and the great marae built for Te Ri'i rere's investiture had been desecrated, destroying the mana (sacred power) of his ancestors. Enraged warriors had thrown down the images of the gods from the marae, demolishing its sacred structures and burning the houses of the local inhabitants. The turkey and goose which they had seen in Matahiapo's district were part of the plunder, as were the jawbones hung up in the houses. Since the battle, however, the marae had been reconsecrated. The sacrifices resting on the pillared altars had been offered in the *raumatavehi* ceremony, which was performed when a district had been despoiled by enemy warriors. In this ceremony, a marae was purified with sea water and incantations, and the gods were ceremoniously put back in their places. Human sacrifices were offered, and when the rituals were completed, the high priest chanted:

> The land is restored as land,
> The temples are restored as temples,
> The gods reign again as gods
> The high chief is restored to his position
> All is well once more
> The sickness of the temples is healed
> The sickness of the altars is healed
> The sickness of the land is healed.
> Extend the peace, great peace
> Let there be deep peace
> Let there be long peace
> Let there be excellent peace![11]

Afterwards, there was feasting and celebrations.

Banks and Cook slept in Purea's small house that night, and the next morning they carried on up the west coast to Atehuru. There they met their 'intimate friends' (no doubt Purea and Amo), who greeted them with pleasure. That night they slept peacefully, and the next morning they boarded the pinnace again. After a brief visit to Tutaha at Pare, Cook came back to Matavai Bay on 1 July, having completed his circuit of the island.

During this journey, Cook realised that the breadfruit season on the island had ended. For the next three months, the people would be living on *mahi* [fermented breadfruit paste], *mape* [Tahitian chestnuts] and a few late-fruiting breadfruit and plantains from the mountains, with no surplus available for his sailors. He decided to leave Tahiti as soon as possible, ordering his men to complete all repairs on the ship, pack up the shore camp and dismantle the fort at Point Venus. The canoes he had confiscated were still in the river, so he began to return these to their owners. His taio Potatau, the chief of Atehuru, claimed one of these canoes, but when he tried to take it away a number of people protested loudly, saying that it was not his. At first he tried to say that he had bought it from Cook for a pig, but when this was denied, Potatau and his wife were covered with shame. For the rest of that day they could scarcely speak or look anyone in the eye, so great was their humiliation.

On 3 July, while the sailors were packing up the shore camp, Banks and Monkhouse walked up the Vaipopo valley. About two miles upriver, they met people coming down with loads of breadfruit on their backs, gathered in the hillside plantations. The trees in the hills, which fruited later than those on the plains, had been planted there to lengthen the breadfruit season. Nevertheless, when the *Dolphin* had visited Tahiti at about the same time, the supplies of breadfruit had been plentiful; so Banks concluded that the timing of the fruiting season must vary from year to year. He and Monkhouse carried on up the valley, passing numerous clusters of houses; and about six miles beyond the last house they came to a place where a high waterfall tumbled from a cliff 100 feet high, into a very deep pool. Although this cliff was precipitous, it was crossed by a pathway with ropes of hibiscus bark strung across the rock face, where people climbed up to the plateau above to collect wild plantains. Banks examined the bare rock carefully, looking for signs of minerals. When he found none, he decided that this high island was either an extinct volcano (a good guess), or an exposed mountain top from the great Unknown Continent, which must have sunk below the sea during some great cataclysm.

The following day, Banks planted watermelons, oranges, lemons and limes on Point Venus, and watched curiously as a young girl had her buttocks tattooed near the shore camp, held down by two older women who alternately coaxed and beat her. The sailors took down the guns from the fort and carried them back to the ship; and the sails were brought up on deck and hoisted. Purea's son Te Ri'i rere came to visit the British again, accompanied by his future wife, although Purea would not allow the girl to enter the tents. During this meeting she warned Banks that the thief who had stolen the quadrant from the fort had vowed to attack their encampment, but instead, the staple and hook of the great gate were taken. Again Banks led the hue and cry, chasing the thief for about six miles up into the forest. The man had concealed himself in some rushes by a stream, however, watching as Banks and his companions ran past him.

During their last days at Tahiti, relationships both on the ship and ashore became increasingly volatile. On 9 July, two of Cook's sailors were attacked when one of them had his knife stolen, and tried to recover it. He was hit on the forehead with a stone, while his companion was slightly wounded. That same morning, two of the marines on duty at the fort deserted from their posts. When they first arrived at Tahiti, there had been murmurings of mutiny among the crew, which had soon settled down, so this was an unpleasant omen. According to Molyneux, one of these men, Clement Webb, 'is a sober man & was steward of the Gunroom which Office he faithfully perform'd but being extravagantly fond of a young woman with whom he has been connected for some time', while the other, Samuel Gibson, 'is a wild young man & a sworn Brother to Webb – he has no other reason than the pleasure of living in a fine Country without controul they both had large Promises from some of the Principal men & was to have Lands & servants assighn'd them.'[12]

Cook waited all that day, hoping that the missing men would return to the ship of their own accord, but the next morning he was forced to take action. He despatched a midshipman, Jonathan Monkhouse, and a corporal of marines to find them; and when Purea, Potatau, Te Pau and his wife, Banks's lover Tiatia and others came to the fort, he ordered his officers to detain them, telling the chiefs that they would be kept under guard until the deserters were brought back to Point Venus. Lieutenant Hicks was sent in the pinnace to fetch Tutaha, and he 'took him or rather stole him from the people', delivering him to the *Endeavour*. As night fell, Te Pau, Potatau and Purea were rowed out to the ship, weeping and loudly protesting their ill-treatment. Banks stayed behind in his tent with the rest of the prisoners until, at about 8 pm, Webb was brought there by some of Purea's people. He delivered a message that Tutaha's followers had captured Monkhouse and the corporal of marines, and were determined to hold them hostage until the Regent was released from captivity.

As soon as this message was brought out to the ship, Cook told the chiefs that unless they ordered their people to release the two men immediately, he would punish them severely. He despatched an armed boat, commanded by Hicks, with Tupaia on board as a voluntary hostage. With Tupaia's assistance, Hicks's armed party was quickly led to the place where Monkhouse and Truslove were held. By now, a large crowd had gathered around the fort, many of them armed, although according to Banks, 'they were very civil and shewd much fear as they have done of me upon all occasions, probably because I never shewd the least of them but have upon all our quarrels gone immediately into the thickest of them.'[13] Early the next morning, the British hostages were delivered to the *Endeavour*, and Cook released Tutaha and the other chiefs. Although he presented them with gifts as they left the ship, as they returned to the beach, Banks saw 'no sign of forgiveness . . . in their faces, they lookd sulky and affronted'.[14] That night, Cook wrote with regret:

Thus we are likly to leave these people in disgust with our behaviour towards them, owing wholy to the folly of two of our own people for it doth not appear that the natives had any hand in inticeing them away and therefore were not the first agressors, however it is very certain that had we not taken this step we never should have recover'd them.[15]

Tupaia had acted as a voluntary hostage during this crisis, siding with the British during the negotiations, and this no doubt caused bitter resentment. Early the next morning he came out to tell Joseph Banks that he had decided to leave the island, and to sail with them to England. Although Tupaia had often talked about joining the *Endeavour* expedition, his decision was unexpected. As Banks noted with pleasure:

He is certainly a most proper man, well born, chief *Tahowa* or preist of this Island, consequently skilld in the mysteries of their religion; but what makes him more than any thing else desireable is his experience in the navigation of these people and knowledge of the Islands in these seas; he has told us the names of above 70, the most of which he has himself been at. The Captn refuses to take him on his own account, in my opinion sensibly enough, the goverment will never in all human probability take any notice of him; I therefore have resolvd to take him. Thank heaven I have a sufficiency and I do not know why I may not keep him as a curiosity, as well as some of my neighbours do lions and tygers at a larger expence than he will probably ever put me to; the amusement I shall have in his future conversation and the benefit he will be of to this ship, as well as what he may be if another should be sent into these seas, will I think fully repay me.[16]

As a sign of their friendship, Banks gave Tupaia a miniature of himself to show to his friends, and some gifts to take ashore. That afternoon Tupaia accompanied Banks's artists to make a few final sketches of Tutaha's marae;

and when he left to farewell his friends, Cook, Banks and Solander walked to Tutaha's house at Pare, where Purea and Potatau were staying. They soon made their peace with the chiefs, who promised to come out to say goodbye the next morning. As the last tents were lowered and loaded on board, the sailors exchanged gifts with their taio. Cook and his companions returned to the ship, accompanied by Tupaia and a young boy, Taiato, his servant; and that night the high priest slept for the first time on board the *Endeavour*.

Early the next morning, Purea, Potatau and his wife, Tiatia (Banks's lover) and their companions came out to the ship. Tutaha, Cook's taio, and Te Pau and his wife did not accompany them, so they must still have been angry about the way they had been treated. There were final exchanges of gifts, and at about 11 am Cook gave the order to raise the anchors. The people in canoes alongside lamented loudly, calling out '*Aue! Aue!*' [Alas! Alas!], while Purea and the others burst into tears. Tupaia tried not to cry, but he eventually broke down as he presented his friends with a shirt to give to Tutaha's favourite wife. When Purea and her companions boarded their canoes, he and Banks went to the topmast head and stood waving until they were out of sight. At dusk, as they sailed in light easterly winds, Tetiaroa, a cluster of islands around a reef to the north (which Tupaia told them had no permanent population, and was owned by the high chief), came into sight, and Tupaia gave Cook sailing directions for Huahine and Ra'iatea, his home island.

An Arioi Voyage through the Society Islands

Tupaia was a high priest of 'Oro, renowned throughout the archipelago for his courage and formidable intellect, and his ritual and navigational knowledge. As Molyneux noted in his journal: '[He] has appear'd always to be infinitely superiour in every Respect to any other Indian we have met with, and he has conceiv'd so strong a Freindship for Mr. Banks that he is Determined to Visit Britannia.'[17] As soon as they set sail, Tupaia began to act as the *Endeavour*'s high priest-navigator. He set the course for Tetiaroa, and when the ship entered a zone of light, variable breezes, he prayed from the stern windows: '*O Tane, ara mai matai, ara mai matai!*' [O Tane, bring me a fair wind!], crying out when the breeze died down, '*Ua riri au!*' [I am angry!], although Banks was dubious about his efforts, remarking that Tupaia 'never began till he saw a breeze so near the ship that it generaly reachd her before his prayer was finished'.[18]

Despite Banks's scepticism, Cook was glad to have Tupaia on board, acting as the ship's pilot. He wanted to cruise around the archipelago for a few weeks, making charts, collecting provisions and allowing his men to recover from their venereal infections, and this would be much easier with Tupaia to guide the expedition through these unknown waters. By now Tupaia (who was a good linguist) had picked up a smattering of English, while Cook had acquired a little Tahitian. Banks and Parkinson, who had studied Tahitian vocabulary and grammar, were more fluent in the language, although their knowledge was still rudimentary. Their communications with Tupaia may have been rough and ready, but anyone who has ventured into strange societies will know the value of such linguistic bridgeheads. Tupaia knew these waters well, and he was familiar with local customs and practices. From this time on, his presence on board the *Endeavour* transformed the voyage.

As soon as they were under way, Cook acted to reassert shipboard discipline by ordering the two marines who deserted in Tahiti to be punished. Early in the morning after their departure the boatswain's whistle shrilled, summoning the ship's company to witness punishment, and the sailors and marines stood by as their comrades were tied to the gratings and each was flogged with two dozen lashes. By sunset that evening the *Endeavour* was sailing in a steady wind, as Huahine and Ra'iatea (the most southerly of the Leeward Islands) appeared on the horizon.

When the sun came up the next morning, some canoes from Huahine came out to inspect the vessel. At first the local people seemed terrified, trembling when they saw the Europeans, but Tupaia soon reassured them. A canoe carrying the high chief of the island and his wife came alongside, and the high chief (a very tall man, six feet four inches high, named Ori[19]) boarded the *Endeavour*, where Ori greeted Cook, exchanging names with him. As they approached the gap in the reef Tupaia sent a local man to dive down beneath the keel to see how much water it drew, guiding the ship safely into the harbour. When he took Cook and his party ashore at Fare, Tupaia stripped himself to the waist, asking Dr Monkhouse to do the same as a sign of respect to the gods of the island. Tupaia and Monkhouse, in his perceived role as *tahu'a* (priest-healer) among the Tahitians, sat bare-chested before Ori's long-house with Cook, Banks and Solander behind them; while Tupaia made a long speech and presented two handkerchiefs, a black silk neckcloth, some beads and two small bunches of feathers to the local people. Two chiefs from Huahine spoke in reply, welcoming the strangers and presenting Tupaia with some young plantain plants and two small bunches of feathers, and a pig and some coconuts. In such rituals, gifts were presented to each other's gods to show that the two groups had come together in friendship. Plantain plants symbolised human sacrifices, the red feathers were prized signs of 'Oro's power, while the pig and coconuts represented fertility and prosperity. When these exchanges were completed, Tupaia sent the feather bunches out to the ship, and then went to the local marae 'to pay his oblations', as Cook put it;[20] performing the rituals of thanksgiving so that the gods would protect them during their voyage.[21]

During their brief stay on Huahine, the high chief Ori told Cook that warriors from the nearby island of Borabora held his people in subjection, arriving every few weeks to take away their possessions, and killing anyone who opposed them. He pleaded with Cook to free his island from these invaders, but Cook refused to get involved in local politics. When Cook asked for fresh supplies of pork and vegetables, Ori replied that it would take some time to gather provisions from different parts of the island, suggesting that they should stay longer. Nevertheless, Sydney Parkinson reported that the land around Fare harbour was fertile and productive, with gardens of bark-cloth and sweet potatoes, and plantations of coconut, plantain trees and breadfruit. The bark-cloth cultivations were laid out with care, edged with stone curbings and drained by ditches planted with taro. The local people were eager to exchange names with the British, regarding this as a mark of great friendship, and generously supplied them with pigs and other provisions. They seemed less afraid, but at the same time less inquisitive than the Tahitians had been, and their women were remarkably delicate and beautiful. During this visit to Huahine, Joseph Banks was disconsolate and frustrated. He was missing his lover, Tiatia, and Tupaia was preoccupied with his friends and estates on Huahine,[22] leaving Banks to wander about with young Taiato. He explored the area around the harbour, noting the large boathouses with their carved pillars and a finely crafted mobile god-house, but complaining that he could find few new species of plants, and that the Huahine people were 'almost exactly like our late friends but rather more stupid and lazy'.[23]

On 19 July, after only three days at Fare, Cook decided to carry on to Ra'iatea, Tupaia's home island. He presented some medals and a small plate to his taio Ori, engraved with the inscription, *His Britannick Maj. Ship Endeavour, Lieut Cook Commander 16th July 1769, Huaheine*, to record the *Endeavour*'s 'discovery' of the island. Tupaia set the course, and at sunrise the next morning, the *Endeavour* sailed into the sacred pass, Te Ava Moa, through the coral reef which encircled Ra'iatea. When the anchors rattled down into the calm waters of the lagoon, they found themselves opposite Taputapuatea marae in the legendary district of Opoa. Tupaia had taken them to the heart of the arioi cult. As the missionary William Ellis explained in 1859:

Opoa is the most remarkable place in Raiatea; of its earth, according to some of their traditions, the first pair were made by Tii or Taaroa, and on its soil they fixed their abode. Here Oro held his court. It was called Hawaii; and as distant colonies are said to have proceeded from it, it was probably the place at which some of the first inhabitants of the South Sea Islands arrived. It has also long been a place of celebrity, not only in Raiatea, but throughout the whole of the Society Islands. It was the hereditary land of the reigning family, and the usual residence of the king and his household.

But the most remarkable object connected with Opoa, was the large marae, or temple, where the national idol was worshipped, and human victims were sacrificed. These offerings were not only brought from the districts of Raiatea and the adjacent islands, but also from the windward group, and even from the more distant islands to the south and south-east. The worship of Oro, in the marae here, appears to have been of the most sanguinary kind; human immolation was frequent, . . . [with] bones and other relics of the former sacrifices, now scattered among the ruins of the temple. A number of beautiful trees grow around especially the tamanu and the aoa.[24]

Soon after the *Endeavour* had anchored, two canoes paddled out from the marae, each carrying a pig and a chiefly woman. At first their crews seemed very frightened of the Europeans, but Tupaia was able to reassure them. When the women ventured on board this strange vessel they were each given a spike nail and some beads, which pleased them, and they warned Tupaia that the Borabora invaders were nearby, and planning to come the next day to attack the strangers. Cook and Banks decided to go ashore at once, before the Borabora warriors arrived. They landed on the beach where Tupaia led them through a ceremony almost identical to the rituals of welcome on Huahine several days earlier. As soon as this was over, the marines went through their ceremonial drill and Cook raised the Union Jack, formally taking possession of Ra'iatea and the adjacent islands – Borabora, Tahaa and Huahine – in the name of His Britannic Majesty.

Once the flag was fluttering on its pole, Tupaia led his companions to Taputapuatea, the most sacred marae in the archipelago. This was an awesome place, shaded by trees, where the world of darkness, *Te Po*, inhabited by gods and ancestors, came into contact with the world of light, inhabited by living people. In the words of a Tahitian text:

Marae were the sanctity and glory of the land; they were the pride of the people of these islands. The ornaments of the land were the marae, they were the palaces presented to the gods.

Terrible were the marae of the royal line: their ancestral and national marae! They were places of stupendous silence, terrifying and awe-inspiring; places of pain to the priests, to the owners, and to all the people . . . When a canoe passed along the shore, it withdrew far off as it approached the point where stood the royal marae, the people lowered their clothes, and paddled lightly until they passed the marae.

It was dark and shadowy among the great trees of those marae; and the most sacred of them all was the *miro* that was the sanctifier . . .

> It was the basis of royalty;
> It awakened the gods;
> It fixed the *'uru* [red feather] girdle of sovereigns.[25]

At this marae, where the most sacred high chiefs of the archipelago were invested, the priests spoke with their ancestor gods, invoking their power to ensure the fertility of the land and sea, and protect their people.

Tupaia had brought his shipmates to this great marae to ask for 'Oro's blessing on their journey, but Banks seemed oblivious to the solemnity of the occasion. Wandering along the long walls of the main marae, edged by massive coral slabs and topped with tall carved planks, past an altar carrying a large roasted pig, he came upon a group of four or five god-houses. Thrusting his hand into one of these shrines he found a parcel about five feet long, wrapped up in mats, which he tore with his fingers until he reached a layer of plaited sinnet, the covering of the god. As he later admitted, 'what I had done gave much offence to our new friends', but offered no comment on Tupaia's reaction. Sydney Parkinson, however, remarked: '[The local people] behaved so coolly that the captain did not know what to make of them. Toobaiah, who was with him, seemed to be quite displeased. We did not know the occasion of their reservedness.'[26] Banks had desecrated the image of a god at Taputapuatea, the height of sacrilege, and Tupaia must have been horrified. The punishment for such an act was death, and it was an ill omen for their voyage. Soon afterwards they went to a long-house in which rolls of cloth were stored, where they saw a model of a canoe about three feet long with eight under-jawbones attached to it, a trophy from the Borabora conquest of the island. As Banks and Solander walked along the beach in the dusk, they came upon a god-house with a row of jawbones hung along its eaves, which according to the local people also belonged to Ra'iatea men who had been killed during the Borabora conquest.

During their brief visit to Opoa, Cook ordered the forge to be set up to make nails for barter, and put Dr Monkhouse and Tupaia in charge of all trade, which greatly annoyed the sailors. As Pickersgill complained, 'this day Trade Oligopoliz'd on Shore by the Surgeon &c whilst the most Triffling Things was not admitted to be Purchas'd on board even by the Petty Officers a Centinal Being Putt on each ganway on Purpus while the 2d Lieutn (Mr

A sketch of Taputapuatea marae, showing the stone slabs of the
main marae with carved plants and an offering of roast pig, by
Sydney Parkinson

Gore) stay'd on the Qr Deck all day.'²⁷ At Tahiti, the sailors had obsessively traded for 'curiosities' and sex, and Ra'iatea offered new opportunities; but Gore was unmoved by their protests. Although he was intent on controlling the terms of trade, Cook wanted to ensure that none of the crew could slip ashore, provoking the sort of drastic measures that had ruined their last days on Tahiti. In addition, at least half of his men were now suffering from VD, and he did not want them to infect the Ra'iatean women. Discipline among the sailors had become lax during their months in Tahiti, but now that they were back at sea, Captain Cook was determined to reassert his authority.

The people of Ra'iatea were expert boat-builders, and when they went ashore, Banks and Solander saw many large boathouses, similar to those at Huahine. Banks watched a large double *pahi* or sailing canoe being built, and Tupaia told him that in such canoes island navigators sailed out of sight of land for twenty days or more, although after that time they had to land to procure fresh provisions. Sydney Parkinson went straight to Taputapuatea, where he made a black and white water-colour sketch of the main marae complex. Later he wrote a vivid description of Taputapuatea, its altar which carried offerings of roasted pig and fish, and a large house nearby which held the large drums whose solemn tones summoned the gods to the great rituals. Near this house a group of 'cages' stood on poles, shaded by thatched roofs of palm leaves, which acted as perches for the sacred birds – grey heron, and blue and brown kingfishers. The marae pavements were made with coral flagstones and edged with flowering shrubs, and on a pavement facing the sea, a pyramid faced with large rough stones had been built which carried many long boards carved with various figures. According to Parkinson, the priests of this marae wore feather capes ornamented with round polished pieces of mother-of-pearl; semicircular breastplates made of wickerwork covered with rows of green pigeon feathers and sharks' teeth and fine white dog's hair; and high hats made of bamboo decorated with stripped quills and feathers. These priests were attended by boys smutted with charcoal, who helped them to place the offerings on the altars. He added that these people worshipped the rainbow, which he called 'Tamaiti no Tane' [Tane's child], although according to local traditions the rainbow was closely associated with the worship of 'Oro.[28]

According to Cook, at the time of the Endeavour's visit the district of Opoa was relatively impoverished. The people were few, and their gardens and plantations had been ravaged during the Borabora conquest. Cook was intent on provisioning the ship for the next stage of their journey, so he decided to look elsewhere for supplies. On 24 July, he tried to take the Endeavour through the pass opposite Fa'aroa to the adjacent island of Tahaa, but the winds were north-easterly and the ship was almost driven ashore on several occasions. Fortunately, early the next morning a good breeze blew up from the north-west, and the Endeavour sailed through the pass and crossed to the east coast of Tahaa, an island which shared its reef with Ra'iatea. As they approached Tahaa, Tupaia indicated a pass through the reef to a large harbour (Hamene Bay), but the winds were unfavourable and they could not reach it. Two days later, tacking back to Tahaa, Cook sent the longboat through the pass to inspect the harbour. When they landed at Hamene Bay, the local people greeted them warmly, lowering their clothes to their waists, the customary sign of respect for ari'i rahi or high chiefs, and presented them with gifts of pigs, chickens, and as many yams and plantains as they could load in the longboat. They were grateful for these supplies, because by now the ship's bread was crawling with vermin. As Banks remarked, boiled plantains and yams tasted much better than weevil-infested ship's biscuits.

After this brief visit to Tahaa, Cook sailed north to the high island of Borabora, where Tupaia warned them against landing, saying that his enemies would attack the ship, although most of the Borabora warriors had gone to Ra'iatea. He told Cook that there was a good passage through the reef on the west side of the island, opposite a deep harbour, but the winds were unfavourable so they sailed on to Maurua (now Maupiti) instead, a

small island with no good passage through its reef for the vessel. On
1 August, having sailed down the western side of Tahaa, the *Endeavour*
finally came to anchor in Hamanino Bay on the rocky north-west coast of
Ra'iatea, where Cook hoped to procure more ballast, and repair a leak in
the ship's powder-room.

Hamanino Bay was Tupaia's birthplace, a snug cove sheltered by an offshore
reef, with a curving river behind it. It has changed very little over the past
two hundred years; the river still winds slowly down through groves of
coconut palms out to the calm waters of the harbour. Before the Borabora
invasion, Tupaia's family had owned numerous estates around this bay,
twenty of which Banks listed in his working vocabulary. They worshipped
at Taputapuatea and Tainuu marae, which still stand on the island.[29] Here
the *Endeavour* was warmly welcomed. Perhaps because this was Tupaia's
home district, the local people came out to the ship in large numbers,
bringing generous gifts of pigs, chickens and plantains. When Banks and
Solander went ashore the next morning, they were given a rapturous
reception:

Everybody seemd to fear and respect us but nobody to mistrust us in the smallest
degree, men women and children came crouding after us but no one shewd us the
least incivility, on the contrary wherever there was dirt or water to pass over they
strove who should carry us on their backs.[30]

In the Society Islands, high chiefs were carried on people's backs to keep
their feet from touching the ground, thus rendering it sacred, a custom they
had previously encountered in Tahiti. In the chiefly houses they visited at
Hamanino, however, they were greeted with an unfamiliar ceremony. The
people rushed into the house, placing themselves on either side of a long
mat, at the end of which one or two pretty, well-dressed children sat waiting
to receive gifts from their visitors. In one of these houses, a girl about six
years old dressed in red bark-cloth, her head decorated with a large quantity
of plaited human hair wound around it, greeted them with great dignity.
Banks was impressed with her demeanour: 'As we walkd up to her, . . . she
stretchd out her hand to receive the beads we were to give, but had she been
a princess royal of England giving her hand to be kissd no instruction could
have taught her to have done it with a better grace. So much is untaught
nature superior to art that I have seen no sight of the kind that has struck
me half so much.'[31]

During Cook's stay at Hamanino, the local people staged a series of
entertainments in his honour. In one house, a man put on a head-dress

Ariori dancers and musicians perform for Cook's men at
Hamanino harbour, Ra'iatear, Tupaia's birthplace

about four feet high, decorated on the front with feathers and edged with
sharks' teeth and the tail feathers of tropic birds, and performed a comic
dance; slowly turning and then suddenly dipping his head so that the feathers
of the head-dress brushed against the faces of the spectators. His audience
laughed uproariously, especially if the victim was one of the British. On
another occasion Cook, Banks, Solander and Parkinson were entertained
by a troupe of arioi who were touring round the island, two women dancers
and six men, who danced to the music of a small group of drummers. These
were fine-looking, aristocratic people, the women wearing pearls in their
ears and large coils of plaited hair on their heads, decorated with gardenias.
Their shoulders and arms were bare, and they wore bodices of black cloth,
with bunches of black feathers on each shoulder. They had thick layers of
pleated bark-cloth around their waists, which shimmered as they rapidly
rotated their hips, sometimes standing, sometimes sitting or resting on their
knees and elbows. They danced on a large mat, moving their fingers at
high speed, twisting their mouths in strange contortions, and sometimes
performing erotic gestures which left the sailors gasping. An old man acted
as their prompter, and the men and women took turns to dance, moving in
strict unison. In between these dances, arioi clowns performed a satire which
depicted the conquest of the island by the Borabora warriors; and in the last
scene of this skit, Parkinson noted primly, 'the actions of the men were very
lascivious'. The next day they were invited to watch a competition where

the men threw light spears at a mark, which they did with more enthusiasm than accuracy.

In this festive atmosphere, Cook and Banks's party wandered freely around the bay, visiting several marae where they saw jawbones hung up in the god-houses, and skulls laid out in rows from the Borabora conquest. There were also numerous boathouses along the coastline, sheltering large canoes with bellied sides and high-peaked sterns, which they were told sailed only at certain times of the year. According to Cook:

In these Pahee's [pahi],᾿ . . . these people sail in those seas from Island to Island for several hundred Leagues, the Sun serving them for a compass by day and the Moon and stars by night. When this comes to be prov'd we Shall be no longer at a loss to know how the Islands lying in those Seas came to be people'd, for if the inhabitants of Uleitea have been at Islands laying 2 or 300 Leagues to the westward of them it cannot be doubted but that the inhabitants of those western Islands may have been at others as far to westward of them and so we may trace them from Island to Island quite to the East Indias.[32]

This was a perceptive observation, foreshadowing the findings of contemporary scholarship on the exploration of the Pacific, which point to migratory voyages from west to east across the Pacific, with the East Indies as one early homeland.

During their stay at Hamanino, the ari'i rahi of Ra'iatea, an unassuming man named Uru,[33] visited the British accompanied by his son, a remarkably handsome young fellow. According to Tupaia, however, most of the people now living in the district were Borabora invaders, who had seized the land (including his own estates) after their conquest of the island. He told his companions that the high chiefs of Tahiti and Ra'iatea had originally used Borabora as a kind of Alcatraz, a place of exile for thieves and other criminals. Over the years, however, its population had grown, and the Boraborans turned to piracy, seizing canoes at sea and confiscating their cargoes. When the high chief Puni came to power on the island, he had forged his warriors into a strong army, inspiring them with imperial ambitions.[34] First they attacked the nearby island of Tahaa, conquering it decisively. Emboldened by this success, they descended upon the sacred island of Ra'iatea, where the people fought bravely in defence of their high chief until, three years later, the Borabora warriors finally killed him. His young son was invested with the red feather girdle and his father's titles, and reigned on the island until Puni gathered a great army and attacked in force, conquering his people. Tupaia, who had fought in this last battle, was wounded and fled to the mountains. As the marauding warriors devastated the island, the young high chief was taken by canoe to his mother's lands in Papara. According to this account, as soon as his wounds were healed, Tupaia joined the high chief and settled down in Papara, where he became Purea's lover, and high priest of 'Oro on the island.[35]

Puni, whom Tupaia cordially detested, was now an old man about 90 years old, and staying in a nearby bay on the island (although his main residence was on Tahaa). On 4 August he sent a gift of three hogs, some lengths of bark-cloth, plantains and coconuts to Cook, saying that he would soon come and visit him. On this occasion Tupaia studiously avoided advising Cook on the proper protocol and no return gift was sent, deeply offending the old warrior. Several days later three pretty young girls arrived out at the ship to ask when Puni's return gift would be delivered. That afternoon Banks and Cook went to see the old chief at his encampment, carrying a small present, but as Banks remarked with chagrin:

The King of the *Tata toas* or Club men who have conquerd this and are the terror of all other Islands we expected to see young lively hansome &c &c. but how were we disapointed when we were led to an old decrepid half blind man who seemd to have scarce reason enough left to send hogs, much less galantry enough to send ladies.[36]

By now Cook had completed his chart of the west side of Ra'iatea, but he still wanted to visit the west coast of Tahaa, so he invited Puni to accompany him. At sunrise the next morning he left Hamanino with the pinnace and the longboat, travelling along the coast to the great lagoon where Puni joined him in his canoe, and they went together to Hurepiti harbour where Puni had his main settlement. The houses in this harbour were large and elaborate, and the canoes were finely crafted, so Cook hoped for generous gifts of pigs and other supplies from Puni's people. When he presented the old warrior with an axe, however, he received nothing in return; so at noon he left the harbour and travelled to the northern end of Tahaa to complete his survey, trading en route for pigs, chickens, plantains and yams with the local people. Banks and Parkinson had stayed behind to attend the arioi Heiva, so that Parkinson could sketch the dancers. The following day Banks visited the Heiva again, this time with Dr Solander. They watched a skit that showed a successful theft (perhaps a depiction of the god Hiro at work), and then went off to search for plants, although new species were now almost impossible to come by.

By this time the ballast had been loaded on board, and the repairs to the powder-room were completed. Cook was happy with the quantities of pigs, chickens, plantains and yams he had procured, and was ready to continue his search for the Great Unknown Southern Continent. Tupaia's homeland was in the hands of his enemies, who rejoiced in their victories over his people; and unknown islands were waiting over the horizon. On 9 August, an easterly breeze sprang up, which took the ship out from the bay. As Cook set a course to the south and the coast of Ra'iatea faded on the horizon, Banks remarked:

We again Launchd out into the Ocean in search of what chance and Tupia might direct us to.[37]

7

Travellers from Hawaiki

As the *Endeavour* sailed from Ra'iatea, Tupaia urged Cook to head to the west, where he said there were plenty of islands. He assured Cook that he had visited some of these islands before, on a voyage which took '10 to 12 days in going thither and 30 or more in coming back'. When Cook asked how this was possible, Tupaia explained that his people used the prevailing easterly trade winds to sail to the west, and the summer westerly wind shifts (which were common in these latitudes between November and January) to sail back to Ra'iatea.[1] Cook had been puzzled about how island navigators could travel eastwards across the Pacific when the prevailing winds blew in the opposite direction, and this answered his question. From Tupaia's description of the islands he had visited, Cook thought that they must be part of the Tongan group visited by Abel Tasman in 1643, 1200 miles west of Tahiti.[2] Despite Tupaia's entreaties, however, Captain Cook set a course south, intent on resuming his search for Terra Australis. As they headed out to sea, Tupaia told Cook that several days to the south-east there was an island called Manu'a; and that shortly afterwards they should see an island called Hitiroa, which he had visited more than twenty years earlier. Over the following days there was no sighting of Manu'a, but on 13 August they came to a small volcanic island (Rurutu), where Cook sent Gore ashore with Banks, Solander and Tupaia in the pinnace.

As they rowed towards the island, several men armed with long spears came down to the shore, where about sixty people were waiting. Gore decided not to risk a landing and told his men to carry on to the next bay, but upon rounding the point they found another group of armed warriors on the beach, who sent a small, ornately carved canoe out to meet them. As they paddled towards the pinnace Tupaia called out to its crew, trying to befriend them; but when the canoe came alongside three of these warriors suddenly leaped into the boat, one of whom seized Banks's powder-horn. Banks struggled with his assailant, trying to retrieve the horn, while Gore ordered the sailors to fire over their heads and the warriors dived into the ocean. When one of these men came up to the surface, a sailor took aim and grazed his forehead with a musket ball.

As the disconcerted warriors swam back to the beach, a challenger armed with a long lance began to gesture angrily at the boat, calling out in a shrill voice and shaking his weapon in defiance. Before long he was joined by another challenger (whom Banks dubbed the 'Harlequin'), wearing a cap decorated with tropic bird tail-feathers and a yellow bark-cloth garment, decorated with red and brown stripes in an intricate pattern. While this man waved his weapon, an elder came down to the edge of the sea where he hailed the pinnace, asking who they were and where they came from. Tupaia told him that they had come from Tahiti, which seemed to pacify him, so Gore ordered his men to keep rowing until they found a suitable landing-place. Soon they came to a shoal where a group of people stood chanting loudly, asking the strangers not to kill them, but although Tupaia responded to these entreaties he warned his companions not to trust these people. Again Gore decided not to risk a landing, because it seemed likely that they would be attacked, and if their powder got wet their weapons would be useless; so they rowed back to the *Endeavour*.

As they headed south once more, Tupaia told Cook that the most southerly island he had visited, a place called 'Moutou' (now Tubuai), lay at two days' distance. His father had also mentioned islands further south, but Tupaia had heard nothing about a Southern Continent. During the long days of their passage, Tupaia often sat in the Great Cabin with Cook and Banks, talking with them and answering their questions. Cook was completing his charts of the Society Islands, while Banks was drafting his description of 'Manners and Customs' in Tahiti, which portrayed the people as 'free from deceit' and sexually attractive, and their islands as a tropical version of the Garden of Eden:

In the article of food these happy people may almost be said to be exempt from the curse of our forefather; scarcely can it be said that they earn their bread with the sweat of their brow when their cheifest sustenance Bread fruit is procurd with no more trouble than that of climbing a tree and pulling it down. Not that the trees grow here spontaneously but if a man should in the course of his life time plant 10 such trees, . . . he would as completely fulfull his duty to his own as well as future generations as we natives of less temperate climates can do by toiling in the cold of winter to sew and in the heat of summer to reap the annual produce of our soil, which when once gatherd into the barn must be again resowd and re-reapd as often as the Colds of winter or the heats of Summer return to make such labour disagreable.[3]

Tupaia worked closely with Banks on the details of his ethnographic account (which Cook largely copied in his journal). He tried to explain the Tahitian system for keeping time, the social hierarchies in the archipelago and the mysteries of island religion, although he used an esoteric language for sacred matters which made many of his comments incomprehensible.[4] The high priest gave Banks a list of the districts in Tahiti with the number of warriors which each could muster, allowing a rough estimate of the island's population to be made; and annotated a sketch of Ra'iatea, Tahaa, Borabora and Maurua, dictating the names of offshire islets, passes and settlements which Banks inscribed around the coastlines. He also talked about his navigational methods, telling Cook about the summer westerlies used by island navigators; and Banks about a method of predicting the winds from the shifting curve of the Milky Way.[5] It is likely that these discussions were conducted in a mixture of Tahitian and English, and it seems safe to assume that during these conversations, both Tupaia's grasp of English and Cook's and Banks's knowledge of Tahitian were extended.

Tupaia's most remarkable contribution, however, was a chart of the islands in the seas around Tahiti. He dictated a list of 130 islands to Banks, and worked with Cook on a chart of their relative positions. Tupaia's original sketch has not survived, but Cook's version of it shows seventy-four islands, laid out in concentric circles from Ra'iatea, although Cook evidently misunderstood some of Tupaia's directions. Tupaia told Cook that he had been to twelve of these islands (eight in the Society Islands, two in the Australs, and two which remain unidentified), in addition to the islands he had visited in Tonga; and that three of the islands on his chart (Tahiti, Ra'iatea and one of the Tuamotus, marked by Cook with images of ships under sail) had previously been visited by European vessels. Johann Forster, who sailed with Cook on his second Pacific voyage, wrote a second-hand account of how this chart was compiled:

Having soon perceived the meaning and use of charts, [Tupaia] gave directions for making one according to his account, and always pointed to that part of the heavens, where each isle was situated, mentioning at the same time that it was either larger or smaller than Taheitee, and likewise whether it was high or low, whether it was peopled or not, adding now and then some curious accounts relative to some of them.[6]

Tupaia's chart (with its accompanying list) includes islands as far-flung as New Zealand ('Pounamu' and 'Teatea' in Cook's rough notes[7]), Tonga, Samoa and Rotuma. It also included islands in the Tuamotus, the Marquesas, the Southern Cooks and the Australs, suggesting that Tahitian navigators had an extensive knowledge of the seas around their archipelago.

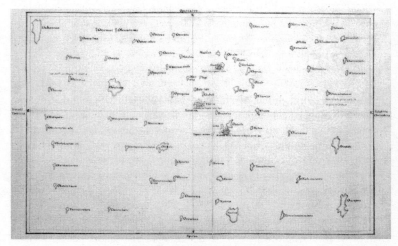

*Tupaia's chart of the South Pacific, centred on his
home island, Ra'iatea*

Of the islands he said he had visited, the most distant from Tahiti were the
two in the Tongan archipelago, and 'Moutou', or Tubuai, in the Australs.[8]
Although inter-island voyaging was no longer routine in Eastern Polynesia,
the arioi travelled under the protection of their gods, and their rituals gave
them the means and motivation to make such journeys.[9]

Unfortunately, neither Cook nor Banks recorded any of Tupaia's descriptions of these islands, their sailing directions, or the expeditions which had
peopled them. In Pacific oral histories, island place-names are often linked
with voyaging narratives; and Tupaia's chart is relatively mute without its
stories. Although Tupaia and Taiato learned to speak some English on
board the *Endeavour* (especially from Charles Green, the astronomer), and
Banks, Parkinson, Gibson – the marine who had tried to desert in Tahiti –
and Cook had all learned some Tahitian, the conversations between Tupaia
and the British were still limited by linguistic difficulties on both sides, and
cultural gaps which led to mutual incomprehension. In many ways during this
voyage, Tupaia and Cook and Banks were on diverging trajectories. The sky
and the seas that they traversed were the same, and yet quite different.

Tupaia must often have spoken with 'Oro in his dreams, and watched the
night voyages of his star ancestors. His advice came with their guidance,
and the authority of a high priest-navigator; and Cook often found him
irksome, and difficult to follow. As John Marra, a sailor from the second
voyage, remarked:

Toobia ... was a man of real genius, a priest of the first order, and an excellent artist: he was, however, by no means beloved by the Endeavour's crew, being looked upon as proud and austere, extorting homage, which the sailors who thought themselves degraded by bending to an Indian, were very unwilling to pay, and preferring complaints against them on the most trivial occasions.[10]

Tupaia was indeed proud, and he let it show. When he was told that King George had many children, for instance, he was quite contemptuous. He remarked that 'he thought himself much greater, because he belonged to the arreoys. In most other countries the name of a parent gives honour and respect; but when an arreoy, at Taheitee, emphatically bestows it, it is meant as a term of contempt and reproach.'[11] Cook and his sailors would not have found this kind of comment endearing.

Over the days that followed, the weather grew colder and the pigs and chickens from Tahiti began to die one by one. The sailors put on their cold-weather gear, and Tupaia donned European clothing, since bark-cloth was not suitable for such conditions. A dog brought from Ra'iatea, which Parkinson described as 'excessively fat' although it had eaten nothing since it was brought on board, was slaughtered and cooked; and the next day Tupaia suffered from stomach pains, although he soon recovered.[12] One of the seamen died in a drunken stupor, and the next night a large comet streaked across the sky. When he saw it, Tupaia exclaimed that the Borabora people would now kill his relatives on Ra'iatea.[13] As the ship sailed further south, there were several sightings of 'land' or 'Cape Fly-away'. Despite these brief flurries of excitement, Banks's scientific party worked industriously on their collections, sketching and describing their specimens, shooting birds and observing new forms of marine life in the ocean. After almost two months at sea, when fresh clumps of seaweed floated past the ship and land birds flew about the masts – sure signs that land was nearby – Banks wrote exuberantly in his journal:

Now do I wish that our freinds in England could by the assistance of some magical spying glass take a peep at our situation: Dr. Solander setts at the Cabbin table describing, myself at my Bureau Journalizing, between us hangs a large bunch of sea weed, upon the table lays the wood and barnacles; they would see that notwisthstanding our different occupations our lips move very often, and without being conjurors might guess that we were talking about what we should see upon the land which there is now no doubt we shall see very soon.[14]

On 6 October, the surgeon's boy, Nicholas Young, finally sighted land from the masthead and was rewarded with a gallon of rum. The sailors crowded up on deck, pointing in all directions around the horizon, while Banks remarked: 'Much difference of opinion and many conjectures about Islands, rivers, inlets &c, but all hands seem to agree that this is certainly the Continent we are in search of.'[15] In fact, the *Endeavour* had arrived on the east coast of New Zealand's northern island, just south of Turanga-nui, or Gisborne.

Te Tai Rawhiti (the East Coast of New Zealand)

| *He iwi ke, he iwi ke* | One strange people, and another |
| *Titiro atu, titiro mai!* | Looking at each other! |

In an uncanny echo of the arrival of the *Dolphin* in Tahiti, it is said that in New Zealand, a priest also predicted the coming of the Europeans. One day, according to tribal traditions, Toiroa, a priest from the school of learning on the Mahia Peninsula, fell into a trance and spoke with his ancestor gods. His back arched, the fingers of his raised hands splayed out, and he darted about like a lizard, chanting:

Tiwhatiwha te po,	Dark, dark is the po (the realm of spirits)
Ko te Pakerewha,	It is the Pakerewha (red and white strangers)
Ko Arikirangi tenei ra te	It is Arikirangi (the high chief from the sky)
haere nei.	that is coming.

After his vision of the coming of the Pakerewha, it is said, Toiroa drew images of these strangers in the sand, with their ships, carts and horses, and wove flax replicas of their clothing.[16]

As the *Endeavour*'s masts and sails appeared over the horizon in October 1769, some thought that Cook's ship must be Waikawa, a sacred island off the Mahia peninsula, sailing into their harbour. According to an early Maori newspaper:

When the old men and women saw Captain Cook's ship, they called out 'It is an island, an island floating from afar. Here it is, coming towards us!' When they saw its sails, they cried out 'Aha, ha! The sails of this travelling island are like clouds in the sky!'[17]

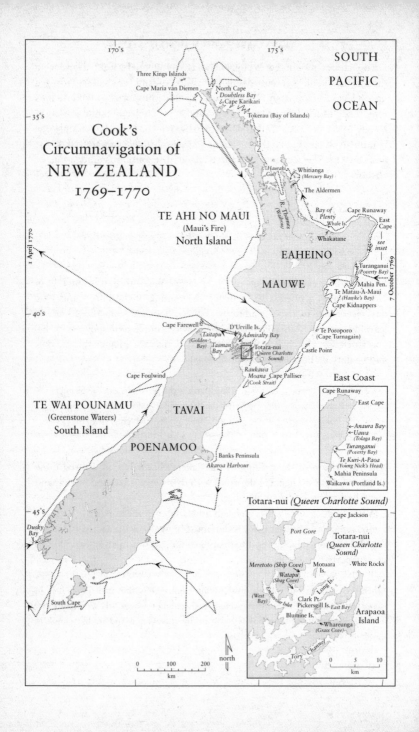

SOUTH
PACIFIC
OCEAN

Cook's
Circumnavigation of
NEW ZEALAND
1769–1770

Three Kings Islands
Cape Maria van Diemen
North Cape
Doubtless Bay
Cape Karikari
Tokerau (Bay of Islands)

Hauraki Gulf
Whitianga *(Mercury Bay)*
The Aldermen

TE AHI NO MAUI
(Maui's Fire)
North Island

R. Thames (Waihou)
Bay of Plenty
Whale Is.
Whakatane
Cape Runaway
East Cape
see inset

EAHEINO

MAUWE

Turanganui *(Poverty Bay)*
Mahia Pen.
Te Matau-A-Maui *(Hawke's Bay)*
Cape Kidnappers

7 October 1769

Cape Farewell
D'Urville Is.
Admiralty Bay
Taitapu (Golden Bay)
Tasman Bay
inset
Totara-nui *(Queen Charlotte Sound)*
Te Poroporo *(Cape Turnagain)*
Castle Point

1 April 1770

Raukawa Moana Cape Palliser
(Cook Strait)

Cape Foulwind

TE WAI POUNAMU
(Greenstone Waters)
South Island

TAVAI

POENAMOO

Banks Peninsula
Akaroa Harbour

Dusky
Bay

South Cape

East Coast

Cape Runaway

East Cape

Anaura Bay
Uawa (Tolaga Bay)
Turanganui (Poverty Bay)
Te Kuri-A-Paoa (Young Nick's Head)
Mahia Peninsula
Waikawa (Portland Is.)

Totara-nui *(Queen Charlotte Sound)*

Cape Jackson

Port Gore

Totara-nui
(Queen Charlotte Sound)

Meretoto (Ship Cove)
Watapu (Shag Cove)
Motuara Is.
White Rocks

(West Bay)
Clark Pt
Pickersgill Is.
East Bay
Long Is.

Blumine Is.

Arapaoa
Island

Whareunga (Grass Cove)

Tory Channel

0   100   200
km

north

0   5   10
km

Others thought that this might be a great bird, perhaps the legendary bird of Ruakapanga from Hawaiki, which had brought the *kumara* (sweet potato) to their district. They saw 'a smaller bird, unfledged (without sails), descending into the water, and a number of parti-coloured beings, but apparently in the human shape, also descending, the bird was regarded as a houseful of divinities. Nothing could exceed the astonishment of the people.'[18]

On board the *Endeavour*, there was also lively speculation. Banks had a copy of Dalrymple's *Account of the Discoveries made in the South Pacifick Ocean* in his library, with its version of Abel Tasman's 1642 brief visit to the South Island of New Zealand, where a boat had been attacked and some of his sailors killed by Maori warriors. In the Great Cabin, he and Cook pored over its sketches of New Zealand's western coast, and of Maori warriors in small double canoes. Back in Europe, many scholars believed that Tasman's coastline was part of Terra Australis; and although Cook was sceptical, Banks was sure that they were about to find the Southern Continent. As they sailed towards a wide, open bay to the north, a fenced enclosure on the summit of a small island appeared which provoked further discussion. Some of the sailors thought that this was a deer park, or a fenced enclosure for sheep or cattle, but Tupaia was sure that it was a marae. It must have reminded him of the marae at home, which usually stood on a point by a sacred passage into a harbour.[19] (In fact, it was a fortified village.)

Turanga-nui is sheltered by Te Kuri-a-Paoa, a white-cliffed peninsula to the south, which Cook named 'Young Nick's Head' after the surgeon's boy who made the first sighting, and Titirangi, a high hill to the north with an offshore island. In the early settlement period, voyaging canoes from the legendary homeland, Hawaiki, including the sacred canoe *Takitimu*, with its cargo of gods, had landed on its long, sandy beaches. Now four different descent-groups occupied the bay, and as the strange vessel approached the coast, signal fires flared up on the hills, summoning their warriors to challenge the new arrivals. Unlike the Society Islanders, however, the local people knew little or nothing about Europeans, and they were astonished by their first sight of the strangers. On the afternoon of 8 October, when Cook, Gore, Monkhouse, Banks, Solander and Green and a party of red-coated marines came ashore in the boats, some people who had been standing on the opposite bank of the Turanga-nui river abruptly vanished. Cook left the pinnace at the river-mouth and told the yawl to ferry them to the opposite bank, where they found a fishing camp that had just been abandoned.

After inspecting this hamlet, Banks and Solander wandered about in delight, collecting new species of plants in flower. This idyll was interrupted when musket shots rang out, and they rushed back in alarm to the river. Cook had left four small boys from the ship in charge of the yawl, who wandered from their post to play on the beach. Soon afterwards, four warriors with long spears appeared from the foothills of Titirangi and marched down the beach towards them. Terrified, the boys rushed back to the yawl, and frantically tried to row to the mouth of the river, as the coxswain in the pinnace, seeing their danger, fired a musket and then a musketoon in the air to try and frighten the warriors. They continued to advance, however, brandishing their weapons; and when one of them lifted his spear to hurl it at the yawl, the coxswain shot him through the heart. His companions carried this man for about 100 yards before they realised he was dead, then put his body down and retreated into the forest. This man was Te Maro of Ngati Oneone, a descent-group which lived in the north-east side of the bay. When Cook's party returned to the east bank of the Turanga-nui river, they left nails and beads on his body.

The next day Cook brought a large armed party back to the east bank, where Te Maro's body was still lying. It was so steeped in sacred power that no one dared to go near it, for his compatriots were not certain whether he had been killed by humans or *atua* (ancestral beings). As Cook, Banks and Tupaia approached the river's edge, a large party of warriors rose up from the western bank, performing a ferocious *haka* (war-dance). A musket was fired into the water of the river, which halted the haka abruptly; and Cook and his companions withdrew, waiting until the marines had landed. The red-coated marines were drawn up along a ridge by the river, carrying a Union Jack, and Tupaia called out to the warriors in Tahitian. According to Monkhouse, the ship's surgeon:

We found they understood his language. A long conversation ensued, which seemd to consist on their part of inquirys from whence we came, of complainings that we had killed one of their people, and of many expressions of doubt of our friendship – their pronunciation was very guttural, however Tupia understood them and made himself understood so well that he at length prevailed on one of them to strip of his covering and swim across – he landed upon a rock surrounded by the tide, and now invited us to come to him. C. Cook finding him resolved to advance no farther, gave his musket to an attendant, and went towards him, but tho' the man saw C. Cook give away his weapon to put himself on a footing with him, he had not courage enough to wait his arrival, retreating into the water, however he at last ventured forward, they saluted by touching noses, and a few trinkets put our friend into high spirits.[20]

This rock in the river, Te Toka-a-Taiau, a famous boundary marker between the tribes of the south and the north, is still often invoked in tribal debates and discussions.

Cook and this man greeted each other with a *hongi* (pressing noses), a precious moment of amity. Unfortunately, it only lasted a moment. Other men swam across the river, where Cook gave them gifts. Soon there were twenty or thirty warriors crowding around the strangers, who performed a haka and tried to exchange weapons with them. When the sailors and gentlemen refused to give up their muskets and swords, the warriors began to snatch at them. In the mêlée, one man who seized the astronomer's short sword was shot with smallshot by Banks, and killed by a ball from the surgeon's musket, while Tupaia fired last, and shot two men in the legs. The man who was killed was Te Rakau, an important chief from the Rongowhakaata tribe, who according to local tradition had come with a party of warriors from Orakaiapu, a large fortified village in the south-west of the bay, to try to seize the *Endeavour*.

Things kept going wrong all through that day. Cook was taken aback by Maori military aggression, for after the *Dolphin*'s attacks, the Tahitians had avoided mass confrontations with his people. Once the warriors had retreated, Cook formally took possession of the country and led his party back to the boats, crossing the bay to examine the shoreline from the water. When several fishing canoes were seen coming in from the sea, he decided to try to intercept them. He hoped to capture some of the crew and take them aboard the *Endeavour*, in order to treat them kindly and try to win their confidence. His plan misfired, however, because when the ship's boats cut the canoes off, their crews vigorously resisted capture, hurling paddles, anchor stones and even a parcel of fish at the sailors. They opened fire, and four more men were wounded. The larger canoe paddled rapidly away, but three young men from the smaller canoe were captured, one of whom dived and swam for some time before they finally pulled him out of the water. Cook took his captives on board the *Endeavour*, where they were fed and given gifts. At first they were terrified, thinking they were about to be killed, but when they realised that they were in no danger, they became remarkably cheerful. That evening they danced and sang for Cook, and talked with Tupaia, telling him their names, and those of some of their gods; and informing him that the people to the north of this bay ate people. In the middle of the night, when one of the boys began to sigh loudly, Tupaia got up to comfort him.

As Cook sat down to write his account of these events that night, he was acutely aware that he had breached his instructions from the Royal Society. In his 'Hints', the Earl of Morton had written:

They may naturally and justly attempt to repell intruders, whom they may apprehend are come to disturb them in the quiet possession of their country, whether that apprehension be well or ill founded.

Therefore should they in a hostile manner oppose a landing, and kill some men in the attempt, even this would hardly justify firing among them, 'till every other gentle method had been tried.[21]

While one man might draft such instructions in his study in London, however, another man caught in a face-to-face confrontation with Pacific warriors might have to ignore them. As Cook reflected:

I am aware that most humane men who have not experienced things of this nature will cencure my conduct in fireing upon the people in this boat nor do I my self think that the reason I had for seizing on her will att all justify me, and had I thought that they would have made the least resistance I would not have come near them, but as they did I was not to stand still and suffer either my self or those that were with me to be knocked on the head.[22]

Banks, too, was unhappy. He had discovered that shooting men was much less entertaining than potting birds, and that night he wrote in his journal, 'Thus ended the most disagreable day My life has yet seen, black be the mark for it and heaven send that such may never return to embitter future reflection.' His remorse, however, could not quell his scientific curiosity; for in the very next line he added, 'I forgot to mention in its proper place that we pickd up a large pumice stone floating in the bay, . . . a sure sign that there either is or has been a Volcano in this neighbourhood.'[23]

The next morning Cook decided to put his captives ashore. He, Banks and Tupaia accompanied them to the west bank of the river, while the marines and a party of armed men went off to cut wood. The boys were very reluctant to leave the *Endeavour* party, saying that this part of the bay belonged to their enemies. They went off and hid in some bushes, but when a party of about 200 armed warriors was seen approaching from the south, they ran back and stayed close to Tupaia. Cook and his companions now returned to the east bank of the river, where the bodies of Te Maro and Te Rakau were still lying. They were intensely tapu (or sacred), because of the way they had died, and Te Rakau had been shot on enemy territory. Again there was a parlay across the Turanga-nui river. The young men called out to the warriors, saying that the strangers had treated them well, and that Tupaia 'was almost one of themselves';[24] and one of them took off a red garment he had been given on board, and laid it on Te Rakau's body. According to Monkhouse:

Topia's name was now ecchoed incessantly – he talked with them – messengers were dispatched to hasten those that were coming up with the good news . . . At length after a teadious harangue on yesterdays transactions and recriminations had been bandied backwards and forwards between Tupia & them an old Man ventured over to us.[25]

As the old man crossed the river he brought a green bough as a sign of peace, which he presented to Tupaia – a gesture which Tupaia would have understood, since plantains were used to convey a similar message in Tahiti. In his conversations with the local people, Tupaia no doubt told them that the *Endeavour* had sailed from their ancestral homelands, Tahiti and Ra'iatea (or Havai'i); that he was a high priest from Ra'iatea, and that this craft, with its white-skinned crew and their fantastic weapons, came from an island, 'Peretane', which lay far across the ocean. His presence, and the things he said about the *Endeavour* and its crew made its arrival seem even more astonishing. After presenting the green bough to Tupaia, the old man performed a ritual over Te Rakau's body, and then summoned his companions to cross the river and collect their dead kinsman. Not surprisingly, given its near-mythical associations, the red coat which the young boy had draped over Te Rakau's body became a prized heirloom among the local people. Red was also a sacred colour in New Zealand, and in the future when this sacred garment, which they called Te Makura, glowed in battle, it was a sign that the Rongowhakaata warriors would win, but if its colour was dull, it was a sign that they would be defeated.[26]

When the corpse was carried back across the river, Cook and his party returned to the ship accompanied by the three boys, who were eager to stay with them. After dinner, however, they were taken back to the beach, where they stood watching for a time. At sunset, they returned to the water's edge, and when the *Endeavour* set sail, they lowered their bodies and then threw their arms up and outwards towards the ship three times, perhaps a gesture of ritual separation. At first Cook thought of naming Turanga-nui 'Endeavour Bay', but as he sailed south he called it 'Poverty Bay' instead, 'because it afforded us no one thing we wanted'.[27]

Over the next few days, the ship ran down the coast towards Te Matau-a-Maui (which Cook named Hawke's Bay, after the First Lord of the Admiralty). Several canoes came out to the *Endeavour*, but their crews refused to board the ship until a canoe joined them from Poverty Bay, whose crew came up the side and eagerly traded clothes, ornaments, painted paddles and weapons (including a whalebone and a greenstone hand-club) for beads, trinkets, glass and white Tahitian bark-cloth. The crew of one carved canoe

A Maori war canoe making a peaceful visit to the Endeavour,
sketched by Sydney Parkinson

even offered their craft to the Europeans, but there was no room for it on board the *Endeavour*. Banks recognised one of their visitors as the warrior who had saluted Cook on the rock in Turanga-nui several days earlier, and asked after the three young fisherboys they had captured. The man said that they were well, and had told everybody about the kind treatment they had received on board the European ship; and invited him to return to Turanga-nui. Cook was intent on exploring the coastline, however, and declined his invitation. Banks wrote in his journal:

[T]he captn chose rather to stand on in search of a better harbour than any we have yet seen. God send that we may not there have the same tragedy to act over again as we so lately perpetrated: the countrey is certainly divided into many small princi- palities . . . and this I am well convincd of, that till these warlike people have severely felt our superiority in the art of war they will never behave to us in a freindly manner.[28]

That night three young men from this group slept on board, although when they woke in the morning and realised how far south they had sailed, they began to weep, saying that if they were put ashore in this district, their enemies would certainly eat them.

As the ship approached the northern end of the Mahia Peninsula two canoes came out, one carrying an *ariki* (high chief), a tall stout man with an elaborate facial tattoo, accompanied by a small group of men and women. The three young men hailed this man, explaining that they had been left on board the ship, but that the strangers 'neither beat nor *eat* their country men, which was farther illustrated by striking with the hand, and afterwards fixing the teeth in the flesh and giving a horrid picture of tearing it from the bone'.[29] Eventually the high chief came on board, where he showed no signs of fear, but 'saluted those next him; and contemplated the objects about him with a kind of look of consequence. He answered the questions put to him with a peculiar indifference.'[30] News of the *Endeavour*'s arrival was spreading along the coast, and the people were transfixed with curiosity, overcoming their fear to come out to the ship. When he left the *Endeavour*, the chief took their three young visitors with him.

The *Endeavour* was now cruising down the Mahia peninsula. At about noon, when a canoe came out from the peninsula with four people on board, a man performed a series of ceremonies, waving a green bough, brandishing his *patu* (hand-club), and singing, dancing, and chanting. According to Banks, Tupaia had a long conversation with this priest, but could not persuade him to come on board the *Endeavour*. When a sudden wind blew up and the ship sailed off, leaving this canoe behind, its crew shouted and brandished their paddles, and one of them 'very civilly turned up his breach and made the usual sign of contempt among the Billingsgate ladies' – the *whakapohane* (or exposure of the anus), a sign of contempt and derision.

Before long they came to Waikawa, the island off the south end of Mahia peninsula where the sacred canoe, *Takitimu*, had left a *mauri* stone (which held the life force of a guardian god) many generations earlier. As they hauled around the southern end of the island, they noticed a great number of armed men lined up along its cliffs, so that the horizon bristled with spears; and when the *Endeavour* was caught in shoal waters, five canoes paddled out, filled with warriors. These men threw spears against the side of the ship, making long speeches and shaking their paddles. Noticing one man who brandished his spear with particular ferocity, Monkhouse stood on the taffrail, and repeated the insulting gesture he had seen earlier that day:

Seeing one man brandish his lance with great fury I was induced to retort the compliment we had recieved in the morning merely to try its effect upon this Quixotic hero – enraged at the insult he instantly threw his lance towards me with all his might, and took up another to try a second effort: he bid his Comrades pull up a little nigher and held his lance poized ready to throw while I put myself in the same attitude with a long telescope – thus full of wrath we both stood staring at each other when C.C. observing these threats begun to be uneasy about the man in the boat astern and therefore ordered a musket loaden with small shot to be fired at the very

Canoe I was engaged with. Mr. – who was below and hearing the order threw a loading of small shot so nigh the ear of my Antagonist that it produced the most ludicrous change in his Countenance that I ever saw . . .

Immediately after the discharge of the muskets a great gun loaden with musket-ball was fired upon the water which threw them into great consternation. Yet in the midst of all this they felt the sting of our laughing at them, and by a kind of involuntary impulse shook their paddles and gave a shout – but their fears instantly succeeded this flash of Courage – they Stared wildly round them for a moment, and then retiring, collected themselves to hold a conference on matters of the most extraordinary nature that they would perhaps allow they had ever seen.[31]

As the *Endeavour*'s great gun roared, the muskets cracked and smoked, and musket balls and smallshot whizzed through the air, the local warriors could be forgiven their astonishment. The presence of a high priest from Ra'iatea on board this astonishing craft, Monkhouse's taunting gesture, the red-coated marines with their muskets, the flash, smoke and thunder of the ship's cannons, and the splashes as the shot hit the water must have seemed like a display of supernatural aggression, directed against the island which held the sacred mauri of their ancestors.

During the encounters that followed in Hawke's Bay, Tupaia led the negotiations with the chiefs and priests who came out to the vessel. On 14 October, for instance, when the ship approached the Ngaruroro River, a large canoe came out whose crew performed an impassioned war-dance. As they brandished their paddles in the air, a challenger hurled a spear against the side of the ship; it bounced off harmlessly and sank into the ocean. This canoe carried a man covered in red paint (*kokowai*, or red ochre mixed with oil) and wearing a red cloak, the local equivalent of the red feather girdles worn by high chiefs in Tahiti. As other canoes gathered around the ship, the British noted that these people seemed to be wealthy. Their canoes were richly carved and decorated with feather streamers, and the crews were either naked or wore striped cloaks, with greenstone ornaments around their necks, and they carried greenstone clubs or 'halberts' (*taiaha*) decorated with red feathers and white dog's hair. At first they seemed intent on attacking the strangers, but when a four-pounder loaded with grapeshot was fired wide of them, they retreated for a time. Eventually the leading canoe came back to the ship, and when it was close enough, Tupaia talked with its crew, asked them about 'the names of the countreys kings &c', invited them to sing and dance, and when they came alongside, he gave them gifts of iron and bark-cloth.

The next morning some fishing canoes came out to the ship, and their small crews of unkempt, poorly dressed men traded fish, lobsters, and fishing tackle for nails and trinkets. As soon as they tried to cheat by loading their baskets with stones instead of fish, they were sent away. Soon afterwards, a small fleet of canoes approached from the north side of the bay. This flotilla was led by a large canoe carrying twenty-two men, including a priest who stood with a large staff in his hand, repeating 'certain sentences in a tone very similar to that in which our Otaheite friends repeat their religious forms or Church liturgy'. Another old man sitting in the stern of this canoe wore a black dogskin cloak, which Cook decided to add to his collection of 'curiosities'. He held up a red piece of baize, offering this in exchange for the cloak, but when the old man received it, he put the red cloth in a basket and coolly offered Cook a paddle instead. His men were infuriated by this attempt at 'cheating', and some of the sailors decided to try and 'trepan' the offender's canoe, i.e. lassooing its prow and hoisting the canoe up the anchor chains.

The local people got in first, however, first grabbing at the captain's steward and then seizing Taiato, Tupaia's boy, as he climbed down the ship's ladder. This canoe paddled rapidly away with Taiato, who was held by two warriors, defended by the large canoe whose crew adopted a fighting posture. According to their descendants, Tupaia was enraged. He called out 'Mai, mate koe' (you will be killed!), to which their ancestors retorted, 'Kahore he rakau o te hunga o Hawaiiki; he puu kakaho, he korari!' (The people of Hawaiki have no weapons; only reeds and flax stalks!).[32] They soon learned their mistake, however, for when the marines lined up on the deck were ordered to fire, several of the abductors were shot. The boy jumped into the sea and was pulled back on board the ship. Later he brought a fish to Tupaia as an offering to his god ('Oro, or perhaps Ta'aroa),[33] and Tupaia told him to throw it into the ocean.

After reaching Te Poroporo, a promontory south of Hawke's Bay which Cook dubbed 'Cape Turnagain', the Endeavour turned back northwards. They retraced their track and sailed past Poverty Bay, arriving on 20 October off a snug cove (Anaura Bay), where several canoes came out to greet them. These canoes carried two high-ranking chiefs, both heavily tattooed, one of whom wore a red feather cloak, while the other wore a finely woven cloak decorated with transverse stripes of white dogskin. These stately men boarded the ship where they invited the strangers ashore, and when a crowd of warriors in canoes began to dance the haka and threaten the British, one of them leaned out the window of the Great Cabin and 'threat'ned them in very warm terms', no doubt reminding them of the shootings in Turanga-nui.

When Cook's party went ashore at Anaura, the local people were peaceful and friendly. For the first time in New Zealand, they could wander about freely, walking through clusters of houses, noting latrines and rubbish heaps with approval, and inspecting the large, finely tilled hillside gardens, which Spöring sketched in his views of the harbour. The next morning when Monkhouse and some others ventured up into the hills, they came to an isolated house whose occupants greeted them, showing them garden tools, weaving, paddles and other possessions. Before they left, the man of this household gave them the mummified body of a child in exchange for a 'trifle' – a strange transaction, since human remains were usually intensely tapu. He probably thought that they were supernatural beings of some kind, for whom such a gift was appropriate. Despite the warmth of their welcome, however, the expedition's members found the local women much less accessible than the women in Tahiti. Although they tried Tahitian-style caresses, pressing noses with them and attempting other familiarities, Banks remarked ruefully that they 'were as great coquetts as any Europaeans could be and the young ones as skittish as unbroke fillies'.[34] If the local women were reluctant to make love with the strangers, however, they were wise, because by Cook's own reckoning several of his men had stubborn venereal infections, and at least half of the rest had contracted venereal diseases in Tahiti.

The next morning the surf threatened to capsize the boats, making it difficult to water the ship, so Cook decided to leave Anaura and sail northwards. The winds were unfavourable, and again the ship was driven to the south. The local people guided them to Uawa (now known as Tolaga Bay), where there was a small sandy cove to the south of the bay, sheltered by an offshore island. At this time Uawa was the home of a high chief named Te Whakatatare-o-te-Rangi (perhaps the man in the red cloak who had greeted them at Anaura), and the location of a famous school of learning – Te Rawheoro – where young men were taught esoteric lore and specialised in the arts of carving. The local leaders had decided to welcome the strangers in peace, and Banks and his companions had a marvellous time at Uawa. They were entranced with the local flora and fauna, finding twenty new species of trees, ferns, parasitic plants, and the flax plant from which Maori made fishing lines, baskets, and many of their garments. Most New Zealand plants were found nowhere else in the world, and almost every specimen they collected was previously unknown to European science. They also found many beautiful varieties of birds, including parrots, pigeons and quail, many unfamiliar species of fish, and a few Polynesian rats and dogs like those in Tahiti.

After wandering about, Parkinson described the countryside around the bay as 'agreeable beyond description, and, with proper cultivation, might be rendered a kind of second Paradise. The hills are covered with beautiful flowering shrubs, intermingled with a great number of tall and stately palms, which fill the air with a most grateful fragrant perfume [the 'cabbage tree' or *kouka*].'[35] When Banks discovered a natural rock arch just north of the watering-place, he was in raptures – 'it was certainly the most magnificent surprize I have ever met with, so much is pure nature superior to art in these cases.'[36] He asked his artists to sketch this rock arch, not realising that it was known as 'Te Kotore o te Whenua' (The Anus of the Land), a cosmographical equivalent of the insult directed at the *Endeavour* several weeks earlier. To add to their pleasure, at least some of the officers and gentlemen (including Tupaia) were offered sexual hospitality in the bay, a gesture of respect for high-ranking visitors.

During their stay at Uawa, Tupaia slept ashore in a cave by the watering-place, which the local people later named after him. According to Banks, he spent a good deal of his time with one of the local *tohunga* (priests):

Tupia . . . had much conversation with one of their preists; they seemd to agree very well in their notions of religion only Tupia was much more learned than the other and all his discourse was heard with much attention. He askd them in the course of his conversation with them many questions, among the rest whether or no they realy eat men which he was very loth to beleive; they answerd in the affirmative saying that they eat the bodys only of those of their enemies who were killd in war.[37]

It would be marvellous to have a detailed account of these conversations. No doubt Tupaia talked with this man about the arioi and their god, 'Oro, traced his genealogical connections with the local people, and gave them news of the homeland, Hawaiki. He collected information about local beliefs, passing some of this on to Banks and Cook for their ethnographic descriptions. He must also have discussed his experiences on board the *Endeavour*, and his views of the British. When he questioned the local people about cannibalism, however, and they told him that they ate their enemies, Tupaia was disgusted. He often urged them to give it up, although this cannot have been out of squeamishness. The priests of 'Oro frequently sacrificed people to their gods, and hung up the jawbones of their enemies on their marae; and they knew about the practice of eating enemies, since their neighbours in a number of the islands around Tahiti (including the Tuamotus) were notorious cannibals. Perhaps he considered the local people blasphemous, however, because in Tahiti, it was the gods who 'ate' the sacrificed bodies.[38]

Tupaia also practised his graphic skills at Uawa. In 1836, Joel Polack was taken to Tupaia's cave, where he was shown a charcoal sketch of a ship and some boats on the rock walls, which the people all said had been drawn by the Ra'iatean.[39] In addition, Tupaia's image of Joseph Banks exchanging cloth for a large crayfish was almost certainly painted at Uawa, because

*Tupaia's sketch of Joseph Banks at Uawa, exchanging bark-cloth
for a crayfish*

exchanges of such goods for crayfish were mentioned only during this visit.
It is not surprising that Tupaia was inspired to draw and paint at Uawa, the
home of Te Rawheoro, where the local people were notable artists, producing finely carved canoes and houses. While they were in the bay, Banks,
Spöring and Parkinson were taken to Pourewa, a small island off the coast,
where they were shown a carved war canoe, and an unfinished house with
carved side panels. Both Spöring and Parkinson sketched the prow of this
canoe, and one of the carved panels was taken out of the house and sent on
board the *Endeavour*. Tupaia is not mentioned in accounts of this visit, but
it seems very likely that he was present. This carving may have been given
to the high priest, since he came from the homeland and such *poupou* (wall
panels) were ancestral portraits. It was taken back to England, where an
image of it was engraved by John Miller in 1771; then it vanished. By a
curious twist of history, it recently re-surfaced in the Ethnological Collection
of Tuebingen University in Germany, and is now being restored in Dresden.
This remarkable poupou, the only surviving carving from the Te Rawheoro
school of learning, is much smaller than contemporary wall panels, with

*The poupou (carved wall panel) collected by Cook's
party at Uawa (Tolaga Bay), recently restored in
Dresden*

traces of black pigment and red ochre in its spirals. For Maori such carvings
embody particular ancestors and are imbued with their power; during a
recent visit to Dresden, it was moving to see this ancestral figure so far from
Uawa, in the heart of Europe.[40]

During his stay in Uawa, Cook's impressions of Maori seem to have
crystallised. In his rough notes he wrote:

1 The Religion of the Natives bear some resemblance to the George Islanders –
2 they have god of war, of husbandry &c but there is one suprem god whom the[y]
   call he made the world and all that therein is – by Copolation

3 they have many Priests
4 The Old men are much respected —
5 they have King who lives inland his name is we heard of him in Poverty Bay
6 They eat their enimies Slane in Battell – this seems to come from custom and not
   from a Savage disposission this they cannot be charged with – they appear to have
   but few Vices – Left an Inscription

Their beheavour was Uniform free from treachery . . .[41]

For years, Cook held fast to these conclusions, that Maori were honourable people with 'few Vices' and that cannibalism was simply a matter of custom. In this judgement he was influenced by Enlightenment ideals rather than British popular culture, which linked cannibalism with witchcraft and demonic possession. Many of the crew, however, held opposite views about Maori, regarding them as 'savage' and 'treacherous', and these differences of opinion sowed the seeds of future dissension between Cook and his men about how Maori and other 'savages' ought to be treated.

On 29 October as the *Endeavour* sailed from Uawa, the winds were unfavourable, but they soon rounded East Cape, entering a wide, open bay whose coastline curved into the distance. The local populations seemed large and prosperous, so Cook named this the 'Bay of Plenty'. As the ship sailed along the shoreline, canoes came out from the beaches carrying priests and warriors who chanted and performed haka, challenging the strangers. Off the Motu River, for example, a fleet of forty-five canoes came out, and a large carved canoe carrying a chief approached the *Endeavour*. This man made an impassioned speech before tossing a stone against the ship's side, as his warriors brandished their weapons. Tupaia warned them that if they attacked the ship, his companions would kill them; and threw Tahitian bark-cloth down into their canoe. This was more effective than his warning had been, for bark-cloth was a rarity in New Zealand; and people sought it eagerly. Eventually, one of the warriors seized a pair of sheets that were being towed alongside in the sea to be washed, provoking a confrontation. Cook ordered musketballs to be fired through the hull of this man's canoe; and when he failed to return the sheets but sat there laughing and plugging up the holes in the hull, he was shot in the back with smallshot. The crews of the other canoes carried on with their haka until a cannonball was fired between them, which bounced several times on the sea before sinking. As the cannonball flew past, as Pickersgill noted, 'they made the most Precipitated retreat I ever saw'.[42]

Again, off Whakatane, a very large double sailing canoe came out to the ship; the crew talked with Tupaia, performing songs and dances, making speeches and then pelting the ship with stones, smashing some of the *Endeavour*'s stern windows. The next morning, the same vessel overtook the ship and confronted them again, pelting the sides with stones and mocking the strangers for running away from them. As they sailed towards the end of this vast bay, the fortified settlements along the cliff-tops and the fleets of canoes on the beaches seemed larger than ever. Banks, who was still convinced that they were sailing up the coastline of Terra Australis, speculated that this was the headquarters of the prince of this great continent.

On 3 November, the *Endeavour* sailed past a cluster of oddly-shaped islands which they called 'The Court of Aldermen', where several dug-out canoes came out to challenge them. These vessels were unadorned and their crews were almost naked, yet as Banks commented, 'these few despicable gentry sang their song of defiance and promisd us as heartily as the most respectable of their countrey men that they would kill us all.'[43] Later that evening they came to a deep, sheltered bay, Whitianga, where Cook decided to anchor. The Transit of Mercury was rapidly approaching, and he was looking for a harbour where he and Green could conduct their astronomical observations, enabling them to accurately fix the longitude of New Zealand. As the ship's anchors splashed down, more dug-out canoes came out to the ship whose crews talked with Tupaia, performed a haka and promised to return the next day to kill the strangers. Cook was unperturbed, although that night he posted sentries to guard the vessel.

Early the next morning a fleet of about fifteen canoes surrounded the ship, threatening the strangers and widening their eyes in the *pukana*, a gesture of defiance. Again, Tupaia persuaded these people to trade, although when they began to 'cheat', musketballs were fired through the hulls of their canoes and two of the culprits were shot with smallshot. These men bled profusely, but their companions ignored them and resumed trading with the strangers until another man tried to keep goods without making any return. A musketball was fired through the hull of his canoe, and then Cook ordered a cannon loaded with round-shot to be fired over their heads, sending the canoes paddling back to shore in a panic.

Such hostile exchanges, which were commonplace around the New Zealand coast, were provoked at least in part by misunderstandings about reciprocity. In Maori gift exchange, return gifts were often delayed in a counterpoint of chiefly generosity. No doubt Tupaia tried to make these matters clear, but when the sailors simply pointed at things in the canoes, expecting people to hand them over at once, Maori were confused or resentful. Sometimes they were defiant, and taunted the strangers for failing to follow the appropriate rituals. After a certain point, however, if they did not get what they wanted, the Europeans decided that these people were 'cheating' and fired upon them to punish their 'dishonesty'.

When they went ashore at Whitianga (which Cook named 'Mercury Bay', after the Transit of Mercury), Cook and his men met a group who were there on a short-term visit. There were middens of shellfish and piles of fern-root by their camp, and they were sleeping on the bare earth with just a few branches over their heads, the women and children encircled by their menfolk, who slept with their weapons stacked up beside them. The local inhabitants, however, were living in fortified villages built on islands and hilltops, protected by palisades, earthworks and fighting stages. They told Tupaia that every now and then, people came from the north to raid their settlements, capturing their wives and children and plundering all their possessions. Because of these constant raids, they were relatively poor, with no carved houses, carved canoes or fine garments.

On 9 November, as Cook and Green prepared to observe the Transit, some strangers arrived in the bay in a flotilla of large carved canoes, who may have been some of these raiders. Their crews seemed to be wealthy, with fine cloaks and weapons, and they knew nothing about the Europeans' weapons, although this was about to alter. When one of them offered Lieutenant Gore his black and white dogskin cloak in exchange for a large piece of cloth and paddled away with the cloth, still wearing his cloak and shouting in triumph, Gore shot him dead with a musketball. Cook, however, was unhappy about this affair, noting in his journal, 'I have here inserted the account . . . just as I had it from Mr. Gore but I must own that it did not meet with my approbation because I thought the punishment a little too severe for the Crime, and we had now been long enough acquainted with these People to know how to chastise trifling faults like this without taking away their lives.'[44]

According to that amiable gossip, Dr Solander, Cook and Gore quarrelled bitterly over this shooting: 'Cooke was jealous of [Gore] . . . Gore had a sort of separate command in the vessel, . . . which gave him superintendance over all the transactions with the Indians. He made use of this sometimes to disobey Cooke; & therefore they hate each other. Gore always blamed severity [on] the Indians, & yet by a sudden emotion shot the man who cheated, but . . . did not recover for 12 days of the shock it gave him.'[45] This is a rare glimpse into the relationships between Cook and his officers. Lieutenant Gore, who had already sailed twice around the globe on the *Dolphin*, could claim the benefit of greater Pacific experience than his captain. As a Pacific 'expert', he was perhaps prone to challenge Cook's authority; and as an avid hunter, too free with his musket. Gore was one of those on board who advocated stern measures when dealing with 'Indians', believing that this was essential to uphold European authority. Cook, on the other hand, considered such instances of 'cheating' to be relatively trivial, and was furious with Gore for flouting the Earl of Morton's instructions. Solander's remark that Cook was jealous of his second lieutenant and that he and Gore hated each other is illuminating, revealing the kind of tensions that were liable to develop on a very small ship during a long, dangerous voyage.

Despite this disagreement, Cook's observations of the Transit of Mercury were successful, and his men collected large supplies of greens, fish and shellfish during their visit to Mercury Bay, including boatloads of succulent oysters. After their initial confrontation with the local people they found them friendly and hospitable. The men assisted the sailors with their work, and the women and children helped Banks and Solander to gather plants and rocks for their collections. One of these children was a young boy called Horeta Te Taniwha, who in later years often reminisced about Cook's visit to Whitianga. According to Horeta, his people were astonished by the Europeans, concluding that they were *tupua* or 'goblins' rather than human beings:

In the days long past, . . . we lived at Whitianga, and a vessel came there, and when our old men saw the ship they said it was an *atua*, a god, and the people on board were *tupua*, strange beings or 'goblins'. The ship came to anchor, and the boats pulled on shore. As our old men looked at the manner in which they came on shore, the rowers pulling with their backs to the bows of the boat, the old people said, 'Yes, it is so: these people are goblins; their eyes are at the back of their heads; they pull on shore with their backs to the land to which they are going.' When these goblins came on shore we (the children and women) took notice of them, but we ran away from them into the forest, and the warriors alone stayed in the presence of those goblins; but, as the goblins stayed some time, and did not do any evil to our braves, we came back one by one, and gazed at them, and we stroked their garments with our hands, and we were pleased with the whiteness of their skins and the blue of the eyes of some of them.

These goblins began to gather oysters, and we gave some kumara, fish, and fern-root to them. These they accepted, and we (the women and children) began to roast cockles for them; and as we saw that these goblins were eating kumara, fish and cockles, we were startled, and said, 'Perhaps they are not goblins like the Maori goblins.' These goblins went into the forest, and also climbed up the hill to our pa (fort) at Whitianga (Mercury Bay). They collected grasses from the cliffs, and kept knocking at the stones on the beach, and we said, 'Why are these acts done by these goblins?' We and the women gathered stones and grass of all sorts, and gave to these goblins. Some of the stones they liked, and put them into their bags, the rest they

Horeta Te Taniwha, printed in later years by Gottried Lindauer

threw away; and when we gave them the grass and branches of trees they stood and talked to us, or they uttered the words of their language. Perhaps they were asking questions, and, as we did not know their language, we laughed, and these goblins also laughed, so we were pleased.[46]

News of these 'goblins' quickly spread to the surrounding districts, and on 15 November, when the *Endeavour* left Mercury Bay and sailed north in fresh breezes up the coast, they found a crowd of people gathered on a bare rocky point, talking earnestly with each other. According to tribal histories, the high priest of the *Te Arawa* canoe had left a mauri stone on the island of Moehau (off the end of the peninsula), and they must have been concerned to protect this sacred island from the strangers. Soon two large carved canoes put out from the shore, where they performed a haka and threw stones at the side of the vessel. Shortly after this they dropped off, but when they returned to confront the British once more, Tupaia warned them that they would be killed unless they stopped this aggressive behaviour. In the

Society Islands, the open sea was regarded as a great marae, where anyone could go to cleanse and comfort themselves in times of trouble; rather than a possession of particular groups.[47] According to Banks:

They answerd him in their usual cant 'come ashore only and we will kill you all.' Well, said Tupia, but while we are at sea you have no manner of Business with us, the Sea is our property as much as yours. Such reasoning from an Indian who had not the smallest hint from any of us surprizd me much.[48]

On 19 November the *Endeavour* entered the Hauraki Gulf, where two canoes came out from the land whose crews greeted Tupaia by name. The ship sailed down the west coast of the peninsula and soon came to anchor, and in the morning these people guided the boats to a wide river, the Waihou, 'as broad as the Thames River at Greenwich'. Cook, Banks and Tupaia were taken to a fortified town on an island about a mile upstream, whose inhabitants welcomed them warmly. After briefly visiting this settlement they carried on up the river, past another swamp pa until they found themselves in the midst of a magnificent forest. These ancient *kahikatea* trees had immense, straight trunks, one which they measured at nineteen feet eight inches round; and as they inspected these trees, Cook and Banks both concluded that 'the Thames' would make an excellent site for a British settlement.

This was Cook's longest excursion inland during any of his visits to New Zealand. Unlike Tahiti, where he and his men had felt free to explore the island, Cook was cautious in his dealings with Maori. His officers were less restrained, however, and the next day, while Cook was away from the ship exploring the west coast of the river, a Polynesian was flogged for the first time on board the *Endeavour*. A local warrior had stolen a half-minute glass from the ship's binnacle cupboard, and when he was caught Lieutenant Hicks had him seized and tied to the shrouds for a flogging. Seeing this, his companions began to call for their weapons, but Tupaia reassured them, saying that he would only be beaten. They watched without resistance while this man was given twelve lashes with the cat-o'-nine-tails, and then an old chief gave him a further thrashing and sent him down to the canoes. Like in the Society Islands, it was shameful to be caught in a theft, and his punishment was evidently felt to be justified. Again, Cook thought that one of his officers had overreacted, commenting in his journal, 'The punishing this Man in this manner might have had some good effect had we been going to stay any time in this place, but as we were going away it might as well have been let alone.'[49]

On 23 November the *Endeavour* weighed anchors, and began to work its way north in torrential rain, with loud claps of thunder. They soon caught a south-westerly gale, and by 25 November found themselves 200 kilometres north of Hauraki. At dusk that evening seven large canoes came out to the ship; the crews said that they had heard of the *Endeavour*. At sea, European vessels were frequently outsailed by large Polynesian canoes, and on the coast of New Zealand, news of Cook and Tupaia often preceded their arrival. There were both men and women on board these canoes, and according to Parkinson they had elaborate body tattoos, with facial tattoos quite different from those further south. Although Tupaia persuaded them to come on board, they soon returned to their canoes where they began to hurl stones at the ship, shaking their spears at the strangers. When they resumed trading, one of these men kept a pair of black breeches without giving anything back, and was fired on with smallshot. As another musket was aimed at him he held up his cloak to try and protect himself (a traditional defence against stones and darts), hastily throwing the breeches into the ocean. At the same time, several canoes were hit with musketballs, and as the splinters went flying, the whole fleet retreated to a safe distance where they broke into a spirited haka. Cook ordered a cannonball to be fired overhead, which terrified them so much that they paddled back to shore 'with the most Amaseing Expedition'.[50]

By now the *Endeavour* was approaching Tokerau, which Cook named the 'Bay of Islands'. On 26 November more canoes came out to the ship, including a carved canoe 70 feet long carrying people who wore fine dogskin cloaks and carried stone and whalebone weapons. The next day as they sailed past a cluster of islands – the Cavallis – a flotilla of canoes came out to offer fish in exchange for European goods. Their crews soon began to chant and throw fish at the sailors, however, pelting the ship with sticks and stones and behaving 'most abominably saucy'.[51] They would not listen to anything that Tupaia said, and when Cook went to the poop they threw stones at him. Cook flew into a rage, aiming his musket at a man who was about to throw a rock, and wounded him in the face with smallshot. As the man clapped his hands to his face and fell flat in his canoe, another canoe raced forward with a load of stones, ready to attack, and several more warriors were hit with smallshot. The following day the wind turned foul, and the *Endeavour* was forced to retrace its track southward. The next morning the ship bore up for a 'most spatious and well shelterd harbour, or rather collection of harbours almost innumberable formd by islands', finally coming to an anchor in the lee of Motuarohia (Arohia island).

The Bay of Islands is a beautiful place, its deeply indented coastline sheltered by clusters of islands which protect its small sandy coves and long beaches.

The district around the bay was densely populated, and soon thirty-seven large and small canoes crowded around the *Endeavour*. Cook invited some of their chiefs on board, who presented him with gifts of large mackerel, and in return he gave the leading chief a length of broadcloth, and presented the others with nails and trinkets. The leader of these people, a high chief named Tapua, was both war-leader and priest for his people. His son, Patuone, later described his father's meeting with Cook:

They went to see the vessel because such a ship had never before visited that place. When the canoes were near the ship, the people on board beckoned to them to come closer. So Tapua's men conferred together, and when they had come to a decision, the canoe commanded by Tapua went alongside the ship. Then they threw the fish from the canoe up on to the ship, as an offering to those strange sea-goblins. The goblins were pleased with the fish, and shouted with joy as they gathered them up.

After this Tapua went on board the ship, and the leader of the goblins presented him with a red garment and with the salt flesh of an animal. It was cooked flesh, with both fat and lean meat on the one piece. Tapua took it and gave it to his son and daughter, Patuone and Tari. Food of this kind had not been known to the Maori; they found it to be sweet, and very good.[52]

When Tapua and his companions returned to their canoes, Cook and most of the officers went below decks to eat dinner. In their absence, the warriors in several of these canoes tried to seize the anchor buoy in a concerted manoeuvre. As they hauled the buoy out of the water, the marines fired smallshot over their heads, and wounded one of the ringleaders in the arm with a musketball. One of the great guns was fired, the warriors threw the buoy back into the sea in consternation, and as the cannonball skipped over the surface and rolled inland, the crews of two or three canoes paddled furiously ashore and ran up the beach to find it. Tupaia called out to these people, and after a while persuaded them to return peacefully to the vessel.

After dinner, Cook decided to land on Motuarohia. He went with Banks, Solander and an armed party of marines in the pinnace and the yawl to a bay on the west end of the island. As they landed on the beach, all of the canoes on the surrounding waters paddled at high speed towards them, landing on either side of the cove and concealing themselves behind the rocky outcrops. On a signal, about 500 to 600 warriors appeared on the beach, surrounding the Europeans. When Cook and Banks marched towards them, they raised their weapons but did not attempt to attack, so Cook drew a line on the sand and signalled that no one should cross it. Some of the warriors began to mingle with their party, however, chanting their war-song; and when three of them tried to haul the boats ashore, the marines shot them with smallshot. They retreated, and as a chief waving his hand-club tried to rally his men, Solander fired his musket and shot him. Cook and his companions now loaded their muskets with ball, and for the next quarter of an hour they held the warriors at bay by firing at them. Luckily for the shore party, the officers on board the *Endeavour* had seen their danger. The ship was warped about to bring the guns to bear, and when a broadside was fired overhead, the warriors finally retreated.

After this confrontation, according to Cook, the inhabitants 'were as meek as lambs';[53] and he would not allow any form of retribution. The next morning, three men who had gone ashore overnight to steal sweet potatoes from their gardens were punished with sentences of twelve lashes each; and when one of them, Mathew Cox, argued that there was nothing wrong with what he had done, he was confined, and given twelve more lashes the following morning. Apparently Cox harboured a grudge against Cook over this episode, because at the end of the voyage he laid a complaint against him with the Admiralty for unfair punishment. As always when they were at anchor, the men were difficult to manage. In the middle of the next night, the gunner and three sailors stole twelve gallons of rum from the cask of spirits on the quarterdeck; and Cook ordered the three sailors to be flogged with twelve lashes each, although as he commented irately, 'the Gunner . . . richly deserved the whole upon his back; from his Drunkenness [he has] become the only useless person on board the Ship.'[54]

Over the next few days Cook and his men explored the bay, finding it densely populated, with many large fortified towns, villages and cultivations. The local people were very afraid of the British and many of them stayed away, although some brave souls sought them out, showing them settlements and houses; gardens of yams, kumara (sweet potatoes) and taro with a few bark-cloth plants; and huge fishing nets 9 metres deep and 1000 metres long, which dwarfed the king's seine on board the *Endeavour*. During their excursions Cook and Banks met several of the warriors who had been shot during the affray on the island (one of whom Parkinson subsequently sketched), and were impressed to find their wounds healing cleanly. Cook was told, however, that the man he shot in the face off the Cavalli Islands had died. Three smallshot had penetrated his brain, wounding him fatally.

Towards the end of their visit Banks reflected upon Maori life, and the differences between the various parts of the country they had so far visited. In particular he mused about cannibalism:

It is now a long time since I have mentiond their custom of Eating human flesh, as I was loth a long time to beleive that any human beings could have among them so brutal a custom. I am now however convincd and shall here give a short account of

A sketch of a fortified hilltop village on Motuarohia Island, by
Herman Spöring

what we have heard from the Indians concerning it. At *Taoneroa* [Poverty Bay] the
first place we landed in on the Continent the boys who we had on board mentiond
it of their own accords, asking whether the meat they eat was not human flesh, as
they had no Idea of any animal but a man so large till they saw our sheep: they
however seemd ashamd of the custom, saying that the tribe to which they belonged
did not use it but that another very near did. Since that we have never faild whereever
we went ashore and often when we convers'd with canoes to ask the question; we
have without one exception been answerd in the affirmative, and several times as at
Tolaga and today the people have put themselves into a heat by defending the
Custom, which Tubia who had never before heard of such a thing takes every
Occasion to speak ill of, exhorting them often to leave it off. They however as
universaly agree that they eat none but the bodies of their enemies who are killd in
war, all others are buried.[55]

Banks's comments give an interesting insight into the debates about cannibalism on board the *Endeavour*. He was horrified even by reports of eating
human flesh, and found it difficult to accept the existence of such a practice.
Cook, on the other hand, was matter-of-fact about cannibalism, considering
it to be the consequence of 'custom' rather than vice or savagery. Like
Banks, Tupaia was appalled by the practice and often urged Maori to
give it up. The young fisherboys in Turanga-nui, however, had excused

themselves by saying that their own tribe did not eat people; while those at Uawa and the Bay of Islands rebutted Tupaia's criticisms, stoutly defending the practice of eating their enemies.

On 5 December Cook decided to leave the Bay of Islands. As a fair breeze blew up, he ordered his men to raise the ship's anchors. They were soon caught in foul winds, however, and that night the *Endeavour* lay becalmed off the heads, where an eddy caught the ship and swept her towards the rocks at the entrance. The pinnace was lowered in order to take the ship in tow, but it got stuck on a gun and had to be manhandled into the water. In the midst of this chaos a land breeze sprang up, carrying the ship away from the rocks, while Tupaia, unaware of their danger, stood on deck talking to some people on the shoreline. At about half past ten, Cook and Banks retired to their cabins, but shortly afterwards the *Endeavour* struck on a submerged rock, bringing Cook running up on deck in his drawers. Fortunately the rock was to windward and the ship came safely off, as Banks drily observed, 'much to our satisfaction as the almost certainty of being eat as soon as you come ashore adds not a little to the terrors of shipwreck'.[56]

Once he was out in the open sea, Cook set a course north, and on 9 December they sighted Tokerau, which he named 'Doubtless Bay'. As they lay becalmed off the Karikari Peninsula, six canoes came alongside the ship, where Tupaia asked these people about their country:

They told him that a distance of three days rowing in their canoes, at a place called *Moorewhennua* [Muriwhenua], the land would take a short turn to the southward and from thence extend no more to the West. This place we concluded must be Cape Maria Van Diemen, and finding these people so intelligent desird him to enquire if they knew of any Countries besides this or ever went to any. They said no but that their ancestors had told them to the NW by N or NNW was a large countrey to which some people had saild in a very large canoe, which passage took them up to a month: from this expedition a part only returnd who told their countreymen that they had seen a countrey where the people eat hogs, for which animal they usd the same name (*Booah*) as is used in the Islands. And have you no hoggs among you? Said Tupia. – No. – And did your ancestors bring none back with them? – No. – You must be a parcel of Liars then, said he, and your story a great lye for your ancestors would never have been such fools as to come back without them.[57]

Cook linked this account of the coastline with the lines on Abel Tasman's chart, identifying the peninsula to the north as Cape Maria van Diemen (named by Tasman). It is not clear, however, which land these people were discussing in their story of an ancestral voyage to the NNW, although it might have been a reference to one of the high islands of West Polynesia.

Over the next few days the *Endeavour* tacked on and off the land, caught in unfavourable winds. On 16 December the ship was driven out to sea by violent westerlies, while the *St. Jean Baptiste*, a French vessel also on a voyage of discovery, was driven around North Cape, its crew stricken with scurvy and its hull leaking badly. The *St. Jean Baptiste* commanded by Jean-François-Marie de Surville, a merchant ship associated with the French India Company, had been sent off into the Pacific after the news had arrived of the *Dolphin*'s discovery of Tahiti. The new island was rumoured to be rich and populated by a colony of Jews, and the French hoped to be the first to exploit it. Surville followed Tasman's chart to the North Cape of New Zealand, where they were caught in the same storm that was battering the *Endeavour*.[58] Thus the first two European ships to visit New Zealand since the seventeenth century sailed past each other in a howling gale, unaware of one another's existence. Two days later, the *Endeavour* sighted Murim-otu, the small island off the end of North Cape, and on 24 December they sailed past the Three Kings Islands, which Abel Tasman had previously visited and named. As the wind died down Banks went alongside in his boat, and shot some gannets which were baked that night as a Yuletide pie in the ship's galley. The next day the pie was served up as the main dish for their Christmas feast, and that night 'all hands were as Drunk as our forefathers usd to be upon the like occasion'.[59]

On 2 January, having finally weathered Cape Maria van Diemen, the *Endeavour* headed south along the west coast of the North Island. Because of the prevailing westerlies, Cook was in grave danger of being caught on a lee shore, but at the same time he wanted to chart the coastline as accurately as possible, and tacked the ship inshore on a number of occasions. As they sailed past Mount Taranaki, Cook named it 'Egmont' after another First Lord of the Admiralty, and on 14 January the ship crossed the entrance of Tasman's 'Murderers' Bay' (Taitapu, now Golden Bay), where several Dutch sailors had been killed in 1642 in a skirmish. Cook was looking for a sheltered harbour where he could careen the *Endeavour*, and collect wood, fresh food and water. On 15 January 1770 they sailed into Totara-nui, a deep sound on the north-east coast of the South Island of New Zealand. This sheltered maze of inlets and islands, which he named 'Queen Charlotte Sound', was to become one of Cook's favourite anchorages in the Pacific.

8

The Owner of These Bones

As the *Endeavour* entered Queen Charlotte Sound, the tide carried the ship towards a reef off the north-western shore. The boats were lowered and towed the ship clear, watched by a curious sea-lion. As they passed a *pa* [fortified town] built on an island in the channel, the people in the pa shouted and brandished their weapons; and an old man came down to the water's edge where he performed a ritual with a mat and feathers. By two o'clock that afternoon, the ship was anchored off Meretoto, a small cove on the west side of the Sound, where four canoes came out to meet them. According to Banks, their crews were dressed in cloaks very like those sketched in the account of Tasman's voyage; and they paddled around the *Endeavour* before throwing some stones at the side of the vessel. After this, Tupaia engaged them in conversation, and a very old man decided to come on board. Although some of his companions tried to hold him back, he climbed up on deck, where Tupaia greeted him with a hongi. When they saw this, his companions laughed uproariously and eagerly climbed up the side of the ship, where they were given a number of presents.

Cook was delighted with Meretoto, which he named 'Ship Cove', and its stream of fine water, thick forest and sandy beaches. As soon as their visitors had left he put the men to work, collecting wood and water, shooting shags, collecting shellfish and taking a huge haul of fish with the ship's seine. Early the next morning, the *Endeavour* was careened at the north end of the beach; and as the sailors began to scrub the hull and paint it with a mixture of tar and oil, three canoes came out from the island pa, bringing about 100 people (including women) to see what they were doing. When the longboat, laden with casks, began to row away from the ship, the canoes set off after it, so a musket loaded with smallshot was fired at them, and they quickly came back to the vessel. These people began to trade dried fish for European goods, and when the master prevented two of the warriors from climbing on board, they threatened him with spears and were physically forced back into their canoe. Shortly after this a man tried to snatch some goods from the deputy purser, threatening him with a hand-club. Seeing this, Cook fired

Fishermen in canoes in Queen Charlotte Sound, sketched by
Sydney Parkinson

a musket loaded with duck-shot at the warrior, wounding him in the knee and the foot. According to Magra, one of the sailors:

His wounds producing a plentiful hemorrhage, [the warrior] bathed them in salt water, and the pain being acute, he angrily threw the fish which he had sold, and for which he had been paid, into the sea. The Indians who were in the other canoes, did not appear surprized either at the report of the gun or the wounds it had made, though they all paddled round and examined them; nor did the wounded Indian retire, but wrapping himself up in mats he continued about the ship several hours.[1]

His companions did not leave the ship, but paddled around it several times before coming under the stern where they talked with Tupaia, 'discours[ing] with him about their antiquity and Legends of their ancestors'.[2]

After dinner, Cook, Banks and Tupaia boarded the pinnace and went to explore another cove about a mile from their anchorage. As they rowed along, they noticed something floating on the surface of the water. At first they thought that it was a dead seal, but as they came closer they realised that this was the corpse of a woman. They carried on to the cove, and when they landed, the members of a small family group who had been cooking on the beach ran off into the forest. After a while these people returned, except for an old man and a child, who lingered at the edge of the woods. They found the Europeans examining their earth oven, and food baskets nearby which held dog meat, and two bones which had been recently picked clean, with a few sinews still clinging to them.

As Cook examined one of these bones, he realised in consternation that it might be from a human forearm. He asked one of the family members if these were not dog bones, but in answer the man took hold of the flesh of his own forearm and pretended to chew it. Joseph Banks noted later:

Tho we had from the first of our arrival upon the [New Zealand] coast constantly heard the Indians acknowledge the custom of eating their enemies we had never before had a proof of it, but this amounted almost to demonstration: the bones were clearly human, . . . and on the grisly ends which were gnawed were evident marks of teeth, and these were accidentaly found in a provision basket.[3]

Nevertheless, Banks was not sure whether these were the remains of a meal of human flesh. Tupaia asked these people, 'What bones are these?' They answered, 'The bones of a man.' 'And have you eat the flesh?' 'Yes.' 'Have you none of it left?' 'No.' 'Why did you not eat the woman who we saw today in the water?' 'She was our relation.' 'Who then is it that you do eat?' 'Those who are killed in war.' 'And who was the man whose bones these are?' '5 days ago a boat of our enemies came into this bay and of them we killed 7, of whom the owner of these bones was one.'[4]

When they returned to the ship, they told their shipmates about what they had seen. Judging from their journals, it made a tremendous impact. No one on board the *Endeavour* was indifferent to cannibalism, although their reactions varied widely. Eating human flesh was not a theoretical matter for sailors during this period, for when ships were wrecked or burnt at sea, and men took to the boats or were marooned, they were known to eat each other.[5] Human flesh was also occasionally eaten in Europe in times of famine, or riot. Many of the sailors, too, believed in witchcraft and were intensely super-stitious, believing that witches and warlocks sacrificed and ate human beings during their rituals. Although cannibalism sometimes happened in eighteenth-century Europe, it was regarded as behaviour at the extreme edges of human possibility; and most of the sailors were aghast to think that Maori might hunt each other casually, for meat. As Pickersgill remarked with horror, 'We saw one of the Bodys and two arms with flesh upon them which we saw them eat this is the first Proof Possitive we have had of the Inhabitants being CANNIBALS and I belive these are the only People who kill their fellow creatuers Puerly for the meat which we are well Assured they do by their laying in wait one for another as a sportsman would for his game and they carry this detestable crime so far as to glory in carrieing in their ears the Thumbs of those unhappy sufferrs who fell in their way.'[6]

Magra added that the people in 'Cannibal Cove' felt no shame about the practice of cannibalism, mocking those philosophers in Europe who thought it impossible that human beings could eat each other:

Perhaps they thought, like a celebrated philosopher, that it was as well to feed on the bodies of their enemies, (for by their own accounts they eat no other) as to leave them to be devoured by crows. It is however certain that they had no belief of any turpitude in this practice, because they were not ashamed of it; but, on the contrary, when we took up an arm for examination, they imagined us to be desirous of the same kind of food, and with great good nature promised that they would the next day spare a human head ready roasted, if we would come or send to fetch it.

Some gentlemen, who never left their own homes, have ventured, on the strength of speculative reasoning, to question the veracity of those travellers who have published accounts of cannibals in Africa and America; treating as falsehoods every relation, which, from their ignorance of human nature, appears to them improbable: but let them not indulge the same freedom on this occasion; the fact will be too well attested to be rendered doubtful by their visionary impertinent objections.[7]

Joseph Banks, on the other hand, was concerned about the implications of cannibalism for the place of humanity in the Great Chain of Being. In his journal he argued that the practice was unnatural and irrational; and that Maori must be driven by a 'Thirst of Revenge' to eat each other. In an eloquent passage, he wrote:

Nature through all the superior part of creation shews how much she recoils at the thought of any species preying upon itself: Dogs and cats shew visible signs of disgust at the very sight of a dead carcass of their species, . . . and were never say'd to eat each other except in cases of absolute nescessity, when the stings of hunger have overcome the precepts of nature, in which case the same has been done by the inhabitants of the most civilizd nations.

Among fish and insects indeed there are many instances which prove that those who live by prey regard little whither what they take is of their own or any other species; but any one who considers the admirable chain of nature in which Man, alone endowd with reason, justly claims the highest rank and next to him are placd the half reasoning Elephant, the sagacious dog, the architect Beaver . . . from these descending through the less informd Quadrupeds and birds to the fish and insects, which seem besides the instinct of Fear which is given them for self-preservation to be movd only by the stings of hunger to eat and those of lust to propagate their own species . . . shading itself away into the vegetable kingdom – whoever considers this will easily see that no Conclusion in favour of such a practise can be drawn from the actions of a race of beings placd so infinitely below us in the order of Nature.[8]

Even dogs and cats, he thought, recoiled from eating their own kind. By this reckoning, dogs and cats were more civilised than Maori.

In many respects, Tupaia shared Banks's views about cannibalism. Although cannibalism was common in the Marquesas and other islands around his homeland, and human sacrifice and infanticide were part of the worship of 'Oro,[9] Tupaia considered the custom barbaric. Of them all, Cook seemed least disturbed, and there is little hint in his journal that he found the habit disgusting. Rather, he seems to have held to his view that 'this seems to come from custom and not from a Savage disposission this they cannot be charged with'.[10] He sought empirical proof that Maori ate each other, and when some warriors offered to trade another human forearm bone to Banks the next morning, they were asked to demonstrate the custom. Until the 'experimental gentlemen' had seen human flesh being eaten with their own eyes, they could not claim incontrovertible proof of the custom. Cook calmly watched this demonstration, noting that when these men 'bit and naw'd the bone [they] draw'd it thro' their mouth and this in such a manner as plainly shew'd that the flesh to them was a dainty bit'.[11] While the sailors might react with horror to such a display, 'enlightened leaders' and 'experimental gentlemen', it seemed, should remain detached and try to understand what they were seeing.

As the killings attested, the Sound was in an uproar at the time of the *Endeavour*'s visit. Totara-nui was a favourite landing-place for northern tribes who came to plunder for southern greenstone, and in January 1769, it was a battleground. The local inhabitants were living in fortified pa, having abandoned their undefended villages, and expected to be attacked at any moment. There had been recent skirmishes, and Cook and his men met women in mourning for their husbands, who slashed at their bodies with flints and chips of greenstone in grief; and spoke of children captured and killed by enemy raiders. On 18 January a second earth oven with human bones beside it was found in a clearing – additional evidence of 'their horrid midnight repasts', according to Parkinson's lurid comment.[12] The sailors became obsessed with acquiring human bones as souvenirs; while Tupaia tried to find out more about Maori warfare, asking the local people whether they collected the skulls of their enemies (as his own people did in the Society Islands):

But where are the sculls, sayd Tupia, do you eat them? Bring them and we shall then be convinced that these are men whose bones we have seen. – We do not eat the heads, answerd the old man who had first come on board the ship, but we do the brains and tomorrow I will bring one and shew you.[13]

Three days later, the old man (whose name was Topaa) came out to the ship with four preserved heads, which Banks concluded had been kept as war trophies. He managed to acquire one of these 'curiosities', the head of a boy about fourteen years old who had been killed by a blow to the temple, exchanging it for an old pair of white linen drawers.

Despite this evidence of violent conflict, Cook and his men had little fear of the local inhabitants. The British had great faith in their muskets and guns, trusting them in almost any situation. Over the following days Banks and Solander wandered around the Sound, observing local fishing methods, visiting a number of the abandoned villages, and searching for new species of plants. The men went out fishing, and on 21 January when a fishing party went ashore at a deserted village, Jonathan Monkhouse found a bunch of human hair tied to a tree, which he took away with him. As he suspected, this was 'a place consecrated for religious purposes', for human hair was used in witchcraft, and as a marker for burial sites and boundaries. It is probable that he was observed, however, because later that day when he and some other sailors rowed towards the island pa, a group of canoes came towards them in a threatening fashion.

According to some reports, Monkhouse shot at these people, first with smallshot and then with musketball, killing a man and wounding another. They rapidly retreated 'as well they might', commented Banks, 'who probably came out with friendly intentions (so at least their behaviour both before and since seems to shew) and little expected so rough usage from people who had always acted in a friendly manner to them, and whoom they were not at all conscious of having offended.'[14] Cook, however, was told nothing about this incident until Topaa reported it to him eight days later. Even then, another local man denied the story, and Tupaia also cast doubt on Topaa's complaints, remarking with asperity that 'Our Friend Topaa is . . . given too much to Lying.'[15] It is quite likely, in fact, that Monkhouse had shot a man, but that knowing how Cook was likely to react, his shipmates had decided to keep quiet about it.

During their three weeks in the Sound, the sailors were kept busy, repairing ironwork, woodwork and rigging, repairing the casks, drying out powder and sails, fishing and gathering shellfish, collecting fresh water, wood and green vegetables, and re-baking the ship's bread to try and kill the weevils which infested it. The weather was pleasant, they had plenty of fish and shellfish to eat, and there were no floggings. As they worked to get the ship ready for sea, Cook set about surveying this deep maze of waterways. He took the pinnace on expeditions to various inlets, and on 22 January climbed a high hill on the south-east side of the Sound, where he saw a magnificent panorama of hills and islands, with a strait running from the east to the west, dividing the North Island from the southern land mass. Four days later he took Banks and Solander up another steep hill on the eastern side of the Sound, to view the strait (now Cook Strait). They built a cairn of rocks on the summit, with some musketballs, shot beads and other small items beneath it, and when they came back down to the boat they found Tupaia waiting for them, chatting with the local inhabitants in a very relaxed and friendly fashion. Cook and Tupaia seem to have been on excellent terms during this period, for as Cook noted gratefully, 'Tupia always accompanies us in every excursion we make and proves of infinate service.'[16]

On 30 January, Cook put up a post in Ship Cove inscribed with the ship's name and the date of its visit to the Sound, and then went with Monkhouse and Tupaia to the island pa, where he asked for Topaa's permission to set up a similar post on the highest point of the island. Topaa agreed, and accompanied them to the top of the peak, where Cook set up the post, hoisted the Union Jack upon it, and named the inlet 'Queen Charlotte Sound', taking possession of this part of the country. He distributed silver threepenny pieces and spike nails marked with the King's broad arrow to several old men who had come with them, toasted the King with a bottle of wine, and then gave the empty bottle to Topaa, who was delighted. Afterwards Cook and Tupaia talked with Topaa, asking him about the Strait through to the eastern sea, and whether this land was part of a great Continent. Topaa told them that 'they knew but of 3 lands one of which lay to the N which they would be 3 months in going round [which Cook identified as 'Aeheino mouwe' – *Ahi no Maui* – Maui's fire, the North Island]; another which we was upon they could go round in 4 days [probably Arapaoa Island on the east side of the South] and a Third lyeing SWtd of which they had but a very Imperfect knollege and called it Towie poe namou [*Te Wai Pounamu* – Greenstone Waters, the South Island].'[17] From Cook's comments, it is obvious that he already had a shrewd idea that New Zealand was not part of the Southern Continent, but was made up of islands, and Topaa's information tended to reinforce that opinion. After this exchange they returned to the ship, where Cook invited the old chief to dinner.

By 3 February, it seemed that the *Endeavour* expedition was depleting local resources. Cook went with Solander and Tupaia to a pa in East Bay to trade for dried fish for the voyage, buying so much that finally the old men told them to leave the island. When he went to the north of the Sound to see if he could do better, he met a similar rebuff. At the same time, the 'gentlemen' were making last-minute efforts to prepare themselves for the rigours of the voyage. As Banks reported with glee:

One of our gentlemen came home to day abusing the natives most heartily whom he said he had found to be given to the detestable Vice of Sodomy. He, he said, had been with a family of Indians and paid a price for leave to make his adresses to any one young women they should pitch upon for him; one was chose as he thought who willingly retird with him but on examination provd to be a boy; that on his returning and complaining of this another was sent who provd to be a boy likewise; that on his second complaint he could get no redress but was laught at by the Indians. Far be it from me to attempt saying that that Vice is not practisd here, this however I must say that in my humble opinion this story proves no more than that our gentleman was fairly trickd out of his cloth, which none of the young lades chose to accept of on his terms, and the master of the family did not chuse to part with.[18]

Banks does not name the unlucky 'gentleman', but from his delight at his discomfiture, it was probably William Monkhouse, the ship's surgeon, with whom he had quarrelled in Tahiti.

On 5 January, Cook ordered the *Endeavour* to be warped out of Ship Cove, and prepared to sail from the Sound. Seeing that they were about to depart, Topaa came on board, where he talked with Tupaia about local traditions. According to Banks:

He knew of no other great land than that we had been upon, *Aehia no Mauwe*, of which *Terawhitte* was the southern part; that he beleived his ancestors were not born there but came originaly from *Heawye* (the place from whence Tupia and the Islanders also derive their origin) which lay to the Northward where were many lands; that neither himself his father or his grandfather ever heard of ships as large as this being here before, but that they have a tradition of 2 large vessels, much larger than theirs, which some time or other came here and were totally destroyd by the inhabitants and all the people belonging to them kill'd. This Tupia says is a very old tradition, much older than his great grandfather, and relates to the two large canoes which came from *Olimaroa*, one of the Islands he has mentiond to us. Whether he is right, or whether this is a tradition of Tasmans ships whose size in comparison to their own they could not from relation conceive a sufficient Idea of, and whoom their Warlike ancestors had told them they had destroyd, is dificult to say. Tupia all along warnd us not to beleive too much any thing these people told us; For says he they are given to lying.[19]

Whether Tupaia really believed that Maori were inveterate liars, or whether he had become a little jealous of Topaa's relationship with Cook, this was a revealing comment. In the event, Cook took little notice of what he said, putting considerable weight on Topaa's geographical information during the next phase of the voyage. On 6 January, as they sailed out of the Sound, the *Endeavour* was at first becalmed, and then carried by a tide which roared 'like a mill-stream' and almost swept them onto one of the sacred rocks, Nga Whatu. After escaping these hazards, Cook set his course south-east, sighting a high, snow-capped mountain in the Kaikoura Range as they headed for the open ocean.

On the evening of 7 January, some of the officers told Cook they thought that the land between the Strait and Cape Turnagain might be joined by an isthmus to a larger land mass. Cook had seen so far up the eastern coast from the high hill in the Sound that he thought this highly improbable, but he tacked north in order to prove that *Te Ahi no Maui* really was an island. Off Cape Palliser, three canoes came out whose crews boarded the ship without any sign of fear, asking for *whau* or nails. When they were given some, they asked Tupaia what these things were, making it plain that they had only heard of nails, not seen them. The chief of this party was a silver-haired, tattooed man with a fine carriage, who wore a finely woven cloak with a decorative border, and a greenstone earring. Parkinson was impressed by his demeanour, commenting:

We observed a great difference betwixt the inhabitants on this side of the land, north of Cook's Straits, and those of the south. The former are tall, well-limbed, clever fellows; have a deal of tataow, and plenty of good cloaths; but the latter are a set of poor wretches, who, though strong, are stinted in their growth, and seem to want the spirit or sprightliness of the northern Indians. Few of them are tataowed, or have their hair oiled and tied up, and their canoes are but mean.[20]

The next day Cape Turnagain came in sight, convincing everyone on board that there was no isthmus in this latitude. Having proved his point, Cook turned south again, sailing back down the eastern coastline.

Over the days that followed, there were few contacts with local Maori. Two canoes came out from Castle Point where their crews traded a few fish and trolling lures; and on 14 February, four double canoes came out to meet them from Kaikoura, about nineteen miles out at sea. These people seemed very timid, however, and Tupaia could not persuade them to come alongside the *Endeavour*. On 16 February Gore thought he saw land to the south-east, but this proved to be another 'Cape Flyaway'; and the next day near Akaroa they saw two people sitting on top of a hill, the last Maori they would see in New Zealand. As they sailed further south, high land was sighted far off in the distance. Banks and the other 'Continents' on board rejoiced, thinking that this was surely part of the coast of Terra Australis. Topaa had told them that they could circumnavigate the southern island in only four days (although he was almost certainly referring to Arapawa Island in Queen Charlotte Sound), and his geographical knowledge now seemed questionable. As Banks wrote cheerfully: 'We were now on board of two parties, one who wishd that the land in sight might, the other that it might not be a continent: myself have always been most firm for the former, tho sorry I am to say that in the ship my party is so small that I firmly believe that there are no more heartily of it than myself and one poor midshipman, the rest begin to sigh for roast beef.'[21]

On 28 February Tupaia told his shipmates that it was New Year's Day in Tahiti, and as the new moon rose above the horizon, they celebrated the occasion with him. Since there was still land as far south as the eye could see, Banks was also celebrating. On 6 March he declared, 'our unbeleivers are almost inclind to think that Continental measures will at last prevail.'[22] By 9 May, however, the *Endeavour* was off South Cape on Stewart Island, with no land visible further south, and a great swell rolling in from the south-west. It was the birthday of one of the petty officers, and the 'no-Continents' were rejoicing, so they marked the occasion by killing and cooking a dog that had been bred on board the vessel. The hindquarters were roasted, the forequarters were made into a pie, and the viscera was turned into a haggis – an exotic combination of British and Tahitian cooking. The next day they sailed around South Cape, 'to the total demolition of our aerial fabrick calld continent', Banks ruefully acknowledged in his journal. New Zealand was two large islands, but it was no Terra Australis, with its 'civilised' inhabitants and its fabled wealth of gold and pearls.

The collapse of his dream of exploring the Unknown Southern Continent made Banks testy, and soon after the ship turned up the west coast of the South Island, he and Cook had a difference of opinion. Banks was eager to land in one of the fiords to look for minerals and plants, but Cook considered it far too dangerous. As he noted in his journal, 'It certainly would have been highly imprudent in me to have put into a place where we could not have got out but with a wind that we have lately found does not blow one day in a month: I mention this because there were some on board who wanted me to harbour at any rate without in the least considering either the present or future consequences.'[23] Banks did not agree, and harboured a grudge against Cook on this score for many years, remarking in 1803: 'Had Cook paid the same attention [as Flinders] to the Naturalists, we should have done more at that time. However, the bias of the public mind had not so decidedly marked Natural History for a favourite pursuit as it now has. Cook might have met with reproof for sacrificing a day's fair wind to the accommodation of the Naturalists.'[24]

The *Endeavour* flew up the west coast of the South Island, and on 26

March they sailed into the west side of Cook Strait, passing Taitapu (now Golden Bay), where Tasman's ships had anchored. They landed in Admiralty Bay, and the next morning the sailors began to collect wood, water and greens, while Tupaia and Taiato went out angling and caught almost a boatload of fish, and Solander and Banks inspected a few abandoned houses and foraged for new species of plants, without finding any. The following day was wet and windy, and on 29 March Banks retired to his cabin with a violent headache and an attack of nausea. By the next day he had recovered, however, climbing a high hill where he found three new species of plants to add to his New Zealand collections. That evening Cook met with his officers to discuss which route they should follow on the return voyage to England. He had hoped to sail in high latitudes from New Zealand around Cape Horn, to prove that there was no Southern Continent, but they all agreed that the ship was in too poor a condition for such a voyage. For the same reason, the officers thought it too risky to go west in high latitudes to the Cape of Good Hope. Instead, they resolved to go by way of the east coast of 'New Holland' (Australia) to the East Indies, a fateful decision. On Saturday 31 March the Endeavour sailed out of the bay, past Onetana (Cape Farewell) and into the Tasman Sea, plunging through the waves in a fresh nor'-easterly gale, leaving a blue and white wake like a peacock's tail behind them.

As they sailed from Cook Strait, Cook and Banks began to draft their 'Accounts' of New Zealand. Although Banks had been shaken by his encounters with Maori cannibalism, he thought that a British colony might be established in the North Island (an idea which he had not raised in connection with Tahiti), perhaps at the River Thames:

The River Thames is indeed in every respect the properest place we have yet seen for establishing a Colony; a ship as large as Ours might be carried several miles up the river, where she would be moord to the trees as safe as alongside a wharf in London river, a safe and sure retreat in case of an attack from the natives ... The Noble timber, of which there is such abundance, would furnish plenty of materials either for the building defences, houses, or Vessels. The River would furnish plenty of Fish, and the Soil make ample returns of any European Vegetables sown in it. I have some reason to think from observations made upon the vegetables that the Winters here are extreemly mild, much more so than in England; the Summers we have found to be scarce at all hotter, tho more equably Warm.[25]

Cook was also in favour of establishing a colony in New Zealand, and spoke highly of the local resources – the timber, fish and native flax in particular. He held fast to his positive impressions of the local inhabitants, concluding that 'all their actions and beheavour towards us tended to prove that they are a brave open warlike people and voide of treachery':

After they found that our Arms were so much Superior to theirs and that we took no advantage of that superiority and a little time given them to reflect upon it they ever after were our very good friends and we never had an Instance of their attempting to surprize or cut off any of our people when they were ashore, oppertunities for so doing they must have had at one time or a nother.[26]

At the same time, there were lively debates in the Great Cabin about how the question of the Southern Continent might finally be settled. Banks admitted, 'That a Southern continent realy exists, I firmly believe; but if ask'd why I believe so, I confess my reasons are weak; yet I have a preposession in favour of the fact which I find it dificult to account for.'[27] Cook held the opposite opinion: 'As to a Southern Continent I do not believe any such thing exists unless in a high Latitude, but as the Contrary oppinion hath for many years prevaild and may yet prevail it is necessary I should say some thing in support of mine . . .'[28] Each man marshalled arguments in support of his own view, finally agreeing that another voyage to the South Seas would be needed to settle the matter. At the end of his 'Account' of New Zealand Banks laid out a plan for such an expedition, to be supported by the Royal Society and King George as a 'Voyage of Mere Curiosity'. In supporting the idea of a second voyage, Cook also acknowledged Tupaia's role on the *Endeavour*:

Should it be thought proper to send a ship out upon this service while *Tupia* lieves and he to come out in her, in that case she would have a prodigious advantage over every ship that have been upon discoveries in those seas before; for by means of Tupia, supposeing he did not accompany you himself, you would always get people to direct you from Island to Island and would be sure of meeting with a friendly reseption and refreshments at every Island you came to.[29]

Although Cook and his officers had decided against continuing their search for the Southern Continent, the greatest trials of the voyage were still before them.

The East Coast of Australia

After crossing the Tasman, on 19 April 1770 they came to the coast of Australia, where Cook's skills as a practical sailor would be tested to the limit. The east coast of 'New Holland' had not previously been explored, and Cook decided to chart it. As they approached 'Point Hicks' on the south-east coast, waterspouts curved and swayed ahead of the ship, and the next day clouds of smoke puffed up from signal fires inland. On 22 April as the *Endeavour* ran up the coast, the sailors glimpsed a group of five naked men standing on a beach whom Banks described as 'enormously black', although he confessed in his journal, 'So far did the prejudices which we had built on Dampiers account influence us that we fancied we could see their Colour when we could scarce distinguish whether or not they were men.'[30] In his *New Voyage* of 1697, which Cook had with him, ex-buccaneer William Dampier had recalled his encounters with Aboriginal people in 1688, describing them as 'the miserablest People in the World . . . setting aside their Humane Shape, they differ but little from Brutes . . . The Colour of their Skins, both of their Faces and the rest of their Body, is Coal-black . . . They all of them have the most unpleasant Looks and the worst Features of any People that ever I saw, tho I have seen a great variety of Savages.'[31] Banks and Cook had read his account as they crossed the Tasman, and had been influenced by this description.

On 27 April Cook made an attempt to land at Bulli on the south-east coast, where four men were seen walking along a beach, two of them carrying a small canoe on their shoulders.[32] Cook, Banks, Solander and Tupaia crammed into the yawl and rowed to the beach to try and make contact with these people; but the surf was too high, and after watching the strangers from the rocks for a while, the men ran away into the bush, leaving four small dug-out canoes on the beach behind them. According to Parkinson, 'The country looked very pleasant and fertile; and the trees, quite free from underwood, appeared like plantations in a gentleman's park.'[33]

From Bulli they sailed on up the coast, and the next morning came to Kamay (now known as Botany Bay), where they saw about ten people by a fire, who climbed up a small hill to gaze at the *Endeavour*. Soon two small canoes landed, and four men went to join the others. Cook ordered a boat to go in and sound the bay, and as they approached the shore, this group (now identified as Gweagal people[34]) retreated further up the hill except for a small group of naked warriors, with white lines painted on their torsos and armed with boomerangs, who stood on the rocks to confront the

Tupaia's sketch of Gweagal fishermen at Kamay (Botany Bay)

strangers. When the sailors found a safe anchorage, another group of warriors armed with spears, throwing sticks and boomerangs gestured for them to come ashore, and signalled the ship to enter the bay. At noon as the ship passed the south head of Kamay, four small canoes paddled past, each carrying one man who speared for fish, virtually ignoring the *Endeavour*. Within an hour they had anchored opposite a small village, where an old woman and three children, each carrying a bundle of sticks, came out of the forest. The old woman, who was also naked, often looked at the ship, but showed no signs of fear or concern. She lit a fire, and when the men came back from their fishing they began to prepare their meal by the fire, 'to all appearance totally unmovd at us, tho we were within a little more than a half a mile of them', as Banks remarked with astonishment.[35] A surviving water-colour by Tupaia showing three Aborigines in two small bark canoes, one man spearing for fish while the two in the other canoe are paddling along, probably depicts these fishermen.

After dinner Cook decided to try and make contact with these people, and boarded the boats with Banks, Solander, Parkinson and Tupaia. As they approached their village, however, two naked warriors, each armed with a spear and a throwing stick, came down to the rocks – perhaps two of the fishermen who had landed earlier. Cook ordered the sailors to lay on their oars while Tupaia called out to these men and the Europeans used sign language, trying to befriend them. If Tupaia was wearing European clothes, he would have looked just like the strangers, however, and his language was just as unintelligible as English. They shook their spears, and 'calld to us very loud in a harsh sounding Language of which neither us or Tupia understood a word', so Cook threw beads and nails on the beach as a gesture of friendship.

When the warriors picked up these gifts and beckoned him ashore, Cook ordered the boat to land, but they quickly resumed their hostile postures. He fired a musket between the two men, trying to intimidate them; and although the younger man dropped his bundle of darts, the older warrior hurled a stone at Cook's party. Cook fired a musket loaded with smallshot, hitting this man in the legs, but he took little notice of his wounds, running to a nearby house and coming out with an oval shield, painted white in the middle with two holes to look through, and a wooden weapon. As Cook's men landed on the rocks, the two men advanced again, throwing stones and darts, one of which fell between Parkinson's feet; and two more muskets loaded with smallshot were fired, wounding one of them. They cried out for help while some women and children who had been watching 'set up a most horrid howl'. When the sailors landed, the warriors ran away yelling, leaving the children in one of the houses, crouching behind a piece of bark and the shield, which the older man had used to hide them. Cook and his companions looked around the encampment for a while, threw some nails, ribbons, cloth and a few strings of beads into the house where five or six small children were huddled, and collected about fifty spears which they took back to the beach, examining three small bark canoes ('the worst I think I ever saw,' said Cook) before embarking in the boats and crossing to the north shore of the bay, where they found some pools of fresh water.

When Cook went back to the village the next morning, its inhabitants had disappeared, and the beads and nails they had thrown to the children lay untouched in the house where they had hidden. Cook boarded the pinnace and explored the bay, sighting another group of Gweagal people cooking mussels over camp-fires who ran away as soon as he approached them. When Lieutenant Hicks went back to the beach that afternoon to collect water, eighteen warriors armed with throwing sticks and darts confronted him, sending two of their number ahead as challengers; although when Hicks sent two of his men to meet them they all retired. As Cook observed later, 'All they seem'd to want was for us to be gone.' The following day some men were heard shouting loudly from the shore, and when the sailors landed to cut grass, another group of warriors armed with boomerangs confronted them. That night a sailor died of consumption, and was buried by the watering-place, and Cook left cloth, looking-glasses, combs, beads and nails in a conspicuous place in the village.

Over the next few days the *Endeavour*'s men ranged about the bay, gathering greenstuffs, collecting wood and water, shooting birds, catching fish and exploring. They had a number of chance encounters with local people, who sometimes followed them, although they stayed at a safe distance. On one occasion Tupaia, who had gone off by himself to shoot parrots, met a group of nine people, who ran off as soon as they saw him. Two days later a midshipman, who was out on his own, met a very old man, a woman and some children who did not run away. When he offered them some parrots he had shot, however, 'they refusd, withdrawing themselves from his hand when he offerd them in token either of extreme fear or disgust'.[36] That same day Dr Monkhouse, who had also left his group, met seven people, one of whom threw a spear at him from up in a tree, but ran away immediately. Banks concluded from these encounters that the local inhabitants were 'rank cowards', not to be feared in any circumstance. Since Tupaia could not speak with the local Aborigines, as Cook noted with regret, 'We could know but very little of [the Aborigines'] customs as we never were able to form any connections with them.'[37] From this time onwards Tupaia, having lost his role as the expedition's interpreter and mediator, found himself marginalised among his shipmates.

As they sailed north, Cook named the harbour 'Botany Bay' after the harvest of new species of plants collected by the botanists. Banks and Solander worked hard on their specimens, and Parkinson completed ninety-four glorious water-colours and sketches. On 19 May Cook sailed past K'Gari Island (now Fraser Island), watched by a curious group of Dulingbara people foraging on the beach. As this 'mysterious white-winged object passing along the face of the ocean like a gigantic pelican' flew past them, heading towards a dangerous shoal called Thoorvoor, they saw people moving upon it. Later they composed a song to commemorate its passing:

> These strangers, where are they going?
> Where are they trying to steer?
> They must be in that place, Thoorvour, it is true,
> See the smoke coming in from the sea.
> These men must be burying themselves like the sand crabs.
> They disappeared like the smoke.[38]

Several nights later, Cook's clerk Orton went to bed dead drunk, and in the dark someone cut his clothes from his body, and cropped his ears. Cook was furious, describing this assault on his clerk as 'the greatest insult that could be offer'd to my authority in this Ship, as I have always been ready to hear and redress every complaint that have been made against any person in the Ship'.[39] The sailors remained silent, however, and Cook never discovered who had perpetrated the mischief, although in Batavia when a reward of 15 guineas and 15 gallons of arrack was offered to anyone who would identify the culprit, one of the midshipmen, Patrick Saunders, promptly deserted.

On 23 May Cook and his men made a brief landing at Bustard Bay to collect fresh water, catch fish and shoot birds. When they found a ring of small fires near a lagoon with some bark shelters nearby, and lengths of bark to sleep on, Tupaia observed to Cook that these people, who had so little, were *Taata Enos* (*ta'ata 'ino* – bad people).[40] After leaving the bay they sailed further up the coast, where their path was beset by shoals, reefs and small offshore islands, and Cook sent the boats out ahead of the ship to take soundings. After a time Tupaia began to complain of swollen gums, livid spots appeared on his legs (symptoms of scurvy), and the surgeon treated him with extract of lemon juice. Many of the supplies had run low, and Tupaia, who was yearning for the fresh fruits and vegetables of Tahiti, found the shipboard staples of salt meat and biscuit inedible. Although they made several more landings, they found little food of this kind, and Charles Green, the astronomer, and some of the sailors also began to suffer from scurvy.

These were treacherous and difficult waters, and on the night of 10 June, the *Endeavour* struck on a coral reef in the darkness. As Banks ran up on deck, he saw sheathing boards floating on the sea in the moonlight. The tide was going out, and they were about eight leagues from the land. It was a terrifying moment. Cook ordered the men to pump the ship, take in the sails, strike the topmasts and lower the boats to take soundings. At daylight, while the men in the boats examined the reef, their shipmates frantically jettisoned ballast, water from the casks, six of the guns, decayed stores and oil jars in a desperate attempt to lighten the vessel. They knew that the boats could not carry them all ashore, and that any survivors would be 'debarred from a hope of ever again seeing their native countrey or conversing with any but the most uncivilizd savages perhaps in the world'.[41] Nevertheless, when Cook decided to try and heave the ship off the rocks, the men worked with the greatest good will, without grumbling or cursing. After hours of gruelling effort they finally managed to free the ship, although as they began to sail her towards the shore, the hull started to fill with water. The officers and gentlemen (including Banks) took their turn at the pumps while Jonathan Monkhouse and a group of sailors prepared a sail as a 'fother'. The sail was coated with oakum and wool stuck on with dung, and then slung under the hull and pulled tight, and the ship was soon pumped dry, to their immense relief and gratitude.

The pinnace went off to find a suitable bay where the ship could be repaired, and as they limped towards the coast, Banks praised the sailors unreservedly:

During the whole time of this distress I must say for the credit of our people that I believe every man exerted his utmost for the preservation of the ship, contrary to what I have universaly heard to be the behavior of sea men who have commonly as soon as a ship is in a desperate situation begin to plunder and refuse all command. This was no doubt owing intirely to the cool and steady conduct of the officers, who during the whole time never gave an order which did not shew them to be per-fectly composd and unmovd by the circumstances howsoever dreadfull they might appear.[42]

It was not until 17 June that the *Endeavour* was finally beached at Whalum-baal Birri, now known as 'Endeavour River', where the sick (including Green and Tupaia, who by now were very ill) were landed. Over the following days Tupaia went angling for fish, shot birds with his musket, collected shellfish, wild bananas and taro (which he cooked in an earth oven to make the roots less acrid) and quickly recovered his health; although Green still had acute symptoms of scurvy. The sailors thanked Providence when they inspected the gaping hole in the hull, which had been partly plugged by a coral rock which broke off in the gap, saving them from sinking. Gore shot a kangaroo and a wallaroo, Banks's greyhound hunted down a wallaby, and quantities of turtles were collected. Tupaia often went off hunting and gathering on his own, and on one of these expeditions he saw a dingo, and several days later came across two people digging for roots, although they ran away as soon as they saw him.

The first exchange with local Aboriginal people, the Guugu-Yimithirr, came after Cook and his men had spent three weeks at Endeavour River. Cook had advised his men not to attempt to initiate contact with these people, but let them make the first move. Eventually a party of four men in a small dug-out canoe with outriggers came fishing near the ship, and hailed the *Endeavour*. The sailors responded, and eventually persuaded these men to come alongside, where they were given some 'trifles'. They received cloth, nails, paper and beads with indifference, but when a small fish was thrown to them they seemed delighted. As they returned to the beach, the Aborigines stood holding their throwing sticks, ready to hurl spears at the strangers. Tupaia signalled to them to put their weapons down, and when they sat

The Endeavour *beached at Whalumbaal Birri (Endeavour River)*

down, Tupaia gave them presents. When Tupaia and the sailors tried to talk
with these men, however, although they repeated words willingly, no one
could understand their language. Tupaia was sleeping ashore in one of
Banks's tents, and after this meeting Guugu-Yimithirr people visited him
often, giving him wild taro and bringing others to meet him and the British.
Parkinson recorded the names of his visitors in his journal, and collected a
vocabulary,[43] noting that they whistled when they were surprised; and that
they kept their women strictly away from the strangers.

After a week of these amiable exchanges several people came out to the
ship, but on the following day a group of ten Aborigines arrived, carrying a
large quantity of spears. They came on board and asked for some of the
turtles which the sailors had collected, and when they were refused, stamped
their feet in anger and pushed the Europeans away. When they tried to
take a couple of turtles from the deck, they were prevented, and soon went
ashore, where one of these men lit some dried grass from a pitch kettle
and set fire to the grass around Tupaia's tent, blaming him for this un-
generous behaviour. As the blaze spread, burning a sow with her litter of
piglets to death, they set fire to the grass where all the ship's nets and some
clothes were piled up, so Cook fired a musket loaded with smallshot at one
of the ringleaders and they ran off into the bushes. They soon returned,
however, led by an old man who looked at the strangers, and told his
companions to put down their weapons. The Europeans took them to the
beach, where they sat looking at the ship for several hours, and then
departed. Several days later one of the sailors lost his way in the bush, and
stumbled upon a group of four Aboriginal people cooking a bird and the
hind leg of a kangaroo on a fire. The sailor was unarmed, and although he
was afraid of being attacked he sat quietly while these people touched

different parts of his body and examined his skin, then gave them his knife as a present. They were friendly and peaceful, and as soon as they had satisfied their curiosity, they showed him how to find his way back to the *Endeavour*.

By now Cook was anxious to leave the bay, because supplies were running low and the repairs to the vessel had been completed. The winds were unfavourable, however, and it was not until 4 August that they finally sailed out of Endeavour River, only to find themselves surrounded by shoals in all directions. They threaded their way through a maze of shoals and islands, narrowly escaping grounding several times before making their way to the open sea ten days later. On 16 August Cook decided to try and get back inside the reef to look for Torres Strait. As he tacked back towards the coast, however, he found his way blocked by a high wall of coral rock, on which a mountainous surf was breaking. Just as the *Endeavour* was about to strike on the reef, driven by an enormous wave, a small breeze from the land blew them back, and then died, and then blew again, and the boats towed them towards a narrow opening where the ebb tide ran furiously, sweeping them safely back out to sea. After a while, they found another channel through the reef, passing into calmer waters. That night, Cook showed some of the appalling strain he had been under:

Were it not for the pleasure which naturly results to a Man from being the first discoverer, even was it nothing more than sands and Shoals, this service would be insuportable especialy in far distant parts, like this, short of Provisions and almost every other necessary. The world will hardly admit of an excuse for a man leaving a Coast unexplored he has once discover'd, if dangers are his excuse he is than charged with *Timorousness* and want of Perserverance and at once pronounced the unfitest man in the world to be employ'd as a discoverer; if on the other hand he boldly incounters all the dangers and obstacles he meets and is unfortunate enough not to succeed he is than charged with *Temerity* and want of conduct.[44]

From this time on Cook decided to keep within the Barrier Reef, and several days later, the *Endeavour* entered Endeavour Strait where they saw small groups of people on the continent and the offshore islands. Cook sailed through the Strait, proving that New Holland was separated from New Guinea, and carried on to the west coast of New Guinea, where his men had a brief but startling encounter with warriors armed with darts and hollow canes filled with burning embers. As Cook and Banks began to draft their 'Accounts' of Australia, Cook described Aboriginal people as 'timorous and inoffensive ... no ways inclinable to cruelty'; countering Dampier's dismissal of these people with an eloquent defence of their way of living:

From what I have said of the Natives of New-Holland they may appear to some to be the most wretched people upon Earth, but in reality they are far more happier than we Europeans; being wholy unacquainted not only with the superfluous but the necessary Conveniences so much sought after in Europe, they are happy in not knowing the use of them. They live in a Tranquillity which is not disturb'd by the Inequality of Condition: The Earth and sea of their own accord furnishes them with all things necessary for life, they covet not Magnificent Houses, Houshold-stuff &c, they live in a warm and fine Clime and enjoy a very wholsome Air. In short they seem'd to set no Value upon any thing we gave them, nor would they ever part with any thing of their own for any one article we could offer them; this in my opinion argues that they think themselves provided with all the necessarys of Life and that they have no superfluities.[45]

James Cook had grown up in the lower reaches of a class-ridden society, and his heartfelt comment about 'Inequality of Condition' was based on personal experience.

From New Guinea, Cook decided to head straight for the East Indies. At once, according to Banks,

the sick became well and the melancholy lookd gay. The greatest part of them were now pretty far gone with the longing for home which the Physicians have gone so far as to esteem a disease under the name of Nostalgia; indeed I can find hardly any body in the ship clear of its effects but the Captn Dr. Solander and myself, indeed we three have pretty constant employment for our minds which I believe to be the best if not the only remedy for it.[46]

As they sailed west, passing the south coast of Timor, the men's rations were increased. Although some of his officers importuned Cook to land there to collect fresh food and water, he knew that this was a Dutch possession and refused, concerned that they might be poorly treated by the Dutch officials. On 17 September the *Endeavour* anchored off the small island of Savu, where Lieutenant Gore went ashore, returning with the Dutch factor and the local Rajah (who had signed a treaty of alliance with the Dutch East India Company). Cook entertained these men to dinner, presenting the Rajah with gifts, including an English sheep and Banks's greyhound; and saluting them with nine guns as they left the vessel. Solander and Spöring were both able to converse with the Dutchman, and when they went ashore the next day, the Rajah entertained Cook and his companions to dinner. Although there were initial difficulties in bartering for fresh meat and vegetables, these were soon overcome by a little bribery, and Cook acquired eight buffalo, 30 dozen chickens, six sheep, three pigs and some vegetables – enough to feed the men during the short voyage to Batavia.

By the time they arrived at Java Head south of Batavia on 1 October, the sailors were well fed, rested and healthy, although both Green and Tupaia were still suffering from scurvy (complicated in Green's case by alcoholic symptoms), and Hicks was in an advanced stage of tuberculosis. Tupaia refused to take European medicines but craved fruit and root vegetables, so Cook tried to buy fresh food for him. As they carried on up the strait to Batavia, they met two Dutch East Indiamen who gave them news of Europe, reporting that the Russians had invaded Constantinople, and that England was in an uproar, 'the people crying up and down the streets Down with King George, King Wilkes [Wilkes, the radical politician] for ever'. On 9 October they sailed into Batavia road where a pilot boat came out to meet them. According to Banks, the officer of this boat and his men 'were almost ... Spectres, no good omen of the healthyness of the countrey we were arrived at; our people however who truly might be calld rosy and plump, for we had not a sick man among us, Jeerd and flouted much at their brother sea mens white faces.'[47]

At first, all went well in Batavia. When they landed, Cook paid his compliments to the Dutch Governor-General, and despatched copies of his journal and charts of the South Seas, New Zealand, and the east coast of New Holland to the Admiralty in London. In his covering letter Cook was full of praise for his men, modestly celebrating the success of his shipboard regime, with its rigorous attention to cleanliness, adequate rest and diet, and the use of anti-scorbutics:

In Justice to the officers and the whole crew I must say that they have gone through the fatigues and dangers of the whole voyage with that cheerfullness and allertness that will always do honour to British Seamen, and I have the satisfaction to say that I have not lost one man by sickness during the whole Voyage.[48]

The few sick men were sent ashore and fed with fresh fruit and vegetables, where they soon began to recover. As Tupaia regained his strength, he and Taiato wandered around Batavia in delight, amazed by the canals and the fine houses (although Tupaia was disgusted to find that every house contained a lavatory, which he considered most unhygienic). They enjoyed the avenues of trees, the marketplace, the Town Hall and the octagonal church; the paved streets, the fine merchants in their laced hats, and velvet and silk garments, who rode about in horse-drawn carriages; and the many different nationalities they encountered. According to Banks, Taiato was 'allmost ready to run mad with the numberless novelties which diverted his attention from one to the other, he danc'd about the streets examining every thing to the best of his abilities'.[49] Tupaia was also enthralled, and when he saw the people in the streets wearing the costumes of their own nationalities, he decided to change from European clothing back into Tahitian bark-cloth. One day as he walked about the streets with Banks, dressed in this fashion, a man came running up to them to ask if Tupaia had ever visited Batavia before. In this way they learned that Bougainville had been there eighteen months earlier with two French ships, accompanied by a Tahitian. When Banks made further enquiries he realised that the 'Spaniards' they had heard about in Tahiti were in fact Bougainville's men, and that the Tahitian who had visited Batavia was Ahutoru, the 'brother' of Reti, the chief of Hitia'a. His informants also told him about the young woman who had been smuggled on board Bougainville's ship, disguised as the naturalist Commerson's assistant.

After several weeks, however, the canals of Batavia (which also served as sewers) and their clouds of malaria-carrying mosquitos began to take their toll. First Taiato and Tupaia fell ill, and although Taiato was a good patient, Tupaia refused all medical attention. Instead, he asked Banks if he could go back to the ship, because he found the air in the houses stifling. This was not possible, so Banks had a tent pitched for them on a small islet in the harbour, where the sea breezes blew. Soon afterwards Banks was stricken with malaria, and then his two servants fell ill; followed by Dr Solander and Dr Monkhouse. After a few days of intense suffering, Dr Monkhouse died, followed by Taiato (who had an acute form of tuberculosis). When he lost his young companion, Tupaia was inconsolable, crying out 'Taiato! Taiato!', weeping bitterly and saying that he wished he had never left his own country. He died several days later, and was buried with Taiato on another islet in the harbour.[50] According to Cook, the scurvy which had affected Tupaia during the last stages of the voyage had weakened him, making him susceptible to the 'unwholesom air' of Batavia. On the coast of Australia, where he could not speak the local languages, Tupaia had been of little use to the expedition, and his resistance to the use of European medicines, his dislike of the shipboard diet and his stubborn loyalty to his own customs had irritated Cook. When he was told of his death, he commented coldly: 'He was a Shrewd, Sensible, Ingenious Man, but proud and obstinate which often made his situation on board both disagreeable to himself and those about him, and tended much to promote the deceases that put a period to his life'[51] – an ungracious obituary, considering Tupaia's contributions to the voyage.

At the time of Tupaia's demise Banks was very ill, and was sent to a house in the country where he was soon joined by Solander, Spöring and Cook's servant, all of whom had malaria. Banks dosed himself with a private supply of chincona bark, which brought his symptoms under control, and Solander also gradually recovered. Meanwhile the sailors fell ill from a variety of complaints (dysentery from drinking contaminated arrack and water; and possibly typhoid fever), and when they were taken to the sick-tents on the islet, they were attacked by swarms of mosquitos and contracted malaria. After a month in Batavia, Cook complained that he had only twenty men and officers left to work on the ship, and during this period he also suffered a bout of fever. The shipyard was very efficient, however, and by 25 December, Cook was ready to leave Java. They did not celebrate Christmas, because there were still forty sick men on board, and every member of the crew had been ill except for Ravenhill the sailmaker, a man in his seventies and a confirmed drunkard. On 27 December, the bronzed, cheerful crew of the *Endeavour*, who had jeered at the white-faced 'spectres' of sailors who greeted them on their arrival at Batavia, crept away from the port in a pitiable condition.

Even after they left Batavia, the diseases of that fatal port still clung to the *Endeavour*. There were mosquitos in the water butts, and the water which they had taken on at Princes Island was contaminated. After a month at sea, the men began to die of dysentery; many of the crew lay listlessly in their hammocks, dangerously ill with fevers and fluxes. Banks became ill again, Spöring died on 25 January 1771, and Parkinson followed him two days later. Ravenhill, the aged sailmaker who had remained healthy throughout the voyage, died soon after, followed by Charles Green, the astronomer, and a succession of sailors. By 5 February when Jonathan Monkhouse died, the men were in a state of deep depression. Two weeks later a sailor was flogged for getting drunk, assaulting the officer of the watch and beating some of his sick shipmates; and more sailors died on 27 February. The muster-roll of the *Endeavour* had become a disastrous list of 'DD' entries ('Discharged Dead'); and Cook, who had kept his men healthy throughout the voyage across the Pacific, was desolate.

On 14 March the *Endeavour* anchored in Table Bay, where Cook sent the sick men ashore. Solander had fallen ill again, this time of dysentery. When he landed, Banks received detailed reports of Bougainville's voyage. Ahutoru had returned from France, and was now at L'Île de France (now Mauritius), where a ship commanded by Marion du Fresne was preparing to take him back to Tahiti. He heard that the French were planning to establish a colony at Tahiti, and feared that Bougainville might try to claim the island by right of discovery, declaring the *Dolphin*'s visit to have been a fiction. He was anxious to get back to England, so that the *Endeavour*'s discoveries could be celebrated. Although Solander recovered during their stay at the Cape, three more men were lost, and when the *Endeavour* set sail on 15 April, the ship's master, Robert Molyneux, also perished.

After a brief visit to St. Helena, where Cook despatched the ship's log and some of the officers' journals to the Admiralty, Lieutenant Hicks died from the tuberculosis that had plagued him throughout the voyage; and Charles Clerke, who had also sailed around the world on the *Dolphin* with Byron, was promoted to third lieutenant. On 4 July 1771, as they approached the English coast, Banks's 'Bitch Lady', the mongrel that had accompanied him around the world, lay down on a wooden stool and died. A week later, 'Young Nick', the boy who had first sighted land at New Zealand, saw Lizard Head from the masthead. Cook had lost more than half of his men on this epic voyage, almost all of them after the *Endeavour*'s arrival at Batavia; and the survivors were longing to be back home in England.

9

Penguins on Wimbledon Common

On 12 July 1771 the *Endeavour* sailed briskly up the English Channel and anchored in the Downs. Almost immediately, Cook set out for London. The journals and charts that he had forwarded from Batavia and St. Helena had not yet arrived in England, and there had been speculation that the *Endeavour* had been sunk by the Spanish after her visit to Rio. The letter in which he announced his arrival to the Admiralty was brief and unassuming: 'I flatter myself that the [Charts, Plans & drawings] will be found sufficient to convey a Tolerable knowledge of the places that they are intended to illustrate, & that the discoveries we have made, tho' not great, will Apologize for the length of the Voyage.'[1]

Cook was unduly modest, however. Although the health of his men had been destroyed by the mosquitos and dirty water of Batavia, his ship had circumnavigated the world, turning much of the 'Unknown Southern Continent' into ocean in the process. He had discovered a series of new islands, each with its own unique culture, produced superb charts of the Society Islands, New Zealand and the east coast of Australia, and demonstrated that there was open sea between Australia and New Guinea. During the three years of the voyage, he and his men had braved many dangers, and discipline on board the *Endeavour* had been good. During the voyage twenty-one men out of the crew of eighty-five had been punished (six of them twice), with five floggings of twenty-four lashes (two for attempted desertion, one for theft, and two for offences against the islanders); nineteen floggings of twelve lashes for more minor offences (especially disobedience); and one of six lashes for disputing a prior sentence – a relatively moderate tally.[2] On the whole, Cook had also managed to restrain his men in their dealings with 'natives', although during his absence on other duties his officers or sailors had on occasion disregarded his instructions, loading their muskets with ball instead of smallshot (in Tahiti and Mercury Bay), capturing a high chief (in Tahiti), or flogging a thief (in Hauraki). Like his men, however, he was glad to be back home, and in no mood to complain about these matters.

As soon as he had delivered his journals and charts to the Admiralty, Cook hurried home to Mile End, where his wife told him about the loss of their baby son, born after his departure, and their daughter, who had died just three months before his return to England. His two older sons were thriving, however, and before long Cook turned his attention back to professional matters. He was soon drafting reports for the Admiralty about the state of his ship, the health of his men, and the efficacy of the anti-scorbutics used on board the *Endeavour* (although his praise of sauerkraut at the expense of lemon and orange juice was seriously misleading[3]). Later he packed up his collection of 'curiosities', forwarding them to Lord Sandwich at the Admiralty, who sent them on to his old college at Oxford University. Cook also wrote letters to the Astronomer General about the Transit of Venus, the variation of the compass and the South Sea tides, which were later published in the Royal Society's *Philosophical Transactions*;[4] and compiled a chart showing the tracks of Tasman, the *Dolphin*, Bougainville and the *Endeavour*, and those oceanic areas which remained to be explored for a Southern Continent.

When a letter arrived from Joseph Banks, a month after his return to England, telling him that he had been promoted to commander, Cook replied with grateful pleasure:

Promotion unsolicited to a man of my station in life must convey a satisfaction to the mind that is better conceived than described ... The reputation I may have acquired by [the Voyage] by which I shall receive promotion calls to my mind the very great assistance I received therein from you which will ever be remembered with most grateful acknowledgements by Dear Sir Your most obliged Humble servt Jams Cook.[5]

A few weeks earlier, Cook had been in command of the *Endeavour* and master of all who sailed on her (including Joseph Banks), but back in England, he was simply a lieutenant from a lowly 'station in life', dependent upon people like Banks in the struggle for advancement. It was typical of the informal processes of patronage that he should hear of his promotion from Banks, who was not even an officer in the Royal Navy. Whether because of Banks's support or his own meticulous journals and charts, his merits were being recognised, however. That afternoon Cook met Lord Sandwich, Banks's intimate friend and now First Lord of the Admiralty, and several days later Sandwich took him to meet the King at St. James's Palace. At the Palace, Cook told King George about the voyage and explained his charts; and the King gave Cook his promotion in person and thanked him for his efforts.

Over the following weeks, Cook met with members of the Royal Society; and he and Banks went to Hitchingbrooke, Lord Sandwich's country home, where he was introduced to Dr Burney, a musician and leading figure in literary and artistic circles in London, whose son James hoped to join a second Pacific expedition. Burney invited him to his home in Queen Square in London, where Cook examined his copy of Bougainville's *Voyage*, annotating it with the track of the *Endeavour*. Burney's young daughter Fanny (who later became a famous novelist) thought that Cook was 'full of sense and thought; well-mannered and perfectly unpretending; but studiously wrapped up in his own purposes and pursuits; and apparently under a pressure of mental fatigue when called on to speak, or stimulated to deliberate, upon any other.'[6] And when he went to visit his aged father and his friends in Yorkshire some months later, they gave him a hero's welcome, greeting him with pride and joy. Captain Walker's housekeeper, who had looked after him during his years in Whitby, threw her arms around him and exclaimed, 'Oh honey James! How glad I is to see thee!'[7]

At the same time, most of the glory of the *Endeavour* expedition went to Banks and Solander. The aristocracy and the scientists flocked to see their collections of plants and curiosities, while the *London Chronicle* announced that they had made 'more curious discoveries in the way of astronomy and natural history than . . . have been presented to the learned world for these fifty years past'.[8] Soon after his arrival in London Banks was presented to the King; and a week later, Sir John Pringle, President of the Royal Society, accompanied Banks and Solander to Richmond to discuss the voyage. King George inspected Parkinson's sketches and suggested that the living plants from their collections should be transplanted to the Royal Gardens at Kew. At the end of August, the newspapers reported that 'Dr. Solander and Mr. Banks . . . have the honour of frequently waiting on his Majesty at Richmond, who examines their collection of drawings of plants and views of different places'.[9] Later, Banks met Dr Johnson, who supplied him with a Latin motto for the *Dolphin*'s goat which had once again sailed around the world on the *Endeavour* ('*Perpetua ambitâ bis terrâ praemia lactis, Haec habet altrici Capra secunda Jovis*': In fame scarce second to the nurse of Jove, This Goat, who twice the world had traversed round, Deserving both her master's care and love, Ease and perpetual pasture now has found[10]).

The young explorer was painted by Joshua Reynolds; and by Benjamin West, wearing a Maori cloak, with a painted paddle and wooden *taiaha* beside him. When he heard about the *Endeavour*'s return to England, the Swedish naturalist Linnaeus wrote in great excitement, addressing him as 'Immortal Banks' and ending his letter with the salutation, '*Vale vir sine*

*Portrait of Joseph Banks in London, cross-dressing in a Maori
cloak and surrounded by 'artificial curiosities' from the Pacific*

pare, Farewell O unequalled man'.[11] In November 1771 Oxford University,
Banks's alma mater, conferred honorary doctorates on him and Solander.
If Cook was spoken of at all, it was as 'Lieutenant Cook, who sailed round
the globe with Dr. Solander and Mr. Banks'; and when the newspapers first
announced in August that 'Mr. Banks is to have two ships from government
to pursue his discoveries in the South Seas, and will sail upon his second
voyage next March',[12] Cook's name was not mentioned.

Unfortunately, this adulation went to Banks's head. He did not visit
Harriet Blosset, the young woman who had waited so faithfully during his
long absence; and when she asked him for an explanation, he answered 'by
a letter of 2 or 3 sheets professing love &c but that he found he was of too
volatile a temper to marry'.[13] At the same time Banks bragged about his
sexual conquests during the voyage. After the *Dolphin*'s voyage, the amorous and beautiful women of Tahiti had become notorious in London, and

when unnamed members of the *Endeavour*'s crew wrote in letters published in the newspapers about their love affairs, saying that a virgin could be purchased in Tahiti for 'three nails and a knife' and that Tahitian women, with their tattooed buttocks, danced with 'obscene gesticulations',[14] this only fuelled the gossip. Banks was a keen advocate of Linnaean botany, which used metaphors of human sexuality to describe plant fertilisation and classified plants by inspecting their sexual organs – an approach denounced by the *Encyclopaedia Britannica* in its first edition (1768) as highly improper.[15] His morality was already suspect, and the satirists had a field day with his indiscretions. To quote one of the milder effusions:

That curiosity which leads a voyager to such remote parts of the globe as Mr B– has visited, will stimulate him when at home to penetrate into the most secret recesses of nature. As nature has been his constant study, it cannot be supposed that the most engaging part of it, the fair sex, have escaped his notice; and if we may be suffered to conclude from his amorous descriptions, the females of most countries that he has visited, have undergone every critical inspection by him. The queens, and women of the first class, we find constantly soliciting his company, or rather forcing their's upon him: at other times we find him visiting them in their bed-chambers, nay in their beds.[16]

At the same time, Banks became embroiled in a controversy with Stanfield Parkinson, Sydney Parkinson's older brother, who was on the verge of a mental breakdown. Stanfield disputed the ownership of Sydney's journal, his collection of curiosities, and the sketches his brother had made of subjects other than plants, animals and insects during the voyage. The two men had angry meetings, and although Banks eventually handed over Sydney's painting equipment and most of his curiosities, and loaned the manuscript of the journal, Stanfield promptly had it copied and published in a pirate edition, complete with a preface accusing Banks of theft, and declaring him to be 'vain' and 'rapacious', an unscrupulous fraud and a bully.[17]

Banks was also disconcerted when members of the Royal Society supported a proposal by Alexander Dalrymple for an expedition to New Zealand. At a Society dinner in their honour, hosted by the President Sir Joseph Pringle, Banks and Solander had delivered a riveting account of their adventures in Tahiti and New Zealand (including the observation, recalled by Benjamin Franklin, that 'The [Tahitians] had no Idea of Kissing with the Lips, . . . tho they lik'd it when they were taught it.'[18]). At a subsequent Society gathering, when Dalrymple volunteered to lead a voyage to New Zealand, the members were fired with enthusiasm. A 'Plan for Benefiting Distant Unprovided Countries' was drafted with a stirring introduction by

Franklin, and subscriptions were sought for a voyage to carry domestic fruits and animals and the arts of Europe to the 'brave and sensible' people of New Zealand. In his introduction to this tract, Franklin delivered a powerful exhortation:

Britain is now the first maritime power in the world. Her ships are innumerable, capable, by their form, size, and strength, of sailing on seas. Our seamen are equally bold, skilful, and hardy; dexterous in exploring the remotest regions, and ready to engage in voyages to unknown countries, though attended with the greatest dangers. The inhabitants of those countries, our fellow men, have canoes only; not knowing iron, they cannot build ships; they have little astronomy, and no knowledge of the compass to guide them; they cannot therefore come to us, or obtain any of our advantages. Does not Providence, by these distinguishing favours, seem to call on us, to do something ourselves for the common interest of humanity?

Many voyages have been undertaken with views of profit or of plunder, or to gratify resentment; to procure some advantage to ourselves, or do some mischief to others. But a voyage is now proposed, to visit a distant people on the other side of the globe; not to cheat them, not to rob them, not to seize their lands, or enslave their persons; but merely to do them good, and make them, as far as in our power lies, to live as comfortably as ourselves.[19]

Despite these noble sentiments, the proposal seemed aimed directly at Banks's second South Seas voyage, announced in the press just two days earlier. Banks and Dalrymple had an uneasy, competitive relationship; and Franklin's preface may have carried veiled criticism of Banks's expedition, with its interest in finding new resources and sites for British settlement. In the event, no significant funds were found for Dalrymple's proposal, and it came to nothing.

The most serious imbroglio, however, surrounded the arrangements for the second Pacific voyage. From the beginning, Banks seems to have assumed that he would have effective command of the expedition, and that shipboard arrangements would allow him to travel with a much larger entourage in relative comfort. At the same time Cook had worked on his own plan for the voyage, and he also had clear views about the appropriate practical arrangements. Although Lord Sandwich, Banks's intimate friend, was now First Lord of the Navy, the Navy was dead set against civilians commanding its vessels, and Cook had been told that if there was a second voyage to search for Terra Australis, he would lead it.[20] As soon as the decision was taken to support a second voyage, the Navy Board asked Cook to find suitable vessels for the purpose. By November 1771 he had selected two sloops, which were soon purchased from a yard in Whitby and renamed

Resolution and *Adventure*. Although Banks had been thinking of much larger, grander vessels, during the *Endeavour* expedition Cook had learned how important it was to carry adequate provisions and supplies on a long voyage of discovery, to survive a grounding, and to be able to careen the vessel for repairs and cleaning.

When Banks first saw the *Resolution*, he thought the sloop far too small, and insisted that it should be altered. He went to Lord Sandwich, who supported him, and orders were given to add an extra upper deck and a raised poop on her superstructure. Although the Navy Board protested, Banks was adamant. He was spending vast sums of money on the voyage, he argued; he needed room for his scientific equipment, trade goods (including forty 'Patopatoes for New Zealand in imitation of their stone weapons') and private supplies; he and Dr Solander required spacious cabins and separate libraries; he had recruited Dr James Lind, a physician from Edinburgh, John Zoffany, and assorted draughtsmen, secretaries, servants and two horn-players, all of whom required reasonable accommodation. He had even invited Dr Johnson to join the expedition, although Johnson later ridiculed the idea, saying that Banks and Solander had 'thought only of culling of simples [herbal remedies]' during their travels, and there was 'little of intellectual in the course'.[21]

Banks also wrote to Lord Sandwich demanding that Captain Cook should be ordered to follow his directions throughout the voyage, and that he (not Cook) should recommend which officers should be promoted; although these requests were not accepted. He invited a stream of visitors to view the alterations, including Lord Sandwich and his mistress Miss Ray, the artist Zoffany, the French ambassador and David Garrick the actor, slowing down the work. When the *Resolution* finally set sail for the Downs on 14 May 1772, she was so top-heavy that she almost capsized; and Cook and all of the officers agreed that she must be altered. Charles Clerke, the second lieutenant, wrote to Banks, 'By God, I'll go to sea in a grog-tub, if required, or in the *Resolution* as soon as you please, but must say I think her by far the most unsafe ship I ever saw or heard of.'[22] A message was sent to the Admiralty, and according to one of the midshipmen, John Elliott, a young midshipman whose merchant uncle had secured him a place on the *Resolution*, 'the next morning at daylight, I believe two Hundred shipwrights were cutting and tearing the Ship to pieces'. When Banks saw the alterations, Elliott reported:

He swore and stamped upon the Warfe, like a Mad Man, and instantly ordered his Servants and all his things out of the Ship. To find himself under the necessity of taking such a step must no doubt have been a very great mortification to him, for he had put himself to very great expence, in all kind of curious things, for use, amusement, and pleasure, as had Dr Solander and Mr Zoffany, both of whom were attached to Mr Banks, and went with him.

This was a loss to me, but upon the whole, it has always been thought that it was a most fortunate circumstance for the purpose of the Voyage that Mr Banks did not go with us; for a more proud, haughty man could not well be, and all his plans seemed directed to shew his own greatness, which would have accorded very ill with the discipline of a Man of War, and been the cause of causing many quarrels in all parts of the Ship.[23]

Unfortunately, Banks did not have the sense to keep quiet about his frustrations. He wrote a furious letter to Sandwich, provoking an angry reply from his friend and a blistering response from the Navy Board. Several of his supporters also wrote scurrilous letters to the newspapers, suggesting that an unnamed naval officer (perhaps Cook) had deliberately designed the alterations to make the sloop unseaworthy.[24] In his letter to Sandwich, Banks suggested that accommodation on board the *Resolution* for the sailors was inadequate, a direct attack on Cook's relationship with his crew; and from that time on he lobbied for another expedition to be organised with another captain, on another vessel. John Gore, who had quarrelled with Cook in New Zealand, had already accepted Banks's invitation to accompany him on another voyage, and now Banks tried to recruit Charles Clerke (whom Cook had promoted to third lieutenant), who amiably refused this invitation, although in the process he made disparaging remarks about Cook's plans for stowage on board the *Resolution*.[25] Despite all the pressure that Banks could bring to bear, however, the Admiralty was unmoved. The *Resolution* and *Adventure* were already equipped with guns, stores, trade goods, provisions and crews, and the Comptroller of the Navy Board, Sir Hugh Palliser, was not impressed by his tantrums. Cook must have breathed a sigh of relief when it finally became clear that Banks would not be sailing with them.

According to John Elliott, 'it was thought it would be quite a great feather in a young Man's Cap, to go with Capt. Cook' on this second Pacific voyage. Nevertheless, many of the sailors appointed to the ships deserted before they sailed, deterred by the dangers of the voyage.[26] In selecting his crew, Cook gave preference to men who had sailed with him on the *Endeavour*, and of the survivors from that voyage, twenty joined the *Resolution*. They included Charles Clerke, described by Elliott as 'a brave and good officer, & a genal favorite', who despite Banks's blandishments joined Cook as his second lieutenant. Richard Pickersgill, a serious, hard-drinking Yorkshireman and former *Dolphin* ('A good officer and astronomer, but liking ye Grog'), was promoted to third lieutenant. John Edgcumbe ('A steady

man and a good officer') became a lieutenant of marines; and Samuel
Gibson, the marine who had tried to desert at Tahiti, rose to corporal. At
the end of the *Endeavour* voyage Cook had made three young men – Isaac
Smith (his wife's cousin), Isaac Manley and William Harvey – midshipmen,
and they joined him on board the *Resolution*, along with thirteen sailors
from the *Endeavour*, six of whom were also promoted.

Of the other officers and sailors, Tobias Furneaux, the third lieutenant
who had sailed with Wallis on the *Dolphin*, described by the *Dolphin*'s
master as a 'Gentele Agreeable well behaved Good man and very humain
to all the Ships company',[27] was appointed captain of Cook's companion
ship, the *Adventure*. Robert Palliser Cooper, a close relative of the Comptroller of the Navy Board and a 'sober, steady good officer'[28] became the
Resolution's first lieutenant; while James Burney, the son of Dr Charles
Burney, joined her crew as an able-bodied seaman with a lieutenant's
commission. Once again, Cook put his two young sons on his ship's
muster-roll.

After Banks's departure, the scientific party shrank to two astronomers,
a naturalist with his assistant, and an artist. William Wales, the astronomer
on board the *Resolution*, was an experienced man who had observed the
Transit of Venus for the Royal Society at Hudson's Bay in 1769; while
William Bayly, who sailed with the *Adventure*, had observed the Transit at
the North Cape. Their role was to fix the position of any new discoveries,
and to test a set of chronometers (including K1, an exact copy by Kendall
of a chronometer by the great John Harrison; and three made by John
Arnold) for their accuracy in determining longitude at sea.[29] Johann Reinhold Forster, a former Lutheran pastor from Germany who replaced Banks
and Solander on board the *Resolution*, was a distinguished naturalist and
an astute and insightful observer with a philosophical turn of mind. He
was also self-important, argumentative and querulous, however; qualities
which drove his shipmates crazy ('A clever but a litigious, quarelsom,
fellow', was Elliott's verdict). His son George, who acted as his botanical
draughtsman ('A clever good young man') was much better liked; as was
William Hodges, the landscape painter who replaced Zoffany as artist to
the expedition.

During the preparations for the voyage, an impressive array of experimental equipment was assembled, including devices for turning sea water
into fresh water, measuring the temperature of layers of the ocean and
sweetening water in the barrels; and a variety of anti-scorbutics, including
sauerkraut, portable broth and carrot marmalade. Unfortunately, after the
Endeavour voyage, Cook's assistant surgeon William Perry had concluded
that malt was a more effective anti-scorbutic than 'robs' of orange and

Johann and George Forster, naturalists on board the
Resolution

lemon juice, a setback for the treatment of scurvy in the Navy, and only a small quantity of boiled citrus juice was included.[30] Banks's friendship with Lord Sandwich ensured that the *Resolution*'s gear and provisions were of the highest quality, however; and his exit from the voyage meant that Cook regained his own living quarters and the Great Cabin.

On 3 July 1772 when Lord Sandwich and Sir Hugh Palliser boarded the *Resolution* at Plymouth, Cook praised the ship unreservedly, and as they disembarked, the crew gave them three hearty cheers. The sailors and officers of the two vessels had been paid their back wages, and in addition the petty officers and sailors received a two months' advance, an unusual act of generosity by the Navy. The men celebrated with an orgy of drunkenness, and when the *Resolution*'s buoy came adrift, the ship almost crashed on the rocks at the entrance to Plymouth harbour. On the morning of 13 July 1772 Cook ordered his men to hoist up the anchors, and as the sun came up, the *Resolution* and *Adventure* sailed in company down the English Channel.

Having farewelled her brother James, who had joined Cook's crew, Fanny Burney exclaimed, 'I should prefer this voyage to any in the world if my ill stars had destined me a sailor!'[31]

During the long months of planning, Cook had polished his strategy for searching for the Unknown Southern Continent. After charting and examining the known tracks of earlier Pacific voyages, he concluded that if there was a southern land mass, it must lie in the high southern latitudes, unless it lay about the meridian of 140 degrees west (which runs through the Tuamotus and Marquesas), where there were stretches of ocean which had not yet been explored. He proposed to sail from England to the Cape of Good Hope, turning south during the summer months and running eastward with the prevailing westerlies across the Indian Ocean and the Tasman to Queen Charlotte Sound in New Zealand, where he could rest his men, repair the ship and collect fresh vegetables and water. After that the sloops might cross the meridian of 140 degrees west, looking for land, and then proceed to Tahiti for the winter months; returning south again the following summer for an eastward run across the Pacific to Cape Horn before sailing back to the Cape of Good Hope and England. This was an ambitious plan, requiring long periods in uncharted, icy waters. In the eighteenth century, sailors in wooden ships rarely ventured beyond 50 degrees south, where the winds could be ferocious and the waters dangerous and freezing.

As they sailed down the Channel in fresh gales, Johann Forster was prostrated by seasickness, which he treated by drinking mulled red wine. Past Cape Finisterre, the ships were challenged by three large Spanish vessels, one of which fired a shot at the *Adventure*. When the sloops brought to, a Spanish officer hailed Furneaux, and when he was told that this was Cook's expedition, the Spaniard replied, 'Oh, Cook, is it? and wished us all a good Voyage.'[32] They sailed on, and on 29 July they reached the pretty town of Funchal at Madeira, its harbour encircled by neat white houses and orange trees, and its high hills green with vineyards. The sailors gorged themselves on oranges and walnuts, and Cook purchased 400 gallons of wine, ordered the water barrels to be filled, and bought fresh beef and strings of onions. Johann Forster went ashore to collect plants and insects, clambering up hillsides, tripping over briars and rocks and cursing at the heat and mud, and when he returned to the ship he wrote an account of the island which argued that the climate made its inhabitants indolent and lazy. During this brief visit to Madeira, Cook was amused to hear that a young 'gentleman' who had recently been at Funchal with a letter of recommendation from Joseph Banks, awaiting his arrival, had proved to be a woman in disguise, and hastened to report this scandalous titbit to Sir Hugh Palliser.[33]

As they sailed away from Madeira, one of the sailors, John Marra, who had attempted to desert at Deptford, was punished with twelve lashes for insolence, the first flogging of the voyage. Cook ordered the sloop cleaned and fumigated below decks with charcoal fires, a practice which became routine, along with pumping sea water through the bilges, and making the seamen wash and dry their clothes and bedding. On 12 August the ships arrived at the island of St. Jago, one of the Cape Verde group, where Lieutenant Pickersgill went ashore to meet the Governor, a Portuguese officer who lived in a dilapidated fort, attended by ragged soldiers armed with antiquated muskets, some with no flintlocks and others with no barrels. Cook managed to acquire one bullock, some pigs, goats and fruit, and collected water from a dirty well, but the Governor refused his invitation to dine on board and did not keep his promise of helping him to purchase more bullocks. While Cook was bartering for supplies, the Forsters went ashore to botanise and the sailors traded at the market. Many of them bought little grey monkeys as pets, but these were dirty and lice-infested, and overran the ship until Cook, in a fit of exasperation, ordered them all thrown overboard. Despite this order, Elliott hid his pet monkey for months, until one day it threw ink over a letter the master's mate, Whitehouse, was writing. In a fit of annoyance, Whitehouse drew his pistol and blasted the monkey out the window – no doubt one reason why Elliott later damned him as a 'Jesuitical, sensible but an insinuating litigious mischief making fellow'.[34]

After leaving St. Jago, a carpenter's mate fell overboard, where he was attacked and torn to pieces by sharks while his shipmates watched transfixed in horror. The Forsters caught fish and dissected them, and the apparatus for distilling sea water into fresh water was tried with some success, although the quantities of fresh water that it produced were too small for practical purposes. During this period, Cook sent his midshipmen aloft, where they learned to hand and reef the sails, and ordered them to steer the ship and exercise with firearms. According to Elliott, he also supervised their lunar observations, while William Hodges taught them sketching in the Great Cabin. Most of the midshipmen developed quickly under this regime, although there was a group of wild, drinking young men on board the *Resolution* whom Cook called his 'black sheep'. His insistence on hygiene and a good diet helped to keep his crew healthy, although after their stop at St. Jago there was an epidemic (perhaps of typhoid fever) on the *Adventure*, which killed two of the midshipmen.

On 9 September, the two sloops crossed the Line and brought to for a celebration. About fifty men were ducked from the *Resolution*'s yardarm, while others were 'lathered' with an unspeakable mix of tar and filth, 'shaved' with rusty iron hoops and drenched with water. The passengers were excused from these ordeals by paying 'Old Neptune' a forfeit of a pound of sugar and a gallon of rum, which the sailors drank with great enthusiasm. Furneaux, who considered ducking too dangerous, forbade his men to perform this ceremony on board the *Adventure*; although his sailors marked the occasion with games, songs and drunken merriment. Several days later, discipline was restored when two of the *Resolution*'s crew were flogged for insolence; although a week later Pickersgill (who liked his grog) complained when Cook gave the crew experimental beer instead of wine, and stopped up the barrel when the men tried to drink it dry, attempting to stop these 'purser's tricks' by forcing him to serve them their daily ration.

On 30 October 1772, as the ships sailed through a storm-tossed, fiery sea, lit by tiny phosphorescent insects, Table Mountain loomed up on the horizon. Upon their arrival in South Africa at the Cape of Good Hope, the *Resolution*'s men were in high spirits and excellent health, which they attributed to Cook's 'great care & attention'. The sailors admired the fine houses, the canals and splendid gardens, and sampled the local wines with enthusiasm, while Cook dined with the Dutch Governor, and purchased fresh bread, beef, mutton and vegetables. During his meetings with local officials, he was told that a French expedition led by Kerguelen had recently reported a sighting of land in latitude 48 degrees south about the meridian of Mauritius; and that Marion du Fresne's expedition had visited the Cape some months earlier, where Ahutoru had died of smallpox. As Cook remarked, all of the Tahitians who had joined European ships thus far had perished, so that their friends and relatives would never hear their tales of the marvels to be seen in European towns and cities.

When Bayly and Wales went ashore at the Cape to check the performance of the chronometers against their own astronomical observations, they were impressed to find that K1, Kendall's copy of John Harrison's famous watch, had gained only about a second a day, although one of the three chronometers supplied by John Arnold had stopped, and the other two were highly inaccurate. At the same time, the Forsters ranged around the countryside, collecting plants and insects; and Johann met Anders Sparrman, a Swedish student of Linnaeus's, persuading him at his own expense to join the expedition. Before leaving the Cape, Cook sent a letter to his mentor, Captain Walker of Whitby, praising his ship and crew; and a conciliatory note to Joseph Banks, telling him about Ahutoru's death and trying to make peace with his former shipmate:

Some Cross circumstances which happened at the latter part of the equipment of the Resolution created, I have reason to think, a coolness betwixt you and I, but I can by no means think it was sufficient to me to break of all corrispondance with a Man I am under many obligations too.[35]

After three weeks at Capetown, Cook was ready to begin his new search for the Southern Continent. On 23 November 1772 he took his ships south, hoping to find Cape Circumcision, the icy headland which Bouvet had seen in 1739. Although the Cape was just part of an island, this sighting lured Cook down towards the Antarctic Circle for his first great sweep across high southern latitudes. The men had been issued with fearnought jackets and trousers, but as the weather grew colder, they were plagued with chills and fevers. Over the following days the animals began to tremble and die, while squalls whipped the sails and battered the hull of the ship, working open its seams and drenching the exhausted sailors. Johann Forster had been allocated a small cabin next to the Master's, and as the sloop rolled and pitched, his bunk was soaked with sea water. During a great storm which began on 29 November, the ship was tossed and battered, and in his misery Forster turned to Virgil's great saga of the wanderings of Aeneas for consolation: 'Then came the cries of the men and the groaning of the rigging. Darkness, like night, settled on the sea, and all the elements threatened the crew with death at any moment.'[36] As he read this text, Forster saw himself (not Captain Cook) as Aeneas, and *The Aenid* became his inspiration for the rest of the voyage.

By 10 December they were among the icebergs, marvelling at their size, colour and formations. Some of these grotesque ice islands looked like the ruins of ancient towns while others reminded the voyagers of Gothic castles. As Pickersgill noted stoically:

Sailing here is render'd very Dangerous, Excessive Cold, thick snows, Islands of Ice very thick sometimes 40 in sight at once, the people Numb'd, ye Ropes all froze over with Ice & Ye Rigging & Sails all covered with Snow; such is the dispossion of ye Crew that every Man seems to try who shall be foremost in ye readiest performance of his duty.[37]

In these freezing, miserable conditions, the ship's water began to run out until the crew collected large hunks of ice, melting them on board to yield pure, fresh drinking water. As the rigging froze and snapped, icicles dripped from the sailors' noses. Whales sounded about the sloops and albatrosses wheeled overhead, and the men watched in amusement as squads of penguins lined up on the icebergs, marching and wheeling in file with such precision that 'they only wanted the use of Arms to cut a figure on Whimbleton Common'.[38]

On 25 December the sailors saluted each other with three cheers as the ships were brought to, and Christmas Day was celebrated with a good hot dinner, extra rations of rum, boxing matches and drunken antics. Three weeks later when the *Resolution* crossed the Antarctic Circle, Cook remarked in his journal that 'we are undoubtedly the first and only Ship that ever crossed that line'.[39] He had found no land, however, and as they sailed along the edge of the ice fields, the constant danger and discomfort was taking its toll. There were signs of scurvy among the crew, and the 'wild & drinking' midshipmen misbehaved so badly that Cook had been forced to send Loggie, one of his 'black sheep', before the mast for arguing with the boatswain, followed soon after by John Coghlan, another of these reprobates, for disputing with the captain's servant. He decided to turn back north, to search for the land that Kerguelen had reported.

On 8 February 1773, shrouded in thick fog, the two ships lost sight of one another. Although the *Resolution* fired her guns and tacked across the area where the *Adventure* had last been seen, they could not find her. Cook's officers, who by now had given up on Kerguelen's land, wanted to head north or east, but Cook decided to turn south again, still looking for the Southern Continent, before heading to the agreed rendezvous at Queen Charlotte Sound in New Zealand. There must have been mutterings among the men, for shipboard discipline was soon tightened. Cook sentenced five men to be flogged for theft, issued the sailors with needles and thread and ordered them to mend their clothing, punishing them by stopping their grog if their hands were found to be dirty. At the same time he kept the ship clean and smoked, ensuring that the sailors were always kept busy, although he frequently changed the men who worked above deck, so that they did not become too exhausted. As icebergs cracked and capsized about the ship, and the Aurora Australis flashed and spiralled, on 24 February Cook finally turned north-east, heading towards Tasmania to discover whether it was an island or part of the Australian mainland, and to collect fresh food and water. The surviving sheep and cattle intended for the Maori in Queen Charlotte Sound were now brought below to protect them from the sleet and snow, huddling in a narrow space next to Johann Forster's cabin. Forster lamented:

I was now beset with cattle & stench on both Sides, having no other but a thin deal partition full of chinks between me & them. The room offered me by Capt. Cook, & which the Masters obstinacy deprived me of, was now given to very peaceably bleating creatures, who on a stage raised up as high as my bed, shit & pissed on one side, whilst 5 Goats did the same afore on the other side.[40]

After a time, finding that the winds were unfavourable for Tasmania, Cook headed for Dusky Bay in the far south of New Zealand, which Banks had been so eager to visit during the *Endeavour* voyage.

As the *Resolution* sailed towards the New Zealand coastline, riding a huge south-westerly swell, the weather was thick and hazy. On 25 March the sun came out, and land was sighted from the masthead. Cook tacked off the coast, looking for the entrance of Dusky Bay, and about noon the following morning, they sailed into the harbour. When the anchors splashed down into the deep, translucent water of the fiord, the sailors were ecstatic. They had been out of sight of land for months, sailing among the icebergs in sleet and snow, and the green luxuriant hills and islands looked wonderful. As George Forster remarked:

The weather was delightfully fair, and genially warm, when compared to what we had lately experienced; and we glided along by insensible degrees, wafted by light airs, past numerous rocky islands, each of which was covered with wood and shrubberies, where numerous evergreens were sweetly contrasted and mingled with the various shades of autumnal yellow. Flocks of aquatic birds enlivened the rocky shores, and the whole country resounded with the wild notes of the feathered tribe ... The sloop was no sooner in safety, than every sailor put his hook and line overboard, and in a few moments numbers of fine fish were hauled up on all parts of the vessel.[41]

Cook sent Lieutenant Pickersgill to look for a safe anchorage, and he soon came back with reports of a deep-water cove with a clear stream, where forest trees rose up from the water's edge. As Pickersgill exclaimed, it was: 'one of the most inchanting little Harbours I ever saw ... surrounded with high Lands intirely cover'd with tall shady trees rising like an ampitheatre; and with the sweet swelling Notes of a number of Birds made the finest Harmony.'[42] While the sloop was being manoeuvred into 'Pickersgill's Harbour', the officers shot a seal on a nearby island for supper, and the men went off fishing and shooting birds in the forest. The sheep and goats were soon landed, but their teeth were so loose with scurvy that they could not chew the greenery, to Cook's intense disappointment.

The next day at noon, two or three small canoes glided around the point, their crews staring at the *Resolution* in astonishment. After a few minutes they retired, but a small double canoe with a crew of eight, led by an old bearded man, soon came back around the point, paddling to about a musket-shot from the ship, where they sat, studying the ship in amazement. When the corporal of marines, Samuel Gibson, stood on the yardarm waving a white cloth and calling out to them in Tahitian, they studiously ignored him. About half an hour later, they paddled away again, and vanished. That afternoon Cook, the Forsters and William Wales, eager to make contact with these people (members of Ngati Mamoe, a migratory group of hunters and gatherers who periodically visited the Sound), took two boats to a cove where a double canoe had been sighted. Behind the beach, they found a small hamlet, but Cook and his party could find no one in the cove, so they examined the canoe and the makeshift shelters, and put ribbons, medals, beads and a looking-glass on a canoe bailer, before returning to the *Resolution*.

Over the following week, there were no further sightings of these people. A gangway was built from the ship to the water's edge, wood was cut, and beer was brewed from rimu and manuka leaves and molasses. A site was cleared on 'Astronomer's Point', where Wales erected his portable observatory, intending to fix the position of the Sound by astronomical observation. He also set up a barometer, a thermometer and an instrument to measure the tides, as the Forsters ranged around the Sound, collecting specimens of plants, fish and animals. Thrilled by these signs of 'progress', George Forster exclaimed:

The superiority of a state of civilization over that of barbarism could not be more clearly stated, than by the alterations and improvements we had made in this place. In the course of a few days, a small part of us had cleared away the wood from a surface of more than an acre, which fifty New Zealanders, with their tools of stone, could not have performed in three months. . . .

Nor had science disdained to visit us in this solitary spot: an observatory arose in the centre of our works, filled with the most accurate instruments, where the attentive eye of the astronomer contemplated the motions of the celestial bodies. The plants which clothed the ground, and the wonders of the animal creation, both in the forests and the seas, likewise attracted the attention of philosophers, whose time was devoted to mark their differences and uses. In a word, all around us we perceived the rise of arts, and the dawn of science, in a country which had hitherto lain plunged in one long night of ignorance and barbarism![43]

Characteristically, however, Johann Forster was less enthusiastic. As he walked into the rain forest, sinking into rotten wood and soft cushions of moss up to his knees, he discovered that the flowering season was over. Without flowers, it was difficult to apply the Linnaean system of classification to these new species of plants, although he consoled himself by shooting huge numbers of birds, some of which were so tame that they perched on the muzzle of his musket. As the specimens piled up in his cabin, he grizzled:

My Cabin was a Magazine of all the various kinds of plants, fish, birds, Shells, Seeds etc. hitherto collected: which made it vastly damp, dirty, crammed, & caused very noxious vapours, & an offensive smell, & being just under the Chain-plates & the Ship lying close in Shore under high trees; it was so dark, that I was obliged to light a candle during day, when I wanted to write something ... My & my Sons accomodations were the worst in the whole Ship, under all circumstances, in hot & cold climates, in dry & moist weather, at Anchor & at Sea.[44]

The sailors, who slept cheek-by-jowl in their hammocks on the lower deck, were heartily sick of Johann's grumblings, however. He was being paid 4000 pounds for the voyage, more than any other man on board (including Cook), and they found his endless complaints infuriating.

On 6 April, as Cook, Clerke and the Forsters were returning from a duck-shooting expedition, an old man hailed them from a rocky point, brandishing a paddle-shaped weapon. As they rowed towards him he cried out angrily, although Cook called him in Tahitian. When he reached the point, Cook approached this man unarmed, holding out two sheets of white paper and two handkerchiefs. After putting the paper on the ground, he gave the man the handkerchiefs and pressed noses with him in greeting. The sailors were filled with admiration at his aplomb. As Elliott remarked:

No man could be better calculated to gain the confidence of Savages than Capt. Cook. He was brave, uncommonly Cool, Humane, and Patient. He would land alone unarmed, or lay aside his Arms, and sit down when they threatened with theirs, throwing them Beads, Knives, and other little presents, then by degrees advancing nearer, till by patience and forbearance, he gained their friendship and an intercourse with them, which to people in our situation was of the utmost consequence.[45]

Two young women stood nearby, watching this encounter, and soon the old man beckoned them over to meet Cook and his companions. Although Cook tried to talk to this group, he found that pidgin Tahitian was useless, so he used sign language to invite them to the *Resolution*. After chattering for a while, the younger of the two women danced for them, while the sailors exchanged ribald comments. The next day Cook, Pickersgill, the Forsters and William Hodges visited this family (the old man, the two women, a young girl, a boy of about fourteen and three small boys) in a nearby cove; where Cook gave them gifts of hatchets, spike nails, necklaces, beads and looking-glasses, receiving two 'staffs of honour' in return. When Hodges sketched their portraits in red pastel, the tapu colour, they were fascinated, calling him 'Tuhituhi' [painter]. The old man offered Cook garments and bird-bone beads in exchange for a boat cloak, but he had no spare cloak with him. That night, however, Cook ordered the sailmaker to make up a boat cloak in red baize, and the next day he took it to the family's hamlet. They had put on their best flax cloaks, decorated with parrot feathers, and wore ornaments of albatross skin in their ears and white feathers on their heads, calling out to him in greeting. They fed Cook and his companions with a delicious meal of fish grilled in kelp, and when Cook presented the red cloak to the old man, he was overjoyed, immediately presenting Cook with his whalebone *patu*.

Over the next two weeks the members of this family visited the shore camp almost every day, although when one of the boys on board tried to make advances to the young girl she burst into tears and avoided him thereafter. One night Cook organised a concert of bagpipes, fifes and drums, and when the corporal of marines, Samuel Gibson, asked the old man if he could 'marry' the girl, they sang and chanted near the ship, gesturing at the sky and seeming to seek the assent of their *atua* [ancestral gods]. Finally, after a violent family argument, the old man agreed to come on board the *Resolution*. On 19 April, when he and the young girl arrived at the gangway, he broke off a green branch from a nearby tree and walking with a stately tread to the main shrouds, struck them with the branch while he recited a *karakia* or incantation. After this they looked over the sloop, marvelling at the sheep and goats, and the girl stroked the ship's cat, rubbing its fur the wrong way, trying to see how long it was. Below decks they examined Cook's chairs and bed, admiring his cabin, and presented him with a feather cloak and a greenstone adze, gifts for a high chief. The young girl gave Hodges a cloak and tried to tie his hair up on his head, a sign of mana (prestige and power), and in return they were given gifts of hatchets, nails and tufts of feathers. Again, some of the sailors attempted to approach the girl, but she spurned their advances. As Clerke observed:

The Gallantry of our People in general made them very anxious to pay some Compliment to the Young Lady, as 'Twas the first Female we had seen for many Months, but the Young Gypsey did not seem at all inclin'd to repay them in the Kind Indian Women in general trade in and indeed the Kind that's most esteem'd I believe by all men after so long an absence from the Sex.[46]

Before they left the ship, the old man fired off a musket several times, while the girl threw herself on the deck in terror. On shore, the man watched the sawyers for a time and took his turn in the saw-pit, then they made their farewells and vanished.

Cook stayed for six weeks in Dusky Sound, while the men went camping, shot birds and seals, fished, and collected wood and fresh water. They did not see this family again, although Cook had one brief encounter with another small group, who used wooden rafts for their journeys across the water. They largely avoided the strangers, however, so Cook's men had the run of the Sound, which they found idyllic (although Cook was plagued for several days by a swelling in his right foot and a pain in the groin, which the ship's surgeon attributed to wading in icy water). The sloop was cleaned and re-rigged; peas, mustard, parsley and strawberries were planted in a garden plot; and a meticulous chart of the Sound was completed. On 28 April Cook ordered the shore tents to be struck; and on 11 May 1773, they sailed for Queen Charlotte Sound to look for the *Adventure*.

On 17 May as they approached the entrance to Cook Strait, the sky darkened and six waterspouts swirled up from the sea, curving around the ship in an uncanny fashion. As one of the waterspouts headed straight for the *Resolution*, the sails were hoisted and they fled in the opposite direction, escaping only when the waterspout spun away at the last moment. The next morning as they arrived at the entrance of Queen Charlotte Sound, Cook signalled with his cannons, and when the *Adventure*'s men fired in answer, the two sloops were reunited. 'Both Ships felt an uncommon joy at our meeting after an absence of fourteen Weeks,'[47] said Furneaux that night in his journal.

After losing sight of the *Resolution* three months earlier, the *Adventure* had searched for several days before heading for Tasmania. The mood on board the *Adventure* had been tense and disconcerted. The men were anxious about being parted from their consort ship, and many of them were suffering from scurvy, which was often attended with strange moods and fits of terror.[48] During this time the Lieutenant of Marines, a passionate, unpredictable man, quarrelled with Furneaux and was forcibly thrown out of the Great Cabin; and several nights later one of the midshipmen who had been standing watch at the forecastle came running aft, white as a sheet, saying that he had seen the ghost of his father walking across the deck towards him. After a short visit to Adventure Bay in Tasmania, where they found several bark shelters on the beach, but saw no Aborigines, Furneaux sailed for the rendezvous at Queen Charlotte Sound, hoping to find the *Resolution*. As they crossed the Tasman Sea, the ship's officers – Kempe the first lieutenant, Burney (who had been transferred to the *Adventure* at the Cape as her second lieutenant), Andrews the surgeon and one of the midshipmen – came to Bayly's cabin late one night to demand rum from the startled astronomer. When he refused, they began to break down his cabin door with a chisel, and there was a violent scuffle. Discipline, as well as hygiene and diet, it seems, was slack on board the *Adventure*.

On 6 April 1773 when the *Adventure* sailed into Queen Charlotte Sound, where the *Endeavour* had anchored three years earlier, they had found the place deserted. William Bayly set up his observatory in the abandoned pa off the end of Motuara, while the rest of the crew camped in empty houses on the island. The local people avoided them until three days later, when a double canoe and a single canoe with an outrigger carrying sixteen people came out. As they approached the *Adventure*, a man holding a green bough stood up and chanted a *karakia* while his companions cried out 'Tupaia! Tupaia!' They had come to meet the high priest from Ra'iatea, hoping that he had returned to visit them, and soon came on board to ask after him. When they were told that Tupaia had died of fever in Batavia, they were dismayed, asking if the British had killed him. Furneaux and his men tried to reassure them, giving them gifts of clothing and trinkets, until one young officer discovered a freshly severed head in one of their canoes, wrapped up in a cloak. This may have been brought out to the ship as an offering, but when the officer tried to take a closer look, the people in the canoe trembled in fear and hid the head, paddling away from the vessel. That afternoon Furneaux, fearing an attack, ordered six carriage guns to be set up on the deck of the *Adventure*; but their visitors soon returned with gifts of fish and fern-root. None of the crew had been to New Zealand before, but there was a Maori vocabulary on board from the *Endeavour* voyage, and when one of the officers used it to try and communicate with these people, they were fascinated and offered large quantities of fish in exchange for this vocabulary.

The next morning, two double canoes carrying a group of about sixty people came out to the *Adventure*, where they exchanged weapons, tools and cloaks for nails and old bottles. These people had arrived to trade with the British, and set up a camp in a nearby cove. Over the following days, the sailors exchanged nails and other items for sex with the women. There were already four sailors on board the *Adventure* with stubborn venereal infections, and over the next few weeks at least five more men showed signs of the disease, which the women had contracted after the *Endeavour*'s visit. News of the *Adventure*'s arrival was spreading, and on 12 April, a flotilla of canoes arrived in the Sound, bringing goods to trade with the British. Their crews immediately came on board, offering women in exchange for spike nails. These exchanges continued for several weeks, until on 24 April, the Europeans' strength was tested. That night, several canoes attempted to ambush Bayly's camp, but were driven off by musket fire; and the next day the ship's jollyboat was chased and almost intercepted by two carved canoes packed with warriors, who were frightened off when the sloop fired a cannon. In response to these skirmishes Furneaux sent two marines with wall-guns[49] to reinforce the observatory, and shifted the shore camp to Ship Cove, under the protection of the ship's artillery.

As the days went by and there was still no sign of the *Resolution*, Furneaux brought the *Adventure* closer in to shore, mooring her for the winter. The decks were cleared for caulking and the hull and rigging were tarred to protect them from the winter weather. Although the sailors were eating plenty of fish, Furneaux did not make his men take greenstuffs with their meals, and many still had symptoms of scurvy – loose teeth, ulcerated gums, swollen limbs and livid spots on their bodies. On 11 May there were two earth tremors, and that night a large meteor streaked across the sky, signs of supernatural power to local Maori. On 18 May cannon-fire was heard out at sea, and as the *Adventure*'s men fired their guns in reply, the *Resolution* sailed into the Sound towards them.

When Cook came on board the *Adventure*, he found that the ship had been battened down for winter and that many of her crew had scurvy. He ordered Furneaux to ensure that his men ate plenty of wild celery and scurvy grass boiled with wheat or oatmeal, and told him to prepare the *Adventure* for sailing. The *Resolution*'s crew were sent ashore to collect wood and water, while Cook and some men planted gardens with European seeds, and the Forsters shot birds and began to gather plants, shells and insects. The two surviving sheep from the *Resolution* were put out to graze and promptly died, as the result of eating poisonous plants, to Cook's intense annoyance; and the *Resolution*'s quartermaster was flogged for 'insolence' to the boatswain.

Four days passed before any of the local people ventured out to the *Resolution*. They asked for nails, hatchets and glass bottles, and enquired anxiously after Tupaia. Apparently, they were convinced that the British had come from Ra'iatea, bringing treasured goods from the homeland. Cook recognised none of these people from his previous visit to the Sound, and speculated that there must have been serious fighting in the interim. The following day a double canoe arrived in the Sound, carrying more strangers who asked after Tupaia, and when they heard that he had died, they lamented. Over the next few days, as more canoes arrived, two young men made it plain that they would like to join the *Resolution*. One of them climbed up to her topgallant mast, and that night they slept on the deck on a sail, until an old man came out to the ship to fetch them. When the officer on duty checked the next morning, he found that one of these young men had taken a hand lead from the quarterdeck, while the other had filched a copy of Henry Fielding's novel *Tom Jones* from his cabin.

Over the days that followed, as the Forsters collected words for an extended Maori vocabulary, they met a group which included a man named Toka and his son Te Weherua ['Taywaherua'], and another man, Te Wahanga ['Towahangha'] with his small son Koa. Te Weherua, a boy about fourteen years old who came on board almost every day, became quite familiar with the British. On one occasion, he asked for Cook's boat cloak, and when he was refused it, he sulked until Johann Forster gave him a glass of Madeira to cheer him up, followed by two glasses of Cape muscatel, which made him very drunk. There were no intoxicating liquors in New Zealand, not even kava (a drink made from the chewed root of the kava plant, grown widely in the Pacific, which made people feel relaxed and euphoric), and Maori had no experience with inebriation. His father Toka also asked for things from the ship, including a tablecloth, and when he was refused, he left the ship in high dudgeon.

Several days later, when Te Wahanga came on board with his small son Koa, Cook gave this boy a white shirt, and he was so thrilled that he immediately put it on and strutted about the deck, showing everybody. Unfortunately, as he walked past 'Old Will', the ship's billy-goat, the goat butted him from behind, knocking him over. According to Cook, who found this episode very funny: 'The Shirt was dirted and he was afraid to appear in the Cabbin before his father untill brought in by Mr. Forster, when he told a very lamentable story against Goure [Kuri] the great Dog, for so they call all the quadrupeds we have aboard, nor could he be pacified until his shirt was wash'd and dry'd.'[50]

Cook was much less amused by the conduct of his sailors, who had joined the *Adventure*'s crew in a riot of debauchery. He remarked that when the *Endeavour* had visited New Zealand, very few of the women would sleep with his men, but now they had lost all sense of discretion. Their menfolk brought them to the ship, where they copulated with the sailors on the decks or in their hammocks. Cook was acutely aware that venereal diseases were being transmitted in these exchanges, but he was powerless to stop them. As for the women, they concluded that the Europeans had only one thing in mind, and one day when a young woman was brought to the Great Cabin to be sketched by Hodges, she took it for granted that he wanted to sleep with her:

Language difficulties at first gave rise to a misunderstanding between the girl and the painter, for she, having been paid well to go down into the saloon, imagined that she ought to give satisfaction, in the way she understood it, as soon as possible in return for her gift; perhaps she had had previous experience with our sailors? She was astonished when signs were made for her to sit on a chair; such a novel way of doing things struck her as absurd, but she promptly volunteered a prone position on the chair for the painter and his companion. To her further surprise she was eventually put in a correct position, just sitting on the chair with nothing to do; wherupon, to the wonderment and entertainment of herself and the two savages with her, she quickly saw her likeness appearing in a red crayon drawing.[51]

Cook was disgusted by these orgies, exclaiming in his journal, 'To our shame [as] civilized Christians, we debauch their Morals already too prone to vice and we interduce among them wants and perhaps diseases which they never before knew and which serves only to disturb that happy tranquillity they and their fore Fathers had injoy'd. If any one denies the truth of this assertion let him tell me what the Natives of the whole extent of America have gained by the commerce they have had with Europeans.'[52]

Cook was now eager to get to sea, so that he could restore discipline among the men and resume his search for the Southern Continent. While final repairs to the sloops were being completed and wood and water were loaded on board, he put some goats and a boar and a sow ashore, hoping that they would breed and multiply. On 1 June another flotilla of canoes arrived from out of the Sound, bringing more strangers who asked for Tupaia and wept when they heard that he had died. As Cook commented, Tupaia's fame had spread far beyond the places he had visited on the *Endeavour*: 'It may be ask'd, that if these people had never seen the Endeavour or any of her crew, how they became acquainted with the Name of Tupia or to have in their possession such articles as they could only have got from that ship, to this it may be answered that the Name of Tupia was at that time so popular among them that it would be no wonder if at this time it is known over the great part of *New Zealand*.'[53] These people also brought quantities of 'curiosities' – a woman's dancing apron decorated with red feathers, white dogskin and pieces of *paua* [abalone] shell; greenstone tools and ornaments, and Polynesian dogs, some spotted, some black and others perfectly white, which they fed on fish and held by the customary string tied around their middles.

Three days later, as Cook and his men were about to celebrate the King's birthday on board the ships, yet another carved double canoe arrived from the north, bringing a group of tall, well-dressed, dignified men with full facial tattoos, one of whom stood and chanted as they came alongside the *Resolution*. Again, these men asked for Tupaia, and lamented when they heard that he had died. George Forster commented:

So much had [Tupaia's] superior knowledge, and his ability to converse in their language rendered him valuable, and beloved even among a nation in a state of

A canoe alongside the Resolution *in Queen Charlotte Sound, a Maori orator chanting for Tupaia*

barbarism. Perhaps with the capacity which Providence had alloted to him, and which had been cultivated no farther than the simplicity of his education would permit, he was more adapted to raise the New Zeelanders to a state of civilization similar to that of his own islands, than ourselves, to whom the want of the intermediate links, which connect their narrow views to our extended sphere of knowledge, must prove an obstacle in such an undertaking.[54]

In New Zealand, it seemed, many Maori thought that the *Endeavour* was Tupaia's ship, a sacred craft from the homeland. As a high priest from Ra'iatea, Tupaia had made a tremendous impact on the people that he met, and he was now spoken of in all parts of the country. Because the *Endeavour* had sailed from Ra'iatea, they concluded that the astonishing things on board came from there as well. Tales of Tupaia's arrival in the *Endeavour*, with its cannons which flashed and thundered, its white-skinned crew with their muskets and their extraordinary cargo, had spread around the country. Tupaia had been the only man on board the *Endeavour* who could readily communicate with Maori, so he could say what he liked about the British. He had become the object of veneration across New Zealand, a near-mythical figure who had brought these strange vessels from the homeland with their loads of marvellous possessions.

When these visitors came on board, led by an impressive, white-haired old chief, Cook gave them gifts, including brass medals stamped with the titles of King George and the name of the *Resolution*, and the young orator who had greeted him from the canoe gave Cook his striped dogskin cloak as a return gift. They seemed affluent, wearing whalebone combs in their hair, fine cloaks and greenstone ornaments, and bringing with them a greenstone adze and musical instruments, including flutes, a shell trumpet and a war trumpet, which they played for the British. After they left the ship, Cook hosted a dinner for the officers in honour of the King. The marines lined up on the beach and fired a twenty-one gun salute, and that night bonfires were lit in Ship Cove and there was a display of fireworks, to the astonishment of the assembled Maori. On the whole, the Europeans' visit to the Sound had been peaceful and tranquil, and on 7 June 1773, as they sailed from the Sound, the astronomer William Wales reflected quizzically upon the Maori reputation for violence and cannibalism:

Before going to leave this land of Canibals, as it is now generally thought to be, it may be expected that I should record what bloody Massacres I have been a witness of; how many human Carcasses I have seen roasted and eaten; or at least relate such Facts as have fallen within the Compass of my Observation tending to confirm the Opinion, now almost universally believed, that the New Zeelanders are guilty of this most detestable Practice. Truth, notwithstanding, obliges me to declare, however unpopular it may be, that I have not seen the least signs of any such custom being amongst them, either in Dusky Bay or Charlotte sound; although the latter place is that where the only Instance of it was *seen* in the *Endeavour*'s Voyage.[55]

Wales, the scrupulous scientist, was making it plain that he had no eyewitness evidence of cannibalism, and could not vouch for the practice. The young midshipman, Elliott, however, had no such reservations:

They are desperate, fearless, ferocious Cannibals, the Men generaly about six feet high, with Limbs and sinews like an Ox, dark copper coloured faces, fine white teeth, and eyes that strike fire, when angry, and I declare that I have seen a couple of them, in giving us the War Song on the Quarter deck, work themselves into a frenzey, foaming at the mouth, and perfectly shaking the whole Quarter deck with their feet ... And in this state they attack their Enemies, and will rush upon Bayonets or anything else.[56]

Along with shipwreck and love affairs with seductive brown-skinned maidens, encounters with wild, tattooed savages were the very stuff of seafaring adventure, and the sailors would not be denied their tales about their meetings with the 'fearless, ferocious Cannibals' of New Zealand.

10

Cannibals and Kings

On 8 June 1773 as the *Resolution* and *Adventure* sailed out of Cook Strait, three large albatrosses circled overhead while the sailors joked that these birds were the spirits of Captains and Chief Mates, banished to these cold seas as a punishment. Cook set his course south-east, looking for the Southern Continent at about 45 degrees south, before heading to Tahiti. The officers decided to celebrate their departure from Queen Charlotte Sound with a feast of roasted meat, and a dog from the Cape, which had grown fat and sleek from hunting birds in New Zealand, was slaughtered and roasted. As he ate his serving of dog roasted with garlic, Anders Sparrman decided that it tasted just like mutton, and laughed a little at William Wales, who had difficulty in even nibbling it. On this occasion, Johann Forster waxed philosophical:

It is really a pity, that in Europe there are such terrible prejudices among mankind, as to think cats, dogs, horse & other Animals (we are not used to eat by custom) to be unclean & an Object of Abomination . . . Were it general to eat these domestic Animals who afford both a wholesome & palatable food, many a poor Man could now & then feast upon flesh, which he but too often must abstain from . . . Many a Lady & Gentleman fond of their Lap-Dogs & favorite Cats will be displeased with this doctrine, but true Philosophy & common sense seems to be on my Side & self interest & prejudice on theirs.[1]

The whole question of what people and dogs would eat had become a major preoccupation on board the *Resolution*. Several weeks later when a litter of puppies were born, one of them dead, Forster watched curiously as a young New Zealand dog eagerly devoured the carcass, although his pet spaniel would not touch it. He decided that, like its masters in New Zealand, the kuri was an inveterate cannibal with a taste for human flesh, for as he observed, 'the Cannibal-Dog having one Day licked off the blood of a cut in a finger of the Capts Servant fell greedily upon the finger & began to bite in good earnest.'[2]

On board the *Adventure*, the officers and crew had other, more pressing concerns. Many of the men were sickly, and after three weeks at sea, there was an outbreak of venereal disease, contracted after their orgies in Queen Charlotte Sound. This was followed by cases of scurvy, which made its victims depressed and irrational. Late one night, for example, the *Adventure*'s Lieutenant of Marines, Lieutenant Scott, came to Bayly's cabin, almost naked and talking incoherently, and accusing the ship's surgeon, his close friend, of poisoning him. The crew of the *Adventure* had refused to eat wild celery and other anti-scorbutics at Queen Charlotte Sound, and were now paying dearly for their obstinacy. On 22 July the ship's cook died of scurvy; and a few days later, Furneaux reported to Cook that twenty-one of his men were seriously ill, so that the remaining sailors were forced to do double duty, making it difficult to work the vessel. Cook sent a boat across to the *Adventure* with a new cook, ordering Furneaux to serve his men spruce beer with wort, sauerkraut and boiled cabbage, and wine instead of spirits.

By this time, Cook had decided that there was no Southern Continent in this part of the Pacific. He turned north for Tahiti, where he knew that he could obtain fresh fruit and vegetables for his men. On 11 August one of the Tuamotu Islands was sighted, which had been found by Bougainville. The archipelago was very dangerous to sail through, however, because the atolls were so low that they were almost impossible to see at night, and Cook railed at Bougainville for not revealing the exact locations of the islands that he had discovered.

On the night of 15 August as they approached Tahiti, Cook gave the duty officer a course to Vaitepiha Bay on the south-east side of the island, and retired to his cabin. When he woke at daybreak, he found the sloop sailing straight for the reef off the south end of Tahiti-iti. He immediately ordered a change of course, and as the ships edged up along the southern coast, a canoe came out with two envoys waving a plantain branch, calling out 'Taio! Taio!' As they came alongside the *Resolution*, the plantain was passed up to one of the officers, who took it and stuck it in the main shrouds. When people on shore saw this sign of peace they climbed into their canoes, and about a hundred canoes came out laden with fish and fruit, while their crews cried out for 'Pane' (Banks) and 'Tolano' (Solander). As soon as they caught sight of Cook and Furneaux, they recognised them and came on board the ships, including a number of beautiful young women who embraced the sailors, opening their shirts and looking at their white skins in astonishment. Near the south-east point of the island, a pass in the reef was sighted, and Cook sent the boats off to investigate it, although the Tahitians told him it was too shallow. Shortly afterwards, however, the wind died, and the *Resolution* was dragged towards this gap by the tide, grounding on the reef with a crash that shook the whole vessel. As Cook roared at his men, Sparrman observed primly: 'I should have preferred to hear fewer "Goddams" from the officers and particularly from the Captain, who, while the danger lasted, stamped about the deck and grew hoarse from shouting.'[3]

Cook was furious because as soon as the Tahitian women came on board, some of his men forgot their duty. One officer, for instance, was about to make love to a girl in his cabin when the *Resolution* hit the reef; and as he rushed up to help save the ship, she vanished with his bed sheets, to his chagrin and disappointment. Up on deck, all was chaos and confusion. While the sailors were heaving on the capstan, dropping the anchors to try and save the *Resolution*, the tide was sweeping the *Adventure* towards the coral. About thirty of Furneaux's men were sick, so Cook had sent some of his own crew across to help work the vessel. Just as it seemed that both sloops were about to be wrecked on the reef, a breeze blew up from the land, and with the help of the boats they pulled clear, leaving their anchors behind them. Once they were safely out at sea, Cook retired to the ward-room, covered with sweat and suffering from terrible pains in his stomach. Sparrman gave him a good dose of brandy, which soon restored him. This was probably an early symptom of the internal disorder which would plague him during the voyage.

Before he retired, Cook ordered all the visitors ashore, but the next morning when they anchored in Vaitepiha Bay, the Tahitians swarmed up the sides of the vessels, exchanging fruit and 'curiosities' for beads and nails. Those who tried to steal from the ships were lashed with a whip, which 'they bore very patiently'. No hogs or chickens were offered to the British, however, because young Vehiatua, the new high chief of Tahiti-iti, had prohibited this kind of barter. It was the season of scarcity in Tahiti, and besides, there had been a war between the island's two main divisions since the *Endeavour*'s visit, during which Cook's taio Tutaha, the regent of Tahiti-nui, and Banks's taio, Te Pau, had been killed by Vehiatua's father, the leader of Tahiti-iti. Vehiatua must have been very apprehensive about Cook's reaction to this news. As Marra noted, taio friendship was a powerful bond of loyalty in Tahiti:

[They show] fidelity to those who condescended to place confidence in them as particular friends. To such there is no service that they will not readily submit, nor any good office that they will not willingly perform; they will range the island through to procure them what they want, and when encouraged by kindness and some small presents and tokens of esteem, no promises or rewards will influence them to break their attachments.[4]

Although Cook's relationship with Tutaha had been marked by ambivalence and misunderstanding, Vehiatua (the old war chief whom Cook met in 1769) had waited until Cook left the island before daring to attack his taio. There had been a series of battles, including one in 1770 in which Purea and Amo's people had allied themselves with Vehiatua. It began out at sea, where the orators worked up the men into a fighting frenzy. The two fleets were lashed together, and so many warriors were killed that the sea ran red with blood. The battle continued on the beach, where Vehiatua's army won the victory; and a huge pile of enemy corpses was built near Taunoa.[5]

After this 'battle of the red sea' there was a period of peace, but eventually Tutaha decided to seek revenge for his defeat. In about March 1773 he and the young high chief Tu led a large army to attack Tahiti-iti; and when Tutaha and Vehiatua confronted each other in battle, Tutaha was killed, along with Banks's taio Te Pau and many of the leading chiefs of Tahiti-nui. Tutaha's body was disembowelled and hung in a breadfruit tree; and several months later a treaty was concluded with Tu, now acknowledged as the ari'i rahi or high chief of Tahiti-nui. Although old Vehiatua died shortly afterwards, his son (who took his father's name) expected Cook to avenge his taio Tutaha's death. When Cook, Furneaux and Johann Forster landed that afternoon and asked to see young Vehiatua, therefore, the high chief avoided them, although his people carried them across the river on their shoulders and treated them kindly, saying that he would visit them shortly.

The next morning, Cook sent two longboats and the *Resolution*'s cutter to try and recover the anchors they had lost on the reef. Although they succeeded in retrieving the *Resolution*'s bower-anchor, the *Adventure*'s three anchors had to be abandoned. Afterwards, Cook went ashore with Furneaux and the Forsters to see if Vehiatua had arrived, but there was no sign of him. The Forsters went off looking for plants, wandering through shady groves of breadfruit trees interspersed with coconut and banana palms, where they found well-tended gardens of cloth-plant, taro, yams and sugar-cane plants, scattered amongst houses surrounded by bushes covered with aromatic flowers.

When Cook came back to the ship for dinner at noon, he brought a chief and his two sons aboard, and although he gave gifts to these men, one of the sons was soon caught stealing a silver knife and a pewter spoon from the Great Cabin. The sailors threw the young man off the sloop, but he swam to a canoe and sat laughing at the Europeans. In exasperation Cook fired a musket loaded with ball over his head, and when he dived into the water, Cook fired again as he surfaced. When the young chief climbed into a double canoe which was quickly paddled towards the shore, Cook ordered a boat to chase him, but upon approaching the beach, the sailors were pelted with stones. Cook boarded his own boat with armed men and quickly rushed to the rescue, while a four-pounder was fired overhead. As the Tahitians fled in panic, two double canoes were seized and taken alongside the *Resolution*. In trying to understand the motive for such 'thefts', one of the sailors mused, 'Is it not very natural, when a people see a company of strangers come among them, and without ceremony cut down their trees, gather their fruits and seize their animals, that such a people should use as little ceremony with the strangers, as the strangers do with them; if so, against whom is the criminality to be charged, the christian or the savage?'[6]

Despite this confrontation, George Forster was enchanted by Vaitepiha Bay:

The harbour in which we lay was very small; . . . the water in it was as smooth as the finest mirrour, and the sea broke with a snowy foam around us upon the outer reef. The plain at the foot of the hills was very narrow, . . . but always conveyed the pleasing ideas of fertility, plenty, and happiness. Just over against us it ran up between the hills into a long narrow valley, rich in plantations, interspersed with the houses of the natives. The slopes of the hills, covered with woods, crossed each other on both sides; and beyond them, over the cleft of the valley, we saw the interior mountains shattered into various peaks and spires, among which was one remarkable pinnacle, whose summit was frightfully bent to one side . . . The serenity of the sky, the genial warmth of the air, and the beauty of the landscape, united to exhilarate our spirits.[7]

On shore that afternoon, Cook's men found that the settlements in the bay had been abandoned. That night, a boat was sent out of the harbour with the body of one of the marines, who had died that morning of consumption; and they buried him out at sea, to avoid further difficulties with Vehiatua's people.

The next morning some people came out to the *Resolution* to ask for the return of the double canoes. Trade ground to a halt, until Cook yielded to their entreaties. Over the next few days the British explored the area around Vaitepiha bay. As they wandered about, the Tahitians offered them hospitality and asked them their names, their country, whether their wives were on board, and how long they would be staying. They often greeted the British with cries of 'Taio, give us a bead!', and when George Forster repeated this phrase back to them, imitating their wheedling tone of voice, they went into peals of laughter. Cook's visit to this district during the *Endeavour* voyage had been brief, and many of these people had never seen Europeans. They were amazed by Hodge's sketches, and by the strangers' white skins, clothing and weapons. They asked them to demonstrate their muskets by shooting birds, although those who had not seen guns before fell to the ground, or ran away in terror when they were fired. There were plenty of pigs in the bay, but the local people hid them in their houses, saying that they all belonged to Vehiatua. During their excursions, the Forsters encountered one extremely corpulent chief, who was being force-fed by an attendant, and another chief who had very long nails as a sign that he did no hard labour. George, who had radical leanings, found these signs of aristocratic decadence disturbing, since he thought such excesses would not occur among people in a 'state of nature'.

About this time, Cook renewed his acquaintance with Tuahu, the man who had guided him on his circuit of Tahiti in 1769. Tuahu gave him a detailed account of the recent wars, including the killing of Tutaha and the death of old Vehiatua. When Cook showed him his engraved chart of Tahiti, Tuahu seemed delighted, pointing at each of the districts in turn and reciting their names. When he came to the district just south of Vaitepiha, he told Cook that several months earlier a ship had arrived there, which he called 'Pahi no Pepe' (Pepe's vessel). The crew of the ship had been given five hogs; and one of the sailors had deserted and was now living on the island. This man had attached himself to Vehiatua, and Tuahu said that it was he who had advised the chief not to give any pigs to Cook and his companions. In this way Cook learned about the brief visit by the Spanish ship *Aguila* under Don Domingo de Boenechea, who had been sent from Peru to examine the island of Tahiti. Boenechea had anchored off the neighbourhood of Vaiurua nine months earlier, and eventually took four Tahitians off to Lima, leaving a virulent epidemic (probably influenza) behind him.[8]

Although his arrival was promised almost daily, Vehiatua had still not arrived in the bay. The sailors were growing unruly, and many of them were sneaking ashore without permission. After waiting a week, Cook declared that he was leaving Vaitepiha to go to Matavai. Stung by this announcement, Vehiatua arrived the following day, and sent a message inviting Cook to meet him. When Cook's party landed on the beach the next morning, he found Vehiatua sitting on a four-legged stool, attended by an enormously fat, heavily tattooed arioi named Ti'i, who acted as his 'Prime Minister'.[9] They were surrounded by a crowd of five hundred people, all uncovered to the waist, guarded by marshals who struck their fellow countrymen with bamboo canes if they crowded too closely. Vehiatua, a young man about eighteen years old, was light-skinned and sandy-haired, with a stiff, solemn demeanour. Although he had met Cook several times in 1769, he seemed afraid of him at first.[10] Nevertheless, he invited him to sit beside him on his stool while 'ava (a ceremonial drink) was being served, and Cook gave him gifts of red cloth, a sheet, a broad-axe and other items.

When Johann Forster presented an aigrette of scarlet feathers to the young 'King', a shout of admiration arose from the gathering. Vehiatua enquired after Joseph Banks, and asked Cook how long he intended to stay at Vaitepiha. When Cook replied that he had decided to go to Matavai since he had been unable to obtain pigs in this district, Vehiatua was not happy to hear this, since Matavai was rival territory. He asked Cook to stay longer with him, and although Cook declined, he ordered a young Scots sailor to play the bagpipes for the high chief, who lit up with pleasure when he heard the lilting music. He examined Cook's watch with intense interest, and when he was told that this instrument told the time, he called it a 'little sun', which 'talked' with its ticking. The counsellor Ti'i asked whether the Europeans had a god, and when he was told that they worshipped an invisible God, he seemed to approve. After these amiable exchanges Cook and Vehiatua walked arm in arm towards the beach, and Cook and Furneaux were each presented with a pig, before returning to their ships to prepare for the passage to Matavai. Johann Forster was sorry to leave this beautiful place, and that night he paid his tribute to Tahiti-iti by quoting Virgil's description of the Elysian Fields in his journal:

'They reached the places of joy and the grassy groves of the Happy Ones, and the homes of the Blessed. Here a more wholesome air clothes the plains in a brilliant light, and they have their very own sun and stars to enjoy. Some were exercising themselves in the grassy fields of sport, playing games and wrestling on the yellow sand; some beat out rhythms with their feet and sang songs . . . He [Aeneas] saw others to left and right feasting on the grass, and singing a joyful hymn in chorus, amid a scented grove of laurel, whence the mighty stream of Erydanus rolls through the woodland to the upper world.'[11]

The next morning Cook took the ships out of the bay, sending Lieutenant Pickersgill ashore in the armed cutter to see if he could procure more pigs from Vehiatua. When he returned to the beach, the young chief greeted Pickersgill, asking him to demonstrate his musket. Pickersgill loaded his musket with ball and fired it at a target, and some of the people fell over in astonishment, although as soon as they discovered it left just one small hole, they seemed rather contemptuous. Seeing this, Pickersgill asked them to set up a mark and fired at it with smallshot, tearing the mark to pieces. Vehiatua, who was deeply impressed by this demonstration, urged Pickersgill to stay with him in Tahiti-iti, offering him women and generous presents. Although Pickersgill refused these inducements, Vehiatua did not seem offended, but stayed to make sure that his people traded fairly with the British.

After acquiring eight pigs at agreed rates, Pickersgill tried to catch up with the *Resolution*, but the cutter was caught in drenching rain and high winds. At dusk that night, several canoes came out from the eastern coast, led by Taruri, a 'brother' of Reti[12] (the chief who had welcomed Bougainville to Hitia'a), who dressed Pickersgill in his own clothes and invited him ashore, promising him that he could sleep that night with his daughter. As Pickersgill remarked, 'this was an offer not to be refused', so he landed at Hitia'a, where a crowd of thousands of people greeted him and his men, picking him up and carrying him on their shoulders to Reti's house, where he met the 'King', a fine, grey-haired man with a deep scar on his forehead and a cheerful, lively demeanour, who introduced him to his council of elders. When he mentioned Ahutoru's name, however, he was surprised to find that neither Reti nor his people seemed particularly interested. That night Pickersgill posted armed sentries in the boat to protect his trade goods, while he and the rest of his party slept blissfully in the arms of local women.

The next morning Pickersgill, accompanied by Taruri, set off to rejoin the *Resolution*. After boarding the sloop they sailed towards Matavai Bay, where two canoes decked with streamers came out to greet them. As they hauled around Point Venus, they saw a huge crowd of people on the beach, their bodies uncovered to the waist, except for a tall, striking figure whom their companions identified as Tu, the high chief of Tahiti-nui. When the ships dropped their anchors, most of these people fled over the hills to Pare, led by Tu who ran away along the rocky shoreline. The few who had stayed on the beach came out to greet the Europeans, and Fa'a, the *Dolphin*'s 'old man', soon boarded the *Resolution*. The men from the *Dolphin* and the *Endeavour* greeted their old friends, and there were many joyous reunions. Samuel Gibson, the marine who had tried to desert from the *Endeavour* and who spoke quite good Tahitian, and Pickersgill, who had now visited the island on three consecutive occasions, were welcomed with particular warmth. Their visitors also asked after Banks, Solander and Tupaia, although Ahutoru (who had sailed with Bougainville) was rarely mentioned.

That afternoon a chief named Marae-ta'ata came on board with his wife, and told Cook that Tu was very afraid of him. Cook was mystified by this, but Tu and Tutaha, Cook's taio, had not always been on good terms, and Tu had stayed away from Cook during his previous visit to the island. As they were showered with gifts, Marae-ta'ata's wife embraced Cook and caressed him fondly, although she offered no further intimacies. That night many of the Tahitians stayed on board, including women who played flutes, danced, and slept with the sailors. Almost all of these women were commoners, however, some of them very young; whereas the married and high-born women were almost inaccessible. They would only sleep with their husbands' taio; and high-born Tahitians would only contract such bonds with officers and gentlemen. As William Wales reflected:

I have great reason to believe that much the great part of these [women] admit of no such familiarities, or at least are very carefull to whom they grant them. That there are Prostitutes here as well as in London is true, perhaps more in proportion, and such no doubt were those who came on board the ship to our People. These seem not less skilfull in their profession than Ladies of the same stamp in England, nor does a person run less risk of injuring his health and Constitution in their Embraces. On the whole I am firmly of opinion that a stranger who visits England might with equal justice draw the Characters of the Ladies there, from those which he might meet with on board the Ships in Plymouth Sound, at Spithead, or in the Thames; on the Point at Portsmouth, or in the Purlieus of Wapping.[13]

Unlike most of his men, Cook remained very concerned about the transmission of venereal diseases, and tried to set an example by refusing to sleep with any women who were offered to him. This did not enhance his reputation among the island women, however, who according to Elliott, jeered and laughed at him, 'calling him *Old*, and good for nothing'.[14] They respected Cook, but felt much more affection for the younger men like Banks, Samuel Gibson and Richard Pickersgill, who joined in the amorous delights they were offered with alacrity.

The next morning, accompanied by Furneaux, Sparrman, the Forsters, Marae-ta'ata and his wife, Cook set off down the west coast in the pinnace to Tu's settlement. At Pare they were greeted by at least a thousand people who cried out in welcome, while the marshals beat them with long poles to keep them back from the 'King' and his European visitors. Tu, a strongly built, curly-haired man about twenty-five years old and six feet three inches high, was seated among a circle of distinguished men and women.[15] All of the people around him had uncovered their torsos as a sign of respect, including his father and his brothers and sisters; except for one man, who seemed to be some kind of courtier. Cook sent some of his sailors forward with a number of valuable gifts, saying that these were for 'Taio' or friendship. During the conversation that followed, Tu asked after Tupaia, and various of the officers and gentlemen who had sailed on the *Endeavour* (although as Cook observed, he had never met any of these people). He told Cook that he was frightened of his guns, and indeed he seemed timid and afraid of the Europeans. When Cook ordered his bagpiper to play for Tu, however, the people were delighted and they parted on excellent terms. Tu promised to come and see Cook at Matavai, bringing him pigs, so Cook made his farewells and went back to the *Resolution* for dinner.

That afternoon the shore camp was set up on Port Venus, on the site of the old fort, and Wales's observatory was landed. Early the next morning, Tu arrived alongside with a large entourage, and gifts of bark-cloth, a cavalli, a tuna, a pig and baskets of fruit, which were sent to the *Resolution* as gifts of welcome. Cook called out to the high chief, inviting him aboard, but Tu would not stir until Cook allowed himself to be wrapped in layers of bark-cloth, as a sign that his intentions were peaceful. Tu then ventured onto the quarterdeck, where he embraced Cook, and sent his young brother below decks to assure himself that it was safe. When he received a favourable report he accompanied Cook to the Great Cabin, although he would not eat any food (since he was under a sacred restriction). Tu was very surprised by the hot tea he was served and the dishes of breadfruit roasted in oil; but as soon as he saw Johann Forster's spaniel, a fine dog but very dirty, he asked for it. The spaniel was gladly handed over to his attendant, who cradled it tenderly in his arms. After breakfast, Cook offered to take him back to Pare, and as they set off Furneaux gave Tu a breeding pair of goats as a gift, indicating that they should be fed on grass and kept in shady places. When they landed at Pare, the people greeted the high chief with acclamation, and an old grey-haired lady ran to embrace Cook. This was Tutaha's mother, who wept over Cook, lamenting the death of his taio. Cook was deeply moved by her tears, admitting later:

I was so much affected at her behaviour that it would not have been possible for me to refrain mingling my tears with hers had not Otoo come and snatched me as it were from her, I afterwards disired to see her again in order to make her a present but he told me she was Mataou [afraid] and would not come, I was not satisfied with this answer and desired she might be sent for, soon after she appeared I went up to her, she again wept and lamented the death of her son. I made her a present of an Ax and other things and then parted from her and soon after took leave of Otoo and return'd aboard.[16]

Tu seemed unhappy about this encounter, however, due to the difficult relationship he had had with Tutaha, and discouraged Cook from prolonging it.

By now, provisions were running short on board the ships. Cook had received only ceremonial gifts of pigs from Vehiatua and Tu, so early the next morning he sent Pickersgill south to see if their old friends in those districts could supply them with pigs and chickens. Pickersgill travelled down the west coast to Punaaiua where he found Potatau, the tall, imposing high chief whom Cook had met in 1769. Pickersgill gave him gifts of a large axe and looking-glasses for his women, and asked whether he had any hogs

*Tu, the ari'i rahi (high chief) of Tahiti and Cook's taio
(ceremonial friend)*

to barter. Potatau seemed hesitant, saying that he was afraid of being shot by the British; and when one of the sailors lost a powder-horn, he sent his men to catch the thief, quickly returning the stolen item to the visitors. Along with Tutaha, Purea and Amo, Potatau was one of the chiefs who had been taken hostage by Cook at the end of his *Endeavour* visit, and he had good reason to be cautious, although he promised to try and procure pigs and other supplies for Cook as soon as possible.

Not long after Pickersgill had left the *Resolution*, Tu arrived alongside, bringing a ceremonial gift of a pig, a large fish and some fruit; and Reti, the chief of Hitia'a and Bougainville's 'friend', who was already on board, lowered his bark-cloth garments to his waist in homage to the high chief. Cook entertained Tu and his retinue on board before taking them back to Pare, where he entertained them with bagpipe music and dancing by the sailors. When the Tahitians danced in their turn, they performed Tahitian dances and then mimicked the hornpipe and some English country dances, which they found hilarious. The following day, Cook returned to Pare to visit Tu, where the royal family entertained him with an arioi performance. Tu's sister danced, dressed in an elegant costume and accompanied by five men and three drummers, who often mentioned Cook's name in their songs. Cook gave Tu a gift of a broadsword, buckling this around his waist, but Tu seemed afraid, insisting that the sword should be taken out of his sight. Soon afterwards, Cook returned to Matavai.

On 30 August, Cook sent Pickersgill south again, to see whether Potatau had kept his promise. When Pickersgill arrived at Punaauia, however, no pigs had been collected, so he carried on to Papara to see whether Purea and Amo could assist him. At the border, however, he found their way barred by a chief who ordered his party to go no further. When the sailors brandished their muskets, the Tahitians held up plantains as a sign of peace, and eventually a messenger was sent to tell Purea to come to meet the Europeans. When she arrived, she seemed very glad to see them, but confessed that she was now very poor, and had little to give them. During the recent wars, Purea had allied herself against Tu and Tutaha, and Tu now counted her as an enemy. She and Amo had parted, and he was now married to another, younger woman. Amo and his new wife also arrived, and as Pickersgill remarked, he now seemed very relaxed and 'indolent'.

Pickersgill and his men slept with Purea and Amo that night, and the next morning they returned to Potatau's headquarters. Pickersgill presented Potatau with a sheep, although when this strange creature stood up and began to bleat, the local people were so frightened that some of them fled into the forest. Nevertheless, the chief decided to accompany the lieutenant back to the ships, but not until he had sworn on a bunch of red and yellow feathers (the sign of 'Oro) that Potatau would not be harmed, and that Cook would be his taio. The promise was duly made, and the next morning Potatau and his two wives climbed on board the pinnace with a gift of four pigs for Cook, two from himself and two from Purea. Although his people wept loudly and begged him not to go, he brushed them aside, declaring that 'Cook will not kill his friends!' before resolutely joining the sailors.

When they arrived at Matavai Bay later that afternoon, Cook was glad to see Potatau again, and Hodges was so impressed by this imposing, good-looking chief that he sketched him in the Great Cabin. While Pickersgill was travelling down the coast, some of the *Adventure*'s men (three marines and a sailor) overstayed their shore leave and got into a fight, after attempting unwanted intimacies with local women. When the men finally straggled back to their ship the next morning, they were tied to a mast where they were each given a flogging, watched by Tu's 'ambassador', Ti'i. Tu was not mollified, however, and stayed away from the ships, so Cook and

Furneaux decided to go and find him. He had fled from Pare, and when they finally tracked him down, he seemed very frightened. In an effort to reassure the high chief, Cook presented him with three sheep from the Cape, axes, cloth and other presents. Again the bagpipes were played, and Tu gave his taio 'Tute' a large pig, another for 'Tono' (Furneaux), and a small one for Johann Forster, who had accompanied Cook on that occasion. Seeing this, Tu's uncle spoke sharply, and the small pig was replaced with a larger animal. Forster gave Tu a bunch of red feathers in return, a gift greeted with a shout of pleasure. When Cook announced that he was about to leave Matavai, Tu embraced him several times, expressing sadness at his departure; as they parted, Cook returned to his ship while Tu carried on to Pare.

When Cook arrived back on board the *Resolution*, a young commoner named Porea, who had often spoken of going to Cook's country, 'Peretane', begged to be allowed to join the *Resolution*. After Cook had agreed, Porea asked for an axe and a nail to be given to his father, who was on board the vessel. While the anchors were being hoisted later that afternoon, however, a canoe came alongside, demanding that Porea should be sent back to shore. Cook, who thought that he was being tricked out of an axe, replied in exasperation that as soon as his father returned the gifts, the boy could leave the vessel. At sunset that night, Cook farewelled Potatau and his wife, saying that he would return to visit them in seven months' time, and with Porea still on board, ordered the anchors to be hoisted. As they sailed away from Matavai, Porea burst into tears and was comforted by Cook and Johann Forster, who promised that they would be his 'fathers'. Like the rest of his shipmates, Elliott was sad to leave Tahiti:

This Island appeared to us to be the Paradice of those Seas, the Men being all fine, tall, well-made, with humane open countenances; the Women beautiful, compaired with all those that we had seen, of the Middle Size, zingy, suple figures, fine teeth and Eyes, and the finest formed Hands, fingers, and Arms that I ever saw, with lively dispositions. And tho the Men were inclined to steal little things from us, yet the Women seemed free from this propensity.[17]

Their visit to Paradise had had its price, however. To Cook's frustration, a number of his men were exhibiting signs of venereal disease (presumably gonorrhoea); and it was all too likely that they would infect any other women they slept with during the voyage.

At dusk on 1 September, as the wind shifted to the east, they sailed from Matavai Bay to Huahine, arriving the following evening off the northern point of the island. Early the next morning as the sloops approached Fare harbour, the *Adventure* grounded briefly in the passage, although they finally got in safely. Soon afterwards Cook went ashore, where he was greeted with pleasure. The people remembered him from his previous visit, bringing numerous pigs, dogs and chickens to barter, although they had few vegetables for the sailors, since both breadfruit and plantains were out of season. A message soon came from Ori, the Regent of Huahine, who had exchanged names with Cook during the *Endeavour*'s visit in 1769, saying that he hoped to see his taio the following morning.

When Cook went ashore at Fare the next day, his boat was guided straight to Ori's house. At the water's edge, five young plantain trees were brought out – the first, with a pig, for the *Ari'i* or high chief [Captain Cook]; the second, with another pig, for the Atua [god] of the Europeans; the third as a sign of welcome; the fourth, with a dog, to represent the *taura* or rope which bound them together; and the fifth, with a pig, for Ori's taio, Captain Cook.[18] These gifts were accompanied by a piece of pewter, engraved with an inscription from the *Endeavour*, which Cook had given to Ori in 1769 to mark their friendship. Their guide instructed Cook and his companions to take up three of these plantain branches, to decorate them with nails, looking-glasses and medals, and give them to Ori. Holding these branches, they walked through a lane through the huge crowd to where Ori was seated. The plantains were presented to Ori one by one, the first for his god, the second for the high chief of Huahine; and the third for Ori himself, Cook's taio.

Ori, a thin, tall man about sixty years old, fell on Cook's neck and wept over him like a father welcoming his long-lost son. Cook gave him valuable presents, and Ori presented his grandson to Cook and asked after Tupaia. After this ceremony the people flocked to the trading-place, where large numbers of pigs, chickens and dogs were bartered for axes, nails and other European items. Young Porea, who had come ashore as Cook's attendant, carrying his powder-horn and shot-pouch and dressed in a linen jacket and a pair of trousers, put on tremendous airs, refusing to speak Tahitian but talking in a kind of gibberish. He insisted on being called 'Tom', which greatly amused his shipmates.

Sparrman and George Forster had not accompanied Cook on this occasion, but walked overland from Fare to Ori's settlement. During this excursion they saw large numbers of pigs and dogs roaming around, and watched curiously as one woman fed a little pig. She offered it a piece of hog's skin, and when it opened its mouth to bite, she pushed in a handful of fermented breadfruit. They also saw a middle-aged woman breast-feeding a little puppy, and as they gazed at her in astonishment, she smiled and said that she had lost her child, and that she also sometimes fed piglets in this fashion. George Forster described the Tahitian dogs as small, with pointed snouts, broad heads, small eyes, upright ears, and long lank hair. They hardly ever barked, but howled, and were 'shy of strangers to a degree of aversion'.[19] They also saw a number of white-bellied kingfishers and grey herons, and shot some of these birds, although they were soon warned not to do this, since these were *atua* or supernatural beings.

The next morning, Ori came out to the *Resolution* with gifts of Tahitian delicacies, bringing his sons to meet his taio. Cook ordered the bagpipes to be played, delighting the old chief, who always insisted on being addressed as 'Tute' or Cook; while Cook was always addressed as 'Ori', as he had been during his first visit to Huahine. Later, the Forsters went ashore and walked to a place where a large double war-canoe was being built. The people working on this canoe asked them about Tupaia, telling them that some months ago a fleet of Borabora warriors had arrived on the island and killed a number of Ori's kinsmen, and asking if the Europeans would help them to fight the invaders. At the same time, Sparrman had wandered off to a large saltwater lagoon where rare plants were growing, guided by a young man who carried his plant-bag, calling himself his taio. When some warriors approached him, intent on taking his things, it was only the fact that he had taken his gun with him, and the presence of his young taio which saved him.

Despite the warmth of their welcome at Huahine, the arrival of Cook's ships was causing tensions on the island. The shooting of the sacred birds was an ill omen, and although the season of scarcity had begun, hundreds of pigs were being bartered to the sailors, along with large numbers of dogs and chickens. Some people clearly thought that Ori should declare a rahui (or prohibition) on the island's livestock, as Vehiatua and Tu had done on Tahiti. In any case, Ori's position was under challenge in the name of the young ari'i rahi [high chief] of Huahine, Te Ri'i taria.[20] When the trading station opened early the next morning, a chief arrived, dressed in a red war-costume and furiously brandishing two wooden clubs, who tried to stop some people from bartering breadfruit (which were very scarce at this time of year), grabbing a bag of nails from the ship's clerk and threatening to knock down the midshipman, one of Cook's 'black sheep', Charles Loggie. Cook told Johann Forster to charge his musket, and walked up to this man, boldly grabbing his weapons. As the chief struggled with him, Cook drew his sword and Forster aimed his musket; and when he sullenly stepped aside, Cook ordered the sailors to smash his clubs to pieces.

The chief was furious, and went off swearing vengeance. Not long afterwards, Sparrman arrived back at the trading station, dressed only in a length of bark-cloth and bleeding profusely from his head and shoulders. Despite his narrow escape the previous day, he had decided to go off botanising on his own. Two men had offered to guide him, who expressed great admiration for his hat, boots and black silk jacket, calling themselves his taio. They led him into the forest, where one man grabbed his belt and took his hunting knife while the other seized him by the throat, almost strangling him. When Sparrman tried to fight back, he was hit on the head with the hunting knife and knocked to the ground; as he lay there half-stunned, they grabbed his coat and tore it off his back, taking his knife and a small microscope. He got up, but when he tried to run away, he tripped over some convolvulus vines and they grabbed him again, trying to wrestle the shirt off his back and hitting him about the head and shoulders. After his assailants finally left him, dazed and bleeding, Sparrman picked up some stones as weapons and walked back to the ship. The people in the houses were afraid when they saw him red-faced with anger and half-naked, but an old man and his young companion took pity on him, wrapping him up in a bark-cloth cloak before guiding him back to the trading-place.

Although Cook ordered clothes to be fetched for Sparrman, he reproached the young naturalist for being so foolhardy. Despite his annoyance, he took Sparrman and the Forsters to Ori's house, where Cook told his friend what had happened. Ori was horrified and wept aloud; then talked to his people, reminding them of Cook's generosity. He asked Sparrman for a detailed account of the things that had been taken, and afterwards walked with Cook to the boat, which he boarded with his taio. When his people saw him getting in the boat, they begged him not to go, weeping loudly, and even Cook urged Ori to stay behind, but the chief was determined to find the thieves and punish them. After rowing along the coast for a time they landed at a bay, where Ori led them inland, stopping at the houses and asking where the thieves had gone. They had fled, so eventually Ori led them back to the boat, where they found his old sister waiting with her daughter. When they saw Ori the two women wept, but seeing that he was determined to visit the ship, his sister decided to go with him.

Cook took them out to the *Resolution* for dinner, and when they returned to Ori's house after the meal, they found that all the chiefly families had gathered, fearing for Ori's safety. They welcomed the old man, weeping over him and presenting Cook with lavish gifts of fruit, pigs and chickens. Eventually some of Ori's people arrived with Sparrman's hunting knife and part of his waistcoat; and various other things which had been stolen from some officers on a hunting party. Cook decided not to pursue these matters, but to leave them to his taio Ori; although Johann Forster vehemently questioned the wisdom of this decision, arguing that 'violent robbery is an act of violence, which ought not to remain unpunished, for it will in future times cause [in]security to British Subjects that land here; & too much lenity is absolutely dangerous.'[21] Cook was more concerned with upholding Ori's authority, however. He was moved by his friend's loyalty, remarking in his journal:

It shews what great confidence this Brave old Chief put in us, it also in a great degree shews that Friendship is Sacred with these people. Oree and I were profess'd friends in all the forms customary among them and he had no idea that this could be broke by the act of any other person, indeed this seem'd to be the great Argument he made use on to his people when they opposed his going into my boat, his words were to this effect: Oree (for so I was always calld) and I are friends, I have done nothing to forfeit his friendship, why should I not go with him?[22]

Nevertheless, it was time to leave the island. Early the next day as the sloops loosed their moorings, Cook returned to Ori's house with the most useful and valuable gifts he had to offer. He also returned the inscribed pewter plate from the *Endeavour*, along with a copper plate engraved with the words, 'Anchor'd here His Britannic Majestys Ships Resolution and Adventure September 1773', placed in a small bag with some engraved medals. Ori gave Cook a pig and traded six or eight more, and as they parted on the beach, the old chief embraced and wept over his taio.

As they said goodbye, Cook asked Ori about the Borabora invaders; and although the high chief had asked for his help during the *Endeavour* visit, he now assured Cook that he had made his peace with Puni, the high chief of Borabora. Cook did not ask about the rest of Sparrman's possessions, but as the *Adventure* was sailing out of the harbour, Ori came out in his canoe to tell Cook that the two thieves had been apprehended, inviting him to return ashore to witness their punishment. He said that four of his people had been taken away on the *Adventure* and asked Cook to send them back, so a boat was despatched to the *Adventure*. By the time the boat returned, Ori had returned to shore, and in any case his information was inaccurate. Only one islander was on board the *Adventure*, a commoner named Mai, whom Cook described as 'dark, ugly, and a downright blackguard' (i.e. of lowly birth, an old meaning of the term), who was now delivered to the *Resolution*.[23] Mai had made no secret of his intention to sail with the British since their first arrival at Huahine, and none of his family or friends had objected. Cook decided to delay his departure no longer, and set sail for Ra'iatea.

On 7 September 1773 the ships headed for Hamanino, Tupaia's birthplace on the island of Ra'iatea, which the *Endeavour* had visited four years earlier. It was a glorious day; the sea sparkling in the sun as a fresh breeze bellied the sails. When they arrived off the west coast of Ra'iatea, however, the wind was blowing straight out of Hamanino harbour, and it took all of the following day to warp the sloops into the anchorage. Canoes came out bringing pigs and fruit, and two burly, heavily tattooed chiefs from Borabora boarded the *Resolution*, presenting plantain branches and little pigs to their visitors.[24] Johann Forster exchanged names with one of these men, who told him that Uru, the high chief of Ra'iatea, was still the titular head of the island, although his authority was restricted to Opoa; while Puni, the high chief of Borabora, had appointed a man called Boba as the regent of Tahaa, the neighbouring island. According to George Forster, Mai, the young man who had just joined the *Adventure*, was a native of Ra'iatea who, like Tupaia, wanted to sail to England to get guns to free his homeland from the Borabora invaders (the first time that this ambition of Tupaia's had been mentioned). Puni himself, however, was nowhere to be found. As soon as he heard of the arrival of the English ships, he had retreated to Maupiti Island, asking anxiously after Tupaia, and enquiring whether the English ships had come to free Ra'iatea and Huahine from his dominion.

When Cook went ashore the next morning, he paid a visit to the Borabora regent of Ra'iatea, a chief named Reo.[25] Reo was a middle-sized, well-built man with a thin reddish beard and a lively, intelligent face, who asked to exchange names with his visitor. He also enquired after Tupaia, and was interested to hear about his death in Batavia. The atmosphere in Reo's house seemed cheerful and relaxed, and he joked and laughed with the Europeans in a very friendly manner. He had an elderly wife and two teenage children, one of them a pretty girl about fourteen years old. Later that day, when the Forsters went off to hunt birds, they shot three kingfishers and a grey heron, although George Forster should have known better, since he had already been reproached for killing such birds on Huahine. When they met Reo and his family shortly afterwards the young girl wept to see the sacred birds dead, and Reo told them very solemnly not to kill any more kingfishers and herons on his island.

Despite this episode, over the following days Reo and his family treated Cook's men with great kindness. They were impressed by this chief, whom Sparrman described as 'wise and order-loving', and much esteemed by his people.[26] Ra'iatea was the headquarters of the arioi, the devotees of 'Oro, and many of its people were skilled performers in dance and drama. Once again Cook and his officers and gentlemen were invited to a series of heiva featuring high-born arioi, staged in their honour. The first, on 10 September, involved seven men and one woman, Reo's niece. This performance included a skit on a daring theft, rather like one which Cook had watched during his previous visit, which celebrated the feats of Hiro, the god of thieves (and son of 'Oro). The next day, the heiva featured Reo's daughter, Poiatua, dressed in a dancing costume with a ruffled skirt and bodice, and a head-dress of plaited human hair, decorated with scented flowers. Although she was an expert in the facial contortions that had astonished Cook's men in the previous voyage, they admired her grace and agility. The men also danced with great rhythm, and their skits about theft and love-making were performed with such skill and conviction that Wales declared, 'I am not certain that I ever saw Mr. Garrick perform with more propriety.'[27] The day after, they were entertained with another heiva, shorter than the others.

In exchange for these courtesies, Cook invited Reo and his entourage to dine with him on several occasions. Reo brought his son to meet Cook, and later brought his close relative Uru, the high chief of the island, out to the *Resolution*. There were further exchanges of gifts, as the officers and gentlemen competed to attract the attention of three beautiful young women who had accompanied Reo and Uru on this occasion. Although 'the ladies very obligingly received their addresses, to one they gave a kind look to another a smile, thus they distributed their favours to all, received presents from all and at last jilted them all.'[28] During one of these visits, Reo and his companions told Cook about a number of islands in the surrounding seas, which he and the Forsters checked against Pickersgill's copy of Tupaia's chart. This proved to include all of the islands mentioned by these people, except for Tubuai and Upolu, islands in the Australs and Samoa respectively.

On 13 September, after five days in Hamanino harbour, a party including Cooper and Clerke (the *Resolution*'s senior lieutenants), the Forsters and several sailors went to the northern part of Ra'iatea to see whether they could find any new species of plants. As they walked along the coast, the Forsters became separated from the rest of their party. After a while, George Forster decided to hire a canoe to take them back to the ships, because neither of them was fit and they were very tired. When George began to bargain with one of the Ra'iateans, however, this man asked for four nails for the journey; and when George refused, he took the one nail that he had left and tried to grab his gun. His father, who was a little way off, thought that George was about to be killed, and aimed his musket at the man, who handed the gun back to George and retreated. As this man was running away, Johann Forster, who had been brooding about Cook's refusal to punish the Huahine men for their attack on Sparrman, shot him in the back with smallshot. When they returned to the ship, he told Cook what had happened.

According to Johann Forster, Cook laughed about this episode at first, but that night, when the matter was discussed over supper with Furneaux and the other officers, Cook rebuked him for shooting a man in the back.

Forster grew angry and attacked Cook for failing to protect his own people, insisting that he was not under his authority, and no doubt repeating his customary refrain of 'I will tell the King!' Cook was furious, 'hot & unguarded Expressions' were exchanged on both sides, and in the end Forster was thrown out of the Great Cabin, having asked for 'Satisfaction & was promissd it' – presumably a challenge to a duel.[29] Cook's journal entry that night was curt – 'Nothing happen'd worthy of note' – a remarkable understatement.[30] If Forster had been a sailor, this would have been mutiny, and it was a gross breach of protocol to challenge the ship's captain in such a fashion.

Cook had already decided to send Lieutenant Pickersgill across the lagoon to Tahaa, since bananas were in short supply on Ra'iatea. In order to get away from the ship, Johann Forster asked if he could join the expedition. Cook let him go, and early the next morning he set off in the cutter with Pickersgill, Sparrman and some sailors, accompanied by John Rowe, master's mate on the *Adventure* (and a relative of Furneaux's) and his men in another boat. When they entered Hamene harbour, the people told them that a heiva was under way, and upon rounding the point to the next bay, they found that a large crowd had gathered for a funeral. The Europeans were conducted to a low stool where the local high chief, an 'elderly mean-looking Man' named Ta, invited Forster to sit beside him. Three very young girls danced, and a group of men performed a skit about a thief stealing from a group of sleeping people. After this skit, the mourners paraded through the crowd in pairs, shining with *monoi* oil and wearing red loincloths, their heads decorated with coils of plaited human hair, and received gifts of rolls of bark-cloth. In the midst of this heiva one of the drummers became involved in a scuffle, but the combatants were quickly pulled apart, and the performance resumed.

Although the weather that night was wet and windy, the Europeans slept comfortably in a large house, with Ta sleeping beside them. In the middle of the night, however, the candle blew out, and the sentry thought that they were being robbed. He reached down and grabbed a head of hair, thinking it was a thief, and began to beat the culprit about the head with the butt end of his musket. The man yelled out in surprise and pain, and when the candle was lit again they realised that the 'thief' was none other than their host Ta, and laughed heartily at his anger and discomfiture.

The next morning Ta, still brooding over this insult, took them around the coast to see Boba, the 'vice-roy' of the island. Boba was nowhere to be seen, but his servants prepared a feast of roasted pork for the visitors. At the end of the meal, however, they found that Rowe's mat-bag, which contained nails, looking-glasses and strings of beads, had been stolen.

Johann Forster was still angry about Cook's 'laxity' towards local people, and he and Pickersgill decided to punish this theft severely. Seizing Ta and another chief as hostages, they ransacked Boba's settlement. They took a pig, a mat and some pearl shells from a man who had brought them to barter with the strangers. As this man struggled with Pickersgill, Forster threatened him with his pistol. Pickersgill now ordered all of his men to arm themselves, and several more pigs and bales of cloth were taken.

When a hostile crowd began to gather, Pickersgill ordered his men to fire over their heads; and as his people fled, Ta was so terrified by their actions that he fouled himself. They took two breastplates and a drum from Boba's house, and then ran towards the storehouse where the costumes and other items for the heiva were kept, and an old man and woman came out, each carrying a dog, half-kneeling and half-crawling in abasement. When they returned to the boat that night to sleep, Pickersgill told Ta that as soon as the stolen things were returned, they would give him back his treasures. Ta asked to be released, and soon returned with the mat-bag and most of the things which had been in it. The following morning when the last of the stolen items were returned, they gave back the things that they had taken, boarded the boat, visited several other bays to trade for bananas, and then returned to Ra'iatea.

During their absence, Cook had gone ashore to Reo's house, where a feast of roast pork and fermented *mahi* (breadfruit paste) had been prepared. His officers brought several bottles of wine, and after the meal, Reo tossed off his Madeira with the best of them. They found this very surprising, because most of the islanders detested strong liquor, preferring to drink the 'ava (the beverage made from the chewed root of the kava plant) which young Porea had begun to serve to visitors in the Great Cabin, often getting himself intoxicated in the process. After this meal, the officers distributed some of their pork to the young women who were present, but insisted that they should remove one item of clothing for each piece of pork that they were given. One of the gentlemen had a small padlock with him, and when one of these women begged for it, he clasped it in her pierced ear and threw away the key. She found the padlock too heavy but could not remove it from her ear, and wept bitterly until another key was found, and she was released from her burden. When they returned to the *Resolution* that afternoon, a man who was caught stealing shirts from the ship was tied up to the shrouds and punished with two dozen lashes. According to William Bayly, such punishments had already been instituted on board the *Adventure*.[31] After Johann Forster's criticisms of Cook's 'lenity', the *Resolution*'s officers were evidently determined to take a tough line with local offenders.

No canoes came out to the ships the following morning; and a rumour flew around the crews that two of the *Adventure*'s men, who had been on shore all night, had been murdered. When the matter was investigated further, however, it emerged that one of the *Adventure*'s crew had quarrelled with a local man, but when the sailor was confronted by three burly warriors, armed with clubs, he had taken to his heels. He and his shipmate found a place to sleep that night, where they were kindly treated. When they returned to the ship, Cook decided to try and calm things down, and went ashore to find Reo. Reo had moved away, but when they finally tracked him down, he embraced Cook, weeping and saying that some of his people had been killed by the Europeans. He had heard about Forster's quarrel with Cook and the rampage on Tahaa, and thought that Forster and Pickersgill had deserted the *Resolution*, and that he and his people would be taken as hostages. Cook assured him that this was not the case, and eventually persuaded him to return home to his settlement.

At the same time, however, Porea, who had accompanied Cook on this expedition, handed Cook's powder-horn to one of the sailors and disappeared. He had met a young woman on Ra'iatea, and had apparently decided that the Europeans were uncomfortable travelling companions. The news of his defection spread quickly, and that afternoon, George Forster was approached by a handsome, high-born young man named Hitihiti (also known as Mahine[32]), a relative of Puni, the high chief of Borabora, who said that he wanted to go with them to England. George told him that the voyage would be long and hard, but he was not deterred, and his friends echoed his entreaties. When George presented Hitihiti to Cook, he agreed that he could go with them, and they went out to the ship together.

The next day Cook and Furneaux visited Reo to invite him to dinner; and when Pickersgill and Forster returned to the *Resolution* that afternoon from Tahaa, Cook announced that he had decided to sail the next morning. Cook told Furneaux that he wanted to make his peace with Forster, and Furneaux privately advised Forster not to pursue the quarrel. As the sloops were being prepared for sailing the following day, Cook and Forster met in the Great Cabin, where they shook hands and agreed to settle their differences – a marked concession from Cook, who had realised on the matter of how to treat 'natives', he had few supporters. Shortly afterwards, Hitihiti's friends came out to say goodbye, weeping and presenting him with balls of fermented breadfruit, a favourite voyaging food.

On board the *Adventure*, however, Mai, the young man from Ra'iatea, was glad to be leaving the island. On shore one night, he had boasted that he was going to England to get guns to kill the Borabora men, and when they heard about this, a group of Borabora warriors stripped him naked

Hitihiti, the young man from Borabora who sailed with Cook on the Resolution

and made him run for his life. Once he got back to the ship, Mai refused to go ashore again; and left his home island with very mixed feelings.

Early on the morning of 17 September, as the ships were being unmoored, Reo came out with gifts of pigs and fruit for his taio Captain Cook. Cook gave him a broad-axe as a farewell present, and Reo asked him when he would return, urging him to bring his sons to Ra'iatea. Shortly afterwards the sloops sailed from Hamanino harbour and Cook set a course to the west, looking for the islands which Tupaia had been so eager to visit during the *Endeavour* voyage.

The sailors had been very impressed by their visit to Ra'iatea, and their encounters with the Borabora warriors. They called the male arioi from that island, with their prolific tattoos and their formidable fighting reputation, 'The Knights of Borabora'; and the *Resolution*'s midshipmen decided to call themselves 'The Knights of Tahiti', and had themselves tattooed with a large star on their chests. When the other sailors saw this insignia it became all the rage, and many of the men took this tattoo as a memento of their stay in the Society Islands. Eating dog became another mark of a Polynesian veteran. The midshipmen ate roasted dog in their mess, as Elliott remarked, 'merely from curiosity, and to say that we had eat dog', even when pork was available.[33] The sailors liked the Society Islanders, and Captain Cook spoke for most of them when he wrote:

The more one is acquainted with these people the better one likes them, to give them their due I must say they are the most obligeing and benevolent people I ever met with.[34]

As they sailed from Ra'iatea, Charles Clerke lamented:

I must own that 'tis with some reluctance I bid adieu to these happy Isles, where I've spent many very happy days; in the first place . . . you live upon and abound in the very best of Pork & the sweetest and most salutary of Vegetables; in the next place, the Women in general are very handsome and very kind, and the Men civil and to the last degree benevolent – in short, in my Opinion, they are as pleasant & Happy spots as this World contains.[35]

Although the men liked the Tahitians, they found their light-fingered ways infuriating, and many of them agreed with Johann Forster that their captain was too lenient with the islanders. On the whole, the sailors were in favour of swift, harsh punishments for theft, since they themselves were flogged for stealing. The officers recognised this, and at Ra'iatea several Tahitians who had stolen from the ship were flogged on board the *Resolution*, despite Cook's view that such thefts should not be taken too seriously. Cook was walking a narrow line on this issue, however, and he made no comment about the rampage on Tahaa when Forster, Pickersgill, and Rowe from the *Adventure* demonstrated their own approach to disciplining unruly 'natives'.

Once they reached the open sea, Hitihiti, the young Boraboran on the *Resolution*, was seasick, although he cured himself by eating raw fish and balls of fermented breadfruit. Their third day at sea was a Sunday and when the crew mustered for Divine Service on board the *Adventure*, Mai, the young Ra'iatean who had joined Furneaux's ship, thought that they intended to offer him as a human sacrifice to their god, until Burney assured him to the contrary. Several days later three small islands were sighted, which Cook named after his friend Augustus Hervey, a dashing naval captain.

On 2 October 1773, after an uneventful passage, the ships came to 'Eua, a small island in southern Tonga which Tasman had charted more than a century earlier. When they anchored off the north-west coast of 'Eua, a place which Cook named 'English Road', a local chief soon came on board and pressed noses with each of the officers, presenting them with gifts including bark-cloth, fine mats and kava. In return, Cook gave him a large piece of red cloth, a hatchet and some nails. When this man, Taione, led Cook ashore with Furneaux, the Forsters, Hitihiti and Mai, a huge crowd of people cried out in acclamation. Taione took them to his house where Cook ordered his bagpiper to play, and a group of women sang to them in harmony, snapping their fingers to the rhythm. Afterwards Cook and his companions walked inland to some plantations, where Taione took them to a house where they were served coconuts, bananas, and bowls of kava.

They were very impressed by the friendliness of the 'Eua people, their tidy houses surrounded by scented bushes and fenced gardens, the elaborate body tattoos of the men (which extended to their private parts, so that the sailors winced as they imagined the operation), and their finely fashioned canoes, war-clubs, spears, musical instruments, mats and other items. After dinner, when they went back on shore, Taione gave them a meal at his house, and loaded the boats with presents. Although Mai and Hitihiti tried to communicate with the 'Eua people, they could not understand Tongan (since Western Polynesian languages are quite different from those of the east), although they could pick up a few words here and there. And as they worked with the Forsters on a vocabulary of Tahitian and their descriptions of customs in the Society Islands, it became obvious that the two young men were at odds with each other. Hitihiti was a close relative of Puni, the high chief of Borabora, whom Mai hated for invading his home island; and one morning when Hitihiti saw a kingfisher in the Great Cabin which the Forsters had shot, greeting it respectfully as 'the god of Puni', Mai laughed and retorted that Puni's god had been eaten by the Europeans.

They could find no watering place on 'Eua, so Cook decided to leave the island. The next morning the sloops sailed to the adjacent island of Tongatapu, the headquarters of the sacred chiefs of the Tongan archipelago. As they sailed up the west coast, people waved to them with little white flags; and Cook anchored off the district of Hihifo on the north-west side of the island. Early the following morning a man named Ataongo[36] came out to the ship, and gave gifts to Cook, exchanging names with him. He guided them ashore at a nearby beach (Pokula), where they were welcomed by another large and rapturous crowd. Cook and Furneaux distributed gifts, and asked to take a walk in the countryside. Ataongo guided them along a lane to a nearby fa'itoka, or chiefly burial place, where a sacred house stood on an oblong mound faced with a stone wall. After a ritual

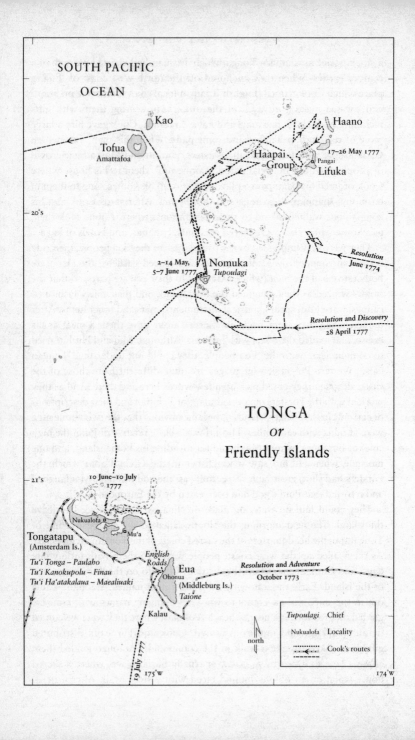

SOUTH PACIFIC
OCEAN

Kao

Tofua
Amattafoa

Haano

17–26 May 1777

Haapai
Group   Pangai

Lifuka

—20°S

Resolution
June 1774

2–14 May,
5–7 June 1777

Nomuka
Tupoulagi

Resolution and Discovery
28 April 1777

TONGA
or
Friendly Islands

—21°S

10 June–10 July
1777

Nukualofa

Mu'a

Tongatapu
(Amsterdam Is.)

Tu'i Tonga – Paulaho
Tu'i Kanokupolu – Finau
Tu'i Ha'atakalaua – Maealiuaki

*English
Roads*

Eua
(Middleburg Is.)

Ohonua

Taione

Resolution and Adventure
October 1773

Kalau

Tupoulagi	Chief
Nukualofa	Locality
	Cook's routes

north

19 July 1777

175°W

174°W

conducted by three elderly men, Cook was shown into the house, where he saw two crude images standing, and an oval mound of bluish pebbles (*kilikili*, a sign of mourning) which marked a burial site,[37] where he placed beads and medals as a sign of respect. Cook considered the landscape of Tongatapu idyllic:

I thought I was transported into one of the most fertile plains in Europe, here was not an inch of waste ground, the roads occupied no more space than was absolutely necessary . . . Nature, assisted by a little art, no where appears in a more florishing state than at this isle.[38]

Afterwards he walked along shady roads between the plantations to another fa'itoka, possibly at Mu'a, the sacred heart of the island, where a second ritual was conducted. Back on the ship for dinner, Ataongo introduced Cook to an elderly, near-blind chief (no doubt a person of superior status, since Ataongo could eat with him, but only by turning his back), who joined Cook and Furneaux for a meal of fish and a glass of wine.

That afternoon Cook and his companions returned inland, where the Tongatapu people offered them 'curiosities'. Mai and Hitihiti were amazed to find that these included garments and lengths of bark-cloth decorated with red feathers, prized items in the Society Islands. They bartered for some of these treasures themselves, and Hitihiti advised Captain Cook to obtain as many red feathers as possible to use as gifts when he returned to Tahiti. Afterwards, the two captains were taken back to the second burial place, where the old chief offered a pretty young woman to Cook, although he refused to sleep with her. It is clear that the sailors had no such scruples, however. That afternoon a number of naked women swam out to the sloops, and when they were persuaded to come on board, as George Forster remarked, 'our seamen took advantage of their disposition, and once more offered to our eyes a scene worthy of the Cyprian temples.'[39]

Next morning when Ataongo came to the ship for breakfast, Cook gave him a sheet and a piece of red baize and Hodges sketched his portrait. As he left the cabin, Ataongo saw a Tahitian dog and clapped his hands on his chest for joy, saying 'Kuli' or dog (there were no dogs on these islands, although the Tongans knew of them from their visits to Fiji), so Cook gave him a dog and a bitch as a present. When Ataongo went ashore, the old chief came up to him and took the dogs away from him, a privilege that went with superior status. Although Cook's initial reception at 'Eua and Tongatapu had been warm, his patience was about to be tested to the limit. When the pinnace rowed ashore to the trading-place, a man dived beneath it and seized the grappling iron, and as they landed, some men tried to wrestle the oars from the sailors. A party of marines was sent to protect the pinnace, but as they rowed ashore, a man stole a jacket from one of the boat's crew, swimming away with it under water. One of the gentlemen on board the *Resolution* cried out a warning, and the men in the boat fired at the thief, but missed him. As he ran ashore, the thief was fired at with smallshot which hit him in the cheek, and several other people were wounded, while their compatriots calmly carried on trading.

While the thief was being chased on the water, George Forster was attacked in the forest. He and Sparrman had gone ashore to look for new species of plants, and when they were separated for a moment, a man tried to take Forster's musket from him. As they struggled, he yelled out for Sparrman and the man ran away; so they decided to go back to the *Resolution*. Soon after they returned to the ship, a man climbed through the scuttle into the master's cabin, where he took some log-books, the *Daily Assistant* and *Nautical Almanack*, a sword, a ruler and a volume of Pope's *Homer*. As soon as he was seen getting back into his canoe, the pinnace set off in hot pursuit, and the thief threw all of these things into the water. When a musketball struck the stern of his canoe, its crew jumped overboard. As the thief was chased in the water he kept diving out of reach, even unshipping the boat's rudder until one of the sailors hooked him in the ribs with a boat-hook and hauled him into the pinnace. Although Ataongo and some other chiefs saw what was happening, they seemed unconcerned. There was little sympathy for thieves in Tonga, especially if they happened to be commoners. The *Resolution*'s men were also unsympathetic, for as William Wales remarked, 'their Audacity and our lenity had been Carried now to such lengths that they had several times attempted to take the Cloaths of our Back';[40] and they wanted to see the offenders punished.

The following morning Cook went ashore, where the officers introduced him to a high-ranking individual, a middle-aged man named 'Latoo-Nipooroo' (Latunipulu).[41] Pickersgill and the others, who had seen the Tongans prostrating themselves before this man, kissing his feet and placing them on their heads,[42] were told he was the '*eiki* of the island. They thought that this meant 'high chief', but in Tonga the term referred to the direct descendants of the sacred chief Tu'i Tonga or their sisters, and Latu was sister's son to the current holder of that title. In Tongan society, which was ruled by a system of hereditary titles, sisters outranked their brothers, and this gave their sons many privileges.[43] Pickersgill took this man by the arms and led him to the landing-place, where he sat in 'sullen and stupid gravity'. When they presented Latu to Cook, and Cook gave him a shirt, a piece of red cloth, a looking-glass and some medals, he sat in absolute silence, not looking to right or left, so that Cook took him for an idiot.[44]

That afternoon, however, Latu sent a gift of pigs, roast bananas, sour bread and yams out to Cook. Cook had already decided to leave the island, but as the sloops were being unmoored the next morning, he went ashore with Johann Forster, carrying farewell gifts for the high chief. Ataongo guided him to a place where Latu was waiting, and Cook greeted him by pressing noses, then presented him with a white shirt, some red cloth, a brass kettle, a saw and a number of other items. Latu sat there impassively, although afterwards when Ataongo and an old woman (Latu's mother, the female Tu'i Tonga) talked to him, he laughed and then left the gathering. Now that the formalities were concluded, Forster began to barter for curiosities, but when a man took a nail without making any return, Forster struck him with a heavy wooden dart he had just purchased, and as the man went to return the blow, he struck him on the back with his hanger, wounding him slightly. As this man ran away, the other Tongans laughed, and did not seem particularly worried.

When Cook made his farewells to the assembled elders, they 'express'd niether sorrow nor joy at our departure'. Ataongo, however, begged him to return, bringing him a uniform like his own. Cook was grateful to this chief for his assistance, and farewelled him with regret: 'He constantly came aboard every Morning soon after it was light and never quited me during the remainder of the day, he was always ready either aboard or a shore to do me all the service that lay in his power, his fidelity was rewarded at small expence and I found my account in having such a friend.'[45] Nevertheless, by changing names with a lesser chief, Cook had diminished his own status in Tongan society. As they sailed away from the island, a canoe carrying four men came out and paddled alongside the *Resolution*, one man drumming furiously. Cook gave these people gifts, and when the canoe turned back to Tongatapu, the two ships headed southwards to New Zealand. Once again, Johann Forster quoted Virgil in his journal:

'Altogether they veered out the sheet, and let the sails out now to port then to starboard: together they turned and turned the yards high above: The winds they wanted carried the fleet along.'[46]

II

A Feast at Grass Cove

After leaving Tongatapu, the sloops cruised past the small island of Ata, in gentle winds and fine weather. On the night of 17 October as they sailed through a school of luminous jellyfish, Johann Forster exclaimed that 'the Sea seems to include Stars in its bosom'.[1] They were still feasting on pork which had been salted in the Society Islands, and the mood on board was cheerful as they headed for the east coast of the North Island of New Zealand. On 21 October 1773 Table Cape was sighted, but no canoes came out, so Cook headed south to Cape Kidnappers, intending to visit Queen Charlotte Sound before crossing the Pacific again in search of Terra Australis Incognita.

When they passed the Cape, two canoes came out, one richly carved and carrying two chiefs whom Cook invited on board the *Resolution*. These people had obviously heard about the shootings off Cape Kidnappers during Cook's visit in the *Endeavour* four years earlier, because the first thing they said when they boarded the sloop was '*Mataku no te pupu!*' ['We are afraid of guns!'] The leading chief, a man named Tuanui, was fascinated by the ship, examining the cabin, the hold, the gun-room and the masts and rigging with great attention; and when Cook presented him with several large spike nails, he was so enthralled that the gifts of livestock and seed he was given next seemed an anticlimax. He presented Cook with his weapon, and he and his companions performed a rousing haka in gratitude. Although Hitihiti tried to talk with this chief, offering him gifts of coconuts and yams, he could not make himself understood, and Tuanui largely ignored him, fixing his attention instead on Cook as the leader of the expedition. Neither Hitihiti nor Mai shared Tupaia's linguistic abilities, which the high priest had developed during his arioi expeditions to various Pacific Islands. They were just adventurous young men who lacked Tupaia's charisma, his deep knowledge of traditional matters and his mana or spiritual power.

As the sloops sailed south, a terrible storm blew up overnight, splitting the sails and battering the vessels. For days, they were beset by high winds and huge waves, which swept across the decks, soaking beds and hammocks.

As Johann Forster was thrown against the sides of his cot, listening to the sailors' volleys of curses and oaths as they struggled with ropes and sails, he regretted that he had ever left England. At the height of the storm, the ships lost sight of each other, and were separated. Cook thought that the *Adventure* must have run for shelter into Queen Charlotte Sound, and on 2 November he took the *Resolution* into Raukawa-moana (Cook Strait), anchoring briefly off Whanganui-a-Tara, now Wellington Harbour. The next morning when they sailed into the Sound, however, there was no sign of the *Adventure*.

On 3 November 1773 when the *Resolution* anchored in Ship Cove, several canoes came out, and Cook recognised some of these people from his *Endeavour* visit three years earlier. He was soon told that the two goats left behind during his last visit in April had been killed and eaten, and that the boar and sow had been carried away to different parts of the country. He found this news frustrating, for as George Forster exclaimed:

By separating the animals, and dividing them as a spoil, these barbarians effectually destroy the possibility of propagating the species. Too preoccupied with the wants of the present moment, they overlook the only means of securing a certain livelihood to themselves, and reject every attempt to civilize them.[2]

Still, the gardens of European plants were thriving, although the people had dug up most of the potatoes, and rats had chewed the peas and beans. Hitihiti visited one of these cultivations with the Forsters, where they found a flock of small birds feeding on the seed-heads of radishes and turnips. Hitihiti, who had never used a musket before, shot a *pipiwharauroa* [shining cuckoo] at his first attempt. As Johann remarked, many of the Society Islanders had remarkable eyesight, and could often discern birds on the water or in the undergrowth which none of the Europeans could detect. Johann was delighted to be back in New Zealand, because it was now summertime and the plants were flowering, and he could finally classify his New Zealand plant collections.

Over the next few days, canoes began to arrive at Ship Cove, bringing fish and weapons to exchange for nails and Tahitian bark-cloth. On 10 November, Te Wahanga and his family (including his small son Koa), who had got to know the British during their previous visit to the Sound, arrived with quantities of greenstone chisels and axes. They had learned which items Cook's men particularly prized, and collected these things in some quantity. The canoes also brought women, and the sailors resumed their nightly revels, which Hitihiti joined in with alacrity. Unlike Tupaia, Hitihiti found it difficult to understand or speak Maori, although he shared Tupaia's chauvinistic attitudes. He delighted in pointing out the disadvantages of the Maori way of life, and recommended various improvements; urging the local people to cultivate yams and coconuts, although these plants were out of their climatic range in Queen Charlotte Sound. This did not endear him to Maori, and his lack of linguistic expertise and his youthful inexperience made him of limited use to Cook during this brief visit to New Zealand.

By 15 November, Cook was increasingly concerned about the *Adventure*, and he and the Forsters climbed a high hill in East Bay to see if they could see the consort vessel anywhere in the Strait, or along the eastern coastline. There was no sign of the *Adventure*, however, so he decided to leave the Sound as soon as possible to try and find her. When the Maori gathered in the Sound were told that the *Resolution*'s departure was imminent, they decided to acquire one last load of trade goods to barter with the sailors. On 21 November, a group of women came to Ship Cove, saying that their menfolk had gone westward to fight in Admiralty Bay. The next morning, a flotilla of seven or eight canoes arrived triumphantly back in the Sound, paddled by warriors with their hair tied up, their faces painted with red ochre, and their canoes laden with cloaks, weapons and greenstone. Soon afterwards, some of these men came alongside and began to barter 'curiosities' with the sailors; and George Forster realised that they had gone raiding specifically for this purpose. Cook had gone to a remote part of the Sound to drop off a pair of pigs, and hens and cocks in the hope they might breed there undisturbed, and when he returned he was told that some of his men had just found chewed thighbones at a shoreline hamlet. He ordered the tents to be struck and everything brought on board, and ordered a sailor who had taken hatchets and other 'curiosities' from a hut to be given a flogging. That night he wrote in his journal:

It has ever been a maxim with me to punish the least crimes any of my people have commited against these uncivilized Nations, their robbing us with impunity is by no means a sufficient reason why we should treat them in the same manner . . .

The best method in my opinion to preserve a good understanding with such people is first to shew them the use of fire arms and to convince them of the Superiority they give you over them and to be always upon your guard; when once they are sencible of these things, a regard for their own safety will deter them from disturbing you or being unanimous in forming any plan to attack you, and Strict honisty and gentle treatment on your part will make it their intrest not to do it.[3]

Despite the debate with Johann Forster and this new evidence of Maori cannibalism, Cook was upholding the disciplinary policies forged during the *Endeavour* voyage. This was perhaps easier when he did not have the

Adventure beside him, with Furneaux's 'rough and ready' approach to discipline (as well as hygiene and diet) to undermine his own regime with the sailors. Nevertheless, many of his men regarded 'savages' as fair game and disagreed with their captain's defence of their rights, resenting his punishment of crimes against the 'natives'.

On 23 November, Cook, the Forsters and William Wales went with Hitihiti for a last-minute check on the gardens on Motuaro. At the same time, Pickersgill and some of the other officers went across to Indian Cove, where they found some women weeping and cutting their foreheads with slivers of obsidian, a sign of mourning. Nearby, a group of warriors was cutting up the body of a young man whom they had killed in the raid on Admiralty Bay. His heart had been stuck on a forked stick and fixed to the prow of their largest canoe, while his head (with its jawbone removed and placed in the canoe), intestines, liver and lungs were lying on the ground. These men explained that some of their party had been killed in the recent raid, and they had been able to bring away the body of only one of their enemies. One of these warriors skewered the discarded lungs with his spear and with 'great gayety' (no doubt teasing the British) brought them up to Pickersgill's mouth, offering him a taste. Pickersgill refused, but offered two nails for the head, which he carried back to the *Resolution*.[4] The head was of a young man about fifteen years old, who had been killed by a blow to the temple. When this grisly trophy was brought on board, Charles Clerke, the ship's humorist, famous for his practical jokes, decided to conduct a mock barbecue. He cut a piece of flesh from the cheek and took it to the galley, where he grilled this 'steak' on a gridiron. He then carried the sizzling meat up to the quarterdeck and offered it to a man from another part of the Sound, who ate it with evident pleasure, 'suck[ing] his fingers half a dozen times over in raptures'.[5]

Shortly after this, Cook and his companions arrived back from Motuaro. When Cook realised what was happening he asked Clerke to repeat the demonstration. Some of the sailors laughed, saying that the warriors had 'been on a hunting party and got a buck', while others cried out in disgust or vomited. Hitihiti, however, stood stock-still, 'as if Metamorphosed into the Statue of Horror', and then burst into tears, telling both Clerke and the warriors that 'they were Vile men, and he was no longer their friend', and ran off when the local people laughed at him. Charles Clerke was unrepentant, however. His parody of a scientific experiment mocked both scientists and cannibals; while in their finger-licking responses, Maori were mocking both Europeans and Hitihiti, the young Polynesian. Most of the witnesses, however, were horrified by this display, which provoked a great outpouring in the journals.

James Cook was relatively cool, concluding that Maori cannibalism was the result of ancestral habit:

That the New Zealanders are Canibals can now no longer be doubted, the account I gave of it in my former Voyage was partly founded on circumstances and was, as I afterwards found, discredited by many people . . . The New Zealanders are certainly in a state of civilization, their behaviour to us has been Manly and Mild, shewing allways a readiness to oblige us; they have some arts a mong them which they execute with great judgement and unweared patience; they are far less addicted to thieving than the other Islanders and are I believe strictly honist among them-selves.

This custom of eating their enimies slain in battle (for I firmly believe they eat the flesh of no others) has undoubtedly been handed down to them from the earliest times and we know that it is not an easy matter to break a nation of its ancient customs . . . As they become more united they will of concequence have fewer Enemies and become more civilized and then and not till then this custom may be forgot.[6]

Cook, who had fought in naval battles and watched men torn to pieces by cannonballs and splinters,[7] was also familiar with naval customs such as flogging and keel-hauling. Like many of the sailors he had a phlegmatic view of military violence (both Polynesian and European).

George Forster, the young German naturalist, on the other hand, who had little direct experience of warfare, compared Maori cannibalism with contemporary practices in Europe. He must have read Montaigne's essay on cannibalism, for he echoed the French philosopher by asking why civilised cruelty should seem virtuous for being detached:

Though we are too much polished to be canibals, we do not find it unnaturally and savagely cruel to take the field, and to cut one another's throats by thousands, without a single motive, besides the ambition of a prince, or the caprice of his mistress! Is it not from prejudice that we are disgusted with the idea of eating a dead man, when we feel no remorse in depriving him of life? A New Zeelander, who kills and eats his enemy, is a very different being from a European, who, for his amuse-ment, tears an infant from the mother's breast, in cool blood, and throws it on the earth to feed his hounds.[8]

Sparrman, his Swedish colleague, cited accounts of European cannibalism during famines and riots to make a similar point; while William Wales, the empirically minded British astronomer, wrote up the episode as though he had been witnessing a Royal Society experiment (as perhaps he had, at least in parody):

From this Transaction the following Corollaries are evidently deducible, viz.

1st) They do not, as I supposed might be the Case, eat them only on the spot whilst under the Impulse of that wild Frenzy into which they have shewn us they can & do work themselves in their Engagements; but in cool Blood: For it was now many Days since the Battle could have happened.

2d) That it is not their Enemies only whom they may chance to kill in War; but even any whom they meet with who are not known Friends: since those who eat the part of the head on board, could not know whether it belonged to a friend or enemy. [Here he underestimated the efficiency of local communications.]

3d) It cannot be through want of Annimal food; because they every day caught as much Fish as served both themselves and us: they have moreover plenty of fine Dogs which they were at the same time selling us for mere trifles; nor is there any want of various sorts of fowl, which they can readily kill if they please.

4th) It seems therefore to follow of course, that their practice of this horrid Action is from Choice, and the liking which they have for this kind of Food; and this was but too visibly shewn in their eagerness for, and the satisfaction which they testified in eating, those inconsiderable scrapts, of the worst part on board the Ship.[9]

By this process of deduction Wales concluded that Maori were cannibal epicures, inspired by a liking for human flesh to kill and eat each other. Hitihiti, though, found Clerke's demonstration agonising. Once again, a Tahitian reacted against Maori cannibalism more strongly than many of the Europeans. Some of the crew considered this funny, although this was probably the last time that any of Cook's men laughed at the custom of *kai tangata* [eating people].

Of them all, Hitihiti had the best understanding of what was going on, because Maori cannibalism had much in common with human sacrifice and the offering of jawbones in the Society Islands. From a Maori point of view, when the warriors cut off the head of their victim, stuck his heart on a forked stick and fixed it to the prow of their canoe, they were completing a victory. In battle, the *mana* [sacred power] of both gods and their descendants was at stake. If they gained the victory, warriors fed the life force or *hau* of their enemies to their ancestor gods in the *whangai hau* [literally, feeding the hau] ceremony, offering up body parts such as the head, liver and heart, where the life force was concentrated, or ritually eating them. This avenged the insult that had sparked off the conflict, and at the same time nullified the power of the enemy gods, who might otherwise spiritually attack them. When Lieutenant Clerke cut some flesh from the cheek of the hapless warrior on the taffrail of the *Resolution* and grilled it on a gridiron, he was joining the power of his ancestors to those of the victors. This complicity was not forgotten by the dead man's friends and relations, and Clerke's joke was to have cruel consequences.

Shortly after this display, Cook and his men left Queen Charlotte Sound, leaving a message in a bottle in Ship Cove for Furneaux; and sailed north as far as Cape Palliser, looking for the *Adventure*. Less than a week later, the *Adventure* sailed south into the Sound, searching for her consort. They had also been blown off the coast, but had sought refuge in Tolaga Bay on the east coast of the North Island, which Cook had visited and charted during the *Endeavour* voyage. There the people had supplied them with crayfish, and asked after Tupaia, whose memory still remained vivid among them. When they were told about his death, they composed a lament, which Lieutenant Burney transcribed in his journal: 'A koe mate aue Tupaia' – 'You have died – alas, Tupaia!' Although Mai, the young Ra'iatean, was on board the *Adventure*, he was just a commoner; and while he may have basked in Tupaia's reflected glory, the local people soon forgot him.

During this brief visit to Tolaga Bay, some of the *Adventure*'s officers came across a canoe which held the body of a woman lying in state, decorated with feathers and ornaments. They inspected the body, breaching the tapu [sacred restriction] on such burials; and the next day a keg of brandy was stolen from the wooding and watering party. Jack Rowe, the hot-headed master's mate who had participated in the escapade on Tahaa, wanted to seize some hostages to ensure its return, but Lieutenant Burney would not allow this. As he remarked unsympathetically in his log, 'this I thought dangerous as the Zealanders were too numerous – and all our Empty casks ashore – if Sailors won't take care of their Grogg, they deserve to lose it.'[10] After three days in the Bay, they headed south to the rendezvous at Queen Charlotte Sound. Although they did not know that the *Resolution*'s men had seen human flesh being eaten, they were about to experience an even more compelling demonstration of Maori cannibalism.

When the *Adventure* came to an anchor in Ship Cove on 30 November, Furneaux was bitterly disappointed to see no sign of the *Resolution*. He sent his men ashore, and they came back with a note which they had found in a bottle buried beneath a stump carved with the message, 'LOOK UNDER-NEATH'. Cook's message was brief, and scrawled in haste. It was dated six days earlier and explained that he intended to cruise off the Sound for several days, looking for the *Adventure*. It ended:

As Captain Cook has not the least hopes of meeting with Captn Furneaux he will not take upon him to name any place for a Rendezvous, he however thinks of retiring to Easter Island . . . about the latter end of next March – it is even probable that he may go to Otaheite or one of the Society Isles but this will depend so much on Circumstances, that nothing with any degree of certainty can be determined upon – James Cook.[11]

Mai was present when the message was unearthed, and was so struck by this method of communication that he decided to learn how to read and write. According to Burney, however, 'so many people gave him paper, pens etc and set him copies & tasks that in a weeks time the poor fellow's head was bothered – too many Cooks spoilt the Broth.'[12] Burney had taken Mai under his wing during the voyage from Ra'iatea, and when the shore camp was set up for the wooding and watering party and Bayly's observatory, Burney was in charge, and Mai slept in his tent and accompanied him on every excursion.

From the outset of the *Adventure*'s visit to the Sound, the inhabitants were hostile. Clerke's mock barbecue had infuriated the family of the young man who had been killed, and there may have been other offences, unreported in the journals. The sailors' goods were also irresistible, inciting daring attempts at theft. On 9 December, for instance, the sentry at the shore camp left his post at midnight to get some tobacco. When he came back, he saw a man sitting by the fire, who crept into the bush as soon as he was noticed. The sentry raised the alarm and woke everybody up. Although they searched the surrounding bush, they found nothing and eventually went back to bed. Bayly told the sentry to wake him if he saw anything else, and before long the sentry roused him again, saying that he had just seen a canoe crossing the bay. It was a bright, moonlit night, and soon they saw two more canoes out on the water, coming to join the first canoe, now hidden under overhanging bushes. Bayly sent the sentry to wake the others, and went down to the beach. The three canoes were coming around the rocks, hugging the shore in the darkness. Bayly called out to their crews in Tahitian, saying that he would kill them if they did not go away. After talking with each other for a moment, one of the canoes came slowly forward, so Bayly fired over their heads, and they paddled off at high speed. Nothing further was seen of the intruders that night, although the camp stayed on alert until daybreak.

On 12 December, the first Lieutenant, Samuel Kemp, Burney, Mai and Jack Rowe, the master's mate, had a 'narrow escape' in Watapu (Shag Cove). Apart from this bare fact, nothing more was reported in the journals, although very likely, it involved some kind of violent confrontation. Two days later a number of canoes arrived at the shore camp, apparently spying on the British. That night Bayly stayed up late, observing the stars. He took some altitudes of stars to the east and then went to bed, setting his alarm for a later observation of stars to the west. Some time later the lid of his tool-box, which he had wedged against the door of his tent, rattled loudly, jolting him awake. He grabbed his gun and jumped out of bed, calling out, 'Who is there?', but nobody answered. Soon afterwards when his alarm went off, he got dressed, but could not find his hat. When he came out of the tent he found the lid of his tool-box lying on the ground, and feeling around in the dark, realised that his hatchet, saw and hammer were missing. He went to the camp-fire, where the sentry was sitting, to accuse him of the theft. Protesting his innocence, the sentry lighted a lantern and went with Bayly to the beach, but they could see no sign of any intruders. As they returned to the camp, however, Bayly saw a man coming out of the ship's tent, holding something in his hands. He couldn't tell whether this was one of his shipmates, so he called out, 'Who are you?' The man started, dropping his load, and ran towards the bush that encircled the clearing. Bayly ran after him, but just as he was about to club him with the butt of his musket, he tripped over a rock in the darkness. Jumping to his feet, Bayly took a shot at the man as he disappeared into the bush.

By now the camp was in an uproar, with people tumbling out of the tents to see what was happening. The musket shot had also alerted the sentry on the *Adventure*, and Furneaux sent two armed boats to investigate. In the meantime, Bayly and one of the sailors were running along the rocky shore, hoping to intercept the intruders. Soon Bayly heard a Maori whisper a warning, 'Hist! Hist!', so he answered and moved towards the sound, but dislodged a stone which rattled on the rocks. As the warrior ran away, Bayly shot at him with his musket loaded with ball, but missed. Further along the shore, he found a pile of things that had been stolen from the camp on the rocks, with a canoe loaded with other stolen goods nearby, which they confiscated. The next morning they found a trail of blood along the beach, indicating that one of the raiding party had been wounded; and that night a large meteor flashed across the sky, warning of death and disaster.

Furneaux now ordered his men to prepare the ship to leave the Sound, and on 17 December, some Maori came out to ask for the return of their canoe. Since they would soon be leaving the Sound, Burney handed it over. Furneaux sent Jack Rowe (his kinsman, whom he had promoted to acting lieutenant) with an armed party to Whareunga Bay (named Grass Cove by Cook) to gather wild greens, with strict instructions to be back by mid-afternoon at the latest. Bayly and another armed party went off in a small boat to collect greens and flax, but when they returned to the *Adventure*, there was no sign of the cutter. That night when the cutter's party failed to return to the ship, Furneaux was worried, and the next morning he sent Burney, the ship's second lieutenant, in the launch with Mai and an armed party of sailors and marines, to search for their comrades. After examining several bays without success, they came to a small cove where a large double canoe was hauled up on the beach. Two men were standing by it, who ran off as the launch approached. Burney searched the canoe and to his dismay, found one of the cutter's rowlock ports in it, a shoe belonging to a midshipman, and a piece of meat, which they thought might be dog's flesh. Nearby on the beach they saw about twenty food baskets, tied up. When they cut these open they found them packed with roasted meat and fern-root, still warm from the fire. Burney hoped that this might also be dog's flesh, but soon they found more shoes and a hand tattooed 'T.H'. This was unmistakeably the hand of Thomas Hill, a sailor who had worn this tattoo since their stay in Tahiti. Behind the beach they saw a circle of freshly dug ground about four feet in diameter, almost certainly an earth oven. As the marines feverishly began to dig with a cutlass, Burney prepared to burn the canoe, but a great plume of smoke billowed up from one of the nearby hills and they hurried back to the launch.

By now it was almost dusk. They rowed the launch to Grass Cove, the adjacent bay, where they found canoes hauled up on the beach and hundreds of people gathered along the shore and on the hillside. According to Burney there was a large fire on the hill behind the cove, and 'the place was throng'd like a Fair'. As the launch approached the beach some people began to taunt the sailors, calling out and gesturing for them to come ashore. Burney ordered his men to fire muskets and musketoons at will into the crowd. At the first volley the people seemed stunned; at the second volley they broke and ran for the trees, howling with fear and pain. The wall-guns were then loaded and fired, and the marines kept on shooting until nobody was left in sight. Burney left Fannin, the ship's master, to guard the boat, and searched the beach with a party of marines. They found one of the cutter's oars broken and stuck upright in the ground, and behind the beach 'such a shocking scene of Carnage & Barbarity as can never be mentiond or thought of, but with horror'.[13] Dogs were chewing at the discarded entrails of four or five men, and they found the eyes, hearts, lungs, livers and heads of their comrades, including the head of Furneaux's black servant, various feet, and Rowe's left hand (identified by its scarred forefinger) roasting on fires or scattered on the ground. Fannin called out that he could hear people shouting in the valley, perhaps preparing to attack, so they hastily gathered up some of these body parts and hurried back to the launch. They fired one last volley at a large crowd of people gathered on a hillside up the valley, and left the cove in darkness as it began to rain and a huge fire flared up further along the Sound. As John Marra said in his retrospective account, 'the Lieutenant

The Adventure's *men find the remains of their comrades at Grass Cove in Queen Charlotte Sound, New Zealand*

not thinking it safe to trust the crew in the dark, in an open boat, within reach of such cruel barbarians, ordered the canoes to be broken up and destroyed; and, after carefully collecting the remains of our mangled companions, they made the best of their way from this polluted place.'[14] Now that Europeans had become the objects of Maori cannibalism, nobody was laughing.

When Burney and his men got back to the *Adventure* at about eleven o'clock that night, they told Furneaux what had happened. It is not difficult to imagine the shock and horror on board the ship. Although Furneaux had lost ten of his best men, including his kinsman Jack Rowe, he decided to carry on across the Pacific in high southern latitudes, still looking for the Southern Continent. Early the next morning the *Adventure* hoisted her anchors and fled to the entrance of the Sound, but could not get out because of contrary winds. The human remains rescued from Grass Cove were tied in a hammock with ballast and shot and buried at sea, and that night 'every Body on board [slept] under Arms expecting the Canibals to be down and board us'.[15] The next day they escaped at last, heading south-east across the Pacific. On 22 December, the clothing and personal effects of the murdered men were sold before the mast, according to the old sea custom. As they headed into the high latitudes, the men began to freeze, and were once again plagued with scurvy. It seemed that there was no end to their sufferings on this interminable voyage; on reaching 56 degrees south, Furneaux gave up and headed for Cape Horn, sailing eastwards across the Pacific. After rounding the Horn and crossing the Atlantic, and a brief stay at the Cape of Good Hope, they turned north and on 14 July 1774, the *Adventure* anchored at Spithead.

Perhaps because Mai captivated King George and his court upon his arrival in England, reaction to the loss of the *Adventure*'s men was muted. Joseph Banks noted in a letter to his mother, 'ten of the Adventure's people have been rosted & Eaten by our friends in New Zeland',[16] while Fanny Burney exclaimed, 'I am heartily glad they *are* returned, & I hope that a Country so savage as New Zealand will never more be visited by my Brother.'[17] For the rest of his life, however, James Burney, that bluff, kind-hearted seaman, could only speak of the terrible events in Grass Cove in a whisper.[18]

A Pacific Odyssey

After leaving Queen Charlotte Sound on 25 November 1773, narrowly missing the *Adventure*, Captain Cook and his shipmates had headed south-east across the Pacific. Although the *Adventure* was on her way home, the *Resolution*'s voyage was just beginning. In the Sound, Cook had decided to spend the summer searching the high Pacific latitudes for the Southern Continent, and after that to sail back to England via Cape Horn, or else head to the tropics for the winter. As the *Resolution* sailed southwards, the daylight hours became longer and temperatures fell sharply, and on 7 December they calculated that they had reached the Antipodes of London. Cook ordered the last cask of beer to be tapped for the crew, who drank 'health to the King and Royal Family, and to all their good friends in England'. As the officers and gentlemen gathered in the Great Cabin, Wales jested that 'the good People of that City may *now* rest perfectly satisfied that they have no Antipodes besides Penguines and Peteralls, unless Seals can be admitted as such; for Fishes are absolutely out of the question.'[19]

On 12 December at 62 degrees south, they saw their first iceberg. Hitihiti was amazed by this 'white land', and by the hail or 'white stones' they met with in the far South. At New Zealand he had collected a bundle of twigs, naming one of these for each island they had visited, and now he added one to his tally for this *whenua teatea* [bright land], which he described as 'white, evil, useless'.[20] On 15 December as the *Resolution* sailed through a field of ice islands, which reminded the men of dragons, wrecked ships or ruined churches, the officer on watch steered windward of a huge mountain of ice, which towered high over the mastheads. When the wind began to drive the ship towards it, he yelled out a warning; Cook rushed on deck, ordering the sailors to grab light spars to try and fend off this iceberg and watching helplessly as the sloop was blown into its backwash. Fortunately they just missed it, by the narrowest of margins.

Several days later, the *Resolution* crossed the Antarctic Circle for the second time. In these high southern latitudes where it sleeted and snowed, the rigging hung with icicles, and working the ship became a nightmare. The ropes were like wires, the sails were frozen stiff, and when the wind blew, the hull and decks leaked, drenching the men's bedding and hammocks. They began to suffer from rheumatic pains, swollen glands and severe headaches. Cook had a fire lit in the Great Cabin, where the officers and gentlemen went to try and thaw out, and Hitihiti sat there unpicking the red feathers from the garments he had acquired in Tongatapu, or working with the Forsters on their vocabulary of Tahitian. According to Johann Forster, conditions on board were intolerable:

The Sea is now tempestuous, the Decks are never dry, all the Ship moist & damp; my Cabin cold & open to the piercing winds, full of unwholesome effluvia and vapours, every thing I touch is moist & mouldy & looks more like a subterraneous mansion for the dead than a habitation for the living. In the Captain's Cabin there are broken panes, the apartment full of currents & smoke, a parcel of damp Sails spread, & a couple of Sailmakers at work, now & then discharging the mephitic Air from the pease & Sower-krout they have eaten, & besides 5 or 6 people constantly in it; so that it cannot be reckoned one of the most comfortable places neither: if to this we add that there the pitching of the Ship is more felt, than any where else it will clearly appear, that these Expeditions are the most difficult task that could be imposed on poor mortals.[21]

He and his son were exempt from the work of running the ship, however, and his shipmates found his grizzling infuriating. They were no doubt relieved when on 23 December Johann took to his bed, and stayed there for most of January.

On Christmas Day 1773, Cook invited his officers and chief mates to dinner, while the crew feasted on a double helping of pudding, washed down with copious draughts of brandy. The wind had died and as they drifted among the icebergs, they joked that if they were wrecked, they would at least die happy, each clutching a keg of brandy. Observing his shipmates, George Forster described the sailors as 'a body of uncivilized men, rough, passionate, revengeful, but likewise brave, sincere, and true to each other' – very like Cook's description of Maori. That night the sun did not set, to Hitihiti's utter astonishment. By now they had reached 65 degrees south, and the drunken sailors reeled and cursed on the deck, surrounded by icebergs which looked like 'the wrecks of a shattered world'.[22] After eighteen months at sea, most of the food on board was rotten or tasteless, and the men had been on reduced rations for weeks. They were pale-faced and exhausted, and Cook himself had lost his appetite, and was suffering from terrible constipation. He had not discussed his plans for the coming year with his officers, and when it became plain that they would not be returning to England, the crew lapsed into sullen indifference. Johann railed from his cabin:

There are people, who are hardened to all feelings, & will give no ear to the dictates of humanity & reason; false ideas of *virtue* & *good conduct* are to them, to leave nothing to *chance*, and future discoverers, by their *perserverance*; which costs the lives of the poor Sailors or at least their healths. These people should be constantly employed by Government upon such Schemes: as for instance the N.W. or NE. Passage; there they will find a career to give to their genius full Scope; but wo! the poor Crew under them.

Quicquid delirant reges, plectuntur Achivi [What mad schemes kings have, the Greeks are punished].[23]

As this mood of despondency spread throughout the ship, Cook's 'black sheep' began to riot once more, and on 2 January 1774 in a drunken spree, Maxwell ('An hypocritical canting fellow') hit his fellow midshipman Charles Loggie, who threatened to stab him. According to John Elliott, Loggie was usually a very good-tempered fellow, but he had been hit on the head as a child and trepanned (an operation in which a hole was drilled through the skull to relieve pressure on the brain), and whenever he drank too much, he went crazy. Maxwell made a game of provoking Loggie, and on this occasion when Loggie scratched him with his knife, he laid a complaint with Cook, who turned Loggie before the mast and had him flogged like a common seaman. This episode caused a good deal of ill-feeling among the crew, and even Elliott, who idolised Cook, thought that he 'had lost sight of both justice and humanity' on this occasion.[24]

Perhaps because Cook himself was eating so little, he did not realise how much the men were suffering. On 11 January the *Resolution* headed south again, and although Cook's bilious symptoms began to ease, morale among the sailors plummeted. On 17 January when the first mate appeared in Cook's cabin, brandishing a portion of crumbling, rotten biscuit and demanding where he could get bread to fill his belly, Cook immediately restored full rations. Nevertheless, he kept the *Resolution* heading towards the Antarctic. After several more weeks of dreadful weather they crossed the Antarctic Circle for the third time. On 29 January the sun came out, warming the air, and Johann Forster ventured out of his cabin; and the next morning, they reached an unprecedented 71 degrees south, where they discovered an immense glittering icefield with high ice mountains stretching away to the horizon. Cook was relieved to find his path blocked by so impenetrable a barrier:

I will not say it was impossible anywhere to get in among this Ice, but I will assert that the bare attempting of it would be a very dangerous enterprise and what I believe no man in my situation would have thought of. I whose ambition leads me not only farther than any other man has been before me, but as far as I think it possible for man to go, was not sorry at meeting with this interruption, as it in some measure relieved us from the dangers and hardships, inseparable with the navigation of the Southern Polar regions.[25]

If there was a Southern Continent in this part of the ocean, it was clearly hidden beneath a sheet of ice; and Cook decided to sail north-east in order to search for the land reported by Juan Fernandez, before heading for Easter Island to spend the winter in the tropics. The ship's last pig was slaughtered for the men, and the officers celebrated by feasting on a dog which had been roasted for them in the galley.

Now that it was clear that the voyage would take at least another year, Cook's 'black sheep' once again began to riot. Mr Maxwell, the midshipman who had caused Loggie to be flogged, cut the main topsail while unbending it, and was ordered off the quarterdeck to do duty before the mast as a common sailor, to the delight of his shipmates. Although Cook remarked in his journal that 'the Seamen were always obedient and alert, and . . . were so far from wishing the Voyage at an end that they rejoiced at the Prospect of its being prolonged another year and soon enjoying the benefits of a milder Climate', this was an overstatement. The thought of returning to the Society Islands gave his men some consolation, however, although on 22 February when some of the sailors celebrated by stealing some liquor and drinking themselves insensible, three of them were flogged for 'drunkenness and neglect of duty'.[26]

That time among the icebergs almost killed Cook. Although his illness had abated during the run south, on 23 February it took a dangerous turn for the worse, 'to the grief of all the ship's company'. He had been suffering acute stomach pains and constipation for weeks, which he had concealed from his shipmates, and when he finally took a purge to try and clear the intestinal obstruction, he was stricken with violent vomiting. The ship's surgeon Mr Patten ('a steady clever Man', according to Elliott) ordered him to bed and treated him with ipecacuanha, camomile tea and castor oil, but this gave him an attack of hiccups which lasted for twenty-four hours,

weakening him severely. Over the following days Patten nursed him devot-
edly, giving him repeated hot baths, opiates, and plasters on his stomach to
try and relieve the obstruction, until he finally gained some relief; and by
26 February he was able to sit up in his bed and take a little nourishment.
Johann Forster offered up his favourite dog, which was killed and turned
into meat broth and steaks for the captain, greatly assisting his recovery.
Cook commented, 'We had no other fresh meat whatever on board and I
could eat of this flesh as well as broth made of it, when I could taste nothing
else, thus I received nourishment and strength from food which would have
made most people in Europe sick, so true it is that necessity is govern'd
by no law.'[27]

Cook's illness, which has been the subject of much speculation, has been
diagnosed as an acute gall-bladder infection[28] or a roundworm infestation
of the lower intestine, although his shipmates associated the symptoms with
scurvy.[29] It had evidently begun before his arrival at Tahiti in August 1773,
when he suffered acute stomach pains, so if this was roundworm, he was
already infected by that time. Although he rarely complained, Cook was
never really well for the rest of the voyage, and over the weeks that followed,
he was weak and emaciated, only gradually recovering his strength and
resilience.

By this stage of the voyage, most of the crew were also in poor physical
condition. Forster's servant and then Patten fell dangerously ill with bilious
symptoms very similar to Cook's, while scurvy was rife among them. Johann
Forster suffered from a terrible toothache, and his son George had acute
scorbutic symptoms – excruciating pains, swollen legs, rotten gums and
livid blotches on his body. As the weather became warmer and Cook set a
course towards Easter Island, the tropical heat brought its own discomforts.
When Easter Island (known as Te Pito o te Whenua to its inhabitants) was
finally sighted on 11 March 1774, George Forster exclaimed that 'the joy
which this fortunate event spread on every countenance is scarcely to be
described'.[30] They had been out of sight of land for 103 days, and every
man on board was yearning for fresh meat and vegetables, shady groves of
trees, and streams of sweet, pure water.

Easter Island proved disappointing, however. As they sailed close to the
coast, it looked rocky and quite barren, although the rows of tall stone idols
which the Dutch navigator Roggeveen had described during his visit in 1722
were clearly visible. Off the southern point of the island, they saw some
houses with thatched roofs like the hulls of upturned canoes, and two men
came out in a small canoe made from small pieces of wood, bringing a large
bunch of ripe bananas and a piece of bark-cloth. They were naked and

covered with body tattoos, and their ear lobes had been stretched so far that they almost reached their shoulders. As they came alongside, everyone tried to talk to them at once, so that Hitihiti could hardly get a word in edgewise. Cook could find no sheltered harbours on the island, and he finally anchored off Hangaroa on the west coast, sending the master off in the boat to take soundings. A brisk, active man of about fifty with long ear lobes named Maru-ahai boarded the boat and was brought out to the ship; and when he asked whether the British would kill him, Cook reassured him and presented him with gifts, including a hat and a jacket. Although Hitihiti made several attempts to talk with this man, they were constantly interrupted; that night Maru-ahai wrapped himself up in a thick piece of Tahitian bark-cloth and went to sleep on a table in the master's cabin.

After breakfast the next morning, Cook went ashore with Hitihiti, Maru-ahai, Sparrman and the Forsters, although George's legs were still so swollen that he could hardly walk. As they approached the shore they saw a massive hewn stone wall, with two huge statues lying shattered beneath it, and when they landed in a snug cove, they were greeted by about 150 Easter Islanders, who walked arm in arm with the sailors and gave them roast potatoes and sugar cane. Their faces were painted with reddish-brown ochre streaked with white or yellow, and they wore feather caps or woven hats on their heads, while a few sported cloaks made of yellow quilted bark-cloth, or jackets of blue woollen cloth acquired during a recent visit by a Spanish vessel. These people bartered sweet potatoes, plantains, sugar-cane and some barbecued chickens for nails and other trinkets. They were terrified of firearms, because the Dutch navigator Roggeveen had shot a number of people during his visit to the island (an episode familiar to Cook from his shipboard copy of Dalrymple's *Collection of . . . Voyages*), and their Spanish visitors had frightened them by firing muskets and cannons.

When Cook and his companions walked inland at Hangaroa, they came across a stone pavement where a great stone idol (or *ahu moai*) about twenty feet high and five feet wide stood gazing out to sea, a round, red stone topknot balanced on its head. The local people treated these monuments with reverence, and seemed uneasy when the Europeans examined them too closely. Further inland they came across a few houses, with gardens of *kumara* [sweet potatoes], paper mulberry, sugar-canes, and bananas grown in holes in the stony ground, a small well with brackish water; but no shady forests or running rivers. Cook decided not to stay too long on this island, since it was clear he would not be able to provision the ship from its limited resources of food and water. The sweet potatoes, bananas and sugar-canes were delicious, however, and the sailors were delighted to find at least a few of the local women who were willing to sleep with them.

After dinner that day, when they returned ashore, the Easter Islanders began to pick their pockets. Soon Hitihiti had a black cap snatched from his head, leaving him speechless with surprise, and later William Hodges, who had walked with William Wales and George Forster towards the south-east coast, had his hat stolen as he sat sketching the countryside. Wales aimed his musket to fire at the thief, but could not shoot him, while Hodges 'Sat like Patience on a Monument, Smiling at Grief'.[31] There was little shade and the harsh sun beat down on their heads, so hats were particularly desirable items on the island. At dusk as they walked back to the boat, they passed a plantation of yams, and George Forster noticed human bones around the base of one of the great statues. At a place where three great stone statues stood on a large pedestal, they met a group of islanders sitting around a fire, who offered them roast potatoes for supper.

The next morning Cook was feeling unwell again, so he sent a party of men including Johann Forster, Sparrman, Hodges and Wales, and led by Pickersgill and Edgcumbe, his lieutenant of marines, to explore the country-side. They set off at about nine in the morning, walking towards the volcanic slopes of Rano-kao followed by a large, curious crowd of people. Soon they were met by a man tattooed from head to foot and carrying a white flag, who kept the people back as he led them on their journey. The countryside seemed very barren and rocky, although they passed large gardens of sweet potatoes and banana plantations on their way to the base of the volcano. The stone village of Orongo, where men waited to swim to the islet of Motu-kaokao in an attempt to become the sacred 'bird-man' for a year, was hidden on the other side of Rano-kao, and they were led away from it. Walking around the volcano to the south-east coast they came to three ruined stone platforms, each of which had formerly held four tall idols, some of which lay toppled and broken around them. The people told them that each of these statues, which they called ariki or 'high chiefs', had a name, so presumably they represented former leaders of the island. From these statues they walked north-east along a narrow rocky pathway at the edge of a cliff, to a much more fertile part of the island (probably Vaihu) where they found large plantations of sweet potatoes, sugar-canes, yams mulched with dry grass, and plantains and taro, planted in holes to preserve the moisture. As they passed a small group of houses, the people came out with water, and a very large bag of roast potatoes and sugar-cane to sustain them on their journey.

When they came to a slight hill, Hodges sat down to sketch some ahu moai at a distance, and the sailor who was carrying Johann Forster's plant bag put it down on the ground to rest for a while. When one of their guides snatched the plant bag and began to run away, Lieutenant Edgcumbe took aim, shooting him in the back with smallshot. The man threw down the bag, but soon afterwards collapsed and was carried away by his companions. Although the people ran away, some returned when they were assured that as long as they did not steal from the sailors, they were in no danger. The tattooed man with the white flag had been left behind, but he and some others came running and circled around Pickersgill and his men, chanting a few words, then hoisted the white flag again and led them on their journey. About midway along the eastern coast, they noticed a group of men standing on a hill, some armed with spears with flint points and one carrying a stone hand-club very like a Maori *patu*. This party was led by a tall, heavily tattooed man dressed in a quilted yellow cape and wearing a cap of long shining black feathers, who greeted them by clasping his hands and raising them over his head. When Pickersgill and Forster approached him and gave him presents, they learned that this man, Tohitai, was the ariki of the district of Vaihu. The man with the white flag gave it to the high chief, who handed it over to another man who became their guide for the rest of their journey.

Tohitai indicated that he wanted the British to go back to the ship, but they carried on with their march until they came across another rank of stone statues. At Rano-Raraku, another site associated with the bird-man rituals,[32] they saw large numbers of isolated statues and statues standing in ranks; and near the eastern end of the island they were led to a freshwater well on high ground, soon afterwards climbing a hill where they had a clear view of the northern and eastern coastlines, but could see no rivers or creeks, nor any sheltered harbours. After returning to the well to refresh themselves, they walked across country back to Hangaroa, and en route Forster and Wales climbed to the crater of Punapau, where they found a number of the red stone topknots lying on the ground in a quarry. They arrived back at the ship very tired and thirsty.[33] During this excursion, according to William Wales, they saw no trees or any kind of wood, but just a few spindly bark-cloth plants.

In the meantime, Cook had gone ashore at Hangaroa with George Forster, Hitihiti, Mr Patten and Charles Clerke, where they met about 200 men, accompanied by a few women who copulated with the sailors in the shade of the stone monuments. Disgusted by this spectacle, George Forster, Hitihiti and the officers walked a little way inland, where they found a few houses and cultivations, and then returned to the landing-place where the people eagerly traded feather caps, small, angular carved human figures, and sweet potatoes that they had dug up without permission from a nearby garden. Hitihiti bartered for these wooden figures, including an elegant carving of a woman's hand, and caps decorated with the feathers from the man-o'-war bird, which he assured George Forster would be highly prized at the Society

Islands. When they returned to the sloop for dinner, several men and one woman swam out from the beach and boarded the *Resolution*, which they examined with 'unbounded admiration'. The islanders were forced to build their boats from small lengths of wood, and one of these men measured the ship from head to stern with his outstretched arms, marvelling at its size and construction. While the man measured the sloop, the woman slept with one sailor after another ('emulating the feats of Messalina' [the Emperor Claudius's nymphomaniac wife], according to George Forster),[34] for a few pieces of Tahitian bark-cloth and English clothing. The next morning there was a downpour, and after collecting fresh water in the sails and bartering for a few more sweet potatoes, bananas and chickens, they left the island. Hitihiti gave his verdict on Te Pito o te Whenua in two succinct phrases – 'Bad land, good people'.[35]

The scurvy sufferers had benefited from the fresh fruit obtained on Easter Island, which were distributed at Cook's expense, and they all felt refreshed, although some of the men had been badly sunburned. The Europeans marvelled at the stonework and the colossal statues on this barren, sun-baked island; monuments whose construction seemed beyond the technical capability of its current inhabitants. Johann Forster concluded that these people had once been more numerous, civilized and powerful, and from their language, material culture and crops that they were closely related to the New Zealanders and Society Islanders. As Cook later remarked in his 'Account' of Easter Island, the ancestors of all of these groups must have migrated across vast stretches of the Pacific Ocean:

In Colour, Features, and Language they bear such affinity to the people of the more Western isles that no one will doubt but that they have the same Origin, it is extraordinary that this same nation should have spread themselves over all the isles in this Vast Ocean from New Zealand to this Island which is almost a fourth part of the circumference of the Globe, many of them at this time have no knowledge of each other than what is recorded in antiquated tradition and have by length of time become as it were different Nations each having adopted some pecular custom or habit &c never the less a carefull observer will soon see the Affinity each has to the other.[36]

Unfortunately, his exertions ashore had aggravated Cook's illness, and he was again stricken with acute bilious symptoms. Over the following days, Forster's servant, Mr Patten and William Wales all suffered from the same complaint; and Johann Forster's last remaining Tahitian dog was sacrificed to make meat broth for the invalids.[37] While Cook was in bed, the first lieutenant, Cooper, ordered one of the marines, William Wedgeborough, to be confined and flogged for 'uncleanliness' (i.e. relieving himself in the lower deck), on the basis of circumstantial evidence. The hands were called to witness punishment, but when the Lieutenant of Marines objected, the marine was sent back to confinement while further proof was sought. Cook was consulted, Wedgeborough had another hearing in which the case against him was considered proven, and he was given a dozen lashes.

Cook now set a course for the Marquesas, found by the Spanish navigator Mendaña in 1595. These islands were given different positions on the various charts on board, and he hoped to accurately fix their location, and to obtain good supplies of fresh food and water. The *Resolution* was sailing in fine weather, her sails curving in fresh easterly breezes, surrounded by sea-birds that dived down on shoals of flying fish, while dolphins frolicked around the vessel. Finally, on 6 April 1774, a small bluff island was sighted, the first of the Marquesas, which Cook named Hood's Island after the midshipman who first saw it. They sailed past this island, St. Pedro (Motane) and La Dominica (Hiva Oa), looking for a safe harbour, until they came to St. Christina (Tahuata), where the high, jagged coastline looked fertile and inviting.

When Cook tried to tack into Vaitahu bay on Tahuata on 7 April, the ship was hit by a sudden squall which sprung the mizzen topmast and almost drove them onto the rocks. On the second attempt, however, he got in and anchored safely, while a shoal of porpoises cruised up the channel. About fifteen canoes came out, but their crews were reluctant to come too close until the offer of a hatchet and some large nails enticed one group to come alongside and barter. These men were almost naked and elaborately tattooed from head to foot in circles, scrolls and squares, with pearl-shell ornaments around their necks, and they had slings tied around their foreheads and piles of stones in their narrow canoes, which were made of thin planks sewn together. They sent up roots of kava as a sign of peace; and a brisk trade for breadfruit, fish and curiosities quickly got under way. Their language appeared to be very close to Tahitian, and when they were asked for pigs they went ashore and got one, which they traded for a knife. At nightfall they retired, as fires flared up around the bay and on the surrounding hillsides.

The next morning Cook and his men had a clear view of the bay, which was sheltered by a craggy mountain on one side, and a high tableland with palisades along the skyline. Soon a number of canoes came out and their crews began to trade for fish and breadfruit, yelling and making a deafening racket. Some of these people came on board, but soon began to 'cheat'. When one man tried to take goods without making a return, Cook fired a musket ball past his ear. Shortly afterwards, as Cook was boarding his boat to go ashore, a man grabbed an iron stanchion from the opposite gangway, dived overboard and swam with it to his canoe. Cook shouted to his officers to fire over the thief's head, so that he could intercept him in his boat, but they could scarcely hear him in the racket. They fired two shots, which the man ignored, and when one of the officers came on deck he fired straight at the thief, killing him with a shot to the head. Hitihiti burst into tears when he saw this, and the dead man's two companions dived from the canoe, which was filling with blood, but soon climbed back in again, and frantically tried to bail the blood out of the canoe. One of these men looked distraught as he did this, while the other laughed hysterically. The other canoes fled ashore, and Cook went after them to give them gifts of nails and trinkets in an effort to calm them. When he returned on board, drums began to beat in the forest as crowds of armed Marquesan warriors gathered on the beach. The sailors carried out a kedge anchor, but as soon as it was lowered a canoe left the shore and its crew tried to seize the anchor buoy. When two musket shots were fired over their heads, they dropped the buoy and fled ashore, making no more efforts to threaten the strangers.

Shortly after this, a canoe came out bringing a distinguished-looking man, who carried a green bough with a white flag and a pig, which he exchanged for a spike nail. Cook presented him with a hatchet and other gifts, and after briefly stepping on the gangway, this man returned to the beach. Cook was determined to get fresh water and food, so he went ashore with a party of armed men, accompanied by Hitihiti, the Forsters and Sparrman. On the beach, they were confronted by about a hundred armed warriors. Hitihiti asked these men to sit down, and they did so, while he and the Forsters explained that the man had only been killed because he had stolen from them. They seemed somewhat mollified by this, and guided them to a fine stream of water where Cook ordered the waterers to start filling the casks, as the Marquesans began to barter plantains, bananas and breadfruit for nails and other iron items, guarded by a line of marines armed with muskets. The Forsters walked a little way inland to collect plants, where they found a number of square stone platforms, the foundations of abandoned houses, and a fine spring of clear water gushing from a rocky hillside. Back on the beach they found the Marquesans trading clubs for iron tools, and bartering pigs and great quantities of fruit; and shortly after this returned to the sloop for dinner. That afternoon George Forster stayed on board, while Johann went ashore with Captain Cook to shoot birds, once again frightening the local inhabitants.

Early the next morning, seven canoes arrived from the neighbouring island, Hiva Oa, while several canoes from Tahuata paddled up the strait between the two islands. They had brought fruit to trade, and when Cook went ashore after breakfast with the Forsters, they were greeted by a man named Honu, the high chief or *haka'iki* of Tahuata, who was surrounded by a large entourage, including a very beautiful older woman, and a lovely little girl who seemed to be her daughter. The high chief, who was dressed in a bark-cloth garment, a feather diadem, a gorget and ear pendants, with bunches of human hair, struck them as a good-natured, intelligent fellow. He presented Cook with some of his ornaments, several pigs and quantities of fruit, although when Cook gave him nails and some other items and invited him back to the ship for dinner, he would not accept the invitation.

Like the Society Islanders, these people placed a high value on red feathers, eagerly exchanging these for head-dresses and other ornaments. When the British returned to the ship, the boat was almost swamped in the surf, leaving the Forsters pale-faced and gasping. Hitihiti, who had been left behind, swam out to the *Resolution* to avoid another dangerous crossing. That afternoon George stayed on board with Sparrman to sketch and describe the specimens they had collected, while Johann went ashore with Cook, where they were taken to the house of the man who had been shot, and presented his male relatives with several gifts as compensation. The Europeans were very struck by the Marquesans, considering them the most attractive people they had met during their travels. As William Wales remarked:

The Natives of these Islands taken Collectively, are undoubtedly the finest Race of People that I or perhaps any Person Else has ever seen. They are not like to the Otahiteans One a great fat Overgrown, unweildy fellow and the next perhaps you meet a poor meagre half starved Wretch, over run with Scabs and blotches, but are, almost without exception all fine tall stout-limbed, and well-made People, neither lean enough for scare-Crows, nor yet so fat as in the least to impede their Activity.[38]

Hitihiti was equally delighted with these people, talking to them in an animated fashion, bartering for ornaments and explaining various Tahitian customs, including a method of making fire by rubbing together dry sticks of hibiscus. They remembered the young Boraboran long after his visit, naming a stone platform after him – 'Hitihiti Paepae'.[39]

When he went ashore the next day, Cook was furious to find that his midshipmen had spoiled the terms of trade by trading red feathers, ribbons and cloth. He decided to leave the Marquesas as soon as possible, and head to the Society Islands to obtain more provisions. While he was trying to acquire a few last pigs, Sparrman, Patten and George Forster with some others decided to climb to the top of the tableland behind the bay to inspect the fortifications, and set off up a path across the stream through spacious plantations of bananas and fruit trees, past a number of houses. After climbing about three miles from the coast, they came to a house where a young woman came out, dressed in bark-cloth, who walked rapidly away from them up the hillside, while some men urged them to return to the ship. Memories of Mendaña's brief visit, when the Spaniards had killed about two hundred people, gave the islanders good reason to be afraid of Europeans. Sparrman and Forster turned back, but Patten and the others carried on about two miles further, before returning to the landing-place.

Although barter had become difficult, the people were now very friendly, and a number of women joined their menfolk at the beach, where several of them agreed to sleep with the sailors. As they were packing up to return to the sloop, Cook struck a sailor several times for neglecting his duty, and when the Marquesans saw this they exclaimed, 'He beats his brother!' They thought that the sailors were all members of one kin group, and that Cook was their high chief and kinsman. In the Marquesas, the people seemed much less affluent than the inhabitants of the Society Islands, and much more egalitarian. Honu, the high chief, was not treated with any particular respect, although he wore a more elaborate costume than any of his fellow islanders.

On their final morning ashore at Tahuata, very few pigs were brought for barter, and the people were demanding china cups, saucers and glasses, and other irreplaceable items for their provisions. That afternoon Cook ordered the anchors to be hoisted, and the *Resolution* sailed towards the southern coast of Hiva Oa, and then turned south-south-west towards Tahiti.

On 17 April they came to Byron's 'Coral Island' (Takaroa), one of the Northern Tuamotus, where Cook sent a boat to sound the entrance through the reef of the atoll. Although some armed men threatened them briefly, they quickly began to trade coconuts for nails, so Cook sent the other boats in under the command of Cooper and Pickersgill, so that the Forsters could go ashore to collect plants. They were met by people who bartered a few dogs and coconuts, and allowed them to examine their houses and boathouses. Hitihiti eagerly traded for these dogs, which had fine, long white hair, much valued in the Society Islands for decorating the breastplates worn by warriors. These people showed them a kind of scurvy-grass which they crushed, mixed with shellfish and threw into the sea among a shoal of fish, intoxicating the fish and making it easy to catch them. When a group of armed warriors began to gather, however, Hitihiti warned his shipmates that they were about to be attacked, so they decided to return to the ship; as the boats rowed back towards the *Resolution*, the men threw small stones after them and then sat on the beach, talking loudly. Once his men were back on board, Cook ordered four or five cannon shots to be fired over these warriors' heads, and they ran away as fast as their legs could carry them.

After this brief visit to Takaroa the *Resolution* carried on in a south-westerly direction, passing three more small atolls and heading for Tahiti, which the sailors now regarded as their 'second home'. They were all longing to return there, for different reasons: Cook wanted to provision his ship; the Forsters hoped to complete their collections of Tahitian plants; Wales was anxious to set up the observatory and check the watches (especially Kendall's timepiece), which he had not been able to do since their last visit to New Zealand;[40] the scurvy sufferers wanted more fresh meat and vegetables; and the sailors were longing for their taio and Tahitian women. Of them all, however, perhaps Hitihiti was the most eager to arrive at the island. He had never been to Tahiti before, although many of his friends and relatives lived there. He was bringing an unprecedented treasure-trove of gifts – red feathers from Tongatapu, carvings and feather hats from Easter Island, white dogs from Takaroa and presents from his shipmates, which he knew would be highly prized among his people. He had lived with the Europeans on their ship for seven months, and could tell marvellous tales about his adventures. He had completed a voyage which made the arioi excursions pale by comparison – from Ra'iatea to 'Eua and Tongatapu in the west, southwards to Te Wai Pounamu in New Zealand, south-east to the ice islands of the frozen 'bright lands', where no island navigator had ever ventured before, northwards to Te Pito o te Whenua, and then north-west to Tahuata in the Marquesas, and south-west to Takaroa in the Tuamotus. Above all, it would be wonderful to be back in his home islands, among people who spoke his own language and who practised the same customs, to dance with the arioi and amaze the young women.

12

The Return of the Native

When the *Resolution* approached the coast of Tahiti on 22 April 1774, several canoes came out bringing two high-born young men, whom Cook invited into the Great Cabin. Upon being introduced to Hitihiti, who was wearing English clothing, they took off their bark-cloth garments and dressed him in these instead, declaring themselves to be his taio. In return, he showed them some of the treasures he had collected and gave them a few red feathers, to their intense delight. As the anchors splashed down in Matavai Bay the ship was surrounded by canoes whose crews bartered quantities of fish, breadfruit, *vi* or Tahitian apples, and coconuts for small nails. It was the season of plenty, and when they went ashore, the sailors found plenty of pigs and lush gardens, and many new houses and canoes under construction. During Cook's previous visits, Tahiti had been suffering from the ravages of war, but now the local economy was recovering, assisted by the iron tools acquired from the British. That afternoon William Wales sent his clock and the astronomical quadrant ashore and set them up in the entrance to the ship's tent on Point Venus, in order to check Kendall's chronometer. When Hitihiti landed on the island, he was greeted with joy. According to George Forster, 'he was courted and looked upon as a prodigy by all the Tahitians who saw him; he was feasted with their choicest meats, he received several changes of dress, and revelled among the nymphs of the land.'[1] That night a number of Tahitian women flocked on board the ship, and as George remarked, 'the excesses of the night were incredible'.[2]

The repairs to the *Resolution* soon got under way, and two days later Cook's taio Tu, the high chief of Tahiti-nui, came to visit the ship, bringing a dozen pigs as presents. He had already talked with Hitihiti, and seemed to have set aside his reservations about the British. Hitihiti had told him about the red feathers Cook had acquired in Tonga, and after an exchange of greetings, the conversation quickly turned to these treasured items. When Cook showed him part of his supply, Tu and his companions were amazed and delighted, and when Cook gave him and his sister two small pieces of bark-cloth with red feathers glued onto them, they accepted these with unfeigned pleasure.

The next morning, there was a terrific thunderstorm in Matavai Bay. Fortunately Cook had ordered a copper chain to be fixed to the main topgallant masthead as a lightning rod, for at the height of this storm the *Resolution* was struck by lightning. Amidst a torrential downpour, there were deafening claps of thunder as a shimmer of blue flame ran down the copper chain into the sea, saving the sloop from certain destruction. In the minds of the Tahitians, this demonstration of supernatural power must have been linked with her cargo of red feathers, which signified 'Oro's power. When his other taio Potatau and his two wives arrived at the sloop with a large number of pigs, they eagerly traded these for a few red feathers. Cook decided to stay on at Matavai for several weeks, resting his men and repairing the ship, knowing that he would be able to obtain provisions without any difficulty.

On 26 April, Cook went to pay a visit to Tu at Pare. As he and his companions rowed along the coast, they noticed a number of large canoes converging on Tu's settlement. When they rounded the point, they were confronted by a fantastic spectacle. A fleet of 160 large double war canoes had lined up along the beach, attended by about 200 smaller canoes as tenders. The fighting canoes in this armada were decorated with flags and streamers, loaded with quantities of spears, clubs and stones, and crewed by armed warriors in fighting costume, most wearing breastplates and some distinguished by towering wickerwork helmets decorated with feathers. Cook estimated that more than 7000 men had gathered on this occasion, and he was both impressed and startled, wondering whether the fleet had been summoned to attack the *Resolution*. Nevertheless he landed and was greeted by Ti'i, one of Tu's uncles who had acted as an emissary during Cook's previous visit.

When Ti'i took Cook by the right hand and went to lead him inland to Tu, there were cries of 'To'ofa is coming!' The leader of the flotilla, To'ofa, a tall, vigorous grey-haired man about sixty years old whom the sailors dubbed the 'Admiral',[3] landed and strode towards them. Seizing Cook's left hand, he began to guide him towards the canoes, while Ti'i tried to take him in the opposite direction. After an undignified tug-of-war, Cook decided to go towards the fleet with To'ofa, passing between two lines of armed warriors but refusing to board his canoe, because he had not met this great fighting chief before and was unsure about his intentions. Angry at this slight, To'ofa stalked off, and soon afterwards Ti'i returned to tell Cook that his friend Tu was afraid and had gone inland. He advised Cook to get

The great fleet of war canoes at Pare in Tahiti

back in his boat, which he did, intently examining the war canoes with their high, curving carved prows and fighting stages before ordering his men to row back to the *Resolution*.

When he got back on board Cook asked his visitors why this great fleet had been summoned. Some said that it would sail to Mo'orea, but according to Potatau, To'ofa wanted to sail against Amo, Purea's ex-husband who had joined Vehiatua (the high chief of Tahiti-iti) in the recent wars, although Tu did not support this intention. According to tribal histories, both the high chief of Mo'orea and Amo were likely targets on this occasion. The high chief of Mo'orea, Mahine, was an arioi, and childless. Supported by his brother-in-law Amo, he had promoted a foster-son as his successor, but Mahine's nephew Mahau, who was Tu's brother-in-law, was claiming the title. There were frequent intermarriages between the chiefly lines in the Society Islands, which led to complex and shifting jealousies and alliances. The fleet had assembled to fight on Mahau's side in this war of succession, but Tu, who was always reluctant to go to war, did not want to join a force commanded by To'ofa. That afternoon Cook went with the Forsters to Pare, where he met Tu, who greeted him with high good humour. It seems likely that Cook's arrival, and his refusal to go with To'ofa had strengthened Tu's hand in a difficult situation.[4]

The next morning, after receiving a gift of two large pigs from To'ofa, Cook went to visit Tu at Pare. He found To'ofa sitting with Tu, and invited them both back to the ship for dinner. The 'Admiral' was fascinated by the *Resolution*, examining its decks, masts and rigging with great care and requesting spares of parts he particularly admired, especially the cables and anchors. Tu was in a jovial mood, showing To'ofa how to eat with a knife and fork, how to salt his meat and drink wine from a glass, jesting that this dark red liquid was human blood. To'ofa tossed off a glass of grog, and both of these chiefs seemed to enjoy their visit immensely. They assured Cook that the fleet would sail against Mo'orea, and when Cook jokingly offered to go with them to fire on Tu's enemies, they seemed eager at first, and then changed their minds and said that the attack on Mo'orea had been scheduled to take place five days after his departure. Cook reflected that he was probably regarded as a dangerous ally, who could dictate the terms of battle, give the victory to whomever he pleased, and claim most of the spoils of conquest. Certainly To'ofa would have been cautious about the prospect of Tu's sworn friend, with his overwhelming firepower, joining the expedition.

Over the following days, Johann Forster and Sparrman explored the inland mountains where they discovered several new species of plants; while people flocked to the *Resolution* with their most valued possessions, hoping to exchange them for red feathers. Vehiatua sent pigs from Tahiti-iti, asking for red feathers, and Cook's taio Potatau came on board with his young wife, offering her to his friend in exchange for some of these treasures. Cook refused, but when they heard about it, George Forster and some others rebuked Potatau for his 'immoral' behaviour. Unperturbed by their disapproval, Potatau bartered his towering war-helmet instead, while other chiefs offered cherished items, including chief mourners' costumes. The women flocked on board, and any sailor who had red feathers could take his pick. As Charles Clerke jocularly noted:

So very solicitous & zealously desirous are our good friends here for the attaining of these red Feathers and so thoroughly convinc'd of their efficacy with their Sovereign Deities that they will very chearfully oblige us in good natur'd but rather unhallow'd rites for the possession of them to render back religious Ceremonies by way of Propitiation to their Jolly Gods.[5]

The Tahitians also sought 'curiosities' from the other Polynesian islands which the *Resolution* had visited, preferring these to English trade goods. They followed Hitihiti everywhere and listened to the tales of his adventures with rapt attention, although they dismissed his accounts of white 'rocks' and 'stones' that melted into fresh water, and the perpetual daylight of summer in the frozen south as fabulous inventions. His stories about the cannibals in New Zealand struck them with horror, and many people came on board to see the young boy's head which Pickersgill had acquired in Queen Charlotte Sound, now preserved in a bottle of spirits. As they marvelled at this gruesome object, they spoke of a legendary period when a

Capt. James Cook of the Endeavour.

1. *A portrait of Captain James Cook (William Hodges)*

2. *Matavai Bay in Tahiti, Cook's favourite Pacific anchorage (William Hodges)*

3. *The war canoes in Tahiti, an ari'i rahi (high chief/priest)
on the platform (William Hodges)*

4. *Vaitepiha Bay in Tahiti-iti, the home of the high chief Vehiatua (William Hodges)*

5. *Papetoai Bay in Mo'orea, Society Islands, where Captain Cook met the high chief Mahine, and rampaged across the island to revenge the theft of a goat (John Webber)*

6. *Fare harbour in Huahine, the home of Cook's*
ceremonial friend Ori (John Webber)

7. *Hamanino Bay in Ra'itea, the birthplace of the high*
priest-navigator Tupaia (William Hodges)

8. *The Resolution at anchor in Pickersgill Harbour,*
Dusky Sound, New Zealand (William Hodges)

9. *The Resolution in Cook's Strait, New Zealand, with waterspouts (William Hodges)*

10. *Captain Cook greets local Maori in Ship Cove, Queen Charlotte Sound, New Zealand, the scene of the trial of the cannibal dog (John Webber)*

11. *Captain Cook's reception at Ha'apai in Tonga, men boxing and duelling with clubs (John Webber)*

12. *The great moai or monuments at Easter Island (William Hodges)*

13. *Resolution Bay in the Marquesas (William Hodges)*

14. *Kealakekua Bay in Hawa'i, where Captain Cook was killed (John Webber)*

15. *John Webber's painting of the death of Cook (John Webber)*

race of man-eaters had inhabited Tahiti, but assured the British that these people had long since vanished.

On 28 April a man who was caught trying to steal a cask from the watering-place was sent on board the *Resolution* and clapped into irons. When Tu and To'ofa came on board the next morning, Tu begged that the culprit be released, but Cook refused, saying that his own men would be flogged for such an offence, and that the thief would certainly be punished. He had turned a blind eye to a number of thefts, and thought that the Tahitians were taking advantage of his leniency; so he sent the man ashore and had him tied up to a post, while a large crowd of Tahitians assembled. Tu and his sister begged again that he should be set free, but To'ofa watched impassively as the man was given two dozen lashes, a punishment which he endured bravely. The spectators were terrified by this spectacle and began to run away, but To'ofa called them back. In a fiery oration, he urged them to steal from their enemies, not their friends, and to stop trying to take the Europeans' possessions.

After the 'Admiral''s speech Cook ordered the marines to go through their exercises, and to load and fire their muskets, a demonstration which greatly impressed the onlookers. To'ofa was fascinated by what he had seen, and that afternoon he came alongside the *Resolution* with his wife on a large double canoe, and invited Hodges and George Forster to accompany him to Pare. As they conversed during the journey, it became plain that the Tahitians thought that Joseph Banks must be the King of England's brother, and that Captain Cook was the high admiral of England. When he was told otherwise, To'ofa was surprised, rapidly readjusting his notions of Cook's social status. The following day, a review of ten war canoes was conducted at Matavai that showed how these canoes were paddled en masse and how landings were handled, and Hodges made sketches for some paintings he was planning of the great war fleet at Pare.

While the repairs to the ship were being completed, people were arriving at Matavai from all over the island. One day Reti, Bougainville's robust, grey-haired taio from Hitia'a, came to ask Captain Cook if it was likely that he would see the French captain upon his return to Britain. When Cook said no, he asked Johann Forster, who replied that he might possibly meet him. Reti asked him to tell his taio Bougainville to come back to Tahiti, since he was longing to meet him again, promising him two pigs if he would deliver this message. Later, Hodges sketched a portrait of Reti, which Johann Forster eventually delivered to Bougainville in Paris. Several days later Hitihiti reappeared on board, bringing his newly-wed wife, the daughter of a chief at Matavai. Tu had taken the young traveller under his protection, offering him land and marrying him to this high-ranking girl, and Hitihiti told the Forsters that he had decided not to go to England, but wanted to stay on in Tahiti. When he heard this, Johann tried to persuade Hitihiti to carry on to Ra'iatea, saying that at Tahiti he had no house or land, and that as soon as the *Resolution* left the island, he would be stripped of all of his treasures.

During this period Tu also visited the ship on several occasions, and on 7 May he brought his entire family. Tu's father gave Cook a mourning costume, receiving red feathers in return; and Tu told Cook that he could cut down as many trees as he pleased for fuel. That evening Tu's younger brother stayed on board. He gave the Forsters a list of all of the members of his family, and a detailed account of recent events on the island, including Vehiatua's attack on Purea and Amo, and Tutaha's revenge attack on Vehiatua, which had led to the death of Tutaha and many of his people. During these amiable exchanges, however, a man stole a musket from a sentry who had dozed on duty at the shore camp. As soon as he heard what had happened, Tu sent Ti'i on board to fetch his brother, alerted the sergeant of marines, and then fled to the mountains with his family. Cook's habit of taking high chiefs (even his own taio) hostage for such thefts had become notorious on the island, and Tu was taking no chances.

Cook went on shore to try and find Tu, but his taio had vanished. Ti'i advised him to return to the ship while he tried to recover the musket. Back on board the *Resolution*, Cook sent Hitihiti with a message for Tu to say that he was still his friend, and only wanted the return of the musket. While Hitihiti was being taken ashore, six large canoes paddled around Point Venus, and when Cook went to meet them in the pinnace, some women whom he knew on one of these canoes told him that Tu had gone to the shore camp. Cook told his men to let the canoes pass, but when he got ashore and found that the high chief was not there, he realised that he had been hoodwinked. He fired shots after the canoes and sent another boat to chase them. Five of these canoes were captured, including one owned by a Tahiti-iti chief known as Marae-ta'ata (whom Cook had met during his previous visit), although the women escaped.

That afternoon when Ti'i came out to the ship, he told Cook that the thief had fled with the musket to Tahiti-iti and could not be captured. Cook restored all of the canoes, except Marae-ta'ata's, to their owners, and when Ti'i and Hitihiti both swore that Marae-ta'ata was innocent of the theft, he eventually released his canoe as well. Cook had almost decided to let the matter drop when at dusk, three men arrived at the shore camp, sweating and dishevelled, who brought back the musket and some other stolen items. They told Cook that Marae-ta'ata had been responsible for the theft of the musket after all, and he concluded ruefully that both Ti'i and Hitihiti had deceived him. They also said that they had beaten the thief severely, and the next day the marine whose musket had been stolen was punished with a flogging of twenty-four lashes.

On 10 May Cook went to Pare to make his peace with Tu, reproaching him for having run away since he was not angry with him, only with the Tahiti-iti people. When Tu asked why Cook had fired on the canoes, he excused himself by saying that one of them belonged to Marae-ta'ata, the Tahiti-iti man who had stolen the musket, and that he wished he had destroyed his canoe while he had it in his possession. Gratified by this declaration, Tu promised that supplies to the ship would be resumed the next day. At about noon, Cook gave Tu a demonstration of the ship's great guns, firing a broadside across the reef into the sea, and that night Tu dined on board and was entertained with a display of skyrockets, serpents and air balloons followed by 'grotesque' singing and dancing, including a hornpipe by the sailors and Swedish songs from Sparrman, which the Tahitians loved, calling this a 'Heiva Peretani' [a British festivity].

Two days later, as Cook was getting ready to leave the island, Purea (formerly revered by the British as the 'Queen' of Tahiti) and her ex-husband Amo arrived alongside the ship. Although Cook greeted Purea kindly, the other members of his expedition virtually ignored her, and both she and Amo soon returned ashore. Shortly afterwards Tu and his father arrived with a large retinue and a great quantity of provisions, and Cook gave him lavish gifts in return. That night Cook entertained Tu and his people with another fireworks display. They marvelled at the skyrockets and air balloons, but when a violent thunderstorm broke out afterwards they were terrified, thinking that 'Oro was offended because the British were challenging his power.

Cook had intended to sail the next morning, but he was forced to wait until Hitihiti returned to the vessel. As Cook noted:

He was very well beloved in the Ship for which reason every one was persuading him to go with us, telling what great things he wou'd see and return with immence riches, according to his Idea of riches, but I thought proper to undeceive him, thinking it an Act of the highest injustice to take away a person from these isles against his own free inclination under any promise whatever much more that of bringing them back again, what Man on board can make such a promise as this.[6]

Early on the morning of 14 May when Hitihiti came back to the *Resolution*, he declared that he wanted to stay at Tahiti, but Johann Forster persuaded him to accompany them to Ra'iatea. He asked if four young men from

Borabora could travel with him; when Cook agreed, he modestly confided that he had made love with Purea the previous evening, showing the officers several pieces of fine bark-cloth that she had given him. Knowing that Hitihiti had decided not to carry on to England, Johann Forster had asked Cook if he could take a young boy named Nuna as his servant, and although Cook agreed at first, this led to so many requests of this kind from the officers that he finally refused them all, provoking another of Forster's outbursts:

I had allways been treated by him in this manner . . . but seeing that this would avail nothing & that it was a premeditated Scheme to cross me in everything: I gave the point up . . . There is no arguing against people, who have no Idea of obliging others, make themselves the center of all their own wishes & gratifications, are come to power from nothing & will others let feel their own importance & Lord & Bashaw it over others.[7]

Shortly afterwards, To'ofa and his wife came out with farewell presents. Cook gave them gifts in return, including an English pennant for To'ofa's canoe, showing him how to hoist it. Later that day, Cook and his companions were treated to another naval review when about forty war canoes gathered at Pare. As they paddled past in strict unison, the canoes lashed together in divisions and guided by a man with a green branch who stood behind the fighting stage of the main canoe, the Forsters were reminded of the fleet of Greek heroes that had fought against Troy. When they landed, Tu ordered some of these warriors to show Cook their fighting techniques, and they began by throwing and parrying spears, then engaged in single combat with clubs. After this demonstration Tu showed Cook a new double fighting canoe about as long as the *Resolution* which was almost ready to launch, and asked him for a grapple and a grappling iron. Cook gave him these items and added an English Jack and a pennant, suggesting that he should call this great canoe 'Peretane' [Britain], a proposal to which Tu gladly assented.

That night the *Resolution* finally set sail from Matavai, and as Tu paddled off in his canoe, they fired three cannons as a salute. While the officers were thus distracted, John Marra, the gunner's mate, slipped overboard and swam towards some canoes which were coming out to meet him. A boat was sent to pick him up, but when they reached him, he dived in an effort to drown himself. The officer in charge promised that he would not be flogged and brought him back to the ship, where he spent a fortnight confined in irons.[8] Shortly after this, a beautiful young girl hesitantly emerged from her hiding-place, and showed herself on deck. She had eloped with a lover to Tahiti from Ra'iatea some years earlier, but was yearning to see her parents again, and had decided to return on the *Resolution* to the island. Cook allowed her to stay on board, and the officers gave her European clothing to wear and invited her to dine with them during the voyage.

On 15 May at daybreak, the island of Huahine appeared on the horizon, and early that afternoon, the ship anchored once more in Fare harbour. Cook's taio Ori, the Regent of Huahine, came out in a small canoe with a little pig and a warrior's breastplate, which he presented to his friend, distributing roots of kava to the officers. Soon afterwards Porea, the young man who had sailed on the *Resolution* from Tahiti earlier in the voyage, came on board. He assured Cook that when he had left the ship at Ra'iatea the previous year, it was not of his own free will. He had been having a love affair with a local girl, and one night when he went ashore to meet her, her father and his people stripped him of his European clothes, beat him soundly, and kept him confined until the *Resolution* had left the island.

When trade began that morning, Cook realised that the prodigal supplies of pigs and other provisions that Ori had made available during his last visit were no longer forthcoming. The local people now expected axes for their pigs, and did not place the same high value on red feathers as the chiefly families in Tahiti. Instead, a mood of resistance and hostility was prevalent. Although many of his people hated the Borabora invaders, Ori had forged an alliance with Puni, the high chief of Borabora; since Cook was Ori's taio, he was included in this resentment. When Cook's men went on shore, it became clear that many of the local people did not welcome their presence. Sparrman and the Forsters went inland looking for plants, and before long Forster's servant (who was suffering from the same bilious disorder as Cook) was seized by a group of men who knocked him over, while one of them tried to grab his trade bag. Sparrman aimed his gun at the thief, but Forster's servant was in the way, and when Forster tried to fire at the attackers, his musket flashed in the pan and they escaped, having learned that firearms were not always effective. When Cook hastened to Ori's house to complain about the assault, Ori assured him that neither he nor any of his fellow chiefs had anything to do with the attack, and that they would be delighted if he would shoot the culprits. That evening when William Wales and his friends attended a heiva, the same mood of hostility was apparent. The arioi mercilessly lampooned the young woman who had joined the British at Tahiti, depicting the harsh reception she could expect when she returned to Ra'iatea and reducing her to humiliated tears with their satire.

The next morning some of the petty officers went ashore, taking two men as guides who offered to carry their trade bags. In an isolated spot, their guides pointed out some birds, and when the officers took aim and fired, they ran off with their booty. That same day, a man tried to steal Charles Clerke's powder-horn, and during the struggle Clerke hit him with his gun, bending the barrel and breaking the stock. Later that morning, the young girl who had sailed with them from Tahiti was invited to a house where she was seized and stripped of her European clothes, until some of the ship's people came to her rescue. As Johann Forster sniffed disapprovingly, 'None is punished for his Audaciousness & Robbing; & they grow bolder every day for this reason: in case one were shot dead, the rest would be so alarmed, that no thefts would be more committed, & it would cause more honesty among them & greater Security for Europeans.'[9] Cook's companions were dismayed by the hostility they were encountering, and when a man came up to Charles Clerke, brandishing a stone and saying, 'This stone is for you!', a rumour flew around among the crew that the people of Huahine were plotting to seize the *Resolution*.

On 20 May Lieutenants Cooper and Clerke, and the master's mate John Burr went to the lagoons to shoot ducks, where they forced a local man to retrieve the birds for them. Although he pleaded exhaustion, they hit him and forced him back into the water, so he swam to the other side and escaped with some of the ducks they had potted. In a fury Lieutenant Cooper aimed his gun at this man, and would have shot him except that his powder was wet, and the musket flashed in the pan and misfired. Seeing this, a number of men grabbed Cooper, and began to strip and beat him. Clerke aimed his gun at them but because Cooper was in the way he could not shoot his assailants, and he was also seized; when Burr was attacked he managed to fire his gun, which was loaded with smallshot, wounding three men in the legs before he was grabbed and beaten unmercifully. In the midst of the struggle a chief arrived and freed Burr and Cooper, and sent his people to retrieve the stolen items.

When Cook heard that his officers had been captured and stripped, he rushed ashore with Johann Forster and a boat's crew, seizing a large house and two chiefs before storming off to find Ori. The chief was nowhere to be found, but early the next morning Hitihiti arrived with a message from Ori saying that there were thirteen of these thieves, who refused to obey him; and asking Cook to come with a party of twenty-two armed men (Hitihiti had been given twenty-two small sticks to remind him of the exact number) to help capture them. According to Hitihiti the thieves came from a district in Huahine which had rebelled against Ori, and would be supported by the warriors of their district in any conflict. When Cook talked with his officers about their next move, Clerke confessed their part in provoking the confrontation the previous day. Nevertheless, Cook decided to go ashore and talk with Ori about this outrage, and went ashore with Johann Forster, where Ori told them that he proposed to go and attack the offenders.

Upon returning to the ship, Cook mustered an armed party of forty-eight men, including Hitihiti, the ship's officers, the Forsters and Sparrman. They marched inland, accompanied by some warriors led by Ori, brandishing a spear tipped with the barbed tail of a stingray. As more men joined the warriors, however, Hitihiti became alarmed, telling Cook that many of them belonged to the dissident group which was planning to ambush their party. When they had walked about two miles inland, Ori wanted to leave them, but Cook insisted that he should stay with their party. After marching about three miles further inland they came to a deep, rocky valley, where Hitihiti warned Cook that he was about to be attacked. After inspecting the lie of the land, Cook decided that it would be imprudent to proceed further, and ordered his men to march back to the *Resolution*. When they arrived back at the beach, he ordered them to fire their muskets in platoons, to show the local people what they were capable of. Despite this demonstration, it had been a futile expedition. As Wales remarked sardonically, 'About 4pm the Armed Party returned; having, according to the strict, literal meaning of some Poet or other; who, I have utterly forgot, March'd up the Hill, and then – March'd down again.'[10]

Early that morning a flotilla of sixty arioi canoes had sailed from Huahine to visit their brethren in the neighbouring islands; and that evening, peace offerings of pigs and fruit were brought out to the *Resolution*. Ori sent more coconuts to his taio the following day, and when he farewelled Cook on 23 May, the old chief wept and told Cook to send his sons to Huahine, where they would be treated with the utmost kindness. As Cook reflected ruefully:

Oree is a good Man to the utmost sence of the word, but many of the people are far from being of that disposision and seem to take advantage of his old age. The gentle treatment they have ever met with from me and the careless and imprudent manner many of our people have rambled about in their country from a Vain opinion that fire Arms rendred them invincible hath incouraged some of the people to commit acts of Violence no man at Otaheite ever dar'd attempt.[11]

Hitihiti's four friends had stayed behind at Huahine, but before he left the ship, Ori asked Cook to take one of his people to Ra'iatea with a message for Puni, the high chief of Borabora, asking for help with the rebels. As the *Resolution* sailed away, the local women wept and lamented loudly in their canoes, before paddling back to Fare.

*

On 25 May when Cook arrived at Hamanino harbour in Ra'iatea (Tupaia's birthplace), his taio Reo, the Borabora regent of Ra'iatea, came out to meet him. He greeted Hitihiti and Ori's ambassador with evident delight, and seemed thrilled by the *Resolution*'s return to his district. A great arioi ceremony had been held on the east coast (no doubt at Taputapuatea marae in Opoa) several days earlier, and arioi from around the archipelago were arriving on the west coast of the island. The shoreline was covered with their canoes, the houses were packed with people, and the women were preparing lavish feasts for their visitors. According to Hitihiti, when arioi visited each other, they were greeted with unstinting hospitality. The young men who had met him at Tahiti were arioi who had adopted him into their society, although he still knew little of their secrets. Sexually explicit dancing, love-making, kava drinking and drama were all part of the arioi festivities, and the arrival of the British added to the excitement. When Cook went ashore he was greeted by Reo and four or five old women, including Reo's mother, who cut themselves with tools made of shark's teeth, weeping bitterly, and embraced Cook tenderly. This was a time of sexual licence and the local women came out to the ship in droves, leaving the sailors enraptured by their welcome.

On 27 May, Reo and his family, accompanied by Boba, the viceroy of Tahaa, came out to visit Cook and his officers. Boba, a tall, handsome young arioi betrothed to Puni's twelve-year-old daughter, was expected to succeed him as high chief of Borabora. His current mistress, a beautiful young arioi dancer, was pregnant, although she made no secret of her intention to destroy the child as soon as it was born. The Forsters pleaded with her, trying to dissuade her from such a terrible act, but she laughingly retorted that although the god of England might not like it, it would please the god of Ra'iatea.

That afternoon Reo took them to a heiva in which his daughter Poiatua took the leading role. She danced beautifully, although they found her facial grimaces disconcerting, and her performance was followed by a series of entertaining interludes. The first of these was a skit depicting Captain Cook and his companions being robbed by Ra'iatean men; the second celebrated the Boraboran invasion of Ra'iatea; while the third was a burlesque carica-ture of childbirth. A large brawny man with a black bushy beard played the part of the expectant mother, and as he sat on the ground with his legs outstretched, he was supported by another man who sat behind him as the midwife. A large white cloth was spread over them both, and after many ludicrous wrigglings, twistings and exclamations, a tall 'lubberly' man crawled out from under the sheet, trailing a straw string with a little mat from his middle representing the umbilical cord and the afterbirth. The

Poiatua, the beautiful daughter of Reo, Cook's taio at Ra'iatea

audience found this hilarious, and as the arioi actor ran about the stage, chased by the 'mother' who squeezed her mock breasts, rubbing them on the 'baby's' face and stroking them up his backside, the sailors joined in their 'immoderate peals of laughter', likening the arioi actors to the 'drolls at St. Bartholomew's Fair'.

After this heiva, Cook invited Reo's pretty daughter, Poiatua, to visit the ship with her family. When they arrived at the gangway the next morning, the young woman who had sailed on the *Resolution* greeted each of their female visitors with a fond embrace. Hitihiti had already told Reo about the islands they had visited during their journey, and in return Reo regaled Cook and his officers with tales of a nearby island called Miromiro which was inhabited by a race of good-natured giants, although if any visitor annoyed these huge men they would pick him up and hurl him far off into the ocean. That afternoon he invited them to attend another heiva, where the dramas depicted arioi warriors being challenged to combat.

Although the people in Hamanino were having a wonderful time, Hitihiti seemed subdued and regretful. His friends and family were happy to see him, but it was nothing like the reception he had received on Tahiti, where he had been courted and lionised. His relatives importuned him for curiosities and red feathers until he had nothing left to show for his travels. His estates had been taken over by his brothers during his absence; and when he invited Cook to visit him at his home at the north-eastern end of the island, promising him pigs and fruit in abundance, it was Hitihiti's elder brother who presented his guests with two small pigs and cooked these for dinner. Cook had brought several bottles of brandy as his contribution to the feast, and they all drank very freely; and Hitihiti was carried back to the ship dead drunk, having mixed his kava with too much brandy. He would gladly have stayed on the *Resolution* for the voyage back to England, if there was any certainty that he could travel home again, but at that stage Cook had no plans to return to the Society Islands.

During their stay on Ra'iatea, the Forsters, Wales and Sparrman travelled around the island, looking for new plants and animals. They walked up the coast to the north, where they saw a marae dedicated to dogs, and travelled by boat to the south, where they visited Tainu'u Marae, a stone structure sixty yards long which still stands on the west coast of the island. The people called this marae 'Tupaia's marae', assuring them that Tupaia was an ari'i. This puzzled Johann, who had been told during his previous visit to Ra'iatea that Tupaia was not high-born, but his informants on that occasion had probably been Borabora people, Tupaia's enemies. The Europeans also walked up various valleys, collecting plants, shooting birds and enjoying glorious views of the ocean; and on 2 June they climbed the valley behind Hamanino, where, to their delight, they discovered some new species of plants and birds. That evening Cook entertained the Ra'iateans with a spectacular fireworks display, staged on a neighbouring *motu* [reef islet].

Cook was now preparing to leave the island, and people flocked to the ship with provisions, which they bartered for iron knives and hatchets made by the ship's armourer. The Forsters had been told about a *ta'ata 'orero* [orator] at Hamanino called Tutavai, who had an expert knowledge of ancestral traditions. On 3 June they interviewed this man at length about the gods of the various islands, the local calendar (which had fourteen lunar months of twenty-nine days each), the creation of the moon, marae ceremonies when gods descended to converse unseen with the priests, and an island called Manu'a, inhabited by tall spirits with fiery eyes, who had a habit of devouring hapless travellers.

Early the next morning, Reo and his family arrived with Boba and Uru, the high chief of the island, who brought lavish farewell gifts for Cook and his companions. As the ship was unmoored, Reo and his family wept bitterly, especially when Cook told them that he would never see them again. Upon hearing this, Reo asked him the name of his marae, and when Cook told him it was Stepney Parish, they all repeated this earnestly – 'Stepney Marae no Tute' ['Stepney, Tute's marae'].[12] Before Hitihiti left the ship, he asked Cook to 'tattoo' some words for him, so Cook wrote a character reference for him to give to future European visitors to the island. Hitihiti helped his shipmates to fire a gun in the farewell salute, then ran speechlessly from one cabin to another, embracing his friends and weeping. After climbing down into his canoe, as it moved away from the ship he 'gave a look up at her of unutterable anguish, burst into tears and droped down in the stern of it'.[13] As the ship sailed away, he stood there silently, and then hung down his head and hid it in his garments; when they cleared the reef they could see Hitihiti still waving his arms, and calling out heartfelt farewells to the Resolution.

Cook was convinced that he would never see the Society Islands again – 'these happy isles on which Benevolent Nature, with a bountiful and lavishing hand hath bestowed every blessing a man can wish'.[14] He had some months to spend in the tropics before attempting a final ice-edge cruise across the Atlantic the following summer. Although most of the places he had visited thus far were already known to Europeans, he was about to make a number of new 'discoveries'. The first of these came just twelve days out from Ra'iatea, when the man at the masthead sighted an uninhabited atoll, which Cook named 'Palmerston Island' after one of the Lords of the Admiralty. Four days later on 20 June, a high island (Niue) was sighted, where Cook decided to land so that the Forsters and Sparrman could gather plants for their collections. The boats took them to the north-western shore, where they began to explore the surrounding area. When several warriors with blackened bodies and feather head-dresses confronted the Resolution party, Cook waved green branches and called out to them in Tahitian. He and his people were pelted with rocks, however, provoking Sparrman and then Johann Forster to fire on these men with smallshot. Cook was annoyed about these shootings, although he was able to raise the Union Jack and ceremoniously take possession of the island. The sharp resistance to his landing may have been partly because he had landed by a ritual site where a number of paramount chiefs had been anointed and tried to raise his standard above it.[15]

After this ceremony, Cook and his companions made another brief landing on the coast, and then rowed to a rocky gully where they found some small carved canoes. While Hodges was sketching these craft, Cook placed nails, beads and medals in each canoe as a sign that they had come in peace, but while he was doing this another group of warriors attacked his party, hurling two spears which narrowly missed him and George Forster. Cook and then the Forsters tried to shoot at their attackers, but their muskets misfired, leaving them vulnerable until George finally managed to discharge his weapon, which was loaded with smallshot, holding the warriors at bay until the rest of their party arrived and opened fire, allowing them to retreat to the *Resolution*. That night Johann Forster exclaimed in his journal, 'Thus we left this *inhospitable* Shore with its still more *inhospitable* inhabitants;' giving expression to his sense of outrage by quoting the *Aeneid*: 'All were of the same opinion, to quit the accursed land, to leave a place where hospitality was defiled and give over our ship to the winds.'[16] For his part, Cook named Niue 'Savage Island'.

Several days later, on 26 June 1774, the *Resolution* came to Nomuka, one of the Tongan islands which Abel Tasman had named 'Rotterdam' during his 1643 visit. As they approached the south coast, several canoes came out and a man asked for Cook by name, having heard of his visit to 'Eua and Tongatapu nine months earlier. While the sloop was anchoring off the north coast of the island, one of the Tongans seized the lead-line just as a sailor was hauling it. Cook told this man to let go of the line, but he cut it instead, and when a musketball was fired through the hull of his canoe he simply paddled to the other side of the *Resolution*, where he was fired on with smallshot. After this he quickly took the lead-line back to the ship, where the other islanders threw him out of his canoe and made him swim back to shore, while they carried on trading coconuts, yams, breadfruit, bananas and shaddocks (a type of citrus fruit) with the British.

Early the next morning Cook landed in a sheltered, sandy cove on the north coast of Nomuka, where he was presented with a pig and offered a lovely young woman by a man and an old woman. High-born women had great authority in Tongan society, especially in respect to their brothers and brothers' children, and this old lady was confident and assertive. When Cook refused to sleep with the girl, she scolded him loudly, 'Sneering in my face and saying, what sort of man are you thus to refuse the embraces of so fine a young Woman.'[17] Discomfited by her tirade, Cook hurried back to the boat, but was followed to the beach, where the old woman tried to make him take the girl on board the *Resolution*. Cook had to refuse, provoking another round of abuse, because he had left strict orders with his officers that all of the men who had become infected with VD in the Society Islands should stay on board, and no women should be allowed on the vessel.

After breakfast Cook went ashore again with Sparrman and the Forsters, where the people helped to fill the casks with water from a brackish pond, loaded the boats with yams and shaddocks, and eagerly traded weapons and other 'curiosities'. As the Forsters walked inland along a path under a long row of high trees, past fertile gardens and thatched houses filled with yams, the local people greeted them courteously. They seemed remarkably friendly, collecting flowers from high trees for the scientists, pointing out plants and telling them their names, and fetching birds that the Forsters had shot in the forest. When they came to a large saltwater lagoon with three small islands[18] covered with flowering trees mirrored on its still surface, the Forsters were enchanted, and when they returned to the ship for dinner, they exclaimed at the beauty of the island and the kindness of its people.

Soon afterwards, however, there was an uproar on the beach. When the trading boats went back to the landing-place, they found Patten, the ship's surgeon, standing there in distress, stripped of his gun and most of his garments. He had gone off on his own shooting ducks with a local man as his guide, and when he returned to the landing-place, he found that the boats had already gone back to the ship without him. Seeing that he was alone, the crowd pressed around him, and several men began to threaten him with spears. The women tried to distract him with alluring gestures but he kept up his guard, offering a man a nail to paddle him back to the *Resolution*. As he climbed into this canoe, however, the people grabbed his fowling-piece and most of the ducks he had shot, and snatched his cravat and the coat from his back. He found a toothpick case in his pocket and waved it threateningly, pretending it was a pistol, keeping them at bay until a beautiful young woman took pity on him. Just then the boats set out from the ship and the crowd dispersed, but the young woman stayed with Patten, exchanging names with him. When Cook arrived and the surgeon told him what had happened, Cook remarked that the loss of his gun was a fair price to pay for his imprudence, and ordered the officers not to punish these people.

As Cook later reflected ruefully, however, 'In this I was wrong and only added one fault to a nother; my Lenity in this affair and the easy manner they had obtained this gun which they thought secure in their possession incourag'd them to commit acts of greater Violence.'[19] When Lieutenant Clerke went ashore the next morning with the watering-party, warriors surrounded the launch, and as the sailors were loading the casks back in the boat, these men closed in, shoving and jostling. The lieutenant's gun was seized and the cooper's adze was stolen, along with various other items. The officers were under strict instructions not to kill anyone, however, and despite this provocation, only one or two muskets were fired.

When Cook arrived shortly afterwards, he ordered the marines to be landed. He harangued the local people, and when the marines arrived on the beach, ordered them to confiscate two large double sailing canoes from their owners. As soon as these people realised what he was doing, Clerke's musket was brought back, but Cook was also determined to retrieve the carpenter's adze, since there were few of these tools on board the vessel. He ordered another canoe to be seized, and when its owner raised his spear, Cook aimed his gun and told him to drop his weapon. The man refused, so Cook shot him with smallshot, hitting his arms and legs and sending him limping off into the forest. He ordered the marines to line up and fire a volley to summon the shore party back to the beach, as three cannons were fired overhead from the *Resolution*.

As the local people fled, Cook called them back, and tried to make peace with them by returning the canoes to their owners. Nevertheless, the women looked at him reproachfully as the wounded man was brought to him on a plank. He sent for the ship's surgeon Patten to treat this man, but insisted that the adze must be returned, infuriating the old lady who had scolded him earlier, who berated him once more for his conduct. Eventually she went off, and shortly afterwards, the adze was brought back to Cook, along with a cartridge box and Patten's fowling-piece. When Patten came ashore he removed the smallshot and dressed the man's wounds, which were obviously very painful. As soon as he had finished, the islanders applied chewed sugar-cane and banana leaves as a poultice, and Cook gave the wounded man a knife and a spike nail, ordering beads to be distributed to the people.

Because Cook and Cooper were detained ashore by these events, Kendall's chronometer was not wound up at noon that day, and Wales forgot to wind it until it had stopped. He felt very guilty, but consoled himself by reflecting that he had taken some good altitudes earlier that morning, and that the situation was easily corrected. For the rest of that day, the Tongans continued to trade curiosities, yams and other goods, and were delighted when one of their number was presented with a pair of dogs. They obligingly gave Cook and the Forsters the names of twenty islands in the surrounding seas, and some of the women slept with the sailors. Early the next morning, the *Resolution* left Nomuka, sailing past the volcanic island of Tofua with a lateen-rigged sailing canoe in hot pursuit, whose crew were eager to trade with the Europeans.

Despite these violent encounters, Cook named the Tongan archipelago the 'Friendly Isles', in recognition of the 'extraordinary courteous and friendly disposition of their inhabitants'.[20] He recognised from the vocabularies that he and the Forsters had collected that the people of Tonga were related to each other, and to the Society Islanders, the Tuamotuans, the Marquesans, the Easter Islanders and the people of New Zealand. The high priest Tùpaia had included two of the Tongan islands (Vava'u and 'Uiha) in the list he dictated to Banks, and on the chart compiled for Cook during the *Endeavour* voyage. He had urged Cook to sail from Ra'iatea to the west, no doubt to extend the outer reaches of his geographical knowledge by visiting these islands. As he headed west from Tonga, however, Cook was sailing off the edge of Tupaia's chart and out of Polynesia, towards new groups of islands inhabited by other kinds of people.

13

Monboddo's Monkeys

On 2 July 1774, a low island was seen on the horizon, which proved to be another new discovery, the small Fijian island of Vatoa. The master took a boat to sound the entrance through the reef, watched intently by twenty armed warriors, who retired as soon as he landed. He left some nails, a knife and a few medals on the beach, and then returned to the ship. Cook, who had seen some breakers to the south-west, decided not to land at Vatoa, leaving Johann Forster fuming with frustration:

Either we stay but a day or 2 on one place, go late ashore, come early off again, are hindered to ramble about by the carelessness of people in guarding their Arms . . . People who know nothing of Sciences & hate them, never care whether they are enlarged & knowledge increases or not. This Age only cares to make the most money [a gibe at the sailors who were acquiring specimens and curiosities to sell upon their return home] . . . But why do I go over these unpleasant things for no purpose?[1]

On 9 July Cook turned to the north-west, heading for a group of islands which Quiros had discovered at the beginning of the seventeenth century. Four days later the *Resolution*'s men celebrated the second anniversary of their departure from Plymouth by getting very drunk. One of the sailors composed a hymn to mark the occasion, and having exhorted his shipmates to repent of their sins, drank so much grog that his legs gave way under him.

On 16 July land was sighted from the masthead, which Cook identified as Del Espiritu Santo of Quiros (in fact it was Maewo, another of the northern islands of Vanuatu). In a roaring gale the *Resolution* tacked around the island, looking for a sheltered harbour. Most of the pigs they had collected in the Society Islands had been killed and eaten, although they still had the yams they had obtained in Tonga, and Cook was anxious to get fresh supplies of food, wood and water. As they tacked along the northern coast of Omba on 18 July, George Forster admired the luxuriant forest and the high cascades that tumbled down the cliffs into the oceans. On 21 July as they reached the island of Malakula, people waded out into the sea with clubs or bows and arrows in their hands, waving green branches, a sign of greeting. After reconnoitring the coast they anchored off a bay sheltered by a coral reef (which Cook called 'Port Sandwich'), where a few men came out in their canoes, waving green branches and dipping their hands in the sea and pouring the water over their heads and faces. Two of these men came briefly on board, and during that night the islanders circled the *Resolution* in their canoes, carrying torches and inspecting the ship carefully.

These people spoke a language unlike any they had previously encountered, constantly using the word '*Tomarr*', meaning 'ancestors'. According to later accounts, they understood the Europeans to be the ghosts of their forebears and approached them with caution, for such spirits could be malevolent.[2] The British, on the other hand, were struck by the fact that Malakulans looked very different from any other Pacific Islanders they had met during their travels. The men had dark skins, black frizzled hair, long slender limbs, and wore conspicuous penis sheaths, and their bellies were tightly restricted by a rope, or 'nipped in with a Cord, like a Wasp', as Elliott put it.[3] When they boarded the sloop early the next morning and climbed rapidly up the rigging, chattering to each other, the sailors likened them to monkeys, although George Forster later added, 'We should be sorry . . . to supply Rousseau, or the superficial philosophers who re-echo his maxims, with the shadow of an argument in favour of the Orang-Outan system.'[4] This was a reference to Lord Monboddo, a Scottish Enlightenment philosopher who had argued that orang-outans were part of the human race, and that men were sometimes born with tails. When Joseph Banks and Dr Solander visited Monboddo after the *Endeavour* voyage in 1772, according to James Boswell (who was present), he quizzed them about the physiognomy of the Australian Aborigines, asking eagerly, 'Have they tails, Dr Solander?' 'No, my Lord, they have not tails.'[5]

Although his remarks about the appearance of the Malakulans were unflattering, George Forster described them as exceptionally acute, quickly deciphering the Europeans' signs and gestures, and teaching them large numbers of words from their language. Nevertheless, this encounter was soon marred by violence. When a sailor refused a man entry to the ship, pushing his canoe off with a boat-hook, the man grabbed a long bamboo cane and shoved at him. The sailor jabbed back with his boat-hook, and the warrior deliberately took an arrow out of his quiver, put it in his bow, and was getting ready to shoot when one of their visitors, who saw what was happening, leaped out of the cabin window into the sea to try and stop him. While they were struggling together, Lieutenant Cooper called for Cook, who ran on deck, aiming his gun at the angry warrior. The man

Cook and his men land at Malakula, by William Hodges

turned and aimed his arrow at Cook instead, so Cook shot him in the face and head with smallshot. The warrior clapped his hand to his head, but quickly recovered and aimed at the captain again, until Pickersgill peppered him in the chest with smallshot, sending him paddling back to shore. Another man who fired an arrow at Cook was shot at with a musket-ball, which missed him. When a cannon was fired overhead, all of these men retreated ashore, as gongs began to sound loudly in the forest.[6] Shortly afterwards Cook took two armed boats ashore with a guard of marines to cut wood, as a crowd of about five hundred warriors armed with barbed spears and bows and arrows (some of which were barbed) assembled around the landing-place.

When Cook landed alone and unarmed, carrying a green branch, their leader gave his weapons to a companion and greeted Cook with open arms, offering him a green branch and a pig as a sign of peace. When the Forsters went ashore, the people willingly gave them new words for their vocabulary and traded weapons for European goods, but would not allow them to walk inland. That afternoon Cook and Forster visited a small village, where there were a few gardens, some yams piled up on platforms, and a number of pigs and chickens. These people had taken a buoy from one of the anchors, but otherwise they seemed remarkably honest, keeping their side of any bargains and making no attempt to steal from the British. As Cook and Forster rowed along the coast they saw people dancing to the beat of drums around a fire. Cook might have been tempted to stay at Malakula, but that night the young midshipman John Elliott caught two large red fish, which his lieutenants and their messmates ate the next morning. These proved to be extremely poisonous, and everyone in the officers' mess was stricken with agonising headaches, vomiting, giddiness, numbed limbs and terrible diarrhoea, and later the skin peeled off their bodies. The dogs and pigs that had eaten the fish guts were extremely ill, and a pet parrot from Tonga which had nibbled some of the fish soon perished.[7] After leaving Port Sandwich, for almost a week as they sailed south down the island group, the gunner and some of the mates had to help Cook to run the ship, because all of the lieutenants, one of the mates and several midshipmen were so sick that they could not carry out their duties.

On 1 August there was a shout of 'Fire!' A piece of bark-cloth had been laid near a lamp and caught on fire, but fortunately it smoked furiously as it burned, giving the alarm, and was quickly extinguished. It was not until 4 August that Cook felt able to risk a landing on the island of Erromango, although once again Johann Forster complained bitterly:

We are to float on the water for ever, to have very few relaxation a shore & it is as if envy would have it so, that lands should be discovered, but none of its productions, because people think that if any man but they themselves makes discoveries, their reputation & fame would decrease in the same proportion, as that of others gets a little addition.[8]

Off the east coast of Erromango, Cook anchored the ship and took two armed boats ashore, looking for a sheltered harbour. After trying unsuccessfully to land on a small, rocky island (known to local people as 'The Place of the Dead'), Cook disembarked in a sandy bay, carrying only a green branch in his hand. Once again he was greeted by a large crowd of armed warriors, who according to their descendants also took Cook and his men to be ancestor spirits.[9] They pressed around until a man who seemed to be their leader told them to step back, arranging them in a semicircle and striking any of them who tried to move forward. Cook gave this man some trinkets, and in return was handed a bamboo full of water, some coconuts and a yam, in so friendly a fashion that he was 'charmed with their behaviour'. The men held on to their weapons, however, and when their leader gestured for the boat to be hauled ashore, Cook climbed back on board with his sailors. As soon as he put his foot on the gangway, some of the warriors grabbed it and tried to take it away, while others seized the oars; and when he pointed his musket at them, they hung back for a moment, then moved to haul the boat forward.

Cook aimed at their leader, whom he felt had betrayed him, but at this critical moment his musket misfired. As the warriors began to shoot their arrows and throw stones and spears at Cook's men, he ordered them to open fire, and they killed at least four of these men (although only two of the sailors were slightly wounded). Half of the muskets in the boat would not fire, which the Forsters blamed on the poor quality of flints supplied by the armoury; but one of the bow-men jabbed and hooked furiously with his boat-hook, giving his comrades time to reload their weapons. When a cannon was fired overhead, most of the warriors ran away, although some stayed in the fringes of the forest to throw spears at the British. Now that these 'ghosts' had shown themselves to be hostile, they wanted to drive them away, and they succeeded. Shortly afterwards Cook left Erromango and his ship vanished over the horizon, en route to Tanna, further south in the Vanuatu archipelago. As far as Cook could tell, the people of Erromango were quite different from the Malakulans, both in their appearance and the language that was spoken among them.

The *Resolution* now headed south past a small island, the Polynesian outlier of Aniwa. As they approached Tanna on 5 August, they realised that the large fire they had seen in the night was in fact an active volcano (Mount Yasur), which spewed out flames and pillars of fiery smoke with explosions that sounded like claps of thunder. At the east end of the island they found a small harbour, Uea, which Cook named Port Resolution. On 5 August two armed boats were sent in to sound the bay, followed by several canoes whose crews watched them curiously. When Lieutenant Cooper signalled that they had found a good anchorage, Cook brought the ship in and anchored in four fathoms of water; a little old man came out as an emissary, paddling his canoe towards the ship and throwing a coconut ahead on the sea as an offering to these ancestral beings. When he was within a stone's throw of the ship Cook approached this man in his boat and gave him some small trinkets, including a mirror.

This old man (whose name was 'Paowang') seemed cheerful and lively, and he was so entranced by the sight of his own face in the mirror that he gazed at it while his canoe drifted out to sea, carried by the outgoing tide. When he finally paddled back to the beach, other canoes came out, some holding more than twenty armed warriors, which surrounded the *Resolution*. After bartering a few coconuts and yams, some of these men tried to tear down the ship's ensign and knock the rings off her rudder with their clubs; while another old man attempted to take salt meat from a net which was being towed overboard, soaking the meat for cooking. They were told to move away from the ship, but shook their spears in defiance, and when one man pointed his bow and arrow at the sailors a cannon was fired overhead, and they all dived into the water. Only one good-looking young

Cook's landing at Tanna

fellow remained standing in his canoe, looking at his fellow warriors with contemptuous amusement.

When they realised that they were unharmed, the warriors laughed ruefully and climbed back into their canoes, returning to the ship, where a bald-headed old man paddled his canoe towards the anchor buoy, trying to tow it away. Cook ordered him to let it go, and when this man ignored him, Cook fired at him with smallshot. He threw away the buoy but soon went to grab it again, and a musketball was fired close to him. The old man dropped the buoy and paddled alongside the ship, where he offered Cook a coconut, looking up at him with a bold, bemused expression. Another man now paddled towards the buoy, and after some hesitation, also decided to try and take it. After several warnings a musketoon was fired close to his canoe, the ball skipping over the surface of the sea to the beach, where it frightened the people who stood there watching. When this man realised that he was uninjured he returned to the buoy, and Cook ordered a musketoon, and then a swivel and a ship's cannon to be fired overhead, as the warriors fled inland.

The *Resolution* was taken further into the bay, and after dinner, Cook landed with his armed party between two groups of armed warriors. As the marines lined up, Cook gave gifts of cloth and medals to several old people who presented him with green coconut fronds, another gesture of appeasement, and ordered his men to fill two casks of water from a nearby pond. Johann Forster talked with some of these people, who told him that the name of their island was 'Tanna' (although this simply meant 'ground' in one of the local languages) and gave him words for his vocabulary, a few of which seemed similar to Tongan. These men were strongly built, with long hair plaited in strings, naked except for penis wrappers and a string around their waists, and armed with spears, clubs, slings and bows and arrows. After the water casks and a load of coconuts had been collected, Cook took his party back to the ship, while the volcano belched clouds of ashes and cinders that showered down on the decks of the vessel. Later that afternoon a barn owl which had been disturbed by the racket flew along the beach, and as the local people pelted it with rocks it tried to fly towards the ship, but soon settled on the surface of the water. A canoe came out to pick it up and brought the owl to the *Resolution*, handing it over to the strangers – a gesture which surely had ritual significance.

Early the next morning, at least a thousand armed warriors assembled in two divisions at the landing-place. At this time the region was dominated by two competing confederations of tribes, one to the east and the other to the west, and as they lined up, more warriors kept coming over the hill on the western side of the harbour.[10] By now the *Resolution* was only a musket shot from the beach, with her guns aimed ashore to cover the landing-party. A few canoes came out with bananas and coconuts and traded peacefully, but when one man accepted some trinkets in exchange for his club and then refused to hand over the weapon, Cook called to him several times to send up the club, and when he was ignored, shot him in the face with smallshot. The canoes paddled rapidly away, chased by several musketoon balls which splashed alongside in the water.

Shortly after this shooting Paowang, the old man who had acted as an envoy during the previous day, came out to the ship with offerings of coconuts, yams and sugar-cane. Cook gave him a fine red Tahitian garment, and indicating that the warriors ashore should put down their weapons, he took several clubs from the old man's canoe and threw them into the water. Paowang seemed to understand Cook's message, because he went unarmed for the rest of the day, although the warriors on the beach held on to their weapons.

When the old man returned ashore, Cook ordered the marines and a party of armed sailors to follow him in the launch and two boats, and as they came close to the beach, Paowang and two other elders piled up some bunches of plantains, a yam and two taro roots marked by four small reeds, as an offering to the white-skinned 'ghosts'. Cook gestured for the two divisions of warriors to move back so that his men could land, but although the elders tried to get them to obey, the warriors kept moving forward. As George Forster remarked, they no doubt thought it 'absurd and unjust that a few strangers should prescribe laws to them on their own ground'.[11] Cook now ordered a musket to be fired over their heads and most of the men ran away, although the old man and his companions stood there calmly. One bold warrior, however, capered and slapped his backside at the strangers; and as the Lieutenant of Marines hit him with smallshot, Cook gave a signal for the ship's artillery to fire over their heads, and five cannons, two swivel guns and four musketoons boomed and flashed all at once, shattering the coconut palms and cutting their fronds to pieces.

All of the warriors now ran away except Paowang, who stood calmly beside his pile of plantains. He indicated that the strangers should stop shooting at his people, and Cook had an area staked out and roped off on the beach, to keep the warriors back from the watering-party. Later that afternoon as the sailors hauled the seine on the beach, catching a huge quantity of fish, Paowang met again with Cook, presenting him with a small pig as an offering and receiving a large nail and a hatchet. When Cook's men landed the next morning to collect wood and water, the elders from the confederation to the east of the bay seemed conciliatory, although warriors from the western confederation continued to threaten the strangers. Finally, one of these men taunted the British, slapping his naked backside and turning it towards them, and was shot in the thigh for his impudence.

From that time on, most of the people who came to the beach were unarmed, and the elders did their best to control the younger warriors. Several days later when Cook took a party inland to explore the volcano, they were turned back by armed warriors (presumably from the western confederation) who blocked their pathway. Over the next two weeks, as the sailors explored the area, Paowang and other men from the eastern confederation steered them away from pathways and areas under the control of their enemies. They entered the forest behind the landing-place, walking along a path across a low neck of land to the eastern coast, where the islands of Aneityum and Futuna were visible in the distance, collecting new species of plants and birds en route, and examining plantations of yam, taro, fig and coconut trees. They also visited the west side of the bay, where hot springs bubbled at the foot of a high hill, and as they climbed up its slopes, they discovered a number of volcanic vents, whose temperature Johann Forster tested with his portable thermometer.

The local people tried to keep the British away from their settlements, and if they encountered women during these excursions, the women refused to look at them and ran off if they were gazed at. When the sailors gave them gifts, they wrapped them up in a leaf and did not touch them with their hands, to avoid being contaminated by the spiritual power of the strangers. Only the people at Paowang's village on the east side of the bay seemed friendly and hospitable, offering them yams, sugar-cane and drinking coconuts; although when Cook sought to look into a house near this settlement where a sick man was lying, they would not allow him to enter.

On his third day at Port Resolution, Johann Forster exchanged names with a man called 'Oomb-yegan'. As George Forster commented: 'this custom of making friendship, by a reciprocal exchange of names, is common in all the southern islands which we had hitherto visited, and in reality has something in it very engaging and affectionate.'[12] The next day Captain Cook met Fannakko, the courageous young man who had laughed when the *Resolution*'s cannons were first fired, and invited him to dinner on the vessel. He told Cook the names of the surrounding islands, and when Cook showed him around the sloop, he was fascinated by the goats, dogs and cats, calling them all *puaka*, the Tongan word for pig. He seemed keen to have a dog, so Cook gave him a breeding pair of dogs and a hatchet; and in return his companions gave Cook some sugar-cane, a cock, and a few coconuts. In general, the Tannese, like the Malakulans, avoided exchanging food with the British, for spirits were not thought to need earthly sustenance; and they procured only ritual offerings of foodstuffs on the island.

Cook tried to foster his relationship with Paowang, the old 'peace-maker' from the eastern confederation, by giving him gifts and inviting him on board the *Resolution*. The old leader regarded the interior of the ship with 'the greatest indifferency', however, and left Cook's gifts lying strewn on the bushes around his dwelling. Towards the end of their stay, Cook also met the 'King or Chief of the Island', a tall, lean old man named 'Yogai' with a bald head, a wrinkled face and a benign, open expression. He was probably a *yeremwanu* or ritual leader, because there were no strong and established systems of authority on Tanna.[13] Yogai was accompanied by his son and another fine-looking young boy whom Cook invited out to the ship, where he gave them presents, and although they ate a meal of yams, they would not touch any of the European food that they were offered.

The Forsters soon realised that a number of different languages were spoken on Tanna, including some with words which seemed very close to Tongan (in fact, the languages spoken on the nearby Polynesian outlying islands of Futuna and Aniwa, settled centuries earlier by back-migrations from West Polynesia). The local men told them about other islands in the nearby seas, including an island called 'Etonga', which George Forster thought might be Tongatapu, and indeed there may have been voyaging contacts with Tonga, since these islands were mentioned in Tongan traditions. During their conversations, the people asked the Europeans to sing for them. They liked the German and English songs, but Dr Sparrman's Swedish tunes had them in ecstasies. As George Forster commented wryly, 'their judgement of music was not influenced by the same rules which regulate the taste of other countries.'[14] George, who thought that Tannese music was more complex and rhythmic than the music of Tahiti or Tonga, missed his 'ingenious and obliging friend' James Burney, and wished that he was there to record it.

As they got to know the Europeans better, the Tannese men told them that they sometimes ate human flesh, and warned that if they strayed onto enemy pathways or tried to walk into enemy territory, they would be killed and eaten. George Forster was dismayed to discover that these people were cannibals:

> Those who contend, that anthropophagy has the plea of the most cruel necessity, will hardly be able to account for its existence in a nation living in a rich and fertile country, having plenty of vegetable food, and likewise well provided with domestic animals. The principle of revenge seems much more likely to have produced this extraordinary custom, whereever it has been observed . . . The natives of Tanna doubtless are engaged, either in civil feuds with each other, or in frequent wars with the adjacent islanders . . . We have therefore, I think, great room to believe, that the violence of resentment has insensibly led them to the customs of eating human flesh, which they practise according to their own confession.[15]

In fact, only a small number of families on Tanna had the right to eat human flesh, and the bodies of slain enemies were carried along ceremonial pathways from one district to another, being exchanged for pigs until a family with this right decided to consume them.[16] This discovery had horrified the sailors, however, since most of them regarded cannibalism with revulsion. On 10 August, when some local boys threw some stones at the wood-cutters, they were fired at by the petty officers. Cook was annoyed, noting in his journal: 'I was much displeased at such an abuse of our fire Arms and took measures to prevent it for the future.'[17]

Shortly after these shootings a rumour flew around among the sailors that the Tannese were sodomites as well as cannibals, because several of them had tried to entice members of the crew into the bushes for sexual purposes. William Wales was convinced that the crew members in question had been mistaken for women, since they were either chubby-faced or carrying bundles (like the local women), and on 13 August he decided to put this hypothesis to the test. He was out walking with the Forsters towards the volcano, and when Johann's servant, who was carrying the plant-bag, went into the bushes, Wales nudged one of the local men who accompanied them, and gave him a sly look accompanied by a graphic gesture. Two of these men jumped up with great glee and followed the servant into the bushes, but soon came out looking shame-faced and abashed, while their companions shrieked with mirth, mocking them and calling out, 'Yeruman, yeruman!'

['It's a man! a man!'], convincing the sailors that they were not homosexuals after all.[18]

About this time, however, other interactions with local people caused tensions among the expedition's members. On 15 August, when Johann Forster was in the forest collecting plants, he came across a nutmeg tree where some pigeons were feeding. He asked his guide the local name of this tree, and thinking that Johann was pointing at the birds, the man told him '*guanattan*' (*yawinatuan* or 'green pigeon' in his dialect).[19] Upon returning to the landing place, Johann showed the leaves from this tree to a group of people, who gave it another name altogether. When Johann testily insisted that this was a 'guanattan', the guide tried to get his fellow islanders to agree, in an effort to placate the stranger. As soon as Johann realised what was going on, he flew into a rage, yelled that he was being cheated, and according to William Wales, shoved the guide with his foot and spat in his face for giving him false information.[20] When Lieutenant Clerke came over to see what was the matter, annoyed by this high-handed behaviour he accused Johann of 'kicking up a Cabal' and ordered him to stop it. Johann retorted that there was nothing wrong with punishing a man who had deceived him, and told Clerke that he had no right to give him orders. Infuriated, Clerke replied that he could force Forster to do as he pleased, and would order the sentry to shoot him if he disobeyed. Forster was so incensed by this remark that he pulled out his pistol, aiming it at the lieutenant.

Afterwards, when both Clerke and Forster told Captain Cook their version of these events, Cook upheld Clerke's right to give Forster orders. Forster was furious, demanding to have this ruling in writing, and when Cook refused, he said that 'he durst not be ashamed to write what he was not ashamed to say' and accused Cook of being afraid of the consequences. Cook was fed up with Forster's obstinacy and rudeness, and regarded his behaviour as stupid and irresponsible, since he might have provoked the local people into an attack on his shipmates. Clerke had been ill and was not as good-tempered as usual, and Forster's attitude was maddening. As for Johann, he persisted in acting the martyr:

This [dispute] only shall serve to shew, what a hard thing it is, to be on board a Man of war, where every petty Officer or boy pretends to command Men, that never were intended to be controuled by such inconsiderable beings: the greater part of these people are so used to command & to bashaw it over other people, that no Man of honour will for the future venture to go on any Errand on board His Majesties Ship, for fear to be ill treated by these imperious people, who cringe ashore for preferment,

& are often thought to be civil, nay polite; but as soon as they return to their Element the Sea, they are as rough & boisterous as it.[21]

Not surprisingly, when the sailors hauled the seine a couple of days later and caught a new species of stingray, Lieutenant Cooper cut off the tail of the ray and threw it away rather than give it to Forster. Charles Clerke was a great favourite among his shipmates, and Forster's open defiance of his authority, and his incessant complaints about the ship and its crew had turned them against him.

During their stay on Tanna, the mood among the *Resolution*'s men was increasingly fractious. On 17 August one of the marines, William Tow, was flogged for trading with the natives while on guard duty. The marines were resentful, and two days later, when another marine, William Wedgeborough, was on guard, he ordered some local men who had stepped across a line drawn on the sand to move back, and to keep away from the sailors. When they ignored him, Wedgeborough shoved one of these men and raised his musket, and when the man aimed his bow and arrow at Wedgeborough in return, the marine shot him. Cook was present, although he did not have a clear view of the confrontation. He was very angry about the shooting, however, which he considered completely unjustified:

At this time I had my eyes fixed on them and observed the sentery present his piece (as I thought at the men) and was just going to reprove him for it, because I had observed that when ever this was done, some or another of the Natives would hold up their arms, to let us see they were as ready as us, but I was astonished beyond measure when the sentry fired for I saw not the least cause . . . The rascal who perpetrated this crime, pretended that a Man had laid an arrow a Cross his bow and was going to shoot it at him, so that he apprehended himself in danger, but this was no more than what they had always done, and I believe with no other view than to shew they were armed as well as us.[22]

The man was shot in his left arm and side, and although Cook called for the ship's surgeon to treat him, he died shortly afterwards. When Cook ordered Wedgeborough to be clapped into irons and taken to the ship, many of the sailors were angry, since they thought that the shooting had been warranted.

According to Johann Forster, this affair provoked a violent argument between Cook and his officers. The Lieutenant of Marines, Edgcumbe, said that 'the man was entitled to believe he was not posted there merely to provide a target for arrows';[23] while Cooper, the first lieutenant, argued that the people on Tanna had often threatened the sentries, and because they were not allowed to retaliate, the marines were being treated with increasing insolence. Charles Clerke brought matters to a head when he told Cook that Wedgeborough was not to blame, since he had instructed the sentries that if a warrior went to throw a spear at them or fire an arrow, they should shoot him. Cook's orders were that the men should never fire their muskets unless they were actually under attack, however, and if Clerke had indeed issued such an instruction, it was a direct challenge to Cook's authority.[24]

Cook's philosophy about how to handle encounters with indigenous peoples was clear and unambiguous. It had been forged during his first Pacific voyage, and was often restated in his journals. Just three months earlier, in Tahiti, he had written:

Three things made them our fast friends, Their own good Natured and benevolent disposition, gentle treatment on our part, and the dread of our fire Arms; by our ceaseing to observe the Second the first would have wore off, and the too frequent use of the latter would have excited a spirit of revenge and perhaps taught them that fire Arms were not such terrible things as they had imagined, they are very sencible of the superiority they have over us in numbers and no one knows what an enraged multitude might do.[25]

His views on these matters were based partly on the Earl of Morton's instructions for the *Endeavour* expedition, and partly on his own inclinations, perhaps shaped by his youthful experiences with the Quakers. Cook was determined not to allow his men to fire their muskets at will, favouring instead a strategy of using smallshot as a first warning, followed by a musketball through a canoe or at a bird; shooting musketoon balls overhead or into the water, or firing the great guns overhead to demonstrate the ship's firepower. Only in the last resort would he allow his men to shoot to kill, for as he reflected during this visit to Tanna:

We enter their Ports without their daring to make opposition, we attempt to land in a peaceable manner, if this succeeds its well, if not we land nevertheless and mentain the footing we thus got by the Superiority of our fire arms, in what other light can they than at first look upon us but as invaders of the Country; time and some acquaintance with us can only convince them of their mistake.[26]

Many of his shipmates, however, utterly disagreed with Cook on this point. They thought that his approach gave 'savages' more rights than his own men, exposing the sailors to undue risk, and allowing the 'savages' to treat them with outright contempt on occasion. They wanted to be able to use their guns more freely (especially on cannibals). The young midshipman, John Elliott, spoke for many of his shipmates when he wrote:

Tho . . . Captn Cook was a Most Brave, Just, Humane, and good Man, and the fittest of all others for such a voyage, yet I must think that here . . . he lost sight of both justice, and Humanity. Now the question was, whether the sentry was to receive a Poisoned Arrow into him (for he was sure to be hit) or to save himself he was to shoot the Man. The sentry choose the latter, and he instantly levelled his Musquet and Shot the Man. For which Capt. Cook ordered him on board and had him brought to the gangway to be flogged, but was induced through the perswasions of all the officers, to forgo the flogging, but kept him in Irons a considerable time.[27]

In his journal, Cook made no mention of this disagreement with his officers. He may have been content to let it pass, since they were still recovering from the terrible effects of fish-poisoning; and he knew that in this matter, shipboard opinion was against him. Wedgeborough was not flogged, but confined in irons for two months as a punishment. Ironically, it seems that Cook's friends from the eastern confederation were gratified by this shooting. During his visit to their main hamlet, he had tried to enter a shelter in a ceremonial clearing (*yimwarem*) where a sick man was lying; many years later when a missionary discussed Cook's visit with some local people, they told him that afterwards Cook had sought out the people who bewitched this man, and shot them:

They say that he went up to a marum [sacred clearing] and saw a chief very ill and people wailing over him, and on being told that certain persons were burning his rubbish and causing all the sickness he sought them out and fired upon them![28]

Although Cook knew nothing of this interpretation of his conduct, he had a shrewd idea about the likely consequences of such a shooting. He ordered the *Resolution* to be prepared for an immediate departure, and sailed from Port Resolution the next morning.

After leaving Tanna, Cook tacked south-east past the Polynesian outlier of Futuna, and then turned north-west to chart the western coasts of Tanna, Erromango, Efate (which he named Sandwich Island 'in honour of My Noble Patron the Earl of Sandwich') and Malakula. Off the northern coast of Espiritu Santo, where three sailing canoes came out to the ship, Cook was able to establish that their crews spoke yet another new language, but there were no further contacts with local people. He sailed around the rest of Espiritu Santo, thus completing his survey of the archipelago, which he named 'New Hebrides' after the islands off the west coast of Scotland. Cook also used this period to improve the 'young gentlemen's' skills in surveying methods, for as John Elliott proudly noted, 'I surveyed this Group Myself, and settled them by my own Lunar Observations, and Capt. Cook told me, they were nearly as correct as his own.'[29]

Several days after leaving the coast of Espiritu Santo, on 4 September 1774, a midshipman sighted high hills from the masthead. This proved to be a very large island not previously seen by Europeans, which Cook named 'New Caledonia'. Although some sailing canoes came out to look at the ship, they stayed at a safe distance and made no contact with the British. Early the next morning Pickersgill took the boats through an entrance in the reef, where he met two fishing canoes and had an amiable exchange with their crews, including a fine young man named Tea Puma, the high chief or ariki of the neighbouring district of Balade. It seems that at this time the chiefs of New Caledonia had close contacts with Polynesian settlers on the Loyalty Island of Ouvea, which helps to explain the use of a Polynesian term for their leaders.[30] Pickersgill gave Tea Puma some medals and other trinkets, and when he offered similar gifts to the rest of the crew, they handed these over to their young leader. In return, Tea Puma gave Pickersgill some stinking fish, which may have been a ritual offering. According to later accounts, these people also thought at first that the Europeans were ancestral spirits 'who . . . had become white and more beautiful in the other world',[31] and the rotting fish may have been an offering intended to bridge the gap between the dead and the living.

After Pickersgill had sounded the gap through the barrier reef, Cook brought the *Resolution* in, anchoring by 'Observatory Island'. Some islanders swam more than a mile to the ship, which was soon surrounded by twenty double sailing canoes, whose crews quickly boarded the vessel. When the officers sat them down to dinner these men watched curiously, eating the yams that had been obtained at Tanna, although they refused to touch salt pork or drink a drop of red wine. They were very robust and tall, with mild features and frizzled hair and dark, swarthy complexions; and their language was different to all of those so far recorded by Cook and the Forsters. These men were eager to acquire red cloth and spike nails, and looked curiously at the goats, pigs, dogs and cats, all of which seemed to be unfamiliar to them.

Later that day when Cook and his companions went ashore, they were guided through a huge crowd of people, many of them unarmed and the men naked except for the customary penis wrappers, although some wore black caps decorated with red feathers. As the marines lined up, when the officers indicated that the people should give them more room, they did so very peacefully. Tea Puma was present, accompanied by some old men, and Cook's guide indicated that he should present his gifts to these dignitaries. After some affable greetings, Tea Puma called for silence and made a short speech, in which he seemed to ask several questions that were answered by three old men in the crowd. He was followed by a man who made another oration, while the old men grunted or nodded their heads in approval.

After the speeches, the Europeans were free to mingle with the gathering. Johann Forster noted that many of these people had elephantiasis in their legs, and examined the genitals of several of the men, noting that their foreskins had been split and tied before being wrapped in a penis sheath. If the men thought he was an ancestor, this may help to explain why they tolerated this conduct, but even so, it must have seemed eccentric. For their part, the British found the local dress code bizarre. When Charles Clerke gave one of the warriors a stocking, for instance, the man pulled it on over his penis sheath; and when he was offered a string of beads and a medal, he tied these onto his sheath as decorations. As Clerke noted quizzically, 'In short let that noble part be well decorated and fine, they're perfectly happy, and totally indifferent about the state of all the rest of the Body.'[32]

Cook was eager to find fresh water, and his guide took him in the boat about two miles along the coast, to a small river with a straggling village beside it. They met the local chief, a man named 'Heebai', who seemed very friendly. The land on one side of this river was planted with sugar-canes and yams, with coconut trees nearby, where Cook could hear a cock crowing. As they rowed up the creek George Forster shot a duck on the wing, greatly impressing their guide, who asked for its body so he could show his countrymen. The water was too far inland for the watering-party, however, so they soon returned to the *Resolution*. That night the ship's butcher, an older man who was very popular among his shipmates, fell down the fore hatchway and fractured his skull, expiring some hours later.

After breakfast the next morning, Cook went with William Wales to observe a solar eclipse from a nearby sandy island, so that they could check Kendall's watch and fix the ship's position. At the same time, George Forster went with several officers to the west of the bay, where they found more irrigated plantations and high rocky ground, and a freshwater river. While they were filling the water casks with the help of some local men, Tea Puma arrived, and they gave him some medals and other small gifts, receiving a sling and some clubs in exchange before returning to the ship for dinner. Johann Forster had spent the morning on board, and, as he sat down to eat, Lieutenant Cooper told him the boats were about to go ashore, and that he should go with them if he wanted to collect plants on the island. Forster was furious, thinking that he was being forced to choose between his meal and his botanical duties, and stayed where he was, but he later complained bitterly to Cook about Cooper's conduct. This episode provoked another outburst in his journal, which showed how far his relationships with his shipmates had degenerated:

The whole of the Affair is this, the greater part of the Men in the Ship have begun to calculate their pay & find that it will not amount to 4000 pounds Sterl., which government allows me, & therefore I am the object of their Envy & they hinder me in the pursuit of Natural History, where they can, from base & mean, dirty principles, beneath any Man of Sense ... But it cannot be otherwise expected from the people who have not sense enough to think reasonably & beyond the Sphere of their mean grovelling Passions.[33]

That night the ship's butcher died, and very early the next morning, before any of the local people came out to the ship, his body was taken out to sea on a boat and buried. Afterwards, Cook took the Forsters inland to find plants, and in the heat of the day he walked so fast that Johann was exhausted. The local people came out of their houses and gave them sugar-canes and cups of fresh water in a very friendly fashion. After dinner George Forster accompanied Cook ashore and wandered off on his own, coming across a small hamlet where he found a man seated with a little girl on his lap, cutting her hair. George gave some black beads to the little girl and the man, who seemed delighted. Later he visited a small living compound in this hamlet, where three women were cooking yams in a large earthernware pot stuffed full of dry grasses and green leaves, and set on a fire. These women gestured anxiously, telling George to leave them at once, and indicating that they would be strangled if their menfolk found them alone with the stranger. When he returned to the watering-place, however, he found several other women mingling with the sailors, beckoning them to join them in the bushes, although as soon as the men came after them, they ran away laughing.

By now, Cook had recovered from his illness and was physically fit again, but that afternoon his clerk purchased a large puffer-fish for his supper. When he sat down with Sparrman and the Forsters that evening, the fish had not been cooked, but Cook's servant brought in the liver and Cook told him to fry it as a delicacy. Cook ate a piece about the size of a crown, Johann ate about twice as much, George took just a little, while Sparrman refused, since he would never eat the liver of any animal. At about four o'clock the next morning, Johann woke up feeling giddy and ill, with numbed, heavy limbs, so that he could not stand or move his arms properly. He called for his servant and tried to throw up, and then woke his son and the captain, both of whom had similar symptoms of poisoning. Cook summoned Patten, the surgeon, who told them to drink warm water to make them vomit, and gave them a mix of wine, lemon juice, sugar and boiling water. They slept well after that, although when they woke they found that one of the pigs which had eaten the fish's entrails had died, and a number of the dogs were also suffering. They still felt giddy and drowsy, and when Johann tried to do some writing, he found that he could not concentrate, and made stupid errors. They took several days to recover from this bout of fish-poisoning, which left them feeling weak and exhausted, and unable to do justice to exploring the new island. The following morning, however, Cook despatched Pickersgill to examine the nearby island of Balabio. Although the cutter sprang a leak and almost sank during the passage, Pickersgill received a friendly welcome from the local people when he arrived on the island. That night when they saw some sailors picking at a large beef-bone for their supper, however, they looked disgusted and soon left, assuming that this was a cannibal meal.

After recovering from the bout of fish-poisoning the Forsters managed several excursions ashore, and on 12 September they accompanied Cook to the river to the east of the bay, to deliver a pig of each sex to 'Heebai', the chief of the first hamlet they had visited. The chief could not be found, so Cook offered the pigs to a grave old man in the village, who told him to take them to the ariki, and sent him to a house where about ten middle-aged men seated in a circle invited him to join them. Cook did so, and endeavoured to explain the virtues of his pigs, and when he finally handed them over, they gave him six yams in exchange for these peculiar animals. During his visit to this village Cook noticed large irrigated plantations of taro and gardens of yams, sugar-cane and plantains, where women and children were working. That afternoon he took possession of New Caledonia in the name of King George III of Great Britain, and had an inscription to that effect carved onto a large tree near the watering-place. When Cook had become ill, Tea Puma made a ceremonial visit to the *Resolution*, bringing yams and sugar-cane, so Cook sent him a dog and a bitch in return, a gift which delighted him. Tea Puma lived over the nearby mountains, and after this visit they did not see him again, so Cook left Balade without saying goodbye to the young high chief. He and his shipmates took away a positive impression of the local inhabitants, however, whom they described as 'charming, benevolent, good People'.[34]

As the *Resolution* sailed towards the northern end of New Caledonia, Cook decided not to try and get around the island. He could see only shoals in that direction, which he thought might stretch all the way to the Barrier Reef off the coast of Australia. Upon heading back down the eastern coast, however, the ship was almost driven onto a reef and the boats had to tow it out of danger. Cook sailed south to the Isle of Pines (Kunie) and the Botany Isles, where they made a brief landing and had several more narrow escapes from treacherous coral reefs. Once the *Resolution* was safely back in the open sea, Cook headed south-east to New Zealand, where he planned to rest his crew and collect fresh supplies of wood and water. After that, he intended to cross the Pacific to Cape Horn and into the high reaches of the Southern Atlantic, completing the search for Terra Australis before sailing home to England.

On 9 October a small rocky island was sighted which Cook named after the Duchess of Norfolk. When Cook took a party ashore, the island proved to be uninhabited. The hills were covered with flax bushes, towering pine trees which seemed ideal for masts and spars, and tangled forests where pigeons and brightly coloured parrots darted through the canopy. Many of the plants (except for the spruce pines) on Norfolk Island seemed very like the species in New Zealand and New Caledonia. The men collected cabbages from the cabbage trees and caught a good haul of fish from the rocks, before returning to the ship for supper. That night they 'ate fish & cabage made into Sallad, & were as happy as possible'.[35] As they sailed from Norfolk Island, George Forster noted that 'the melody of the birds was very pleasing in this little deserted spot, which if it had been of a greater size, would have been unexceptionable for an European settlement.'[36]

By now they were yearning to get to New Zealand and their familiar anchorage, Ship Cove, where they knew they could get fish and greens in plenty. The salt meat on board was unappetising and the biscuits were mouldy and rotten, and they had only been able to procure a few pigs, root vegetables and fruit at the New Hebrides and New Caledonia. As George Forster remarked:

All our officers, who had made several voyages round the world, and experienced a multiplicity of hardships, acknowledged at present, that all their former sufferings were not to be compared to those of the present voyage, and that they had never before so thoroughly loathed a salt diet ... It was owing to our having such an excellent preservative as sour-krout on board, that the scurvy did not at this time make any considerable progress amongst us; but our situation was indeed wretched enough, without the additional horrors of disease.[37]

Five days later, tossed by a gale which tore the jib sail to tatters, they sighted Mt Egmont on the west coast of New Zealand, and on 18 October the *Resolution* sailed into Queen Charlotte Sound, where Cook hoped to find news of the *Adventure*.

*

As soon as they anchored in Ship Cove, Cook looked around eagerly for his consort ship, and sent some men ashore to check on the message which he had left for Captain Furneaux. The glass bottle with its message was gone and the marker tree had been cut down, but shags were nesting in the cove, suggesting that no one had been there over the winter. Other trees had been felled with saws and axes, indicating that the *Adventure* must have stayed in the Sound, although Cook was surprised that Furneaux had left him no message. As the work on refitting the ship began and birds were shot and greens were gathered, Cook went with the Forsters to 'Cannibal Cove' to see if they could find any of the local people. When they returned to Ship Cove later that day, one of the ship's cannons was fired as a signal to any people in the vicinity. No one appeared, and the next few days were chilly, stormy and miserable, so they stayed on board the ship, feeding on fish, celery and scurvy grass and resting from their exertions.

On 21 October, the sun came out again and birds sang loudly in the forest. Cook went with the Forsters to Motuara to check on the cabbages they had planted during their last visit, and lit a fire to summon the local people. Still no one appeared, but that night they feasted on birds, fish and fresh greens, which 'contributed to make a kind of festival in the ship, which the levity of the mariners rendered the more chearful, as every past discomfort was already forgotten.'[38] The Sound seemed strangely quiet, although on 24 October at daybreak two canoes sailed past the point of Shag Cove then paddled off at high speed as soon as they saw the *Resolution*. Cook decided to go and find these people, so after breakfast he took the boats with the Forsters and Sparrman to Shag Cove, where they heard shouting in the forest. Three or four people dressed in old, shaggy cloaks stood on a knoll near some houses, and when Cook and his companions landed in the cove, they seemed very apprehensive. Cook knew nothing about the killing and eating of the *Adventure*'s men at Grass Cove, but these people were well aware of those events, and expected a swift retribution.

When Cook beckoned them over and pressed noses with them, 'Joy took the place of fear, they hurried out of the woods, embraced us over and over and skiped about like Mad men.'[39] Cook and his companions recognised some of these people, but when they asked them for news of their old friends, they could barely understand what they were saying. All that Johann Forster could gather was that there had been killings, and that some of their old friends were dead, while others had gone to Te Rawhiti on the other side of Cook Strait. Despite these garbled exchanges, their leader, a middle-aged man called 'Pitere' (whom the sailors nicknamed 'Pedro'), seemed delighted when Cook gave him a piece of red cloth, a nail and some bark-cloth, presenting him with a large quantity of fish in return.

The next morning Pedro and his people came alongside the *Resolution* in their canoes, bringing 'curiosities' and fish to barter for iron tools, bark-cloth, English cloth and mouldy biscuits. Over the next few days they camped near the ship, supplying the sailors with fresh fish while the men worked to refit the vessel. On 28 October Cook visited West Bay, looking for the pigs and chickens he had landed there during his previous visit. When he returned to the ship, however, one of the marines, who had been talking with some of his friends from previous visits, told him a chilling story:

A ship had been lately lost in the Straits, that some of the people got on shore and that the Natives stole their Cloathes &c for which several where shot: but afterwards when they could fire no longer the Natives got the better and killed them with their Pata-patoos and eat them. But that they had no hand in the affair, which they said happened at Vanua Aroa near Teerawhitte which is on the other side of the Strait. One man said it was two Moons ago; but another contradicted him and counted on his fingers about 20 or 30 days. They discribed by actions how the Ship was beat to pieces by going up and down against the Rocks till at last it was all scattered abroad.[40]

As soon as he heard this account, Cook feared that it referred to the *Adventure*, and that his consort ship had been wrecked, and her crew killed and eaten. When some people repeated the story to William Wales the following morning, pointing to the east side of the Sound (no doubt towards Grass Cove itself), Cook asked him to find out whether they were talking about the *Adventure*. As soon as they were asked the direct question, however, these people clammed up, saying '*Kaore!*' ['No!'], flatly denying the story. There was no one on board the *Resolution* who could speak fluent Maori, so Cook could not establish the truth or otherwise of these rumours. Different people were told different stories, with conflicting details. Finally, Cook decided that their accounts probably referred to a fight among different kin-groups in the Sound, in which a canoe had been wrecked on the rocks and destroyed.

On 30 October, Pedro and his people abruptly left Ship Cove, and several days later, a party of affluent strangers arrived alongside the *Resolution*, bringing large pieces of greenstone, cloaks, bone hand-clubs and women to barter with the British. They controlled the trade with the ship over the following days, while Cook and the Forsters carried on with their explorations. On 5 November Cook decided to go to the southern end of the inlet, to see whether it opened to the ocean. En route they met Pedro and his people, and as they rowed down Tory Channel, they found the shoreline crowded with people. When Cook and his companions landed, they were met by a short, lively old man, his face heavily tattooed in spirals, who tried to hold his people back as they jostled the sailors. Cook exchanged trade goods for weapons, cloaks and fish; and when the old man, whose name was Te Ringapuhi, told him that this channel opened to the sea, he decided to carry on up the inlet. He and the Forsters climbed back into the pinnace and were rowed past high mountains, green coves and sandy beaches out to the sea, where they could see the North Island far off in the distance. There was a fortified village on a rock near the northern heads of the inlet, with double-crested shags wheeling overhead and high waves tumbling and crashing on the rocky coastline.

The next day, Pedro and his family arrived back on board the *Resolution*. Cook took Pedro to the Great Cabin where he dressed him in a shirt, coat, breeches and stockings before taking him to Long Island for a shooting expedition. At dinner, after they had all drunk a good deal of wine, Cook asked Pedro and another man if any harm had come to the *Adventure*. Again they answered '*Kaore!*'; and when Cook showed them a chart of the Sound, using two pieces of paper to represent the *Resolution* and the *Adventure* and sliding these over the paper to represent the ships' movements, Pedro took the paper representing the *Adventure* and slid it out of the Sound, counting on his fingers to indicate that ten months had passed since its departure. Cook accepted Pedro's assurances, noting that 'soon after we were gone, she arrived, that she stayed between ten and twenty days and had been gone ten Months. They likewise asserted that neither she or any other Ship had been stranded on the Coast as reported.'[41] All of this was true, except for the Grass Cove killings. The local people had evidently agreed that Cook should be told nothing about the deaths of his men, for several days before, when a man had mentioned the *Adventure* in front of the sailors, his ears had been roundly boxed by his companions.

Despite the rumours that were circulating about the fate of the *Adventure*, on 3 November John Marra, the gunner's mate who had attempted to desert first in England and then at Tahiti, went ashore without leave, chasing a local woman. Although he was flogged for drunkenness and leaving the ship without permission, on 6 November John Keplin left his boat, 'declareing that he would go with the Indians', and was also flogged for attempted desertion.[42] By now Cook had lost all patience with Marra, commenting that 'if he was not well assurd that the fellow would be killd and Eat, before Morning, he would have let him go.'[43] Over the following few days, a boar and a sow were put ashore and birds were shot and fish were salted, while the Forsters completed their botanical collections.

On 9 October when the *Resolution* was being unmoored, Pedro brought out a large load of fish, and Cook gave him an oil jar 'which made him as happy as a prince', since glass looked like translucent greenstone, a treasured possession. The next morning while the ship was being taken out of the cove, Cook went ashore to a small bay where two families were camping. Some of these people were asleep, others were making mats or cooking, and a little girl was making a steam bath for an old woman, who seemed to have an internal disorder. Cook commented of the people in the Sound, 'Notwithstanding they are *Cannibals*, they are naturaly of a good disposission and have not a little share of humanity.'[44] The next morning as the *Resolution* sailed out of Queen Charlotte Sound, Johann Forster quoted Virgil's *Aeneid*:

'The same frenzy gripped them all at once. They seized the tackle and hurried off. They left the shore; the sea lay beneath the ship.' [*Aeneid* IV. 581.][45]

Homeward Bound

By now, they had all had enough of this interminable voyage. Fortunately, their crossing to South America was uneventful and rapid. Once the *Resolution* reached about 50 degrees south, she flew along in a steady westerly gale, making 183 sea miles during one memorable twenty-four-hour period. To the sailors' delight, after a sea passage of only forty-two days they arrived off the west coast of Tierra del Fuego, where Cook declared with satisfaction: 'I have now done with the SOUTHERN PACIFIC OCEAN, and flatter my self that no one will think that I have left it unexplor'd, or that more could have been done in one voyage towards obtaining that end than has been done in this.'[46]

At Tierra del Fuego they spent a few days charting the coastline, and on 21 December 1774 the *Resolution* anchored in a fine sheltered cove with a freshwater stream, a wooded valley and sea-birds nesting along the rocky shoreline. Cook set off to explore the nearby inlet with the botanists, and when they went ashore, every plant they collected seemed to be a new species. They came across a few uninhabited huts, and quantities of celery that they gathered to take back to the ship. When he arrived back on board that evening, Cook was told that William Wedgeborough, the marine who had shot a man in Tanna, was missing. He had got drunk during the crew's celebrations the previous evening, and must have fallen overboard when he went to the head – the third and last fatality of the voyage.

On the day before Christmas, Cook and the botanists went off in the pinnace, while Pickersgill took some of the officers in the cutter to go shooting. Later Cook and his companions returned to the ship with sixty-one geese, while Pickersgill and his party had shot fourteen, all of which were roasted, boiled and turned into goose patties for their Christmas dinner. During their absence, some Fuegians had arrived alongside in their canoes, and on Christmas morning they came back to see Cook, who gave them some knives and medals. The Europeans pitied these people, who seemed half-starved, half-frozen and apathetic. As Sparrman remarked:

The inhabitants of this country are the filthiest, most miserable and pitiable of all the children of men. Although they live in a severe climate, both sexes were quite naked, except for a modest sealskin over the shoulder, and the women in addition had a small piece of sealskin to conceal the private parts. The savages kept a small fire in their bark boats, of which they occasionally made use, but we had hardly imagined we should encounter such naked beings in the cold that reigned here . . . They are small in stature, though squarely built, but seemed to be thin owing to starvation . . . Their eyes were small, brown and lifeless; the nose squat, cheekbones prominent, the chin beardless, the hair smeared with grease and stinking; the whole face, like the body, was olive brown and soiled with dirt; taken all round, they were distressed, amazed, stupid and even idiotic in appearance.[47]

The Fuegians left the ship before Christmas dinner, to the sailors' relief, because they were so dirty and smelly. That day they sat down to a feast of roast and boiled geese, goose soup, goose pies, and Madeira wine that had greatly improved during its long sea voyage. With his customary goodwill, Johann Forster remarked that 'the Sailors had every thing good to eat & drink in Plenty & could now, as their Expression is, celebrate the Feast & live *like Christians*, or as people of Sense would call it, *like Beasts*: for the little sense they have, was soon lost in Liquor: & clamour & fighting was all over the Ship seen & heard.'[48] The next day Cook sent all the drunken sailors ashore until they sobered up and were fit to return to the vessel.

On 28 December the *Resolution* sailed from 'Christmas Sound', as Cook called it, heading south to Success Bay on the eastern point of Tierra del Fuego, to see whether the *Adventure* had been there. As they approached the point, the ship was surrounded by a school of whales that spouted and sounded, leaping out of the water and beating the sea with their fins as they landed. Cook sent Pickersgill ashore, where he encountered a few of the Ona people, dressed in sealskins and bracelets of silver wire, but found no trace of the *Adventure*. From Success Bay they carried on to Staten Land, an island off the eastern end of Tierra del Fuego, landing at 'New Year

Harbour' to shoot seals and birds for the passage across the South Atlantic. The first boat ashore found the beach crowded with several hundred sea-lions, some of which weighed 1000 pounds, and armed with muskets, bayonets and Tahitian clubs, they shot and clubbed these monsters as they fled into the ocean. Over the next two days the sailors indulged in an orgy of killing, shooting, bayoneting and clubbing sea-lions and seals, firing on geese, ducks and shags, and knocking down penguins. The seals were butchered and skinned, and their blubber collected and boiled down for oil for the ship; and great quantities of meat were taken aboard for the rest of the voyage. After their brief stay in New Year Harbour they headed eastwards across the Atlantic, still searching for Terra Australis.

On 16 January Thomas Willis, one of the 'wild and drinking midshipmen', sighted land, an islet at the tip of a much larger island. This high, rocky land was covered with ice, with mountains looming up into the clouds, valleys filled with snow and bays packed with icebergs that cracked off the face of the glaciers. Cook landed and took possession of this new discovery, which he called 'South Georgia' after King George III, where the sailors shot more sea-lions and some very tall penguins. The botanists found only three types of plants on South Georgia, which they considered the very worst place they had visited. As Johann wrote, 'If a Captain, some Officers & a Crew were convicted of some heinous crimes, they ought to be sent by way of punishment to these inhospitable cursed Regions, for to explore & survey them. The very thought to live here a year fills the whole Soul with horror & despair. God! what miserable wretches must they be, that live here in these terrible Climates.'[49] As they sailed along the eastern coast of South Georgia, Cook named one bay after Lord Sandwich, another for First Lieutenant Cooper, some rocks off Cooper Isle 'Clerke's Rocks' after his second lieutenant Charles Clerke, and a small island to the west of South Georgia 'Pickersgill Island' after his third lieutenant, Richard Pickersgill.

From South Georgia they carried on further south, and on 31 January three rocky islands were sighted. Cook named the southernmost island of this group Southern Thule, after the *Ultima Thule* of the ancient navigators; and the passage between this and the next island 'Forster's Passage'. Having dubbed the archipelago the 'South Sandwich Islands' in honour of Lord Sandwich, they headed east, looking for Cape Circumcision, a land reported by the French explorer Bouvet and named after a Catholic feast day. As the ship sailed right through the supposed location of this land, Cook decided to turn north, heading for the Cape of Good Hope and England. As he observed with satisfaction, it was time to head for home, since the Admiralty's plan for the voyage had now been completed:

I had now made the circuit of the Southern Ocean in a high Latitude and traversed it in such a manner as to leave not the least room for the Possibility of there being a continent, unless near the Pole and out of the reach of Navigation; by twice visiting the Pacific Tropical Sea, I had not only settled the situation of some old discoveries but made there many new ones and left, I conceive, very little more to be done even in that part. Thus I flater my self that the intention of the Voyage has in every respect been fully Answered, the Southern Hemisphere sufficiently explored and a final end put to the searching after a Southern Continent, which has at times engrossed the attention of some of the Maritime Powers for near two Centuries past and the Geographers of all ages.[50]

As the *Resolution* turned northwards, the mood on board was jubilant. The men were still healthy, although many of the ship's provisions had long since been exhausted. Despite bouts of scurvy and fish-poisoning, and Cook's near fatal intestinal obstruction, the death-toll had been low during this long and hazardous voyage. One man had been drowned, another had died of consumption and a third of a fall down a hatchway, and no one had died of illness. The tally of punishments had also been relatively light, even less than on board the *Endeavour*. Only twenty sailors had been punished during their three years at sea; one of them, the incorrigible gunner's mate John Marra, four times, two of them three times, and six men twice, with a total of 288 lashes (compared with twenty-one men punished with 354 lashes on the *Endeavour*).

Although there had been disagreements about how natives should be treated, the *Resolution* was reckoned to be a happy ship. As the midshipman John Elliott wrote, 'No Men could behave better under worse circumstances than they did. The same must be said of the Officers, and I will add that I believe there never was a Ship where for so long a period, under such circumstances, more happiness, order, and obedience was enjoyed – and yet we had Two or Three troublesome characters on board.'[51] By now, Cook had made his peace with Johann Forster (one of these 'troublesome characters') and his senior officers, naming places in his most recent discoveries after them. By this stage in their journey, the success of his disciplinary regime was obvious. As they sailed towards the Cape of Good Hope, heading for England at last, one of the men, Thomas Perry, composed a shanty which expressed the sailors' pride in their marvellous voyage:

> We are hearty and well and of good constitution
> And have ranged the Globe round in the brave *Resolution*
> Brave Captain Cook he was our Commander
> Has conducted the Ship from all eminent danger

We were all hearty seamen no cold did we fear
And we have from all sickness entirely kept clear
Thanks be to the Captain he has proved so good
Amongst all the Islands to give us fresh food

And when to old England my Brave Boys we arrive
We will tip off a Bottle to make us alive
We will toast Captain Cook with a loud song all round
Because that he has the South Continent found

Blessed be to his wife and his Family too
God prosper them all and well for to do
Bless'd be unto them so long as they shall live
And that is the wish to them I do give.[52]

As the *Resolution* sailed towards the Cape of Good Hope on 16 March 1775, two ships were sighted to the north-west, the first European vessels they had seen since parting from the *Adventure* eighteen months earlier. There were celebrations on board, and that afternoon Cook's 'black sheep', the midshipmen Maxwell, Loggie and Coghlan, got drunk and entered the ship's galley with knives drawn, threatening to kill the cook, so Cook had them clapped into irons. He made an eloquent speech urging his men not to gossip about their discoveries, took all of their journals, logs, charts and sketches and sealed them for the Admiralty, and had the seamen's chests searched for documents, in an effort to avoid the publication of illicit 'Accounts' after the voyage. The next morning he sent a boat across to one of the ships, a Dutch Indiaman, where his men learned that the *Adventure* had arrived at the Cape twelve months earlier from New Zealand, where the crew of one of her boats had been killed and eaten. When Cook heard this report, he refused to jump to any conclusions about who was to blame, observing that 'I shall make no reflections on this Melancholy affair untill I hear more about it. I must however observe in favour of the New Zealanders that I have allways found them of a Brave, Noble, Open and benevolent disposition, but they are a people that will never put up with an insult if they have an oppertunity to resent it.'[53]

The following morning the second ship, an English Indiaman, bore up to the *Resolution*. Lieutenant Clerke and Johann Forster took a boat across and went on board, where they were given a mouthwatering dinner of roast goose and fattened Chinese quails. When her captain and officers heard how long they had been at sea, they pressed their own meals on their visitors and gave them a fat pig, several geese and tea to take back to their shipmates, along with a bundle of old English newspapers. Cook sent a letter for the Admiralty across to the British vessel, and during this visit Johann Forster wrote a letter to Banks's friend Daines Barrington, telling him about the voyage, although Cook had ordered that no news of their discoveries apart from his official despatches should be sent back to England. After being battered by a gale, the *Resolution* sailed into Table Bay on 21 March 1775, her bleached rigging, patched and tattered sails and leaking sides betraying the hardships of a long and arduous voyage.

Cook was given a warm welcome at the Cape, where the Dutch Governor went out of his way to help him procure fresh supplies, although Cook found the cost of spare rigging and spars at the Dutch shipyard exorbitant. The Forsters went ashore and collected an array of exotic animals, and farewelled Anders Sparrman, who had decided to make an expedition into the African interior. When the sailors were given shore leave, they celebrated with joyful carousing. As Elliott reported:

It was no uncommon thing in our rides in the Country, to see three of the Sailors on a Horse, in full sail, and well fed with grog. At other times I have seen them laying asleep by the roadside, and the Horse standing over them. All this must not be wondered at, when it is considerd how long they had been confined.[54]

Cook enjoyed hospitable exchanges with other ships at the Cape, in particular a French Indiaman commanded by Julien Crozet, who had been second-in-command to Marion du Fresne during his fatal visit to New Zealand in 1772. When Cook invited the French captain back to the *Resolution*, Crozet gave him and his officers a graphic account of how Marion and some of his men had been killed and eaten by Maori warriors in the Bay of Islands. He added that when he had discussed these killings with Jean-Jacques Rousseau upon his return to France, the great Enlightenment philosopher had exclaimed, 'Is it possible that the good Children of Nature can really be so wicked?'[55] Crozet also gave Cook a copy of his world chart, from which he learned that Marion had discovered some new islands in the Indian Ocean and others in the Tongan archipelago, and that Kerguelen Island was located just where he and Furneaux had unsuccessfully searched for it.

At the Cape, when Cook received a copy of Hawkesworth's edition of the *Endeavour* voyage, he was mortified by its mistakes and blunders. He despatched a letter to Lord Sandwich giving a summary of the *Resolution*'s voyage, sent copies of the ship's journals to the Admiralty in London, and resolved to write the official account of the expedition himself when he returned to England. On 27 April 1775 as the *Resolution* sailed from the Cape, she was accompanied by an English and a Spanish ship on one side and a Danish craft on the other, who fired cannons in tribute to Cook while music played from the decks of the Danish vessel. By now, Cook had implicit faith in Kendall's chronometer, and a day out from St. Helena, when the English ship sent him a message that they were worried about their longitude, he laughed heartily and declared that 'he would run their jibboom on the Island if they chose'.[56]

The Governor of St. Helena proved to be the brother of the squire who had paid for Cook's early education, and Cook and his companions were fêted at dinners and balls, at which there was much good-humoured raillery about Hawkesworth's account of the *Endeavour*'s visit to the island. In particular, comments (taken from Banks's journal) about the treatment of slaves, and the lack of wheelbarrows on the island were greeted with amused indignation, and night after night, wheelbarrows and other wheeled carts were lined up outside Cook's lodgings. From St. Helena, the *Resolution* sailed to the barren island of Ascension where they caught a number of turtles before heading west to Fernando de Noronha, an island off the coast of Brazil, in order to determine its longitude. When one of the forts on this island fired at his ship, Cook headed for the Azores, landing at the island of Fayal to collect water and fresh provisions. At Fayal, his officers visited the mother of one of the sailors who had been killed at Grass Cove, and the ship sailed for England. The *Resolution* finally anchored at Spithead on 30 July 1775 after an absence of three years and an extraordinary voyage of more than twenty thousand leagues, equivalent to sailing three times around the equator.

14

A Tahitian at the Opera

Upon his return to the Downs, Cook met with a heart-warming reception. 'Glorious voyage!' wrote Solander to Joseph Banks, who was cruising on the Admiralty yacht with Lord Sandwich and Mai, inspecting the royal dockyards. Sandwich was thrilled, Mai (who had been brought to England on the *Adventure*) was eager to hear news of his homeland, but Banks, who had been sharply critical of Cook before the voyage, was a little shamefaced, and still smarting that he had not been part of the expedition.

During Cook's absence from England, Joseph Banks had kept himself busy. On the same day that the *Resolution* sailed from England in 1772, Banks had left Gravesend on a journey to Scotland and Iceland with Dr Solander, John Gore and Nicholas Young, the boy who sighted the first land in New Zealand. When he returned to England, he set up a museum at his London home in New Burlington Street and hired artists and scientists to work on his collections. Afterwards, he made brief trips to Holland and Wales and toyed with the idea of joining an expedition to find the Northwest Passage. When John Hawkesworth's edition of the *Endeavour* voyage was published in June 1773, it brought Banks back into the limelight. The Hawkesworth *Account*, based on Banks's and Cook's journals embellished with literary flourishes, took Tahiti as its centrepiece, and its portraits of Joseph Banks, the young gentleman-botanist with a penchant for native women, and 'Oberea' (Purea), the amorous 'Queen of Otaheite', added piquancy to a tale that otherwise focused upon Captain Cook, the brave and superbly competent naval commander.

The literary elite were scathing about Hawkesworth's *Account*, however. Horace Walpole wrote that its 'entertaining matter would not fill half a volume; and at best is but an account of the fishermen on the coasts of forty islands';[1] Dr Johnson harumphed that he 'can tell only what the voyagers have told him; and they have found very little, only one new animal, I think';[2] while Alexander Dalrymple, who was still aggrieved that he had not been permitted to command the expedition, castigated Cook for failing to find the Southern Continent. Nevertheless, the *Account* was a huge popular success, serialised in *The Gentleman's Magazine* and selling a vast number of copies. It made Joseph Banks notorious in Britain, inspiring a flurry of satirical cartoons and poems which portrayed him as a libertine who had betrayed an English maiden by falling into the tattooed embraces of Oberea, the Queen of Tahiti. To quote one of the less salacious lampoons:

> ATTEND, ye swarms of MODERN TOURISTS
> Yclept, or Botanists or Florists:
> Ye who ascend the cloud-capt Hills,
> Or creep along their tinkling Rills; . . .
> Ye who o'er Southern Oceans wander
> With simpling B–ks or sly S–r;
> Who so familiarly describe
> The Frolicks of the wanton Tribe,
> And think that simple Fornication
> Requires no kind of Palliation . . .
>
> Behold, a Queen her Gul o'er-reaches;
> First steals, and then she wears his Breeches . . .
> Such luscious Feats, when told with Ease,
> Must Widows, Matrons, Maidens please;
> Yet though ye strive to dress your Story,
> And make (what is your Shame) your Glory,
> Still is it simple FORNICATION
> Whether in DRURY'S ROUNDS ye sport
> Or frisk in OBEREA'S COURT.[3]

Fortunately for Banks, these satires and the ribald laughter they provoked did no lasting harm to his reputation. During this period he became close to King George III, serving as his botanical advisor at Kew, and donated plants from the Pacific to the Chelsea Physic Garden. This walled oasis, which still survives in the heart of London, is full of memories of the young Joseph Banks. His bust sits in the central rockery, which was built from volcanic ballast from his voyage to Iceland and adorned with a large white clam-shell from Tahiti; and a *kowhai* tree grows against the walls of the curator's house, descended from a specimen that Banks had collected in New Zealand. In 1774, Banks's generosity and his contributions to science were recognised by his election to the Council of the Royal Society, of which he would later become the long-serving, imperious President.

In July 1774 the *Adventure* arrived back in London, bearing the grim news that a boatload of its men had been killed and eaten in New Zealand. Her

Portrait of Mai by Sir Joshua Reynolds

captain Tobias Furneaux took Mai to the Admiralty, where Lord Sandwich summoned Banks and Dr Solander to meet the young islander. As soon as he saw Joseph Banks, Mai remembered him, although he recognised Solander only by his voice, since 'the good doctor' had put on a lot of weight since his return to England. Shortly afterwards Dr Burney joined them, seeking news of his son James, the *Adventure*'s second lieutenant, and later gave an account of the meeting to his daughter Fanny:

[Mai] was dressed according to the fashion of his Country, & is a very good looking man – my father says he has quite an *interesting* Countenance. He appeared to have uncommon spirits, & laughed very heartily many Times. He speaks a few English words – & Capt. Furneaux a few Otaheite words. – They had got Mr Banks there, on purpose to speak with him – but Mr Banks has almost forgot what he knew of that language. But you must know we are very proud to hear that our *Jem* speaks more Otaheite than any of the Ship's *Crew*. – this Capt. F. told my Father, who was

Introduced to this Stranger, as Jem's Father – he laughed, & shook Hands very cordially, & repeated with great pleasure the name thus *Bunny*! O! *Bunny*! immediately knowing who was meant. & the Capt. says that he is very fond of *Bunny*, who spent great part of his Time in Studying the Language with him.[4]

James Burney, who had often talked with Mai during the *Adventure*'s journey from Tahiti to England, described him as a very intelligent young fellow, with a good memory; strong and robust, and well able to endure the hardships of the voyage.[5] According to Mai's own account, he had been born on Ra'iatea, but his father was killed during the same Borabora invasion which drove Tupaia from the island. Mai was taken captive by the Borabora warriors, but his life was saved when an old woman interceded on his behalf. Like Tupaia, he fled to Tahiti, although he settled in the district of Haapape. Mai was among the spectators at Matavai Bay when the Tahitian fleet attacked the *Dolphin*, and was wounded in the bombardment that followed. After Wallis's visit Mai became an acolyte to one of the priests of 'Oro. When Mai met the *Endeavour*'s crew during their visit, he became so fascinated by the Englishmen that he decided to travel to England to meet King George, the high chief of 'Peretane'. After their departure, he spent some time on Huahine, and it was there that he met James Burney and joined the *Adventure*.

Mai's arrival in London was reported by the British press, who delighted in this exotic visitor. For Banks, who had hoped to bring Tupaia to Britain, his advent was a godsend. He carried Mai off and lodged him in his town house, and only three days after his arrival in England, presented him to the King and Queen at Kew. According to the *Gentleman's Magazine*, Mai was a 'tall, genteel, well-made' man, although when he was introduced to the King, he forgot the salutations that he had been taught, greeting the monarch by saying, 'How do you do?' King George took him by the hand, asked him about his health and way of living, and recommended to Banks that Mai should be inoculated against smallpox, so that he would not be carried off by the disease like the other 'savages' who had recently been brought to Britain.[6] The *St. James Chronicle* added that when Mai was told to kneel before King George, he exclaimed, 'What, won't he *eat me* when he has got me down?' – an unlikely elaboration. After this meeting with the King and Queen, the Duke of Gloucester invited Mai, Banks and Solander to dinner, before Banks took Mai off to Hertford for his smallpox inoculation.

Mai survived this ordeal in good shape, and when he returned to London, was quickly caught up in a round of social engagements. He dined at Sir John Pringle's, with Lord Sandwich, and at a Royal Society dinner at the Mitre Tavern. Soon afterwards Sandwich invited Mai, Banks, James Burney and Dr Burney to a house party at Hinchingbrooke, his country mansion, where they sailed on Whittlesea Mere, attended a grand oratorio and took part in a fox-hunt, and Mai cooked delicious dishes for his host in an earth oven. He was beginning to learn English, and when he was stung by a wasp, Mai exclaimed that 'he had been wounded by a soldier bird'. His fellow guests were very impressed by his courtesy and good nature; as one remarked, 'Wherever he goes he makes Friends & has not I believe as yet one Foe.'[7] They also found the young Polynesian amusing; and during a visit to the Duke of Manchester's, when he was shocked by an electrifying machine to see how he would react, Mai ran away and refused to return until James Burney promised that they would play no more tricks upon him.

When the house party broke up, Banks took Mai to the Leicester races. They attended a performance of Handel's *Jephtha*, where the celebrated Giardini led the orchestra and Lord Sandwich gave a virtuoso performance on the kettledrums, filling Mai with admiration. He learned to dance, and at tea parties gracefully handed around cake and bread-and-butter to the ladies. In October Mai was taken to Cambridge, where he visited the Senate house and watched the doctors and professors processing. He was greatly struck by Cambridge, which reminded him of the ritual centre at Taputapua-tea, speaking of its professors (who seemed to him like high priests) with the utmost veneration. When he and Banks returned to London, they visited the theatre at Sadlers Wells and attended the opening of the House of Lords, where they heard King George deplore 'a most daring spirit of resistance' in the colony of Massachusetts. Mai also dined with the Royal Society and visited the opera, later imitating this style of singing to amuse his English friends and acquaintances.

In November, when Mai visited Dr Burney at his home in London, Fanny Burney penned a vivid portrait of the young islander. Mai, who had just been to hear the King make his speech from the throne at the House of Lords, was wearing court dress, a suit of Manchester velvet lined with white satin, lace ruffles and a sword that the King had given him. He bowed gracefully when he was introduced to the ladies, and behaved very politely throughout the dinner. When Mai was asked how he had liked King George's speech, he replied, '*Very well, King George!*'; and when Mrs Burney proposed a toast to his majesty, according to Fanny Burney, Mai bowed and said, ' "*Thank you, Madam,*" and then *tost off "King George!*"' After the meal when Mai told James Burney in Tahitian that he was to go with Solander to meet twelve ladies, James translated for his family, and afterwards Mai laughed and counted on his fingers in English, '1. 2. 3. 4. 5. 6. 7. 8. 9. 10. – *twelve – Woman!*' In her letter, Fanny observed that the young Ra'iatean seemed graceful and well bred, comparing him with Lord

Chesterfield's son, who for all his education was 'a meer *pedantic Booby*', adding, 'I think this shews how much *Nature* can do without *art*, than *art* with all her refinement, unassisted by *Nature*.'[8]

Although Banks had introduced Mai to English society, some observers felt that he was simply amusing himself with the young man, rather than giving him useful skills to take back to the Society Islands. As a scholarly divine who met Mai at a Royal Society dinner remarked: 'I do not find, that any Steps have been taken towards giving him any useful Knowledge, Mr. Banks seeming to keep him, as an Object of Curiosity, to observe the Workings of an untutored, unenlightened Mind.'[9] It also seemed that Banks was getting bored with Mai, because when Lord Sandwich invited him and Mai to Hinchingbrooke for Christmas, although the young islander arrived as expected, Banks sent his excuses. Sandwich was upset, writing to Banks to ask how Mai would fare in lodgings in London if his friends did not keep him out of trouble, adding, 'I should think we were highly blameable if we did not make use of all the sagacity & knowledge of the world which our experience has given us, to do every thing we can to prove ourselves his real friends – your most obedient & most faithful servant *Sandwich*.'[10]

At the end of 1774 Mai returned to London, where he was put into lodgings close to Banks's house, and the surgeon of the *Adventure*, Mr Andrews, was paid a stipend to keep him company. Over the following months, Mai attended plays, learned to play chess and to ride a horse, and watched the launching of a frigate. It was reported that he was learning to read and write English, and the *London Chronicle* added that 'he is going to be married to a young Lady of about 22 years of age, who will go with him to his own country.'[11] By now it was widely rumoured that when Captain Cook arrived back in England, Mai would be taken home by another South Seas expedition; and when Bruce, a Scottish traveller, visited the Burneys, he discussed the proposed voyage, and how Mai would be received back in Tahiti:

'But,' said Mr. Bruce, 'This poor fellow, Omai, has lost all his Time; they have taught him Nothing; he will only pass for a consummate Lyar when he returns; for how can he make them believe half the Things he will tell them? He can give them no idea of our Houses, Carriages, or any thing that will appear probable.'

'Troth, then,' cried Mrs. Strange [one of the company], 'they should give him a set of Dolls' Things and a Baby's House, to shew them; he should have every Thing in minature, by way of mode; Dressed Babies, Cradles, Lying In Women.'[12]

Although Banks's interest in Mai had waned, Lord Sandwich kept an eye on the young islander, and in June he invited him and Banks on a tour of inspection of the Royal Naval dockyards. At Chatham their yacht was greeted by a party of marines and a brass band; and Mai was shown over the *Victory*, a 100-gun ship, and was amazed by the size of the vessel. They visited Greenwich, Portsmouth and the Isle of Wight, and while they were away on this excursion, inspecting ships, shooting birds, attending plays and examining mechanical devices, a satirical poem entitled *An Historical Epistle, from Omiah, to the Queen of Otaheite*, was published in London, reflecting upon Mai's experiences in England, and the prospect of his return to Tahiti:

> Know, through the town my guide S-L-ND-R goes,
> To plays, museums, conjurers and shows;
> He forms my taste, with skill minute, to class,
> Shells, fossils, maggots, butterflies, and grass . . .
>
> O'er verdant plains my steps OPANE leads,
> To trace the organs of a sex in weeds;
> And bid like him the world for monsters roam,
> Yet finds none stranger than are here at home . . .
>
> Sick of these motley scenes, might I once more
> In peace return to *Otaheite*'s shore,
> Where nature only rules the lib'ral mind,
> Unspoil'd by art, by falsehood unrefin'd;
>
> There fondly straying o'er the sylvan scenes,
> Taste unrestrain'd what Freedom really means:
> An glow inspir'd with that enthusiast zeal,
> What *Britons* talk of, *Otaheiteans* feel.[13]

While Banks and Mai were still at Portsmouth, letters finally arrived from Captain Cook and Johann Forster, announcing the *Resolution*'s safe arrival at the Cape of Good Hope. Solander sent Banks a breathless summary of the voyage:

260 new Plants, 200 new animals – 71 degrees 10' farthest Sth – no continent – Many Islands, some 80 Leagues long – The Bola Bola savage [Hitihiti] incorrigible Blockhead – Glorious voyage – No man lost by sickness.[14]

Although Solander stayed in London to await the *Resolution*'s arrival, Banks set off with Mai, Lord Sandwich and his mistress, Miss Ray, on another yachting excursion. On 1 August 1775, he received a note from Solander which declared, 'This moment Captain Cook is arrived!', adding '[Cook] expressed himself in the most friendly manner towards you . . . He has some Birds for you. He rather looks better than when he left England.'[15] Solander also enclosed an exuberant letter from Charles Clerke, announcing his return to England:

God bless you send me one Line just to tell me you're alive and well . . . if I recieve no intelligence from you I shall draw bad conclusions and clap on my suit of black; but you know I never despair, but always look for the best, therefore hope and flatter myself this will find you alive and happy . . . Excuse the Paper, its gilt I assure you, but the Cockroaches have piss'd upon it. – We're terribly busy – you know a Man of War. I'll write to [the good Doctor] as soon as possible – here's too much damning of Eyes and Limbs to do any thing now.[16]

Two weeks later, Lord Sandwich and Miss Ray went with Solander to visit the *Resolution* at Woolwich. This was a high-spirited occasion, during which Sandwich offered Cook a captaincy at Greenwich Hospital, and promised a number of his crew that they would be promoted. As Solander wrote to Banks:

We had a glorious day and longd for nothing but You and Mr. Omai . . . Providentially old Captn Clements died 2 or 3 days ago, by which a Captains place of Greenwich was made Vacant – This was given to Capt Cook – and a promise of Employ whenever he should ask for it. – Mr. Clerke was promised the command of the *Resolution* to carry Mr. Omai home; Mr. Pickersgill to be his 1st Lieutenant. 3 Midshipmen were made Lieutenants . . .

I was told that Mr. Anderson one of the Surgeons Mates, has made a good Botanical Collection . . . There were on board 3 live Otaheite Dogs, the ugliest most stupid of all the Canine tribe. Forster had on board the following Live Stock: a Springe Bock from the Cape, a Surikate, two Eagles, & several small Birds all from the Cape. I believe he intends these for the Queen.

If I except Cooper & 2 of the new made Lieutenants I believe the whole Ship's Company will go out again. Pickersgill made the Ladies sick by shewing them the New Zealand head of which 2 or 3 slices were broiled and eat on board of the Ship. It is preserved in Spirit and I propose to get it for Hunter, who goes down with me to morrow on purpose.[17]

Banks, however, was still avoiding his old shipmates. Instead of visiting the *Resolution*, he took Mai to York for the races, and then to Scarborough, where Mai went swimming, amazing the bathers with his tattoos. After that they went shooting at Mulgrave, the country house of a school friend, where Mai befriended the young son of another guest, who helped him to improve his English in exchange for instruction in Tahitian.

Meanwhile Cook had returned to his home in Mile End, where he was reunited with his family. He began to prepare papers for the Royal Society on fish-poisoning in the Pacific and the methods used to keep the *Resolution*'s men healthy during their long voyage; and contemplated his new role at Greenwich Hospital. Cook had been too long at sea to find the transition easy, however. Less than three weeks after his return to England, he was already restless. He wrote to his friend and patron John Walker in Whitby with more than a hint of regret – 'The *Resolution* . . . will soon be sent out again, but I shall not command her, my fate drives me from one extream to another a few Months ago the whole Southern hemisphere was hardly big enough for me and now I am going to be confined within the limits of Greenwich Hospital, which are far too small for an active mind like mine, I must however confess it is a fine retreat and a pretty income, but whether I can bring my self to like ease and retirement, time will shew.'[18]

During this period, Cook sought solace in his contacts with the Royal Society. At one of their dinners, he and Joseph Banks met and were reconciled; and when Cook was proposed as a Fellow of the Society later that year, Banks was one of his sponsors. The King promised to send Mai home to Tahiti, and during this period Cook was often consulted about the choice of ships for the expedition and other practical matters. In December, Mai visited the Burneys and discussed the voyage, saying that he hoped that James would be back from America (where he had been sent by the Navy) in time to go with them to the Pacific. As Fanny Burney reported:

'Lord Sandwich write one, two, three' ([said Mai] counting on his fingers) *monts* ago – Mr. Burney, – come home.'

'He will be very happy,' cried I, 'to see *you*.'

He Bowed, & said, 'Mr. Burney very *dood* man.'

We asked if he had seen the King lately?

'Yes; King George *bid me*, – "Omy, you go home." Oh, very *dood* man, King George!'

He then, with our assisting him, made us understand that he was extremely rejoiced at the thought of seeing again his Native Land; but at the same Time, that he should much regret leaving his friends in England.

'Lord Sandwich,' he added, '*bid me*, "Mr. Omy, you two ships – you go home." – I say (making a fine bow) "Very much *oblige*, my Lord." '[19]

Over the latter months of 1775, as the splendour of Cook's achievements during his previous voyages became clear, the idea of appointing him to lead the expedition seemed increasingly appealing. The Admiralty and the Royal Society agreed that the ships which took Mai home to Tahiti should carry on to the coast of North America to search for the Northwest Passage, another icon of speculative geography. It was thought that such a passage through the American continent must exist, but although Parliament had offered a reward of twenty thousand pounds and a number of ships had set out to find it, none had so far succeeded.

Any search for the Northwest Passage would involve an exploration of the north-west American coast and the Arctic ice-edge, reminiscent of Cook's survey of the east coast of Australia on the one hand, and his search for Terra Australis along the Antarctic ice-edge on the other. By now Cook was recognised as an exceptionally determined commander as well as a brilliant surveyor, and perhaps he could succeed where others had failed. He knew the South Pacific well, his ships were well disciplined and handled, and he would have a better chance than most of delivering Mai safely to Tahiti. Although Charles Clerke was good-natured and popular and had been promised the command, this voyage demanded sterner qualities. Cook was approached, and according to his biographer, Kippis, at a dinner hosted by Lord Sandwich in February 1776 attended by Cook and key figures from the Admiralty and the Navy Board, the importance of the voyage was spoken of in such glowing terms that Cook leapt to his feet and volunteered to lead it.

Within a few days, Cook was formally appointed to command the expedition. He was given the *Resolution*, which was being refitted at Deptford, while Charles Clerke was made captain of her consort ship, the *Discovery*. As Cook wrote to his old friend Captain John Walker in Whitby:

I expect to be ready to sail about the latter end of Apl with my old ship the Resolution and the Discovery . . . I know not what your opinion may be on this step I have taken. It is certain I have quited an easy retirement, for an Active, and perhaps Dangerous Voyage. My present disposition is more favourable to the latter than the former, and I imbark on as fair a prospect as I can wish. If I am fortunate enough to get safe home, theres no doubt but it will be greatly to my advantage.[20]

It took longer than Cook had expected to get the ships ready for the voyage, however. He began to prepare his account of the previous voyage for publication, but found himself at odds with Johann Forster, who believed that he had been promised the commission. Lord Sandwich attempted to mediate, asking Forster to produce a sample chapter describing the *Resolution*'s visit to Dusky Bay, with a promise that if this was approved, he could write the account, although Cook would share equally in the profits. When the text was produced, the Admiralty did not like it, and Sandwich suggested that two accounts should be written, one by Cook dealing with the voyage, and the other by Forster, describing its scientific aspects. When Forster tried to procure the astronomical findings of the voyage from William Wales for this purpose, however, Wales was unco-operative:

When I meet a person capable of taking every means, fair or unfair, to scrape together the knowledge of every one else, and that in matters whereof he is totally ignorant and with an avowed design to publish them as his own, I think it behoves me to be private.[21]

Forster had alienated most of his shipmates during the voyage, and his scathing comments about Cook and many of the *Resolution*'s crew upon his return to London had annoyed Sandwich and his associates. When Johann turned on Sandwich himself, whom he accused of endeavouring 'to ruin me by the weight of His power and opulence', his relationship with the Admiralty came to an end, and he worked instead with his son George on an unauthorised narrative of the voyage, as well as his own more philosophical *Observations*. Although these two publications, along with Johann's original journal, give acute insights into the *Resolution*'s adventures, Forster's journal, with its self-pitying soliloquies, shows him to have been an uncomfortable shipmate. His arrogance and lack of self-knowledge cost him dearly, both during and after the voyage.

While Cook was preoccupied with these matters, he could not give his undivided attention to preparing for the expedition. Much of the work on refitting the *Resolution* was completed by the time he took command, and it had been scandalously skimped, although this was not evident until they sailed from England. Rotten wood had been used in some of the repairs, and the caulking was completely inadequate. Lieutenant Gore, who had sailed on the *Dolphin* and the *Endeavour*, but went with Banks to Iceland when the *Resolution* sailed to the Pacific, was appointed Cook's first lieutenant, and he did his best, but he was the only Pacific veteran among the ship's officers, and lacked a captain's authority.

The *Resolution*'s crew included a number of men who had previously sailed with Cook – five who had gone on his first and second voyages; and eight more from the second Pacific expedition (including William Anderson, the *Resolution*'s intelligent and capable Scottish surgeon's mate during that voyage, now the ship's surgeon). Apart from Gore, the officers included James King, the second lieutenant, a clever and thoughtful man who had studied science at Paris and Oxford, described by Trevenen (a promising Cornish midshipman who wrote a lively account of the voyage) as 'one of the politest, genteelest, & best-bred men in the world'; and John Williamson, the third lieutenant, a bully and coward, later damned as 'a wretch, feared & hated by his inferiors, detested by his equals, & despised by his superiors; a very devil, to whom none of our midshipmen have spoke for above a year'.[22]

The *Resolution*'s master was William Bligh, who later became notorious as the hot-tempered commander of the *Bounty*, a fine practical sailor but harsh in speech and manner, an unfortunate combination with Williamson. The commander of the marines, Molesworth Phillips, was a close friend of James Burney's, a brave but disorganised officer whose contingent included Samuel Gibson, the Tahitian-speaking sergeant of marines who had sailed on two previous voyages with Cook, and John Ledyard, a young American who had recently spent some time among the 'six nations of Indians on the borders of Canada'. David Samwell, a lively Welshman who supported Anderson as surgeon's mate, was a better ethnographer than a medical man, and an ardent lover of the 'dear Ladies'. With such a combination of characters, the shipboard dynamics during the *Resolution*'s voyage were bound to be interesting.

After Joseph Banks's tantrums and Johann Forster's incessant grumbling, Cook had become averse to taking civilian scientists to sea. As he exclaimed during a discussion with James King, 'Curse the scientists, and all science into the bargain!'[23] He was not entirely serious, however, for Cook himself was now a Fellow of the Royal Society, King had a scientific training and was a capable astronomer, and the ship's surgeon William Anderson, whom Cook respected and admired, was a marvellous observer. Instead of the 'experimental gentlemen' of his previous voyages, the *Resolution*'s super-numeraries included John Webber, a fine landscape artist, and Mai, the young Ra'iatean who had had a wonderful time in England, learning to ice-skate and play chess, dining with the nobility and flirting with the ladies.

Charles Clerke, the high-spirited captain of Cook's consort ship, the *Discovery*, had his own difficulties to deal with. Clerke had acted as guarantor for his brother's debts, and when his brother sailed to India he was pursued by the 'Israelites' and eventually thrown into the King's Bench prison, where he contracted tuberculosis. James Burney, Mai's friend from the *Adventure*, was appointed first lieutenant of the *Discovery*, and had to take command of the ship until Clerke was released from jail. Despite his misfortunes, Clerke had a likely group of midshipmen and master's mates on board his ship, including Edward Riou, George Vancouver (who had sailed with Cook on his second voyage, and later became a famous Pacific explorer in his own right), Nathaniel Portlock and Alexander Home, the ringleaders in the trial of the cannibal dog. His supernumeraries included William Bayly, the astronomer who had sailed on the *Adventure* during Cook's second expedition, and David Nelson, a gardener from Kew sponsored by Joseph Banks as a botanical collector.

Although the period leading up to the third Pacific expedition was frustrating, Cook had some great moments. He met the King and was made post-captain, and Joseph Banks commissioned Nathaniel Dance to paint his portrait. The members of the Royal Society fêted him, and many of this circle, who admired his honesty and modest demeanour, treated Cook with respect and kindness. When James Boswell, the Scots diarist and biographer of Dr Johnson, met Cook at a dinner in April hosted by Sir John Pringle, the President of the Society, he described him as 'a plain, sensible man with an uncommon attention to veracity. My metaphor was that he had a ballance in his mind for truth as nice as scales for weighing a guinea.' Apparently Sir John Pringle had informed Lord Monboddo that Cook had found a 'nation of men like monkeys' in the Pacific, which thrilled the Scottish philosopher, but when he reported this conversation to Cook, Cook firmly put him right – 'No, I did not say they were like Monkeys. I said their faces put me in mind of monkeys.'[24]

During this dinner, Boswell became inspired with the idea of joining Cook's next Pacific expedition. He recorded in his diary how curious it had been to see Cook, 'a grave steady man, and his wife, a decent plump Englishwoman, and think that he was preparing to sail round the world';[25] and confided to Dr Johnson that he wanted to live 'three years at Otaheite, or New Zealand, in order to obtain a full acquaintance with people, so totally different from all that we have ever known, and be satisfied what pure nature can do for man'. If he had carried out this plan, Boswell would have become the father of ethnographic fieldwork, but Samuel Johnson was quelling. He had already tried to put his young friend off the voyage by saying that shipboard life was like being in jail, only worse, because there was a chance of being drowned, and 'a man in jail has more room, better food, and commonly better company'. Now he retorted:

'What could you learn, Sir? What can savages tell, but what they themselves have seen? Of the past, or the invisible, they can tell nothing. The inhabitants of Otaheite and New Zealand are not in a state of pure nature; for its plain they broke off from some other people. Had they grown out of the ground, you might have judged of a state of pure nature.'[26]

Despite Johnson's discouraging remarks, Boswell went to visit Cook at his home in Mile End to discuss the expedition. They drank tea and a blackbird sang in the garden, and Boswell remarked that it was 'quite pleasant. Was in *perfect* London spirits.' Still bruised from his experiences with Johann Forster, however, Cook did not give him the encouragement he had hoped for. Sadly for posterity, when Cook sailed for the Pacific, James Boswell did not go with him.

As the arrangements for the voyage reached a crescendo, anti-scorbutics, provisions, slops, barrels, guns, tools and gifts for the natives were packed into the vessels. Cook received his instructions from the Board of Longitude, and an array of scientific instruments, including Kendall's faithful watch, were loaded on board the *Resolution*. Lord Sandwich despatched an ark-load of animals for delivery to the Pacific – cattle, sheep, goats, hogs, rabbits, turkeys, geese, ducks, and a peacock and a peahen. At least some of these creatures were intended for New Zealand, in the hope that if they had more large animals, Maori would give up eating each other.[27] Other items included loose-leaf engravings for the official publication from the second voyage, some of which were later presented to the Governor of Kamchatka and now rest in the Museum of Anthropology and Ethnography in St. Petersburg.[28] By now Cook was on board his ship, and in early June when Lord Sandwich, Sir Hugh Palliser and other Admiralty potentates visited the *Resolution*, they were greeted with a salute of seventeen guns and three cheers, given a dinner of Westmoreland ham, pigeon and strawberries, and cheered again at their departure. The crews were paid an advance, and soon afterwards Clerke was given permission to travel to London to sort out his financial affairs, where he was arrested and thrown into a debtors' prison.

In Clerke's absence, Lieutenant Burney was given temporary command of the *Discovery*. He was ordered to sail her to Plymouth, and Mai, who had contracted a pox from one of his lady friends and received a crash course in reading, writing and Christian principles from the philanthropist Granville Sharp, came on board the *Resolution*. He had asked for quantities of port wine and gunpowder to take back to Tahiti, which were loaded in the hold; along with a suit of armour commissioned by Lord Sandwich and made in the Tower of London, a globe of the world, some elegant clothing, an array of iron tools and domestic utensils, miniatures of European soldiers, animals and vehicles, magnifying glasses, chessboards, umbrellas, silver

Captain Charles Clerke, by Nathaniel Dance

watches, an electrifying machine, and portraits of King George III and Queen Charlotte.

On 25 June 1776 the *Resolution* sailed to Plymouth, where Cook learned that his wife and family would be paid a generous allowance during his absence. There, Sir John Pringle informed him that he had been awarded the Royal Society's prize medal for his contributions to the health of seamen. On 12 July Cook farewelled his family and sailed for the Cape of Good Hope, leaving the *Discovery* behind at Plymouth, waiting for her commander Charles Clerke to be released from prison. War had just broken out with the American colonies, and the port was packed with armed ships preparing to fight the rebels.

Back to the Pacific

As soon as they left Plymouth Sound, Cook discovered that the *Resolution*'s repairs were defective.[29] The ship leaked, sailrooms and storerooms dripped, and rain poured into the officers' cabins, ruining their bedding and possessions. Cook did not have enough fodder on board to feed the livestock, so he decided to head for the Azores to buy corn and hay, and wine for the voyage. At Tenerife, where his men feasted on fresh fruit, Cook purchased fodder for the animals, and wine, pumpkins, onions, potatoes and bullocks for the sailors. Samwell, the Irish surgeon's mate, heartily disliked the inhabitants of Tenerife, describing them as 'a sett of gloomy, bigotted, praying Priest ridden Miscreants',[30] although Mai could scarcely tell the difference between Tenerife Spaniards and the English, simply noting that 'they seem'd not so friendly & in person they approach'd those of his own country'.[31]

As they left the Azores, one of the sailors was given six lashes for 'neglect of duty', the first punishment of the voyage. Cook and King made an error in their calculation of the longitude of Tenerife, and when the island of Bonavista appeared earlier than expected, the ship almost crashed into the rocks off the south-eastern point of the island. Fortunately Cook had sensed that something was amiss. When he came on deck and saw the breakers, he ordered a change of course just in time to avoid a collision, but it had been a careless mistake, and he and King were mortified. They carried on to Porto Praya where there was no sign of Clerke, so Cook headed straight for the Cape of Good Hope. By now the *Resolution* was leaking worse than ever. The seams on the decks, which had not been properly caulked, opened in the heat, and water poured in through the upper works of the ship, drenching clothes, sails, instruments, books and bedding. On 1 September they crossed the Equator, celebrating the occasion with the customary duckings and merriment. Ten days later when a bright meteor streaked across the sky, Mai declared that it was his god, heading for England, arguing furiously with anyone who questioned this assertion.

On 17 October 1776, the Cape of Good Hope was sighted. The local inhabitants greeted Cook with joy, for as Samwell declared, 'The Governor & all at the Cape pay Captn Cook extraordinary Respect, he is as famous here & more noted perhaps than in England.'[32] The livestock were landed, tents for the sailmakers and coopers were erected, and the caulkers began to repair the shoddy work done in England. Cook dined with the Governor, but despite his local fame he found the Cape tedious, writing to one of his friends, 'I arrived here . . . after as favourable a passage as I could wish, but nothing new or entertaining happened, and I am now at one of the worst places in the world to find either one or the other.'[33] As always, it was difficult to maintain discipline in port, and nine of the *Resolution*'s men were punished during their stay at the Cape for a variety of offences (neglect of duty, absenting themselves without permission, selling their 'necessaries'), which Cook found depressing. He waited at the Cape for almost a month before the *Discovery* arrived, having narrowly escaped being wrecked on the coast in a recent gale. Clerke had finally managed to escape from England, despite his bout of consumption and an outbreak of smallpox on board the *Discovery*, announcing his arrival at the Cape in a cheerful letter to Banks, 'Here I am hard and fast moor'd alongside my Old Friend Capt Cook so that our battles with the Israelites cannot now have any ill effects upon our intended attack upon the North Pole.'[34]

Cook set his caulkers to work on the *Discovery* and helped Clerke to load water and provisions on board the vessel. He sent Anderson, Gore and Mai inland on an exploring expedition, where Gore and Mai blazed away with their guns, but shot just a few small birds which they preserved in spirits for Joseph Banks. Some more animals were brought on board the *Resolution* – two young bulls, two heifers, two young horses, two mares, two rams, several ewes and goats, several monkeys, and some rabbits and poultry for New Zealand and Tahiti. Charles Clerke's arrival had lifted Captain Cook's spirits, and as he prepared to leave the Cape, he wrote cheerfully to Lord Sandwich:

Nothing is wanting but a few females of our own species to make the Resolution a Compleate ark, for I have taken the liberty to add considerably to the number of animals your Lordship was pleased to order to be put on board . . . The takeing on board some horses has made Omai compleatly happy, he consented with raptures to give up his Cabbin to make room for them, his only concern now is that we shall not have food for all the stock we have got on board. He continues to injoy a good state of health and great flow of Spirits and on every occasion expresses a thankfull remberence of your Lordships great kindness to him.[35]

During the *Discovery*'s passage to the Cape, Clerke and Burney had quarrelled, but on board the *Resolution*, the mood was excellent. The men were in good health and looking forward to a visit to Tahiti. According to John Gore, '[We] have hitherto agreed verry Will and there is a fair Prospect of its Continuing To the End of our Voyage.'[36]

Cook sailed south-east from the Cape on 30 November 1776, looking for the islands discovered by Marion du Fresne and Kerguelen, and marked on the chart which Crozet had given him at the Cape eighteen months earlier. Despite hard gales and cold weather, he found Marion Island on 12 December, and sailed through thick fog, firing the guns hourly to keep in touch with the *Discovery*. They sighted Kerguelen Island twelve days later, and upon entering a large harbour, found the shore lined with tall penguins, standing like soldiers on parade. These birds were quite tame, and the sailors amused themselves by knocking them on the head. Cook set the men to work hauling the seine, cutting grass and collecting water, and butchering seals for their blubber, delaying their Christmas celebrations until 27 December, when this work of provisioning the ship was completed. One of the sailors found a bottle fastened with wire to a rock, holding a document which recorded a French visit to the island in 1772. Cook added a note to the other side of the document commemorating his own visit, put it back in the bottle, and hoisted a flag taking possession of the island for King George III of Britain. The island was so rocky and desolate, with only wild cabbage, a couple of cresses and grasses, mosses and lichens as vegetation, that many of the sailors thought it was scarcely worth the trouble. As Burney remarked, 'Nature seems to have designed this spot solely for the use of Sea Lions, Seals, penguins and Sea fowls.'[37] Cook carried out a survey of the east coast of the island, but the shoreline was fringed by shoals and shrouded with fog, making this a dangerous exercise. After an overnight stay in another harbour, which Cook called Port Palliser, they sailed down the coast the next morning, finally farewelling this 'Cold Blustering Wet Country of Islands, Bays & Harbours', as Gore described it.

The ships made a brisk passage to Tasmania and on 27 January 1777 they anchored at Adventure Bay, first visited by Furneaux during Cook's previous voyage. The observatory tent was sent ashore and the men fished with the seine, but the marines on guard duty managed to smuggle liquor onto the boats, and drank themselves into a stupor. Five of these men had to be carried back to the ship and hoisted up the side, and the ringleaders were flogged with eighteen lashes and the rest with twelve lashes the next morning. Annoyed by this breach of discipline, Cook ordered the tent to be brought back on board, and decided to shorten his stay at Tasmania. The next afternoon, a party of Nuenonne men and boys armed with pointed sticks appeared out of the woods in the bay, as a marine on guard duty cried out, 'Here they are! Here they are!', and fled to the boat in a panic. The wood-cutters advanced on these men with their axes, but since the Aborigines put down their spears and seemed friendly, the midshipman told his men to fall back, and gave these visitors a few trinkets. Cook and Mai soon arrived and tried to make friends with these people, offering them bread and fish, which they disliked, although they accepted some birds they were given. The local inhabitants, who seemed inoffensive and friendly, were fascinated as they watched the wood-cutters felling trees, and willingly helped to pull the cross-saw. One of these man had picked up his spear, and when Cook urged him to throw it at a mark, he obliged but missed the mark by a wide margin. Mai, intending to demonstrate the superiority of European weapons, raised his musket and fired it at the target, blowing it to pieces. The Aborigines were astonished, stood stock-still for a moment and then turned and fled back into the forest, abandoning the things they had been given. Soon afterwards, they went to the place where the *Discovery*'s launch was anchored and tried to haul it up on the beach, but ran off when a musket was fired in warning.

Cook was annoyed with Mai, fearing that he had frightened these people away, but at sunrise the next morning they found a group of about twenty Nuenonne people sitting on the beach, who came to meet the boats when they landed. Again, they were naked and unarmed, and when Cook tied medals, strings of beads and ribbons about their necks, they seemed to place no value on these things, although when one man took a fancy to Cook's striped waistcoat and was given it, they seemed delighted. These men stood with one hand behind the back, the other playing idly with their genitals, and when they urinated, they stood there unconcerned; so that Samwell decided that these were people in the 'rudest State of Nature'. They seemed extremely cheerful, however, 'burst[ing] out into the most immoderate fits of Laughter & when one Laughed every one followed his Example Emediately'.[38] When some women joined them, who were naked except for slings which they used to carry their children on their backs, they let the Europeans touch their genitals, although they refused any sexual intimacies. An old, humpbacked man who led the group saw this, became angry and sent the women and children away. As Cook commented:

This conduct to Indian Women is highly blameable, as it creates a jealousy in the men that may be attended with fatal consequences, without answering any one purpose whatever, not even that of the lover obtaining the object of his wishes . . . This observation I am sure will hold good throughout all parts of the South Sea where I have been, why then should men risk their own safety where nothing is to be obtained?[39]

Time was passing, so Cook decided not to carry out a coastal survey of Tasmania, assuming that Furneaux was correct in thinking that it was joined to the Australian mainland. The Admiralty had asked him to collect flax seeds and plants in New Zealand if possible, so instead of sailing directly for Tahiti, he headed towards Queen Charlotte Sound, where he now knew that the *Adventure*'s men had been killed and eaten by local Maori.

The Trial of the Cannibal Dog

On 11 February as Cook's two ships sailed with a gentle breeze into Totara-nui (Queen Charlotte Sound), three or four canoes approached, but seemed reluctant to come alongside. Once the ships had anchored at Ship Cove, the canoes paddled forward in a group, their leader waving a white garment and singing a song of friendship. When they came closer, Mai talked with these people about the killings at Grass Cove, although his European companions could not really follow what he was saying. Cook also talked with them, assuring them of his friendly intentions, and Te Weherua, a chief's son and a 'good natured honest young fellow' whom they knew well from their previous visits, came on board, although 'Pedro', whom Cook had befriended during his last stay at the Sound, refused to leave his canoe. As Cook remarked, 'It appeared to me that they were apprehensive we were come to revenge the death of Captain Furneux's people: seing Omai on board whose first conversation with them generally turned on that subject; they must be well assured that I was no longer a stranger to that unhappy affair, and I did all in my power to assure them of the continuence of my friendship, and that I should not disturb them on that account.'[40]

The local people were nonplussed by Cook's friendly overtures. From a Maori point of view, the killing and eating of his men was an attack on the mana of his people, which demanded immediate retribution. If Cook, with his ships full of weapons and warriors, did nothing to avenge his men, then he and his companions must be *taurekareka* [slaves, people without mana or spiritual power]. He might have some trick in mind, so they decided to watch until they could work out whether or not he was trying to beguile them. In the meanwhile, Cook sent empty casks and two tents ashore, and ordered his men to cut wood, collect water, brew spruce beer and collect grass for the livestock, and despatched parties of marines to protect them from ambush by the local warriors.

That evening a number of families arrived at Ship Cove, where they quickly erected temporary shelters. When they awoke the next morning, these people saw an astonishing assortment of animals coming ashore. Samwell gave a vivid account of this zoological disembarkation:

Today our Ship, which for the variety of living Things she contained might be called a second Noahs Ark, poured out the Horses, Cattle, Sheep, Goats &c. with peacocks, Turkeys, Geese & Ducks, to the great Astonishment of the New Zealanders, who had never seen horses or Horned Cattle before; these being all feeding & diverting

*The Shore Camp in Ship Cove, Queen Charlotte Sound,
New Zealand*

themselves about the Tents familiarised the Savage Scene & made us almost forget that we were near the antipodes of old England among a rude & barbarous people.[41]

The Maori who had gathered in the cove marvelled at these strange sights, and then produced fish and curiosities, and girls to sleep with the sailors. Although venereal diseases had been established in the Sound since the *Endeavour*'s visit in 1770, Cook still disliked this kind of barter:

A connection with Women I allow because I cannot prevent it, but never encourage tho many Men are of opinion it is one of the greatest securities amongst Indians, and it may hold good when you intend to settle amongst them; but with travelers and strangers, it is generally otherwise and more men are betrayed than saved by having connection with their women, and how can it be otherwise sence all their View are selfish without the least mixture of regard or attatchment whatever; at least my observations which have been pretty general, have not pointed out to me one instance to the contrary.[42]

These women were rather ugly, and daubed with red ochre; as Te Weherua explained to Samwell, they were 'mere refuse & outcasts' (probably war captives), while the 'fine Girls' were kept well away from the British. Because of their repugnance over the killing and eating of their shipmates at Grass Cove, some of the sailors refused to sleep with the women, although one man formed a close attachment with a girl who tried to persuade him to stay at Totara-nui, and become a leader among her people.

Four days after Cook's arrival in the Sound, Kahura, a strong, middle-aged man with a fierce, tattooed face, came out to the *Resolution*. Some of the Maori on board told Cook that he was a 'very bad man', urging that he should be killed; but so many people in the Sound had asked Cook to destroy their enemies that he took little notice. Soon after this encounter, Cook went off to Motuara to collect grass, where an old man stood on the shore with a green bough in his hand, delivering a speech which ended with a chant. Cook landed and pressed noses with the elder, and then went with him to look at the gardens he had planted on the island, finding them overgrown with weeds, although the cabbages, onions, leeks, parsley and potato plants were flourishing.

The next morning, 16 February, Cook, Mai, several officers and a party of armed men set off in five boats to collect grass for the livestock. They rowed to Grass Cove, where Cook was met by his acquaintance 'Pedro' and another man, each armed with a spear and a patu. They seemed very apprehensive, although Cook offered them gifts before questioning them about the killings. Through Mai, they told him that during the *Adventure*'s last visit, a boatload of her men had visited this cove to cut grass. When one of the sailors traded with a local man for a stone adze, the sailor had refused to hand over anything in return. The warrior was furious and snatched some of the European's bread, and when he tried to get it back, there had been a scuffle. Jack Rowe, who was in command of the grass-cutters, fired his musket loaded with ball, killing the owner of the adze. At the same time, Furneaux's black servant, seeing another warrior taking a jacket from the boat, hit him with a stick while Rowe reloaded his musket, then shot and killed him. When Kahura saw this, he had called out to the men at a nearby hamlet for help, and before Rowe could reload his musket again, Kahura and the other men jumped on him. Rowe had slashed Kahura's arm with his sword before he was killed. Some of the other sailors were slaughtered on the spot, while the rest were killed later that day. According to Pedro, who had not participated in the attack, Furneaux's black servant was the last man to be executed.

While Cook was at Grass Cove listening to this story, an old chief visited the shore camp in Ship Cove. When he tried to enter the tent, Samuel Gibson, the Maori-speaking sergeant of marines, thinking that he was trying to steal something, refused him entry. In a fury, the old man challenged Gibson to a fight, and then promised to seek revenge for this insult. He leaped into his canoe and paddled to a nearby hamlet; soon all of the canoes in the Sound headed off at high speed for Grass Cove, where the old chief upbraided Cook for Gibson's conduct. Soon afterwards the fleet of canoes set off for Long Island, where a party of grass-cutters was working, although they quickly changed direction when Cook sent the pinnace chasing after them.

By now Cook had some understanding of the affray at Grass Cove, but he still held his own men responsible for what had happened. As he remarked, 'if these thefts had not, unfortunately, been too hastily resented no ill consequence had attended, for Kahoura's greatest enemies . . . owned that he had no intention to quarrel, much less to kill.'[43] Now that Cook knew the identity of their killers, however, the local people expected him to take revenge, and when he did nothing, they were contemptuous. They began to demand gifts without offering anything in return, as though the British were indeed taurekareka. According to Lieutenant Gore, they seemed 'Confident of their own Power', expecting a 'Tribute for their friendship'; while Lieutenant Burney, smarting from his own memories of the Grass Cove killings, wrote:

It seemed evident that many of them held us in great contempt and I believe chiefly on account of our not revenging the affair of Grass Cove, so contrary to the principles by which they would have been actuated in the like case . . . As an instance how little they stood in fear of us, one man did not scruple to acknowledge his being present and assisting at the killing and eating of the Adventure's people.[44]

Here, and in other comments by the sailors, Cook's handling of local people was being questioned. Although his men greatly admired Cook, they found the attitudes of local Maori galling, and he and his officers had often disagreed about how disrespectful 'natives' should be treated. Cook would not allow his men to shoot to kill unless they were in imminent danger, punishing them for thefts or violence against local people, and he got very angry if this policy was flouted. He had quarrelled with Lieutenant Gore during the first voyage over the shooting and killing of a Maori at Mercury Bay; with Johann Forster over a shooting in Ra'iatea early in the second voyage; and with Charles Clerke and his fellow officers at Tanna later in that voyage, when a sentry shot and killed a man who had aimed an arrow at him. His views on this matter were obviously deeply felt, since he held to them even at the expense of his own popularity. The sailors, on the other hand, felt that on such occasions, their commander favoured 'savages' over his own men, and were aggrieved that the 'barbarians' who had killed and eaten their comrades at Grass Cove went unpunished. After the visit to

Grass Cove the *Resolution*'s quartermaster was flogged for 'Insolence and Contempt', which may hint at their mood. This feeling of resentment was particularly strong among those men (including Lieutenant Burney and Mai) who had sailed on the *Adventure*, and had vivid memories of how their shipmates had perished.

Registering his men's disaffection, Cook decided to leave the Sound as soon as possible. On 23 February he ordered the tents to be struck, and everything loaded back on board the vessels. Te Weherua, the chief's son who had lived on board the *Resolution* during her stay, realised that they were about to sail off into the Pacific and asked if he could go with them. Mai, who hoped that this young man would act as his attendant, added his entreaties, and Cook agreed. Te Weherua brought his things to the ship, where his mother wept over him, and a small boy named Koa, whom Cook had met during his earlier visits, came on board as Te Weherua's companion. On the following morning when they set sail, the winds were unfavourable, so the ships anchored off Motuara, where Cook landed some rabbits. That afternoon the local people came out in several canoes loaded with cloaks, greenstone ornaments, adzes and Polynesian dogs, trading these for hatchets. Kahura was on one of these canoes, and came on board the *Resolution*. When Mai saw Kahura, he was infuriated. He pointed at the chief and urged Cook to shoot him, telling Kahura that he would shoot him himself if he dared to return to the vessel. Kahura was defiant, and the next morning he returned to the ship with his family, about twenty people in all; again Mai exclaimed in a fury to Cook, 'There is Kahura – kill him!'

Cook had promised Kahura that he would do him no harm, however, and took him into his cabin to hear his account of the Grass Cove killings. Kahura told a story that was almost identical to the tale that Cook had heard in Grass Cove; then, noticing a sketch by Webber in the cabin, asked whether his portrait could be painted. While Webber was being summoned, Mai returned to the Great Cabin once more to implore Cook to kill this man, exclaiming, 'Why do you not kill him, you till me if a man kills another in England he is hanged for it, this Man has killed ten and yet you will not kill him, tho a great many of his countreymen desire it and it would be very good!'[45] Cook ignored the young islander's protests, and when Webber arrived, told him to sketch Kahura's portrait.

Although Cook was trying to act like an enlightened leader, from a Polynesian point of view he was behaving like a man without mana. Many of the sailors, feeling the sting of Maori contempt, shared Mai's disbelief and frustration. On board the *Discovery*, at a safe distance from Cook, where James Burney was the first lieutenant, the midshipmen and master's mates found a way of expressing their views. One of them, Edward Riou, had acquired a kuri from Kahura's people, which went around nipping his shipmates. While he was ashore, his messmates took this dog and put it on trial for cannibalism. After the mock court martial, the dog was convicted, sentenced, executed, cooked and eaten. When Riou came back on board, his friends put the bloody dog's skin over his shoulders, its head resting on his head and its tail dangling down his back, and he rushed below in a huff. His messmates soon relented and served him his share of cooked dog meat, for there was little fresh meat to be had in New Zealand, and like most young men they were ravenously hungry. With its mockery of naval discipline, this prank turned the world upside down – a fitting thing to do at the Antipodes. 'Ah, those were the glorious days!', exclaimed one of the men, Alexander Home, recalling this episode many years later. It was a great way of showing their captains how cannibals ought to be handled, and the sailors found it both satisfying and hilarious. Cook was cut to the quick by his men's disaffection, however, and this visit to Queen Charlotte Sound proved to be a key turning-point in his relationships both with his crew, and with Polynesians.

15

The Glorious Children of Te Tumu

When the *Resolution* sailed from Queen Charlotte Sound, Te Weherua and Koa were in high spirits, but as the land faded behind them on the horizon, they began to cry, singing a song of farewell to their country and kinsfolk. They were sailing to Tahiti, the ancestral homeland, a marvellous adventure, but they were both seasick and Koa, who was only ten years old, missed his parents. Cook ordered red jackets to be made to cheer them up, but this was little consolation. For the next few days, Koa sat in the anchor chains every day, crying and singing his lament, while Te Weherua came and wept with him. They were the first Maori to leave New Zealand on a European ship, sailing towards unknown horizons. Once Koa settled into life on board the *Resolution*, however, he proved to be a lively, cheerful boy, very popular with the sailors; and Te Weherua, a chief's son, was a sensible and sedate young man, well respected on board, who spent most of his time with the officers.

After leaving New Zealand, Clerke mused upon their dealings with Maori, and the wider question of how 'Indians' ought to be handled:

Whilst you keep the command in your own hands you are at leisure to act with whatever lenity you please, but if you relax so far as to lay yourself open to their machinations, you may be deceiv'd in your expectations. There are few Indians in whom I wou'd wish to put a perfect confidence, but of all I ever met with these shou'd be the last, for I firmly believe them very capable of the most perfidious & most cruel treachery, tho' no People can carry it fairer when the proper superiority is maintain'd.[1]

At the same time, a new note had crept into Cook's journal. Although he felt kindly towards Te Weherua and Koa, his attitude towards their people had shifted. He, who had so often described Maori people as 'brave, noble, and open', insisting that 'they are no more wicked than other men', now spoke sharply about their cruelty in warfare, saying that they 'kill every soul that falls in their way, not even sparing the Women and Children, and then either feast and gorge themselves on the spot or carry off as many of the dead as they can and do it at home with acts of brutality horrible to relate.'[2]

The shift in Cook's behaviour during the third voyage has been described as '"the loss of hope", an "increased cynicism", or "familiarity breeds contempt", and "power tends to corrupt and absolute power corrupts absolutely".'[3] This transformation began at Queen Charlotte Sound, in the aftermath of the Grass Cove killings. Cook realised how far he had been hoodwinked during his previous visit, and felt the sting of disrespect not only from local people, but from his own sailors. As an 'enlightened' leader, he had tried to act with calm detachment, even in the face of cannibalism. Most of his men had no such scruples, however. They wanted to revenge their shipmates, and kill the cannibals. When Cook did nothing to punish Kahura, their faith in their commander was undermined and discipline was threatened. Almost as soon as the *Resolution* sailed from the Sound, there were rumblings on board the ship. According to Lieutenant King, there was an 'appearance of general disobedience among the people' and a rash of minor thieving during which meat was stolen from the messes. The men would not identify the offenders, so Cook put them on two-thirds salted rations until the culprits had been punished. The crew refused to co-operate and would not eat their reduced allowance, which he considered 'a very mutinous proceeding'.[4] Captain Cook's authority had been undermined, affecting his own morale as well as that of the sailors. Although it has been claimed that his conduct was influenced by the illness which had almost killed him during the second voyage,[5] there is no evidence that Captain Cook was unwell at this time. It was rather his belief in himself and his men that had been shaken.

As the ships headed into the Pacific, the winds were light and flukey. Cook had been hoping for strong westerlies to carry them to Tahiti, but instead they met south-easterly breezes. By now they were short of fodder for the livestock, and Cook was keen to find an anchorage where grass and greenery could be collected. On 29 March the *Discovery* signalled that land had been sighted, and a high island (Mangaia, one of the Cook Islands) appeared on the horizon, its hills covered with breadfruit trees, coconut palms and flowering bushes which sent out a tropical fragrance. As they approached the island, small groups of warriors gathered on the reef, shouting and brandishing their spears and clubs in a threatening manner. Two of these men launched a small canoe and paddled out to the ships, chanting, where Mai called out that the ships had come in friendship. In response, they asked where had they come from and who was their leader? Mai answered their questions and offered them gifts, but one of these men, a robust, fine-looking fellow named Mourua, demanded an offering for his god; so Mai tied a spike nail, some beads and red cloth to a stick and threw it into the sea beside the canoe. When Mai asked Mourua whether his people were cannibals, he indignantly denied it, and when he was asked how he had got a livid scar on his face, he replied that it had happened during fighting on an island to the eastward. Cook threw this man a shirt, which he tied around his head like a turban, grimacing and pulling faces (probably a ritualised challenge). He would not come on board the *Resolution*, although when Cook put off in his boat, Mourua readily joined him.

By now about two hundred people had gathered on the reef, and some of them swam out to the boats where they grabbed at muskets, beads, iron rings and other objects. The sailors offered them hatchets, but when looking-glasses were produced they took these instead, looking at themselves in astonishment. After failing to find a safe passage through the reef Cook took the boats back to the ships, and Mourua decided to go with him. Upon boarding the *Resolution*, however, he was so uneasy that he seemed quite distracted, so Cook ordered a boat to take him back to the island. As Mourua left the Great Cabin he tripped over a goat and stopped in amazement, asking Mai what kind of *manu* [living creature] this was. When he was dropped off near the surf he swam to the beach, where a large crowd surrounded him, agog to know what he had seen on this extraordinary vessel.

The ships carried on to the north, and at noon the next day, another high island (Atiu) was sighted. The winds were still light and contrary, however, and it took another day to get close to the island. Cook sent Lieutenant Gore with three armed boats to look for a safe harbour, but just as they were about to leave the ship, several canoes paddled out and some islanders, including a large, corpulent man, a chief named 'Otenouhoora [Tinohura?]', came on board the *Discovery*, where Gore and Mai soon joined them. They were unarmed, and carried a plantain branch as a sign of greeting. According to their descendants, these people asked Gore, 'Are you one of the glorious sons of Tetumu?'[6] – a precise echo of the phrase used by the priest Vaita in his chant which foretold the coming of Europeans to the Society Islands:

> The glorious offspring of Te Tumu
> will come and see this forest at Taputapuatea.
> Their body is different, our body is different
> We are one species only from Te Tumu.
> And this land will be taken by them
> The old rules will be destroyed
> And sacred birds of the land and the sea

Will also arrive here, will come and lament
Over that which this lopped tree has to teach
They are coming up on a canoe without an outrigger.[7]

It seems that people in the Cook Islands knew about the arioi in Tahiti, for there was a marae called Taputapuatea and an arioi house on the north-west coast of Atiu.[8] Later, when the missionary John Williams visited Rarotonga (another of the Cook Islands) in 1838, the local inhabitants asked a Ra'iatean sailor on the ship why his people had killed the priests Paoa-tea and Paoa-uri at Taputapuatea, and what had happened to the sacred drum, Taimoana, which they had sent as a gift for 'Oro?[9] This was a reference to a great quarrel at Taputapuatea in Ra'iatea, in which the high priest Paoa-tea had been killed on the marae, and his counterpart, the high priest Paoa-uri, had been slain in retribution. After these killings the canoes had fled through the southern pass (Te Avarua), breaking the tapu as they left the island. This quarrel, which had destroyed the voyaging network which brought arioi from many islands to Taputapuatea at Ra'iatea, was also vividly remembered at Tahiti.[10] The story was known in New Zealand as well, where there are a number of sacred sites known as 'Taputapuatea', although this name may have been very ancient.[11] If they had heard about the rituals at Ra'iatea, however, then it is no surprise that Tupaia's arrival in New Zealand was so momentous for Maori, and why it was Tupaia, the high priest from Taputapuatea, rather than Captain Cook, whom they later remembered.

During this meeting with the people of Atiu, the frond of a coconut palm was produced, and Mai and Tinohura went through a ritual, chanting in turns and alternately pulling leaves from it. After this ceremony they crossed to the Resolution, where Tinohura gave Cook a bunch of plantains sent by one of the three high chiefs of the island, and Cook handed over an axe and a length of red fabric as a return present. A double canoe came alongside, and an orator (who presumably represented one of the other two high chiefs) stood and made a speech before sending up a pig, some coconuts and a fine mat to Captain Cook. When these people came on board the ship, they looked at the Europeans in astonishment, touching them and smelling their skin, and exclaiming aloud at each new discovery. They examined the ship's cattle, horses, sheep, goats and peacocks with amazement, but left disappointed because they had hoped to acquire a pair of dogs, which had become extinct on Atiu. When he returned to the ship, Gore reported to Cook that the surf had been too high for a landing and he could find no good harbour, but suggested that since the local people seemed friendly, Mai could persuade them to send out provisions to the vessels.

The next morning more canoes brought out gifts for Cook, and the envoys asked for a dog as a return present. One of the gentlemen on board the *Resolution* had a pair of dogs but would not give them up, so Mai parted with a favourite animal and their visitors went away happy. These men offered to guide Lieutenant Gore and his three boats ashore, and he and Mai set off accompanied by Dr Anderson and Lieutenant Burney, both of whom could speak some Tahitian. Just beyond the surf, Anderson and Burney boarded a canoe which took them to the beach, where they were surrounded by a huge crowd of people. A man covered with black dye used a small stick to keep the crowd back, as a group of armed warriors led the Europeans inland, chanting a short sentence over and over. When they arrived at the meeting-ground, they were saluted by two elders who pressed noses with them before presenting them to Atirau, one of the island's three leading chiefs, an elderly, corpulent man with an intelligent, grave face and bunches of red feathers in his ears who sat under a tree, cooling himself with a ceremonial fan. After this encounter, they were taken to meet the other high chiefs, each of whom wore red feather ear ornaments as a mark of their status. A group of women, also wearing.red feathers, sang and danced for their guests, directed by a man who prompted each movement.

Soon afterwards there was a loud rattling noise as three ranks of armed warriors danced forward with clubs and pointed spears. Mai and Lieutenant Gore had arrived, and Mai sat down about four yards away from the high chiefs and made a speech of greeting. When Atirau answered, he sent him a small bunch of red feathers. The dances began again, and Mai took an ornamental dagger and broke open a coconut, presenting this gallantly to one of the female dancers. Atirau and his companions examined this weapon, exclaiming in admiration. Lieutenant Gore wanted to barter for local produce, but when he suggested that trade should begin, he was told that he would have to wait until the next morning. The people began to crowd around their visitors, not allowing them to move from the meeting-place, picking their pockets and snatching at their possessions, including Mai's dirk and a fan which Atirau had given to Burney. When Mai complained to the high priest about this behaviour, however, he was simply told that he and his companions would not be allowed to return to the ships before nightfall.

Every time they attempted to leave the meeting-place, their way was barred by warriors with clubs, so they decided to sit down and talk with these people. Upon his arrival on the island Mai had been greeted by a group of Tahitians, whose canoe had been driven to Atiu during a storm many years earlier, losing all but five of the crew during the ordeal. These people, who had been on Atiu for more than a decade and knew nothing about

Wallis's arrival at Tahiti, now told him that they had been very kindly treated. They talked eagerly with Mai, their presence on Atiu no doubt explaining how the local people knew about Vaita's prophecy at Taputapua-tea. They told him that the island was called 'Whenua no te atua' [The Island of God], because so many of the Atiuans were possessed by ancestral spirits.

After talking with his countrymen, Mai presented gifts to several high-born women, and the people entertained them with wrestling matches and dancing, first by the men and then by the women. When some oven fires were lit, Mai became anxious, fearing that he and his companions were about to be killed and eaten, and decided to divert the locals with a demon-stration of Tahitian fighting methods. He stood in the middle of the crowd and went through his weapon drill; and when he performed a heiva as his finale, the chiefs burst out laughing, teasing him about some of his actions. The people crowded around, eagerly asking Mai about the Europeans and their country, and he answered with some fabulous stories, telling them among other things that the British had ships larger than their island, with guns which could destroy Atiu with one shot. When the chiefs seemed sceptical, Mai took a musket cartridge, removed the ball and threw a live coal onto it, causing a loud explosion. He warned them that unless he and his companions were allowed to leave the island before nightfall, the ships would fire their guns without fail, killing everybody on Atiu. After this exchange, a large number of coconuts, baked plantains and a roasted pig were produced, and the visitors were feasted, although they were so anxious about their safety that they could barely eat. Mai was given kava to drink, and then to their intense relief Gore's party was led back to the beach, where a canoe took them out to the *Resolution*. As Gore noted in his journal, these people were almost indistinguishable from Tahitians, except for their tattoos and ornaments:

The People of Wautiew . . . have Black Bellies Privities included and black Leggs reaching To Just above their Calf . . . Their Weomen have only Black Leggs, In one thing more these Differ from the Otahiteans in, is the Holes in their Ears are Larger and instead of Poees they ware Roses made Of red Feathers with the Rose forward resting on their Temples which in their Ladies looks Pretty Enuff, and there Are some Verry Pretty Lasses Here I'll Ashure You.[12]

The next morning the ships sailed to Takutea, a small uninhabited island north-west of Atiu in the Cook Islands. When Gore went ashore to collect greenery for the animals, and coconuts and scurvy grass for the sailors, he found several old houses and burial grounds. After this Cook decided to carry on to Hervey's Island (Manuae), a larger uninhabited atoll discovered during his previous voyage. When they arrived there on 6 April, however, they found to their surprise that the island was now occupied. Several canoes came out to look at the ships, and their crews conversed with Mai but refused to come on board, although they eagerly accepted nails and paper from the sailors. A fine red feather cap was seen in one of these canoes, which made Cook think that there was a chief on board, although these people told Mai that they paid tribute to the high chiefs of Atiu. They also said that they had seen two great ships like these before, presumably the *Resolution* and *Adventure* during the second voyage. These men were bold and acquisitive, grabbing a coat from a sailor and taking some meat that was being towed behind the ship, which they traded to Koa, the young Maori lad, for a piece of brown paper. They tried to seize the *Discovery*'s cutter and when one of the sailors fended them off, they hit him on the head with a paddle and grabbed the astronomer's servant, who had gone on board the cutter to help his shipmates. As soon as two armed boats were lowered they let him go and fled in their canoes, while Te Weherua and Koa remarked in surprise that 'of so many people within reach of our power, we have neither killed or made prisoners of any'.[13]

   Cook had failed to find enough fodder in the Cook Islands to keep the cattle alive while he waited for the westerly winds to take him to Tahiti. The ships were running out of water, and it was already autumn in the southern hemisphere. He had been late in leaving the Cape of Good Hope, and because he had spent several months in Tasmania, Dusky Sound and Queen Charlotte Sound, the season for exploration was almost over. He was also tired of dealing with aggressive, unfriendly 'natives'. Instead of heading directly for the north-west coast of America, therefore, he decided to sail to the Tongan archipelago, which he had named the 'Friendly Islands' during the *Endeavour* voyage, where the people were welcoming, he had reliable friends, and he could get everything that he needed.

On 13 April 1777 the ships sighted Palmerston Island, which Cook had located during his previous voyage. Over the next few days, the boats rowed to the islets around the reef, fishing and collecting coconuts and fodder for the cattle. Among the trees the sailors found a few Polynesian rats, and large numbers of sea-birds nesting by the shore. The sea inside the reef was crystal clear, its white sand floor edged with coral outcrops where bright fish darted in shoals, their brilliant colours flashing in the sunlight. There was no sign of any inhabitants, although they found parts of a wrecked canoe on the beach and a carved piece of wood, painted yellow, which the sailors thought was part of a ship, although Mai said it was part of a burial marker. Mai camped ashore on the atoll with some of his shipmates and taught the sailors how to catch fish on the reef and birds in the forest, cooking these for them in an earth oven. As Burney remarked gratefully, the young islander 'was a most usefull companion for a party of this kind; being a keen sportsman, and excellent cook and never idle. Without him we might have made a tolerable shift, but with him we fared sumptuously.'[14] Mai was thrilled with this island, saying that he would like to return there by canoe with his family from Tahiti and Ra'iatea. With the ships loaded with coconuts for the men, and palm fronds, pandanus branches and scurvy grass for the livestock, Cook headed west again. On 24 April they sailed past Niue (which Cook had named 'Savage Island' during his previous voyage) without attempting a landing.

Four days later in squally, wet weather, they arrived at the Nomuka group, at the heart of the Tongan archipelago. As they anchored amidst the islands, there were flashes of lightning and loud claps of thunder – signs of ancestral power. Cook had visited Nomuka three years earlier, and when two canoes came alongside their crews showed no great surprise, but immediately began to exchange coconuts, breadfruit, plantains and sugar-cane for knives and small nails. An old chief named Tapa, his torso scarred from past battles, came on board and spoke vehemently to the Europeans, pointing towards Nomuka, although they could not understand what he was saying. Because he often made speeches and seemed very active in directing his countrymen, the sailors nicknamed this man 'Lord North', after the Prime Minister of Britain. At sunrise the next morning Lieutenant King went to the nearby island of Mango to procure provisions, returning several hours later accompanied by this old man and a chief named Tupoul-angi, a stout, robust man about thirty years old with an agreeable, open countenance, who brought a large hog for Cook as a present. As soon as the boats had been hoisted back on board they sailed for Nomuka, followed by canoes from the surrounding islands loaded with fruit, pigs, chickens and 'curiosities', including cloth, fish-hooks, baskets, weapons, musical instruments and specimens of local birds, to barter with the Europeans.

The next morning Tupoulangi (the leading chief of Nomuka) and Tapa came off with more hogs, and Cook exchanged gifts with other Nomukans who came out to the ship with pigs and large quantities of provisions. They refused to enter into exchanges with any of his subordinates, however, including Captain Clerke; for in this rank-ridden society, this would have diminished their own status. During the day a hatchet was stolen from the galley, and Cook ordered the man in charge, Richard Young, 'a quiet and good man', to be punished with a flogging of six lashes. On 1 May the ships anchored off the northern coast of Nomuka by Cook's former landing-place, where they were soon surrounded by canoes, including two large voyaging canoes with crews of forty to fifty men each. Cook stopped the ship's provisions, serving fresh pork and vegetables instead, and forbade his men to trade for curiosities until the ships were fully provisioned. When one of the sailors flouted this order, he also was punished with half a dozen lashes.

Upon their arrival at Nomuka, Tupoulangi took Cook and Mai to his own house, offering it to his guests for their use during their stay on the island.[15] The horses, cattle, sheep and other livestock were landed, and water was collected from a large stagnant pool, for fresh water was difficult to find on the island. Some of Tapa's men carried a shelter on their shoulders from a quarter of a mile away and erected it next to Tupoulangi's house, so that he could stay next to Cook and his companions. Mai sat with the chiefs, regaling them with stories about Britain, and impressing them with the power of the King of England. A market was established on the beach, where the gunners controlled the trade, and the chiefs kept their people in order by pelting them with stones and coconuts or hitting them with clubs if they crowded too close, or disobeyed their instructions.

The sailors had no difficulty in attracting women to the ships, bartering hatchets, shirts and nails for red feathers and sex; although they soon found that venereal diseases had already been introduced to Nomuka, presumably during Cook's previous visit. The Tongan men willingly helped the sailors cut wood and fill the water barrels, although they demanded payment for every service they rendered. Cook's men loved this idyllic island, where they had plenty to eat and could wander ashore without fear, shooting ducks on the inland lagoons and eating fruit from the trees, enjoying the lush scenery and the friendliness of the people. As Samwell remarked:

Nothing can be more agreeable than the Inclosures in which their Houses stand, round which the bread fruit & Plantain Trees grow & extend their friendly Shade over the Natives . . . Such enchanting Prospects does this little Isle afford that it may be said to realize the poetical Descriptions of the Elysian Fields in ancient Writers, it is certainly as beautiful a Spot as Immagination can paint.[16]

On 6 May a chief called Finau arrived in a large sailing canoe from Tonga-tapu with his retinue, which included half a dozen beautiful young women. Finau was a tall, slender, active man about thirty-five years old, with a handsome face, a commanding presence and an alert, vivacious expression. He became a great favourite with the British, who found him intelligent, generous and charming.[17] According to Queen Salote, Finau probably held the title of Tu'i Kanokupolu at this time, and had great secular power in the

Ashore at Nomuka, in the Tongan archipelago

archipelago.[18] In Tonga during this period, there were three ruling titles with complementary roles; the Tuʻi Tonga, a sacred chief descended from the god Tangaloa; the Tuʻi Haʻatakalaua, appointed by the Tuʻi Tonga, who exercised secular authority, ensuring that appropriate tribute was paid to the Tuʻi Tonga; and the Tuʻi Kanokupolu, appointed by the leaders of his own lineage, to whom much of this power had been delegated.[19] This system thoroughly confused Cook, who was bewildered by the succession of 'Kings' whom he encountered in Tonga. Power and status did not go hand in hand in these islands, for the Tuʻi Tonga had the highest ceremonial status, followed by the Tuʻi Haʻatakalaua, while the Tuʻi Kanokupolu had the greatest political authority. To make matters more complicated, they were each outranked by their father's sisters, for while power and authority usually passed through males, sacred status passed through the female line in Tonga.

When Finau landed on the beach, Tupoulangi bowed his head to his feet and Tapa made a long speech, listing 150 islands over which Finau exercised authority. When he came on board the *Resolution*, an inferior chief ordered the people ashore, and when some of them came back to the ship without permission, he beat them unmercifully with a large stick, so that one man fell down in convulsions, blood gushing from his mouth and nostrils. When one of the officers reproached the chief, he simply laughed, showing no remorse, for in Tonga at this time, if commoners flouted chiefly commands, harsh physical punishment was taken for granted.[20] In the Great Cabin, Finau presented Cook with gifts of red feathers, pigs and fruit, while Cook gave him a printed linen gown, hatchets and beads. Afterwards he entertained Finau with bugles and drums and firing the great cannons, which amazed him with their loud explosions and the splash of the cannon-balls far off in the ocean. Although Finau managed to maintain his composure during the salute, his followers clapped their hands over their heads in astonishment.

After this visit, Finau dined on board the ship with Cook every day, although only Tapa was allowed to eat with him in the Great Cabin. When he went ashore the local people crowded on board, and the women ate with the men, a practice which was strictly forbidden in the Society Islands. Like the Society Islanders, however, the Tongans were irrepressibly acquisitive, taking anything from the ships they could get their hands on. Although Cook refused to have them shot for these offences, the punishments on board the *Resolution* became increasingly severe. On 9 May a chief who came on board with Finau was given a dozen lashes for taking an iron bolt, and confined with his hands tied behind his back until a large hog was delivered for his ransom. William Anderson, the *Resolution*'s surgeon, was uneasy about this punishment, remarking that 'I am far from thinking there was any injustice in punishing this man for this theft, . . . but that he should be confin'd in a painfull posture for some hours after, or a ransom demanded after proper punishment for the crime had been inflicted I believe will scarcely be found consonant with the principles of justice or humanity upon the strictest scrutiny.'[21] At the same time on board the *Discovery*, Clerke ordered local thieves to have their heads shaved, a mark of great humiliation.[22] That night there was a torrential downpour of rain, with flashes of lightning and claps of thunder like the roar of a large cannon firing.

Finau had urged Cook to accompany him to his headquarters at Lifuka, north-east of Nomuka, where he could entertain him in chiefly style, and on 11 May, having exhausted the supply of provisions on the island, Cook decided to accept this invitation. As the tents were brought back on board, three of the marines were punished for negligence. Few canoes came out that day, but after dusk they heard a large gathering of people singing and dancing. When the *Discovery* weighed anchor, a cable parted and one of its anchors fell to the sea floor, and it took several days to recover this irreplaceable piece of equipment. On 14 May they finally left Nomuka, heading north and sailing past Tofua, a smoking volcanic island which Cook had sighted during his previous visit to Tonga. Finau, a noted navigator, led the way in his own sailing canoe, which sailed much faster than the European ships (covering three miles for each two sailed by the *Resolution* and *Discovery*). He guided them while they were out of sight of land, stretching out his arms to indicate the depth of the water.

During this passage Finau and Mai slept on an island each night, and every morning they presented Cook with gifts of pork, fresh fruit and vegetables. While they were camped ashore, Mai regaled Finau with tales of his experiences on the European ships, and his adventures in England. Although Mai liked to elaborate on the power of the Europeans, Finau quickly learned that Captain Cook was not the head of his own society, but a commoner who had risen to be a famous navigator, subordinate to the King and the naval authorities in Britain. In an island society which (like Britain) was obsessed with rank, this made a huge difference to how Cook and his men were regarded.

On 17 May 1777 the ships anchored off the northern end of Lifuka, where they were surrounded by a milling crowd of canoes whose crews exchanged pigs, fowls, fruit and root crops for hatchets, knives, cloth and nails. At daylight Finau and Mai took Cook ashore, leading him to a house by the beach where he sat down with the chiefs, in front of a vast crowd of people who arranged themselves in a circle. When Cook was asked how long he intended to stay on this island and replied, 'Five days', Tapa (who had accompanied them to Lifuka) announced this to the gathering. Reassured by this response and prompted by Finau, Tapa made a long speech to the crowd, urging them to treat the Europeans as their friends. They should not steal from them or molest them, but bring plenty of pigs, chickens and fresh fruit and vegetables to their market. When he indicated that Cook should make a presentation to the chief of the island, Cook gave generous gifts to this man, two other chiefs and finally Tapa himself; after which the chief of Lifuka, again prompted by Finau, made a speech urging his people to treat their visitors with all possible kindness. When Cook returned to the landing-place, he found a baked hog and some piping-hot yams waiting for him on the beach, and invited Finau and his companions to dine on board the *Resolution*.

The next morning, Mai and Finau came to conduct Cook to a great ceremony of welcome. They took him to the house on the beach, where a crowd of at least 3000 people had gathered. Soon about a hundred men arrived in procession, laden with yams, breadfruit, plantains, coconuts and sugar-cane which they stacked in two piles to Cook's left, topping these with six pigs and two turtles. A second procession brought in more vegetables and fruits, laying these in two piles to his right, topped with two pigs and six chickens. The crowd arranged themselves in a circle, and soon a number of men armed with clubs appeared in the arena, engaging in single combat which ended only when a weapon was broken or one of the antagonists could carry on no longer. Each victor squatted before the chiefs, where he was congratulated by the old men and cheered by the gathering.

In the intervals there were wrestling and boxing matches, including a contest in which two lusty young women boxed with each other, applauded by the spectators. When one of the gentlemen, shocked by this display, tried to break up the fight, the spectators thought this hilarious. Some of the sailors who fancied themselves at wrestling and boxing challenged the Tongans to fight, but were roundly defeated except when their opponents let them win for diplomatic reasons. When some of these men refused to retire with a good grace, the people laughed at their ill-humour. As these entertainments concluded, Finau told Cook that the larger pile of food on the left was for him, while the smaller pile on the right was for Mai, whom the Tongans also wished to honour.

Cook was gratified by these gifts, remarking that they 'far exceeded any present I had ever before received from an Indian Prince'. It took four boats to carry the provisions back to the ships, and when Finau came on board, Cook gave him such rich presents (including a sword and a linen gown) that as soon as he returned to shore, Finau despatched two more large pigs, some yams and a quantity of bark-cloth. On board the *Discovery*, however, the festive mood was spoiled when Tapa's son was clapped into irons for stealing a cat. The ships were infested with rats, and as Clerke remarked ruefully, the Tongans had taken 'all my Cats, which were very good ones, & as they did not take the Rats with them, of which the ship was full, I felt this proof of their Dexterity very severely.'[23] When Clerke asked Finau how he could stop the thefts, Finau told him to kill the offenders, or he would do it for him. Cook still insisted that local people should not be killed for theft, however, and Clerke had decided to make an example of the young chief by keeping him confined until two of the stolen cats were brought back to the vessel, angering his people.

The next day, Anderson and some companions strolled the length of Lifuka, past large, well-cultivated fenced plantations linked by wide roads. On their way, they passed a tall man-made mound with a stone monolith at its base, shaded by an arbour of low trees where people sat to catch pigeons. Later they came to a very large house with a clearing in front which served as a ceremonial ground, and a mound two or three feet high, covered with gravel, carrying a group of small houses where high-ranking people were buried. The following morning Cook ordered the marines to go ashore to perform their drill and fire volleys as a compliment to Finau. Thousands of Tongans gathered to watch but the marines were not very well trained, and when they fired at a canoe, only one musketball hit its mark, although it went right through the hull, which left Finau and the other chiefs very thoughtful. In reply, Finau led about 200 chiefs in an impressive display of weapon-handling, each of them brandishing a weapon shaped like a paddle.

They moved with absolute precision, lined up in ranks, posturing slowly and then with great rapidity, accompanied by hollow bamboos and two wooden drums and singing in rich harmony. According to Cook, this performance 'so far exceeded any thing we had done to amuse them that they seemed to pique themselves in the superiority they had over us', and he hastened to instruct the gunner to prepare a fireworks display for that evening.

After dark, a vast crowd gasped with astonishment when a water-rocket was fired into the sea, diving under the water and then rising up in the air, ending with a loud and unexpected explosion. This was followed by skyrockets which burst high in the sky, amazing the Tongans, and by a stunning variety of fireworks, including flower-pots, roses and fire-serpents. When some balloons exploded like a clap of thunder, the people cried out 'Mate! Mate!' ['We'll be killed!'], begging Cook to end the display immediately. According to Lieutenant King:

Such roaring, jumping, & shouting, . . . made us perfectly satisfied that we had gaind a compleat victory in their own minds. Sky & water rockets were what affect'd them most, the water rocket exercis'd their inquisitive faculties, for they could not conceive how fire shoud burn under water. Omai who was always very ready to magnify our country, told them, they might now see how easy it was for us to destroy not only the earth, but the water & the Sky; & some of our sailors were seriously perswading their hearers, that by means of the sky rockets we had made stars.[24]

In return for this entertainment, the local people performed an impressive series of dances. The first was accompanied by a group of eighteen men who sat in the middle of a torchlit arena, beating the ground with long bamboos and singing while women with crimson hibiscus garlands on their heads stepped rhythmically back and forth in unison, snapping their fingers, clapping their hands and leaping quickly, gyrating their hips as they sang with the chorus. As they left the arena each woman placed her garland on the head of her sweetheart, many of whom handed these to their visitors. They were followed by a group of fifteen men, some of them elderly, who stood in a circle, moving their hands in elegant gestures, inclining their bodies to one side and the other, clapping their hands and then moving their feet much more quickly. After this a party of men exercised their wit in a kind of farce, making comic remarks about the fireworks, and then other dancers performed, singing and dancing to shouts of admiration. Finally, a small group of dejected-looking women came out and sat in front of the chief's house, where a man rose up and began to hit each of them hard on the back with his fists, astonishing the Europeans. When he struck the fourth

*A night dance by men at Lifuka, Ha'apai, in Tonga, when the
warriors plotted to kill Cook and his men*

woman hard on her bare breasts, a man rose from the crowd and knocked
him flat with a blow, and he was carried away. As Samwell remarked
indignantly:

To see this unmerciful Beadle punished was no small Pleasure to us all, as it was
really more than we could well bear to be inactive Spectators of so many beautiful
Girls receiving such heavy blows from his villainous Hands. Had a spark of the Spirit
of La Mancha's Knight inspired us we would have rescued them from the Hands of
their Tormentors; but we sat still.[25]

After each of these women had been beaten they danced, but their performance was uneven and they were forced to repeat it twice over. After the
dancing an old chief ordered the people to disperse, and the Europeans were
given supper while Finau scoured the woods for stragglers, almost killing
one man who had lingered in the forest. As Charles Clerke remarked, 'We
clearly perceive that [the high chiefs] can & will order a Man to be put to
death instantaneously, & there is not the least Appeal from their Commands.
What is very extraordinary on these Occasions, the Standers by look on
with the utmost indifference, just as tho' they were Matters of course, and
in 5 minutes afterwards are as facetious as if nothing of the kind had
happen'd.'[26]

According to William Mariner, the first European to live in Tonga, a plot
had been hatched to kill Cook and his officers on this occasion. The Ha'apai
chiefs intended to catch them unawares while they were distracted, watching

the night dances. They were angry about the insult to Tapa's son, and planned to seize the ships as plunder. Finau was not a ringleader in this plot but was aware of its details, urging the chiefs not to attack the Europeans at night but during the daytime. In the event, no signal was given, perhaps because the fireworks had caused such consternation. This story, however, explains the marked interest which the Tongans had taken in the marines' drill, and their muskets. Apparently Finau had finally ordered that the attack should not proceed, and when he scoured the forest that night, he must have been making sure that all of the warriors had left the area.[27]

Early the next morning Cook found Latu alongside in his canoe, the impassive 'idiot' of an 'eiki [aristocrat] introduced to him during his previous visit as the 'King' of Tongatapu. Latu stayed there all afternoon, ignored by Finau and his companions, until he eventually left for one of the islands. By now there was incessant pilfering from the ships, and that day and the next Clerke flogged several of his men for negligence, put two Tongans in irons for theft, and ordered a chief to be given fifteen lashes as a deterrent. Martin, one of the *Discovery*'s midshipmen, commented, 'Had we made an Example of every one of these people that deserved it, Punishment would have been Endless, for their Skill in Pilfering is almost past conception, & had any man of less Humanity then the Captn.s Cook & Clerke Commanded, many of these people must have lost their life, from the daring attempts they were hourly making on us.'[28]

As always, when his relationship with local people began to deteriorate, Cook was keen to leave the island, but Finau and Tapa urged him to stay a few days longer so that they could go to Vava'u to fetch red feather head-dresses for him and Mai. When Cook offered to accompany them, however, Finau refused, saying that there was no suitable anchorage there – a thumping lie, since there was an excellent harbour at Vava'u. The next day a rumour reached Cook that a European vessel had arrived at Nomuka, although when Mai checked this with a chief from that island, he flatly denied it. By now the provisions on Lifuka were almost exhausted, so Cook decided not to wait for Finau. He sailed to a bay at the south of the island, ordering the master, William Bligh, to take soundings while he and Gore explored the southern coastline.

At noon on 27 May while the ships were still anchored off Lifuka, three sailing canoes arrived, bringing a man called Paulaho, whom the Tongans assured Cook was the 'King of all the Isles'. Having met one 'King' of Tonga after another, Cook was sceptical, but when the people insisted that this man out-ranked Finau, he sent a boat to bring him to the *Resolution*. Paulaho was massively corpulent, a sedate, sensible man about 40 years old who asked many astute questions about the Europeans and their intentions.

When Cook showed him a map of his track across the Pacific, he seemed to understand it, explaining the chart to his people. As Cook soon discovered, Paulaho was indeed the highest-ranking chief in the archipelago. He was the Tu'i Tonga, the sacred head of the archipelago, descendant of the god Tangaloa, and it was true that he outranked Finau, although Finau's secular authority as the Tu'i Kanokupolu was greater.

When Paulaho was invited to dine in the Great Cabin, his attendants objected on the grounds that if he went below decks, people might walk over his head (which was intensely tapu). To allay their concerns, Cook ordered that no one should walk on that part of the deck during his visit. Mai, who was furious to hear that this man was of a higher rank than Finau, with whom he had exchanged names, examined him closely about his status. Paulaho presented Cook with two large pigs, a head-dress and a quantity of red feathers; and when he ate his dinner, two men fed him while the rest turned their backs in respect. Cook gave him a sword, some printed linen and other valuable objects; when he invited Cook and Mai to accompany him ashore, Mai excused himself in a fit of pique, but Cook went with him in his own boat, watching curiously as Paulaho was carried ashore on a piece of shaped wood like a hand-barrow.

On the beach, the Tu'i Tonga invited Cook to sit beside him in a shelter that had been especially built for his use, where the people brought all the goods they had acquired by barter with the Europeans. He examined each of these objects, returning all of them except for a glass bowl, which he kept for himself. The people greeted Paulaho with deep respect, silently bowing their heads to the soles of his feet, and impressing Cook with their politeness. 'I was quite charmed with the decorum that was observed,' he remarked; 'I had no where seen the like, no not even amongst more civilized nations.' When Paulaho came out to see Cook the next day, he brought him a red feather head-dress, a highly prized item. He told Cook that if he did not play his proper role of resolving differences among the different islands, Finau had the power to kill him; and that although he himself was the sacred ruler of Tonga, he was outranked by a woman named 'Sinaitakala'.[29] Sinaitakala was in fact Paulaho's father's sister and thus his senior in rank, although she had little real power; while Latu, the impassive and 'idiotic' chief whom Cook had met several times, was her son, which meant that he had very high status in the islands.[30] Paulaho's brother and some of his companions stayed on board the ship that night, although apparently without Paulaho's permission, because when he returned the next morning and found them there, he rebuked them sharply, reducing them to tears. Cook's men paid their lovers a hatchet each night and traded eagerly for curiosities, until local supplies were exhausted.

Cook decided to touch at Nomuka on his way to Tongatapu, and the ships headed south, led by Paulaho's canoe, which guided them through a labyrinth of islands. On 31 May, when Cook was below for dinner, leaving Bligh in charge, the *Resolution* almost struck on a low, sandy islet north of Kotu. Fortunately the crew had just been mustered to put the ship about, and they threw the sails aback, just missing the reef by two or three ship-lengths. The next morning when the boats went ashore at Kotu, they found the place largely empty, since most of its inhabitants had been following the ships, and had not yet returned from Lifuka. Many of those who remained had a violent cough and a sore throat, an ailment which had also afflicted most of the sailors. On 5 June when they arrived back at Nomuka, most of the local population were suffering from this illness, which they must have contracted from the Europeans. During their absence the Nomukans had been busy planting yams, and some melons and pineapples which Cook had planted were already sprouting.

On 7 June, Finau arrived in his canoe, telling Cook that several canoes that had accompanied him from Vava'u, loaded with pigs and other provisions, had been lost in a storm, so that he could not give him the supplies he had promised. When he met Paulaho, Finau was forced to perform the obeisance, bowing his head and touching the sole of Paulaho's foot, which left him visibly chagrined. Paulaho, the son of a secondary wife, was married to Finau's sister, whom many people considered of a higher rank than her husband. As the Tu'i Tonga, however, he was entitled to Finau's homage, although Finau obviously found this galling. As the Tu'i Kanokupolu, the main secular authority, Finau continued to assist the Europeans with practical matters. That afternoon when some Nomukans stole three glasses from the astronomer's quadrant, Finau soon had them brought back to the vessel. The next morning the ships weighed anchor and sailed for Tongatapu, the home of the high chiefs of the archipelago, accompanied by Finau and Paulaho in their large voyaging canoes, each carrying about fifty people and their luggage, which soon outsailed them.

On the approach to Tongatapu the *Resolution* touched on a flat coral shoal, and then the *Discovery* also struck and stuck fast for a while. Fortunately the breeze carried them off, and that evening they anchored in deep water. Early the next morning, 10 June, Paulaho arrived in his canoe, distinguished by a bunch of red grass hanging from a pole at its stern. As he sailed around the ships, he ran over and sank two small canoes during his passage. Ataongo, Cook's 'friend' from his previous visit to Tongatapu, came out to the ship, along with Tupou, who had changed names with Captain Furneaux, bringing out gifts of pigs and yams, and Cook gave them return

The Tuʻi Tonga's kava ceremony, with Paulaho receiving homage

presents. When Cook and Clerke landed on the island, Paulaho met them on the beach, taking them to a small house at the edge of the woods, where a large circle of people had gathered for a kava ceremony. A kava root was produced, and Paulaho ordered it split into pieces and chewed by some attendants. A baked pig and two baskets of cooked yams were brought into the house, divided into ten portions and distributed. When the kava was served, the first cup was presented to Paulaho, who handed it to the chief beside him. He drank the second cup himself, and handed the third to Cook, who gave it to Mai. After Paulaho's brother had been served, he took the kava and his food away, because he could not eat or drink in the Tuʻi Tonga's presence. Some other people, who seemed to be of lower rank, were able to eat with him, however, probably because they were *matapule* or ceremonial attendants of foreign origins, perhaps from Fiji or Samoa, who were not bound by such restrictions.

After the Tuʻi Tonga's kava, the tents and the astronomers' observatories were taken ashore, and all of the livestock were unloaded. As the pigs, turkeys, geese, peacocks, horses, cattle, goats and sheep arrived on the beach, like 'a Collection of wild Beasts at a Country fair in England',[31] the people looked at them in astonishment. Paulaho's people supplied the ships with heaps of provisions, including some baked puddings made from pounded root vegetables, banana and coconut cream, Cook's favourite island delicacy. Paulaho had told Cook about a man named Maealiuaki (his wife's paternal uncle) who was even more powerful than himself, but when Cook asked to meet this potentate, he was told that this was only possible if he and Clerke were prepared to strip their clothes to the waist, so great was his mana. Maealiuaki was a former Tu'i Kanokupolu who had taken on the less demanding but higher status role of Tu'i Ha'atakalaua in his old age. Although at this time he was probably the most influential man in Tonga,[32] Cook and Clerke were affronted by this suggestion. Clerke retorted that they would be happy to doff their hats, as they would to the King of England, but argued that 'it was highly preposterous in King Mallawogga [Maealiuaki] to think of more respect from us than King George, who was so infinitely a greater Prince, whose Subjects were so numerous; and yet we trifling handfull of King George's subjects cou'd with all ease dispossess or even destroy King Mallawogga and every subject he had got.'[33] Swayed by these arguments, Paulaho finally agreed to take them to meet Maealiuaki, dressed in their naval uniforms.

On 12 June, Cook, Clerke, Mai and some of the ships' officers, escorted by the Tu'i Tonga in his canoe, were taken to Mu'a, the Tu'i Tonga's sacred headquarters. They rowed across the lagoon to an idyllic village on the east side of the island where the highest aristocrats in Tonga lived in clusters of houses, each set in its own plantation. Kava plants grew in many of these gardens, which were neatly fenced, with wooden doors for privacy. When they landed, they were greeted by a large crowd who shouted out in greeting, and led them into a house decorated inside with finely woven grass panels, where they were seated in front of a large semicircle of people. After waiting for a while, Mai was told that Maealiuaki was either ill, or had gone to the ships, and Cook was so angry about this apparent affront that he immediately rose up and returned to the boats. Although three men with leaves strung around their necks came to the beach and sat with Paulaho, talking to him earnestly, and others came with gifts of pigs, yams and cloth, he would not accept their presents.

The following day, Maealiuaki and a large entourage arrived at the landing-place. Cook and Clerke went with Finau to see this old man, who seemed to be in his sixties. A chief named Tupou (possibly Tupou'ila, Maealiuaki's younger brother), about fifty years old, corpulent and almost blind, sat at the upper end of a long length of bark-cloth, with Maealiuaki sitting to one side of it. This slender, dignified, grey-haired old man, whom the people called 'Motu'a Tonga' [the father of Tonga],[34] greeted Cook in a kindly manner, inviting him to sit beside him. Mai gave a speech explaining why they had come to Tongatapu, and Cook presented Maealiuaki with a sword and some printed cloth, and with some gauze for Tupou; while Clerke gave him a large bead necklace. When Clerke fired off a pistol he had brought, the two chiefs seemed delighted; and when Cook invited them to dine on the *Resolution* the next day, they presented him with a length of bark-cloth.

Maealiuaki visited the shore camp the next morning, where Lieutenant King showed him around. He examined the observatories and the cattle with acute interest, and the cross-cut saw that the wood-cutters were using. When Paulaho came out to the ship, he brought his son, a fine boy about twelve years old, who stayed at his side but was not allowed to eat with him. After this meeting Paulaho dined with Cook almost every day, savouring the wine which was served in the Great Cabin; while when Cook went ashore to dine with Paulaho, he learned to enjoy the local kava. That afternoon some men paddled out to the ship's boats where they stole an iron pin, and one of them was seized and put into irons until the pin was returned. Over the following days, despite Cook's friendly relationships with the Tongan chiefs, thieving rose to new heights, and Cook and Clerke punished these offences with unprecedented severity. Over the days that followed, Tongans were routinely flogged for theft, and any chief who stole was forced to pay a ransom of pigs in addition to this punishment.

As William Bayly remarked, in some instances Cook was 'guilty of great cruelty'.[35] There were sentences of two dozen, three dozen and four dozen lashes, and blood flew across the decks as the backs of these men were flayed with the cat-o'-nine-tails. After seeing how the high chiefs treated their own people, Cook had decided that mild measures would be worse than useless. This was probably fair, because like Maori, the Tongans had little respect for people who allowed themselves to be insulted with impunity.[36] Nevertheless, this marked a radical shift in his conduct, for up until this time, Cook had been a strong advocate for the policy of turning a blind eye to minor offences, and winning over the islanders with kindness. By punishing chiefs as well as commoners, he alienated their kinsfolk. As Burney noted, 'Scarce a day afterwards passed without some of our people being robbed and insulted on shore, instead of asking us into their houses which they had hitherto done whenever we passed by, the doors of their plantations were shut and fastened against us. Most of the Sailing Canoes left the Bay and it was evident they began to think we had staid long enough.'[37]

At the same time, Cook was very harsh with his own men, flogging eight of them for disobedience or neglect of duty during his stay in Tongatapu.[38] Furthermore, any punishments recorded from this time are likely to be an underestimate, since they were not routinely entered in the official records of this voyage. All the same, the violence on board Cook's ships may have also been taken as a sign of mana. As Cook remarked, after one or two chiefs had been flogged for stealing, they sent their servants instead, knowing that they would be harshly punished if they were caught in the act:

After this we were not troubled with thieves of rank, their servants or slaves were employed in this dirty work, on which a floging made no more impression than it would have done upon the Main-mast; their masters so far from making intrest for them when they were caught would very often advise us to kill them, and as this was a punishment we did not chouse to inflect they generally escaped unpunished, because we could inflict nothing which they thought a punishment.[39]

During Cook's visit to Tongatapu, Paulaho was trying to ensure that Fatafehi (also known as Fuanunuiava), his son by a secondary wife, would succeed him as the Tu'i Tonga. Eventually, he decided that Cook would be a useful ally,[40] and on 15 June he invited Cook to come ashore, where Mai and the young chief were waiting. Cook landed, and found them seated under a bark-cloth canopy before a long piece of bark-cloth on the ground, with Maealiuaki and other high-born people sitting beside it. According to Mai, since Paulaho and Cook had become friends, the Tu'i Tonga wanted his son to be joined in this friendship. Cook agreed, some gifts were exchanged, and he invited Fatafehi and the assembled chiefs to dine with him on board the *Resolution*. Maealiuaki, who was dressed in a new bark-cloth garment decorated with six large patches of red feathers, presented his costume to Cook in honour of the occasion.

When the Tongan dignitaries came out to the ship and entered the Great Cabin, they refused to eat or drink, saying that it was tapu. They looked over the ship with great interest, however, and when they returned to the beach, as the young chief landed from the ship's boat, his father the Tu'i Tonga, Maealiuaki and a high-born old lady saluted him by bowing their heads to the ground and touching the soles of his feet, a tribute to the boy's sacred mana. When Cook came ashore, the Tu'i Tonga presented him with a large pig and some yams, while the people entertained them with drumming and singing.

On Tongatapu every year, there was a great round of ceremonies to ensure the fertility of the island. In late June or early July, when the seed yams were cut, there was a succession of planting rituals (*'inasi 'ufi mui*) in which the Tu'i Tonga was presented with very young yams and other offerings. In October, mature yams were brought to him from throughout the archipelago to thank the ancestor gods for their bounty (*'inasi 'ufi motu'a*).[41] It was now June, a good time for Paulaho to announce that his son would follow him as Tu'i Tonga. Just as the young yams were being planted to replace the previous season's crop, the young chief would be installed as his father's successor; and if the Europeans gave him their support, his position would be greatly strengthened.[42] On 17 June, thousands of people gathered at a ceremonial ground in front of Maealiuaki's house, where Cook and his officers were seated. Hundreds of people arrived in a procession, each carrying a pole with a small yam at each end, or two or three breadfruit. Others brought small fish stuck onto sharp twigs on dry branches, and they laid these offerings down on each side of the clearing, one heap for Cook and the other for Clerke. Later that morning, seventy men arrived with wooden drums who acted as a chorus, drumming and singing for the dancers.

John Webber took his sketch-book to this ceremony, and recorded the dances. They began with four ranks of twenty-four men each, who postured in various formations with their paddle-shaped weapons (or *paki*). After this performance Finau, dressed in English cloth with a dozen strings of beads around his neck, led thirty men in a dance accompanied by chanting. The third dance, which was greeted with loud acclamation, was led by Tupou, wearing a garment covered with red feathers, and accompanied on the drums by Maealiuaki, Finau and Paulaho's brother. This group of thirty men twirled their paki with great dexterity, followed by two men carrying battle-clubs, each wearing a piece of white cloth tied around their heads, who took over the arena, brandishing their clubs, throwing them in the air and making vigorous strokes; succeeded by a man who rushed in with a spear, looking about eagerly and putting himself in threatening attitudes, his body trembling with anger. The last dance began with a prologue accompanied by gestures with the paki, and was followed by a performance by two club-wielding warriors which was greeted with murmurs of approbation. The dancing, which was watched by about 4000 people, lasted until three in the afternoon, followed that evening by *Po me'e* or night dances. This sequence of dances included some by the women and some by the men, including one led by Finau, dressed in linen with some pictures (perhaps some of the second voyage engravings which Cook had brought with him as gifts) hung about his neck. During these celebrations the thefts on board the ships and from the sailors continued unabated, including the theft of a pewter bowl, which was quickly retrieved, and a bold attempt to steal an anchor from the waist of the *Discovery*.

In return for this entertainment, the next morning Cook ordered his marines to perform their drill, with a band playing drums, fifes and French horns in the intervals. The crowds were pleased when the marines fired in platoons, although they did not think much of the music, and laughed in derision when the manoeuvres were clumsily executed. As William Bligh observed sourly, 'A most ludicrous performance for the Marine Officer was as incapable of making his Men go through their exercise as C. Cook's Musicians or Musick was ill adapted.'[43] This was followed by wrestling and boxing matches, where once again the Tongans soundly thrashed any sailor who challenged them. The Europeans were losing face, so Cook ordered the gunner to prepare a fireworks display that night, which made a much better impression. As water-rockets and false-fires darted about underwater, the people were astonished. That night Mai announced that Cook intended to distribute many of his animals the next morning, and a huge crowd gathered to watch the presentations. Cook gave a bull, a cow and a pair of goats to Paulaho, a Cape ram and two ewes to Maealiuaki, and a horse and a mare to Finau. Although Mai had hoped that the animals would be kept for him to distribute in Tahiti, he made a speech explaining their uses to the Tongans, urging the chiefs to look after them, and urging them not to kill them until they had bred and multiplied.

During their first two weeks on Tongatapu, relationships between the members of Cook's expedition and the chiefs had been affable. During this period, Maealiuaki, Latu and Finau erected temporary huts near the shore camp so they could spend all their time with the Europeans. Mai and his Tongan girlfriend were given a small house to live in beside the observatories, and the officers were provided with lovers, who slept with them at the house in the shore camp. Although there was little room for modesty in this situation, the men were startled and amused by the Tongans' openness about sex. One night, for example, when one of these girls was woken by a rustling of mats and bark-cloth and cried, 'What is it?', another woman called out 'Misimisi!' ['Just love-making!']. Sometimes these girls would dance stark naked on the ships, using the most 'lascivious Gestures', to the sailors' surprise and gratification.[44]

Te Weherua and Koa, Mai's two young Maori companions, who also lived on shore, soon became great favourites with the Tongans. After performing a haka at one of the night celebrations, they were often asked to repeat the war-dance, and were much admired and petted (indeed, Te Weherua contracted venereal disease during his stay in Tonga). The Tongans treated Mai with such marked respect that he began to give himself airs. One day he got into an argument with the corporal of marines, and became so heated that he struck the man, who hit him back. Mai was furious and complained to Cook, but Cook declined to punish the corporal. Mai went off in a huff with Te Weherua and Koa, threatening to stay behind on the island, although he quickly relented when Cook sent a man after him with a conciliatory message.

Despite his friendship with the chiefs, on 20 June when one of the kids and two turkey-cocks went missing, Cook thought that they had instigated the theft, and ordered three large canoes alongside the *Resolution* to be confiscated. He stormed ashore in a rage, where he commanded the marines to arrest Paulaho, his brother and Finau until the animals were returned to the shore camp. When they saw the Tu'i Tonga and the Tu'i Kanokupolu under guard, the people began to cry out loud, and Paulaho's little grandson begged that his grandfather should be freed. With great dignity, Paulaho saluted Cook, ordering that some red feathers should be brought and the stolen property returned to him immediately. When Cook asked the chiefs to go on board the *Resolution* for dinner, Paulaho insisted on leading the way. Some armed warriors had gathered behind the house, but when Cook ordered the marines to surround the Tu'i Tonga with their bayonets drawn, Paulaho ordered his people to fall back, assuring them that he was in no danger. Later that afternoon when the kid and one of the turkey-cocks was brought out to the ship, the chiefs told Cook that the other cock would be returned the next morning. He took them at their word, releasing them and their canoes. The Tongatapu people were already short of food, since so many of their yams and other supplies had been given to the Europeans, and when Paulaho and Finau ordered them to arrange another huge presentation for Cook they were extremely resentful.

Early the next morning Paulaho, his head smeared with red ochre, arrived alongside the *Resolution* to take Cook to a ceremony of propitiation.[45] When Cook and his officers landed by the house, dressed in full uniform, they found the people busy putting up poles on either side of the ceremonial ground, where they began to pile up yams, which were delivered by a long procession. These men used poles with crosspieces to build two towering stacks of food about thirty feet high, one of which was named 'Paulaho' and the other 'Finau'. Paulaho's men, who were very numerous, topped their stack with a roasted pig, while Finau's men, wearing gorgeous aprons and cloaks decorated with red and yellow feathers, lashed a live pig on top, and another about halfway up their tower. Beside these they heaped up yams and breadfruit, topped by fine mullet and a small turtle. This presentation of food was followed by gifts of quantities of red feathers, and a series of dances. When dinner was served, Cook ate heartily, but Paulaho could neither eat nor drink, since his father's sister was present. He greeted her by putting his hands to her feet, and when she retired, he dipped his fingers in a glass of wine, and then received the obeisance from all her followers. The feast was followed by night dances, and a display of fireworks from the *Discovery*, most of which had been spoiled and failed to ignite. These celebrations were lavish, but muted. The ritual presentations helped to wipe out the insult to the high chiefs, but the people were still very angry about the way that their leaders had been treated.

Over the following days, the flow of provisions to the ships dried up, and there was a rash of thefts from the sailors. Samwell was attacked and robbed in the forest, and on 23 June when the master, William Bligh, and Lieutenant Williamson went on an expedition inland, the people showed their hostility by refusing to give them any provisions. They took some supplies at gunpoint and carried on their way, but when Bligh stopped to put a new flint in his musket, three men attacked him, knocking him flat and grabbing his weapon, while the boy who was carrying Williamson's musket ran off into the forest. Upon returning to the shore camp, Williamson reported their losses to Lieutenant King, and Mai went to complain to Paulaho. Paulaho and Finau, fearing how Cook might react, immediately left the area, and Cook, infuriated with Mai's meddling, ordered him to go at once and persuade the chiefs to come back to the shore camp. Williamson had already given Finau several gifts in order to get his gun back, but Cook told Mai that Finau could keep the weapon. When they finally returned to the shore camp, the chiefs reproached Cook for letting his men wander about the island, saying that they could not protect them under such circumstances, and suggesting that they should stay on the ships. Cook agreed that their protests were reasonable, but when he reprimanded his officers for going inland without seeking permission, Lieutenant Williamson was bitterly resentful:

I cannot pass over the strange conduct of Captn. Cook upon this occasion . . . If a small nail was stolen from Captn. Cook, the thief if taken was most severely punished, if of a little more consequence than a nail, then the Chiefs were immediately seized until the things stolen were return'd; I was much more affected by such arbitrary proceedings, than with the loss of my gun, although it was great, as I could have no redress.[46]

On 25 June a sharp earthquake shook the island, a sign of ancestral power. During that day, in an effort to make peace with Paulaho, Cook agreed to accompany him to the ritual centre at Mu'a, and the following day they set off together. After crossing the lagoon, they visited the Tu'i Tonga's family burial place, where there were three mounds encircled by a wall of stone. Each mound was strewn with pebbles and topped by a house, and guarded by wooden images. That night they slept in Paulaho's house, and when the Tongans woke well before dawn, the high chief entertained them with anecdotes about the Europeans. After another kava ceremony, Paulaho went outside and changed into an old, ragged mat, a sign of mourning, and led them in a procession to a small house where more kava was drunk in memory of a chief who had died some months earlier.

While Cook was at Muʻa, there were no thefts or provocations on the ships or at the shore camp, but soon after his return, relationships deteriorated. Stones and hunks of wood were thrown at the sailors, who were teased and taunted by the Tongans. Cook instructed the sentries at the shore camp to load their muskets with smallshot, and to fire if the people became too insolent. On 28 June, one of the marines, infuriated by some insults, loaded his gun with ball instead, and when a man tried to snatch a tool from one of the carpenters, he shot him in the shoulder. At the same time some officers who were pelted with coconuts chased the offenders, catching three men whom they brought to the camp, where they were given a severe flogging. One of them was an attendant of Paulaho's, and although Paulaho pleaded to have him released, Cook ordered this man to be tied to a tree, flogged with seventy-two lashes and his arms scored with a knife below the shoulders. Paulaho and the other high chiefs were horrified, and the wives and relatives of these men watched the punishment aghast, wailing and cutting the tops of their heads with sharks' teeth. As one of the midshipmen, George Gilbert, remarked in dismay, at this time Cook was sometimes seized by fits of fury:

This vice which is very pervilent here, Capt Cook punished in a manner rather unbecoming of a European viz: by cutting off their ears; fireing at them with small shot, or ball, as they were swimming or paddling to the shore and suffering the people (as he rowed after them) to beat them with the oars, and stick the boat hook into them where ever he could hit them; one in particular he punished by ordering one of our people to make two cuts upon his arm to the bone one accross the other close below his shoulder; which was an act that I cannot account for any otherways than to have proceeded from a momentary fit of anger as it certainly was not in the least premeditated.[47]

In this respect, Cook was not unlike local leaders, for in Tonga, chiefly violence was commonplace. As Lieutenant King remarked, however, this was coupled with an atmosphere of peace and tranquillity: 'We saw instances, where present Passion seem'd to be their only guide, & where had they killd the Objects of their wrath they woud have been amenable neither to justice nor to a superior; but as the common people by no means appear dispiritd or any way broken by harsh or cruel treatment, It seems pretty certain that the mildness & benevolence of their masters, insures them against an ill use of their Authority. Upon the whole the Friendly Islanders have the appearance of enjoying most of the Advantages aris'ing from a regular Government, few even surpass them in the great order they observe on all Occasions, in their ready compliance with the Commands of their Superiors, & the great harmony which subsists amongst all ranks; & none in the general sweetness and mildness of their tempers.'[48]

A crisis seemed to be brewing, so Cook decided to leave Tongatapu, and on 1 July he ordered the crews to get ready for sailing. Two days later the anchors were raised, and the ships were shifted to a place where they could catch a favourable wind out of the channel. Hearing that Cook's departure was imminent, Paulaho came out to the *Resolution* where he was given a pewter bowl, to use instead of his sacred wooden bowl for ritual purposes.[49] Paulaho was delighted, and told Cook that when he was away from the island, he could wash his hands in this bowl and then leave it behind, and the people could touch it instead of his feet if they wished to lift a tapu. He could also use it to punish a thief; for when his people lined up and each touched the bowl, the culprit would drop dead on the spot, killed by its mana. When Cook heard this, he must have been struck by the contrast between the Tu'i Tonga's absolute authority, and his own recent difficulties with his men on board the *Resolution*.

On 5 July Cook had hoped to impress the Tongans by predicting an eclipse of the sun, but in the event the sky was cloudy, and the eclipse was only visible at intervals. The winds were still contrary, so instead of leaving the island, Cook decided to accept Paulaho's invitation to attend a great ritual at Mu'a. The time had arrived for the *'inasi 'ufimui* ceremony, marked by the rising of the Mataliki constellation,[50] which inaugurated the planting of a new crop of yams, a ritual that was so tapu that only chiefs and priests could be present. At this ceremony, Paulaho intended to announce that his son would be his successor, and lift the ritual prohibition that prevented them from eating together. In the Palace Archives in Tonga, a manuscript has been found which explains Paulaho's intentions:

When the fono (gathering) was being prepared [Paulaho] said to bring his son Fatafehi and the green banana leaf and install him so that the chiefs would know that the son of the Tu'i Tonga had already been installed.[51]

The Tu'i Tonga invited Cook to attend the 'Inasi so that his gods could enhance the mana of the occasion, just as Purea and Amo had been anxious for Wallis to attend the installation of their son as the paramount chief of Tahiti. On 7 July a stream of canoes set off to Mu'a, followed by Cook, Clerke and Mai in two boats which took them across the lagoon to the ceremonial centre, where they found Paulaho in the midst of a kava ceremony. Telling them that the 'Inasi was about to begin, he implored them to take off their hats and let down their hair, or his god would kill him for their impiety.

Later that morning, Cook and Mai went to the ceremonial ground in front of Paulaho's meeting-house, where they watched a procession of about 250 people, each carrying yams or bunches of plantains suspended from a pole, and followed by a man carrying a live pigeon on a perch, heading for a nearby royal grave. After taking off their hats and untying their hair, they were invited to sit with Paulaho and Fatafehi. After dinner, the Tu'i Tonga warned Cook to stay off the roads leading back to the boats, or he would be killed by the club-wielding warriors. Soon a larger procession of about 600 men filed past with sticks (which they were told represented yams), very small yams or fish tied to poles, staggering as though they were carrying very heavy burdens. Mai, Cook and Clerke were told that they could not watch the rituals unless they stripped to the waist as well as letting down their hair. Cook refused to do this, but stole out to try and see what was happening at the burial shrine, ignoring several warriors who cried out 'Tapu!' ['Forbidden!'] in warning. He was turned back twice, eventually rejoining his companions at Paulaho's compound. Here they had a good view of the procession, which was now heading towards the Tu'i Tonga's family burial mound, although they had to cut holes through a bamboo fence to see it.

As they watched, a few men carrying old coconut leaves tied to poles arrived at the foot of the shrine and built a small shelter in front of it, where an old priest chanted solemnly. Shortly afterwards, the young high chief appeared, led by four or five men, and followed by about thirty high-ranking women who walked in pairs, each pair carrying a narrow length of white bark-cloth. After they had swaddled Fatafehi in bark-cloth, Paulaho arrived, led by four men, sitting at a distance from his son as the main procession arrived, laying down their sticks before him. During this presentation an orator kept talking, every now and then breaking one of the sticks that had been placed before the young man, probably to break a tapu. After this ritual the people dispersed, although Cook was told that the proceedings would resume the next morning. They sat down to dine with Paulaho, but soon afterwards Latu, his father's sister's son, arrived unexpectedly with Lieutenant King, and all of the food had to be removed or covered with cloth, since Paulaho could not eat in his presence. The Tu'i Tonga stared fixedly at Latu until at last Lieutenant King took him away and they could resume their dinner, which was followed by boxing and wrestling matches.

Cook and Mai slept in Paulaho's house that night. At daybreak most of the people rose and went away, and Cook watched curiously as the Tu'i Tonga was woken with a massage, a woman beating lightly on his thighs

'The Natche, a Ceremony in Honour of the King's Son, in
Tongataboo', engraving by J. Webber

with her clenched fists. Soon afterwards Mai and Cook went to find the
young high chief, who was in his own house with a group of young boys his
own age, supervised by an old man and woman. When they returned to
Paulaho's compound, they found a kava ceremony in full swing, and were
served baked pig and yams for breakfast. Afterwards Cook took gifts of
English clothes and beads to Fuanunuiava, dressing him in European costume, which he showed proudly to his parents before resuming his bark-
cloth garments. After dinner when the ceremony got under way again,
Paulaho asked Cook to stay in his house until it was over. Frustrated by this
restriction, Cook stole out of the plantation and walked towards the burial
mound, where a number of Tongan men were sitting by the road, surrounded
with small bundles of coconut leaves, tied to sticks in the form of hand-
barrows.

Cook sat down amongst these people, and although they asked him to
leave several times, he refused to budge. More groups of people arrived with
their offerings and more speeches were made, some of which they obviously
found very amusing. They repeatedly told Cook to go back to the house,
but when he would not move, the men ordered him to strip to the waist and
let down his hair. He obeyed, and sat there for an hour with his eyes
downcast, waiting for the young high chief, his female companions and the
Tu'i Tonga. When the high chief's party arrived they sat down in the shelter,
and people ran in groups to sit before them. Cook ran with his companions,
and as they sat there, another long procession of men arrived, carrying poles
with coconut leaves or empty provision baskets tied to them, or with fish

stuck on forked sticks, symbolising the resources of the island. As these offerings were piled up, Cook went with his party to sit in a place where they were told to turn their backs to the young high chief, and not to look at him. Cook disobeyed this injunction, and glimpsed a piece of roasted yam being handed to the Tu'i Tonga and his son, although he could not tell whether or not they ate together. After an interval the assembled chiefs formed into a large semicircle, and some men carrying long poles on their shoulders arrived, singing and waving their hands. When some other men leaped up with heavy sticks and ran towards them, they fled, leaving their sticks on the ground, which these men beat unmercifully. This was followed by wrestling and boxing matches, which brought the 'Inasi to its conclusion.

Cook had done his best to discover the meaning of this ceremony. It seemed to him that the leading people were offering both the produce of the island, and their oaths of allegiance to Paulaho's son as his successor. He was told that in about three months' time there would be another cycle of rituals in which ten human sacrifices would be offered; and remarked on the intense religiosity of these ceremonies. Cook had made extraordinary efforts to observe the 'Inasi, compromising his own dignity in the process. When he removed his captain's hat, let down his hair and stripped to the waist, his men were disconcerted. As Lieutenant Williamson observed:

We . . . were not a little surprised at seeing Capt Cook in ye procession of the Chiefs, with his hair hanging loose & his body naked down to ye waist; not person being admitted covered above ye waist, or with his hair tyed; I do not pretend to dispute the propriety of Capt Cook's conduct, but I cannot help thinking he rather let himself down.[52]

At the same time, the Tongans were horrified by Cook's breaches of tapu, which risked the anger of the gods, endangering both the new crop of yams and the Tu'i Tonga and his successor. As John Thomas, an early missionary who worked in Tonga for more than forty years, commented:

Although [Cook] was checked again and again and told it was tabu or unlawful for him to be present as he was with clothes, yet he persisted. The wonder is that he was not killed then, as the Inaji was the most sacred ceremony possible and only certain select persons were allowed to be present, and those with head and shoulders all bare. Only priests were present for a certain part of the ceremony, and being full of fear for their gods, the wonder is, that the Captain escaped being struck, or killed by some of them.[53]

Cook was determined to see what was going on, and his detailed account of the 'Inasi shows an avid ethnographic curiosity.[54] There were no civilian scientists on this expedition, and he wanted to do justice to the rituals. The absence of these independent observers may also have contributed to Cook's loss of constraint during this voyage, for while they were on board, Cook had to be very careful of his conduct. That restraint was now gone, for both Cook and his officers, which may partly explain the escalation of violence during the third voyage. Although Paulaho pressed Cook to stay for one last ceremony, the wind and tide were now favourable, and he decided to leave Tongatapu. He gave the chiefs some last gifts, and on 10 July in a steady gale, took his ships out of the channel, heading for the nearby island of 'Eua.

When they anchored off 'Eua the next morning, Taione, the local chief who had changed names with Cook during his previous voyage, came out to greet him. Cook had hoped to find fresh water on the island, but all of the streams proved to be brackish. He gave his friend a ram and two ewes; and traded for pigs, yams and shaddocks, acquiring large supplies of these provisions. The next morning he and a party of his men climbed the highest hill on the island, seeking a good view of the interior. They found a round wall of coral and earth on the summit that had been raised in honour of Paulaho, the Tu'i Tonga, where the local chiefs sometimes gathered to drink kava. Mai was a great favourite with these people, and Taione offered to make him a chief if he would stay with them, but Cook disapproved on the grounds that he would do better on his own home island. Cook thought that both cattle and sheep would thrive on 'Eua, where there were no dogs; and on the following day he planted a pineapple for Taione, and sowed European seeds in his garden.

On 15 July, a local man who had tried to rape a high-born girl was attacked at the 'Eua market, and beaten to death with clubs until his body was almost flattened. The following day, Taione presented Cook with some yams and fruit, and entertained him with wrestling and boxing matches. There was supposed to be dancing that night, but during the afternoon two of the *Resolution*'s crew, who had gone inland after women, were stripped of their clothes, returning to the landing-place stark naked. Cook ordered two canoes to be seized and the marines to be landed, and Taione ordered his people to bring back the clothes, and delivered up one of the thieves for punishment. This man was carried out to the ship in irons, but Cook allowed him to be ransomed for a large pig the next morning. Before leaving the island, Cook presented his friend with some gifts, attending a kava ceremony in his honour before returning to the *Resolution*.

Although the Tongans often told him about the nearby island groups of Samoa and Fiji, and their voyages to these places, Cook showed no inclination to explore and chart these new islands. According to the Tongans, the people of Fiji were 'great Warriors & masters all the world as far as they know, & that they eat the men they either kill or take in Battle', but Cook had had his fill of warlike cannibals.[55] Although the Tongans urged Cook to go and fight these people, and to kill as many of them as possible, he showed no interest in pursuing this suggestion. Gilbert remarked, 'It is somewhat surprizing that Capt Cook did not go in search of [them] according to His usual practise. His reasons for not doing it I can't account for; as we certainly had time while we were lying at Tongataboo,'[56] but given the warlike character of its inhabitants, Cook's decision to avoid Fiji was prudent. It was time to take Mai home and get on with the voyage, and on 16 July 1777 the ships sailed east in a light breeze, heading towards the Society Islands.

16

Farewell to Elysium

Cook's ships had an uneventful passage from Tonga, until on 29 July 1777 a sudden gale blew up, splitting the *Resolution*'s staysails and throwing the *Discovery* on her beam ends. The topmast was smashed, so Clerke rigged up a jury-topmast and headed straight for Tahiti. As they passed Tubuai, one of the Austral Islands, two small canoes came out to the ships where their crews brandished their paddles and spears, sang songs in time to blasts from a conch-shell, and then talked with Mai, beckoning the British to come ashore. These canoes were finely built, and decorated with small flat semicircles of pearl-shell below the gunwales. There was no good passage through the reef, so they carried on to the Society Islands.

On 12 August when Cook arrived off the south-east end of Tahiti, at Vaitepiha Bay, several fishing canoes came out whose crews greeted him with evident pleasure. They virtually ignored Mai, apparently not realising that he was a fellow countryman. When another canoe came alongside bringing Mai's brother-in-law and a Borabora chief named Tai, Mai embraced them warmly. They seemed cold and indifferent, however, until Mai took them down into the cabin and opened the drawer where he kept his red feathers. All at once Tai begged Mai to become his taio or ceremonial friend, and sent ashore for a hog to exchange for these items. As Cook observed ruefully:

It was evident to every one that it was not the Man but his property they were in love with, for had he not shewed them his red feathers, which is the most Valuable thing that can be carried to the island, I question if they had given him a Cocoanut.[1]

The Tahitians informed Cook that since his last visit in 1774, two ships from Lima, much larger than his own vessels, had twice visited Vaitepiha Bay. During their first stay the Spaniards had built a house ashore and dropped off four men – two priests, their servant and a man named 'Matimo' [Maximo], who made a great impression on the islanders. Matimo had spent most of his time with the Tahitians and gained some fluency in their language. When the ships left, they took four men with them to Lima. Ten months later the Spaniards had returned to pick up the priests and their companions, bringing only one of the travellers back to Tahiti. Before they left the island, they erected a cross to mark the burial site of their Commodore, Boenechea, who had died during this second visit. The Spaniards had assured the Tahitians that the English were a nation of pirates and slaves, much inferior to the Spanish and of little consequence in Europe; and the Tahitians believed them, since their ships were much bigger than Cook's sloops and their officers wore magnificent uniforms, whereas Cook and his officers dressed informally in the islands. The Tahitians spoke warmly of Matimo, who had joined in Tahitian rituals with gusto and slept with local women, but they condemned the priests 'for that self denial which may be deemed meritorious in Cells & Cloisters, but will be always looked upon with contempt by the lovely & beautiful Nymphs of Otaheite'.[2] Nevertheless, they admired the Spanish officers for their discipline and benevolence, although they had kept strictly aloof from the local people.

As soon as the canoes returned from the *Resolution*, news of Cook's cargo of red feathers spread like wildfire. Early the next morning the ships were surrounded by craft of all sizes, their crews clamouring to barter for feathers. At first a tiny bunch of red feathers purchased a large pig, but since almost all of the sailors had some feathers to trade, these fell five times in value by nightfall. Although the high-born Tahitian women would never look at the seamen before, some succumbed to the lure of these powerful items. In the midst of the hubbub, Mai's sister arrived alongside in a canoe loaded with pigs and fruit, weeping and calling out his name. When she came on board, he embraced her and took her below decks to hide his emotion.

Once the ships were safely anchored, Cook ordered the livestock to be landed. Casks of beef and pork were brought up on deck for inspection, and the caulkers got to work on the hull, since the *Resolution*'s seams had worked open again during the passage from Tonga. Cook presented small bunches of red feathers to several chiefs who came on board, and allowed one of these men to try on a red feather Tongan head-dress. He was thrilled, preening proudly as he showed himself to his fellow-islanders through a gallery window. When Cook and Mai went ashore they paid their respects to an old man on the beach, who was known as 'Oro, the 'God of Bolabola'. This elder, who was thought to be the god's medium, had lost the use of his legs and was carried in a 'hand-barrow'. Plantain branches had been laid at his feet, representing human sacrifices; and Mai gave him a small bunch of red feathers tied to a stick as a tribute.

While they were talking to the 'God of Bolabola', Mai's mother's sister arrived and threw herself weeping at his feet. Mai picked her up and greeted her, while Cook went to look at the Spanish house, a prefabricated structure built of numbered oak pieces with two small rooms and loopholes as windows, which held a table, a bench, a bedstead, a few casks, an old gold-laced hat, and a mahogany chest containing old clothes and some documents in Spanish. The house stood under a thatched roof on a stone pavement, surrounded by a palisade. Nearby stood a large wooden cross about nine feet high carved with the inscription *Christus Vincit Carolus III imperat 1774*. Annoyed by its implied claim of Spanish sovereignty over the island, Cook had the cross taken down and carved on the other side, *Georgius tertius Rex Annis 1767, 69, 73, 74, & 77*, an inscription that claimed Tahiti for King George and gave the dates that English ships had visited the island. He was also chagrined to find fine Spanish pigs, goats, dogs and a bull already ashore, since it had cost him infinite pains to carry English livestock all the way to Tahiti.

The newcomers to Tahiti were enchanted by Vaitepiha Bay, with its high, jagged mountains covered in flowering and fruiting trees, its wide river running down to the sea, and its beautiful, beguiling women. The people were friendly and hospitable, bringing large quantities of provisions and curiosities out to the ships, and girls to exchange for red feathers. Since Cook's last visit the high chief of Tahiti-iti, Vehiatua II, had died from an illness, which his people thought had been caused by the Spaniards' constant breaches of tapu,[3] and his younger brother had succeeded him as the leader of Tahiti-iti. Purea, once famed as the 'Queen of Tahiti', had also died, but Tu and his other friends were still living. Although Vehiatua III was away from the bay, the people assured Cook that he would return shortly. Mai was keen to impress them and as soon as the horses were landed, he and one of the officers went riding. The local people were astonished by this spectacle, although Mai was tossed off almost as soon as he mounted. When Cook came ashore, he was showered with lavish gifts of provisions, and upon returning to the *Resolution*, he summoned all hands on deck and addressed them, suggesting that as they still had a long voyage ahead they should save their grog, since they could drink coconut milk instead during their stay at Tahiti. By now most of the sailors knew that the ships were on their way to search for the Northwest Passage, but when Cook told them about the twenty-thousand-pound reward and the share they would receive if the voyage was successful, they were delighted, willingly agreeing to go on half rations of grog, and Clerke's men did likewise. The officers were amazed, for as Williamson remarked, 'a Seaman in general would as soon part with his life, as his Grog.'[4] Grog was still served on Saturday nights, however, mixed with coconut milk, and with this exotic cocktail the sailors proposed toasts to their wives and girlfriends back in England.

On 16 August Vehiatua returned to the bay, where Cook, attended by Mai dressed in a bizarre mix of English, Tongan and Tahitian clothing, went ashore to meet him. The young high chief, a 'fine sprightly youth about 13 years of Age', sat beside his mother with several elders. One of these chiefs made a speech on Cook's behalf, and was answered by Vehiatua's orator. After this the 'God of Bolabola' spoke, followed by Mai, who produced a maro 'ura, a girdle of red and yellow feathers which he had painstakingly fashioned during the passage from Tonga. Although he had made the feather girdle for Tu, Mai gave it to Vehiatua instead, asking him to send it on to his rival in Tahiti-nui; while Cook presented the young high chief with a sword, a rich cotton robe and a quantity of red feathers. When the orators told Cook that the Spanish had warned them not to receive the English, he angrily retorted that the Spaniards had no right to restrict him in any way. They agreed, and ceremonially handed over the district to Cook, instructing the boy to embrace and exchange names with him. Later that day the sailors were entertained by a heiva, performed by a young woman, two little girls and two men, which featured 'a very obscene part perform'd by ye ladies'.

The next morning Vehiatua sent Cook a gift of a dozen pigs, bark-cloth and a large supply of fruit, and Cook ordered a fireworks display for his entertainment. This impressed the Tahitians, who remarked approvingly that 'the Lima ships had neither red feathers nor fireworks'.[5] While the Tahitians were comparing Englishmen with Spaniards, not always to the Britons' advantage, the British were making their own cross-cultural comparisons. They judged the plantations and roads, and the dancing in Tahiti to be much inferior to those in Tonga, although Tahitian girls were more beautiful and elegant than their Tongan counterparts. By contrast with Tongan warriors, however, they found most Tahitian men effeminate – as King remarked, 'If we want'd a Model for an Apollo or a Bachus we must look for it at Otaheite, & shall find it to perfection, but if for a Hercules or an Ajax at the Friendly Isles.'[6]

Cook was eager to see his taio Tu again, and on 23 August he left Vaitepiha for Tahiti-nui. As he farewelled Vehiatua, the 'God of Bolabola' stood beside the high chief, squeaking and warning him not to sail on the British ships, although no such thing had been contemplated. That evening when the Resolution anchored at Matavai Bay, they were surrounded by a milling crowd of canoes, their crews frantic with joy, calling out to their friends,

Mai goes riding on the beach at Vaitepiha Bay

beating their breasts, tearing their hair, and cutting themselves with sharp instruments. Many of their old friends came on board, warmly greeting Cook and Gore, and affectionately embracing their taio. When Cook landed, he marched with Mai and his officers to a long house about half a mile away, led by a guard of red-coated marines carrying a Union Jack, and a band playing martial music. They found his taio Tu in the midst of a huge and excited crowd, attended by his father, his two brothers and three sisters, whom Ellis described as 'very plain women'. Cook saluted the high chief, and Mai fell at Tu's feet, embracing his legs. Although Mai was dressed in an elegant suit of English clothes, he was ignored at first, even when he gave Tu two or three yards of gold cloth and a large bark-cloth piece covered with red feathers. The news of Mai's gift of a red feather girdle to Vehiatua must have already reached Tu, and when Mai gave a speech extolling the magnificence of the King of England, Tu was annoyed by his effusive praise of the monarch. According to Rickman:

Omai began by magnifying the grandeur of the Great King; he compared the splendor of his court to the brilliancy of the stars in the firmament; the extent of his dominions by the vast expanse of heaven; the greatness of his power, by the thunder that shakes the earth. He said, the Great King of Pretanne had three hundred thousand warriors every day at his command, clothed like those who now attended the Earees of the ships, and more than double that number of sailors, who traversed the globe, from the rising of the sun to his setting . . . He said, the ships of war of Pretanne were furnished with poo-poos [guns] each of which would receive the largest poo-poo which his Majesty had yet seen within it; that some carried 100 or more of those poo-poos, with suitable accommodation for a thousand fighting men, and stowage for all sorts of cordage and war-like stores, besides provisions and water for the men and other animals for 100 or 200 days . . . That in one city only on the banks of a river far removed from the sea, there were more people than were contained in the whole group of islands with which his Majesty was acquainted.[7]

When he was presented to Tu, Cook gave his taio a fine linen suit, a gold-laced hat, tools, a large piece of cloth with red feathers and a Tongan red feather head-dress, which he placed on Tu's head to shouts of admiration. Afterwards Tu and his family accompanied him on board the *Resolution* for dinner, followed by canoes laden with provisions. The high chief ate with Cook and Mai in the Great Cabin, while his sisters dined in another apartment, attended by their own servants. After dinner they all went together to Pare, where Cook presented Tu with a turkey-cock and a hen, four ducks and a drake, and three geese and a gander. In return Tu offered Cook his youngest sister as a bedmate during his stay at Matavai, a gesture which Cook declined as gracefully as possible. When Cook asked Tu whether he had received the feather girdle from Vehiatua, Tu answered that the chief had kept all but a few red feathers for himself, although he had offered Tu a human sacrifice to replace it.

While Cook was away at Pare, his men erected the tents and observatories on Point Venus, and landed the *Discovery*'s mainmast for repairs. Hitihiti soon arrived at the shore camp, overjoyed to see his old shipmates again, although he was stupefied with kava. Samwell remarked in disgust, 'We had been told by those who had been in the Resolution last Voyage that he was a fine sensible young fellow, much superior to Omai in every respect, which made it some disappointment to us to find him one of the most stupid Fellows on the Island, with a clumsy awkward person and a remarkably heavy look.'[8] When Cook returned to the *Resolution*, he gave Hitihiti some clothes, a chest of tools, and a silk dressing-gown which had been sent for him from England. If the officers found Hitihiti unimpressive, they were also disappointed with Mai, whom Cook had hoped to marry to Tu's youngest sister, placing him under Tu's protection. Mai refused this girl, however, disliking her plain looks, and further annoyed the high chief by saying that if he was to stay, Tu would have to get rid of all the Borabora people on the island, including his arioi warriors. After that, Tu and his supporters treated Mai with disdain, and he spent his time with the commoners, boasting about his adventures, dressing up in masks and fancy-dress costumes he had brought from England, giving himself airs and squandering his wealth of European goods and red feathers.

Over the next few days Cook planted melons, potatoes, two pineapples and some shaddock trees ashore, and Mai was delighted to find some grapevines that the Spaniards had planted. He took some cuttings, hoping to make his own wine. Their old friends brought lavish supplies of food and plied Cook and his men with entertainments. As Rickman exclaimed:

We had not a vacant hour between business and pleasure, that was unemployed. We wanted no coffee-houses to kill time, nor Ranelaghs or Vauxhalls for evening entertainments. Every nightly assembly in the plantations of this happy isle, is furnished by beneficent nature with a more luxuriant feast than all the dainties of the most sumptuous champetre . . . Ten thousand lamps, combined and ranged in the most advantageous order by the hands of the best artists, appear faint, when compared with the brilliant stars of heaven, that unite their splendor to illuminate the groves, the lawns, the streams of Oparree. In these Elysian fields, immortality alone is wanting.[9]

Red feathers, trinkets and iron tools flooded ashore, and Tu's rivals in Tahiti-iti were deeply envious. On 27 August a rumour reached Cook that two Spanish ships had arrived at Vaitepiha Bay with Maximo on board, intending to attack the English vessels. The messenger assured Cook that he had been aboard the ships himself, showing him a new piece of blue cloth which he said that the Spaniards had given him. Convinced by his detailed account, Cook mounted the guns on his ships and had the decks cleared for action. When he sent Lieutenant Williamson in an armed boat to check this man's tale, however, it proved to be completely fictitious. Fortunately for the culprit, he jumped overboard and escaped before he could be punished for his lies, which were intended to persuade the English ships to leave Matavai, thus depriving Tu and his people of access to their riches.

When Cook mounted the cannons on his ships, the people of Matavai feared that he was about to attack them, and abruptly left the bay. The next day a barrel, a coat and a hammock were stolen from the ship's tent, and one of the surgeon's mates who had gone inland to barter for curiosities was robbed of his hatchets. That night in the darkness, Bayly woke with a start in the observatory tent, and found a man sitting beside his astronomer's clock. He grabbed him by the hair and yelled for help, but the sentry ran away and none of the officers came to assist him. In the struggle, the barometer was knocked over and the man got away, taking a small box of red feathers and leaving a handful of his hair in Bayly's grip. He was convinced that the man was Tu, but the next morning Cook assured the high chief that he did not intend to punish the theft, although he gave the sentry a flogging for neglect of duty. The atmosphere in the bay at this time was tense and uneasy, and not solely because of Cook's presence. He had arrived in the midst of an inter-island war; on 30 August some messengers arrived from Mo'orea with news that Tu's relatives and friends there had been attacked, and were forced to fly to the mountains.

As Cook soon discovered, this was yet another episode in the war of succession on Mo'orea, which had been raging during his previous visit to Tahiti. At that time, the high chief Mahine, a childless arioi, had attempted to nominate his adopted son as his successor instead of his nephew Mahau, who was linked by marriage with both Tu and Vehiatua. To'ofa, a leading chief of Atehuru (whom the sailors had dubbed the 'Admiral') gathered a great fleet in support of Mahau, but Tu would not join them. After Cook's visit in 1774 the fleet sailed to Mo'orea, but the Mo'oreans had retreated to the mountains, declining to fight, so the canoes had returned to Tahiti. Now, the messengers from Mo'orea were asking their allies to set sail again, and imploring Captain Cook to join them.

During a gathering of chiefs the following day, there was a heated debate. Tu sat there in silence while Cook was asked what part he would play in the war. Mai was absent, so Cook replied in halting Tahitian, saying that since the people of Mo'orea had never offended him, he would not fight against them. The following day, To'ofa sent a message to Tu saying that he had killed a human sacrifice, and demanding the high chief's presence at a ceremony at Atehuru (where the maro 'ura and the image of 'Oro from Papara had been kept since the conquest of Purea and Amo). In the Society Islands at this time, human sacrifices were often offered to the gods in times of war or misfortune. The hapless victim was usually a war captive or someone who had offended the chiefs, who was ambushed without warning and delivered to the marae. When they heard about this sacrifice, some arioi women danced by the river, chanting and exposing themselves to provoke and awaken the gods, led by an old woman who urged them on, dancing with 'uncommon vigour and effrontery'.

On the day before the ceremony, Cook set off in the pinnace with Tu and his other taio Potatau, followed by Mai, Dr Anderson and Webber in a canoe. En route to the marae which held the sacred relics, they stopped at a

A human sacrifice at Utu'aimahurau marae in Tahiti

small island off the district of Fa'a'a, where the 'Admiral' and his entourage were waiting. When To'ofa asked Cook to join them in the war, Cook refused again, making him extremely angry. Nevertheless, To'ofa gave Tu a tuft of red feathers and a half-starved dog as an offering, and after a priest had boarded the pinnace, they set off again to Atehuru. When they came near the great marae of Utu'aimahurau, which stood on a small promontory jutting out into the sea, Tu asked Cook to order the sailors to stay in the boat, and to instruct his companions to remove their hats before landing. Cook obliged, and they set off for the marae complex, accompanied by a crowd of men and boys, but no women, since women did not join in these rituals.[10] When they arrived, they found four priests waiting with their attendants, two priests beside the great marae at the heart of the complex, and two by the human sacrifice, which was lying trussed to a pole in a small canoe in front of the marae, which lay partly on the beach and partly in the water.

As Cook and his companions stood beside Tu, an attendant laid a young plantain tree (a representation of a human body) at the high chief's feet; and another came and touched his feet with a small tuft of red feathers. A priest stood and chanted for some time, holding up red feathers in one hand and 'ava leaves in the other, summoning the gods. A man stood beside him, holding up two bundles wrapped in bark-cloth which proved to hold the maro 'ura (or red feather girdle) and the image of 'Oro brought by Tupaia from Ra'iatea many years earlier. All of the priests, including the man holding the bundles, now sat beside the sacrifice, chanting and lifting the body onto the beach, first with its feet near the sea, and then parallel to the ocean. Some hair was pulled from its head, and one of the eyes was taken out, wrapped in a green leaf and offered to Tu, who opened his mouth towards it in a ritual gesture of eating. As James Morrison, one of the *Bounty* mutineers explained in 1792:

The King is the Head of the People, for which reason the Head is sacred: the Eye being the most valuable part is the fittest to be offered, and the reason that the King sits with his Mouth open, is to let the Soul of the Sacrafice enter into his Soul, that he may be strengthened thereby, or that he may receive more strength of discernment from it.[11]

After this the eye and the hair were taken back to the priests who sat on the beach. When a kingfisher cried out in the trees around the marae, Tu seemed pleased, remarking to Cook, 'That's the Atua [god] speaking.'

After these rituals, the sacrifice was taken to a small marae nearby, decorated with forty-nine human skulls and marked by several carved pieces of wood or *unu* [resting-places of the gods]. Tufts of red feathers were laid at the feet of the corpse, and the cloth bundles were placed on the stone platform. After a prayer imploring the destruction of Tu's enemies, a piece of the victim's hair was pulled out and laid on the platform. The head priest prayed to 'Oro, and the feathers were laid on the sacrifice. Afterwards it was carried to the Great marae, an oblong stone pyramid or *ahu* about fourteen feet high, with a square area on one side loosely paved with pebbles where the high chiefs were buried. One face of this marae was decorated with carved wooden *unu*, overlooking a large pavement, with two sacrificial scaffolds and small standing-stones, some with cloth tied to them and others covered with bark-cloth.[12] After prayers had been chanted, the sacrificial victim was carried back to the small marae where the attendants dug a shallow grave in front of its stone platform, and his body was buried.

When the corpse went into the ground a boy squeaked out loud, which Mai told Cook was the god talking. The dog was now killed by twisting its neck and suffocating it; its hair was singed, the entrails removed and burned, and its organs laid on the hot stones to cook briefly. Its own blood was smeared on the dog, which was presented to the priests; two men drummed loudly as a boy squeaked out three times, calling for the god to consume the sacrifice. When the remains of the dog were placed on a small scaffold along with the stinking corpses of two other dogs and three pigs, the ceremony for that day was over, so Cook went with Tu and Mai to Potatau's house, where they spent the evening. As he had done in Tonga, Cook wrote a detailed account of the ritual, while Webber sketched the proceedings.

Cook was fascinated by this ceremony. The next morning he woke early and walked back to the marae, where two double canoes lay on the beach, each carrying an altar with offerings of food. Later that morning a pig was sacrificed, and Tu took Cook to the main marae, where the priests and a large group of men had assembled. The bundles holding the maro 'ura and the image of 'Oro were still lying on the marae, with two tall drums standing before them. When Tu stood between the two drums, beckoning Cook to stand beside him, the priests sent a young plantain tree to be placed at the high chief's feet and recited incantations, holding up tufts of red feathers and some ostrich feathers that Cook had given Tu for this purpose. It seems that the priests were trying to summon up Cook's gods as well as Tu's, joining the power of the English deities to those of 'Oro to ensure a victory over Mahine. All of the feathers were ritually placed on the bundle that held the image of 'Oro, as four pigs were sacrificed and the maro 'ura was brought out and unrolled on the ground before them.

Cook estimated this famous girdle to be about five yards long and fifteen inches wide. It was covered with bright yellow feathers interspersed with a few red and green ones, set in squares, pasted on to bark-cloth and stitched on to the upper end of Captain Wallis's red pennant. One end of the girdle was scalloped and fringed with black pigeon feathers, while the other end was forked and incompletely covered with feathers. As well as the girdle, there was a red feather bonnet, which seemed to be much older. After the prayer of the maro 'ura was recited, the image of 'Oro was unwrapped from its coconut-fibre container, although Cook and his companions were not allowed to see it. One of the sacrificial pigs was cleaned and its entrails were laid before the priests, who inspected them intently, deducing omens from their spasmodic twitchings. The entrails were thrown into the fire, the pig was put on the platform, and all the feathers except the ostrich plume were placed with 'Oro in his bundle. Cook was told that the sacrificial victim, a middle-aged man, had been killed by blows to the head, and that he was a commoner. He also learned that after a battle, the jawbones of the enemy dead were cut out and taken to the marae, where their bodies were buried in a mass grave. The bodies of the enemy chiefs were disembowelled in front of the marae, and their bodies buried in particular places; a fate which had befallen Tutaha and Te Pau at this marae after their conquest by Vehiatua. Despite the solemnity of this occasion, the people chatted casually during the ritual, and when Mai arrived they talked with him eagerly, only half attending to the proceedings.

On their way back to Matavai Bay, Tu and Cook stopped again at the small island off Fa'a'a where they met the fighting chief To'ofa, who asked Cook what he had thought of the ceremony. Using Mai as his interpreter, Cook told the 'Admiral' that far from pleasing the god, the human sacrifice would anger him, and that their attack on Mahine was destined to failure. When Mai added that in England, if a chief put a man to death in this way, he would be hanged, To'ofa fell into a rage, crying out in disgust, '*Ma 'ino, ma 'ino!*' ['Bad! bad!'] His followers listened attentively to Mai's account, however, seeming to approve of the English custom. To'ofa was already angry with Cook for refusing to join the expedition and now he was outraged, particularly when he realised that Tu might not join him either, and declared that he would sail without them. When they returned to Pare, they found an old man and two women drumming softly in a nearby dwelling, the women chanting as about a hundred people listened with rapt attention; that night at Tu's house his three sisters danced a *heiva ra'a* or sacred heiva, between interludes performed by four men who reduced the audience to helpless laughter with their antics and witticisms.[13]

During the days that followed, Mai invited Cook and the officers to a feast that included baked puddings, Cook's favourite island food, made of breadfruit, ripe bananas, taro and pandanus nuts, mixed with coconut cream and cooked with hot stones from the oven. In return, Cook ordered a display of fireworks, terrifying the Tahitians when a rocket flew into the crowd, instantly dispersing them. The following day Hitihiti gave a feast for his former shipmates, and Tu took Cook to his father's house, where two girls swaddled in vast quantities of bark-cloth, topped by two breast-plates, were sent to the ships with several pigs and fruit, a presentation from Tu's father. The next night Tu gave Cook a large gift of bark-cloth, wrapped around the waists of two women; and Mai dressed in his suit of armour in honour of the occasion.

By now temporary dwellings had been erected near the shore camp, and Tu and his entourage slept there each night, guarding the camp and its treasures from thieves and marauders. Because of Tu's protection, there were very few violent clashes with the Tahitians, and there had been no floggings since their arrival at Tahiti. Mai and the two New Zealand boys also lived ashore, and young Koa, who was a great tease, often got into fights with his Tahitian age-mates. When one girl reproached him with being a cannibal, chewing on her arm, he burst into tears; but when he remembered that the Tahitians ate hair lice he mimicked this in sign language, sending her off in confusion. As the work on the ships was completed, however, the sailors became unruly, and on 10 September, the floggings began again when a boatswain's mate on the *Resolution* was given twelve lashes for neglect of duty and breeding disturbances with the natives; two days later one of the marines and a sailor were each given twelve lashes for theft, stealing iron to barter for sex with local women.

On 12 September when Cook heard that Tu had gone off without him to

Atehuru to offer up the human sacrifice sent by Vehiatua, he was vexed that he had not been invited. When Tu returned to Matavai two days later, Cook and Clerke rode their horses along the coast to meet him, followed by a huge crowd who marvelled at their equestrian prowess. Although Mai had tried to ride once or twice, dressed in his armour, he always fell off before he was properly mounted. As King commented, 'I believe they had never before seen any object which so highly rais'd their conceptions of our superiority over them: We want'd all these helps to give us a consequence in the Eyes of these people equal to the Spaniards.'[14] The officers had begun to quarrel, and on 17 September Lieutenant Williamson fought a duel with Molesworth Phillips, the Lieutenant of Marines, although when they shot at each other, both missed their aim. As one of the sailors, Griffin, commented, 'Many persons would have rejoyced if Mr. Williamson our third Leutenant had fell, as he was a very bad man & a great Tyrant.'[15] That same afternoon, Cook was told that To'ofa's thirty canoes had been surrounded by Mahine's fleet off Mo'orea, although neither side had risked an engagement. Behind the scenes, many of the chiefs were accusing Tu of being a coward for not joining the battle. Cook, who 'had a mighty Friendship for Ottow [and] was a good deal Affected'[16] by these criticisms, gave an impassioned speech to a gathering the next day. He declared that if any of them dared to attack Tu, or kill the livestock that he had given his taio, either he would return and kill them himself, or another British ship would come to destroy them.

By now, Cook was anxious to leave Tahiti. The ships had been caulked, the rigging was renewed, and as always when the men were idle, discipline was suffering. Tu was still hoping to involve Cook in the war with Mo'orea, and on 21 September, he invited Cook to attend a review of his fleet of canoes at Pare. When Cook went ashore, led by marines playing drums and a fife and carrying the Union Jack, he was greeted by Tu, who had assembled about seventy canoes, decorated with streamers and carrying 1000 warriors dressed in red and black feather cloaks, feathered breastplates and head-dresses. When Cook asked Tu to show him how they fought at sea, Tu invited him and Lieutenant King into his canoe. Mai boarded another, and the two craft paddled towards each other at high speed, advancing and retreating as the warriors on the fighting stages gestured and played 'a hundred Antick tricks', flourishing their weapons. When Mai's canoe came alongside his warriors boarded Tu's canoe, capsizing the vessel, but Tu and his men escaped by swimming. After this mock fight, Mai donned his suit of armour and stood on a stage of a fighting-canoe as it was paddled along the coast, although the Tahitians did not seem particularly impressed by this demonstration. Later, when he appeared on horseback in his suit of armour, one of the knee-joints broke, making the leggings useless.

Cook had told Tu that he intended to visit Mo'orea en route to Huahine, and Tu and his father asked if they could go with him. Cook agreed, but soon the news came that To'ofa had been defeated in a battle with Mahine, and had already returned to Atehuru. A truce had been concluded on terms unfavourable to the Tahitians, and a messenger was sent to Tu, summoning him to Atehuru for the peacemaking ritual. Tu had to go, for his presence as ari'i rahi was mandatory on such occasions. He invited Cook to accompany him, but Cook had a rheumatic pain down one side of his body and declined, although he sent Lieutenant King to represent him. When he returned to the *Resolution* that night, Tu's mother and sister gave Cook a vigorous massage, 'squeez[ing] me with both hands from head to foot, but more especially the parts where the pain was, till they made my bones crack and a perfect Mummy of my flesh . . . However I found immediate relief from the operation.'[17]

This peacemaking ritual was a tense affair. King and Tu left Pare at sunset, and on their way to Atehuru, they met To'ofa in his canoe. To'ofa asked King if Cook was angry with him, but King assured him that on the contrary, he remained a firm friend of the 'Admiral'. Kava was made the next morning, and To'ofa's wife and daughter came to greet him, slashing their foreheads with sharks' teeth; when Te Ri'i rere, Purea and Amo's son, arrived, the girl slashed herself again as a sign of greeting. After these ceremonies they carried on to Utu'aimahurau marae, where the sacred canoes were drawn up on the beach, with offerings of pigs lying on their platforms. When Mahine's brother arrived he laid a plantain and a small pig at Tu's feet and they had an animated conversation. Although they had been on opposite sides during the war, neither man seemed particularly angry with the other.

On the following day, 24 September, eight large canoes arrived by the marae, one of which brought the defeated 'Admiral', To'ofa, who was lame and did not stir from his vessel. The other chiefs carried plantains ashore and laid them at Tu's feet, and the priests produced the two bundles containing the image of 'Oro and the sacred feather girdle, placing these by a standing-stone on the pavement. The priests chanted for about an hour, holding up and laying down plantain branches while Tu stood with the feather bonnet in his hand, and the maro 'ura was wrapped around his waist. After more incantations, a man cried out 'Heiva!', and the crowd shouted 'Ari'i!' very loudly, repeating this exchange three times over. The high chief was led to the square pavement in front of the Great marae, facing the carved planks of wood, and after more chanting the cries were repeated. The priests untied the feather girdle and carefully folded it away, with a small bunch of red feathers which Tu had placed on it. Mai told Cook that at this same marae, the paramount chiefs of Tahiti were invested, with a ceremony very similar to the one which King had just witnessed.

After this ritual, the priests and chiefs went to Tu's house, where a chief from Tahiti-iti made a stiff, cold speech, followed by a chief from Atehuru, who gave an animated oration. Potatau gave a very elegant address, followed by Tu's orator, who seemed to speak very ironically. There was a stir of anger during his speech, and Mahine's brother gave a loud, spirited reply, while a man from Atehuru paraded about with a large stone on his shoulder and a sling around his waist, chanting musically at intervals. He was followed by an old man from Mo'orea, whose speech was heard with rapt attention, and when the man from Atehuru threw down his stone, the speeches ended. The plantain branches at Tu's feet were carried to the marae, where the head priest prayed over them. According to Mai, this ritual ratified a six-month truce; although afterwards Tu's father berated the Atehuru warrior, saying that To'ofa had been a fool to rush off to Mo'orea without waiting for Tu and Cook to join him. At the same time, however, To'ofa was furious with Tu for not coming to his aid, and according to Alexander Home, 'He would Curse Ottou for an Hour together and foam at the mouth with rage.'[18]

Determined to leave Tahiti, Cook ordered his ships prepared for sailing. Mai had acquired one of To'ofa's double canoes in exchange for red feathers, since he wanted to make his own way to Mo'orea. On 28 September Tu arrived on board the *Resolution*, presenting Cook with a canoe that he wanted him to take to the King of Britain. It was a small, elaborately carved craft about sixteen feet long, but too big to carry as cargo. The following day the ships sailed from Matavai Bay, accompanied by Mai's canoe, flying an ensign and four pennants. Cook saluted Tu with seven guns, bidding him an affectionate farewell, while Tu's mother and other women wept bitterly. As a parting gift Cook gave his friend a portrait of himself painted by Webber, and a large wooden chest with locks and bolts to protect his most cherished possessions, for even the paramount chief suffered from thieves in Tahiti; and Tu asked him to tell the King of Great Britain to send him another ship, with red feathers, axes, half a dozen muskets with powder, and horses. Several of the sailors wanted to stay on in Tahiti, but although Tu begged Cook to allow this, he refused, fearing that it would encourage his men to desert from the vessels.

During this visit there had been little violence against the Tahitians. Tu and Cook parted on the best of terms, having avoided any major altercations. As he left Tahiti, Cook warned Tu's enemies against any thought of attacking his taio. This was perhaps Cook's happiest stay on any Pacific island, despite the inter-island skirmishing. As Samwell commented, 'no Man could be more esteemed & dreaded than Capt Cook was among them, who upon all Occasions preserved his Consequence with an admirable address, & the Name of Toottee will be handed down to Posterity as the greatest Chief & a man of the greatest Power that ever visited their Island.'[19]

On 30 September 1777 when the ships arrived at the nearby island of Mo'orea, they anchored in Opunohu Bay, a deep, sheltered harbour backed by misty mountains. A large freshwater river ran into this harbour, shaded by hibiscus trees and navigable by the ships' boats for a quarter of a mile. The sloops were soon surrounded by canoes, bringing out women, pigs and provisions to exchange for hatchets, beads and nails. They were told that the high chief, a young boy about eleven years old, would not come out that day, but might visit them several days later. He did not appear, but on 2 October Mahine, the Regent of the island, arrived in his canoe, accompanied by his wife, Amo's sister. The famous fighting chief was about forty years old, corpulent, one-eyed and bald-headed, and covered with battle scars. According to Alexander Home:

We were much disappointed in Our Notions of this Champion of Liberty. We Expected to see A youthful Sprightly Active fellow But Instead of that he Turned out An Infirm Old man more than half Blind. However he was Royaly Attended & Apeared to have the good will & Affection of all the people.[20]

Mahine had never been on a European ship before, and he seemed terrified of Cook, whom he knew was Tu's taio. He hastened to assure him that 'Otoo was his Chief to whom he would submit'. When Cook gave him gifts and exchanged names with him, he was baffled; for according to Lieutenant King, 'it was beyond his comprehension to conceive that we coud be his friend & also that of his enemy.'[21] After staying with Cook for about a half an hour, Mahine and his wife went to visit Clerke on the *Discovery*, and later sent out a large pig to each of the captains. That evening when Mai and Cook rode ashore, they saw the devastation caused by To'ofa's recent attack on Mo'orea. All the trees in the bay had been stripped of their fruit, and the houses had been burned or demolished.

Cook sent his remaining livestock ashore to graze, and on 6 October, when one of the goats disappeared, he was told that the animal had been taken to Mahine at nearby Paopao harbour. Mahine had asked Cook for two goats the previous day, and although Cook had none to spare, he had taken the trouble to send some red feathers to Tu at Tahiti, asking him to send two goats to Mo'orea. Certain that Mahine had arranged the theft of the goat, Cook was furious and sent him a message threatening severe reprisals unless the animal was returned to the *Resolution*. Instead, another goat went missing. The local people assured Cook that it must have strayed into the woods, but although ten or twelve men volunteered to search for the goat, none returned to the ship, and Cook thought that they were simply trying to distract him while the goat was being taken to the far side of the island. That evening the ship's boat returned with the first goat and the man who had taken it. He assured Cook that he had only seized the animal because its keeper had taken his breadfruit and coconuts without payment. Nevertheless, he was put in irons, to his amazement, and none of his friends were allowed to bring him food or drink while he was imprisoned on the vessel.

When Cook awoke the next morning, he found the bay completely deserted. Mahine and his people had fled to the far end of the island. Cook sent a boat with two petty officers and armed men to the south, where he was informed that a chief named Hamoa had the missing goat in his possession. When they returned to the ship that night, however, the officers reported that although they had visited Hamoa and he agreed to give up the goat, it had not been produced, despite repeated promises. Cook was sure that the Mo'oreans were taunting him, and sought advice from Mai and two elders who had accompanied him from Tahiti. They told him to march across the island, shooting 'every Soul I met with'. Although Cook considered this course of action too extreme, he nevertheless decided to make an example of Mahine and his people.

At daybreak the next morning Cook set off with thirty-five armed men, guided by Mai, one of the elders from Tahiti and three or four of his people. At the same time he sent Lieutenant Williamson with three armed boats to the west coast to pick them up once they had crossed the island. They marched across the hills to Maatea, and as they approached Hamoa's settlement, Cook and Mai were pelted with rocks, and some warriors were seen running in the woods with clubs and bundles of darts. According to Bayly, Cook ordered the marines to fire at a man who had hit him with a stone; five or six muskets were fired, the culprit was killed and the bystanders fled into the mountains. When they reached Hamoa's village, the people denied that they had ever seen the goat and Cook flew into a rage, saying that if the goat was not returned, he would scour the mountains for Mahine and capture him dead or alive. He ordered his men to burn the houses and some canoe-sheds with war canoes still in them, and then went on a rampage along the coast, burning war canoes and houses while Mai and his companions seized canoes and filled them with provisions and plunder. As Gilbert, the young midshipman, remarked:

Where ever Capt Cook met with any Houses or Canoes, that belonged to the party (which he was informed) that had stolen the goat, he ordered them to be burnt and seemed to be very rigid in the performance of His orders, which every one executed with the greatest reluctance except Omai, who was very officious in this business and wanted to fire upon the Natives . . . Several women and old men, still remained by the houses whose lamentations were very great, but all their entreaties could not move Capt Cook to desist in the smallest degree from those cruel ravages . . . and all about such a trifle as a small goat . . . I can't well account for Capt Cooks proceedings on this occasion as they were so very different from his conduct in like cases in his former voyages.[22]

At Varari, on the north-west corner of the island, a group of men came forward with plantain branches, imploring Cook not to burn a canoe that was hauled up on the shoreline. He agreed, and spared this craft and all the others at Varari, since he was told that these people were Tu's friends and allies.

Early the next morning Cook sent one of Mai's men with one last message to Mahine, saying that if the goat was not returned, he would destroy all of the remaining canoes on the island. Williamson and the carpenters were sent ashore at Opunohu Bay where they began to break up the canoes hauled up on the beaches, and Cook led an armed party to Paopao, where they demolished houses, killed hogs and dogs and smashed more canoes, taking away the planks to build Mai a house in Huahine. Although he had refused to join To'ofa's attack on Mo'orea, Cook seemed determined to make a demonstration of his power, probably to deter Tu's enemies from attacking Tu or Mai after his departure. In effect he was taking sides in an inter-island war, and although some of his officers supported this, most deplored it, considering his actions unjust and excessive. Lieutenant King, for instance, wrote in his journal:

Not being able to account for Captn Cooks precipitate proceeding in this business, I cannot think it justifiable; less destructive measures might have been adoptd & the end gain'd, whether it was simply to get what was of little value or Consequence back again or in future to deter them from thefts; I doubt whether our Ideas of propriety in punishing so many innocent people for the crimes of a few, will be ever reconcileable to any principle one can form of justice. I much fear that this event will be a very strong motive not only to these Islanders, but to the rest, to give a decided preference to the Spaniards, & that in future they may fear, but never love us.[23]

Lieutenant Williamson added, 'I cannot help thinking the man totally desti-tute of humanity, that would not have felt considerably for these poor &

before our arrival among them probably a happy people, & I must confess this once I obey'd my Orders with reluctance. I doubt not but Captn Cook had good reasons for carrying His punishment of these people to so great a length, but what his reasons were are yet a secret.'[24] Once again, Cook was at odds with his officers, but on this occasion, it was his own violence that was being criticised. When Cook returned to the *Resolution* that night to discover that Mahine had sent back the goat, he penned an epitaph to this episode in his journal: 'Thus this troublesome, and rather unfortunate affair ended, which could not be more regreted on the part of the Natives than it was on mine.'[25]

On 11 October 1777, Cook sailed from Mo'orea for Huahine. There were still many Tahitian women on board the ships, and Mai followed the *Resolution* in his canoe, guided by a local pilot. Early the next morning they heard a musket shot fired from Mai's canoe, which had nearly capsized in a squall. After fleeing from Ra'iatea after the Borabora conquest many years earlier, Mai had spent some time on Huahine, and he now thought that he might like to settle there. When he sighted the island he raised the Union Jack on his canoe as a signal to the ships. Just before they came into Fare harbour, a Mo'orea man was caught stealing on board the *Resolution*; Cook flew into a rage and ordered the barber to shave his head and cut off his ears. One of the officers, convinced that Cook was not serious, stopped the punishment after one of his ears had been cropped, and made him swim to the island. Soon after anchoring at Fare, Cook learned that since his last visit his taio Ori, the former Regent of Huahine, had been deposed, and that the rightful ari'i, a young lad named Te Ri'i taria, had been installed as high chief of the island. He was only twelve years old, and his mother, an elderly, intelligent woman, was acting as his Regent. Ori's sons, who were the first to come out to the ship, presented Cook with lavish presents, no doubt hoping that he had come to reinstate their father as the island's leader.

As soon as they heard that Cook's ships had returned, the principal people of Huahine assembled at Fare. Cook had decided not to take Mai back to Ra'iatea, since he would not hear of living quietly with the Borabora invaders, but was hellbent on expelling them from the island. Huahine was at peace with Puni, the high chief of Borabora; and Cook seized the opportunity to keep Mai out of trouble by settling him there. When the young high chief of Huahine came to meet them, Mai, dressed in an elegant English suit, presented Te Ri'i taria with red feathers and bark-cloth, laying each item at the feet of a priest as one of the Tahitian elders recited the names of Toote (Cook), Tatee (Clerke), Lord Sandwich and the King of Britain. The local priest received each gift with a prayer before sending it off to the main marae, which lay at a distance. After presenting his own gifts, Cook explained how he expected his men to be treated, warning the people sternly not to attempt any robberies, or he would punish them severely.

During the speeches that followed, Mai gave an animated account of his adventures in Britain, and then asked in Cook's name for a piece of land upon which he might settle. The chiefs had hoped that Cook would go with Mai to Ra'iatea to drive out the Borabora invaders, but when Cook explained that he could not do that, they nevertheless welcomed him to Huahine, ceremonially handing over the island and all that it contained, and saying that he could give whatever part of it he liked to Mai and his servants. When Cook asked them to point out a site for Mai's house, they indicated about an acre and a half of coastal land, for which Cook gave them hatchets, saws, nails, knives and axes. Cook ordered his men to erect the ship's tents and the observatories nearby, while the carpenters built a small house for Mai with local wood, and the planks from Mo'orea. This house, which had a locking door, held Mai's treasures from England – a bed, a table and a hand-organ, cooking utensils, a globe of the world, a compass and maps, pictures of his friends in England, toys (which included regiments of tin soldiers, miniature coaches and animals), three swords and some firearms (including a musket with a bayonet, a fowling-piece, two pairs of pistols, 500 cartridges, 300 balls, canisters of powder and a keg of gunpowder). It was surrounded by a deep ditch, with enclosures for Mai's livestock – a horse and a mare, a cow with a calf, sheep, goats, turkeys, geese, a pair of rabbits, two cats and a monkey. Some of the sailors helped the two New Zealand boys, Te Weherua and Koa, to dig and plant a garden inside the ditch with melons, vines, pineapples and shaddocks. Cook advised Mai to give much of his property to the principal chiefs of the island in return for their protection, warning them that if Mai was harmed in any way, he would return to punish them severely.

During their stay in Huahine, Cook was indisposed; although the nature of his illness is not mentioned in the journals, it does not appear to have been serious.[26] Clerke, on the other hand, was very ill with tuberculosis, which he had probably originally contracted either in the debtors' prison or from Lieutenant Hicks during the *Endeavour* voyage. Mai was also unwell, since he had been infected with a venereal disease at Tahiti, but Anderson treated him and soon pronounced him cured. Cook quickly recovered from his ailment, but Clerke got worse until he rarely left the *Discovery*. Dr Anderson was also showing symptoms of tuberculosis, which he must have caught from Clerke. Since they knew that another stint of Arctic exploration would probably kill them, these two men got together and asked Cook

Mai's house in Fare harbour, Huahine

whether they could stay on at Huahine, where they had some chance of recovering their health. Clerke's papers and accounts were in a shambles, however, and Cook was unwilling to release him until they had been put in order. In the event, both Clerke and Anderson carried on almost to the end of the voyage.[27]

On several occasions at Huahine, Cook and his officers dined at Mai's new house, where the young Ra'iatean entertained them by playing his organ and demonstrating his electrifying machine. There were feasts and entertainments, and the high chief and his mother sent a lavish supply of pigs, fruit and vegetables to the British vessels. The atmosphere was relaxed and affable, until on 22 October, a sextant was stolen from Bayly's observatory. When he was told about the theft, Cook was attending a grand heiva, performed by some travelling arioi who had just arrived from Ra'iatea. He flew into a rage, commanding Mai to tell the chiefs that the sextant must be returned instantly. When no action was taken, Cook ordered the dancing to stop, and Mai pointed his sword at a Borabora chief whom he accused of taking the sextant. Although the man hotly denied this, Cook had him taken to the *Resolution* and put into irons until he confessed where the sextant had been hidden. As soon as the man was seized, people began to flee from the bay in their canoes, so Cook sent armed boats to intercept them, and several of these craft were fired on and captured.

When the sextant was retrieved the next morning, Cook released the canoes, but decided to make an example of his captive. He ordered his head to be shaved and his ears cut off, and had him flogged so severely that 'particles of his skin came away in shreds'.[28] The Borabora chief grumbled and groaned, but did not cry out under this punishment. When he was sent ashore, his head and back streaming with blood, he vowed to kill Mai and burn his house as soon as Cook's ships had left the island; and that night he went to Mai's garden and tore up all the grapevines Mai had planted. Cook was furious, and had him captured again and brought back to the ship, where he was once again clapped into irons. When his friends protested, Cook told them that he had no intention of killing the chief, but would take him to Ra'iatea, where he could not hurt Mai; although others were urging Cook to kill him, saying that he was a troublemaker. It is quite possible that Mai had accused this man of theft simply because he was one of the hated invaders from Borabora.

Over the week that followed, although the 'thief' was kept in irons, trade with the ships returned to normal. Cook held a dinner in Mai's house during which the ship's band played, followed by a fireworks display, and he told the island leaders that if Mai came to any harm, he would return with his ships and lay waste to the island. On 29 October at night, the Borabora captive escaped from his irons and swam ashore. As soon as Cook heard about this, he was enraged and interrogated the marines and the petty officers who had been on watch, certain that they had conspired to free him. The sentry confessed that he had fallen asleep on watch, leaving the keys in the binnacle drawer, but resolutely denied any complicity in the escape, and the petty officers on watch also denied any involvement. The sentry and the quartermaster were put in irons in the captive's place, and each day for three days they were flogged with twelve lashes.[29] The mate on watch, William Harvey, was disrated and discharged into the Discovery, and the midshipman was sent before the mast, since both of them had been sleeping on watch. Cook offered a reward of twenty hatchets for the return of the escapee, but he had fled to a distant part of the island. According to the Huahine people, one of the 'young gentlemen', pitying the Borabora man, had unlocked his irons and freed him.

As always, when relationships with the local people and his own men came to a head, Cook decided to leave the island. Mai had not endeared himself to his shipmates over the past few months, giving himself airs, behaving like a fool, and distributing his wealth to anyone who would flatter him. On the whole, they were not sorry to leave him behind. As Rickman observed:

When he was feasting the chiefs, and had nails to give to one, red feathers to another, glass and china-ware to a third, and white shirts to the ladies; Who but Omai? but when they found he had expended most of what he had brought from abroad, and had just enough left by the bounty of his friends to buy him a plantation and to stock it, the chiefs, while they partook of his entertainments, paid him little or no respect; and, had it not been for their deference to Capt. Cook, would probably have treated him . . . with the utmost contempt. Such is the disposition of mankind throughout the world. Men, sprung from the dregs of the people, must have something more than accidental riches to recommend them to the favour of their fellow-citizens; they must have superior sense to direct their conduct, and superior acquirements to render the virtues they possess conspicuous. Such was not the case with Omai . . .[30]

The *Resolution* was crawling with cockroaches, 'so thick you would think the Ship [was] Alive';[31] so in preparation for sailing, Cook had all of the sailors' chests taken ashore and smoked the ship with gunpowder in an attempt to destroy the vermin. As the ships set sail from Huahine on 2 November, Cook ordered a salute of five guns to be fired, and Mai stayed on board as long as possible. When they cast off, he farewelled the officers, and when he came to say goodbye to Cook, he hugged him and burst into tears, saying that he regretted having wasted so much of his time in England, and that he was afraid that as soon as the ships had sailed, his enemies would kill him.

During the voyage, Cook had become quite fond of Mai. He commented that 'whatever faults this Indian had they were more than over ballanced by his great good Nature and docile disposition, during the whole time he was with me I very seldom had reason to find fault with his conduct. His gratifull heart always retained the highest sence of the favours he received in England nor will he ever forget those who honoured him with their protection and friendship during his stay there.'[32] He did not think that the young Ra'iatean would be able to introduce English arts or customs among his fellow islanders, however, because despite repeated visits by the British ships, they showed no signs of imitating any British habits. In fact, Cook doubted whether Mai had learned anything useful during his visit to Great Britain, or whether anything of value to the Tahitians would come from his adventures.

The two New Zealand boys, Te Weherua and Koa, had thought that they were sailing to England with Cook, and when it became plain that he intended to leave them on the island as attendants for Mai, they were distraught. Despite attempts to restrain him, young Koa jumped twice out of the canoe that took him ashore and swam after the ships, crying piteously to the sailors, while Te Weherua stood in another canoe, weeping silently. The sailors admired Te Weherua for his mild, noble demeanour; and Koa, who had shown a real aptitude for life at sea, had endeared himself to them with his wit and clever mimicry. In his journal that evening, Samwell remarked:

If ever I felt the full force of an honest Heart Ache it was at that time . . . [Te Weherua] was a modest sensible young fellow, he always behaved with the greatest Propriety during his Stay with us & was much esteemed by us all. [Koa] was very humorous & lively, by his many Drolleries he used to create no small Diversion on board. He was a favourite with all, & every one of the Jacks took a delight in teaching him something either in Speech or Gesture, . . . he became a diligent Student and in a short time was a perfect adept in Monkey-tricks & the witty Sayings of Wapping & St. Giles. In short they were both universally liked and we should have been much pleased to have taken them with us to England.[33]

Their fears and premonitions proved to be accurate. According to later accounts, in a skirmish between the people of Huahine and the Borabora invaders of Ra'iatea, Mai used his musket and pistols to great effect, winning the victory for the Huahine warriors. After this he was much respected on the island, but did not live long to enjoy his popularity. Several years after Cook's departure, Mai died from a fever. After his death his house was burnt, and his belongings were taken by his relatives from Ra'iatea. Except for the mare, his animals had all died, including the monkey, which was killed by a fall from a coconut tree. With the loss of their protector, Te Weherua and Koa lost heart and died shortly afterwards, still grieving for their own country.

After leaving Huahine, Cook headed for Ra'iatea, where he hoped to get more provisions. On 3 November 1777 when the ships anchored in Hamanino harbour, Cook's old friend Reo, the Boraboran regent of the island and his son, came out to greet them. The canoes flocked out bringing pigs, fruit and vegetables to exchange for red feathers, iron and trinkets. The ships' tents were erected on shore, the forge was set to work, the ships' hulls were scrubbed, wood and water were collected, and there were feasts and arioi dancing and sketches. The hereditary high chief of the island, Uru, did not come to see Cook at first, since most of his lands had been confiscated and he was too poor to make the appropriate gifts, but Cook sent a message telling him not to worry about such matters. According to the local people, when Puni, the elderly chief of Borabora, died, Uru would once again rule Ra'iatea, and he still wore the red feather girdle and presided over the ceremonies at Taputapuatea. Cook was also visited by Reo's gorgeous daughters Poiatua and Tainamai (now married to Boba, the regent of Tahaa), to whom he gave lavish gifts of red feathers, gauze, ribbons, beads and handkerchiefs. Most of the sailors found lovers among the women at Ra'iatea, and considered themselves to be in Paradise. According to Alexander Home:

The Natives were Constantly Inviting us to Stay Amongst them. Their promise was a Large Estate and A Handsome Wife and Every thing that was fine and Agreeable . . . It was Not to be Wondered at that Such proposals were Listened to by many and some of good Sense too for it was by No Means Visionary Dreams of happyness but absolutely real yet the pleasure of it Seemed So Exquisite that one Could Scarcely Believe its reality . . . It seemed Exactly the paradise of Mahomet in Every thing but Immortality.[34]

The men knew that Cook would not give them permission to stay in the islands, and that they were about to set off on a long and arduous voyage towards the Arctic Circle. Some of them found the prospect intolerable, and on 13 November, a marine named John Harrison left the shore camp without leave, taking his musket with him. When Cook heard that Harrison had gone missing, he despatched the sergeant and four marines to find him. That same day, a Ra'iatean who had been caught stealing a nail from a sailor's pocket was brought on board the *Resolution*. As he lay on the deck, Lieutenant Williamson tried to jump on his head, and when the man managed to dodge, he stamped on the side of his face, bruising it badly and smashing several of his teeth. Apparently Williamson was incensed about the theft of his breeches, which had been stolen several days earlier when they were hung out to dry, although his shipmates were sure that no Ra'iatean had taken them. He was a brutal, bad-tempered man, who had little compunction about violence towards subordinates or 'natives'.

When the marines returned to report that they could not locate the deserter, Cook took two armed boats around the island to find him. Reo and his family had fled from Hamanino Bay, but Cook tracked them down and took Reo on his boat, threatening him with dire consequences if Harrison was not located. Reo talked with his people, and then led Cook to a house where they found the marine sitting between two women, his musket at his feet, wearing a loincloth and his head decorated with flowers. His female companions began to cry, imploring Cook not to hurt him, but Cook frowned at them sternly and commanded them to be silent. Harrison immediately surrendered, telling Cook that the older woman, a chiefly landowner about thirty years old, had enticed him to go with her. He was carried back to the *Resolution* where he was put in irons and flogged with twenty-four lashes, although Cook forgave him further punishment on the grounds that he had finished his watch before he left the shore camp. On this occasion Cook made an impassioned speech to his men, telling them that they might run off if they pleased, but he would always get them back, because he had only to seize one of the chiefs, and 'although they Might Like them very well to Stay Amongst them Yet he knew for Certain that they liked their Chiefs far better, with sich a degree of partiality that they would Not give A Chief for A Hundred of us, and that they all Must know that his Authority over these Isles was so great that Never Man had a people more under his Command or At his Devotion.'[35] The next day Harrison's lover came on board the ship, bringing him a gift of a fine pig and vegetables, weeping bitterly when she heard how he had been punished.

After this there was a rash of thefts from the British. Despite Cook's dire warnings, a week later two men from the *Discovery*, a midshipman named Mouat, and the gunner's mate, Thomas Shaw, also deserted. They were helped by a local man who took them off the island in his canoe, taking them first to Tahaa and then to Borabora, where the high chief Puni made them welcome, giving them passage to Tubuai in the Australs. Mouat had asked Cook's permission to stay on Ra'iatea but had been refused, and Cook was incensed that one of his officers had deserted. Clerke set off with two armed boats to find the men, but the Ra'iateans sent him on one false trail after another, apparently determined to protect the deserters and amused by Clerke's fruitless chase around the island. Cook was aware that if the deserters were not captured, half of the men on the ships might join them. The chiefs were offering them land and a life of ease, and the sailors were entranced by the local women, whom they called 'Angels'. Edgar spoke for many of his shipmates when he declared this visit to the Society Islands 'the happiest three months I ever spent'. The temptation to prolong their stay in the islands was almost irresistible.

Cook decided to hunt for the deserters himself, and set off the next morning with two armed boats, accompanied by Reo. When they arrived at the east side of Tahaa, however, they were told that the men had gone to Borabora. Cook decided not to chase them, but to take some chiefs captive until the deserters were brought back to him. The following morning, Clerke invited Reo's son, his beautiful daughter Poiatua and her husband on board his ship to collect a gift of knives, beads and other trinkets, and when they were in the Great Cabin he told them that he intended to detain them until the deserters were brought back to his vessel. They wept when they heard this, and Poiatua in particular was distraught, lamenting loudly. They were put under guard, with battens hammered across the windows of the cabin where they were confined. As the news of their capture spread, the local people came to the beach opposite the ship, where the women tore their hair, cutting their heads with sharks' teeth and weeping inconsolably as the blood ran down their faces.

At first Reo was certain that Clerke must have acted without Cook's knowledge, since Cook was his taio, but when he asked Cook to free his children, Cook told him that they had been taken hostage with his approval, and would not be freed until the deserters had been brought back to the *Discovery*. If the men were not returned, he declared, he would take Reo's children with him to England and destroy everything on the island. Reo was bitterly angry with Cook for his treachery, vowing to kill him and Clerke in revenge for their betrayal. Cook had the habit of bathing in a freshwater river each evening, and Clerke sometimes joined him, so Reo and his men laid a plan to ambush them in the water. That evening when Cook went with Clerke, King, Gore and Anderson for a walk by the river, Reo urged Cook to bathe. He was so pressing, however, that Cook became suspicious, and refused to undress. He warned Clerke not to walk too far, and pulling out his pistol, pointed it at the trees and talked about hitting marks with a bullet. A group of chiefs who had gathered dispersed when they saw that Cook was on his guard, and as King and Anderson walked back to the shore camp, a messenger from the *Discovery* came to warn them of the impending attack. A girl from Huahine, who learned of the plot to kill the captains, had warned her lover on the vessel. King summoned an armed guard to protect Cook and Clerke and sent the ships' boats to intercept the canoes, stopping them from leaving the harbour, and taking more high-born people hostage. When Reo realised that his plan had been foiled, he set off to Borabora in his canoe to bring back the deserters.

Reo returned to the *Resolution* on 29 November, bringing Mouat and Shaw with him. At his request, Puni's men had gone to Tubuai, where they captured the deserters while one was asleep, and the other was on guard with a pistol. Both men were put in irons and disrated. Shaw was given a flogging of twenty-four lashes, and Mouat was sent before the mast. Mouat's father, a captain in the Navy, was a good friend of Clerke's, and Clerke was deeply distressed by his desertion. Cook was also concerned about the young man; according to Williamson, he 'had on this occasion all ye feelings of a parent, & often with great tenderness & concern us'd to say, how soon a young man, even without ye least propensity to Vice (& such was this young man) might by one boyish Action, make a worthy family miserable.'[36] After Shaw had suffered his first flogging, the ship's company petitioned Clerke to excuse him from further punishment, promising 'to behave exceeding well, & not to Atempt to escape or desert any more . . . , but they are still both in Irons & are to continue so till we get clear of the Islands.'[37]

As soon as the deserters were back on the *Discovery*, the hostages were set free, and their people welcomed them with rapturous joy. Reo, who was much liked by the sailors, resumed his friendly relations with Cook; and Ori, the former regent of Huahine and another taio of Cook's, soon paid him a visit. A large stock of pigs, plantains and breadfruit was loaded on board the ships, and when Cook announced that they were leaving and would never return to Ra'iatea, there were loud lamentations, especially among the women. Although many of the sailors were now suffering from venereal diseases and Cook and Clerke scarcely had enough hands to work the ships, on 7 December they sailed for Borabora. Cook intended to make a brief visit to Puni to barter for an anchor that Bougainville had lost at Tahiti, which the local people had sent to Borabora as tribute, since he was running out of iron goods to exchange for local produce.

Reo accompanied Cook on this excursion. When the ships arrived off Borabora, they took some armed boats into a fine harbour, Teveiroa, where the great warrior Puni greeted them affably. Cook asked Puni for the anchor, presenting him with gifts of a ewe, a linen nightgown, a shirt, a looking-glass, some handkerchiefs and six large axes. The anchor was soon produced, to Cook's delight, and after a brief exchange of courtesies, Cook farewelled Puni and Reo and set his course north, heading for America. The sailors left 'these happy Isles' with marked regret, although in his journal, Lieutenant King cautioned against seeing the archipelago as an 'Elysium'. He described the Society Islands as a 'rich wilderness' where civil wars were common and even the paramount chief was not secure in his property; comparing them unfavourably to the islands of Tonga, where the people were superior in 'Industry, Steadiness of conduct, vigour of mind & body, Sweetness of disposition, Elegance of amusements public or private, & in most things that give one set of People the preference over another.'[38]

After an uneventful sea passage, the ships crossed the Line on 22 December, arriving three days later at a low sandy atoll, which Cook named Christmas Island. The men were sent fishing and spent the rest of the day in 'feasting and mirth', and a number of turtles were discovered on the island. They stayed there for several days, relaxing and gathering live turtles for the voyage, although on 29 December two of the *Discovery*'s men got lost on one of these excursions and almost died of thirst, surviving on turtles' blood and plunging into the sea to cool themselves.

After loading 200 green turtles on board the ships, on 2 January 1778 they headed north-east. By now Cook and all of his men were fit and well, except for the two consumptives, Charles Clerke and Dr Anderson. Two weeks later, a hazy peak loomed up on the horizon – Oahu, one of the

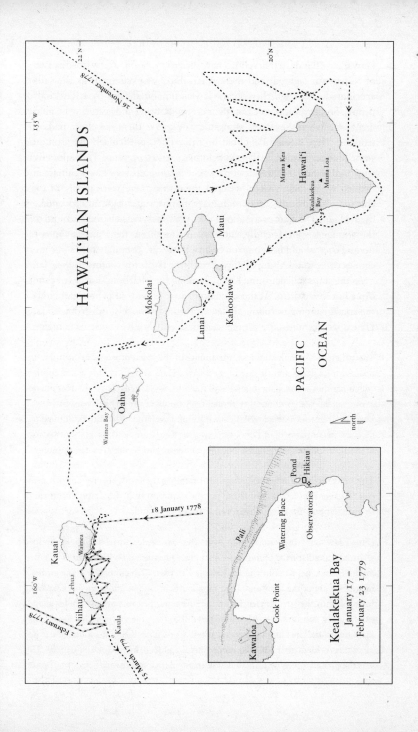

HAWAI'IAN ISLANDS

26 November 1778

22 N

20 N

155 W

Mauna Kea

Hawai'i

Mauna Loa

Kealakekua Bay

Maui

Mokolai

Lanai

Kahoolawe

PACIFIC

OCEAN

Oahu

Waimea Bay

north

18 January 1778

160 W

Kauai

Waimea

Lehua

Niihau

Kaula

2 February 1778

15 March 1779

Kealakekua Bay
January 17 –
February 23 1779

Pali

Pond

Hikiau

Watering Place

Observatories

Cook Point

Kawaloa

Hawai'ian islands, a marvellous new discovery. Soon afterwards the island of Kauai was sighted, and there was a buzz of excitement as the sailors speculated about whether or not it was inhabited, and by what kind of people. Some canoes came out, their crews shouting and gesturing in amazement, and when they came alongside Cook gave them red cloth, nails and trinkets. They seemed delighted by these gifts, particularly the iron, and some of them handed up their loincloths as return presents. The sailors were surprised to find that these people spoke a language very like Tahitian, and thrilled when their visitors assured them that there were plenty of pigs, chickens, breadfruit, sweet potatoes, plantains, sugar-cane and coconuts on their island. The canoes contained piles of stones, but when they found that the strangers were friendly, the Hawai'ians threw their missiles into the ocean. They would not come on board, however, although later some more canoes came out with small pigs, a traditional gift for visitors to the island.

As the ships sailed around Kauai, looking for a harbour, hordes of canoes came out to see them. At the same time, huge crowds of people gathered on the coast, running to follow these extraordinary vessels. According to later Hawai'ian accounts, the people were beside themselves with excitement:

The valley of Waimea rang with the shouts of the excited people as they saw the boat with its masts and its sails shaped like a giant sting-ray, One asked another, 'What are those branching things?' and the other answered, 'They are trees moving about on the sea.' Still another thought, 'A double canoe of the hairless ones of Mana!' A certain kahuna [priest] named Ku'ohu declared, 'That can be nothing else than the heiau [temple] of Lono, the tower of Ke-o-lewa, and the place of sacrifice at the altar.' The excitement became more intense, and louder grew the shouting.[39]

The next morning when the ships stood in for the land, several canoes came out to greet them. Some of these people came on board, gazing about them in amazement. As later Hawai'ian sources reported:

[They] saw many men on the ship with white foreheads, sparkling eyes, wrinkled skins, and angular heads, who spoke a strange language and breathed fire from their mouths. The chief Ki'ikiki and the kahuna Ku-'ohu, each clothed in a fine girdle of tapa cloth about the loins and a red tapa garment caught about the neck, stepped forward with the left fist clenched and, advancing before Captain Cook, stepped back a pace and bowed as they murmered a prayer; then, seizing his hands, they knelt down and the tabu was freed. Captain Cook gave Ku-'ohu a knife, and it was after this incident that Ku-'ohu named his daughter Changed-into-a-dagger. This was the first gift given by Captain Cook to any native of Hawaii.[40]

According to Cook, 'I never saw Indians so much astonished at the entering a ship before, their eyes were continually flying from object to object, the wildness of thier looks and actions fully express'd their surprise and astonishment.'[41] They touched the Europeans and opened their shirts to see the colour of their skins; when one of these men picked up the lead and line, sending it down into his canoe, a sailor stopped him and he looked at him in bewilderment, exclaiming, 'I am only going to put it into my boat!' Another of his companions, who sat on the *Resolution*'s taffrail and tried to take the iron clamp off the driver boom, also seemed to have no idea that he was doing anything improper. When the sailors offered these men beads, they asked if they should eat them, and returned the looking-glasses they were given, considering them useless. They asked for iron, which they acquired by exchange from another island (later identified as 'Orreehoua'), although they had never seen European vessels before. They thought that china cups were made of wood, and could not understand what the ship's sails were made of. It was all very strange, and when a window slammed shut in Clerke's cabin, his visitors leaped up in terror and jumped overboard. According to Lieutenant King, 'in their behaviour they were very fearful of giving offence, asking if they should sit down, or spit on the decks &c, and in all their conduct seemd to regard us as superior beings.'[42]

Because these people had had no previous contact with Europeans, Cook was determined that they should not be infected with venereal diseases. He ordered all women to be banned from the ships, and all men who were infected with VD to stay on board the vessels. Nevertheless, he commented that 'it is also a doubt with me, that the most skilfull of the Faculty can tell whether every man who has had the veneral is so far cured as not to communicate it further.'[43] Perhaps in compensation, at the same time he instructed grog to be served again on board the ships. Three armed boats went ashore under Williamson's command to look for a landing-place, and when Williamson returned, he reported that he had found a large freshwater pond behind a beach near one of the villages along the coast, with a very good anchorage in front of it. They had tried to land on another beach where the people came in great numbers and tried to carry the boat through the surf, taking hold of the oars as they did so. In the course of this encounter, however, there was a shooting, which Williamson tried to conceal from his captain. When these islanders picked up the boat, one of the men laid his hand on Williamson's gun, and he shot and killed him. The islanders dropped the boat, picked up his body and fled wailing into the forest. When Cook finally heard about the shooting, he was furious with Williamson. The third lieutenant had a reputation for brutality, and Cook had already reprimanded him about his treatment of local people on several occasions.

Once the boats were hoisted back on board, the ships anchored in Waimea bay, about a mile from the village.

Several hundred people had gathered on the beach, and when Cook went ashore, accompanied by a guard of marines, they fell flat on their faces – the *kapu moe*, or ritual prostration. They remained in this position until he signalled to them to rise, and then presented him with a great many small pigs, and plantain branches. According to Samwell, as Cook, Anderson and Webber walked through plantations of taro, sugar-cane, plantain and paper mulberry up a nearby valley, the people again fell flat on their faces. Some young women tried to entice them into their houses, doing everything they could to get the sailors to sleep with them.

Along the coast, every village they had seen from the ship seemed to have its own sacred site or *heiau*. Cook was keen to see one of these structures, and so his guide took him to a heiau up the valley which was enclosed by a wall of stone about four feet high, with a high wooden tower decorated with fine grey bark-cloth and carved boards, very like those on the marae in the Society Islands. At this heiau, there was a large house beside the pyramid with an entrance on one side, and a kind of altar on the other, carved with the figures of women, with a stone-edged grave before it. While they were inland on this excursion, quantities of pigs, chickens, sweet potatoes, plantains and red feathered caps and cloaks were taken out to the ships, and women came alongside who 'usd lascivious Gestures and wanted to come [on board] and seemed much chagrined on being refused'.[44] Although the officers tried to prevent them, some of these women dressed up as men and managed to sleep with the sailors. According to the later Hawai'ian histories:

They saw the people with white foreheads, bright eyes, loose garments, corner-shaped heads and unintelligible speech . . . Guns and rockets were fired. They thought it was a god, and they called his name *Lonomakua*, and they thought there would be war. Then a chiefess named *Kamakahelei* . . . said, 'Let us not fight against our god; let us please him that he may be favourable to us.' Then *Kamakahelei* gave her own daughter as a woman to *Lono* . . . and *Lono* slept with that woman, and the . . . women prostituted themselves to the foreigners for iron.[45]

Samuel Kamakau, an early Hawai'ian historian, explained that the high priest Ku-'ohu had proposed a test: if these strange visitors slept with local women, 'opening the sacred gourds', they were men, not gods; and when one of the sailors slept with a woman at this heiau, he decided they were human.[46] It is extremely unlikely that this man was Captain Cook, however. Such an act would have fatally undermined his authority, after his admonitions to the sailors, and the journals from the voyage indicate that he resolutely refused to sleep with island women.

Although there had been prophecies that people with bright, shiny eyes were coming to the island with animals to ride on,[47] the Europeans seemed puzzling in many respects, and this time there were no Polynesians on board to explain them to the local people. Some argued that this was a visitation by 'Ku from Kahiki' or 'the hairless ones of Mana', while others thought that these were simply foreigners from other islands. Some remembered La'a-i-Makahiki [the sacred one from Tahiti], a remote ancestor who had arrived from Tahiti many generations earlier, bringing a small hand-drum and the flute of the hula dance with him and leaving a number of children behind when he finally returned to his homeland;[48] while others speculated that the British were beings from beyond the horizon associated with Lono-i-ka-Makahiki, an ancestral high chief from Kealakekua Bay who had struck his wife in a fit of jealousy and sailed away on a voyage to Tahiti, before returning to rule the island.[49] The sailors must have told the Hawai'ians that they had sailed from Tahiti [Kahiki], and according to the Hawai'ian authorities, including Kamakau, the Lono story eventually prevailed.[50] A famous song was sung in the Hawai'ian islands about Lono's attack on his wife, the institution of boxing and wrestling matches in memory of his violent remorse, and his departure for a foreign country. As he sailed away, Lono had uttered a prophecy:

> I will return later
> On an island bearing coconut-trees,
> And pigs, and dogs.[51]

When the British arrived on their 'floating island' with its tall masts, and with pigs and dogs on board, it is said, this prophecy was remembered, and Cook was identified as Lono.

The next morning the surf was running high and Cook could not get ashore, but the local people came out in their canoes with more gifts of provisions and 'curiosities', including highly polished spears, and red and yellow feather fans, necklaces, bracelets, cloaks and helmets. When a strong wind blew up the next day, Cook raised his anchors and shifted further off shore, but could not get back to his anchorage. While he was tacking off the island, the high chief of the island, Kaneoneo, a young man in his twenties,[52] tall, long-haired, strongly built and dressed in beautifully decorated and coloured bark-cloth, came out to the *Discovery*, accompanied by many of the leading people of the island. As he approached, the people in the other canoes alongside prostrated themselves. His attendants would let him go no further than the gangway, but helped him carefully up the side, and then stood around him protectively as he pressed noses with Captain Clerke and presented him with a fine carved wooden kava bowl. When Clerke tried to reassure the young man by clapping him heartily on the shoulder, his attendants gently lifted off his hand, indicating that the high chief was too sacred for such a gesture. Clerke gave him a large nail, several yards of red baize and a glass bowl in return for his gift, which delighted him. Later that afternoon when the high chief's canoe returned to the *Discovery* with his second-in-command, the Hawai'ians leaped off their canoes into the sea, and any canoe which got in its way was rammed and run over. When the chief returned ashore, the sailors saw huge crowds sitting on either side of a small river valley, gazing at the ship, and they were still there when he came out again to ask Cook not to leave the island.

Over the next few days, however, the ships were frustrated by contrary winds, so Cook decided to land on the neighbouring island of Niihau. On 29 January 1778 he sent William Bligh to sound the coast, anchoring in front of the village of Kamalino at the west end of the island. Later Gore took three armed boats and landed at the village, where he was shown a small well of fresh water. The next morning the boats went ashore again to barter for provisions, but the wind got up and Gore and twenty of his men were stranded ashore, where they slept with local women. Some of these men had VD, and as Cook exclaimed in frustration: 'Thus the very thing happened that I had above all others wished to prevent'[53] – the women were infected with venereal diseases.

The winds remained unfavourable, and it was not until the morning of 1 February that Cook could go ashore to pick up his men. When he landed he was met by Gore's party, accompanied by a local chief to whom Cook presented a billy-goat, two ewes, an English boar and sow, and seeds of onions, pumpkins and melons. While the sailors filled the water casks from a nearby stream, Cook walked inland, led by the chief and followed by two men carrying two little pigs. As soon as they got onto rising ground, Cook stopped, and an old woman on the other side of the valley called out to his companions. The chief muttered a prayer, and the men carrying the pigs walked around Cook in some kind of ritual. Afterwards this woman, a priestess named Walako'i came across and sacrificed the small pigs as an offering by knocking their heads on a stone. She had stayed with Gore's men all the time they were ashore, sacrificing small pigs and performing many rituals with 'Extravagant Gestures like the Thracian Priestesses of old as if possessed with some fury'. She also ensured that they had plenty to eat, and according to Samwell, led the women in sleeping with the sailors, 'almost us[ing] violence to force you into their Embrace'. Rather than an expression of rampant sexuality, however, this was partly an experimental exercise, in which the women tried to assess whether their visitors were supernatural or human. Lieutenant Williamson realised what was going on, commenting that 'ye extreme reservedness of the party excited so great a curiosity in the women, that they were determined to see wether our people were men or not & us'd every means in their power to provoke them to do that, which ye dread of punishment would have kept them from.'[54]

When Cook returned to the ship that evening, a gale blew up and the *Resolution* dragged her anchors. Cook took the *Resolution* out to sea, and the next morning headed north, signalling the *Discovery* to follow him. As Cook sailed away from the Hawai'ian islands towards the coast of North America, he marvelled at the voyaging feats of the Polynesian ancestors:

How shall we account for this Nation spreading it self so far over this Vast ocean? We find them from New Zealand to the South, to these islands to the North and from Easter Island to the Hebrides; an extent of 60 degrees of latitude or twelve hundred leagues north and south and 83 degrees of longitude or sixteen hundred and sixty leagues east and west, how much farther is not known, but we may safely conclude that they extend to the west beyond the Hebrides.[55]

Cook had good reason to admire the Polynesian star navigators. In Tahiti, Tonga and New Zealand, they had outsailed his ships in their double canoes, and he had seen their seafaring skills demonstrated on many occasions. Tupaia, the arioi high priest-navigator who piloted the *Endeavour* through the Society Islands, had produced a chart for Cook which included islands as far east as the Australs and as far west as Tonga; while Finau (the Tu'i Kanokupolu in Tonga) was another fine sailor. Cook's men had met islanders in New Caledonia who talked about Tonga, and Tahitian travellers in Atiu. Most recently, Ra'iatean sailors had carried the deserters from the *Resolution* by canoe to Tahaa, from Tahaa to Borabora, and from Borabora to Tubuai. Like Cook, they were completely at home on the ocean, sailing the sea-paths from island to island.

Killing Kuki

Cook's search for the Northwest Passage proved to be futile and frustrating. As the ships sailed north from Hawai'i and the temperatures dropped, Clerke remarked in his journal, 'We have been so long Inhabitants of the torrid Zone, that we are all shaking with Cold here with the Thermometer at 60. I depend upon the assistance of a few good N:Westers to give us a hearty rattling and bring us to our natural feelings . . . , or the Lord knows how we shall make ourselves acquainted with the frozen seasons of the Ar[c]tic.'[1] True to his wish, when they reached the coast of Oregon in North America the ships were hit by icy westerly gales, making their passage difficult and dangerous. Cook had some charts on board the *Resolution*, drafted by earlier explorers, but as the ships sailed further north, their coastlines proved to be speculative and misleading. Conscious that he had already missed one season of Arctic exploration, Cook found these conditions very trying. Plagued by long periods of poor visibility and unfavourable winds, he could not be sure that his own running survey was accurate, and that they had not missed the opening to the Northwest Passage.[2]

During this part of the voyage Cook was often harsh and irascible, making the midshipmen carry out the tasks of ordinary sailors, working the sails and rowing the ship's boats. It was only on his 'marooning' expeditions, charting inlets such as Nootka Sound or Prince William Sound by boat, that he recovered his good humour. As James Trevenen noted, Cook 'would sometimes relax from his almost constant severity of disposition and condescended now and then to converse familiarly with us. But it was only for a time; as soon as on board the ship he became again the despot.'[3] The sloops were in poor repair, with rotting, sprung masts, ragged sails and inadequate caulking; supplies were running low, and he was forced to put the men on restricted rations. In late May, Lieutenant Gore urged Cook to explore a promising inlet (now named Cook Inlet), which proved to lead nowhere. When they finally emerged from the bay, two weeks of favourable winds had been wasted.

As they coasted the Aleutian Islands off Alaska, the land was shrouded in fog; and on 19 June when some Aleuts came out in their kayaks to the *Resolution* to deliver a note written in Russian, Cook refused to go ashore, although his men were convinced that this was a plea for help, written by shipwrecked Russian sailors. On the night of 25 June, off the north-west coast of Unalaska, the sound of breakers was heard, and Cook immediately ordered the ships brought to. In the morning, they realised that they had escaped shipwreck by a miracle:

We could not help being struck with horror at the sight of the dangers we had escaped, having 3 or 4 patches of rocks above water about a third of a mile from one another on one side of us and the land half a mile distance on the other. So that even after clearing the rocks, had we stood on only six minutes longer we should have run on shore; and from the rate of our going must inevitably have been lost; a more providential escape from instant destruction being scarce to be met with.[4]

This escape filled his men with awe. As Alexander Home commented, 'In the Midst of the greatest Jeopardy, [Captain Cook] Could Judge and Reflect Calmly and allways had the Skill and good Fortune to Extricate himself and his people . . . By Degrees a Habit grew upon us of placing Such Confedence in him, that although Surrounded with Dangers in Shallow Seas, Fogs and Storms we could go Calmly to rest placing our Safty in the Skill and Fortune of Our Leader.'[5] During this passage Cook's men came to revere their commander, despite his severity. In these cold, damp conditions, however, Captain Clerke's and Dr Anderson's tubercular symptoms worsened, and on 3 August 1778, Anderson died of consumption. Cook, who had a high regard for this young man, was greatly grieved by his death. At a time when Clerke was very ill, many of his men were sick and he was stretched to the limit, he had lost his most trusted medical advisor.

On 18 August, as they were sailing north, the ships found their way blocked by a high wall of ice which stretched between Asia and America. Cook sent some men onto the pack ice to kill walruses, and both he and Clerke declared that this was excellent meat, serving it to the crews instead of their salt rations. Some of the sailors claimed that the walrus meat made them sick, and complained so loudly that their rations were eventually restored; and when the spruce beer that Cook had had made in King George's Sound ran out, grog was once again served on the vessels. The ships edged westwards along the ice barrier, looking for a way through, finally reaching the Asian mainland and sailing south along the coast of Siberia. By the time Cook turned east again and headed back to Norton Sound in Alaska, many of the men were emaciated and suffering from scurvy. The crews, who had been pushed to the very edge of endurance, were 'fatigued to death with Labour, pinched with Cold and Starved with hunger'.[6] They were sent ashore to pick berries, more spruce beer was brewed, and Cook charted the inlet. After a brief rest in the Sound they headed back to the Aleutian Islands, where they met a resident group of Russians with whom he exchanged charts of the region.

This is not the place to discuss Cook's contacts with the inhabitants of Nootka and Prince William's Sound, Unalaska and Siberia. Although he produced excellent descriptions of these meetings, his relationships with these people seemed relatively detached and formal. Apart from the Russians, Cook mentioned no individuals by name; and except at Nootka Sound, where they arrived after Hawai'i and stayed for a month, he forged no friendships with local leaders. There was one violent exchange with the people at Nootka Sound, where he shot several Indians in the back with smallshot for stealing iron, and three sailors were flogged for various offences; but otherwise during these seven long months off the north-west coast of America, there were few punishments, either for Cook's men or local people. During times of real seafaring hardship, discipline on board the ships remained tight. It was when they were tempted by the sensuous delights of Polynesia that the sailors became turbulent and unruly.

As winter began to close in, Cook decided to leave America's north-west coast. He knew that he could not find adequate supplies for his men, and disliked the thought of spending long, idle months in these icy regions. As Trevenen remarked, 'This indefatigability was a leading feature of his Character. If he failed in, or could no longer pursue, his first great object, he immediately began to consider how he might be most useful in prosecuting some inferior one. Procrastination & irresolution he was a stranger to. Action was life to him & repose a kind of death.' He added:

He who once revolves in his mind the immense extent of the coast that Captain Cook has in this voyage surveyed, the earliness of the season when he began it, and the advanced state of it when he left off, the badness of the provisions which had already been three years from England, the intricacies of the coast, the inlets, rocks, and shoals that would make, when well known, the boldest pilot tremble to venture on it, the length of time which his crew remained in and bore with the consequent fatigue of such uncommon and accumulated circumstances of distress, passed among rocks and fields of ice in thick fogs, with the entire privation of fresh meat and such necessary comforts as alone can render men capable of undergoing extreme hardships, with the allowed hazard of navigating among ice, must wonder at and admire [his] boldness of daring and skill in executing projects big with every danger.[7]

As they headed south for Hawai'i the crews rejoiced, but when Cook anounced he intended to return next summer to complete his search for the Passage, many of them balked at the prospect. The sailors regarded the islands of Polynesia, with their swaying coconut palms, coral reefs, high, forest-clad mountains, balmy tropical nights, good food and sensuous women as Paradise on earth; exploration in the bleak Northern wastes seemed hellish by comparison.

Cook's Arrival at Hawai'i

On 26 November 1778, after an uneventful passage, a high mountain was sighted. This proved to be Maui, the second-largest island in the Hawai'ian archipelago – another marvellous discovery. These islands were spectacular and fertile, and as they approached Maui, which they called 'the Promised Land', the men gazed longingly at its sandy beaches, luxuriant gardens, deep valleys and waterfalls. Cook read the Articles of War, a recital of dire punishments for offences at sea, ordered his officers to admit no woman to the ships without his permission, and made a 'very sensible speech' explaining why those sailors who were infected with venereal diseases were forbidden to sleep with Hawai'ian women. When several canoes came out, however, bringing cuttlefish and crabs, it soon became obvious that these precautions came too late, since some of these men already had venereal diseases. When they came on board, showing their swollen, inflamed organs to the ship's surgeon, asking about the affliction and blaming it on the British, Cook realised to his dismay that during his visit to Kauai and Niihau earlier that year, his prohibition on sex with the local women had been flouted.

That afternoon Kahekili, the high chief of Maui, approached the *Discovery* in a large double canoe, attended by tall warriors dressed in red feather cloaks and helmets, two of whom were armed with long iron daggers. They had picked up a black cat which had fallen overboard, and brought it back to the vessel. When one of these men stood up and waved a cloak about his head, the others sang, and Kahekili, a middle-aged man with his head shaven except for a vertical band of hair, and his scalp tattooed in half-circles, boarded the *Discovery* with several attendants, bringing two small pigs as a ceremonial gift for the ship's captain. Clerke greeted him in the Great Cabin and gave him presents, while canoes loaded with beautiful young women crowded around the ship, trying to entice his men with 'many lascivious Motions & Gestures'. Cook's orders were strictly observed on this occasion, however, much to the sailors' frustration. Not only were they forced to send these glorious women ashore, but they were abused for refusing their enticements. The following morning when the ships tacked back towards the island, they were surrounded by canoes that brought out quantities of breadfruit, taro, sweet potatoes and a few pigs, enough to feed the crews for several days. Cook was running out of iron goods, and wanted to control the terms of trade as long as possible. He knew that once the men were ashore, they would barter iron for sex and the price of provisions would soar. Clerke was ill, and they had more than 200 men to feed and keep under control. He headed out to sea, tantalising the crews by staying offshore until their supplies of fresh provisions were almost exhausted.

On 30 November Kalani'opu'u, a famous fighting leader and the high chief of Hawai'i, the largest island in the group, came out to the *Resolution*. He was a slender man, about sixty years old, with a dignified, amiable expression, who wore a superb feather cloak and a helmet of black and yellow feathers.[8] Although his demeanour was impressive, Kalani'opu'u seemed weak and debilitated. His body shook violently, his eyes were reddened, and his skin white and scaly from drinking too much kava. When they met in the Great Cabin, Kalani'opu'u took off his feather cloak and presented it to Cook, along with three small pigs and some fruit. He stayed on board for only a few hours, but when he returned ashore he left four of his companions on the ship to check out these strange visitors, including a young warrior named Kamehameha (whom Kalani'opu'u treated as a son, and who later succeeded him as the high chief of Hawai'i). At this time Kalani'opu'u and his army were locked in combat with Kahekili, the high chief of Maui and his long-time antagonist, and he was anxious to ensure that Kahekili did not recruit the British as allies. No doubt he also wanted to see their ships for himself, because after Cook's visit to Kauai and Niihau earlier that year, there had been much talk of these extraordinary vessels. As noted earlier, according to Hawai'ian histories some people had thought that because some of the Europeans slept with local women, they must be human, but most identified Cook with their ancestor Lono-i-ka-Makahiki, a former sacred high chief of Hawai'i, returning from his visit to the far-off land of Kahiki.[9]

As it happened, on this occasion Cook had arrived in the Hawai'ian islands early in the Makahiki, a ritual cycle which celebrated the return of the *akua* [ancestor god] Lono. A few days earlier the Pleiades had appeared on the horizon at sunset, the signal that Lono would soon appear;[10] and fishing from the sea had been banned, explaining why after their first arrival off Hawai'i, no fish were brought out until five weeks later.[11] Although this identification of Cook with Lono has been hotly contested,[12] the weight of supporting evidence from Cook's journals, the accounts of subsequent European visitors and early Hawai'ian accounts is overwhelming. As in other parts of Polynesia, Hawai'ians believed that their ancestors could return to earth, coming to rest in images, mediums or lineal descendants. In the case of the Makahiki rituals, Lono came to bring peace, prosperity and fertility to his people, before handing them back to Ku the god of battle, and Cook, like Lono, had all the signs of ancestral power. Nevertheless, a man had been shot during Cook's visit to Kauai and venereal diseases had been introduced. It is not surprising that some Hawai'ians thought he was a man, while others identified him with Ku, the god of war, rather than with Lono, the god of peace and fertility.

On 1 December, when Cook headed for the island of Hawai'i, Kamehameha and his companions left the *Resolution*. As his ships approached the northern coast, Cook saw white flags flying from the shore, a sign that sacred restrictions were in force, where thousands of people stood gazing at these extraordinary vessels. Over the following days, as they stood on and off the island, tacking windward around the coast, canoes flying white flags brought out large quantities of pigs, breadfruit, taro and sugar-cane. Cook, concerned that his supply of spirits would not last for another season of Arctic exploration, ordered sugar-cane beer to be brewed and served to the sailors; a move which infuriated his men, who were already frustrated since they were not allowed to go ashore to rest, and sleep with the local women. Although no safe harbour had been found, they blamed their captain for keeping them at sea after all their trials and sufferings, and when their beloved grog was stopped, this added insult to injury. Furthermore, the ships were in urgent need of repair, with leaking sides, rat-eaten sails and rigging that was constantly breaking. As one of the marines, John Ledyard, remarked bitterly:

This conduct of the commander in chief was highly reprobated and at last remonstrated against by the people on board both ships, as it appeared very manifest that Cook's conduct was wholly influenced by motives of interest, to which he was evidently sacrificing not only the ships, but the health and happiness of the brave men, who were weaving the laurel that was hereafter to adorn his brows.[13]

On 7 December, the men drafted a letter protesting against the sugar-cane beer and a shortage of fresh provisions, and sent it to their captain. In response, Cook raged against his 'mutinous, turbulent crew', and ordered that their grog should be stopped immediately. According to Watts, one of the midshipmen:

Ye Captn order'd the Hands aft, & told them, that it was the first time He had heard any thing relative to ye shortness of ye Allowance, that he thought they had had the same Quantity usually serv'd them at the other Islands, that if they had not enough, they should have more & that had He known it sooner, it should have been rectified. He likewise understood He said they would not drink the Decoction of Sugar Cane imagining it prejudicial to their Healths, he told them it was something extraordinary they should suppose the Decoction unwholesome when they could steal ye Sugar Cane & eat it raw without Scruple he continued to tell them that if they did not chuse to drink the Decoction he could not help it, they would be the Sufferers as they should have Grog every other day provided they drank ye Sugar Cane, but if not the Brandy Cask should be struck down into ye Hold & they might content themselves with Water, intimating to them that He did not chuse to keep turning & working among these Isles without some Profit. He gave them 24 hours to consider of it.[14]

The hint of 'purser's tricks' angered the men, who steadfastly refused to drink the new decoction, so Cook ordered the brandy cask to be struck down into the hold. While they were locked in this contest of wills, the ships continued to tack on and off the coast, sailing clockwise around the island. On 12 December one of the *Resolution*'s sailors was flogged for emptying the cask of sugar-cane brew, which had gone sour in the hot weather. As the man was tied to the gratings, Cook addressed the crew, 'telling them He look'd upon their Letter as a very mutinous Proceeding & that in future they might not expect the least indulgence from him.'[15] He was at logger-heads with his men, and the mood on board the *Resolution* was defiant.

By this stage of the voyage, the sailors called Cook 'Toote' (the Tahitian transliteration of his name), as in this snatch of doggerel by the young midshipman, Trevenen:

> O day of hard labour! O Day of good living!
> When TOOTE was seized with the humour of giving –
> When he cloathd in good nature his looks of authority,
> And shook from his eye brows their stern superiority.[16]

The nickname had more than a hint of mockery about it. 'Toote' was prone to violent rages, which the sailors linked with his experiences in Polynesia. As Trevenen wrote of the Tahitian term heiva:

Heiva: the name of the dances of the southern islanders, which bore so great a resemblance to the violent motions and stampings on the Deck of Captain Cook in the paroxysms of passion, into which he threw himself upon the slightest occasion that they were universally known by the same name, and it was a common saying amongst both officers and people: 'The old boy has been tipping a heiva to such and such a one.'[17]

Far from being 'cool' and 'rational', Cook had become 'hot-tempered' and 'passionate' (in anger, at least). Unrestrained passion, however, was the way that 'savages' were thought to behave, and Cook's tantrums were at odds with his reputation for rigorous self-discipline. Soon after this episode, the *Resolution* was caught in a squall that almost drove her on to the eastern point of the island, and as they tried to sail the ship to safety, the leach-rope of the main topsail broke, splitting the maintop and topgallant sails and putting her in grave danger. Cook was furious, and that night he vented his anger in his journal, damning the quality of the tackle and rigging supplied by the Admiralty shipyards.

If Cook had become 'Toote' to his men, however, this was scarcely surprising. Over the past ten years he had exchanged gifts, including his own clothing, and sometimes his name, with a series of Polynesian leaders. In the course of these exchanges, according to Pacific understandings, something of the life force of those people had entered his being. Such relationships, especially between ariki, were often turbulent and dangerous. When high chiefs came together, their ancestor gods also met. Ariki were the living representatives of the gods, and imbued with their power. A man caught between two sets of gods was 'two-sided', and could be torn in contradictory directions.

Indeed, by this time, many of his men thought that Cook cared far too much for the islanders. As Lieutenant Williamson noted, there was a long-standing difference of opinion between Cook and many of his officers about how 'Indians' ought to be handled: 'Cn Cook & I entertain'd very different opinions upon ye manner of treating indians, He asserts that he always found upon his first going among them, that ye firing with small shot answers ye purpose, but Cn Clerke & many of ye Officers that have sail'd with him declare, that ye firing with small shot always had bad effects.'[18] His efforts to prevent the spread of venereal diseases had also put him at odds with the sailors. Cook's efforts to save the lives of the 'Indians', although they might be admired back in Europe, had won little support among his crew; while among the islanders, his chastity and refusal to use maximum force looked like weakness. In order to maintain discipline, Cook turned to severe floggings and other forms of violence, both against his crew and the local people. Since his visit to Queen Charlotte Sound in New Zealand early in the voyage, when Cook had refused to punish Maori for killing and eating his men, there had been a remarkable escalation of violence on board the ships. By its end, forty-four of the *Resolution*'s crew had been flogged with a total of 684 lashes, compared with twenty men and a total of 288 lashes during her second Pacific expedition; an extraordinary total compared with Cook's previous record.

Lono's Return

On 24 November, the two ships became separated off the eastern end of the island and did not meet again for a fortnight. On Christmas Day Cook ordered a double ration of brandy and provisions for the men, and they celebrated with drunken revelry. The ships continued to tack on and off the coast of Hawai'i, and on 5 January 1779 the *Discovery* reached Puna on the east side of the island, where a great crowd of people gazed at the vessel. They brought out seven large albacore tuna, a sign that the Makahiki ban on fishing had ended; and many beautiful young women came on board to sleep with the sailors. The next morning the two sloops were reunited off the south point of Hawai'i and carried on together around the coast, searching for a safe harbour. The winds were shifting and often unfavourable, however, often driving them offshore. It was not until 16 January at daybreak that they sighted a small bay on the western coast, Kealakekua [the pathway of the gods], where another huge crowd had gathered on the rocky beaches and along the towering cliff-tops.

It seems that Cook's arrival was expected, and as he sailed towards the bay, he and his men were given a tumultuous welcome. Perhaps Cook had a sense of homecoming, for Kealakekua Bay is very like the havens around Whitby in Yorkshire, where the land dives steeply into the sea from high, stone-walled moorlands.[19] After all their trials, it must have been a marvellous moment. A thousand canoes flocked around the ships, carrying ten thousand people. People paddled out on surfboards and canoes, swarming on board, up the rigging and under the decks, where the women made love with the sailors. They 'swam off in great numbers, and remained along side in the water, . . . men, women and children for four or five hours, without seeming tired; the decks both above and below were entirely covered with them, so that . . . we could not come at the ropes without first driving the greatest part of them overboard; which they bore with the utmost cheerfullness and good nature.'[20] The mood was one of unbounded joy, and when one young woman, 'the most beautiful Girl that we had hitherto seen at these Islands', was given a mirror, she gazed at herself and cried out in delight 'Wahine maika'i au!' ['How beautiful I am!'][21] These people brought out vast quantities of pigs, fruit and vegetables, but when one man stole a bunch of keys from Cook, and another paddled off with a boat's rudder, he had three muskets and several of the four-pounders fired overhead, to add to the uproar and confusion. William Bligh completed his soundings in the bay, and that evening he returned with a favourable report. They had found their anchorage at last, and the sailors were ecstatic.

So were the Hawai'ians, who seemed mad with excitement. The next morning when Cook's ships entered Kealakekua Bay, they were surrounded by 1500 canoes, and men, women and children who swam like shoals of fish about the vessels. They brought little children out to the ships, passing them around in the water when they became tired. According to Ledyard:

The crouds on shore were still more numerous. The beach, the surrounding rocks, the tops of houses, the branches of trees and the adjacent hills were all covered, and the shouts of joy, and admiration proceeding from the sonorous voices of the men confused with the shriller exclamations of the women dancing and clapping their hands, the overseting of canoes, cries of the children, goods on float, and hogs that were brought to market squealing formed one of the most tumultuous and the most curious prospects that can be imagined.[22]

So many of these people came on board the ships and climbed up the masts that it became impossible to work the sails, and according to Ellis, the women were 'remarkably anxious to engage themselves to our people'.[23] The Makahiki was a fertility ritual, celebrated with exuberant hulas and love-making; and the sailors were agog at these demonstrations. When a crowd of women clung to one side of the *Discovery*, the ship heeled right over. Fortunately a young chief named Palea soon arrived with another man named Kanina and ordered most of their countrymen and women to dive overboard, seizing those who refused to go and throwing them into the water.

Palea, a handsome young man who soon confided that he was Kalani'op-u'u's *'aikane* [male lover], seemed to exercise considerable authority. After restoring order on the decks of the ships, he escorted a small, emaciated man named Koa'a on board, whose eyes were reddened and his skin covered with a white scurf from excessive kava drinking. Koa'a, a priest and a distinguished warrior, approached Captain Cook reverently, presenting him with a length of red bark-cloth which he wrapped around his shoulders. Next he held up a small pig and two coconuts, chanting for a time before giving him a large pig and quantities of fruit and root vegetables. After dinner in the Great Cabin, Koa'a and Palea conducted Cook, Lieutenant King and an unarmed party ashore, where they were met by four heralds carrying long white poles tipped with dogs' hair, who as King observed, 'kept repeating a sentence, wherein the word Erono [Lono] was always mention'd, this is the name by which the Captn has for some time been distinguish'd by the Natives.'[24] Cook's bargemen hoisted him on their shoulders and carried him onto the beach, and as they lowered him to the ground the crowd scattered. Koa'a took Cook by the hand and led him past the sacred settlement of Kealakekua in the south corner of the bay, to a stone *heiau* [shrine] known as Hikiau. As they walked towards the temple, the heralds cried out – 'the great Orono [Lono] is coming!' and all of the people except the priests fell flat on their faces, prostrating themselves before him.

Hikiau temple was a large stone structure, forty yards long, twenty yards broad and about fourteen feet high, with a flat, paved top surrounded by a wooden rail, decorated with twenty skulls of enemy warriors from Maui. There was a half-ruined wooden building on top (the drum house), linked to the railing by a stone wall that divided the paved area in half. On the side towards the land, there were five poles about twenty feet high supporting a rickety wooden oracle tower, where the priests spoke with the gods; on the side towards the sea, there were two small houses with a covered way between them. Koa'a led Cook and King up an easy ascent to the summit, where they were confronted by two large images, their torsos wrapped in old cloth, their features violently distorted. Here Koa'a and a tall, bearded young priest presented Cook to the images, chanting, and then led Cook and King to the foot of the scaffold, where twelve more images, each about six feet high, stood in a semicircle in front of a stage for offerings. A rotting hog lay on this stage, which had a pile of sugar-cane, coconuts, breadfruit, plantains and breadfruit lying beneath it.

Koa'a led Cook under the stage and held up the rotting hog, chanting loudly. He then dropped the pig and led Cook up the tower, which they climbed together as ten men arrived in procession on the summit, carrying a live pig and a large piece of red bark-cloth. As they prostrated themselves on the pavement, the bearded young priest, Keli'ikea, collected the cloth, brought it up and gave it to Koa'a. Koa'a wrapped it around Cook, and Keli'ikea collected the pig, which he presented to the old priest. As Cook stood on the tottering wooden tower, wrapped in red cloth, Keli'ikea and Koa'a chanted alternately. According to Queen Lili'uokalani, a descendant of Kalani'opu'u, they were chanting the Kumulipo, a great cosmological chant composed in honour of the birth of Kalani'opu'u's father. This recounted the origins of the world, from its beginnings through the succession of ancestor gods to the child, whom his mother had named Lono-i-ka-Makahiki after his famous forebear.[25] When they had finished this part of the ritual, Koa'a dropped the pig and he and Cook climbed back down to the stone pavement, where he led Cook to the semicircle of images, speaking to each of these in a taunting tone and snapping his fingers at them.

When Koa'a came to the central image, however, a small effigy wrapped in a red cloth, he prostrated himself and then kissed it, asking Cook to do the same, while King, Bayly and Palea sat watching. According to Palea, this image was called 'Ku-nui-akea' [the great god Ku], the god of battle. After this Cook was led to the centre of the sacred area where there was a sunken terrace about ten feet square, where he was seated between two tall idols, Koa'a holding up one of his arms while King held up the other. While Cook was sitting in this position a second procession of men approached, carrying a baked pig, a pudding, breadfruit, coconuts and other vegetables which Keli'ikea presented to Cook, chanting while the other men periodically cried out 'Lono!'

This part of the ritual lasted for about a quarter of an hour, and when it was over the men cut up the pig, peeled the vegetables and prepared a bowl of kava. Keli'ikea chewed some coconut that he wrapped in a piece of cloth, rubbing it over Cook's face, head, arms and shoulders, repeating this performance for King and Bayly. After Cook and King had tasted the kava, Koa'a and Palea broke off pieces of pork and fed it to them by hand, although Cook could not swallow his portion. Cook then presented the priests with gifts of iron and left the temple, led by two heralds with white wands who cried out 'Lono is coming!'[26] Again the crowds dispersed, and those who remained prostrated themselves until Cook had passed, returning to his ship for supper. As he and his companions were rowed back to the *Resolution* they gazed around the bay, which was intensively cultivated, with gardens separated by stone walls and sugar-cane hedges. A forest of breadfruit grew halfway up the slopes, and above the great cliffs there was a plateau covered with gardens. Four settlements were visible along the shore, including two of about a hundred houses each, built along winding alleyways, one of which stood on its southern corner and the other on the northern point, Ka'awaloa. On the north-east side of the bay, the surf crashed against the base of the towering black lava cliffs that sheltered the north side of the harbour.

Today, Kealakekua is reached by a long, winding road that plunges down the side of the cliffs, past a sprawling factory where coffee beans are roasted. Beside the road and along the beaches is a scatter of houses. At the northern end of the road, Hikiau heiau still broods over the bay, overlooking a beach of sea-rolled boulders exposed by a hurricane. Although the ancient stone

monument is still intact, in 1928 an obelisk was built before it to commemorate Captain Cook's visit. The heiau bristles with signs, including a metal
plaque on a post, placed by the Department of Land and Natural Resources,
which declares, *This site is sacred to the Hawai'ian people. Do not move,
remove or wrap the rocks.* Other signs stuck on a rusting metal stake
prohibit launching kayaks from the beach, and warn of the dangers of
swimming without a lifeguard. A small, home-made sign on the steps of the
temple states *Kapu. Sacred Site. No Trespassing.* The stone walls enclosing
the sacred village are still visible, and although the ancient pond is silted up,
its spring-fed waters seep through the sand in puddles. Despite its majestic
setting, Kealakekua is now quiet, almost a backwater. There are few echoes
of the huge, exuberant crowds which once thronged its cliffs and beaches
to welcome Cook, and watched as the priests ritually installed him as Lono.

The morning after the ceremony at Hikiau, Cook's ships were surrounded
by a milling crowd of canoes which brought out quantities of pigs and
vegetables. A fight broke out when a man in one of the larger canoes tried
to throw a sweet potato to one of the sailors but hit a chief instead, who
responded angrily. Blows were exchanged with paddles and clubs, although
when some senior people arrived, the scuffle quickly ended. Soon a stately,
corpulent old woman named Kaheana, wearing red and white striped cloth
around her waist, arm bracelets made from boars' tusks and a plaited bunch
of human hair as a neck ornament, came out in her canoe and paid Cook a
ceremonial visit. She carried a fly flap in one hand and a cock in the other,
which she presented to him. She told Cook that Kalani'opu'u would come
to see him in three or four days' time, although he was presently on the
island of Maui.

Later that morning Lieutenant King went ashore, accompanied by a
detachment of marines in their red uniforms. The local leaders gave Cook
permission to erect the ships' tents in a sweet potato garden on the south
side of Hikiau temple (for sweet potatoes were associated with Lono). They
insisted, however, that none of their people could enter the area, and that
after dark, his men must stay in the tents. They also allocated two of the
houses on the heiau to the sick and the sailmakers, and the priests stuck
white wands around the encampment. Although a huge crowd gathered to
watch the sailors erect the tents, not one Hawai'ian entered the *kapu* (or
tapu) zone. The men who were posted at the shore camp found this extremely
frustrating, because despite all their pleas, none of their sweethearts would
visit them there, saying that the *akua* [gods] and their high chief, Kalani'-
opu'u, would kill them if they broke the kapu. That night, however, some
of the officers sneaked out of the camp to meet local women, and when the

men realised what was happening, they followed their example. The kapu had been broken, and soon the white rods were removed and the people began freely to visit the camp, intently watching the sailors at their daily tasks, learning how to use their firearms, wrestling and making love with the sailors.

Palea had been deputed by Kalani'opu'u to keep his compatriots in order, and when a man stole a large knife from the butcher, he chased him in his canoe and recovered it. He drove all of the women off the *Discovery* during the day, allowing them to stay on board only at night, and stopped his people from thieving, while his friend Kanina performed the same duties on board the *Resolution*. Palea often pelted unruly visitors with stones, and confiscated a thief's canoe, and once when he found a man stealing from the *Discovery* he chased the thief overboard, dragged him underwater and drowned him. These two chiefs were intensely curious about the British. According to Lieutenant King, they 'asked after our King; the nature of our government; our numbers; the method of building our ships; our houses; the produce of our country; whether we had wars; with whom; and on what occasions; and in what manner they were carried on; who was our God; and many other questions of the same nature, which indicated an understanding of great comprehension.'[27]

On 19 January, Palea and Koa'a left the bay to meet Kalani'opu'u, who had landed on another part of the island. By this time the caulkers were busily working on the ships, and the rigging had been dismantled. The pigs offered as tribute by the Hawai'ians were butchered, salted and preserved in brine. The shore camp stood close to the sacred village, Kealakekua, inhabited by the priests of Lono. This village, which the sailors called 'the Cloisters', was built around a pond with several private bathing pools to the north of the stone temple, sheltered by groves of coconut trees. During that day Cook decided to visit the priests with several of his lieutenants, taking Webber to sketch the rituals of welcome. When he came ashore at Hikiau, he was conducted to a building called the Hare o Lono [Lono's house] just behind the temple, and seated in front of an idol which stood at its entrance. Once again Lieutenant King was asked to lift up one of Cook's arms, and after wrapping him in red cloth, Keli'ikea, assisted by twelve of his fellow priests, presented him with a pig. The pig was strangled, singed over a fire, held under Cook's nose and then laid with a coconut at his feet. After this coconut meat was chewed, put in a rag and touched to Cook's head and body, kava was brewed and passed around; a large hog was produced, and Keli'ikea fed Cook and King by hand. After this ceremony, he was taken to another shrine about five miles away, where a similar ritual was conducted. According to Samwell, 'In their Way thither a Herald went

*Captain Cook is honoured at Hare o Lono, Lono's house, in
Kealakekua Bay, Hawai'i*

before them singing, and thousands of people prostrated themselves as they
passed along and put their Hands before their Faces as if it was deem'd
Vilation or Sacrilege to look at them.'[28]

From that time onward, whenever Cook went on shore one of these
priests (whom the sailors dubbed 'the taboo man') went before him, crying
out that Lono had landed, and the people prostrated themselves. When he
went in one of the ship's boats, the priest accompanied him carrying a white
wand, and as they passed the canoes in the bay the people stopped paddling
and lay down on their faces. If he visited the observatory beside the stone
temple, Cook was presented with lavish gifts of pigs, fruit and vegetables,
and no return gift was expected. Sometimes the inferior chiefs were allowed
to present their gifts to Cook in person, gazing at him with fear in their faces
while the priests chanted and carried out their rituals.

According to Lieutenant King, the priests at Kealakekua had an uneasy
relationship with the warrior chiefs, who had their headquarters at Ka'awaloa on the opposite side of the harbour. Ka'awaloa was located in a different
district from Kealakekua, and had its own sacred sites, chiefs and boundaries.[29] The priests associated with Hikiau were led by Keli'ikea's grandfather, a high priest named Kauu who had commanded them to look after
the Europeans, although at present he was on Maui with Kalani'opu'u.
Cook's men became very friendly with these priests, who seemed modest

and obliging and presented them with large quantities of food; unlike the chiefs at Ka'awaloa, who sometimes acted arrogantly and took things from the vessels. Over the following days the local people sent large tributes of food out to the ships, although they also swam beneath the vessels with flints fixed to short sticks, prizing nails loose from the sheathing. When they were fired on with smallshot, they simply dived beneath the water. The sailors also stole nails from inside the ships, and as Samwell commented drily, 'between them both was there not a strict Eye kept over them we should have the Ships pulled to pieces.'[30]

On 21 January, Palea returned to the bay. Two days later, Captain Clerke, who had been too ill to go ashore, decided that he felt fit enough to visit Ka'awaloa with Dr Samwell. When they arrived at the chiefs' settlement, Palea hurried out to meet them. He was accompanied by an attendant carrying a pig, a chicken and a coconut, and as he greeted them he draped a piece of red cloth around Captain Clerke's neck, and put a piece of white cloth around Samwell's shoulders. While his attendant slaughtered two pigs and cooked them for their breakfast, Palea went off and soon returned with a splendid red and yellow feather cloak which he put around Clerke's shoulders, tying a piece of red cloth around his waist. He set the table himself, spreading plantain leaves on the ground and a piece of fresh white bark-cloth, with five coconuts stripped of their rind, two wooden dishes filled with pork and two platters of cold sweet potatoes. He tore the pork to pieces, chewing it and offering to feed them by hand, but Clerke and Samwell refused, indicating that they would rather feed themselves. He also offered them kava, which they declined as politely as possible.

On 24 January, a kapu was placed on the bay. Palea ordered all the women off the ships and no canoes were allowed out to sea, because Kalani'opu'u, their 'Lono Lahi' [Great Lono] was coming.[31] While most of the Hawai'ians were ashore, the following morning Cook ordered a number of his men to be flogged, two with twelve lashes for absenting themselves without permission, one with twelve lashes for disobeying orders, and another with twenty-four lashes for 'having connections with women knowing himself to have the Venereal Disorder on him'.[32] As Rickman remarked soberly, 'There are [those] who have blamed Capt. Cook for his severity to the Indians; but it was not to the Indians alone that he was severe in his discipline. He never suffered any fault in his own people, tho' ever so trivial, to escape unpunished: If they were charged with insulting an Indian, or injuring him in his property, if the fact was proved, the offender was surely punished in sight of the Indians. By this impartial distribution of equal justice, the Indians themselves conceived so high an idea of his wisdom, and his power too, that they paid him the honours as they did their Et-hu-a [*akua*], or good spirit.'³³ Later that day when the officers tried to encourage some canoes to come alongside in breach of the kapu, a chief drove them away, and muskets were fired over his head to stop him. On board the *Resolution*, when Palea spoke sharply to a man who had brought out a large pig to barter, the gunner struck him, to his great fury.

That afternoon Kalani'opu'u arrived in the bay, and visited the *Resolution* 'in a private manner', attended by only one canoe. When the high chief came on board, accompanied by Palea, two of his young sons and his senior wife, Captain Cook greeted him and gave him rich presents. He entertained him to dinner in the Great Cabin until late that night, when Kalani'opu'u went ashore to sleep at the chiefly settlement of Ka'awaloa. The next day at noon, while the kapu was still in force, a stately procession of canoes left the town. Kalani'opu'u and his chiefs stood in the leading canoe, impressive in their red and yellow feather cloaks and helmets. They were followed by a canoe carrying the head priest Kauu (Keli'ikea's grandfather)³⁴ with his chanting followers, and four gods made of basketwork, shells and feathers. The third canoe carried pigs and vegetable foods. The procession paddled out to the ships and then turned, and came back to the heiau. There they landed, and Cook followed them ashore, meeting them at Hikiau temple.

After greeting the high chief, Cook led him into the observatory beside the heiau, where the astronomers were working. Kalani'opu'u and his companions were afraid of the telescopes, which they mistook for guns, but were fascinated by the quadrants. According to Ledyard, they thought that the Europeans must have come from the sky, since they had skins which were red like the sun, and white like the moon and stars. After gazing about for a while, the old man took off his red feather cloak and wrapped it around Captain Cook's shoulders. He put his own feathered helmet on his head and gave him a feathered whisk, the insignia of a great ali'i (ariki, or high chief). Five or six more feather cloaks were piled at his feet, and four large pigs; and then the two men exchanged names. Henceforward, Kalani'opu'u was called 'Kuki', and Cook was called 'Kalani'opu'u'.

Cook had been through similar rituals before, with aristocratic chiefs in other parts of Polynesia. In the Society Islands he had exchanged names with Tu, the high chief of Tahiti, with Tutaha, the Regent of the island, and with Ori and Reo, the Borabora governors of Huahine and Raiatea. In Tonga, when he exchanged names with the lesser chief Ataongo at Tonga-tapu, his status in Tongan society had been diminished. In such a ceremony, the leaders exchanged their names and insignia (for Cook later gave Kalani'-opu'u his own naval sword), their genealogies, and their life force and mana. In Hawai'i, the most sacred (or *niaupi'o*) high chiefs were treated with

Kalani'opu'u's flotilla, with his priests and ancestor gods, visits Captain Cook

extraordinary veneration, and spoken of as akua or ancestor deities.[35] By exchanging names with Kalani'opu'u, Cook had thus acquired part of his mana, or power.[36] From that time on, his men noted, they showed an 'uncommon attachment' for each other. It is notable that like Cook, this sacred high chief carried the title of Lono Lahi and was honoured with the rituals of extreme veneration. As Samwell noted, 'The Title of Orono which is esteemed sacred among them belongs only to Kariopoo [Kalani'opu'u] & his Family; the common people always prostrate themselves before Kariopoo and other Chiefs of the first rank.'[37]

In recent debates over Cook's death, it has been argued that the Hawai'ians honoured Cook as a high chief, not a god or akua,[38] but this is based on a misunderstanding. In Hawai'i the sacred high chiefs (of whom Kalani'opu'u was one) were also regarded as akua. And while it has been claimed that at this stage in the Makahiki cycle, Kalani'opu'u, representing the god Ku, was encompassing the powers of the god Lono,[39] this seems too simple. Kalani'opu'u as well as Cook was addressed as Lono; with the exchange of names, their life forces were mingled. It appears that Lono was a family title, for when Kalani'opu'u's father was born during the Makahiki time, his mother Lono-ma-'I-kanaka had named him 'Lono-i-ka-Makahiki', and the great name chant, the Kumulipo, was composed in his honour. And when Kalani'opu'u's father died, the priest prophesied that 'Lono would come again, that is, Ka-'I-'i-mamao [his true name], and would return by sea on the canoes 'Auwa'alalua. That was why Captain Cook was called Lono.'[40] This suggests that the Hawai'ians identified Captain Cook with a whole line of sacred ancestors – from the original Lono, the god of fertility, to Lono-i-ka-Makahiki, his namesake who had fled on a voyage to another island, to Kalani'opu'u's father, born at Makahiki time, down to Kalani'-opu'u himself, whose names Cook now carried. Along with Kalani'opu'u, Cook had become associated with these great ancestors, and was touched by their mana or sacred power.

After the ritual of name exchange, the old high priest Kauu (whom the sailors dubbed 'the Bishop') appeared at the head of a procession of priests carrying large pigs and a quantity of plantains and root vegetables. He wrapped Captain Cook in a piece of cloth, presented him with a small pig and seated him beside Kalani'opu'u, while Keli'ikea and the other priests chanted loudly. After this Kauu presented red feathers and iron adzes to Kalani'opu'u and went off to the priests' houses, while Kalani'opu'u accompanied Cook to the *Resolution*. There Cook gave his new friend a linen shirt, belted his own sword around his waist and presented gifts to his entourage which 'made them happy'.[41] That night Kalani'opu'u's eldest son stayed on board all night, a sign of the new friendship between his family and the British.

Over the next few days, Kalani'opu'u conducted ceremonial exchanges with both Cook and Clerke. There were feasts, dancing and boxing displays on the sandy beach, where the Makahiki standards (coloured bark-cloth and bird-skins hung from two poles) were displayed; and a violin was played to a hilarious audience of Hawai'ians. During these entertainments, they learned more about Kalani'opu'u. According to Samwell, the high chief had many wives and sexual partners, some of whom were male. A number of attendants in his entourage, not only Palea, were his *'aikane* or male lovers:

Their business is to commit the Sin of Onan upon the old King. This, however strange it may appear, is fact, as we learnt from frequent Enquiries about this curious Custom, and it is an office that is esteemed honourable among them & they have frequently asked us on seeing a handsome young fellow if he was not an Ikany to some of us. The Queen ... was with him, who has had several Children by him notwithstanding the old Boy keeps a number of such Ikany's, and they say he has many concubines.[42]

During this time, Cook received a cloak from Kauu's son 'Omeeah' (his father's successor as high priest, who also carried the title of Lono), and a Hawai'ian was flogged on board the *Discovery* for thieving. Samwell

*Captain Cook is honoured by a boxing match, with Makahiki
standards flying*

reported that despite the kindness of their welcome, some of the sailors
treated the Hawai'ians with disrespect:

As these people behave to us on all occasions when we are rambling on shore and
entirely in their Power, with the utmost kindness and Hospitality, it must hurt every
benevolent Mind to be informed that notwithstanding all this, some among the
lower Class of our People often behave in a brutal Manner towards them. A poor
Indian today for some trifling offence on board the *Discovery*, such as not moving
quick enough out of the way when he was ordered, had a blow given to him by one
of the Captain's servants which made a large Wound on his forehead. Had any of
our Men received such Treatment we should have a number of Epithets to bestow
upon them such as savage, barbarous &c., when at the same time some among us
are found capable of acting in the above base & cruel Manner & yet call themselves
Christians and a civilized People.[43]

As tensions grew between the sailors and the Hawai'ians, Cook prepared to
leave the island. He sent some of his officers to explore the interior, and
ordered the crew to collect loads of firewood. When they reported that no
dry wood was readily available, on 1 February Lieutenant King asked
permission for the sailors to demolish the fence around Hikiau heiau.
According to King, this permission was granted, although when the men
unceremoniously grabbed the carved images from the shrine and carried

them off to the ship, he consulted Kauu, the head priest, who asked that the small image of Ku-nui-akea should be returned, but did not seem unduly concerned about the other idols. This may well have been the case, since such *ki'i* [images] were resting-places for the gods, not their permanent homes, and were only sacred when the gods were present.

That same morning, William Watman, an old gunner's mate and veteran of Cook's second voyage, died on board the *Resolution*. He was a loyal follower of Cook's, much loved and respected by his shipmates. On his deathbed Watman had asked if he could be buried on the heiau; and as soon as he heard that he had died, Keli'ikea offered to inter the old man at Hikiau, the burial ground of the high chief's family. Later that day Watman was placed in a coffin draped with colours and carried ashore by the *Resolution*'s bargemen, followed by Cook, the officers and a number of his shipmates. A guard of marines marched ahead, with a fifer playing the Funeral March. When the procession reached the heiau the marines performed their drill and Cook and his officers read the funeral prayers while Kauu, Keli'ikea and their fellow priests watched attentively. As the coffin was lowered Keli'ikea took a little pig, killed it by beating its head against the stones and threw it into the grave, which had been dug at the foot of Ku's image. Cook intervened before more offerings could be thrown onto the coffin, and it was covered with earth. A carved post inscribed in Latin with Watman's name and the year of his death was attached to Ku's image with wooden pegs, and Cook marched his men back to the *Resolution*. That afternoon more boxing displays were held, and that night, the priests went in a torchlit procession, carrying bark-cloth banners, to carry out their ceremonies by Watman's graveside.

The next day Kalani'opu'u and the chiefs asked Cook when he was planning to leave the island. When he told them that it would be soon, they were pleased and sent out their heralds to call in gifts of food, feathers and clothing for Lono. They also asked him to leave Lieutenant King behind, whom they thought was his son. Cook replied he could not part with King at that time, 'but that he should return to the island next year, and would then endeavour to settle the matter to their satisfaction'.[44]

On 3 February, the tents and the observatory were dismantled and taken on board, and the *Resolution*'s launch went ashore to collect the ship's rudder. When the Hawai'ians were asked to help haul the rudder across the beach, they did so in burlesque fashion, laughing at the sailors. During the carnival atmosphere of the Makahiki, Lono was sometimes mocked, but the British resented such antics. Several people were struck, the Hawai'ians retaliated with stones, and there was a scuffle.[45] Out on the *Discovery* while the ship was being packed up, the sailors reported to Clerke that the jolly-boat was missing. Clerke came up on deck and ordered the canoes alongside to be seized, and their crews taken captive. When Palea appeared and asked what was the matter, Clerke told him that his people had stolen the jolly-boat. After speaking with the Hawai'ians, Palea assured Clerke on his honour that this was not true. Just as Clerke swore at him angrily, the jolly-boat was discovered under the bows of the ship, where the carpenter's mate had left it. Later that day Kauu offered a great tribute of bark-cloth, iron, pigs, vegetables and red and yellow feathers to Kalani'opu'u, who handed over most of the vegetables and pigs to his namesake Cook. This was followed by more wrestling and boxing matches, and when Cook entered the circle of spectators there was a great murmuring of 'Lono', and all the people lay flat on their faces.

That evening, Cook ordered the gunner to arrange a display of fireworks. The people gathered on the beach and out in the bay on their canoes, and when nothing happened, they began to mock the sailors. When a skyrocket was fired, however, they fled in terror, some towards the town and some into the hills, while others dived pell-mell into the water. Almost helpless with laughter, Cook and his officers managed to restrain Kalani'opu'u and his family, reassuring them of their safety. Once the high chief had recovered his composure he summoned his people back to the beach where the rest of the fireworks were let off, to the Hawai'ians' amazement and gratification. That night there was a series of rituals at Hikiau, great drums and large bundles of feathers were put under an image (presumably the small image of Ku); and later that night a fire was seen on the heiau. Early the next morning it was found that the house occupied by the sailmakers had been burned to the ground. It was the practice in Hawai'i, when the chiefs were displeased with the gods, to burn their houses and images,[46] and it is possible that this fire involved a similar process of cleansing.

On the morning of 4 February 1779, the ships sailed from the bay, guided by Koa'a, who had now changed his name to 'Brittanee' (Britain). He brought with him the great drums and the bundles of feathers dedicated at Hikiau, and was accompanied by a number of women. The next morning Kalani'opu'u paid Cook one last visit, bringing him ten large pigs, many chickens, a small turtle, and large quantities of fruit and vegetables as a farewell present. Cook intended to visit Maui before exploring the rest of the archipelago, and after the high chief and his entourage had departed, Lieutenant King reflected:

They regard us as a Set of beings infinitely their superiors; should this respect wear away from familiarity, or by length of intercourse, their behaviour may change; but the common people which are generally the most troublesome, are I am afraid here kept in so slavish a subordination to their Chiefs, that I doubt whether they would venture to give us offence without great encouragement in doing so from their Masters.[47]

Killing Kuki

During his visit to Hawai'i, Cook had been treated with great veneration. The tribute, the rituals at the heiau, the prostration (*kapu moe*) when he approached were all honours accorded to sacred high chiefs. Only such people acted as living representatives of the ancestor gods, and the experience must have been heady. A hero at home, a high chief in the Pacific – Cook could allow himself some satisfaction. Unfortunately, since his journal for this visit has not survived, we lack good evidence of his reactions. One can note, though, that during this visit, things were relatively tranquil on board the *Resolution*. There had been four floggings on board just before Kalani'opu'u arrived in Kealakekua Bay, and after that everything was quiet. The ships sailed from Kealakekua on the exact day set for Lono's departure, and the farewell was conducted with good humour. The Makahiki proprieties had been faithfully observed, and the Hawai'ians could carry on the ritual cycle.

On 6 February, while they were off Kawaihae Bay, Koa'a and the master went ashore, but Koa'a did not return to the *Resolution*. Soon afterwards the ships were caught in a gale which lasted for several days, trapping their female visitors on board the vessels. Many of them were seasick, while others were distraught because they had left their children behind at Kealakekua. On the night of 7 February, the *Resolution*'s foremast was wrenched by a blast of wind and the ship sprang a serious leak. According to Lieutenant King, 'The Captn was for sometime doubtfull, whether to run the Chance of meeting with as good a bay as Karakacooa in the Islands to Leeward, or to return thither: that bay was not so good as not only better might be found, but in others good water might be got; & it was also suppos'd that we had draind (immediately about) Karakakooa pretty well of roots.'[48] On balance, though, it seemed the safest option, and with 'all hands much chagrin'd and damning the foremast',[49] the ships turned back to Kealakekua, over a sea that seemed strangely turbulent. After narrowly escaping shipwreck off the west point of the island, they arrived off Kealakekua Bay where Koa'a came out to greet them, presenting the captains each with a small pig and coconuts. Shortly afterwards the chief Kamehameha came on board, exchanging a fine feather cloak for a quantity of iron daggers and stayed overnight on the *Discovery* with his entourage, which included his *'aikane* or male lover.

At daylight on 11 February 1779 when they anchored in Kealakekua Bay, almost no one came out to welcome them. As Ledyard commented in disgust, 'Our return to this bay was as disagreeable to us as it was to the inhabitants, for we were reciprocally tired of each other. They had been oppressed and were weary of our prostituted alliance, and we were agrieved by the consideration of wanting the provisions and refreshments of the country.'[50] Although Cook was 'chagrined and his people were soured' by this muted reception, they were mollified when it was explained that 'it was Taboo for the Canoes coming until Terreeoboo [Kalani'opu'u] returnd, who was to pay us a Visit soon.'[51] All day, the men worked hard to unstep the *Resolution*'s foremast, and the next day it was sent on shore, with the carpenters and sailmakers. Bayly and King set up the observatories on the heiau where the houses had been burnt, and asked the priests to make a house available for the sailmakers. Once again, the priests seemed friendly, and reinstated the kapu on the shore camp, which was guarded by a corporal and six marines.

That same morning, Kalani'opu'u arrived. He came out to the ships, and 'was very inquisitive, as were several of the Owhyhe Chiefs, to know the reason of our return, and appeared much dissatisfied at it'.[52] Cook's unexpected return seemed inexplicable, and contrary to the assurances he had been given:

The King, whose name was Kurriaboo ask'd Cap Cook what brot him back again. Cook said his mast was broke. The King told the Capn that he had amused them with Lies that [when] he went away he took his farewell of him and said he did not know he should ever come again. It was plain the King suspected Cook had evil intentions and his Countenance Changed towards him and we did not find the people so fond of us as before. They were constantly asking what brought us back for they could form no notion of our distress or what was the matter with our mast.[53]

Kalani'opu'u clearly feared that Cook had come back to settle in the bay, and was angry with the priests for allowing the shore camp to be re-erected. Nevertheless, the kapu was lifted, and the next morning a fleet of large canoes landed at the chiefs' village, Ka'awaloa, where some temporary shelters had been erected. The harbour was once again thronged with canoes that brought out pigs and root vegetables to the ships, but when their crews came on board, they soon began to steal from the British. One man took the armourer's tongs from the *Discovery*'s forge (which he may have associated with the fire gods) in order to try to work iron and was tied to the main shrouds and flogged with forty lashes, a brutal punishment. This man was a high chief, and as Alexander Home remarked, he was not the only one to be flogged:

The Natives were more Bent upon theft then Before and . . . they were unusualy Bold and careless . . . Several of those who called themselves Eris [ari'i – high chief] were Detected in Roberyes. They were punished with the Cat and Nine Tails but never Adequate to their crime for their constitution are Naturally so Robust and their Hides so thick that scarely any Impression Could be made upon them So they Dispised our punishment.[54]

About five o'clock that afternoon, Palea came back on board the ship, and while he was in Clerke's cabin, another man seized the same tongs and leaped overboard with them. A canoe immediately took him on board, and was fired at and chased by the *Discovery*'s unarmed small cutter, commanded by Edgar, the ship's master, while Palea raced ashore to Hikiau in another canoe.

Meanwhile, on the beach, the Hawai'ians were becoming 'insolent' and 'troublesome'. Some chiefs appeared at the watering-place, where they drove away the people who were helping the sailors, and piled up stones in preparation for an attack. Cook was on shore with King, and noting these disturbances, he instructed that 'on the first appearance of throwing stones or behaving insolently, [the men should] fire ball at the offenders.'[55] This order was a departure from Cook's usual rule that the marines should always fire first with smallshot, but the situation was very dangerous. The *Resolution*'s foremast had been lifted and lay on the beach; the sailors were dispersed; Charles Clerke was extremely ill and his men were not under tight control; and the local population was numerous and agitated. Soon, there was a burst of musket-fire out at the *Discovery*, and a small canoe came racing towards the stone temple, chased by the *Discovery*'s cutter. Cook hurried along the shore to intercept it. King outran him, and when he looked around for his captain, he saw Cook with two marines heading up the beach. He joined them, and led by some local people, they ran south along the coast until nightfall. Every time the marine brandished his musket and asked their guides to produce the thief, the crowds just laughed and taunted them. 'Omiah', the priest who also held the title of Lono, was present, and seemed to be co-ordinating some of the action. Finally Cook and King decided to return to the shore camp, led by their guides, who took them away from the sea along a circuitous route, making their expedition as exhausting and frustrating as possible.

When Cook got back to the tents, his coxswain told him what had happened during his absence. The cutter had chased the small canoe ashore, where another canoe, which had already secured the tongs and some other stolen items, brought them back to Edgar. The cutter was returning to the ship when the *Resolution*'s pinnace left its station and joined them, so they decided to go back and confiscate 'the Thief's Canoe'. When Edgar climbed into a canoe which was beached in front of the temple, Palea told him that this was his canoe, seizing its paddle and holding onto the gunwales. Edgar refused to listen and snatched the paddle, and when he began to push the canoe off, Palea grabbed him around the body and held him by the hair.[56] One of the pinnace's crew hit Palea on the head with an oar. In a fury, Palea grabbed the oar and broke it in half. About 300 people were watching, and when they saw Palea struck they were enraged. They picked up stones and pelted the pinnace's crew, driving them into the water, where they were picked up by the cutter. Neither Edgar nor Vancouver, the midshipman who had tried to help him, could swim, so they retreated to a small rock in the water where they were attacked with stones and oars, and beaten until Palea arrived and stopped the thrashing. The warriors began to plunder the pinnace, and when Vancouver climbed on board he was beaten again and had his cap stolen. Palea sent his assailants away, and told Edgar and Vancouver to row back to their vessel. Later, when Cook heard this tale, he reprimanded Edgar for trying to seize a canoe when he and his men were unarmed, and the pinnace's crew for leaving their station without orders.

From Cook's first arrival in Hawai'i, Palea had been on board the ships, particularly the *Discovery*, keeping the Hawai'ians in order. On several occasions, however, Clerke and the sailors had treated him with contempt, refusing to recognise his authority. Since Palea was Kalani'opu'u's lover and attendant, this conduct was insulting and provocative. Several weeks earlier, Palea had punished a thief on board the *Discovery* by thrashing him and confiscating his canoe.[57] Now, however, Edgar disputed his right to 'the Thief's Canoe' in front of the Hawai'ians, and one of the sailors had struck him on the head, a terrible violation of his personal kapu (or sacred power). Despite his anger, Palea stopped the warriors from taking their revenge, and when he returned Vancouver's cap to the boats, he asked 'if Co-kee would kill him for what had happened'.[58]

Palea's apprehensions were well founded. Upon hearing that some of his men had been thrashed, Cook 'expressd his sorrow, that the behaviour of the Indians would at last oblige him to use force; for they must not . . . imagine they have gaind an advantage over us.'[59] Clerke agreed, saying that 'this was an unfortunate stroke as matters now stood, as it increas'd the confidence of these People which before was too much bordering upon insolence.'[60] They ordered all the Hawai'ians, including the women, to leave the ships at once, a sign of imminent hostilities. Overnight, there was an attempt at surprising the shore camp, and the *Discovery*'s large cutter was taken from its buoy (no doubt in revenge for the attack on Palea). When Clerke reported the loss of the cutter early the next morning, Cook told him to send a party of armed men in the *Discovery*'s launch and small cutter to the south-east side of the bay, and to take the *Resolution*'s boats himself to Kaʻawaloa, where Kalaniʻopuʻu was staying. In this way he could cordon off the bay and capture all the canoes, and take Kalaniʻopuʻu hostage for the return of the cutter. If the high chief had fled into the hills, however, the canoes and the houses should be destroyed. Clerke asked to be excused from this action on the grounds of ill health, saying that 'the least rough usuage from the natives would shake him to pieces'.[61] Cook decided to fetch Kalaniʻopuʻu himself, ordering Lieutenant Rickman of the *Discovery* to take the ship's launch and small cutter to the south of the bay, and his third Lieutenant Williamson to take the *Resolution*'s launch and small cutter to the chiefs' settlement at Kaʻawaloa.

Before the boats set out, a large sailing canoe headed out of the bay and was fired on. The *Resolution*'s great cutter was sent off to intercept it, and when the cutter's crew asked what to do if the Hawaiʻians fought back, Cook assured his men that 'there could be no great difficulty, for he was very positive the Indians would not stand the fire of a single musket'.[62] Williamson's two boats soon reached the north-west point of the bay, and Cook followed in the pinnace. Cook left the armed boats on their station and went ashore at Kaʻawaloa with ten marines (including Lieutenant Phillips, Sergeant Gibson and Corporal Thomas). When he marched through the town, however, the people were reluctant to tell him where Kalaniʻopuʻu was staying (although he was almost certainly in his compound on the beach at ʻAwili, which included several dwellings and a men's house).[63] On his way people prostrated themselves on the ground, and the chiefs gave him pieces of red cloth. Finally Kalaniʻopuʻu's two sons, who had often stayed with Cook on board the *Resolution*, led him to their father. Kalaniʻopuʻu had been sleeping. When Lieutenant Phillips went into the house and informed him that Cook was outside, he came out to meet his friend, although his compound was highly sacred and the summons had been unceremonious. A high chief should never be startled awake in this fashion, for his spirit might wander while he was asleep and he could die if he was abruptly woken.[64]

When Cook and Kalaniʻopuʻu spoke with each other, Cook became convinced of his friend's innocence. All the same, he said to Phillips, 'I must get the King on board', and invited the high chief to come out to the *Resolution*. A large crowd had gathered by the house, and followed them as they walked arm-in-arm to the boats, accompanied by Kalani'opu'u's sons, who went ahead to the pinnace. Now, however, a messenger came with news that a chief called Kalimu had been shot on the south-east side of the bay, where the *Discovery*'s boats were stationed. A confused murmur ran through the crowd, and Kalani'opu'u's senior wife, weeping bitterly, begged her husband not to go with Cook. Her young son Keoua was already in the pinnace, and Cook may have tried to urge Kalani'opu'u forward.[65] As his people pleaded with Kalani'opu'u to stay ashore, the ali'i embraced Cook and told him that he could go no further. Two chiefs took his arms and made him sit down, where he stayed 'with the strongest marks of terror and dejection on his countenance'.[66] At this point Lieutenant Phillips suggested that his marines should line up along the water's edge, facing the town. Cook agreed, and the marines marched through the crowd of two or three thousand people, who let them through. Near the water, a priest approached Cook and Kalani'opu'u, offering them a coconut and chanting at the top of his voice, as the warriors began to arm themselves. Although Lieutenant Phillips tried to warn him of their danger, Cook seemed to be oblivious. Seized by 'an infatuation which is altogether unaccountable' he had decided to force matters no further, and said to Phillips, 'We can never think of compelling him to go on board without killing a number of people.'

When the crowd began to jostle them, Cook shouted 'Get away, get away!' A warrior, who was 'exceedingly saucy and behaved in a very insolent manner',[67] threatened him with his iron dagger. When he went to throw a stone, Cook lifted his musket and shot him with the barrel which was loaded with smallshot. The warrior was wearing his war mat, however, which protected him from the pellets. Contemptuously, he gestured to his comrades that he was unhurt and a general attack began on Cook's party. Lieutenant Phillips and several of the marines were attacked with daggers, and they were all pelted with stones. Cook loaded his gun with ball to shoot the man who had threatened him but killed another chief beside him instead, while Kalani'opu'u's son scrambled out of the pinnace, and the men in the boats and the marines on the rocks opened fire on the Hawai'ians.

When Cook waved to the boats, which were just a few yards off-shore, to stop firing and come in and assist them, Lieutenant Williamson, the much reviled third lieutenant who had his own ideas about how to handle 'natives', said later that he mistook this for a command to retreat.[68] Although Williamson ordered the boats to row away from the beach, and threatened the sailors in the launch with his musket if they disobeyed him, the *Resolution*'s cutter and the pinnace ignored his instructions, and went in to assist their comrades. Cook, who could not swim, stood on the beach, and during the lull in the firing, one man struck him on the back of the head with a club, while another stabbed him in the neck with one of his own iron trade daggers. Cook cried out, 'My God!', staggered and fell into a channel in the rocks, where he was stabbed and beaten to death. A confused retreat followed, and four marines and many Hawai'ians were killed. The ship's guns were fired and most of the Hawai'ians retreated, although some remained behind, battering and mangling the dead bodies of the Europeans. Bligh said later, 'The whole affair from [the O]pening to the End did [not] last 10 minutes, or [was] their a spark of cour[age] or Conduct shown in [the] whole busyness.'[69] As Samwell remarked, when Williamson finally ordered in the cutter:

They went close in but could hardly find an Indian to fire at, there being only a few Stragglers thinly scatter'd here & there, & the dead Bodies of Captn. Cook and the four Marines lying on the rock close to the water's edge with only two or three Indians about them, so that there could be no manner of difficulty in taking them in. However one or two muskets having got wet in the Launch & abt as many men saying their Cartridges were almost expended, this was thought a sufficient excuse for returning to the Ship & leave the dead body of their great Commander exposed on the beach to the insults & Barbarities of the Indians. What can be said to this! they did return on board with the Boats with about forty men in them, the major part of whom according to their own declaration, had their boxes nearly full, not having expended above 3 or four Cartridges; as they were pulling off, the Coxswain of the Pinnace fired at a few Indians on the Beach and killed one of them on which the rest immediately fled & left the Place clear.[70]

Cook's corpse was left to the Hawai'ians, who delivered it to their chiefs. In the rituals that followed, his body was stripped and dismembered at a mortuary site above Ka'awaloa, and the pieces (including his bones) were ceremonially distributed.[71]

It has been argued that Cook was killed because he returned to Hawai'i at the wrong time in the Makahiki cycle.[72] On this occasion, however, the Hawai'ians had many reasons for their anger. During the previous day, at least one chief had been viciously flogged for taking the armourer's tongs, and when the tongs were seized a second time, the attack on Palea inflamed local anger. When cannons were fired and a sailing canoe was chased that morning, tensions were greatly heightened. And when another chief was shot and Cook tried to take Kalani'opu'u, despite the protests of his people, onto the *Resolution*, he provoked an explosive confrontation. Nor was this the first time such a thing had happened during this voyage. In Tonga when some livestock were stolen, Cook had confiscated some canoes and took the

Tu'i Tonga and the Tu'i Kanokupolu hostage. At Mo'orea he had destroyed houses and canoes, as he had planned to do at Hawai'i if necessary. At Ra'iatea, when two of his men deserted, he took a high chief's children hostage and cordoned off a bay to seize the local canoes. On that occasion, too, the local people tried to kill him. Seizing a sacred high chief was a terrible offence, and his people were bound to seek vengeance.

During the third voyage, as Cook and his men became increasingly violent, local people often wanted to try and take their revenge; and this was a key factor on this occasion. Cook's relationship with his men during the voyage also influenced that final altercation. Lieutenant Williamson, whom Cook had rebuked for excessive violence towards local people earlier in the voyage, and who had fought a duel in Tahiti with Phillips, the leader of the marines,[73] held the launch back when the Hawai'ians attacked, and when Cook was struck the marines failed to stand their ground, but dropped their muskets and fled into the water. There were suggestions that if they had stood firm, reloaded and fired in sequence, Cook might have been saved. There may be grounds for these accusations of cowardice. Williamson, who evidently panicked when the Hawai'ians attacked, cared little for either Phillips or his captain; and during the voyage, the marines on the *Resolution* had been punished more severely than their other shipmates. Of seventeen marine privates, eleven were flogged during the voyage, one four times, one three times, and two twice, with a total of 216 lashes; and they may have been disinclined to sacrifice their own lives for a commander who had treated them so harshly. At the same time, the Hawai'ians had become familiar with the marines' drill, and knew that if they attacked as soon as the muskets had been fired, they might overwhelm them while they were reloading their weapons. According to Alexander Home:

The very Instant they had Discharged [their muskets] they crowded in upon our Men in Such Numbers that they jostld Several of their firearms our of their Hands and Captain Cook and his people Retreated Close to the waters Edge. Most of them were so sore Bruzed with Blows from Speares and Clubs that they could Not use their Arms, and so Endeavoured to gain the Pinnice, whose Bow had got aground and could Not Come Higher in.

Captain Cook Stood on the Edge of the Rock waiting for the Boat for [he] Could Not Swim and when he Stood in that Possition one of the Chiefs Came Behind him and Stabed in the Back with an iron dagger ... which had been Forged on Board the Ships ... Captain Cook being thus Mortily wounded Tumbled down the Rock into the Sea and his head fell into a gully Betwixt two Narrow Rocks. He attempted to get up could not and I Believe was Suffocated in the water.[74]

Pihere, a man who claimed to have struck the fatal blow,[75] later insisted that the Hawai'ians had not planned to kill Captain Cook. Rather, it happened in the heat of the moment:

I had been in another part of the Island to Collect Hogs for the Ships by Tereaboo's [Kalani'opu'u's] order & had come back only that morning. I arrived just as the disturbance began and heard my Countrymen crying out that the White Men were going to kill the King – If they got him onboard the Ships – great numbers of them were armed and I pressed forward to where the King then was, very near the Boats.

I have a Parhoavah ([*pahua*] or rough Dagger) in my Hand – all was Confusion and in a short time I think Capt. Cook fired, but as nobody was hurt we thought it was only Harmless Thunders, shortly after a number of men fired & killed several of my Countrymen. We then rush'd on & I being near the Oroner [Lono] his Back turn'd towards me struck him quite thro' with the Dagger and he fell – I had scarcely drawn back the Dagger & was thinking which Way I should Run for I was very much frighten'd, when turning round I met the Sword of a White Man which went in here (pointing to his Breach) & I fell. This all I can recollect of that fatal day.[76]

Despite recent controversies, there is no good morality play, colonial or post-colonial, to be made of Cook's killing. Over a decade in Polynesia, he was caught in intractable contradictions. As the trial of the cannibal dog at Totara-nui showed, when he acted with calm restraint, he invited humiliation – his sailors and the islanders alike considered him to be weak and irresolute. When he acted in anger and sought mana by force, he invited retaliation. His men became mutinous, and the islanders sought to kill him. At Lifuka and on Ra'iatea during this voyage, when Captain Cook took high chiefs captive, efforts were made to destroy him. At Hawai'i it happened, but there was no one cause. It was a cross-cultural combination of forces that killed him.

Conclusion

Our Ancestor Captain Cook

According to the official record of the voyage, when he heard that Cook was dead, Kalaniʻopuʻu 'retired to a cave in the steep part of the mountain, that hangs over the bay, which was accessible only by the help of ropes, and where he remained for many days, having his victuals let down to him by ropes.'[1] The intensity of this response is not surprising. When Captain Cook was killed, he carried Kalaniʻopuʻu's own name, as well as the title Lono-i-ka-Makahiki. At the same time, Kalaniʻopuʻu carried the name of 'Kuki'. With this exchange of names, their identities had become entwined. When his ceremonial namesake died, Kalaniʻopuʻu's kapu (or tapu) was breached. It was necessary to try and repair the damage.

Out on the ships, the sailors were stunned when they heard that Cook was dead. According to Gilbert:

When on the return of the boats informing us of the Captains Death, a general silence ensued throughout the ship for the space of near half an hour: it appearing to us somewhat like a Dream that we could not reconcile ourselves to for some time. Greif was visible in every Countenance; some expressing it by tears and others by a kind of gloomy dejection, more easy to be conceived than described, for as all our hopes centred in him, our loss became irrepairable and the sense of it was so deeply impressed upon our minds as not to be forgot.[2]

When they began to recover, Lieutenant Phillips and some of the men clamoured against Williamson for abandoning Cook, but none of the boats' crews would make a formal complaint against him. As the men cried out for revenge, Lieutenant Gore urged Clerke to fire the ships' cannons on Kaʻawaloa. Although Clerke was so ill that he could scarcely stand, he shared their fury. According to one of the sailors, he said, 'Yes damn me boys you shall [take your revenge], and by God I'll head you myself, but in the mean time we must get our foremast and boats off, that's the first thing boys for by God we are ruined if we don't get our foremast.'[3] He sent the master William Bligh with all of the ships' boats to pick up the men from the shore camp, and retrieve the foremast from Kealakekua, where the Lono priests had their settlement.

Because Clerke had hardly been ashore, he had little idea of the nature of the relationships that had developed between his shipmates and the Hawai'ians. Lieutenant King, who commanded the shore camp beside Hikiau temple, where the foremast was lying, had forged a close association with the Kealakekua priests, and when fighting broke out near the chiefs' settlement on the opposite side of the bay, he assured them of his friendship. The people at the priests' village seemed baffled by the turmoil, but when Clerke looked through his telescope and saw a large crowd gathering near Hikiau, he thought that the shore camp was under attack, and fired at them with the ship's cannons. Although a coconut palm was smashed and a rock was shattered by the barrage, no one was injured. Aghast, King sent off a hasty message to the ship, assuring Clerke that the Kealakekua priests had shown no signs of hostility. When Bligh arrived with the news that Captain Cook had been killed, however, he told King to evacuate the shore camp immediately. Keli'ikea, who also received the news, asked King in dismay if it was true that Cook was dead. King answered that he did not know, but requested the young priest to gather his fellow priests in a house near Hikiau, while he posted the marines on top of the heiau. Not long after King left with Bligh to report to Captain Clerke, warriors came running along the cliff-top from Ka'awaloa, and began to pelt the sailors with stones from their slingshots. When one of these men was wounded, his companion braved the musket-fire to try and rescue his body, and was shot several times before he succeeded.

When he saw his men under attack, Lieutenant King hastened back from the ship to the shore camp. He talked with the priests, asking them to assure the Ka'awaloa warriors that if they stopped throwing stones, he would order his men to stop firing. A truce was agreed, and the sailors were allowed to float off the mast and carry the sails, the tents and the astronomical instruments back to the vessels. Back on the *Resolution*, King urged a show of force against the Ka'awaloa chiefs, but some of his fellow officers felt that Cook had provoked the confrontation with the Hawai'ians by attempting to take Kalani'opu'u hostage. Eventually they agreed that there would be no immediate attack, but that they should try to recover Cook's body by conciliatory means. His corpse had been carried up the cliff to the north of the bay, and they hoped to retrieve it to give their commander a decent burial.

At three o'clock that afternoon, the old warrior priest Koa'a (or 'Britanee', as he called himself) came alongside the *Resolution*. Infuriated by his effrontery, the sailors could barely be restrained from shooting him. Shortly afterwards Lieutenant King took the ships' boats and a large contingent of armed men to parley with the chiefs, in an attempt to recover Captain Cook's body. As they rowed towards Ka'awaloa, a huge crowd gathered on the beach. The warriors had thrown up stone breastworks, and the women and children retreated while the men put on their war mats, and began to hurl rocks with their slingshots. Lieutenant King decided to go on alone in a small boat, carrying a white flag. As soon as the Hawai'ians saw this, the women and children flocked back to the beach, the warriors took off their mats and sat down, stretching out their arms in welcome. Koa'a swam to King's boat with a white flag, and clambered on board to embrace him, still holding his dagger. Mistrustful of the old man, King pushed his dagger aside and demanded Cook's body, saying that unless it was returned his soldiers would attack the Hawai'ians. Koa'a assured him that Cook's body would be returned very soon and swam back to the beach, calling out to his people that 'we were all friends again'.

While the boats lay off Ka'awaloa, the chiefs called out to Lieutenant King, telling him that if he came ashore, they would hand over Cook's body. King refused this invitation, however, suspecting that if he landed, he too would be killed. Before long another man, a close associate of Kalani'opu'u's, told him that Cook's body had been cut into pieces and sent away from the bay. King ordered the boats to return to the ships and as they rowed away, the warriors jeered at them. One strutted about in Captain Cook's jacket and trousers; another brandished the sword he had been wearing; others waved cutlasses and bayonets taken from the bodies of the marines; while several exposed their bare buttocks. The sailors were so enraged by these insults that the officers had great difficulty in stopping them from firing their muskets. Back at the ships Clerke ordered all the guns loaded, the boats moored alongside with top-chains, guarded by armed sentries, and the cutter to be rowed around the vessels. That night they could hear loud wailing ashore as a great number of fires flared up on the hills. As they listened to these cries in the dark, they feared that their comrades were being sacrificed. In fact, it seems likely that their bodies were being burned in mortuary rituals, for as the Hawai'ian scholar Kamakau later remarked: 'Those who broke the kapus of the chief or his sacred things were burned in fire. One who broke the kapu of the god became a burned offering for the god.'[4]

Although Clerke was desperately ill, he assumed command of the *Resolution*, handing over the *Discovery* to Lieutenant Gore. Clerke was supportive of Williamson, and despite the outcry against him, he immediately promoted him to second lieutenant. Although Phillips's written accusations against Williamson, backed by depositions from three of the *Resolution*'s mates, were circulating among the crews, Clerke's version of Phillips's eyewitness account of Cook's death made no mention of these matters. It is interesting to note that Clerke later destroyed Phillips's written complaint against Williamson and the mates' depositions; and he may also have destroyed the last three weeks of Cook's journal, since those entries are missing. Perhaps these included compromising material, which Clerke thought should be expunged from the official record.

Shortly after daybreak the next morning, a man came out to the *Resolution* to tell them that Cook's body had been brought back to the beach, and Koa'a arrived alongside shortly afterwards to invite Lieutenant King to Ka'awaloa. By now the crews hated the old warrior priest, but the officers thought it prudent to treat him politely. Koa'a visited the ships several times that day and looked around carefully, assessing the sailors' ability to defend themselves. As large parties of warriors marched over the hills and conches sounded, Clerke set the sailors to work lifting the foremast onto the *Resolution*'s deck. The launch was moored alongside with a top-chain, and guard-boats continued to row around the two vessels. That afternoon the officers gathered to attend an auction of Cook's clothes and belongings in the *Resolution*'s Great Cabin. Although it was customary to sell a deceased sailor's effects in this way, it was unusual for a commander's belongings to be 'sold at the mast'. Such a ceremony was a gesture of respect and support for the dead man's family (who received the money that was raised), while keeping his relics among his shipmates. Perhaps his journal for their time in Hawai'i was lost or destroyed at this time, for it has never been found. The atmosphere on board the ships during this ritual must have been electric. At about eight o'clock that evening when the *Resolution*'s sentries heard a canoe paddling through the dark, they fired their muskets. Two men, who proved to be Keli'ikea and the 'taboo man', cried out 'Tini!' (King's Hawai'ian name) in alarm, and King quickly ordered the sentries to stop shooting.

When they came aboard these men wept, lamenting the death of 'Orono' [Lono]. Keli'ikea presented Captain Clerke and King with a small bundle wrapped up in bark-cloth. When they opened it, they found to their dismay that it contained a hunk of flesh from Cook's thigh. As they gazed at this in horror, the young priest told them that Cook's body had been dismembered and parts of it burned, while the rest had been divided among the high chiefs. This piece had been given to Kauu, the high priest of Lono, who had sent it out to the ships as a proof of his friendship. When he was asked whether his people had eaten Cook's body, Keli'ikea was aghast. He assured King that his people were not cannibals, but asked urgently when the *Orono* would come again, and what he would do to them? The priests had identified

Cook with Kalani'opu'u's father, Lono-i-ka-Makahiki, and with the god Lono; now they supposed that he would come back again, furious about the way he had been treated. When the sailors saw Cook's flesh, they were maddened. As Roberts recorded:

It is impossible to express, the feelings, that every Officer, & seamen, suffered, on this occasion, a sight so horribly shocking; distraction & madness, was in every mind, and revenge the result of all.[5]

Keli'ikea told King and Clerke that he did not want his people to see him visiting the ship, because they would regard him as a traitor. Seventeen Hawai'ians had been killed at Ka'awaloa, including five chiefs, and their friends and families were burning to kill the British. He also warned them against Koa'a, saying that he was their implacable enemy, and on no account to trust him. At about eleven at night Keli'ikea and his companion paddled back to the beach in the dark, accompanied by the guard-boat in case they were intercepted.

Early the next morning, Cook's thigh was buried in the ocean. When Koa'a came out to the *Resolution* in a canoe flying a white flag, he was allowed on board, despite Keli'ikea's warning. Soon after he had returned ashore two boys swam out from Hikiau temple carrying spears in their hands. Treading water under the stern of the *Resolution*, they sang a long lament to Lono, sometimes gesturing to Ka'awaloa where he had been killed, and sometimes pointing towards Kealakekua. They were invited on board, where they presented their spears to Clerke, and then swam back to Hikiau. Soon afterwards a canoe came out from Ka'awaloa on the opposite side of the bay, carrying a warrior who wore Captain Cook's hat. This man brandished the hat, threw stones at the ships and smacked his backside in derision. Although the sailors tried to shoot him, he was just out of range, which sent them mad with frustration. They went en masse to Captain Clerke, demanding to be allowed to go ashore to avenge their commander. Clerke promised that on the following day, he would warp the *Discovery* off Ka'awaloa to cover them with the guns, and they could take the boats ashore and burn down the town. A huge crowd had gathered on the beach, watching the Europeans, and Clerke ordered the *Resolution*'s gun crews to fire on them. Later that evening Koa'a came out and told them that a woman's arm had been torn off and some people had been killed by the cannonballs, including one of Kalani'opu'u's close relatives.

For some reason, the boats did not go to Ka'awaloa the next morning. Instead, they were sent to the priests' settlement at Kealakekua to fetch water. Lieutenant King, who was ill, did not accompany them on this occasion, although he had been in charge of the shore camp and knew the local people. As they approached, the ship's guns were fired to disperse a crowd that had gathered on the beach. When they landed, a party of warriors on the cliffs rolled rocks down on them and pelted them with stones. They fired at them, shattering a calabash carried by a young man who had been fetching water from the pond. He ran to a nearby cave, and when he was chased he tried to repel his pursuers with volleys of stones. They shot him, but he kept hurling stones until he had been shot again through the chest and the head; when they dragged him out of the cave he was still fighting. As Samwell remarked, 'He was a fine young Fellow & no Lion could have defended his Den with greater Fierceness & Courage than he did his, which was probably owing to these people neither giving nor receiving quarter from their Enemies.'[6] After this the sailors rampaged through the settlement and set it on fire, including the houses belonging to Keli'ikea and the other Lono priests, faithful friends of the British. As the villagers ran from their burning houses, six of them were killed and an old man and woman were captured, and in their fury some sailors cut the heads off two of these corpses and stuck them on poles, tying one to the prow of the *Resolution*'s large cutter, and waving the other under the noses of their captives.

As the boats were preparing to leave Kealakekua a large party came down the hill, each man carrying a white flag in his hand and carrying a bundle on his back. Not trusting these people, the officer ordered his men to fire at them, and they fell flat on their faces. It was fortunate that none of these people were hurt, because this was a party of the Lono priests, led by Keli'ikea. When they recognised him they apologised to Keli'ikea for firing on his group, and invited him out to the ship. His party included the 'taboo man' and a number of boys, who had been carrying provisions on their backs as gifts for the sailors. When he saw the decapitated bodies on the beach Keli'ikea wept aloud, and on board the ship he reproached James King for the attack on his settlement. Relying on his assurances of friendship, he and his party had put all their possessions in a house near the temple, which the sailors had burned to the ground. He begged King to have the heads of his compatriots thrown overboard and to free the captives. These things were done, and King expressed his dismay about the attack on Kealakekua, assuring Keli'ikea that if he had been ashore, the destruction of the priests' houses would not have been permitted.

Early the next morning when Koa'a came out to the ship, bringing gifts of a pig and a bunch of plantains, King told the old warrior priest angrily that if he did not bring Captain Cook's body, he would be killed the next time he came out to the *Resolution*. During the day Keli'ikea despatched canoes full of provisions, and a message that Captain Cook's body had been distributed among the chiefs. His hair had been given to Kamehameha, his legs, thighs, arms and lower jaw to Kalani'opu'u, and the rest of his body had been burnt to avenge the breach of the high chief's sacred power. Kalani'opu'u and his attendants had not taken part in the rituals of sacrifice, but were still secluded in their caves on the cliffs behind Ka'awaloa. That evening Hiapo, a close relative of Kalani'opu'u's, came out to the ship, bringing gifts from the high chief. He told Clerke and King that Kalani'opu'u was very sorry that Captain Cook had been killed, and wanted to be friends again with the Europeans. Clerke gave him presents and told him that if he brought back Cook's body to the ship, the hostilities would end. The following day, Clerke and Kalani'opu'u exchanged more messages and gifts, with Hiapo acting as an envoy.

On 20 February two canoes came alongside, each bringing out an offering of a pig and some coconuts. Later that morning a great procession assembled and came down the hills, each man carrying pieces of sugar-cane on his shoulders, and carrying breadfruit, taro or plantains. They were accompanied by two drummers, and when they arrived at the beach these men sat down by a white flag, still beating their drums, while the men heaped up their offerings in a large pile. Halfway along the beach, a man sat alone under another white flag. When the offerings were piled up, Hiapo stood on a rock in his long feathered cloak, beckoning to the boats. Clerke and King approached him in the pinnace and Hiapo stepped on board, presenting them with a large bundle draped in a black feather cloak spotted with white feathers, containing some of Captain Cook's remains wrapped up in bark-cloth.

When they opened the bundle in the *Resolution*'s Great Cabin, they found bones with burnt flesh attached, which included Cook's thighs and legs, but not his feet, both arms with the hands separated from them, but joined to the skin of his forearms, and his skull and scalp with one ear attached, although the facial bones were missing. They recognised his right hand, which had a large scar from an old wound (when a powder-horn had blown up in his hand in Newfoundland), separating the thumb from the forefinger. His lower jaw and feet were not in the bundle, although Hiapo assured them that Kalani'opu'u was doing his utmost to recover them. Captain Clerke was also given Cook's hanger, the barrels from his musket, beaten flat, and a gift of thirteen pigs from Kalani'opu'u. During Hiapo's visit the previous day Clerke had given the chief a red baize cloak, which he asked to have edged with green cloth. This had been done, and the cloak was now handed over. When Hiapo went ashore, Kalani'opu'u's son Keoua came out to the ship, where he was greeted with great respect. The men were busy rigging the masts, and that afternoon the bones were put into a coffin, the ships' colours were flown at half-mast, the yards were crossed and the funeral service was read, ten guns were fired, and Cook's remains were buried in the sea with full military honours.

Zimmermann, one of the *Resolution*'s crew, wrote in his journal that 'the general consternation caused by the death of our Commodore is the finest tribute to Captain Cook. Everyone on the ships was stricken dumb, crushed, and felt as though he had lost his father.'[7] His faults were forgotten, and as his body slid over the side into the bay, almost all of the sailors wept. Afterwards, Zimmermann penned a memorable account of his captain. He described Cook as strict with his men, but frugal with food and chaste with women. He never swore or got drunk, and loved equality, dividing the ship's provisions fairly among his officers and the sailors. He would tolerate no priest on board his ships, and seldom observed the Sabbath. He was fearless, and in moments of greatest danger was merry and serene. He had an instinct for danger, and could sense an imminent shoreline. He cared for his men's health, insisting that they eat plenty of green vegetables and stay busy and active. The ships were kept clean, and well aired, and he cared for the sick.[8] According to Zimmermann, Captain Cook was very strict with his own men, but relaxed and happy with the islanders:

Captain Cook was a tall, handsome man, of somewhat spare build, slightly bent but strong, dark brown in complexion and stern of visage. Starting as a common sailor he worked his way up to such a height through his services that he became one of the most famous navigators.

He was very strict and hot tempered, so much so that the slightest insubordination of an officer or sailor upset him completely. He was unyielding where the ship's rules and the punishment inflicted for breaches of the same were concerned . . . Perhaps no sea officer has ever had such supreme authority over the officers serving under him as he, so that not one of them dared to contradict him. He would often sit at the table with his officers without saying a word, and was always very reserved. In small matters he was more strict with the crew than the officers, but at times was very affable.

He was born to deal with savages and he was never happier than in association with them. He loved them and understood the languages of the different islanders and had the art of captivating them with his engaging manner. This was probably the reason that they honored him and at times even worshipped him, and also further reason that when they ceased to honor him, or sometimes even ridicule him, he burned with rage.[9]

At Kealakekua, this rage had proved fatal. Cook stormed ashore in a fury, determined to use force if necessary – a mood that had often seized him during the third voyage. Faced with Kalani'opu'u, however, he was disarmed and no longer wanted to use violence. In the midst of deadly danger, Cook was possessed 'by an infatuation that is altogether unaccountable [and] trifled away his time', while Kalani'opu'u, his ceremonial friend, sat disconsolately in similar hesitation. While they dithered, the leaders lost control of their people. When the news came that a chief had been killed on the opposite side of the bay, Cook was attacked, the marines fired without warning, people were killed on both sides, and Cook was slaughtered.

On 22 February 1779, as the ships prepared to leave the bay, the chiefs came on board to say how sorry they were for what had happened. Hiapo came out bringing Cook's underjaw and his feet, one of his shoes and a piece of his hat, which he presented to Charles Clerke. When Kalani'opu'u's son Keoua, who had spent a lot of time with Cook, came on board, he wept in memory of 'the Orono'. Nevertheless, Keli'ikea warned the Europeans against the chiefs, saying that despite their fair words they were still hostile. At eight o'clock that night the ships were unmoored and sailed away from Kealakekua Bay, leaving their commander behind them.

Our Ancestor Captain Cook

'To tatou tipuna, ko Kapene Kuki' ['Our ancestor, Captain Cook'],
   from a letter by Te Rangihiroa to Sir Apirana Ngata.[10]

In the islands of Polynesia, the power of a great leader came from his or her ancestors, through strategic marriages and first-born children. These ancestors were thought to dwell in places known as the Po (the darkness), Hawaiki (the homeland) or Tahiti (the far-off country), which lay beyond the horizon, and their mana could be harnessed for human purposes. As their direct descendants, the high chiefs had intimate access to that power. In order to preserve it for a kin group, their lives were surrounded by ceremonial restrictions, and when the ancestor gods were invoked, they were pivotal.

When the European ships first arrived at the islands, it made sense to suppose that these marvellous vessels had sailed through the sky from another dimension. When they came from places such as Havai'i (or Ra'iatea) and Tahiti, the homelands for other islands, it made sense to suppose that those who sailed them might be ancestors. When they fired their cannons, the flash and crash of the guns seemed to be signs of extraordinary power. The vessels were understood as floating islands, whose arrival had been foretold in prophecies and visions. Their leaders, like the high chiefs, were assumed to be atua or akua, beings with superhuman abilities. Time and again the priests came out to greet the Europeans with chants and ritual offerings, and led them to shrines to meet local ancestors. Aristocratic chiefs became their exchange partners, offering pigs, dogs, vegetables and sexual hospitality in return for iron, red and white cloth, tools and trinkets. And when Captain Cook became ceremonial friends with a paramount chief – as he did with Tu in Tahiti, and Kalani'opu'u in Hawai'i, exchanging ritual regalia, including cloaks, helmets and swords, and even names, he became linked with the most senior genealogical lines, and the ancestor gods of the islands.

It is intriguing to note that it was only in those islands where Captain Cook had forged a ceremonial friendship with a paramount chief that he later became a focus of ancestral veneration. In New Zealand, where no such friendship was forged, the Rai'iatean high priest Tupaia made a much greater impression on Maori. In the Cook Islands, Easter Island and the Marquesas, where Cook did not go ashore, his Tahitian companions were the centre of local interest. In Tonga, where he was accompanied by Hitihiti and later Mai and two young Maori attendants, he made the mistake of exchanging names with a junior chief, and later abased himself in the 'Inasi rituals. The main oral tradition which survived in the Tongan archipelago about Cook's visits, recounting the plot to kill him at Lifuka, is far from reverential.

In Hawai'i, however, as successive European visitors reported, Cook was regarded with veneration. According to Andrew Taylor, who visited Kealakekua Bay with Colnett in 1788, he was remembered as 'Lono-nui'.[11] Colnett reported that the Hawai'ians asked anxiously how long Cook would be angry with them. Ever since he had been killed, they had constantly been at war with other islands, and many of their people had died of new diseases. Two new volcanoes had erupted on the island, burning day and night with explosions, which they attributed to Cook's rage.[12] Dimsdell, a European who arrived in Hawai'i in 1792, noted that the Hawai'ians revered Cook as an ancestral being:

There are a Variety of Morais built to his Memory in Several parts of the Island & the Natives sacrifice to him in Common with their other Deities – it is their firm Hope and Belief that he will come again & forgive them. He is never mentioned but with the utmost reverence & Respect. After the affray was over they took the Body back about a mile amongst the Rocks where they dissected it on a large flat Stone. This Stone is still preserved with Great Care. The flesh was even taken by the Priests

& the Bones were divided amongst the Chiefs. Those that fell to [Kalani'opu'u] and now in possession of [Kamehameha] his Successer Dimsdell has seen. They are preserved as Relics & were shewn him as a great favour.[13]

The Hawai'ians greeted English ships with cries of 'Britanee! Britanee!', and according to Edward Bell in 1793:

The Natives seem to consider [Cook's death] as one of the most remarkable events in their History, almost every child able to prattle can give you an account of it – at that time they look'd up to him as to a supernatural being, indeed called him the 'Orono' or great God, nor has he to this day lost any of his character or consequence with the Natives they still in speaking of him style him the Orono and they are to be believ'd, most sincerely regret his fate.[14]

Lieutenant Puget, another member of the 1793 Vancouver expedition, was told that Cook's bones were kept with those of Kalani'opu'u (another Lono-nui) at Hikiau temple: 'Capt Cooks Remains were in the Morai [heiau] along with those of Terreobo [Kalani'opu'u], which faces the place where the above skirmish happened.'[15]

When Kamehameha succeeded Kalani'opu'u as the leading chief of Hawai'i, Cook's mana seems to have grown, not diminished. In fact, Cook's reputation spread across the Pacific. William Mariner, an early European resident in Tonga, was told by Hawai'ians on Vava'u that the people at Kealakekua in Hawai'i were astonished when Cook was killed, since they considered him a superhuman being. They kept his bones as relics, which they used for ceremonial purposes: 'His bones (the greater part of which they have still in their possession!) they devoutly hold sacred. They are deposited in a house consecrated to a god, and are annually carried in procession to many other sacred houses, before each of which they are laid on the ground, and the priest returns thanks to the gods for having sent them so great a man.'[16]

The Rarotongans also heard about Cook, regaling the first European visitors to the island with stories about him.[17] During a visit to Kealakekua in 1823, when the missionary William Ellis visited the cave in the cliffs where Cook's remains were deposited when they were first taken from the beach, the Hawai'ians wept when they spoke about Cook's death, saying that when he arrived at Kealakekua Bay, they thought he was their ancestor, the high chief Lono, returning from Kahiki. Among many other details, he was told that Cook's bones were still held in a temple on the opposite side of the island and cared for by the Lono priests, although nobody would tell him its location. The bones were kept in a small wickerwork basket covered with red feathers, and the priests annually carried these in a procession around the island to collect tributes for Lono.[18]

This awestruck treatment of Cook's remains eventually provoked a sharp reaction, however. As Hawai'i gradually came under the sway of the United States, not Britain, Cook's reputation was attacked, especially by the Calvinist missionaries. He was accused of the sin of hubris, and blamed for introducing venereal diseases and other evils to Hawai'i. This view was influential among young Hawai'ians in particular, and by 1838 the *Moolelo Hawaii*, a compilation of Hawai'ian traditions published by the Lahainaluna Seminary, declared:

If Cook went ashore many of the people ran away in fright and the rest bowed down in a worshipful manner. He was led to the house of the gods and into the temple also and he was worshipped there. He allowed the worshipping like Herod did. He did not put a stop to it. Perhaps one can assume that because of this error on the part of Lono – Cook – and because he caused venereal disease to spread here, God struck him dead.[19]

In 1855 Hiram Bingham, a leading Calvinist missionary, wrote:

How vain, rebellious, and at the same time contemptible, for a worm to presume to receive religious homage and sacrifices from the stupid and polluted worshippers of demons and of the vilest visible objects of creation . . . – to encourage self-indulgence, revenge, injustice, and disgusting lewdness as the business of the highest order of beings known to them, without one note of remonstrance on account of the dishonor cast on the Almighty Creator![20]

Samuel Kamakau, an early Hawai'ian historian, echoed this argument in his book, *The Ruling Chiefs of Hawai'i*:

It was not the fault of the Hawaiian people that they held [Cook] sacred and paid him honor as a god worshiped by the Hawaiian people. But because he killed the people he was killed by them without mercy, and his entrails were used to rope off the arena, and the palms of his hands used for fly swatters at a cock-fight. Such is the end of a transgressor. The seeds that he planted here have sprouted, grown, and become the parents of others that have caused the decrease of the native population of these islands. Such are gonorrhea, and other social disease; prostitution, the illusion of his being a god; fleas and mosquitoes; epidemics. All of these things have led to changes in the air which we breathe; the coming of things which weaken the body; changes in plant life; changes in religion; changes in the art of healing; and changes in the laws by which the land is governed.[21]

Not surprisingly, given this onslaught, the reverential treatment of Captain Cook's remains came to an end in Hawai'i. Instead, he became a demonic figure, blamed for the ills and woes of colonisation.

On the island of Tahiti, where Cook had forged a ritual friendship with the paramount chief Tu, he was also venerated at first. For many years, successive British ships were greeted with joy, and the people asked eagerly when 'Tute' would be returning. Their captains were introduced to Cook's portrait, painted by Webber and presented to his ritual friend Tu, the paramount chief of the island. It was held by the chief of Matavai Bay, who acted as its guardian and brought it out on ritual occasions. Chants were performed and offerings presented to Cook's image. English captains were asked to sign the back of the portrait with their own names, the names of their ships and the dates of their visits. According to James Morrison, one of the *Bounty* mutineers who spent some time in Tahiti, the rituals included arioi performances:

Every thing being ready Captain Cooks picture was brought (by an Old Man who has the Charge of it) and placed in front, and the Cloth with which it was covered being removed, evry person present paid the Homage of striping off their Upper Garments, the Men bareing their bodys to the Waist, Poeno not excepted, and the Weomen uncovering their Shoulders. The Master of the Ceremonies then made the Oodoo (or usual offering) making a long speech to the Picture, acknowledging Captain Cook to be Chief of Maatavye and placing a young Plantain tree with a sucking pig tyed to it before the Picture. The Speech running to this purpose 'Hail, all hail Cook, Chief of Air Earth & Water, we acknowledge you Chief from the Beach to the Mountains, over Men, Trees & Cattle over the Birds of the air and Fishes of the Sea &c &c.'

After which they proceeded to perform their dance, which was done by two young weomen Neatly and elegantly dressd, and two Men, the whole was conducted with much regularity and exactness, beating drums, and playing flutes to which they kept true time for near four Hours. On a signal being given the Weomen Slip'd off their Dresses and retired, and the whole of the Cloth and Matting which was spread to perform on, was rolld up to the Picture and the old man took posession of it for the use of Captain Cook.[22]

As in Hawai'i, Cook had become an atua in a Polynesian pantheon, greeted with incantations and offerings. Eventually, however, his portrait was lost, and the rituals ceased. Again, his posthumous reputation shifted with the vagaries of imperial history. When Tahiti became a colony of France, much of its British history was forgotten. Like ancestors throughout the Polynesian islands, Cook's mana depended on the success of his inheritors. When they were triumphant, he was revered; if they were under attack, he was vilified; and if they were marginalised, his memory faded.

Conclusion

During his first two voyages, Captain Cook had tried to act as an exemplar of enlightened reason. These were scientific expeditions, equipped for systematic observation and enquiry. During the Enlightenment, science was understood as 'enlarging of the bounds of Human Empire', based on a power relation (between mind and matter, reason and nature) that put reason in charge of reality, and made this rule seem natural and right. The man of reason was 'objective', detached and dispassionate, free from emotion and weakness. And the epitome of such men was the great discoverer – 'I whose ambition leads me ... farther than any man has been before me', bringing the edges of the unknown into the light of rational understanding.

For the last decade of his life, though, James Cook had spent much of his time in Polynesia, where the cosmos and the self were understood quite differently. Mind and heart were not split, nor mind and matter – they had a generative relation. And from them came the World of Darkness or Po and then the wind of life, generating forms of the phenomenal world – the World of Light – through aeons of genealogical exchanges. From earth and sky the gods were born, and from the gods came people. The world was patterned by spiralling lines of relationship, named in a genealogical language. In the case of the chiefs, the life-force of the ancestor gods was the source of their power. It could be transferred by descent, the pressing of noses, or the gift of personal possessions. This life-force went with their things – their cloaks, chiefly ornaments and insignia; and with their names, so that to name something was also to claim it. With this went tapu or kapu, the presence of their ancestor gods, and mana, ancestral efficacy. The exemplary Polynesian leader was the man of mana, who mastered the art of successful exchange in the relational networks.

Success in exchange meant revenge for insults, however, as well as generous gifting. As Cook said of Totara-nui Maori in 1775: 'I have allways found them of a Brave, Noble, Open and benevolent disposition, but they are a people that will never put up with an insult if they have an oppertunity to resent it.' During his first two voyages to the Pacific, Cook had often spoken of Tahitians or Maori as his 'friends', and advocated 'Strict honisty and gentle treatment'. After his experiences at Totara-nui, however, he began to lose his faith in the power of reason. Maori had killed and eaten his men, and then deceived him about what had happened. Cook became increasingly cynical, and prone to violent outbursts of anger. He was now known as 'Toote' on board his ships, a passionate, unpredictable character.

Mana and honour, revenge and utu, tapu and the sacred all had points of coincidence, out of which working relationships between Europeans and Polynesians could be constructed. By such rough understandings, cultural edges were sometimes bridged, and people found common ground to stand on. The philosophies were not the same, however, and that was a source of confusion. It was often difficult to know how to act. The rules were no longer certain. When Cook became 'Tute' in Tahiti, and 'Kuki', 'Kalani'opu'u' and 'Lono' in Hawai'i, he became enmeshed in contradictions. As a Polynesian high chief he was descended from the gods; as a Briton, he was the son of a lowly farm labourer. As a naval commander Cook was expected to stay aloof and restrained, asserting his superiority over the 'natives'; as a high chief, he was expected to be loyal to his friends, showering them with gifts and respecting their customs. When Cook forged close associations with a number of island leaders, his relationships with his own men came under pressure, putting shipboard discipline at risk and undermining his authority. After his death, these contradictions continued. At first, he was honoured as both European hero and Polynesian ancestor; later, he was reviled as an imperial villain.

In order to understand these complex, equivocal zones of action, a two-sided historical ethnography is needed. The dynamics on board his ships led to Cook's death, as much as the situation in Hawai'i. It was a tragic event of epic proportions, and a purely local explanation will not serve, for all that it might seem pretty. By the time of the crisis in Kealakekua Bay, Cook had quarrelled with his men, Clerke was seriously ill, and shipboard discipline had been weakened. When Cook was attacked, the marines panicked and ran, and Lieutenant Williamson held back the boats rather than trying to save his commander. In many ways it was a classic case of the 'collapse of command', when a leader's authority is undermined over time by severe stress and undue familiarity. At the same time, Hawai'ian beliefs about Lono, the Makahiki, the quarrels between the priests and the chiefs in the bay, and Cook's friendship with Kalani'opu'u were crucial to what happened. Polynesian as well as European thinking – the World of Light as well as the Enlightenment – played their part in James Cook's death, just as Kuki's and Kalani'opu'u's bones were mingled. Polynesian as well as

European thinking is needed again, to illuminate those cross-cultural exchanges. As my mentor, the Maori tribal expert Eruera Stirling, used to chant:

Whakarongo! Whakarongo! Whakarongo!	Listen! Listen! Listen!
Ki te tangi a te manu e karanga nei	To the cry of the bird calling
Tui, tui, tuituiaa!	Bind, join, be one!
Tuia i runga, tuia i raro,	Bind above, bind below
Tuia i roto, tuia i waho,	Bind within, bind without
Tuia i te here tangata	Tie the knot of humankind
Ka rongo te poo, ka rongo te poo	The night hears, the night hears
Tuia i te kaawai tangata i heke mai	Bind the lines of people coming down
I Hawaiki nui, I Hawaiki roa,	From great Hawaiki, from long Hawaiki
I Hawaiki paamamao	From Hawaiki far away
I hono ki te wairua, ki te whai ao	Bind to the spirit, to the day light
Ki te Ao Maarama!	To the World of Light!

APPENDIX

Calendar of Punishments during Captain Cook's Three Pacific Voyages

Endeavour 1768–72

16 Sept 1768   H. Stephens, Seaman (12 lashes) and Thos. Dunister, Marine (12 lashes) for disobedience – refusing to eat fresh beef.

12 Oct 1768   R. Pickersgill, Master's mate (sent before mast) for disobedience – refusing to scrape between decks.

19 Nov 1768   J. Thurman, Seaman (12 lashes) for disobedience – refusing to assist with repair of sails.

30 Nov 1768   R. Anderson, Seaman (12 lashes) for attempted desertion; W. Judge, Marine (12 lashes) for insolence; J. Readon, Boatswain's mate (12 lashes) for neglect of duty in punishing these two men.

12 Apr 1769   S. Jones, Seaman (12 lashes) for disobedience.

16 Apr 1769   R. Hutchins, Seaman (12 lashes) for disobedience.

29 Apr 1769   H. Jeffs, Ship's butcher (12 lashes) for aggression towards Tahitian woman.

4 Jun 1769   A. Wolf, Seaman (24 lashes) for theft of spike nails.

12 Jun 1769   J. Thurman, Seaman (24 lashes) and J. Nicholson, Seaman (24 lashes) for theft from natives.

19 Jun 1769   J. Tunley, Seaman (12 lashes) for theft of rum.

21 Jun 1769   R. Anderson, Seaman (confined) for disobedience.

4 Jul 1769   C. Webb, Marine (24 lashes) and S. Gibson, Marine (24 lashes) for desertion.

13 Nov 1769   S. Jones, Seaman (confined and 12 lashes) for disobedience.

30 Nov 1769   M. Cox, Seaman (12 lashes), H. Stephens, Seaman (12 lashes) and M. Paroyra, Seaman (12 lashes) for stealing potatoes from natives.

1 Dec 1769   M. Cox, Seaman (confined and 6 lashes) for disputing sentence.

2 Dec 1769   A. Simpson, Seaman (12 lashes), R. Littleboy, Seaman (12 lashes), and T. Rossiter, Marine (12 lashes) for theft of rum.

23 May 1770   Mr Marra, Midshipman (dismissed the quarterdeck), on suspicion of cropping the clerk's ears.

7 Apr 1770   J. Bowles, Marine (12 lashes) for disobedience.

21 Feb 1771   T. Rossiter, Marine (12 lashes) for drunkenness and assault.

Total: 354 lashes; 21 men punished (6 twice).

Resolution 1772–5

3 Aug 1772   J. Marra, Gunner's mate (12 lashes) for insolence.

11 Sept 1772 R. Lee, Seaman (12 lashes) and F. Taylor, Marine (12 lashes) for insolence.

6 Jan 1773   Mr Loggie, Midshipman (sent before the mast) for dispute with Boatswain.

1 Feb 1773   Mr Coglan, Midshipman (sent before the mast) for dispute with Captain's servant.

16 Feb 1773   W. Briscoe, Tailor (12 lashes), F. Taylor, Marine (12 lashes), W. Atkinson, Seaman (6 lashes), J. Buttal, Marine (6 lashes) and P. Brotherson, Marine (6 lashes), all for theft.

20 Jul 1773   J. Keplin, Seaman (12 lashes) for putting old tobacco into ship's meal.

30 Aug 1773   Go. Woodward, Marine (in irons, 18 lashes), J. Buttall, Marine (in irons, 18 lashes) and E. Peterson, Seaman (in irons, 12 lashes) for rioting on shore; J. Marra, Gunner's mate (6 lashes) for insolence.

22 Nov 1773   R. Lee, Seaman (12 lashes) for stealing from Maori.

2 Jan 1774   C. Loggie, disrated Midshipman (12 lashes) for fighting.

6 Feb 1774   Mr Maxwell, Midshipman (sent before mast) for cutting sail.

22 Feb 1774   J. Innell, Seaman (12 lashes), J. Leverick, Seaman (6 lashes) and R. Lee, Seaman (6 lashes) for drunkenness and neglect of duty.

18 Mar 1774   W. Wedgeborough, Marine (confined and 12 lashes) for dirtiness and drunkenness.

6 Apr 1774   J. Innell, Seaman (12 lashes) for insolence.

8–9 May 1774 R. Baldie, Marine (24 lashes) for neglect of duty and having musket stolen.

14 May 1774   J. Marra, Gunner's mate (confined) for desertion.

28 May 1774   C. Williams, Cooper's mate (12 lashes) for losing his tools.

18 Aug 1774   W. Tow, Marine (12 lashes) for trading with natives when on duty.

19 Aug 1774   W. Wedgeborough, Marine (confined) for shooting native.

3 Nov 1774   J. Marra, Gunner's mate (12 lashes) for going ashore without permission.

6 Nov 1774   J. Keplin, Seaman (12 lashes) for going ashore without permission.

18 Mar 1775   Mr Maxwell, Mr Loggie, Mr Coglan, Midshipmen (confined) for threatening to stab the cook.

               Total: 288 lashes; 20 men punished (1 man – J. Marra – four times; 2 three times; 6 twice).

Resolution 1776–9

5 Aug 1776   W. Herold, Seaman (6 lashes) for neglect of duty.

21 Oct 1776   J. King, Seaman (6 lashes), T. Price, Seaman (6 lashes), E. Evans, Seaman (6 lashes) and R. Ervin, Seaman (6 lashes) for absenting themselves without leave.

22 Oct 1776   W. Hunt, Armourer (12 lashes) for attempting to pass counterfeit money and defraud the natives.

31 Oct 1776   J. Smith, Seaman (6 lashes) and W. Nash, Seaman (6 lashes) for neglect of duty.

14 Nov 1776   J. Perkins, Marine (12 lashes) and R. Young, Cook's mate (12 lashes) for neglect of duty.

26 Nov 1776   W. Bradley, Seaman (12 lashes) for absenting himself without leave.

1 Dec 1776   T. Harford, Marine (6 lashes) for selling his necessaries.

23 Dec 1776   J. Jackson, Marine (6 lashes) for fighting.

3 Jan 1777   E. Cawn, Seaman (12 lashes) for leaving his bed on deck all night.

10 Jan 1777   J. Allen, Marine (6 lashes) for drunkenness and neglect of duty.

18 Feb 1777   P. Whelan, Quartermaster (6 lashes) for insolence and contempt.

1 May 1777   G. Barber, Carpenter's mate (6 lashes) for disobedience; J. James, Boatswain's mate (6 lashes) for neglect of duty.

2 May 1777   R. Young, Cook's mate (6 lashes) for neglect of duty.

5 May 1777	T. Garratty, Marine (12 lashes) for neglect of duty.
11 May 1777	Three marines punished on shore for negligence.
11 Jun 1777	W. Butler, Seaman (12 lashes) for accidentally dropping overboard the mouthpiece of Capt. Cook's French horn; and J. King, Seaman (6 lashes) for drunkenness and neglect of duty.
19 Jun 1777	T. Griffiths, Cooper (6 lashes) for disobedience and neglect.
23 Jun 1777	J. Brown, Seaman (12 lashes) for striking an Indian chief.
6 Jul 1777	T. Garratty, Marine (12 lashes) for neglect of duty.
14 Jul 1777	T. Harford, Marine (12 lashes) for disobedience.
16 Jul 1777	J. Clay, Cook's mate (12 lashes) for neglect of duty.
17 Jul 1777	T. Harford, Marine (6 lashes), T. Scruse, Marine (6 lashes) and J. McDonald, Marine (6 lashes) for neglect of duty.
10 Sept 1777	W. Doyle, Boatswain's mate (12 lashes) for neglect of duty and breeding disturbances with the natives.
12 Sept 1777	J. Allen, Marine (12 lashes) and J. Dermot, Seaman (12 lashes) for theft.
28 Sept 1777	T. Price, Seaman (12 lashes) for theft.
29 Sept 1777	W. Doyle, Boatswain's mate (6 lashes) for striking an Indian chief.
12 Oct 1777	M. Spencer, Seaman (12 lashes) for theft.
28 Oct 1777	B. Whitton, Carpenter's mate (18 lashes) for theft.
30 Oct 1777	T. Morris, Marine (12 lashes) for sleeping at his post; J. Harrison, Marine (12 lashes) for neglect of duty.
31 Oct 1777	T. Morris, Marine (12 lashes) for letting native prisoner escape.
1 Nov 1777	T. Morris, Marine (12 lashes) for letting native prisoner escape.
2 Nov 1777	I. Carley, Marine (12 lashes) for sleeping at his post; W. Bradley, Seaman (6 lashes) for insolence and contempt.
16 Nov 1777	J. Harrison, Marine (confined and 24 lashes) for desertion.
24 Nov 1777	T. Hinks, Marine (12 lashes) for sleeping at his post.
21 Jan 1778	S. Bishop, Butcher's mate (6 lashes) for neglect of duty.
7 Feb 1778	J. Clay, Seaman (6 lashes) for neglect of duty.
5 Apr 1778	P. Whelan, Quartermaster (6 lashes) for refusing to take goods into his care.

6 Apr 1778   T. Harford, Marine (12 lashes) for sleeping at his post.

24 Apr 1778   J. Dermot, Seaman (12 lashes) for theft.

8 Jun 1778   W. Crotch, Seaman (6 lashes) and J. Boyd, Seaman (6 lashes) for theft.

27 Aug 1778   M. Dailey, Seaman (12 lashes) for theft; and J. Boyd, Seaman (6 lashes) for neglect of duty.

29 Aug 1778   R. Lee, Butcher (12 lashes) for drunkenness and neglect of duty.

28 Sept 1778 J. Allen, Marine (12 lashes) for theft.

11 Dec 1778   Stopped grog except on Saturday nights.

12 Dec 1778   W. Griffin, Cooper (12 lashes) for starting cask of sugar-cane beer.

24 Dec 1778   J. Grant, Seaman (12 lashes) for disobedience.

5 Jan 1779   J. Dermot, Seaman (12 lashes) for defrauding natives.

25 Jan 1779   J. Grant, Seaman (12 lashes) and B. Lyon, Seaman (12 lashes) for absenting themselves without permission; W. Nash, Seaman (12 lashes) for disobedience; W. Bradley, Seaman (24 lashes) for having connections with native women, knowing himself to have the venereal disorder.

3 Apr 1779   J. Davis, Quartermaster (12 lashes) for neglect of duty.

1 Jun 1779   J. Clay, Seaman (12 lashes) for insolence.

31 Aug 1779   M. Beach, Seaman (12 lashes) for insolence.

7 Sept 1779   J. McDonald, Marine (12 lashes) for insolence.

14 Sept 1779 J. Fisher, Seaman (12 lashes) for drunkenness and insolence.

Total: 684 lashes; 44 men punished (1 man – T. Harford – 4 times; 5 three times; 11 twice).

Selected Bibliography

(see other sources cited in the notes)

Beaglehole, J.C., ed., 1955, *The Journals of Captain James Cook on His Voyages of Discovery, Vol. 1: The Voyage of the* Endeavour *1768–1771* (Cambridge, at the University Press, for the Hakluyt Society).

Beaglehole, J.C., ed., 1962, *The* Endeavour *Journal of Joseph Banks 1768–1771, Vols. I and II* (Sydney, Angus and Robertson).

Beaglehole, J.C., ed., 1969, *The Journals of Captain Cook, Vol. 2: The Voyage of the* Resolution *and* Adventure *1772–1775* (Cambridge, at the University Press for the Hakluyt Society).

Beaglehole, J.C., ed., 1967, *The Journals of Captain Cook, Vol. 3: The Voyage of the* Resolution *and* Discovery *1776–1780*, Parts I and II (Cambridge, at the University Press, for the Hakluyt Society).

Beaglehole, J.C., 1974, *The Life of Captain James Cook* (London, the Hakluyt Society).

Beaglehole, J.C., 1979, *The Death of Captain James Cook* (Wellington, Alexander Turnbull Library).

Bligh, William [1787–9], ed. Owen Rutter, 1937, *The Log of the* Bounty, *Vols. I and II* (London, Golden Cockerel Press).

Bligh, William [1791–3], ed. Douglas Oliver, 1988, *Return to Tahiti: Bligh's Second Breadfruit Voyage* (Honolulu, University of Hawai'i Press).

Boswell, James, 1992, *The Life of Samuel Johnson* (New York, Alfred A. Knopf).

Bott, Elizabeth, 1982, *Tongan Society at the Time of Captain Cook's Visits: Discussions with Her Majesty Queen Salote Tupou* (Wellington, The Polynesian Society).

Brewer, John, 1997, *The Pleasures of the Imagination* (Chicago, University of Chicago Press).

Burney, Fanny, ed. Lars E. Troide, 1990, *The Early Journals and Letters of Fanny Burney, Vol. II: 1774–1777* (Oxford, Clarendon Press).

Burney, James, 1819, *A Chronological History of North-Eastern Voyages of Discovery* (London, Payne and Foss).

Burney, James, in McNab, Robert, 1914, *Historical Records of New Zealand, Volume II* (Wellington, John Mackay, Government Printer).

Carter, Harold B., 1988, *Sir Joseph Banks 1743–1820* (London, British Museum (Natural History)).

Cook, James, and King, James, 1784, *A Voyage to the Pacific Ocean . . . on His Majesty's Ships* Resolution *and* Discovery (Dublin, Chamberlaine et al.).

Cordy, Ross, 2000, *Exalted Sits the Chief: The Ancient History of Hawai'i Island* (Honolulu, Mutual Publishing).

Darnton, Robert, 1985, *The Great Cat Massacre and Other Episodes in French Cultural History* (New York, Vintage Books), 75–104.

David, Andrew, ed., 1988, *The Charts and Coastal Views of Captain Cook's Voyages, Vol. I: The Voyage of the* Endeavour *1768–1771* (London, the Hakluyt Society).

David, Andrew, ed., 1992, *The Charts and Coastal Views of Captain Cook's Voyages, Vol. II: The Voyage of the* Resolution *and* Adventure *1772–1775* (London, the Hakluyt Society).

David, Andrew, ed., 1997, *The Charts and Coastal Views of Captain Cook's Voyages, Vol. III: The Voyage of the* Resolution *and* Discovery *1776–1780* (London, the Hakluyt Society).

Ellis, William, 1859, *Polynesian Researches during a Residence of Nearly Eight Years in the Society and Sandwich Islands, Vols. I–IV* (London, Henry G. Bohn).

Ellis, William, 1782, *An Authentic Narrative of a Voyage Performed by Captain Cook and Captain Clerke, Vols. I and II* (London, G. Robinson).

Evans, E.P., 1987, *The Criminal Prosecution and Capital Punishment of Animals: The Lost History of Europe's Animal Trials* (London, Faber and Faber Ltd).

Forster, George, ed. Nicholas Thomas and Oliver Berghof, 2000, *A Voyage Round the World, Vols. I and II* (Honolulu, University of Hawai'i Press).

Forster, J.R., in Michael Hoare, ed., 1982, *The* Resolution *Journal of Johann Reinhold Forster 1772–1775, Vols. I–IV* (London, the Hakluyt Society).

Forster, J.R., ed., 1772, *A Voyage round the World . . . by Lewis de Bougainville* (London, J. Nourse and T. Davies).

Forster, J.R., ed. Nicholas Thomas and Oliver Berghof, 1996, *Observations Made During a Voyage Round the World* (Honolulu, University of Hawai'i Press).

Gascoigne, John, 1994, *Joseph Banks and the English Enlightenment: Useful Knowledge and Polite Culture* (Cambridge, Cambridge University Press).

Hammond, L. Davis, ed., 1970, *News from New Cythera: A Report of Bougainville's Voyage 1766–1769* (Minneapolis, University of Minnesota Press).

Henry, Teuira, 1928, *Ancient Tahiti* (Honolulu, Bernice P. Bishop Museum Bulletin 48).

Holmes, Christine, ed., 1982, *Captain Cook's Final Voyage: The Journal of Midshipman George Gilbert* (London, Caliban Books).

Holmes, Christine, ed., 1984, *Captain Cook's Second Voyage: The Journal of Lieutenants Elliott and Pickersgill* (London, Caliban Books).

Home, George, 1838, *Memoirs of an Aristocrat* (London, Whittaker & Co.).

Hooper, Beverley, ed., 1975, *With Captain James Cook in the Antarctic and Pacific. The Private Journal of James Burney, Second Lieutenant of the* Adventure *in Cook's Second Voyage 1772–1773* (Canberra, National Library of Australia).

Howay, F. W., ed., 1929, *Zimmermann's Captain Cook* (Toronto, the Ryerson Press).

Joppien, R., and Smith, Bernard, 1985, *The Art of Captain Cook's Voyages, Vol. I: The Voyage of the* Endeavour *1768–1771* (Melbourne, Oxford University Press).

Joppien, R., and Smith, Bernard, 1985, *The Art of Captain Cook's Voyages, Vol. II: The Voyage of the* Resolution *and* Adventure *1772–1775* (Melbourne, Oxford University Press).

Joppien, R., and Smith, Bernard, 1987, *The Art of Captain Cook's Voyages, Vol. III: The Voyage of the* Resolution *and* Adventure *1776–1780*, Parts I and II (Melbourne, Oxford University Press).

Kaeppler, Adrienne, 1978, *'Artificial Curiosities': being an exposition of native manufactures collected on the three Pacific voyages of Captain James Cook R.N.* (Bernice P. Bishop Museum Special Publication 65, Honolulu, Bishop Museum Press).

Kirch, Patrick, and Green, Roger, 2001, *Hawaiki, Ancestral Polynesia: An Essay in Historical Anthropology* (Cambridge, Cambridge University Press).

Ledyard, John, ed. James Kenneth Munford, 1963, *John Ledyard's Journal of Captain Cook's Last Voyage* (Oregon, Oregon State University Press).

Lysaght, A.M., 1980, *The Journal of Joseph Banks in the* Endeavour (Adelaide, Rigby).

McCormick, Eric, 1977, *Omai, Pacific Envoy* (Auckland, Auckland University Press, Oxford University Press).

Magra, James, 1967, *A Journal of a Voyage Round the World in H.M.S.* Endeavour (Amsterdam, N. Israel).

Marra, John, 1775, *Journal of the* Resolution's *Voyage in 1772, 1773, 1774, and 1775 on Discovery to the Southern Hemisphere* (London, F. Newbery).

Martin, John, ed., 1991, *Tonga Islands: William Mariner's Account* (Tonga, Vava'u Press).

Morrison, James [1787–92], ed. Owen Rutter, 1935, *The Journal of James Morrison, Boatswain's Mate of the* Bounty (London, Golden Cockerel Press).

Obeyesekere, Gananath, 1992, '"British Cannibals": Contemplation of an Event in the Death and Resurrection of James Cook, Explorer', *Critical Inquiry*, 18, 630–55.

Obeyesekere, Gananath, 1992, *The Apotheosis of Captain Cook: European Myth-making in the Pacific* (New Jersey, Princeton University Press).

O'Brian, Patrick, 1988, *Joseph Banks: A Life* (London, Collins Harvill).

Oliver, Douglas, 1974, *Ancient Tahitian Society, Vols. I–III* (Canberra, Australian National University Press).

Oliver, Douglas, 1988, *Return to Tahiti: Bligh's Second Breadfruit Voyage* (Honolulu, University of Hawai'i Press).

Parkin, Ray, 1999, *HM Bark* Endeavour: *Her Place in Australian History* (Melbourne, Melbourne University Press).

Parkinson, Sydney, 1773, *A Journal of a Voyage to the South Seas in His Majesty's Ship* Endeavour. *Faithfully transcribed from the Papers of the late Sydney Parkinson* (London, Richardson and Urquhart, for Stanfield Parkinson).

Porter, Roy, 1982, *English Society in the Eighteenth Century* (London, Penguin).

Reay, Barry, 1998, *Popular Cultures in England 1550–1750* (London, Longman).

Rickman, John (attributed), 1785, *Journal of Captain Cook's Last Voyage to the Pacific Ocean on* Discovery (London, E. Newbury).

Robertson, George, 1948, *The Discovery of Tahiti* (London, the Hakluyt Society).

Robson, John, 2000, *Captain Cook's World: Maps of the Life and Voyages of James Cook R.N.* (Auckland, Random House).

Rodger, N.A.M., 1986, *The Wooden World: An Anatomy of the Georgian Navy* (Annapolis, Maryland, Naval Institute Press).

Sahlins, Marshall, 1985, *Islands of History* (Chicago, University of Chicago Press).

Sahlins, Marshall, 1989, 'Captain Cook at Hawaii', *Journal of the Polynesian Society*, 98/4, 371–423.

Sahlins, Marshall, 1995, *How 'Natives' Think, About Captain Cook, For Example* (Chicago, University of Chicago Press).

Salmond, Anne, 1991, *Two Worlds: The First Meetings of Maori and Europeans 1642–1772* (Auckland, Penguin NZ).

Salmond, Anne, 1997, *Between Worlds: Early Exchanges Between Maori and Europeans 1773–1815* (Auckland, Penguin NZ).

Smith, Bernard, 1984, *European Vision and the South Pacific* (Sydney, Harper and Row).

Smith, Bernard, 1992, *Imagining the Pacific: In the Wake of the Cook Voyages* (Melbourne, Melbourne University Press).

Sparrman, Anders, 1953, *A Voyage Round the World with Captain James Cook in H.M.S.* Resolution (London, Robert Hale Limited).

Thomas, Nicholas, 1997, *In Oceania: Visions, Artifacts, Histories* (Durham, Duke University Press).

Thompson, E.P., 1993, *Customs in Common: Studies in Traditional Popular Culture* (New York, the New Press).

Trevenen, James, ed. Christopher Lloyd and R.C. Anderson, 1959, *A Memoir of James Trevenen* (London, Spottiswoode, Ballantyne and Co. Ltd, printed for the Navy Records Society).

Troide, Lars, ed., 1990, *The Early Journals and Letters of Fanny Burney, Vol. II: 1774–1777* (Oxford, Clarendon Press).

Valeri, Valerio, 1985, *Kingship and Sacrifice: Ritual and Society in Ancient Hawaii* (Chicago, University of Chicago Press).

Villiers, Alan, 1967, *Captain Cook, the Seamen's Seaman: A Study of the Great Discoverer* (London, Hodder and Stoughton).

Warner, Oliver, ed., 1955, *An Account of the Discovery of Tahiti, from the Journal of George Robertson, Master of H.M.S.* Dolphin (London, the Folio Society).

Weibust, Knut, 1969, *Deep Sea Sailors: A Study in Maritime Ethnology* (Stockholm, Nordiska Museets).

Theses and Research Essays

Driessen, H.A.H., 1991, 'From Ta'aroa to 'Oro' (unpublished Ph.D. thesis, Australian National University).

Eddowes, Mark, unpublished paper (Eddowes, pers. comm. 2001).

Emory, Kenneth P., 1932, unpublished ms. of Bernice P. Bishop Museum Bulletin, Traditional history of maraes in the Society Islands, in Bishop Museum Library; assorted other mss. by Kenneth Emory in the same collection.

Ryan, Tom, 1993, 'Narratives of Encounter: The Anthropology of History on Niue' (Ph.D. thesis in Anthropology, University of Auckland).

Taonui, Rawiri, 1994, 'Haerenga Waka: Polynesian Origins, Migrations and Navigation' (M.A. thesis, University of Auckland).

Notes

Preface

1. Zimmermann, Henry, in F.W. Howay, ed., 1929, *Zimmermann's Captain Cook* (Toronto, The Ryerson Press), 100–101.

I

How Englishmen Came to Eat Dogs

1. George Home recorded his father Alexander's account of the mock trial in his autobiography – Home, George, 1838, *Memoirs of an Aristocrat* (London, Whittaker & Co.), 271–3.

2. Cook in J.C. Beaglehole, ed., 1969, *The Journals of Captain Cook, Vol. 2: The Voyage of the* Resolution *and* Adventure *1772–1775* (London, the Hakluyt Society), 653.

3. Cook in J.C. Beaglehole, ed., 1967, *The Journals of Captain Cook, Vol. 3: The Voyage of the* Resolution *and* Discovery *1776–1780*, Part I (Cambridge, at the University Press, published for the Hakluyt Society), 59.

4. Cook in Beaglehole, ed., 1967, I, 62.

5. Cook in Beaglehole, ed., 1967, I, 68.

6. Cook in Beaglehole, ed., 1967, I, 69.

7. Burney in Robert McNab, ed., 1914, *Historical Records of New Zealand*, Vol. II (Wellington, John Mackay, Government Printer), 199.

8. Darnton, Robert, 1985, *The Great Cat Massacre and Other Episodes in French Cultural History* (New York, Vintage Books), 75–104.

9. In Evans, E.P., 1987, *The Criminal Prosecution and Capital Punishment of Animals: The Lost History of Europe's Animal Trials* (London, Faber and Faber Ltd), 108–9. For other accounts of animal trials, see Cohen, Esther, 1986, 'Law, Folklore and Animal Lore' in *Past and Present* 110:6–37. For fascinating commentaries on 'rough humour' see Bakhtin, Mikhail, 1984, *Rabelais and His World* (Bloomington, Indiana University Press), especially 196–277; and Thompson, E.P., 1993, *Customs in Common: Studies in Traditional Popular Culture* (New York, the New Press), 467–531.

10. Evans, 1987, 175.

11. Evans, 1987, 285.

12. In 'The Trial of Farmer Short's Dog Porter'; see Keane, J., 1995, *Tom Paine: A Political Life* (London, Bloomsbury Publishing), 70–71. Such trials of animals had antecedents in ancient Greece, where animal malefactors were tried at the common hearth of the city. For a parody of those proceedings, see Barrett, D., ed., 1964, *The Wasps* by Aristophanes (London, Penguin Books).

13. Banks in J.C. Beaglehole, ed., 1962, *The* Endeavour *Journal of Joseph Banks 1768–1771* (Sydney, Angus and Robertson), Vol. I:176.

14. See for instance the discussion in Levi-Strauss, Claude, 1962, *The Savage Mind* (Chicago, Chicago University Press), 204–8. For English attitudes to dogs see also Thomas, Keith, 1983, *Man and the Natural World* (London, Allen Lane); for Polynesian attitudes to dogs, see Titcomb, Margaret, in collaboration with Mary Kawena Pukui, 1969, *Dog and Man in the Ancient Pacific, with Special Attention to Hawaii* (Honolulu, Bernice P. Bishop Museum Special Publication), 59.

15. For accounts of eighteenth-century witchcraft in England, see Gijswijt-Hofstra, M., *et al.*, eds., 1999, *Witchcraft and Magic in Europe: The Eighteenth and Nineteenth Centuries* (London, the Athlone Press); Davies, Owen, 1999, *Witchcraft, Magic and Culture 1736–1951* (Manchester, Manchester University Press).

16. Levi-Strauss, 1962, 205.

17. Beaglehole, J.C., ed., 1955, *The Journals of Captain James Cook on His Voyages of Discovery, Vol. 1: The Voyage of the* Endeavour *1768–1771* (Cambridge, at the University Press, published for the Hakluyt Society), ccvi and 103.

18. Beaglehole, ed., 1969, 419–20.

19. Parkinson, Sydney, 1773, *A Journal of a Voyage to the South Seas in His Majesty's Ship, the* Endeavour (London, for Stanfield Parkinson), 122.

20. Beaglehole, ed., 1969, 333–4.

2

Rule Britannia!

1. Taussig, Michael, 1987, *Shamanism, Colonialism and the Wild Man: A Study in Terror and Healing* (Chicago, University of Chicago Press), 101. 'It is that space of wondering where doubt locks horns with fantasy – the next attack, hidden things, the multiplicity of signs'.

2. Voltaire, trans. Leonard Tancock, 1980, *Letters on England* (London, Penguin Books), 51.

3. For accounts of the Great Chain of Being, see Lovejoy, Arthur O., 1950, *The Great Chain of Being: A Study of the History of an Idea* (Cambridge, Mass., Harvard University Press); and Hodgen, Margaret T., 1964, *Early Anthropology in the Sixteenth and Seventeenth Centuries* (Philadelphia, University of Pennsylvania Press).

4. Defoe in Asa Briggs, ed., 1969, *How They Lived, Vol. III: 1700–1815* (London, Blackwell), 113.

5. Hay, D., and Rogers, N., 1997, *Eighteenth Century English Society* (Oxford, Oxford University Press), 20.

6. For accounts of life in eighteenth-century Britain and England, see Briggs, Asa, ed., 1969. *How They Lived, Vol. III: 1700–1815* (London, Blackwell); Colley, Linda, 1992, *Britons: Forging the Nation 1707–1837* (London, Pimlico); Hay, D., and Rogers, N., 1997, *Eighteenth Century English Society* (Oxford, Oxford University Press); Olsen, Kristin, 1999, *Daily Life in Eighteenth Century England* (London, Greenwood Press); Owen, John B., 1974, *The Eighteenth Century 1714–1815* (London, Nelson); Porter, Roy, 1982, *English Society in the Eighteenth Century* (London, Penguin); Scott, A.F., ed., 1970, *Everyone a Witness: The Georgian Age* (London, Martins).

7. Quoted in Porter, 1982, 118.

8. In Randall, A., and Charlesworth, A., 1996, *Markets, Market Culture and Popular Protest* (Liverpool, Liverpool University Press), 77.

9. Quoted in Porter, 1982, 31.

10. Quoted in Thompson, E.P, 1993, *Customs in Common* (New York, the New Press), 77. For further accounts of the 1768 sailors' riots, see the London newspapers, including *Public Advertiser, St. James's Chronicle, The British Evening Post* and *The Gentlemen's Magazine* for 5–20 May 1768; Rudé, George, 1971, *Hanoverian London 1714–1808* (London, Secker and Warburg), 193; and Shelton, Walter J., 1973, *English Hunger and Industrial Disorders: A Study of Social Conflict during the First Decade of George III's Reign* (London, Macmillan).

11. *The British Evening Post,* 17 May 1768.

12. Quoted in Hay and Rogers, 1997, 136.

13. For accounts of criminality during this period, see McLynn, Frank, 1989, *Crime and Punishment in Eighteenth-Century England* (London, Routledge); Hay, Douglas, *et al.,* 1975, *Albion's Fatal Tree* (London, Allen Lane); Brewer, John, 1980, 'Law and Disorder in Stuart and Hanoverian England', *History Today* 30:18–27.

14. *Grub Street Journal,* 21 October 1731, quoted in Scott, A.F., ed., 1970, *Everyone a Witness: The Georgian Age* (London, Martins), 283. As Glyn Williams notes, transportation was overwhelmingly the most common penalty for serious offences (pers. comm. 2002).

15. Quoted in Brewer, John, 1997, *The Pleasures of the Imagination* (Chicago, University of Chicago Press), 629.

16. For discussions of eighteenth-century English sexuality, see Bouce, P.-G., ed., 1982, *Sexuality in Eighteenth-Century Britain* (Manchester, Manchester University Press).

17. Quoted in Scott, 1970, 25.

18. Quoted in George, M. Dorothy, 1965, *London Life in the Eighteenth Century* (London, Penguin), 76.

19. Quoted in George, 1965, 25. For life in London see also Rudé, George, 1971, *Hanoverian London 1714–1808* (London, Secker and Warburg).

20. For accounts of witchcraft in eighteenth-century England, see Davies, Owen, 1999, *Witchcraft, Magic and Culture 1736–1951* (Manchester, Manchester University

Press); Gijswijt-Hofstra, M., *et al.*, *Witchcraft and Magic in Europe: The Eighteenth and Nineteenth Centuries* (London, The Athlone Press).

21. Quoted in Thompson, 1993, 54.

22. Quoted in Reay, Barry, 1998, *Popular Cultures in England 1550–1750* (London, Longman), 157–8. For further accounts of eighteenth-century 'rough music' see Ingram, M., 1984, 'Ridings, Rough Music and the "Reform of Popular Culture" in Early Modern England', in *Past and Present* 105:79–113; Thompson, 1993, 466–531; Fox, Adam, 1994, 'Ballads, Libels and Popular Ridicule in Jacobean England', in *Past and Present* 145:47–83.

23. Thompson, 1993, 509.

24. Quoted in Brewer, 1997, xix.

25. Quoted in Porter, 1982, 310.

26. Quoted in Brewer, 1997, xix.

3

The Wooden World of the *Endeavour*

1. For accounts of James Cook's life and the *Endeavour* voyage, see Beaglehole, J.C., ed., 1955, *The Journals of Captain James Cook on His Voyages of Discovery, Vol. I: The Voyage of the* Endeavour *1768–1771* (Cambridge, at the University Press, for the Hakluyt Society); Beaglehole, J.C., 1974, *The Life of Captain James Cook* (London, the Hakluyt Society); Hough, Richard, 1995, *Captain James Cook: A Biography* (London, Hodder and Stoughton); Villiers, Alan, 1967, *Captain Cook, the Seamen's Seaman: A Study of the Great Discoverer* (London, Hodder and Stoughton); and Rae, Julia, 1997, *Captain James Cook Endeavours* (London, Stepney Historical Trust). Beaglehole gives an excellent description of the crew, and a meticulous account of the preparations for the voyage in these two works. For primary sources see also Cook, James PRO Adm 55/40; BM Add Mss 27955, 27885; Ship's Log BM Add Ms 8959; Hick, Zachary PRO Adm 51/4546/147-148; Log in Alexander Turnbull Library, Wellington; Monkhouse, W.B. BM Add Ms 27889; Molyneux, Robert PRO Adm 51/4546/152, Adm 55/39; Pickersgill, Richard Adm 51/4547/140-141; Wilkinson, Francis Adm 51/4547/149-150; Forwood, Stephen Adm 51/4545/133; Bootie, James Adm 51/4546/134-135; Monkhouse, Jonathan, Mitchell Library *Log*; Clerke, Charles Adm 51/4548/143-144; Anon Adm 51/4547/153; Adm 51/4548/154; Adm 51/4548/155; Banks, Joseph ML *Journal*; Auckland Public Library *Grey Mss* 47-75; Green, Charles PRO Adm 51/4545/151; Marra, James, 1967, *A Journal of a Voyage Round the World in H.M.S.* Endeavour (Amsterdam, N. Israel); and Parkinson, Sydney, 1773, *A Journal of a Voyage to the South Seas in His Majesty's Ship* Endeavour (London, for Stanfield Parkinson).

2. Quoted in Hough, 1995, 3.

3. For an account of the beliefs of the founding father of the Quakers, see Nickalls, John L., ed., 1997, *The Journal of George Fox* (Philadelphia, Religious Society of Friends). The Quakers first censured slavery in 1727, and spoke out against the treatment of the afflicted and unduly harsh criminal punishments from their

seventeenth-century beginnings. (See *Quaker Faith and Practice*, 1995 (United Kingdom, The Yearly Meeting of the Religious Society of Friends).) My thanks to John and Judith Warren of Countersett, Yorkshire, for taking Jeremy and me to the Countersett Meeting House, and for fascinating discussions about the possible influence of Quakerism on Cook. In his 1694 preface to Fox's journal, William Penn enumerated Fox's personal virtues as 'sobriety, plainness, zeal, steadiness, humility, gravity, punctuality and charity' – a fair description of Cook's conduct during the first two voyages (p. xliii). More work is needed on Cook's relationship with John Walker and his family to assess the extent of the Quaker influence, however.

4. Quoted in Beaglehole, 1974, 59.

5. For life in the Georgian Royal Navy, and details of naval customs and routines, the following sources should be consulted: Bassett, Fletcher S., 1885, *Legends and Superstitions of the Sea and of Sailors, in all Lands and at all Times* (London, Sampson Low, Marston, Searle & Rivington); Earle, Peter, 1998, *Sailors: English Merchant Seamen 1650–1775* (London, Methuen); Henningsen, Henning, 1961, *Crossing the Equator: Sailors' Baptism and other Initiation Rites* (Copenhagen, Munksgaard); Kemp, Peter, 1970, *The British Sailor: A Social History of the Lower Deck* (London, J.M. Dent and Sons); Lewis, Michael, 1960, *A Social History of the Navy 1793–1815* (London, George Allen & Unwin Ltd); Lloyd, Christopher, and Coulter, Jack, 1961, *Medicine and the Navy 1200–1900: Volume III, 1714–1815* (Edinburgh and London, E. and S. Livingstone Ltd); Lloyd, Christopher, 1968, *The British Seaman 1200–1860: A Social Survey* (London, Collins); Pope, Dudley, 1981, *Life in Nelson's Navy* (Annapolis, Maryland, Naval Institute Press); Rediker, Marcus, 1987, *Between the Devil and the Deep Blue Sea: Merchant Seamen, Pirates, and the Anglo-American Maritime World 1700–1750* (Cambridge, Cambridge University Press); Rodger, N.A.M., 1986, *The Wooden World: An Anatomy of the Georgian Navy* (Annapolis, Maryland, Naval Institute Press); and Weibust, Knut, 1969, *Deep Sea Sailors: A Study in Maritime Ethnology* (Stockholm, Nordiska Museets).

6. Cook in Beaglehole, J.C., ed., 1969, *The Journals of Captain Cook, Vol. II: The Voyage of the* Resolution *and* Adventure *1772–1775* (Cambridge, at the University Press, for the Hakluyt Society), 2.

7. Quoted in Beaglehole, 1974, 124.

8. Joseph Banks recorded the full sequence of Royal Society decisions in a holograph manuscript entitled 'Transactions of the Royal Society relative to the sending out people to Observe the transit of Venus in 1769', now held among the Banks papers in the Mitchell Library, Sydney.

9. Quoted in O'Brian, Patrick, 1988, *Joseph Banks: A Life* (London, Collins Harvill), 63. See also a poem by a sailor on board the *Dolphin*, published in *The Gentleman's Magazine* (1768), XXXVIII:390.

10. Quoted in Beaglehole, ed., 1955, cxxxii.

11. Weibust, 1969, 275.

12. For the life of Joseph Banks, and the part he played in the *Endeavour* expedition, the following works are invaluable: Banks, R.E.R., Elliott, B., *et al.*, 1993, *Sir Joseph Banks: A Global Perspective* (London, The Royal Botanic Gardens, Kew); Carter,

Harold B., 1988, *Sir Joseph Banks* (London, British Museum (Natural History)); Gascoigne, John, 1994, *Joseph Banks and the English Enlightenment: Useful Knowledge and Polite Culture* (Cambridge, Cambridge University Press); Miller, David Philip, and Reill, Peter Hanns, *eds.*, 1996, *Visions of Empire: Voyages, Botany, and Representations of Nature* (Cambridge, Cambridge University Press); and O'Brian, Patrick, 1988, *Joseph Banks: A Life* (London, Collins Harvill).

13. Quoted in Carter, 1988, 69.

14. Quoted in McCormick, E.H., 1959, *Tasman and New Zealand: A Bibliographic Study* (Wellington, Government Printer), 23.

15. Beaglehole, ed., 1955, cxxxvi.

16. Beaglehole, ed., 1955, cclxxxii.

17. For details of the *Endeavour*'s construction and layout, see Parkin, Ray, 1999, *HM Bark* Endeavour: *Her Place in Australian History* (Melbourne, Melbourne University Press).

18. O'Brian, 1988, 65.

4

High Priest of 'Oro

1. I am indebted to Roger Green for checking this paragraph, and for this estimate, based on dates of 950 BC for the first Lapita settlement in Tonga; and AD 871–1001 for the Vikings (who settled Iceland in 871 AD. Bjami Herjolfsson discovered north-eastern America by accident in 985, when his ship was blown off course on a voyage to Greenland; and in 1001 Leif Eriksson sailed to America).

2. Kirch, Patrick, and Green, Roger, 2001, *Hawaiki, Ancestral Polynesia: An Essay in Historical Anthropology* (Cambridge, Cambridge University Press).

3. For accounts of Polynesian navigation, see Finney, Ben R., ed., 1976, *Pacific Navigation and Voyaging* (Wellington, Polynesian Society); Finney, Ben R., 1979, *Hokule'a: The Way to Tahiti* (New York, Dodd, Mead); 'Nautical Cartography and Traditional Navigation in Oceania', in Woodward, D., and Lewis, G. Malcom, eds., 2000, *Cartography in the Traditional African, American, Arctic, Australian and Pacific Societies* (Chicago, University of Chicago Press); Gladwin, Thomas, 1979, *East is a Big Bird: Navigation and Logic on Puluwat Atoll* (Cambridge, Mass., Harvard University Press); Irwin, G., 1994, *Prehistoric Exploration and Colonisation of the Pacific* (Cambridge, Cambridge University Press); Levison, M., Ward, R.G., and Webb, J.W., 1973, *The Settlement of Polynesia: A Computer Simulation* (Canberra, Australian National University Press); Lewis, David, 1967, *Daughters of the Wind* (London, Gollancz); Lewis, David, 1972, *We, the Navigators* (Canberra, Australian National University Press); Lewis, David, 1978, *The Voyaging Stars: Secrets of the Pacific Island Navigators* (London, Collins); and Taonui, Rawiri, 1994, 'Haerenga Waka: Polynesian Origins, Migrations and Navigation' (M.A. thesis, University of Auckland).

4. Henry, Teuira, 1907, 'Tahitian Astronomy. (Recited in 1818 at Porapora, by Rua-nui (Great-pit), a clever old woman). Birth of the Heavenly Bodies', *Journal of*

the Polynesian Society 16:101–4 (Wellington, Polynesian Society). For substantial accounts of early Tahitian beliefs and society, in approximate chronological order of original contact, see the *Dolphin* accounts cited below; the Bougainville accounts ditto; the Cook accounts cited in successive chapters in this work; Corney, Bolton Glanvill, ed., 1919, *The Quest and Occupation of Tahiti by Emissaries of Spain during the Years 1772–1776*, Vols. I–III (London, the Hakluyt Society); Bligh, William [1787–9], ed. Rutter, Owen, 1937, *The Log of the* Bounty, Vols. I–II (London, Golden Cockerel Press); Morrison, James [1787–92], ed. Rutter, Owen, 1935, *The Journal of James Morrison, Boatswain's Mate of the* Bounty (London, Golden Cockerel Press); Mortimer, Lieut. James [1789], ed. Cox, John Henry, 1791, *Observations and Remarks made during a Voyage . . .* (London, T. Cadell); Hamilton, George [1791], *A Voyage Round the World in His Majesty's Frigate* (Pandora, London, Hordern House); Vancouver, George [1792], ed. Lamb, W. Kaye, 1984, *George Vancouver: A Voyage of Discovery to the North Pacific Ocean and Round the World 1791–1795* (London, the Hakluyt Society); Bligh, William [1791–3], ed. Oliver, Douglas, 1988, *Return to Tahiti: Bligh's Second Breadfruit Voyage* (Honolulu, University of Hawai'i Press); Wilson, James [1796–8], ed. Moschner, Irmgard, n.d., *A Missionary Voyage to the Southern Pacific Ocean 1796–1798* (New York, Frederick A. Praeger); Oliver, Douglas, missionary sources index, in Anthropology Library, University of Auckland; Davies, John, ed. Newbury, C.W., 1961, *The History of the Tahitian Mission 1799–1830* (Cambridge, the Hakluyt Society); Ellis, William, 1859, *Polynesian Researches during a Residence of Nearly Eight Years in the Society and Sandwich Islands*, Vols. I–IV (London, Henry G. Bohn); Williams, John, 1838, *A Narrative of Missionary Enterprises in the South Sea Islands* (London, J. Snow); de Bovis, Edmond [1843–53], ed. Craig, Robert D., 1976, *Tahitian Society Before the Arrival of the Europeans* (Laie, Hawaii, Institute for Polynesian Studies); Henry, Teuira, 1928, *Ancient Tahiti* (Honolulu, Bernice P. Bishop Museum Bulletin 48); Adams, Henry Brook [1891–3], 1968, *Tahiti: Memoirs of Arii Taimai* (Ridgewood, N.J., The Gregg Press); Handy, E.S. Craighill, 1930, *History and Culture in the Society Islands* (Honolulu, Bernice P. Bishop Museum Bulletin 79); Emory, Kenneth P., 1932, 'Traditional History of Maraes in the Society Islands', unpublished ms. of Bernice P. Bishop Museum Bulletin, in Bishop Museum Library; assorted other mss. by Kenneth Emory in the same collection; Oliver, Douglas, 1974, *Ancient Tahitian Society*, Vols. I–III (Canberra, Australian National University Press); Driessen, H.A.H., 1991, 'From Ta'aroa to 'Oro' (unpublished Ph.D. thesis, Australian National University); and Babadzan, Alain, 1993, *Les Dépouilles des dieux: essai sur la religion tahitiene a l'époque de la découverte* (Paris, Maison des Sciences de l'Homme).

5. Quoted in Oliver, Douglas, 1974, *Ancient Tahitian Society, Vols. I–III* (Canberra, Australian National University Press), II:666.
6. An excellent account of the arioi in Tahitian and English is given by Rev. John Orsmond in his unpublished manuscript, ML Ms A2608, Vol. 4, *The Arioi Wars in Tahiti*.
7. Ellis, 1859, I:237.
8. My thanks to Roger Green and Marshall Weisler for generous assistance with

matters relating to prehistoric long-distance voyaging in Polynesia. For an excellent discussion of these matters, see Weisler, M., ed., 1997, *Prehistoric Long-Distance Interaction in Oceania: An Interdisciplinary Approach* (Monograph 21, Dunedin, New Zealand Archaeological Association); and Weisler, M., 2002, 'Centrality and the Collapse of Long-Distance Voyaging in Early Polynesia', in Glascock, Michael, ed., *Geochemical Evidence for Long-Distance Exchange* (Westport, Ct., Greenwood Publishing Group).

9. It is possible that the introduction of the 'Oro cult to Tahiti was much earlier than this, as the archaeologist Mark Eddowes has suggested in an unpublished paper. Eddowes also argues that the Tahitian aristocracy had previously resisted a number of attempts to bring 'Oro, a Rai'iatean ancestor god, to their island. It is also possible, as Eddowes suggests in another paper, that Taputapuatea marae had been the dwelling place of successive ancestor gods, each new atua being added to the pantheon, so that the name was much older than its association with 'Oro. (Eddowes, pers. comm. 2001.) I am greatly indebted to Eddowes for a series of insightful discussions of the *arioi* cult, and associated sites in the Society Islands.

10. For an account of these migrations, see the unpublished manuscript history of Tahiti by Rev. R. Thomson, an English missionary in Tahiti, who died in 1857 (pp. 13–17). Since he was able to interview old people who were alive at the time of the *Dolphin*'s arrival at Tahiti, his account of events from the 1740s onward is one of the most reliable available; although the even earlier account given by Morrison, one of the *Bounty* mutineers, is also very valuable. Thomson names Tupaia as the priest of 'Oro who took the image of the god and the red feather girdle to Papara (p. 16 of the mss.); who later became Purea's 'paramour' (p. 36), describing him as 'Tupaia, the priest of Oro who had accompanied the God from Raiatea, and who is reputed by the people themselves, as well as by Cook to have been one of the cleverest men of the island' (p. 38, Reference ATL Micro Ms Coll 2 Reel 169, London Missionary Society M660). Somewhat confusingly, there is also a woman named 'Tetupaia', born to the highest line in Ra'iatea, who married a man named Teu from Tahiti, thus giving their son Tuu (discussed in the following chapters) the right to wear the red feather girdle – but the maro 'ura she brought from Ra'iatea was taken to a marae named Taputapuatea at Tarohoi, especially built for the purpose. (See Adams, 1968, 86.)

11. See also Oliver, 1974, III:1202 for information on Tupaia. According to Anders Sparrman, who sailed with Cook on his second Pacific voyage, Tupaia was also known as 'Parua'. Tahitians frequently changed their names, at significant life crises or by name exchange with a bond brother; and in being able to follow the career of any individual through genealogies, oral histories and kin group traditions, it is important to keep track of all the names they were known by. (Sparrman, Anders, 1953, *A Voyage Round the World with Captain James Cook in H.M.S.* Resolution (London, Robert Hale Limited), 63.)

12. For background information on Purea (who was also known as Airoreatua i Ahurai i Farepua) and Amo (who was also known as Tevahitua i Patea), and their son Te Ri'i rere see Oliver, 1974, III:1198–203. For a discussion of the introduction of the 'Oro image to Papara, see Oliver, 1974, III:1214.

13. See Thomson, n.d., 16; Henry, 1928, 253; and Oliver, 1974, III:1199.

14. Driessen, Hank, 1982, 'Outriggerless Canoes and Glorious Beings', *The Journal of Pacific History* XVII:8–9. My thanks to Hank Driessen for access to his excellent unpublished thesis, 'From Ta'aroa to 'Oro', Australian National University, 1991.

15. For accounts of the *Dolphin*'s voyage, see Robertson, George, ed. Oliver Warner, 1955, *An Account of the Discovery of Tahiti, From the Journal of George Robertson, Master of H.M.S.* Dolphin (London, Folio Society); Rowe, Newton, 1955, *Voyage to the Amorous Islands: The Discovery of Tahiti* (London, André Deutsch); Public Record Office London – Mss Adm 55/35 Captain Wallis's Journal; Adm 51/4538/97 Lieutenant William Clarke; Adm 51/4541/95-6 Francis Wilkinson; Adm 51/4541/107-108 William Luke; Adm 51/4541/123-4 Anonymous; Adm 51/4541/125 Benjamin Butler; Adm 51/4542/109-10 George Pinnock; Adm 51/4542/111-2 Henry Ibbott; Adm 51/4542/113-4 Tobias Furneaux; Adm 4542/126-7 William Hambly; Adm 51/4539/102-6 George Robertson, Master; Adm 51/4543/115-6 Pender; Adm 51/4543/117-9 Samuel Horsnail; Adm 51/4543/128 Thomas Coles; Adm 51/4544/129 John Nichols; Adm 51/4544/131 Anonymous; Adm 51/4544/132 West; and Adm 36/7580 Muster Roll of the *Dolphin*. Many of the men were ill during their stay in Tahiti (including Captain Wallis) and their journal entries for Tahiti were written after the events described, so that dates and details given for particular episodes are often in disagreement. On the whole, I have relied on the excellent account given by George Robertson, the ship's master, for the basic chronology of events during the *Dolphin*'s stay on the island.

16. Robertson, 1955, 24.

17. Robertson, 1955, 32.

18. For instance Thomson, n.d., 27.

19. Ellis, 1859, I:302.

20. See Ellis, 1859, I:279–320 and Henry, 1928, 301–22 for descriptions of war ceremonials.

21. As Meredith Filihia reminds me, when Tahitian warriors exposed their genitals, they were showing their virility and readiness for battle; so the women may also have been getting their male companions ready for action (but why then did they expose themselves to the Europeans?). (Filihia, pers. comm. 2001.)

22. Wilkinson Adm 51/4541/96:48.

23. Robertson, 1955, 43.

24. See Ellis's account of ceremonies of peacemaking in Tahiti (Ellis, 1859, I:318–20).

25. Adams, 1901, 12–13; see also Henry, 1928, 192, and Handy, 1971, 34, 89, for accounts of the shark gods and two sacred sharks which greeted each new high chief of Opoa as they were installed, and farewelled them when they died. Gunson also discusses Hotutu, the chieftainess concerned, who slept with this 'Shark God' who is said to have come from Opoa in Ra'iatea. According to tradition, he left her because she preferred her husband's dog to him, a reference to the zooerastic bent of some Tahitian aristocrats. As Gunson remarks, this inclination is amply attested by the early missionaries (Gunson, 1964, 59–60). For other accounts of sacred sharks, see Henry, 1928, 389–90, 403–4, 414.

26. Robertson, 1955, 68.

27. For this sequence of events see Thomson n.d., 26–7.

28. Ellis, 1859, I:84. There was a kind of scrofulous disorder among the Tahitians known as 'o'ovi or 'chief's leprosy', which turned the skin white; and yaws could have a similar effect, which must have led to this speculation.

29. Henry, 1928, 232; Oliver, 1974, II:894–5; see also Handy, 1971, 62.

30. See Gunson, Neil, 1964, 'Great Women and Friendship Contract Rites in Pre-Christian Tahiti', Journal of the Polynesian Society, 73:53–69, especially 61–3.

31. Francis Wilkinson Adm 51/4541/96:51.

32. Cleats were pieces of wood of different shapes nailed or bolted on any particular part of the ship, often for belaying a rope to: WWW/Nautica Etymology/English/ Hedderwick 1830:5.

33. Watt, Sir James, 'Medical Aspects and Consequences of Cook's Voyages' in Robin Fisher and Hugh Johnston, eds., 1979, Captain James Cook and His Times (Canberra, Australian National University), 150.

34. See Smith's discussion of eighteenth-century medical knowledge of venereal diseases, the confusion between yaws and syphilis, and the failure to realise that syphilis could remain infectious for years after all visible symptoms had vanished (Smith, Howard, 1975, 'The Introduction of Venereal Disease into Tahiti: A Re-examination', Journal of Pacific History 10:38–47). In any case, it seems that some of the Dolphin's men were still visibly infectious, and that the surgeon must have known this. According to George Robertson, the ship's master, 'We carried Ten Men ashoar [at Tahiti] to the Sick Tent, three of them Very Bad, and has Been so Ever since we Left England, with Damn'd veterate Poxes and Claps.' (Robertson quoted in Smith, 1975, 41.) In blaming the British, the Tahitians thought that these diseases 'originated in the displeasure of some offended deity or were inflicted in answer to the prayers of some malignant enemy' (Ellis, 1859, II:66).

35. Ellis, 1859, I:331; Henry, 1928, 227.

36. Robertson, 1955, 125.

37. Henry, 1928, 140, trans. Anne Salmond.

38. Bougainville, quoted in L. Davis Hammond, ed., 1970, News from New Cythera: A Report of Bougainville's Voyage 1766–1769 (Minneapolis, University of Minnesota Press), 44.

39. ibid., 44–5. For a less felicitous translation of Bougainville's journal, see J.R. Forster's 1772 edition, A Voyage round the World . . . by Lewis de Bougainville (London, J. Nourse and T. Davies).

40. Bougainville, 1772, 274, 285–6.

41. Scholarly opinion has concluded that VD was introduced by the Europeans to the South Pacific, although they often mistook the symptoms of yaws for those of venereal diseases (see for instance Smith, 1975; Watt, 1979, 150–51).

42. For the ceremonies which surrounded the building and consecration of major marae, and the building of Maha'iatea in particular, see Henry, 1928, 131–41.

43. 'Itia married Tu, who later became the paramount chief of all Tahiti; and perhaps this explains her willingness to challenge her father's older sister. See Oliver, 1974, III:1187–8 for more information on this powerful woman.

44. For an excellent later account of these events see Adams, 1901, 40–46; but see Gunson's caveats in his 1964 article, 62–4. Other, slightly different, versions are given by Morrison, one of the *Bounty* mutineers (Morrison, 1935, 171–3); see also Thomson, n.d., 26–7. The most authoritative general discussion is in Oliver, 1974, III:1217–25.

45. The *pararaa Matahiti* ritual, which celebrated the 'ripening of the year', was generally held between the end of December and the beginning of January in Tahiti, although the timing could vary according to when the main crop of breadfruit ripened. The chiefs and people of the various districts presented lavish gifts of food, which were ceremoniously redistributed; and there were rituals, feasting, arioi performances and revelry as spirits of deceased ancestors and friends were summoned up to join the festivities (Henry, 1928, 177; Oliver, 1974, I:259–62). See also Ellis, 1859, I:351–2: 'The most singular of their stated ceremonies was the *maoa raa matahiti*, ripening or completing of the year. This festival was regularly observed in Huahine: although I do not know that it was universal, vast multitudes assembled. In general, the men only engaged in pagan festivals, but men, women and children attended at this . . .' See Bligh and Portlock (in Oliver, Douglas, 1988, *Return to Tahiti: Bligh's Second Breadfruit Voyage* (Honolulu, University of Hawai'i Press), 116–31) for an account of such a ceremony at Pare in Tahiti in 1792; and also Henry, 1928, (187–96) and Green, Roger C. and Kaye, 1968, 'Religious Structures (*Marae*) of the Windward Society Islands: The Significance of Certain Historical Records', *New Zealand Journal of History*, II:66–89.

46. Banks in Beaglehole, ed., 1962, I, 376. See Ellis, 1859, I:287 and Henry, 1928, 299, 306, for descriptions of the activities of the Rauti [battle orators]; and their principal weapon, the *airo fai*, the sharp, serrated and barbed tail of the stingray.

47. See Oliver, 1974, III:1217–28; and 1988, 159–60, for reconstructions of this episode.

48. In 1865, at the instigation of a French planter, Maha'iatea's stone steps were demolished to build a bridge over a nearby river, although this was soon swept away by a flood (Henry, 1928, 141).

5

Tupaia's Paintbox

1. Beaglehole, ed., 1955, 514–15.
2. Banks in Beaglehole, ed., 1962, I:158.
3. Banks in Beaglehole, ed., 1962, I:160.
4. Cook in Beaglehole, ed., 1955, 10fn.
5. Banks in Beaglehole, ed., 1962, I:177.
6. Banks to Perrin, quoted in Carter, 1988, 76.
7. Banks in Beaglehole, ed., 1962, I:207.
8. Banks in Beaglehole, ed., 1962, I:213.
9. Cook in Beaglehole, ed., 1955, 44.
10. Cook in Beaglehole, ed., 1955, 45.

11. Banks in Beaglehole, ed., 1962, I:240.

12. Cook in Beaglehole, ed., 1955, 74.

13. Banks in Beaglehole, ed., 1962, I:247–8.

14. Cook in Beaglehole, ed., 1955, 75.

15. Parkinson, 1773, 13.

16. Ellis, 1859, III:77; Henry, 1928, 206–7. Tahitian thieves often used incantations to persuade the gods not to notice them when they went stealing, presumably because divination was used to reveal their identities.

17. Banks in Beaglehole, ed., 1962, I:252.

18. See Oliver, 1974, III:1182–3 for Tutaha's genealogy and background.

19. Banks in Beaglehole, ed., 1962, I:254.

20. See Oliver, 1974, III:1192 for information about Te Pau, and a genealogy which shows the relationships among many of the key figures in Tahitian society at this time.

21. Banks in Beaglehole, ed., 1962, I:256.

22. Parkinson, 1773, 15.

23. Banks in Beaglehole, ed., 1962, I:258.

24. As the missionary William Ellis explained in 1859: The institutes of Oro and Tane inexorably required, not only that the wife should not eat those kinds of food of which the husband partook, but that she should not eat in the same place, or prepare her food at the same fire. This restriction applied not only to the wife, with regard to her husband, but to all the individuals of the female sex ... The men, especially those who occasionally attended on the services of idol worship in the temple, were considered *ra*, or sacred; while the female sex was considered *noa*, or common (Ellis, 1859, I:129).

25. Cook in Beaglehole, ed., 1955, 99.

26. According to the English missionaries, the Tahitians blamed the British for bringing many virulent diseases to their island: 'They say, that captn. Cook brought the intermitting fever, the humpbacks & the scrofula which breaks out in running sores in their necks, breasts, groins and armpits' (Elder and Wilson 21.2.1804, in Oliver missionary sources index, card 160) – perhaps a description of tubercular lesions. My thanks to Linda Bryder for the information about tuberculosis (Bryder, pers. comm. 2002).

27. Cook in Beaglehole, ed., 1955, 84. See Ellis, 1859, I:403 for an account of the pollution or *mahuruhuru* which came from touching the corpse or garments of a deceased person.

28. Banks in Beaglehole, ed., 1962, I:264.

29. Molyneux in Beaglehole, ed., 1955, 554.

30. Banks in Beaglehole, ed., 1962, I:266. See Molyneux's account of the meeting with Purea and Tupaia, in Beaglehole, ed., 1955, 554.

31. Cook in Beaglehole, ed., 1955, 85.

32. See Henry, 1928, 90–91, when she discusses two dolls given by a Russian navigator to a high chieftainess, who treasured them as the representations of two deceased women from her own family.

33. Banks first described Tiatia as a 'fine Grecian girl' (Banks, 1769, 'Observationes

de Otaheite', Marsden Collection ms. 12892, School of Oriental and African Studies, London) and later as 'my flame'.

34. Banks in Beaglehole, ed., 1962, I:271.

35. Solander notebook Marsden ms. 12023, Library of the School of Oriental and African Studies, University of London.

36. Banks, 1769, 'Observationes de Otaheite'.

37. Ellis, 1859, I:204–8.

38. See Wilson, James, 1799, *A Missionary Voyage to the Southern Pacific Ocean, 1796–1798, in the Ship* Duff (London), 331–2, for an account of the rahui. For a description of the seasons, see Henry, 1928, 332–3. According to Henry, there were two main seasons in Tahiti: *MataRi'i -i-ni'a*, or the season of plenty, which began with the acronitic rising of the Pleiades [Mata-Ri'i] in the month of Tema, on about November 20; and *MataRi'i -i-raro*, the season of scarcity, which began when the Pleiades descended beneath the horizon in the month of Au-unuunu, on about 20 May, and ended in Tema, when they rose again to the acronitic position.

'Each year had 13 months, which varied slightly in their timing on each island of the archipelago:

Rehu – Levelling – when the harvest is coming in; between December and January. The Matahiti [Ripening of the Year] festival was held at this time, usually in December.

Fa'ahu-nui – Great Repose – the sound sleep of plenty, between January and February.

Pipiri – Parsimony – scarcity begins, between February and March.

Ta'aroa – Departing Joy – breadfruit is scarce – between March and April.

Au – unuunu – Suspension – the fisherman's paddles are put away, it is stormy; between April and May.

'Apa'apa – Severed in twain – scarcity of food, the leaves of plants yellow and fall off, between May and June.

Paroro-mua – First fall – Turmeric and wild ginger die out, between June and July.

Paroro-muri – After fall – the last of the fruit season, between July and August.

Muri-'aha – Prayer behind – between August and September.

Hia'ia – Cravings – descent into the greatest scarcity of food; between September and October.

Tema – The clearing – When the old crops are gone and the new crops are developing, the season for planting, between October and November.

Te'eri – Scarcity – most of November – then the inflorescence of the breadfruit begins.

Teta'i – The cry – the epicure's great forage for food; the breadfruit is developing; wild foods of all kinds are brought out to eat, in December.

There was also an alternative [but rarely observed] system, with three main seasons – '*Tetau*, autumn, or season of plenty, the harvest of breadfruit, which began in Tetai, or December, and continued till Fa'ahu. This was not only the harvest, but the summer of the South Sea Islands. It was also the rainy season. The next was *Te tau miti Rahi*, the season of high seas, which began in Tieri, November, and continued until January. The last was *Te Tau Poai*, the winter, or season of drought and scarcity. It generally began in *Paroromua*, July, and continued till Tema, October.' (Ellis, 1859, I:87.)

For a cross-Polynesian comparison of calendrical systems, see Kirch, Patrick, and Green, Roger, 2001, *Hawaiki, Ancestral Polynesia: An Essay in Historical Anthropology* (Cambridge, Cambridge University Press), 260–73.

39. Carter, pers. comm. 1997.

40. See Henry, 1928, 236. It could be worth checking whether Tahitian dyes, rather than English water-colours, were used for any of Tupaia's paintings.

41. See Parkinson's account of dyeing cloth (Parkinson, 1773); his descriptions of the use of 'taihinnoo' and 'e tau' leaves (37) and those from 'e pooa' (38) along with the figs of the 'mattee' tree (46) to make red dye or 'mattee'; the roots of 'e nono' (38) to dye bark-cloth yellow; the juice of 'e peereepeeree' (40) to produce an 'indifferent' brown dye; the juice of its fruit and leaves of 'tamanno' (41) to give a pale yellow; the bark of 'e tootooe' to give a glossy substance to finish the cloth, and a black dye (44); and 'doodooe-awai' and 'oheparra' to dye cloth brown. See also his Tahitian vocabulary, which names different coloured bark-cloths – white, buff, reddish and russet (56). Parkinson also had himself tattooed (25), so his interest in Tahitian art was genuine. It is also interesting to note William Wales's comment after his first visit to Tahiti during the second voyage: 'Since Europeans have come amongst them they sometimes print [bark-cloth] in diverse figures by diping the End of a Bambo, cut properly, into the juice, in imitation of our Handkerchiefs; but they seldom ever wear it thus printed (in checkers?) themselves, at least I never saw them do it.'(Wales quoted in Beaglehole, ed., 1969, II:799.)

42. Banks in Beaglehole, ed., 1962, I:290.

43. It is possible that his time in John Walker's household was influential here. The Quakers did not believe in formal religious rituals or in the role of priests, and Cook rarely conducted Divine Service on board his vessels.

44. Bligh in Rutter, ed., 1937, I:403; see also Bligh quoted in Oliver, 1988, 107: 'The Men now began their performance which of all things that was ever beheld I imagine was the most uncommon and detestable. They suddenly took off what cloathing they had about their Hips and appeared quite Naked. One of the Men was prepared for his part, for the whole business now became the power and capability of distorting the Penis and Testicles, making at the same time wanton and lascivious motions. The Person who was ready to begin had his Penis swelled and distorted out into an erection by having a severe twine ligature close up to the Os Pubis applied so tight that the Penis was apparently almost cut through. The Second brought his Stones to the head of his Penis and with a small cloth bandage he wrapt them round and round, up towards the Belly, stretching them at the same time very violently untill they were near a foot in length which the bandage kept them erect at, the two stones and head of the Penis being like three small Balls at the extremity. The Third

person was more horrible than the other two, for with both hands seizing the extremity of the Scrotum, he pulled it out with such force, that the penis went in totally out of sight and the Scrotum became Shockingly distended. In this Manner they danced about the Ring for a few minutes when I desired them to desist and the Heivah ended, it however afforded much laughter among the Spectators.'

45. Morrison in Rutter, ed., 1935, 225.

46. See for instance Porter, Roy, 1982. 'Mixed Feelings: The Enlightenment and Sexuality in Eighteenth-century Britain' in Paul-Gabriel Bouce, ed., *Sexuality in Eighteenth-century Britain* (Manchester, Manchester University Press), 1–27.

47. Morrison in Rutter, ed., 1935, 192.

48. Banks in Beaglehole, ed., 1962, I:283.

49. Banks in Beaglehole, ed., 1962, I:286.

50. See Ellis, 1859, I:398–414 and Henry, 1928, 289–96 for accounts of the rituals surrounding death; and Ellis, 1859, I:412–14 and Henry, 1928, 293–4 for the activities of the chief mourner and his attendants.

51. Banks in Beaglehole, ed., 1962, I:289.

52. Cook in Beaglehole, ed., 1955, 101.

53. This was a form of sacrilege punishable with death (Henry, 1928, 143, see also 149); but first the Spanish, and then the English missionaries followed this practice of demolishing marae, as a deliberate act of desecration.

54. Cook in Beaglehole, ed., 1955, 103.

55. Parkinson, 1773, 32.

56. See Ellis, 1859, III:103–5 for an explanation of this custom.

57. Oliver gives this man's name as Pohuetea and his (first) wife as Purutihara (Oliver, 1974, III:1195).

6

Cook's Tour of Tahiti

1. For a masterly account of these divisions and districts, see Oliver, 1974, II:965–1073; and for a list of the districts with their proverbial recitations of mountains above, assembly ground below, point outside, river, marae, harbour, high chief, arioi house, school of learning etc., see Henry, 1928, 70–95.

2. Banks in Beaglehole, ed., 1962, I:297.

3. See Oliver, 1974, III:1174–5 for material on Vehiatua and his wife.

4. Mark Eddowes has written a fascinating unpublished paper on the life and death of this young man (Eddowes, n.d., 'Vehiatua TeRi'i ta'ata 'ura 'ura: An *ari'i nui* of Vaitepiha Tautira as Described in the Journals of the Spanish Padres Resident there from 1774–1775').

5. Apart from his battles with Purea and Amo, Vehiatua was also locked in a running war with the chiefs of Mo'orea, and they may have recently attacked his headquarters. See Thomson's manuscript history for this background.

6. Banks in Beaglehole, ed., 1962, I:297.

7. 'Matahiapo' means 'firstborn' in both Tonga and Tahiti, and it was a common and fitting name for a chief (Meredith Filihia, pers. comm. 2001).

8. Banks in Beaglehole, ed., 1962, I:300–301.

9. Banks in Beaglehole, ed., 1962, I:302.

10. For a discussion of the Papara war, see Oliver, 1974, III:1217–25; see Cook in Beaglehole, ed., 1955, 112–13, and Banks in Beaglehole, ed., 1962, I:303–4 for descriptions of Maha'iatea.

11. Henry, 1928, 319–22.

12. Molyneux quoted in Beaglehole, ed., 1955, 562–3.

13. Banks in Beaglehole, ed., 1962, I:312.

14. Banks in Beaglehole, ed., 1962, I:312.

15. Cook in Beaglehole, ed., 1955, 116.

16. Banks in Beaglehole, ed., 1962, I:312–13.

17. Molyneux quoted in Beaglehole, ed., 1955, 564.

18. Banks in Beaglehole, ed., 1962, I:314.

19. For background information on Ori see Oliver, 1974, III:1211–1212.

20. Cook in Beaglehole, ed., 1955, 141.

21. For accounts of such rituals, see Morrison, 1935, 189–90; Ellis, 1859, I:95–6, II:336–7; Henry, 1928, 177.

22. Banks, 1769, 'Observationes de Otaheite', lists Tupaia's estates or *whenua* on Huahine as 'Taleu, o Maeva, Ohaeti, Owhale'; and his Marae as 'Manunu, Mataitea'.

23. Banks in Beaglehole, ed., 1962, I:315.

24. Ellis, 1859, II:315–16.

25. Henry, 1928, 150–51.

26. Parkinson, 1773, 69.

27. Pickersgill quoted in Beaglehole, ed., 1955, 144.

28. Parkinson, 1773, 70.

29. Banks, 1769, 'Observationes de Otaheite', lists Tupaia's Raiatea estates or *whenua* as 'Otaitua, Opunarei, Oaoala, Ohualu, Tetoaraa, Oheanua, Autuala, Ohamanino, Ohawha, Oulhupai, Outuroa, Tuboa, Oneu, e Ninohuapai, Paeyalua, Oham..?, Matawera, Oharhoa, Oeida.., Ohaleba.'

30. Banks in Beaglehole, ed., 1962, I:323.

31. Banks in Beaglehole, ed., 1962, I:324.

32. Cook in Beaglehole, 1955, 154.

33. For background information on Uru (who was properly known as Vetea Uru) see Oliver, 1987, III:1210.

34. For more information on Puni, see Oliver, 1974, III:1211.

35. See Parkinson, 1773, 73, and Magra, 1775, 61–5.

36. Banks in Beaglehole, ed., 1962, I:327.

37. Banks in Beaglehole, ed., 1962, I:329.

7

Travellers from Hawaiki

1. Cook in Beaglehole, ed., 1955, 139fn.

2. On the basis of extensive research, including experiments using canoes built to traditional Polynesian designs and navigated by traditional methods, Ben Finney has concluded that 'Sailing back and forth between archipelagos within West Polynesia and the central core of East Polynesia would not seem to have presented any insurmountable problems, although it would have been easier to sail back and forth between islands aligned north and south than those aligned east and west, since voyagers on the eastward leg would either have to tack against the trades or wait for westerly winds.' For an excellent discussion of the current state of research on inter-island voyaging in Polynesia see Finney in Weisler, Marshall, ed., 1997, *Prehistoric Long-distance Interaction in Oceania: An Inter-disciplinary Approach* (Monograph 21, Otago, New Zealand Archaeological Association), 38–52; and other papers in this volume which use lithic sourcing among other methods to document links between the Southern Cook Islands and Samoa, Tonga and the Society Islands; between the Society Islands, the Southern Cook Islands and the Marquesas; and within the various archipelagos of Polynesia.

3. Banks in Beaglehole, ed., 1962, I:341.

4. As Banks commented, 'Religion has been in ages, is still in all Countreys Cloak'd in mysteries unexplicable to human understanding. In the South Sea Islands it has still another disadvantage to present to any one who has a desire to investigate it – the Language in which it is conveyd, at least many words of it, are different from those usd in common conversation, so that tho Tupia often shewd the greatest desire to instruct us in it he found it almost impossible.' (Banks in Beaglehole, ed., 1962, I:379.) An extensive account of Polynesian mythology was evidently written at this time, referred to in a letter from Abbé José Francisco Correia de Serra to Joseph Banks, April 7 1805, who had 'found amongst his belongings the last sheet of Tupaia's account of the mythology of the South Sea islanders which B. had lent him, the rest of which he has already returned.' (BM Add MS 8099:384.)

5. Banks in Beaglehole, ed., 1962, I:368.

6. Forster, ed. Thomas, 1996, 310.

7. Beaglehole, ed., 1955, 294fn. In 1912, Teuira Henry published a brief paper on the names Ra'iatea and Taputapu-atea, which explained that the ancient name of Ra'iatea was Havai'i; and all the islands to the east were called Te-ao-uri (the dark land), while all those to the west were called Te-ao-tea (light, or white land). Aotearoa is thus a name of ancient Tahitian origins; she also quoted an ancient chant: 'Na nia Te-ao-uri, Na raro Te-ao-tea, E to roa te manu e, E hi'o i te hiti o te ra' – Above (east) is dark-land; Below (west) is light-land; All encompassed by birds, As they look towards the rising sun' (Henry, Teuira, 1912, 'The Tahitian Version of the Names Ra'iatea and Taputapu-atea', *Journal of the Polynesian Society*, 21:78).

8. Cook in Beaglehole, ed., 1955, 157. John Beaglehole, Greg Dening and, most

recently, Nicholas Thomas, Ben Finney and David Turnbull have all discussed Tupaia's chart at length, pointing out a basic misunderstanding over Polynesian directional terms in its construction, identifying the islands and assessing its accuracy and significance. (Thomas, Nicholas, 1997, *In Oceania: Visions, Artifacts, Histories* (Durham, Duke University Press), 4; Finney, Ben, pers. comm. and 1998, 'Traditional Cartography in the Pacific Basin', in *Cartography in the Traditional African, American, Arctic, Australian and Pacific Societies* (Chicago, Chicago University Press); Turnbull, David, 1998, 'Cook and Tupaia, a Tale of Cartographic *Méconnaissance*?' in Margarette Lincoln, ed., *Science and Exploration in the Pacific: European Voyages to the Southern Oceans in the Eighteenth Century* (Woodbridge, Suffolk, National Maritime Museum), 127–8; Turnbull, David, 2000, '(En-)countering Knowledge Traditions: The Story of Cook and Tupaia' in *Humanities Research* I (Canberra, Australian National University).) In his article, Thomas asks why this chart, 'an extraordinary … document that fuses an indigenous perception of the world with the moralizing cartography of the Enlightenment', has been so little remarked on; claiming that it presents 'Tupaia's vision … in its integrity'. The chart, though, incorporates Cook's understanding of the locations of some Pacific islands in addition to what Tupaia had to say, and is thus much more mediated than his paintings.

9. Current archaeological scholarship suggests that although in the period of early settlement, long-range inter-island voyaging had been commonplace in East Polynesia, this fell away in about the fifteenth century. It has been argued that given the difficulty of such voyages, and the expense of building and maintaining voyaging canoes, there were strong reasons to stay at home; and that once warfare became endemic in some archipelagos, these reasons became even more compelling. At the same time, however, the stories which surround Tupaia's migration from Ra'iatea suggest that a priest who carried a new and powerful god with him might be welcomed on a new island, even in times of war; and that arioi rituals and practices gave members of the society the wealth and motivation to build and maintain voyaging canoes, and to travel to other islands. Certainly such voyages were technically feasible. For an excellent account of lithic evidence for long-range inter-island voyaging in Polynesia, see Weisler, Marshall, 1998, 'Hard Evidence for Prehistoric Interaction in Polynesia', *Current Anthropology*, 39/4:521–32; and for its decline, Weisler, 2002 (in press), 'Centrality and the Collapse of Long-Distance Voyaging in East Polynesia' in Michael Glascock, ed., *Geochemical Evidence for Long Distance Exchange* (Westport, Ct., Greenwood Publishing Group).

10. Marra, John, 1775, *Journal of the Resolution's Voyage in 1772, 1773, 1774, and 1775 on Discovery to the Southern Hemisphere* (London, F. Newbery), 219.

11. Forster, George, in Thomas and Berghof, eds., 2000, I:389.

12. Banks in Beaglehole, ed., 1962, I:388.

13. Banks in Beaglehole, ed., 1962, I:389.

14. Banks in Beaglehole, ed., 1962, I:396.

15. Banks in Beaglehole, ed., 1962, I:399.

16. Binney, 1995, 11: although the dates are too late for this prophecy to apply to Cook's arrival. For more detailed reconstructions of the encounters between the

Endeavour expedition and Maori in New Zealand, see Salmond, Anne, 1991, *Two Worlds: The First Meetings of Maori and Europeans 1642–1772* (Auckland, Penguin NZ), 87–296.

17. Salmond, 1991, 62.

18. Salmond, 1991, 124.

19. Henry, 1913, 26; Green and Green, 1968, 70.

20. Beaglehole, ed., 1955, 566–7.

21. Earl of Morton in Beaglehole, ed., 1955, 514.

22. Cook in Beaglehole, ed., 1955, 171.

23. Banks in Beaglehole, ed., 1962, I:403.

24. Beaglehole, ed., 1955, 570.

25. Beaglehole, ed., 1955, 570.

26. Salmond, 1991, 134.

27. Cook in Beaglehole, ed., 1955, 172.

28. Banks in Beaglehole, ed., 1962, I:408.

29. Monkhouse in Beaglehole, ed., 1955, 575.

30. Monkhouse in Beaglehole, ed., 1955, 575.

31. Monkhouse in Beaglehole, ed., 1955, 576.

32. Salmond, 1991, 150–51.

33. Banks in Beaglehole, ed., 1962, I:413.

34. Banks in Beaglehole, 1962, ed., I:417.

35. Parkinson, 1773, 97.

36. Banks in Beaglehole, ed., 1962, I:419.

37. Banks in Beaglehole, ed., 1962, I:420.

38. My thanks to Paul Tapsell for this suggestion. See also a discussion of Tahitian attitudes towards cannibalism by the missionary William Ellis in 1859: 'Their mythology led them to suppose, that the spirits of the dead are eaten by the gods or demons; and that the spiritual part of their sacrifices is eaten by the spirit of the idol before whom it is presented. Birds resorting to the temple, were said to feed upon the bodies of the human sacrifices, and it was imagined the god approached the temple in the bird, and thus devoured the victims placed upon the altar . . . The king, who often personated the god, appeared to eat the human eye. Part of some human victims were eaten by the priests. The Marquesians are known to be cannibals; the inhabitants of the Palliser or Pearl Islands, in the immediate neighbourhood of Tahiti, to the eastward, are the same. The bodies of prisoners of war, or enemies slain in battle, appear to have been eaten by most of the Hervey Islanders, who reside a short distance to the west of the Society group . . . In the little island of Tapuaemanu, between Eimeo and Huahine, tradition states that there were formerly cannibals.' (Ellis, 1859, I:358–9.)

39. Polack, Joel, 1838, *New Zealand: Being a Narrative of Travels and Adventures*, Vols. 1 & 2, 135–6.

40. My grateful thanks to Dr Volker Harms of the Institute of Ethnology at the University of Tuebingen, and Anke Sharrahs for arranging this visit to the poupou in Dresden. For an excellent account of the most likely European provenance of the carving, see Harms, 1996, 'A Maori Ancestor Panel which was brought to

England from the first Voyage of Captain Cook (1768–1771), rediscovered in the Ethnographical Collection of Tuëbingen University', unpublished ms. Harms thinks that the noted geologist Ferdinand von Hochstetter, who had visited New Zealand in 1858–9, and who later became director-general of the Imperial Museum in Vienna, must have purchased the artefact in England from a private collector or dealer, and brought it to Germany for display in his museum. After his death, it seems likely that his daughter Emma gave the carving to the Ethnographical Collection at Tuebingen University.

41. Cook in Beaglehole, ed., 1955, 538–9.

42. Pickersgill Journal Adm 51/4547/140-141, 1769:54a.

43. Banks in Beaglehole, ed., 1962, 425.

44. Cook in Beaglehole, ed., 1955, 196.

45. Charles Blagden, recounting a conversation with Solander; quoted in Carter, Harold, 1988, *Sir Joseph Banks 1743–1820* (London, British Museum (Natural History)), 86.

46. Horeta as told to John White, quoted in Salmond, 1991, 87–8.

47. Henry, 1928, 143–4; although lagoons were claimed by the occupants of the adjacent coast, as were some near-shore areas of reefless ocean. My thanks to Douglas Oliver for this caveat.

48. Banks in Beaglehole, ed., 1962, I:435.

49. Cook in Beaglehole, ed., 1955, 208fn.

50. Gore 1769 Adm 51/4548/145-6:140.

51. Banks in Beaglehole, ed., 1962, I:439.

52. White quoted in Salmond, 1991, 221.

53. Cook in Beaglehole, ed., 1955, 215–16.

54. Cook in Beaglehole, ed., 1955, 217fn.

55. Banks in Beaglehole, ed., 1962, I:443.

56. Banks in Beaglehole, ed., 1962, I:446.

57. Banks in Beaglehole, ed., 1962, I:446–7.

58. For a detailed account of the *St. Jean Baptiste*'s visit to New Zealand, see Salmond, 1991, 299–356.

59. Banks in Beaglehole, ed., 1962, I:449.

8

The Owner of These Bones

1. Magra, 1967, 93–4.

2. Banks in Beaglehole, ed., 1962, I:454.

3. Banks in Beaglehole, ed., 1962, I:455.

4. Banks in Beaglehole, ed., 1962, I:455.

5. Obeyesekere, Gananath, 1992, ' "British Cannibals": Contemplation of an Event in the Death and Resurrection of James Cook, Explorer', *Critical Inquiry*, 18, 630–55.

6. Pickersgill 1769 Adm 51/4547/140-141:60a.

7. Magra, 1967, 95–6.

8. Banks in Beaglehole, ed., 1962, II:19–20.

9. Tahitian histories tell of enemies who were skinned alive; and their skins worn as 'ponchos' in the field of battle; of women and children being killed in a horrible fashion; of captives being towed behind fleets of canoes until they drowned; of the first man wounded in battle being tightly bound around the head with sinnet until he suffocated; and so on. Tupaia's reaction to Maori cannibalism cannot have been based on squeamishness.

10. Cook in Beaglehole, ed., 1955, 539.

11. Cook in Beaglehole, ed., 1955, 236–7.

12. Parkinson, 1773, 116.

13. Banks in Beaglehole, ed., 1962, I:456.

14. Banks in Beaglehole, ed., 1962, I:459.

15. Banks in Beaglehole, ed., 1962, I:460.

16. Cook in Beaglehole, ed., 1955, 240.

17. Pickersgill 1770 Adm 51/4547/140-141:61a.

18. Banks in Beaglehole, ed., 1962, I:461.

19. Banks in Beaglehole, ed., 1962, I:463.

20. Parkinson, 1773, 119.

21. Banks in Beaglehole, ed., 1962, I:470.

22. Banks in Beaglehole, ed., 1962, I:471.

23. Cook in Beaglehole, ed., 1955, 265–6.

24. Banks in Beaglehole, ed., 1955, 266fn.

25. Banks in Beaglehole, ed., 1962, II:4.

26. Cook in Beaglehole, ed., 1955, 281, 282.

27. Banks in Beaglehole, ed., 1962, II:38–9.

28. Cook in Beaglehole, ed., 1955, 288.

29. Cook in Beaglehole, ed., 1955, 291.

30. Banks in Beaglehole, ed., 1962, II:50.

31. Dampier in Gray, ed., 1937, 312–13.

32. I am very grateful to Dr Fiona Powell for giving me access to her 'Report on the Response of the Europeans and Aborigines to one another during the *Endeavour*'s Journey along the Eastern Coast of Australia' (Powell, pers. comm. 2001), prepared for the CD-Rom *Endeavour: Captain Cook's Journal 1768–71* (National Library of Australia and the National Maritime Museum, 1998); to David Martin, Deborah Bird Rose, Bryce Barker, Peter Sutton, Gillian Cowlishaw, Kate Glaskin and Chris Gregory for their generous responses to an e-mail query about the *Endeavour* contacts with Aboriginal people; and to John Macdonald for detailed and helpful comments on the Australian section of the manuscript.

33. Parkinson, 1773, 134.

34. John Macdonald tells me that the Gweagal people were part of the Dharawal nation whose territory extended from Kurnell Peninsula to Nowra and the Shoalhaven River (pers. comm. 2002); see also Robson, John, 2000, *Captain Cook's World: Maps of the Life and Voyages of James Cook R.N.* (Auckland, Random House), map of Botany Bay.

35. Banks in Beaglehole, ed., 1962, II:54.

36. Banks in Beaglehole, ed., 1962, II:59.

37. Cook in Beaglehole, ed., 1955, 312.

38. Evans, Raymond, and Walker, Jan, 1997, '"These strangers, where are they going?" Aboriginal–European Relations in the Fraser Island and Wide Bay Region 1770–1905, *University of Queensland Anthropology Museum Occasional Papers in Anthropology*, 8, 39–105; and Glaskin, Katie, pers. comm. 2001, citing a letter from Edward Armitage to the Chief Protector of Aborigines in 1925, reporting the collection of a phonograph record of a story about the sighting of the *Endeavour* (although the details of the story seem to have been mixed up with memories of the 1799 visit by Mathew Flinders in the *Investigator*); and Walmsley, Cherise, 1995, *K'Gari Island of Paradise: A Cultural History of Fraser Island* (Kingfisher Bay Nature Notes (pamphlet)).

39. Cook in Beaglehole, ed., 1955, 324.

40. Cook in Beaglehole, ed., 1955, 325.

41. Banks in Beaglehole, ed., 1962, II:78.

42. Banks in Beaglehole, ed., 1962, II:81.

43. Burkitt, Horace, 1900, *Aboriginal Dialect, Endeavour River 1885–1895, Compared with Vocabulary Compiled by Captain Cook, 1770* (Corinda, Queensland); Ling Roth, 1901, 'The Structure of the Koko-Yimdir Language', *North Queensland Ethnography Bulletin* 2 (Brisbane), 6–7; De Zwaan, Jan Daniel, 1969, 'An Analysis of the Gogo-Yimidjir Language', Ph.D. thesis, University of Queensland; Breen, Gavan, 1970, 'A Re-examination of Cook's Gog-Yimidjir Word List', *Oceania* 44, 30; Haviland, John B., 1974, 'A Last Look at Cook's Guugu Yimidhirr Word List', *Oceania* 41(1), 28–38. For a fascinating discussion of Captain Cook stories among Aboriginal people, including those who did not see his ships, see Mackinolty, Chips, and Winburranga, Paddy, 1998, 'Too Many Captain Cooks', in Tony Swain and Deborah Bird Rose, eds., *Aboriginal Australians and Christian Missions: Ethnographic and Historical Studies* (Adelaide, The Australian Association for the Study of Religions), 355–60; Rose, Deborah Bird, 1984, 'Saga of Captain Cook: Morality in Aboriginal and European Law', *Australian Aboriginal Studies* 2, 24–39; and 1994, 'Ned Kelly Died for Our Sins', *Oceania* 65(2), 175–86.

44. Cook in Beaglehole, ed., 1955, 380.

45. Cook in Beaglehole, ed., 1955, 399.

46. Banks in Beaglehole, ed., 1962, II:145.

47. Banks in Beaglehole, ed., 1962, II:184.

48. Cook in Beaglehole, ed., 1955, 501.

49. Banks in Beaglehole, ed., 1962, II:186–7.

50. This was Eadan, a small island which was used to harbour European criminals.

51. Cook in Beaglehole, ed., 1955, 442. See also Parkinson, 1773, 182fn.

9

Penguins on Wimbledon Common

1. Cook in Beaglehole, ed., 1955, 505.

2. A study of Royal Navy ships on the Leeward Islands station from 1784–1812, for instance, shows a frequency of punishments about triple that on board the *Endeavour*. On average there were 3–4 floggings a month on each ship, with more than 12 lashes being awarded in a third of the cases. See Earle 1998:146.

3. Sauerkraut, unlike lemon and orange juice, contained relatively little Vitamin C, and Cook's recommendations helped to delay the effective treatment of scurvy in the Navy. (Lloyd, Christopher, and Coulter, Jack, 1961, *Medicine and the Navy 1200–1900, Vol. III: 1714–1815* (Edinburgh, E. & S. Livingstone Ltd), 302.)

4. *Philosophical Transactions of the Royal Society*, 1771, 61:XLIII:397; XXLIV:422; XLV:433; 62:XXV:357.

5. Cook in Beaglehole, 1974, 275.

6. Burney, Fanny, 1832, *Memoirs of Doctor Burney* (London, Moxon), I:270–71.

7. Quoted in Beaglehole, 1974, 284.

8. *London Chronicle*, 6–8 August 1771, 131a.

9. *London Chronicle*, 27–29 August 1771, 206b.

10. Quoted in Boswell, James, 1992, *The Life of Samuel Johnson* (New York, Alfred A. Knopf), 407.

11. Quoted in O'Brian, Patrick, 1988, *Joseph Banks: A Life* (London, Collins Harvill). Although Solander had written to Linnaeus from Rio, promising that on returning to Europe he and Banks would travel to Uppsala, 'humbly to ask you, Sir, to be the Master Inspector of our recruits [specimens]'; and Banks wrote to Linnaeus in May 1772, proposing that he would come to Uppsala with Solander, this never happened; nor did they send any specimens to Sweden. (Koerner, Lisbet, in D.P. Miller and P.H. Reill, eds., 1996, *Visions of Empire: Voyages, Botany and Representations of Nature* (Cambridge, Cambridge University Press), 129.)

12. *London Chronicle*, 24–27 August 1771, 194b–c.

13. Quoted in O'Brian, 1988, 66.

14. *The General Evening Post* (London), Saturday 20 July to Tuesday 23 July, 1771, 2.

15. The *Encyclopaedia* declared that 'Obscenity is the very basis of the Linnaean system.' Linnaeus had written of plant fertilisation as a marriage, for example, and of the male and female organs as 'husbands' and wives': 'The calyx then is the marriage bed, the corolla the curtains, the filaments the spermatic vessels, the antherae the testicles, the dust the male sperm, the stigma the extremity of the female organ, the style the vagina, the germen the ovary, the pericarpium the ovary impregnated, the seed the ovula or eggs.' Quoted in Browne, Janet, 'Botany in the Boudoir and Garden' in Miller and Reill, eds., 1996, 155–6.

16. *Town and Country Magazine; or, Universal Repository of Knowledge, Instruction, and Entertainment,* September 1773, 457. After the official account of the

voyage by Hawkesworth was published in 1773, there was a flurry of such parodies, including a number of salacious verses about Banks's sexual exploits in Tahiti.

17. Stanfield Parkinson in Parkinson, Sydney, 1773, *A Journal of a Voyage to the South Seas in His Majesty's Ship* Endeavour. *Faithfully Transcribed from the Papers of the late Sydney Parkinson* (London, Richardson and Urquhart), v–xxiii.

18. Benjamin Franklin to Bishop Shipley, 19 August 1771, ATL Ms 196A.

19. Franklin, Dr, and Dalrymple, Dr, 1771, 'Plan for Benefiting Distant Unprovided Countries', in Smyth, Vol. V, p. 340, ATL Ms 196A.

20. In August 1771 Cook wrote to his old friend and patron Captain John Walker, saying that: 'Another Voyage was thought of, with two Ships which if it takes place I believe the command will be confer'd on me'; quoted in Beaglehole, 1974, 277.

21. Boswell, James, 1992, *The Life of Samuel Johnson* (New York, Alfred A. Knopf), 410.

22. Quoted in Beaglehole, ed., 1969, II:xxx.

23. Elliott in Holmes, Christine, ed., 1984, *Captain Cook's Second Voyage: The Journal of Lieutenants Elliott and Pickersgill* (London, Caliban Books), 7–8.

24. For this correspondence, see *The London Chronicle*, 9–11 June 1772, 559; *Annual Register for the Year 1772*, 108; *The Monthly Chronicler*, June 1772, 291; and especially *London Magazine*, July 1772, 341–2: 'The public are already acquainted with the naked inventions, which were used to give birth to this pitiful trick; that it was planned by the miserable pride of a naval officer, who was unluckily connected with the business, but whose advice was not judged necessary to carry it into execution; and that, in the true spirit of a mean mind, he afterwards endeavoured to conceal his real design by the most frivolous and quibbling evasions.'

25. Clerke to Banks, 31 May 1772, in McNab, Robert, ed., 1914, *Historical Records of New Zealand* (Wellington, John Mackay Government Printer), II:95–6. His comments to Banks were openly disloyal to Cook: 'Captain Cook never explained his scheme of stowage to any of us; we were all very desirous of knowing, for it must have been upon a new plan intirely; know he kept whatever scheme he had quite a secret, for Cooper asked my opinion, and repeatedly declared he could form no idea how it was possible to bring it about ... They're going to stow this major part of the cables in the hold to make room for the people even now. I asked Gilbert [the master] if such was the present case, what the devil should we have done if we had all gone. "Oh, by God, that was impossible," was his answer.'

26. Of the original 94 men who set out on the *Endeavour*, only 41 survived the voyage, a mortality rate of 40%, a formidable total; and the public debate over the suitability of the ships for so long a voyage may also have been a factor. On the *Resolution*, 48 men ran before she sailed from England, compared with 18 men from the *Endeavour*; and Cook was forced to hire boatmen at Madeira to patrol the ship, to prevent more men from running.

27. Robertson, George, 1948, *The Discovery of Tahiti* (London, the Hakluyt Society), 202.

28. These quotes are taken from 'The Memoirs of the Early Life of John Elliott, of Elliott House', who sailed on the *Resolution* as a young AB. In these lively,

retrospective memoirs, written for his family, Elliott briefly sketched the characters of some of his *Resolution* shipmates (Holmes, ed., 1984, xxx–xxxi.)

29. See Sobel, Dava, 1999, *The Illustrated Longitude* (London, Fourth Estate), 165–77.

30. For excellent discussions of Cook's use of anti-scorbutics, and the effect of his promotion of malt rather than lemon, lime or orange juice (which contain quantities of Vitamin C) see Lloyd, Christopher, and Coulter, Jack, 1961, *Medicine and the Navy 1200–1900* (Edinburgh, E. & S. Livingstone), 293–325; and Watt, 1979, 144–7.

31. Fanny Burney, quoted in Manwaring, G.E., 1931, *My Friend the Admiral* (London, Routledge), 13.

32. Elliott in Holmes, ed., 1984, 11. For manuscript accounts of Cook's second voyage, see British Museum: Cook's Second Voyage Fragments, Add Ms 27889; South Sea Voyages Drawings and Prints, Add Ms 23920; Charts of Cook's Voyages, Add Ms 31360; Logbook of *Resolution*, Add Ms 27887; Logbook of *Resolution*, Add Ms 27956; James Cook's holograph *Resolution* Logbook, Add Ms 27886; Cook's draft *Resolution* Journal, Add Ms 27888; Charles Clerke's *Resolution* Logbook, Vol I Add Ms 8951, Vol II Add Ms 8952, Vol III Add Ms 8953; Charts, Add Ms 31360; William Hodges's Views, Add Ms 15743; John Elliott's *Resolution* Memoirs, Add Ms 42714; Charts Add Ms 15500; Cook's *Resolution* Journal, Eg Ms 2178; James Cook's *Resolution* Journal, Eg Ms 2177A and B. *Public Record Office:* James Cook's *Resolution* Journal (copy), Adm 55/108; James Cook's *Resolution* Letters, Adm 1/1610; Robert Cooper's *Resolution* Journal, Adm 55/104; Robert Cooper's *Resolution* Log, Adm 55/109; Charles Clerke's *Resolution* Log, Adm 55/103; Richard Pickersgill's *Resolution* Log, Adm 51/4553/5,/6; Joshua Gilbert's *Resolution* Log, Adm 55/107; Isaac Smith's *Resolution* Log, Adm 55/105; John Burr's *Resolution* Log, Adm 55/106; Thomas Willis's *Resolution* Journal, Adm 51/4554/199,/200,/201,/202; William Harvey's *Resolution* Journal, Adm 51/4553/185,/186,/187; Joseph Price's *Resolution* Log, Adm 51/4556/189; Joseph Price's *Resolution* Journal, Adm 51/4556/190; Anon. *Resolution* Log, Adm 51/4555/218; John Elliott's *Resolution* Log, Adm 51/4556/208; Alexander Hood's *Resolution* Log, Adm 51/4554/182,/183; Charles Loggie's *Resolution* Journal, Adm 51/4554/207; James Maxwell's *Resolution* Log, Adm 51/4555/206; Bowles Mitchel's *Resolution* Log, Adm 51/4555/194,/195; Tobias Furneaux's *Adventure* Log, Adm 55/1; Tobias Furneaux's Captain's Letters, Adm 1/1789; Arthur Kempe's *Adventure* Log, Adm 51/4520/1,/2,/3; James Burney's *Adventure* Journal, Adm 51/4523/2,/5,/6; Constable Love's *Adventure* Log, Adm 514520/7,/8; Henry Lightfoot's *Adventure* Log, Adm 51/4523/5; Anon. *Adventure* Journal, Adm 51/4524/17; Robert Browne's *Adventure* Journal, Adm 51/4521/9,/10; Thomas Dyke's *Adventure* Log, Adm 51/4521/12; John Falconer's *Adventure* Log, Adm 51/4524/1; William Hawkey's *Adventure* Log, Adm 51/4521/11; Richard Hergest's *Adventure* Journal, Adm 51/4522/13; John Wilby's *Adventure* Journal, Adm 51/4522/14. National Maritime Museum: James Cook's Journal copy; Richard Pickersgill's *Resolution* Journal, JOD/56. Royal Greenwich Observatory: William Wales's *Resolution* Logbook. National Library of Australia: letter to Cook from Sir Phillip Stephens, 20 July 1776, Mss 688.

Mitchell Library, Sydney: James Cook Log Leaves, Safe PH 17/2; Cook holograph fragments, Safe PH 17/2, 4, 12; William Wales Safe PH 18/4. Alexander Turnbull Library: Sandwich Family papers, WTU Ms Papers 841.

33. See Elliott in Holmes, ed., 1984, 11–12; and Cook's letter in Beaglehole, ed., 1969, II:685.

34. Elliott in Holmes, ed., 1984, xxxi.

35. Cook in Beaglehole, ed., 1969, II:688–9.

36. Forster, Johann, in Michael Hoare, ed., 1982, *The* Resolution *Journal of Johann Reinhold Forster 1772–1775, Vols. I–IV* (London, the Hakluyt Society), II:187.

37. Pickersgill in Beaglehole, ed., 1969, II:57–8.

38. Pickersgill in Beaglehole, ed., 1969, II:69.

39. Cook in Beaglehole, ed., 1969, II:80.

40. Forster, Johann, in Hoare, ed., 1982, II:233.

41. Forster, George ed., Nicholas Thomas and Oliver Berghof, 2000, *A Voyage Round the World, Vols. I and II* (Honolulu, University of Hawai'i Press), I:79. For a detailed account of Cook's visits to New Zealand during his second and third Pacific voyages, see Salmond, Anne, 1997, *Between Worlds: Early Exchanges Between Maori and Europeans 1773–1815* (Auckland, Penguin NZ), 36–160.

42. Pickersgill in Holmes, ed., 1984, 68.

43. Forster, George, in Thomas and Berghof, eds., 2000, I:105–6.

44. Forster, Johann, 1982, II:251.

45. Elliott in Holmes, ed., 1984, 17–18.

46. Clerke in Beaglehole, ed., 1969, II:123.

47. Furneaux in Beaglehole, ed., 1969, II:741.

48. Lloyd and Coulter, 1961, III:294.

49. My thanks to Michael Phillips for the following account of wall-guns: 'A wall-gun is the army name for a swivel gun. Too big to be hand held like a musket, it needed the support of a spigot which went into a hole in the bulwark. The standard Admiralty pattern looked like a small scale cannon, was muzzle loading, and fired a ball weighing about half a pound. They made ideal boat guns, and were big enough to sink a canoe.' (Phillips, pers. comm. 2002.)

50. Cook in Beaglehole, ed., 1969, II:170.

51. Sparrman, 1953, 56.

52. Cook in Beaglehole, ed., 1969, II:175.

53. Cook in Beaglehole, ed., 1969, II:172.

54. Forster, George, in Thomas and Berghof, eds., 2000, I:127–8.

55. Wales in Beaglehole, ed., 1969, II:790.

56. Elliott in Holmes, ed., 1984, 18.

10

Cannibals and Kings

1. Forster in Hoare, ed., 1982, II:303–4.

2. Forster in Hoare, ed., 1982, II:318–19.

3. Sparrman in Rutter, ed., 1953, 50.

4. Marra, John, 1775, *Journal of the* Resolution's *Voyage in 1772, 1773, 1774, and 1775 on Discovery to the Southern Hemisphere* (London, F. Newbery), 43.

5. For a discussion of these events, see Oliver, 1974, III:1225–32. In an unpublished paper about Vehiatua TeRi'i Ta'ata 'Ura'ura, Eddowes gives a detailed account of these battles from a Vaitepiha perspective (Eddowes, pers. comm. 2001).

6. Marra, 1775, 45.

7. Forster, George, in Thomas and Berghof, eds., 2000, I:150.

8. See Spate, O.H.K., 1988, *Paradise Lost and Found* (Rushcutters Bay, Pergamon Press), 122–4 for a brief account of Boenechea's two visits to Tahiti in November–December 1773, and November–January 1775.

9. Eddowes suggests that this man was Ti'itorea, a high-ranking 'black leg' arioi, the lover and possibly the second husband of young Vehiatua's mother Purahi (Eddowes, pers. comm. 2001).

10. For an account of Vehiatua II, see Oliver, 1974, III:1175–6; and Eddowes, unpublished paper, 2001.

11. Forster, Johann, in Hoare, ed., 1982, II:336.

12. For Reti's background, see Oliver, 1974, III:1176–7.

13. Wales in Beaglehole, ed., 1969, II:796–7.

14. Elliott in Holmes, ed., 1984, 31. As Cook noted of his encounter with Maraeta'ata's wife, 'this Lady wanted neither youth nor beauty, nor was she wanting in useing those charms which nature had given her to the most advantage, she bestowed her caresses on me with the utmost profusion and before I could get clear of her I was obliged to satisfy all her demands, after which both she and her husband went away and I was never troubled with either the one or the other afterwards, she no doubt thought I should expect some other favours for the presents I had made her than bare caresses and this was what she never meant to bestow.' (Cook in Beaglehole, ed., 1969, II:207fn.)

15. For detailed information on Tu's background, see Oliver, 1974, III:1179–86.

16. Cook in Beaglehole, ed., 1969, II:207.

17. Elliott in Holmes, ed., 1984, 19.

18. Ellis, William, 1859, *Polynesian Researches* new edn (London, Bohn), II:336–7.

19. Forster, George, in Thomas and Berghof, eds., 2000, I:206.

20. For a discussion of the background politics, see Oliver, 1974, III:1211–13.

21. Forster, Johann, in Hoare, ed., 1982, II:355.

22. Cook in Beaglehole, ed., 1969, II:220.

23. Cook in Beaglehole, ed., 1969, II:428fn.

24. Sparrman described one of these men, Ruhera, as having broad black bands of tattoo on his chest, belly and back; squares on his arms; with his thighs and hands tattooed black – obviously one of the top-ranking 'black-leg' arioi; while the other, Hiria, was statuesque, being measured at 44 inches around the chest and 32 inches around his muscular thighs. (Sparrman in Rutter, ed., 1953, 82.)

25. For background information on Reo (or 'Oreo') see Oliver, 1974, III:1210.

26. Sparrman in Rutter, ed., 1953, 82.

27. Wales in Beaglehole, ed., 1969, II:805.

28. Cook in Beaglehole, ed., 1969, II:225fn.

29. Forster, Johann, in Hoare, ed., 1982, II:365.

30. Cook in Beaglehole, ed., 1969, II:225.

31. Bayly 1773 ATL fMS-015:91,98.

32. According to George Forster, the young man had been called Mahine, but had taken the name of a taio from Mo'orea called Hitihiti (Forster, George, in Thomas and Berghof, eds., 2000, I:228). Cook always referred to him as Hitihiti, and the Forsters as Mahine. Society Islanders changed their names quite often, after some particularly significant life crisis, or in name exchange.

33. Elliott in Holmes, ed., 1984, 20.

34. Cook in Beaglehole, ed., 1969, II:236.

35. Clerke in Beaglehole, ed., 1969, II:230fn.

36. Queen Salote identified this man as Siale'ataongo, son of Tangata-'o-Lakepa, the eldest son of Mumui, the younger brother of Maealiuaki, an important chief whom Cook met during the third voyage. He was thus not of the highest rank. (Queen Salote, in Bott, Elizabeth, 1982, *Tongan Society at the Time of Captain Cook's Visits: Discussions with Her Majesty Queen Salote Tupou* (Wellington, The Polynesian Society), 11–12). Siale'ataongo, who lived in Hihifo, belonged to the Ha'a Ngata line and owed his allegiance to the Tu'i Kanokupolu, the secular leader of Tongan society, who headed that descent group (Kaeppler, Adrienne, 1970, *Eighteenth Century Tonga*. Ms. in Beaglehole collection, Alexander Turnbull Library).

37. See William Mariner in Martin, John, ed., 1991, *Tonga Islands: William Mariner's Account* (Tonga, Vava'u Press), 228, for an early account of these grave decorations.

38. Cook in Beaglehole, ed., 1969, II:252.

39. Forster, George, in Thomas and Berghof, eds., 2000, I:249.

40. Wales in Beaglehole, ed., 1969, II:813.

41. Salote in Bott, 1982, 18.

42. See Mariner, ed. Martin, 1991, 145fn and 247fn, for an account of such greetings in Tonga.

43. For an explanation of the term *'eiki*, see Kaeppler, Adrienne, 1971, 'Rank in Tonga', *Ethnology* 10 (2), 174–93; Bott, Elizabeth, 1981, 'Power and Rank in the Kingdom of Tonga', *The Journal of the Polynesian Society*, 90/1, 10–11; for investigations of the complexities of gender, rank and power in Tongan society at this time see Herda, Phyllis, 1987, 'Gender, Rank and Power in 18th century Tonga',

The Journal of Pacific History, XXII/4, 195–208; Rogers, Garth, 1977, ' "The Father's Sister is Black": Considerations of Female Rank and Power in Tonga', *The Journal of the Polynesian Society*, 86/2, 157–82.

44. In her account of Cook's visit to Tongatapu, Queen Salote says that this man may indeed have been weak-minded, since he had a son who was known to be afflicted in this fashion. (Salote in Bott, 1982, 18.)

45. Cook in Beaglehole, ed., 1969, II:259.

46. Forster, Johann, in Hoare, ed., 1982, III:405.

11

A Feast at Grass Cove

1. Forster, Johann, in Hoare, ed., 1982, III:406.

2. Forster, George, in Thomas and Berghof, eds., 2000, I:271.

3. Cook in Beaglehole, ed., 1969, II:292.

4. According to Anders Sparrman, Pickersgill intended to present this head to the Hunter Anatomical Collection in London, and indeed it eventually ended up in that collection. (Sparrman in Rutter, ed., 1953, 105.)

5. Clerke in Beaglehole, ed., 1969, II:293fn.

6. Cook in Beaglehole, ed., 1969, II:294.

7. Baynham, 1969, 79–80, for instance, quotes this sailor's description of a fight at sea: '. . . The din of battle continued. Grape and canister shot were pouring through our port-holes like iron hail, shaking her to the very keel, or passing through her timbers and scattering terrific splinters, which did a more appalling work than even their own death-giving blows . . . I now went below to see how matters appeared there. The first object I met was a man bearing a limb which had just been detached from some suffering wretch. Pursuing my way to the wardroom I necessarily passed through the steerage which was strewn with the wounded; it was a sad spectacle, made more appalling by the groans and cries which rent the air. Some were groaning, others were swearing most bitterly, a few were praying, while these last arrived were begging most piteously to have their wounds dressed next. The surgeon and his mate were smeared with blood from head to foot: they looked more like butchers than doctors.' One could multiply such accounts of the results of battle in eighteenth-century Europe ad nauseam.

8. Forster, G., in Thomas and Berghof, ed., 2000, I:280–81.

9. Wales in Beaglehole, ed., 1969, II:819.

10. Burney in Hooper, Beverley, ed., 1975, *With Captain James Cook in the Antarctic and Pacific. The Private Journal of James Burney, Second Lieutenant of the* Adventure *in Cook's Second Voyage 1772–1773* (Canberra, National Library of Australia), 87.

11. Burney in Hooper, ed., 1975, 88.

12. Burney in Hooper, ed., 1975, 89.

13. Burney in Adm 51/4523/2:82.

14. Marra, 1775, 96; quoted in preview by See, *Monthly Miscellany*, December 1774, 298–9. Marra was not an eyewitness, however, although he was drawing from an eyewitness account, and there may have been some creative editing.

15. Browne in Adm 51/4521/10:48.

16. Banks, Joseph, 21 July 1774, Mitchell Library.

17. Burney, Fanny, in Lars Troide, ed., 1990, *The Early Journals and Letters of Fanny Burney, Vol. II: 1774–1777* (Oxford, Clarendon Press), 42.

18. Burney in Hooper, 1975, 92fn.

19. Wales in Beaglehole, ed., 1969, II:302fn.

20. Sparrman in Rutter, ed., 1953, 111.

21. Forster, Johann, in Hoare, ed., 1982, III:438.

22. Forster, George, in Thomas and Berghof, eds., 2000, I:291.

23. Forster, Johann, in Hoare, ed., 1982, III:444.

24. Elliott in Holmes, ed., 1984, 43.

25. Cook in Beaglehole, ed., 1969, II:322.

26. Cook in Beaglehole, ed., 1969, II:331; and Clerke in fn. ibid.

27. Cook in Beaglehole, ed., 1969, II:333–4.

28. Thrower, W. R., 1951, 'Contributions to Medicine of Captain James Cook, F.R.S., R.N.', *Lancet*, CCXLI, II:218.

29. Watt, Sir James, in Robin Fisher and Hugh Johnston, eds., 1979, *Captain James Cook and His Times* (Canberra, Australian National University), 129–57.

30. Forster, George, in Thomas and Berghof, eds., 2000, I:298.

31. Wales in Beaglehole, ed., 1969, II:822.

32. See Métraux, Alfred, 1971, *Ethnology of Easter Island* (Bernice P. Bishop Museum Bulletin 160), 294–7.

33. Métraux, 1971, 303. See also his discussions of this expedition on pp. 13, 37–8.

34. Forster, George, in Thomas and Berghof, eds., 2000, I:315.

35. Forster, George, in Thomas and Berghof, eds., 2000, I:324. Forster quoted him in Tahitian, '*Ta'ata maitai, whenua 'ino.*'

36. Cook in Beaglehole, ed., 1969, II:354–5.

37. Sparrman in Rutter, ed., 1953, 118.

38. Wales in Beaglehole, ed., 1969, II:832–3.

39. Dening, Greg, 1980, *Islands and Beaches: Discourse on a Silent Land: Marquesas 1774–1880* (Honolulu, Hawaii, University of Hawai'i Press), 102.

40. As Wales noted, he 'represented to Capt. Cook that it would be of considerable use to get the rate of the Watches going at this Place, and the longitude shewn by it; as it would tend greatly to corroborate the Longitudes of Many Places which we have lately passed more especially as this is now so well determined.' (Wales in Beaglehole, ed., 1969, II:834.)

12

The Return of the Native

1. Forster, George, in Thomas and Berghof, eds., 2000, I:351.
2. Forster, George, in Thomas and Berghof, eds., 2000, I:351.
3. For To'ofa's background see Oliver, 1974, III:1192–3, 1197.
4. See Oliver, 1974, III:1237–55 for an account of the intricate relationships between Tahiti and Mo'orea in this period.
5. Clerke in Beaglehole, ed., 1969, II:383fn.
6. Cook in Beaglehole, ed., 1969, II:400.
7. Forster, Johann, in Hoare, ed., 1982, III:509.
8. According to his own account, Marra had 'flattered himself, as a man of enterprize and courage, with being made king of the country, or at least prime minister'. (Marra, 1775, 236.)
9. Forster, Johann, in Hoare, ed., 1982, III:517.
10. Wales in Beaglehole, ed., 1969, II:841.
11. Cook in Beaglehole, ed., 1969, II:418.
12. Cook in Beaglehole, ed., 1969, II:425.
13. Wales in Beaglehole, ed., 1969, II:845.
14. Cook in Beaglehole, ed., 1969, II:428.
15. By a careful inspection of the ship's chart and sketches by Hodges and Elliott of the island, and by undertaking a boat trip to check the western coast of Niue, Tom Ryan has located the site where Cook raised the Union Jack as immediately below the village of Hikutavake, where a number of paramount chiefs had been anointed and bathed. The second and third landings were close to each other, on the reef below the modern village and national capital of Alofi. The residential and ritual complex associated with the paramount chiefs of Niue, and known as Fatuaua, or Uhomotu – the 'heart of the island' – was located north of Alofi, at Tuapa. Ryan, Tom, pers. comm. 2002, revising his reconstruction in 1993, 'Narratives of Encounter: The Anthropology of History on Niue'. Ph.D. thesis in Anthropology (University of Auckland), 69–90; 161–93.
16. Forster, Johann, in Hoare, ed., 1982, III:538fn.
17. Cook in Beaglehole, ed., 1969, II:444.
18. This lagoon is located on Smith's and Gilbert's charts of Nomuka; see David, Andrew, 1992, *The Charts and Coastal Views of Captain Cook's Voyages, Volume II: The Voyage of the* Resolution *and* Adventure *1772–1775* (London, the Hakluyt Society), 230, 233.
19. Cook in Beaglehole, ed., 1969, II:442.
20. Cook in Beaglehole, ed., 1969, II:449fn.

13
Monboddo's Monkeys

1. Forster, Johann, in Hoare, ed., 1982, III:550–52. See his reference to the sailor who offered him six shells for half a gallon of brandy; and the gunner and the carpenter 'who have made vast Collections, especially of Shells, . . . who have several 1000 Shells: some of these Curiosities are neglected, broke, thrown over board, or lost.' (IV:557.) After quoting from Virgil on this occasion, Forster mocks conversations he had overheard between two of the crew, one an Irish sailor and the other a Welsh carpenter's mate, both of whom had learnt Latin as children, quarrelling over which of them had the best knowledge of that language. It is quite likely that Forster paraded his knowledge of the Classics in the Great Cabin as well as in his journal, at the expense of Cook and his officers as well as the sailors.

2. Forster, George, in Thomas and Berghof, eds., 2000, II:481; Adams, Ron, 1984, *In the Land of Strangers: A Century of European Contact with Tanna, 1774–1874* (Canberra, The Australian National University), 25–6. See Cheesman, Evelyn, 1949, *Camping Adventures on Cannibal Islands* (London, George G. Harrap and Company Ltd), 28, for an account by a woman naturalist who lived on Malekula in the 1940s, where many people still thought that whites were ghosts. See also Schieffelin, Edward, and Crittenden, Robert, eds., 1991, *Like People You See in a Dream: First Contact in Six Papuan Societies* (Stanford, Stanford University Press), for a superb cross-cultural reconstruction of first meetings with European patrols in the Papua New Guinea highlands during the 1930s, when the Europeans were routinely understood to be ghosts or spirits.

3. Elliott in Holmes, ed., 1984, 34.

4. Forster, George, in Thomas and Berghof, eds., 2000, II:480–81.

5. Cited in McCormick, Eric, 1977, *Omai, Pacific Envoy* (Auckland, Auckland University Press, Oxford University Press), 73. My thanks to Amiria Salmond for alerting me to Banks's visit to Monboddo in Scotland.

6. These carved gongs were erected in clearings in the bush, and were used for signalling ritual occasions in Malakula; see Cheesman, 1949, 36–8, 50.

7. According to Michael Hoare, these fish were probably red snapper (*Lutjanus Bohar* Forksal), which had eaten herbivorous fish which in their turn had eaten fine algae, the source of the toxin which caused this ciguatera poisoning. The toxin is about as poisonous as rattlesnake venom. (Hoare, 1982, IV:570fn.)

8. Forster, Johann, in Hoare, ed., 1982, IV:578.

9. Cheesman, 1949, 146–9 recounts local oral histories of Cook's arrival at Erromango: 'When the Erromangans, who had never seen white men before, saw two boat-loads of them apparently coming from the Place of the Dead one can picture their panic! It was natural that they should think these were beings from the other world, the ghosts of a former tribe, come back on a visit. Their only idea was to destroy them before they could do any harm.' See also Robertson, H.A., 1903, *Erromanga, the Martyr Isle* (London, Hodder and Stoughton), 14–19: 'The great

white *nobu* or gods . . . came to their land long ago, and struck terror into the hearts of the people by their wonderful fire and the huge floating *lo* or kingdom in which they lived. Potnilo said that one man only – Narom, the chief – was killed outright by the whites, the other natives who were wounded soon recovered . . . A woman who was gathering food in her plantation . . . *had a finger shot clean off by a cannon ball!*'

10. According to Jean Guiart, at the time of Cook's visit there was fighting going on between the Karumene and their Neraymene allies on the eastern side of Port Resolution, and the more numerous and powerful Enekahi on the western side, who were backed by the Kasurumene who lived near the volcano. Guiart, Jean, 1956, *Un siècle et demi de contacts culturels à Tanna (Nouvelles-Hebrides)* (Paris, Musée de l'Homme), 11–14, 90–92.

11. Forster, George, in Thomas and Berghof, eds., 2000, II:512.

12. Forster, George, in Thomas and Berghof, eds., 2000, II:519.

13. Adams, Ron, 1984, *In the Land of Strangers: A Century of European Contact with Tanna, 1774–1874* (Pacific Research Monograph Number Nine, Australian National University), 14–15.

14. Forster, George, in Thomas and Berghof, eds., 2000, II:534.

15. Forster, George, in Thomas and Berghof, eds., 2000, II:533–4.

16. Adams, 1984, 10–11, 18.

17. Cook in Beaglehole, ed., 1969, II:490.

18. Wales in Beaglehole, ed., 1969, II:859–60.

19. Hoare, ed., 1982, 605fn.

20. Note George Forster's flat denial that his father kicked and spat at the man; although by his own admission, Johann had struck 'natives' on other occasions.

21. Forster, Johann, in Hoare, ed., 1982, IV:606–7.

22. Cook in Beaglehole, ed., 1969, II:499.

23. Sparrman in Rutter, ed., 1953, 151.

24. It is worth noting that Clerke had been disloyal to Cook before, although in private, when he corresponded with Joseph Banks before the *Resolution* left England, criticising his plan for loading the ship, and hinting that Cook might have allowed the sloop to be altered in such a way as to make it impossible to take Banks and his entourage on the voyage.

25. Cook in Beaglehole, ed., 1969, II:398.

26. Cook in Beaglehole, ed., 1969, II:493.

27. Elliott in Holmes, ed., 1984, 34.

28. Adams, 1984, 31.

29. Elliott in Holmes, ed., 1984, 32.

30. Douglas, Bronwen, 1970, 'A Contact History of the Balad People of New Caledonia 1774–1845', *Journal of the Polynesian Society*, 79, 180–200. Bronwen Douglas explains that Ouvea is not a Polynesian outlier but one district of the island which was settled by people from Wallis Island (Urea), who then called the island by the name of their homeland (Douglas, pers. comm. 2002).

31. Douglas, Bronwen, 1994, 'Discourses on Death in a Melanesian World' in Donna

Merwick, ed., *Dangerous Liaisons: Essays in Honour of Greg Dening* (Melbourne, History Department, University of Melbourne), 362.

32. Clerke in Beaglehole, ed., 1969, II:763.

33. Forster, Johann, in Hoare, ed., 1982, IV:647.

34. Clerke in Beaglehole, ed., 1969, II:764.

35. Forster, Johann, in Hoare, ed., 1982, IV:670.

36. Forster, George, in Thomas and Berghof, eds., 2000, II:600.

37. Forster, George, in Thomas and Berghof, eds., 2000, II:597.

38. Forster, George, in Thomas and Berghof, eds., 2000, II:604.

39. Cook in Beaglehole, ed., 1969, II:571.

40. Cook in Beaglehole, ed., 1969, II:572.

41. Cook in Beaglehole, ed., 1969, II:577.

42. Cook in Beaglehole, ed., 1969, II:576fn.

43. Elliott in Holmes, ed., 1984, 36.

44. Cook in Beaglehole, ed., 1969, II:578.

45. Forster, Johann, in Hoare, ed., 1982, IV:684.

46. Cook in Beaglehole, ed., 1969, II:587.

47. Sparrman in Rutter, ed., 1953, 192–3.

48. Forster, Johann, in Hoare, ed., 1982, IV:697.

49. Forster, Johann, in Hoare, ed., 1982, IV:713.

50. Cook in Beaglehole, ed., 1969, II:643.

51. Elliott in Holmes, ed., 1984, 44.

52. Cook in Beaglehole, ed., 1969, II:870.

53. Cook in Beaglehole, ed., 1969, II:653.

54. Elliott in Holmes, ed., 1984, 44.

55. Quoted in McCormick, 1977, 151.

56. Elliott in Holmes, ed., 1984, 45.

14

A Tahitian at the Opera

1. Walpole quoted in Carter, 1988, 120.

2. Boswell, James, 1992, *The Life of Samuel Johnson* (New York, Alfred A. Knopf), 476–7.

3. Anon., 1778, *Transmigration: A Poem* (London), 29–32. A number of satirical poems and cartoons on this theme were published at about this time; see McCormick, 1977, 73–187, and Miller and Reill, eds., 1996, 153–93 for examples.

4. Burney, Fanny, ed. Lars E. Troide, 1990, *The Early Journals and Letters of Fanny Burney, Volume II: 1774–1777* (Oxford, Clarendon Press), 41.

5. Burney, James, in Hooper, ed., 1975, 70–72. For accounts of Mai's life, see also *The Gentleman's Magazine and Historical Chronicle*, vol. XLIV, 388; letter from Solander in Beaglehole, ed., 1969, II:949.

6. *The Gentleman's Magazine and Historical Chronicle*, vol. XLIV, 330.

7. Quoted in McCormick, 1977, 112.

8. For Fanny Burney's account, see Burney, ed. Troide, 1990, 59–63.

9. Revd. Sir John Cullum, quoted in McCormick, 1977, 129.

10. Lord Sandwich, quoted in McCormick, 1977, 132.

11. *London Chronicle*, 20–22 April 1775, 382.

12. Burney, Fanny, ed. Troide, 1990, 91–2.

13. Anon, 1775, *An Historic Epistle, from Omiah* (London).

14. Solander in Beaglehole, ed., 1969, II:953.

15. Solander in Beaglehole, ed., 1969, II:957.

16. Clerke to Banks, 30 July 1775, in Beaglehole, ed., 1969, II:953.

17. Solander to Banks, 14 August 1775, in Beaglehole, ed., 1969, II:959.

18. Cook to Capt. John Walker, 19 August 1774, in Beaglehole, ed., 1969, II:960.

19. For Fanny Burney's account of this visit, see Burney, ed., Troide, 1990, 193–7.

20. Cook to John Walker, 14 February 1776, in Beaglehole, ed., 1967, II:1488.

21. Wales quoted in Hoare, 1982, I:71.

22. Trevenen, James, ed. Christopher Lloyd and R.C. Anderson, 1959, *A Memoir of James Trevenen* (London, Spottiswoode, Ballantyne and Co. Ltd, printed for the Navy Records Society), 36.

23. Cook quoted by Johann Forster, in McCormick, 1977, 178.

24. Boswell, James ed. Ryskamp, 1962, *Boswell: the Ominous Years 1774–1776* (Melbourne, William Heinemann Ltd), 308.

25. Boswell, 1962, 309.

26. Boswell, 1962, 659–60.

27. See Williamson: 'Whoever was the Occasion of sending these Animals out, merits much Praise, & could New Zealand be properly stock'd with them, It's more than probable, it would make a most pleasing Alteration in their Customs & Manners, some of which are so shocking, & contrary to Nature that it is horrid to think of, what secret Pleasure must they feel whose Humanity had extended to ye Relief & Rescue of those unhappy People from these dreadful & offensive Customs.' (Williamson in Adm 55/117:1.)

28. These engravings are now held in the library of the Peter the Great Museum of Anthropology and Ethnography in St. Petersburg. For an account of their provenance see Ivanova, L.A., 2000, 'J. Cook's Collection: Engravings of Drawings by artist W. Hodges held in Peter the Great Kunstkammer'. My grateful thanks to Mariya Vladimirovna Stanyukovich and Yuri K. Chistov, the Director of the Museum, for allowing me to visit this collection (which includes a number of feather capes and helmets, a tabooing wand, a boar tusk bracelet and a glorious makaloa mat from Hawai'i; a shell chest apron, a breast gorget and several fish-hooks from Tahiti; and two combs and a basket from Tonga in addition to the Hodges engravings), presented by Captain Clerke to the Governor during his visit to Kamchatka near the end of the third voyage.

29. For manuscript records of Cook's third Pacific voyage, see British Museum: James Cook's *Resolution* Journal, Eg. Ms 2177A, B; 2178-2179; James Burney's *Discovery* Journal, Add Ms 8955; John Webber's Drawings, Add Ms 15513; John Webber's Drawings, Add Ms 17277; George Gilbert's *Discovery* Journal, Add Ms 38530; David Samwell's *Discovery* Journal, Egerton Ms 2591; Thomas Edgar's

Discovery Journal, Add Ms 37528; John Law's *Discovery* Journal, Add Ms 37327; Public Record Office: James Cook's *Resolution* Journal (copy), Adm 55/111; Charles Clerke's *Discovery* Log, Adm 55/22, 23; Charles Clerke's *Log and Observations*, Adm 51/4561/217; Adm 55/124; John Gore's *Resolution* Log, Adm 55/120; Adm 51/4532/49; James King's *Resolution* Log, Adm 55/116; Adm 55/122; James Burney's *Discovery* Journal, Adm 51/4528/45; John Williamson's *Resolution* Log, Adm 55/117; John Rickman's *Discovery* Log, Adm 51/4529/46; Thomas Edgar's *Discovery* Log, Adm 55/21; Adm 55/24; George Gilbert's *Resolution* Log, Adm 51/4559/213; William Lanyon's *Resolution* Log, Adm 51/4558/196-198; William Harvey's *Resolution* Log, Adm 55/110; William Charlton's *Resolution* Journal, Adm 51/4557/191-193; John Martin's *Discovery* Journal, Adm 51/4531/47; George Gilbert's *Resolution* Journal, Adm 51/4559/213-215; Mathew Paul's *Resolution* Log, Adm 51/4560/209; Nathaniel Portlock's *Discovery* Log, Adm 51/4531/67-69; Adm 51/4532/70; Edward Riou's *Discovery* Log, Adm 51/4529/41-44; William Shuttleworth's *Resolution* Journal, Adm 51/4561/210-211; Adm 51/4531/48; William Taylor's *Resolution* Log, Adm 51/4561/216; John Watt's *Resolution* Log, Adm 51/4559/212; Anonymous, Logs Adm 51/4528/64; Adm 51/4530/65-66, 71-72; Adm 51/4561/220; Adm 51/4561/221; Adm 55/114, 123; William Bayly's *Discovery* Log and Journal, Adm 55/20; William Anderson's *Resolution* Journal, Adm 51/4560/203-204. Dixson Library, Library of New South Wales: James King's *Resolution* Log Ms; Henry Robert's *Resolution* Log Ms (Ms Q/51-51); William Griffin's Narrative; J. Dimsdell, Account of the Death and Remains of Capt. Cook – at Owhyhee recd from Joshua Lee Dimsdell Quarter Master of the Gunjara Capt. James Barber. 1801 (MS Q 154); Mitchell Library: James Burney's *Discovery* Journal; Anonymous, 1781. Copy of Letter to Mrs Strachan of Spithead, 23 January 1781 (Safe 1/67); National Library of Australia: Alexander Home's *Discovery* notes and typescript (Ms 690); Anonymous, Account of the Death of Cook, 9–22 February 1779, by an Eyewitness; Alexander Turnbull Library: William Bayly's *Discovery* Journal; James Trevenen's *Resolution* notes.

30. Samwell to Mathew Gregson, 22 October 1776, quoted in Beaglehole, ed., 1967, II:1515.

31. Cook in Beaglehole, ed., 1967, II:734.

32. Samwell to Mathew Gregson, 22 October 1776, quoted in Beaglehole, ed., 1967, II:1515.

33. Cook to William Strahan, 5 November 1776, in Beaglehole, ed., 1967, II:1516.

34. Clerke to Joseph Banks, 23 November 1776, in Beaglehole, ed., 1967, II:1518.

35. Cook to Lord Sandwich, 26 November 1776, in Beaglehole, ed., 1967, II:1520.

36. Gore to Joseph Banks, 27 November 1776, in Beaglehole, ed., 1967, II:1522.

37. Burney in Adm 51/4528/45:178.

38. Martin in Adm 51/4531/47:14.

39. Cook in Beaglehole, ed., 1967, I:55–6. See the account of this meeting in Mulvaney, D.J., 1989, *Encounters in Place: Outsiders and Aboriginal Australians 1606–1985* (St. Lucia, University of Queensland Press), 33–5.

40. Cook in Beaglehole, ed., 1967, I:59.

41. Samwell in Beaglehole, ed., 1967, II:995.

42. Cook in Beaglehole, ed., 1967, I:61–2.

43. Cook in Beaglehole, ed., 1967, I:64.

44. Burney, James, in McNab, Robert, 1914, *Historical Records of New Zealand*, II:198–9.

45. Cook in Beaglehole, ed., 1967, I:68.

15

The Glorious Children of Te Tumu

1. Clerke quoted in Beaglehole, ed., 1967, I:69.

2. Cook in Beaglehole, ed., 1967, I:71.

3. Smith, Bernard 1992, *Imagining the Pacific: In the Wake of the Cook Voyages* (Melbourne, Melbourne University Press), 207.

4. King quoted in Beaglehole, ed., 1967, I:77fn.

5. Watt, Sir James, in Robin Fisher and Hugh Johnston, eds., 1979, *Medical Aspects and Consequences of Cook's Voyages*, 152–7.

6. Gill, Rev. William Wyatt, 1880, *Historical Sketches of Savage Life in Polynesia* (Wellington, George Didsbury, Government Printer), 187.

7. Driessen, Hank, 1982, 'Outriggerless Canoes and Glorious Beings', *The Journal of Pacific History*, XVII, 8–9.

8. Jukka Siikala, pers. comm. 1999.

9. Williams, John, 1838, *A Narrative of Missionary Enterprises in the South Sea Islands* (London, J. Snow), 57, 104.

10. Henry, 1928, 126–8; see also Finney, Ben, 1999, 'The Sin at Avarua', *The Contemporary Pacific*, 11/1, 1–33.

11. There was a sacred site called Taputapuatea at Whitianga (Mercury Bay), which was also the ancient name of Mokoia Island (Paul Tapsell, pers. comm. 2000) in the middle of Lake Rotorua. According to Judge Joe Williams of the Maori Land Court, there are many other sites with this name scattered around New Zealand, including one on Mangonui Bluff, and another in Tauranga; which suggests that if such sites had any association with the arioi cult, it had spread at least throughout the northern North Island (pers. comm. 2002). There is also a heiau called Kapukapuakea in the Hawai'ian islands.

12. Gore quoted in Beaglehole, ed., 1967, I:87fn.

13. Burney in Adm 51/4528/45:193.

14. Burney in Adm 51/4528/45:194.

15. When a trading ship called the *City of Edinburgh* visited Nomuka in 1808, an elderly chief took the captain and his officers to sleep in the house used by Cook and his men during this visit (Salmond, 1997, 377).

16. Samwell in Beaglehole, ed., 1967, I:1014.

17. Ledyard, for example, described Finau as 'one of the most graceful men I ever saw in the Pacific ocean . . . He was open and free in his disposition, ful of vivacity, enterpizing and bold, expert in all the acquirements of his country, particularly in their art of navigation . . . He was besides extremely handsome. With all these

accomplishments he was extremely popular among the people.' (Ledyard, 1963, 28.)

18. Queen Salote in Bott, 1982, 19, 49. According to Queen Salote, Finau was also known as Tu'i halafatai; and the missionary John Thomas, in his manuscript history of Tonga, also made this identification. Although John Beaglehole, drawing on evidence from William Mariner, the first European to live in Tonga, identified him as Finau Ulukalala Feletoa, the son of the Finau who was Mariner's patron and protector, this is probably mistaken (Martin, ed., 1991, 279). According to Queen Salote, Mariner's patron may have been trying to elevate his ancestor by claiming this association with Cook.

19. See Queen Salote in Bott, 1982, 89–164 for an expert insider's account of the 'three King' system. For further information on the Tongan ranking system, see Gifford, Edward Winslow, 1929, *Tongan Society* (Honolulu, Bernice P. Bishop Museum Bulletin 61). I am greatly indebted to the anthropologist Meredith Filihia for her writings on Tongan rituals in this period, and her advice on Tongan ethnography.

20. William Mariner, the first European to live on Tonga, gave many examples of arbitrary chiefly behaviour, including a high chief who ordered twelve of his serving men to have their arms amputated, simply to distinguish them from other men; and another who ordered a man to be shot to test the accuracy of a musket, and who answered when he was rebuked that the man 'was only a low, vulgar fellow; and that neither his life nor death was of any consequence to society'. (Martin, John, ed., 1991, *Tonga Islands: William Mariner's Account* (Tonga, Vava'u Press), 70, 62–3.)

21. Anderson in Beaglehole, ed., 1967, II:865–6.

22. Heads were shaved as a sign of mourning when the Tu'i Tonga died; but it was degrading to have this done as a punishment. (Mariner in Martin, ed., 1991, 61.)

23. Clerke in Beaglehole, ed., 1967, II:1310.

24. King in Beaglehole, ed., 1967, II:1361–2.

25. Samwell in Beaglehole, ed., 1967, II:1020–21.

26. Clerke in Beaglehole, ed., 1967, II:1310.

27. Mariner in Martin, ed., 1991, 279–80.

28. Martin in Adm 51/4531/47:34.

29. Anderson in Beaglehole, ed., 1967, II:881.

30. See the genealogy in Bott, 1982, 86.

31. Samwell in Beaglehole, ed., 1967, II:1024.

32. Queen Salote in Bott, 1982, 50.

33. Clerke in Beaglehole, ed., 1967, II:1304.

34. See Queen Salote in Bott, 1982, 28.

35. Bayly, William, Log on HMS *Discovery*, 11 June 1776–29, April 1779. ATL fms-016:105.

36. William Mariner, for instance, quotes Finau, his Tongan patron, as saying, 'Oh, that the gods would make me King of England! There is not an island in the whole world, however small, but what I would then subject to my power. The King of England does not deserve the dominion he enjoys. Possessed of so many great ships, why does he suffer such petty islands as those of Tonga continually to insult his people . . . ? Were I he, would I send tamely to *ask* for yams and pigs? No, I would come with the *front of battle*, and with the *thunder of Bolotane*. I would show who

ought to be chief. None but men of enterprising spirit should be in possession of guns. Let such rule the earth, and be those their vassal who can bear to submit to such insults unrevenged!' (Mariner in Martin, ed., 1991, 230.)

37. Burney in Adm 51/4528/45:203–204.

38. See the 'Calendar of Punishments' (pp. 433–7) for 11 June–17 July 1777. While they were at Tongatapu, one of the marines, Thomas Harford, was flogged twice in one week; three other marines were punished for neglect of duty; a cooper for disobedience and neglect; a sailor for striking an Indian chief; and a cook's mate for neglect of duty.

39. Cook in Beaglehole, ed., 1967, I:101.

40. See Herda, Phyllis, 1987, 'Gender, Rank and Power in 18th Century Tonga', *The Journal of Pacific History*, XXII/4, 195–208.

41. See Herda, 1987, 200; Kirch and Green, 2001, 267–73; Perminow, Arne, 2001, 'Captain Cook and the Roots of Precedence in Tonga', *History and Anthropology*, 12/3, 289–314. Perminow also quotes the Tongan ritual expert Havili Hafoka: 'They did not start the planting of the new yam crop haphazardly . . . but looked for the time when the rise of the *Mataliki* (the Seven Sisters) corresponds with the early dawn, and they cut the seed yam of the first yam-crop on that day . . . With the rise of the *Mataliki* all growing things were made free to grow, and corresponding to the name of this cluster of stars the small buds of the yam crop start growing in this month, and by the same means all growing things awaken.' Meredith Filihia has sent me her translation of the text of an old Tongan calendar:

> I am Hilinga-Kelekele
> The leaves take shelter in me
> The yam harvest takes place.
> The time of celebration of plenty takes place.
> The reason I am called thus
> Is because of the new yam harvest
> Its skin is still covered in soil.
> Build a new shelter and place them there;
>
> I am 'Uluenga
> Starvation has been pushed away.
> The early yam crop begins to grow.
> Hope comes with me.
> The land has grown leaves.
> All things work together in its shade.
> The fishermen look for their nets.

When there's not much food on land, complete it from the sea. (Filihia, pers. comm. 2002.)

42. See Perminow, 2001. Meredith Filihia (pers. comm. 2001) argues that the installation of Fatafehi was conducted alongside the 'Inasi, but was not strictly part of that ritual cycle, which I find persuasive. John Thomas referred to the ritual installation of Fatafehi as a *fakahikihiki* [lit. 'to raise'; ML typescript:246].

43. Bligh quoted in Beaglehole, ed., 1967, I:133fn.

44. Samwell in Beaglehole, ed., 1967, II:1042.

45. See Mariner in Martin, ed., 1991, 94–6 for a description of a very similar ceremony which was held to raise a tapu.

46. Williamson in Adm 55/117.

47. Gilbert in Holmes, Christine, ed., 1982, *Captain Cook's Final Voyage: The Journal of Midshipman George Gilbert* (London, Caliban Books), 33–4.

48. King quoted in Beaglehole, ed., 1967, I:174fn.

49. Wooden bowls dedicated to the gods were used for divination in Tonga. See Mariner in Martin, ed., 1991, 106, and 355 for an account of how successive Tu'i Tonga used Cook's pewter bowl for these purposes.

50. John Thomas, a missionary who worked in Tonga for many years after 1825, wrote in his unpublished journals: 'a solemn yearly gathering of chiefs and priests ... to present the ... first young yams to the gods at Tu'i Tonga's house in Mu'a, ... to bless the seed now about to be put into the ground that the yam set may bring forth a crop.' (Thomas, John, Journals 1825–59, Mitchell Library FM 4/1439:262.)

51. Fakaheheua e Tala mei Kauhala'uta – The Straying of the Tradition of the Kauhala'uta, Palace Office File No. 120/2B. This manuscript was located and translated by Meredith Filihia.

52. Williamson quoted in Beaglehole, ed., 1967, I:151fn.

53. Thomas, 1825–59, 67.

54. For later information about the 'Inasi ceremony, see Mariner in Martin, ed., 1991, 147, 289 and 342–6.

55. Bayly, 1778, 107.

56. Gilbert in Holmes, ed., 1982, 35.

16

Farewell to Elysium

1. Cook in Beaglehole, ed., 1967, I:186.

2. Samwell in Beaglehole, ed., 1967, II:1054–5.

3. See Eddowe's unpublished paper on Vehiatua II for a detailed account of the breaches of tapu, the consternation they caused, and their impact on the young high chief (Eddowes, pers. comm. 2001).

4. Williamson in Adm 55/117, Aug 12 1777.

5. King in Beaglehole, ed., 1967, II:1372.

6. King in Beaglehole, ed., 1967, II:1373.

7. Rickman, John, 1785, *Journal of Captain Cook's Last Voyage to the Pacific Ocean on Discovery* (London, E. Newbury), 131–3.

8. Samwell in Beaglehole, ed., 1967, II:1058–9.

9. Rickman, 1785, 139–40.

10. Although according to Tupaia, they had their own marae in Tahiti (see Banks, ed. Beaglehole, 1962, II:383).

11. Morrison, 1935, 117.

12. See the excellent account of this sacrifice by Roger and Kaye Green, in which texts, images and archaeological information are used to unravel some muddles (Green, Roger C. and Kaye, 1968, 'Religious Structures (*Marae*) of the Windward Society Islands: The Significance of Certain Historical Records', *New Zealand Journal of History*, II, 66–89).

13. According to the astronomer Bayly, the ariki women would not sleep with the junior officers: 'Otoo's Sisters would almost do any thing with us except Cohabiting with us – and that was not to be done under any consideration whatever – Either with them or any other Aree Woman – or a woman that was to be married – but they most of them Cohabit Peeree-peeree [piripiri] as they term it – which is performed thus the man sits down on his backside & the woman lays down on her back with her thighs over his & by contracting her selfe passes up & Down the penis & the girls are so dextrous in the management of the operation that our people have lain several times with a girl without discovering the deception.' (Bayly, 27 September 1777, 15.)

14. King in Beaglehole, ed., 1967, II:1376.

15. Griffin quoted in Beaglehole, ed., 1967, I:210.

16. Home, 1778, 1.

17. Cook in Beaglehole, ed., 1967, I:214.

18. Alexander Home NLA Ms, 25 September 1777.

19. Samwell in Beaglehole, ed., 1967, II:1055.

20. Home quoted in Beaglehole, ed., 1967, I:227fn.

21. King in Beaglehole, ed., 1967, II:1382.

22. Gilbert in Holmes, ed., 1982, 46–7.

23. King in Beaglehole, ed., 1967, II:1383.

24. Williamson in Adm 55/117.

25. Cook in Beaglehole, ed., 1967, I:231–2.

26. According to Bayly, 13 October 1777, 'Omi is very ill at present & Capt Cook is a little indisposed at present . . . We have half of our people ill with the fowl disease [VD] & 4 or 5 has had the Yellow jaundice' (Bayly 1776–1779 Log on H.M.S. *Discovery* ATL fms 016:23); while Rickman noted on 26 October that 'Capt. Cook, though he rode out every day, attended by Omai, still continued in a very weak condition'; adding on 28 October that Captain Cook was 'now pretty well recovered' (Rickman, 1785, 162, 163).

27. Burney, James, 1819, *A Chronological History of North-Eastern Voyages of Discovery* (London, Payne and Foss), 233.

28. Zimmermann, 1929, 58.

29. Samwell in Beaglehole, ed., 1967, II:1070; although Rickman claimed that the sentry was sentenced to a flogging of 24 lashes each day for six days, but forgiven after the first day's flogging. (Rickman, n.d., 167.)

30. Rickman, 1785, 166.

31. Bayly, 31 October in Log on H.M.S. *Discovery* ATL fms 016:27.

32. Cook in Beaglehole, ed., 1967, I:240–41.

33. Samwell in Beaglehole, ed., 1967, II:1072–3.

34. Home typescript NLA Ms 690: 25–26 November 1777.

35. Home NLA Ms: 25–26 November 1777.

36. Williamson in Adm 55/117.

37. Bayly quoted in Beaglehole, ed., 1967, I:251fn.

38. King in Beaglehole, ed., 1967, II:1390–91.

39. Kamakau, Samuel, 1992, *Ruling Chiefs of Hawai'i* (Honolulu, The Kamehameha Schools Press), 92. For Hawai'ian accounts of Cook's first arrival, see Kamakau, 1992, 92–5.

40. Kamakau, 1992, 93.

41. Cook in Beaglehole, ed, 1967, I:265.

42. King quoted in Beaglehole, ed., 1967, I:265fn.

43. Cook in Beaglehole, ed., 1967, I:266.

44. Samwell in Beaglehole, ed., 1967, II:1084.

45. Fornander, Abraham, 1969, *An Account of the Polynesian Race* (Rutland, Tuttle), II:168–9.

46. See Kamakau, 1992, 94–5.

47. Cited in Kamakau, Samuel, 1964, *Ka Po'e Kahiko: The People of Old* (Honolulu, The Bishop Museum Press), 54.

48. Beckwith, Martha, ed., 1951, *The Kumulipo: A Hawaiian Creation Chant* (Honolulu, University of Hawai'i Press), 20–21.

49. For an excellent critical examination of the various stories about Lono-i-ka-Makahiki, see Cordy, Ross, 2000, *Exalted Sits the Chief: The Ancient History of Hawai'i Island* (Honolulu, Mutual Publishing), 225–39. Cordy dates Lono-i-ka-Makahiki's rule to AD1640–1660.

50. For accounts of these debates and their conclusion, see Bingham's journal of the American mission 19 September 1822, ABCFM/M; Hawai'ian text collected by Hiram Bingham in 1824 in J.S. Emerson Collection of the Bishop Museum – HEN 1: 648–52; account from Kekupuohi, wife of Kalaniopu'u, collected by Laura Judd at Kealakekua in 1829 in Judd, Laura Fish, 1966, *Honolulu: Sketches of Life in the Hawaiian Islands from 1828 to 1861* (Chicago, Lakeside Press), 64–5; Kamakau, 1992, 94–103; Kahananui, Dorothy, ed., 1984, *Ka Moolelo Hawaii*, trans. and ed. from the 1838 edition by Dorothy Kahananui (Honolulu, University of Hawai'i), 171–3; Hawai'ian text: 12, 18.

51. See Byron, Capt. the Right Honourable Lord Byron, 1826, *Voyage of H.M.S. Blonde to the Sandwich Islands in the Years 1824–1825* (London, John Murray), 21.

52. Although this man has been identified as Kumahana, Herb Kane points out that Kumahana was an old man at that time, and that it is much more likely to have been Kaneoneo, a much younger high-born leader. (Herb Kane, pers. comm. 2002.)

53. Cook in Beaglehole, ed., 1967, I:276.

54. Williamson in Adm 55/117.

55. Cook in Beaglehole, ed., 1967, I:279.

17

Killing Kuki

1. Clerke quoted in Beaglehole, 1967, I:288fn.
2. See the excellent discussion of this survey in David, Andrew, ed., 1997, *The Charts and Coastal Views of Captain Cook's Voyages. Vol. III: The Voyage of the Resolution and Discovery 1776–1780* (London, the Hakluyt Society), xlv–liv.
3. Trevenen, 1959, 20.
4. Gilbert, 1982, 83.
5. Home, Alexander, 1778–9, 'The Account of Ottihiti and our Transactions' by Captain Alexander Home, R.N., typescript manuscript, NLA Ms690, in Log Book:4.
6. Anon., letter to Mrs Strachan of Spithead, Mitchell Library ML Safe 1/67:5b.
7. Trevenen, 1959, 26–7.
8. For an account of the sacred high chief Kalani'opu'u, his ancestors and his battles, see Kamakau, 1992, 34–104. See also Charles Ahlo and Jerry Walker, eds., 2000, *Kamehameha's Children Today* (Honolulu, J. Walker), 21–42.
9. For stories of Lono-i-ka-Makahiki, see Fornander, 1919, 256–363; Kamakau, 1992, 47–63.
10. Sahlins, Marshall, 1995, *How 'Natives' Think, About Captain Cook, For Example* (Chicago, University of Chicago Press), 22, 17–84; see also Sahlins, Marshall, 1989, 'Captain Cook at Hawaii', *Journal of the Polynesian Society*, 98/4, 371–423, and a number of other articles (cited in these works) which outline the evolution of his thinking about Cook's death in Hawai'i.
11. See Sahlins, 1989, 406–9 for an analysis of the Makahiki tapu on fishing.
12. See Bergendoff, Steen, Hasager, Ulla, and Henriques, Peter, 1988, 'Mythopraxis and History: On the Interpretation of the Makahiki', *Journal of the Polynesian Society*, 97, 391–408; Obeyesekere, Gananath, 1992, *The Apotheosis of Captain Cook: European Myth-making in the Pacific* (New Jersey, Princeton University Press); and ripostes by Sahlins in Sahlins, 1989, 1995. Despite these critics, my own reading of sources suggests that the identification of Cook with Lono-i-Makahiki, a former high chief, was indeed one of the ways in which Hawai'ians sought to explain their strange visitors; and that this identification became an orthodoxy promoted by the priests at Kealakekua, as Sahlins has argued.
13. Ledyard, 1963, 102.
14. Watts, quoted in Beaglehole, ed., 1967, I:480fn.
15. Watts in Cook, 1967, I:480fn.
16. Trevenen, 1959, 27–8.
17. Trevenen, 1959, 21.
18. Williamson in Beaglehole, ed., 1967, II:1348–9.
19. There is a striking resemblance between the precipitous cliffs at Kealakekua Bay, and those at Runswick Bay, just south of Staithes, for example.
20. Gilbert in Holmes, ed., 1982, 101.

21. Samwell in Beaglehole, ed., 1967, II:1158.

22. Ledyard, 1963, 103.

23. Ellis, William, 1782, *An Authentic Narrative of a Voyage Performed by Captain Cook and Captain Clerke* (London, G. Robinson), II:85.

24. King in Beaglehole, 1967, I:504.

25. Beckwith, ed., 1951, 18–24.

26. For an interesting interpretation of this ritual, see Valeri, Valerio, 1991, 'The Transformation of a Transformation: A Structural Essay on an Aspect of Hawaiian History (1809–1819)' in Biersach, A., ed., *Clio in Oceania: Toward an Historical Anthropology* (Washington D.C., Smithsonian Institute Press), 101–64 (especially pp. 133–7; for Valeri's account of the Makahiki and the *luakini* temple rituals, see Valeri, Valerio, 1985, *Kingship and Sacrifice: Ritual and Society in Ancient Hawaii* (Chicago, University of Chicago Press), 191–339.

27. King in James Cook and James King, 1784, *A Voyage to the Pacific Ocean . . . on His Majesty's Ships* Resolution *and* Discovery (Dublin, Chamberlaine *et. al*), II:131.

28. Samwell in Beaglehole, ed., 1967, II:1162.

29. Herb Kane, pers. comm. 2002; see also Cordy's excellent account of the layout and political context in the bay in 1779 (Cordy, 2000, 248–58; 292–308).

30. Samwell in Beaglehole, ed., 1967, II:1164.

31. Ledyard, 1963, 111.

32. Charlton in Beaglehole, ed., 1967, I:511fn.

33. Rickman, 1967, 300–301.

34. Unfortunately the European journalists persistently confused 'Koa' or 'Koah' [Ko'a'a] and 'Kao' or 'Kaoo' [Kau], since the names sounded similar to them; and Beaglehole's edition of the journals offers 'corrections' of these name switches which may not always be accurate.

35. For a Hawai'ian account of high chiefs as gods, see the explanation by John I'i, a former priest, in 1841: 'Another sort of kapu that I have seen [is that of the] high chiefs, and especially the king. They were called gods by some, because their houses were sacred and everything that pertained to their persons. Many, very many were the deadly kapus connected with the persons and properties of the chiefs . . . If anything was carried to or from the chief, the carrier cried out aloud to all, to fall prostrate, which all did, throwing off their kapas . . . If they had something they could not get rid of at once, the only way was to fall prostrate. It would have been death to have stood up. So you see, our chiefs used to be gods.' (In Thrum, Thomas, 1889, *Hawaiian Almanac and Annual for 1890* (Honolulu, Press Publishing Company Steam Print), 59.) See also Beckwith: 'The child of a *pi'o* union was an *akua*, a god' (Beckwith, ed., 1951, 13). Beckwith goes on to explain that Kalani'opu'u's father, Ka-'I-'i-mamao, as the first born of his mother, 'was held to be a god among men, with from infancy the rank of a *niaupi'o* chief entitled to the strictest of taboo rights, the *kapu moe* or prostrating taboo, the *kapu wela* or burning taboo. Commoners must fall on their faces before him, chiefs of low rank must crouch in approaching him. If he went abroad by day he was preceded by the cry *Tapu! moe!* . . . The prostration taboo with the penalty for its infraction of death by burning, the

terrible *Kapu wela o na li'i*, tradition says was brought from the island of Kauai . . . into Maui at the time of the ruling chief Kekaulike, who must have been a near contemporary of Ka-'I-'i-mamao, since his daughter Kalola became wife to that chief's son [i.e. Kalanio'opu'u].' (Beckwith, ed., 1952, 16). Kalani'opu'u, as the eldest son of their marriage, was honoured with the same *kapu* as his father.

36. In Tahiti, for example, when Maximo Rodriguez, a very early Spanish resident on the island, changed names with Tu, he was expected to grieve for Tu's uncle as if he was his own. Tu's mother explained 'that I must share in their sorrow, because I was related to all the deceased ari'i, inasmuch as he was related to all the chiefs' (Corney, 1919, III:31).

37. Samwell in Beaglehole, ed., 1967, II:1184.

38. Obeyesekere, 1992, 3–22.

39. Sahlins, 1985, 69–71.

40. For Kalani'opu'u's ancestry see Kamakau, 1992, 78–9; for the story of Kalani'opu'u's grandmother, Lono-ma-'I-kanaka, giving his father, Ka-'I-'i-mamao, the title Lono-i-ka-Makahiki at the time of his birth, see Beckwith, ed., 1951, 8, quoting Liliuokalani. Note also Beckwith: 'In each human birth of a *niaupi'o* child there lived anew a Lono to preserve and carry forward the sacred stock.' (Beckwith, ed., 1951, 21.) This identification with Kalani'opu'u's father may explain why the Hawai'ians greeted Cook as 'Lono-makua' [Lono the parent].

41. King in Beaglehole, ed., 1967, I:513.

42. Samwell in Beaglehole, ed., 1967, II:1171–2.

43. Samwell in Beaglehole, ed., 1967, II:1171.

44. King in Beaglehole, ed., 1967, I:519fn.

45. Ledyard, 1963, 135. For the comic aspect of the Makahiki and Lono as a 'god of the carnival', see Valeri, 1985, 222–5.

46. Portlock, Nathaniel, 1789, *A Voyage Round the World; but More Particularly to the North-West Coast of America, Performed in 1785, 1786, 1787, and 1788* (London, John Stockdale), 166.

47. King in Beaglehole, ed., 1967, I:525.

48. King in Beaglehole, ed., 1967, I:527.

49. King in Beaglehole, ed., 1967, I:527.

50. Ledyard, 1963, 141.

51. King in Beaglehole, ed., 1967, I:528.

52. Burney in Beaglehole, ed., 1967, I:528.

53. Anon., letter to Mrs Strachan of Spithead, Mitchell Library ML Safe 1/67:14b.

54. Home, 1779, in Log Book:1.

55. King in Beaglehole, ed., 1967, I:529.

56. Edgar was said to have been a hard-drinking man, who was not on good terms with his captain, Clerke: 'He was a good sailor and navigator, or rather had been for he drank very hard, so as to entirely ruin his constitution. He and the captain often quarrelled, especially at night.' (Hamilton and Laughton, 1906, quoted in Kennedy, 1978, 14.)

57. See for instance Ledyard, 1963, 137–9, recounting the incident when Clerke accused Palea's people of stealing the *Discovery*'s jolly-boat, which was under the

bows all the time. Palea protested their innocence, but 'was answered only by a strut across the deck, and a couplet of genteel curses and imprecations.' See also Burney in Beaglehole, ed., 1967, I:511, on the *Resolution*'s gunner striking Palea.

58. Samwell in Beaglehole, ed., 1967, II:1193.

59. King in Beaglehole, ed., 1967, I:530.

60. Clerke in Beaglehole, ed., 1967, I:533.

61. Anon. in 'An Account of the Death of Captn Cook of the *Resolution* on making the discoverys round the World in 1779', NLA Ms 8:3.

62. Burney in Beaglehole, ed., 1967, I:549-50. See also Samwell in ibid., 1194.

63. Cordy, 2000, 300, 304. See also Home, 1779, 2: 'Captain Cook landed Directly and Marched through the Town, inquiring as he went Along for Kuriabou, and the people were very Shy of telling him in what House the King was . . . He arrived at Last at the House where the King was But he would not come out to him and it was perceived that he had a great Number of Chiefs about him who . . . Restrained him Contrary to his Inclination, upon this Captain Cook ordered Mr. Phillips and some of his people to Enter the House and persuade him to Come out, which they affected but No Force was used or any offensive Manner.'

64. My thanks to Herb Kane for this insight. In addition, as John I'i reported in 1841, the high chief's house was intensely sacred: 'Neither dare I approach his [the high chief's] shadow in the forenoon or afternoon, not even the shadow of the house in which he lived. No common man could approach that place with their kapas on.' (In Thrum, Thomas, 1889, 61.)

65. According to Zimmermann, 'Captain Cook endeavoured to drag him along by force [and] the people pelted him with small stones . . . Then, he who a short time previously had been honored by these people as a god, became angry and fired into their midst with his double-barrelled shot-gun which was loaded with buckshot, seized the king once more by the hand and dragged him over the outspread cloth' (Zimmermann, 1929, 92) – but Zimmermann was not an eyewitness. A recent account by Hawai'ian experts in traditional history has identified Kalani'opu'u's two sons by his senior wife Kanekapolei as Keoua-a-ku'ahu'ula and Keoua-pe'ale (Ahlo and Walker, eds., 2000, 26). The son who sat in the pinnace was one of these boys, perhaps Keoua-pea'ale.

66. Cook and King, 1784, quoted in Sahlins, 1995, 84.

67. Edgar Ms. Log, quoted in Kennedy, 1978, 74.

68. It seems to be generally agreed by the men (see, for instance, Watts, Harvey, Samwell, Zimmermann, Ledyard and Bayly) that Cook waved for the boats to cease firing and come in, but that Williamson forebade his men to go in and rescue their comrades, although the pinnace and the cutter went in anyway. Williamson, third lieutenant of the *Resolution*, was widely accused of cowardice and heartily hated by his shipmates. As Trevenen wrote at the end of the voyage, 'Our first Lieutenant, Williamson, is a wretch, feared & hated by his inferiors, detested by his equals, & despised by his superiors; a very devil, to whom none of our midshipmen have spoke for above a year; with whom I would not wish to be in favour, nor would receive an obligation from, was he Lord-High-Admiral of Great Britain.' (Beaglehole, ed., 1967, III:lxxix–lxxx). There were also tales of a second duel between Williamson

and Phillips (they had previously fought each other in Tahiti), who called him out for his cowardice in this action (Ledyard, 1967, 148, 231–2). According to Alexander Home, 'it was the intention of the whole of us to bring him to court martial upon our arrival in England but after Cook's death he came to be first Lieut. of the *Resolution*, and on our arrival at Kamschatka, he very knowingly established a mason's lodge, got all of the men to become full masons by bribing them with brandy, and got them to promise as brothers, they would say nothing of his cowardice when they came to England, so by this trick he saved his bacon.' (Quoted in Kennedy, 1978, 86.) He was subsequently court-martialled for cowardice in a later action; Nelson thought he should have been shot.

69. Bligh, quoted in Kennedy, 1978, 81.

70. Samwell in Beaglehole, ed., 1967, II:1200.

71. I would like to thank Herb Kane, the Hawai'ian artist and scholar, for a series of illuminating discussions about the bay in 1779, the rituals Cook was put through, Hawai'ian understandings of his identity, the detailed events surrounding his killing, and an unforgettable visit to Kealakekua in March 2002, in which the precise locations of many of these events were identified in the landscape.

72. Sahlins, 1995, 78–84.

73. In his journal, Williamson was critical of Cook's behaviour on a number of occasions during the voyage. He was angry with his captain in Tonga, on 22 June 1777, when Cook allowed the chief Finau to keep possession of Williamson's musket, which a Tongan had taken. It is plain, too, that at Kauai on their first landing, Cook had rebuked Williamson for shooting a local man dead – 'The first boat that was sent on shore to reconitre (Leutenant Williamson) on the natives flocking round the boat though with no hostile intent, he shot one of them a Cowardly, dastardly action for which Captn. Cook was very angry as he himself generaly acted very humanely towards the natives by which we got much better supply'd.' (Griffin in Beaglehole, ed., 1967, I:267fn.)

74. Home, Alexander, 1778, 'The Account of Ottihiti and our Transactions' by Captain Alexander Home, R.N., typescript manuscript, in Log Book:3.

75. Samwell gave this man's name as 'Noo-ah' [Nu'a] – in Beaglehole, ed., 1967, II:1202. Hawai'ians commonly had more than one name, however, and it is just possible that Pihere and Nu'a were the same person.

76. Pihere, 1792, in 'Some Acct of the Death & Remains of Capt Cook at Owhyhee recd from Joshua Lee Dimsdell Quarter Master of the *Gunjara* Capt. James Barber.' Ms held in Dixson Library, Library of New South Wales, Ms Q154.

Conclusion

Our Ancestor Captain Cook

1. Cook and King, 1784, 66.

2. Gilbert, ed. Holmes, 1982, 107–8.

3. Anon. letter to Mrs Strachan of Spithead, 1781. Mitchell Library Safe 1/67.

4. Kamakau, Samuel, 1976, *The Works of the People of Old* (Honolulu, Bernice

Bishop Museum Press), 130. See also Filihia for an illuminating discussion of human sacrifice in Polynesia (Filihia, Meredith, 1999, 'Rituals of Sacrifice in Early Post-European Contact Tonga and Tahiti', *The Journal of Pacific History*, 34(1), 5–22).

5. Roberts in Beaglehole, ed., 1967, I:542fn.

6. Samwell in Beaglehole, ed., 1967, II:1212

7. Zimmermann, 1929, 102.

8. See also James King's obituary of James Cook, which paints a very similar portrait of his captain (King in Cook and King, 1784, 48–9).

9. Zimmermann, 1929, 98–100.

10. This phrase is taken from a letter from the Maori anthropologist Te Rangihiroa (Sir Peter Buck) while he was working at the Bernice Bishop Museum in Hawai'i, to his close friend Sir Apirana Ngata, the eminent Maori politician, discussing the 150 year commemorative ceremonies for Cook in Hawai'i in 1928 (Sorrenson, M.P.K., 1986, *Na To Hoa Aroha: From Your Dear Friend: The Correspondence between Sir Apirana Ngata and Sir Peter Buck 1925–50* (Auckland, Auckland University Press), I:112–13).

11. Taylor, Andrew, 1786–1788, Journals of A.B. Taylor on the *Prince of Wales* Commanded by J. Colnett, ML (A2106): 17 January 1788.

12. Colnett, James, 1968, *Colnett's journal aboard the* Argonaut (New York, Greenwood Press), 220.

13. Dimsdell, 1801.

14. Bell, Edward, 1929, Log of the *Chatham, Honolulu Mercury*, November, 80; see also September 1929, 10; October, 64. For later accounts of Cook's death and burial place see Bloxam, Andrew, 1925, *Diary of Andrew Bloxam, Naturalist on the* Blonde *on Her Trip to the Hawaiian Islands from England 1824–25* (Honolulu, Bishop Museum), 72–8; Little, George, 1846, *Life on the Ocean; or, Twenty Years at Sea* (Boston, Waite, Peirce and Company), 131–2.

15. Puget, Peter, A Log of the Proceedings of His Majesty's Armed Tender *Chatham*, PRO Adm 55/27, 27 February 1793. See also Manby, Thomas, 1929, Journal of Vancouver's Voyage to the Pacific Ocean (1791–1793) in *The Honolulu Mercury*, July 1929, 42–5. It is interesting to note, however, that Kalani'opu'u's bones were taken to a number of mortuary shrines, including Hale o Keawe ('House of Keawe' – Keawe being his grandfather] at the great ritual site at Honaunau, where it briefly lay before being taken to a cave in Ka'u, also south of Kealakekua. (Cordy, 2000, 270.)

16. Mariner, 1991, 280–81.

17. Williams, 1838, 105–6: 'A heathen woman had, by some means or other, been conveyed from the island of Tahiti to Rarotonga, and on her arrival she informed the Rarotongans of all the wonders she had seen; stating that *they* were not the only people in the world; that there were others entirely white, whom they called Cookees; that Captain Cook had been to her island;' and 199–201: 'Although Captain Cook did not discover the island, we found that the inhabitants had a knowledge of him before our arrival, which they received partly from the heathen woman of whom I have previously spoken, and partly from some natives who were drifted from Tahiti down to Rarotonga in a canoe . . . [who informed them] that a race existed entirely

different from themselves, who were quite white, and were called Tute or Cook; that they traversed the ocean for months together as on dry land, that their canoes were immensely large, and instead of being tied and lashed with cinet, were held together with "*kurima*" or iron; and that though they had no outrigger, they did not overturn. All this was astonishing information; but the Cookees were moreover represented by the trumpeters of their fame as a very impious people, who cared not for the gods, but walked with the greatest unconcern about the maraes, and even eat the sacred food. On hearing this, the astonished inhabitants exclaimed, "Why do you not drive them away, and seize all their property?" To which it was replied, that they were like the gods, and were out of their power; adding, "If we attempt to hurt them, they blow at us." "What," said the Rarotongans, "will blowing at you hurt you?" When they were informed that it was not "blowing at them with the mouth, but with long things they call *pupuhi*, out of which comes fire and a stone, which kill us in an instant, before we can get near our spears." '

18. Ellis, 1859, IV:131–44.

19. Kahananui, Dorothy, ed. 1984, *Ka Moolelo Hawaii, Hawaiian Language Reader based on Sheldon Dibble, Ka Moolelo Hawaii* (Honolulu, University of Hawai'i Press), 173.

20. Bingham, Hiram, 1855, *A Residence of Twenty-One Years in the Sandwich Islands* (New York), 35.

21. Kamakau, Samuel, 1961 (revised edition), *Ruling Chiefs of Hawaii* (Honolulu, The Kamehameha Schools Press), 103–4.

22. Morrison, 1935, 85–6.

Index

Figures in italics indicate illustrations

DISCOVERIES: THE VOYAGES OF CAPTAIN COOK
NICHOLAS THOMAS

Captain James Cook was one of the greatest sea explorers of all time. His epic voyages charted the islands of the Pacific, defined the coasts of New Zealand and eastern Australia, and ventured into both Arctic and Antarctic ice. His men suffered near shipwreck, were ravaged by tropical diseases and survived frozen oceans.

Cook's voyages are remarkable and enduringly controversial for their meetings with peoples. Aboriginal Australians, Maori, Hawaiians and many others encountered Europeans – often for the first time. These meetings were charged with mutual curiosity, animated by pleasure, and disturbed by violence. Contact meant mutual knowledge, but also trade, sex, and disease. Cook became steadily more intrigued by Islanders' lives, arts, and rituals, and at the same time more troubled by the consequences of his own voyages. He wrote copiously and sometimes passionately, trying to find the words for what was novel and curious, trying to define himself and his mission as essentially humane.

Nicholas Thomas draws on twenty years' research into Pacific art, culture and history to explore the drama of Cook's expeditions. Central to the story is Captain Cook's curiosity. A brilliant map-maker even before he entered the Pacific, Cook would journey emotionally and intellectually into unknown waters, and meet people on beaches who were used to voyaging themselves. Tahitians, Maori, and Hawaiians would position this enigmatic visitor on their own maps, in ways he could neither understand nor control. Their meetings would be sometimes rewarding, sometimes dangerous, always strangely rich and unpredictable. *Discoveries* re-imagines these encounters for a new audience, overturning the familiar images of Cook as both hero and as ruthless colonizer, and exploring the fascinating and far more ambiguous figure beneath.

'Rich, vivid and deeply provocative, Thomas's work combines premiere adventure story with thorough history and intensive sociology' *Publishers Weekly*

'A fabulous new book . . . focuses on the extraordinary encounters between Cook's salt-encrusted mariners and the colourful Pacific islanders' Giles Milton, *Living History*

MORE PENGUIN

THE JOURNALS   CAPTAIN JAMES COOK

'They crowded so thick round the boat ... that it was some time before we could get room to land'

These Journals record the historic meeting between two worlds as Europe's greatest navigator made the first contact with many of the peoples of the Pacific. In three extraordinary expeditions, Cook chartered the entire coast of New Zealand and eastern Australia, and made detailed descriptions of Tahiti, Tonga and many previously unknown islands. Cook's journals display the skill and courage with which he faced the continuous dangers of uncharted seas and endeavoured to firm relationships with the peoples he encountered. While he had an eighteenth-century Englishman's imperial assurance, Cook writes of 'native' cultures with striking sympathy and respect to create a truly compelling and revealing account of these momentous voyages of discovery.

This edition, abridged from the Hakluyt Society's definitive four-volume collection and preserving Cook's idiosyncratic spelling, makes this inimitable personal account of his nine years of voyaging accessible to the general reader. Philip Edwards provides an introduction to each voyage and a postscript on the controversy surrounding Cook's death.

MORE PENGUIN

EMPIRE MADE ME: AN ENGLISHMAN ADRIFT IN SHANGHAI   ROBERT BICKERS

The highly charged, evocative story of one ordinary man's life and death as a servant of the British Empire.

Shanghai in the wake of the First World War was one of the world's most dynamic, brutal and exciting cities, rivalled only by New York and Berlin. Its waterfront crammed with ocean freighters, gunboats, junks and a myriad coastal craft, it was the great focus for trade between China and the world creating, for Chinese and foreigner alike, immense if precarious opportunities. Shanghai's great panorama of nightclubs, opium-dens, brothels, racetracks and casinos was intertwined with this industrial powerhouse to create a uniquely seductive but also terrifying metropolis.

Into this maelstrom stepped a tough and resourceful ex-veteran Englishman to join the Shanghai police. It is his story, told in part through his rediscovered photo-albums and letters, that Robert Bickers tells here. Aggressive, bullying, racist, self-aggrandizing, Maurice Tinkler was in many ways a typical Briton-on-the-make in an empire world that gave authority to its citizens purely through their skin colour. But Tinkler was also very much more than this – for all his bravado, he could not know that the history that packed him off to Shanghai could just as readily crush him.

A detective story, a recreation of a lost world and a meditation on loss, *Empire Made Me* is both a moving account of one man's life and a fascinating insight into how the British Empire *really* worked.

'A fascinating and dispassionate portrait of how the British Empire kept afloat for so long. In the process he vividly brings to life the forgotten multitude of ordinary British who oiled its wheels, arrested its enemies, fed off its fat, and sometimes died for its cause' Matthew Kneale

'Bickers' detailed recovery of an obscure and "unimportant" policeman's life gives a valuable street-level view of a complex scene. A fascinating book' *FT Magazine*

'Superb' Giles Foden

MORE PENGUIN

EMPIRE: HOW BRITAIN MADE THE MODERN WORLD   NIALL FERGUSON

The British Empire was the biggest empire in all history. At its peak it governed a quarter of the world's land and people and dominated all its seas.

Though little now remains of the Empire as a political power, its legacy is all around us. It laid the foundation for the global triumph of capitalism. It gave the world its common language, English. It exported both Protestantism and parliaments. And it defeated a succession of rival empires from the Habsburgs' to Hitler's.

In the twenty-first century another English-speaking superpower seems to bestride the globe. But today's American empire was yesterday's British colony. For better and for worse, the world we now know is in large measure the product of Britain's Age of Empire.

How did a rainy island in the North Atlantic manage to achieve all this? What were the special factors that enabled Britain to make the modern world – and made the modern world so British? These are the crucial questions addressed by Niall Ferguson in *Empire*.

This was the first age of globalization. But it was, says Ferguson, globalization with gunboats. *Empire* shows how the British wrested power from their rivals by a combination of imitation and intimidation. It shows how mass migration from Britain turned the American and Australian continents white – and how the missionary movement sought to enlighten the 'dark' continents of Africa and Asia. Above all, *Empire* explains how the British Empire rose – and why it finally fell. Ferguson's answers are controversial but compelling.

There has never been a better time to reassess the achievements – both good and evil – of the British world order. With unrivalled verve and clarity, *Empire* unfolds the imperial story for a new generation of readers.

'Professor Ferguson is the most brilliant British historian of his generation' Andrew Roberts, *The Times*

'Marvellous' *The Sunday Times*

'Elegant and thoughtful' *Sunday Telegraph*

'Excellent' *FT Weekend*

MORE PENGUIN

SPAIN'S ROAD TO EMPIRE: THE MAKING OF A WORLD POWER 1492–1763   HENRY KAMEN

How did an impoverished, thinly populated country, isolated from the rest of Europe, become the world's first superpower?

Henry Kamen's superb book sheds fascinating new light on Imperial Spain's journey to power, from the capture of Moorish Granada to the opening up of the frontiers in Texas and California. Drawing on extensive research and eye-witness accounts, he overturns our traditional view of the all-conquering enemy of Protestant Europe, demonstrating that the Spanish Empire was above all a global, collaborative venture, which depended as much on the cooperation (willing or otherwise) of native Americans, Africans and Asians as that of Europeans for its success. It was, he argues, this diversity of resources and peoples that made Spain's impact on world history so overwhelming.

'Brilliant . . . lucid, scholarly and perceptive . . . a revelation'
Peter Preston, *Observer*

'The best as well as the boldest existing book on the subject . . . This is salutary revisionism, which Kamen tackles with his usual virtues: forthright language, vigorous pace, vivid examples, resilient thinking, critical intelligence, robust scholarship, uninhibited audacity . . . At last Henry Kamen has given us a history which . . . looks at "the untold story"'
Felipe Fernandez-Armesto, *Literary Review*

'A splendid new book' Paul Kennedy, *Guardian*

'Kamen, an expert on imperial Spain ... pulls off a considerable achievement. He changes our perception of the Spanish empire'
Ann Wroe, *Daily Telegraph*

MORE PENGUIN

NEW PENGUIN HISTORY OF THE WORLD
J. M. ROBERTS

A book of breathtaking range by the pre-eminent giant-scale historian of our age. One of the most extraordinary history bestsellers on the Penguin list, John Roberts's book has now been completely updated to the end of the last century and revised throughout to make sure it keeps its amazing appeal to a new generation of readers. The entire text has been overhauled to take account of the great range of discoveries that have changed our views on early civilizations and to bring it fully up-to-date. The book has also been completely redesigned and reset. The result is a book that is both an essential work of reference for anyone with the slightest historical interest and a great reading experience.

'A stupendous achievement – the unrivalled World History for our day. It extends over all ages and all continents. It covers the forgotten experiences of ordinary people as well as chronicling the acts of those in power. It is unbelievably accurate in its facts and almost incontestable in its judgements' A. J. P. Taylor, *Observer*

'A work of outstanding breadth of scholarship and penetrating judgements. There is nothing better of its kind' Jonathan Sumption, *Sunday Telegraph*

'This is a book I would like to put into the hands of anyone interested in the past' Alan Bullock

'Anyone who wants an outline grasp of history, the core of all subjects, can grasp it here' *The Economist*

CLICK ON A CLASSIC

THE WORLD'S GREATEST LITERATURE AT YOUR FINGERTIPS

↗ Constantly updated information on over 1600 titles, from Icelandic sagas to ancient Indian epics, Russian drama to Italian folktales, American greats to modern African masterpieces

↗ The latest news on recent additions to the list, updated editions and specially commissioned translations

↗ Scholarly essays by leading critics: Elaine Showalter on Zola, Tom Paulin on Hazlitt, Frank Kermode on Shakespeare, Lisa Appignanesi on Tolstoy

↗ A wealth of background material, including biographies of every classic author from Aristotle to Zamyatin, plot synopses, readers' and teachers' guides, useful web links

↗ Online inspection copy ordering for academics

↗ Trivia quizzes, competitions, giveaways, news on forthcoming screen adaptations

↗ eBooks available to download